Canadian Profile

Profil canadien

Alcohol, Tobacco & Other Drugs

L'alcool, le tabac et les autres drogues

1997

Canadian Centre on Substance Abuse

Addiction Research Foundation of Ontario

Centre canadien de lutte contre l'alcoolisme et les toxicomanies

Fondation de la recherche sur la toxicomanie de l'Ontario

Canadian cataloguing in publication data

McKenzie, Diane

 Canadian profile: alcohol, tobacco & other drugs = Profil canadien: l'alcool, le tabac et les autres drogues

Text in English and French.

Includes bibliographical references and index.

ISBN 1-896323-20-0

1. Drug abuse—Canada—Statistics
2. Substance abuse—Canada—Statistics.
3. Drug abuse and crime—Canada—Statistics.
4. Drug abuse—Economic aspects—Canada—Statistics
I. McKenzie, Diane (Diane Margaret), 1953-
II. Single Eric, III. Canadian Centre on Substance Abuse. IV. Ontario. Addiction Research Foundation. V. Title. VI. Title: Profil canadien.

HV5000.C3S46 1994 362.29'0971'021
C95-900283-9E

Données de catalogage avant publication (Canada)

McKenzie, Diane

 Canadian profile: alcohol, tobacco & other drugs = Profil canadien : l'alcool, le tabac et les autres drogues

Texte en anglais et en français.

Comprend des références bibliographiques et un index.

ISBN 1-896323-20-0

1. Toxicomanie—Canada—Statistiques.
2. Polytoxicomanie—Canada—Statistiques.
3. Toxicomanie et criminalité—Canada—Statisques.
4. Toxicomanie—Aspect économique—Canada—Statistiques.
I. McKenzie, Diane (Diane Margaret), 1953-
II. Single Eric, III. Centre canadien de lutte contre l'alcoolisme et les toxicomanies. IV. Ontario. Fondation de la recherche sur la toxicomanie.
V. Titre. VI. Titre: Profil canadien.

HV5000.C3S46 1994 362.29'09'71'021
C95-900283-9F

Tables compiled and text edited by
Diane McKenzie, CCSA
Bob Williams, ARF
Eric Single, CCSA

Cover concept and design by
Eric Single and Heather McAfee

Compilation et rédaction
Diane McKenzie, CCLAT
Bob Williams, ARF
Eric Single, CCLAT

Couverture
Eric Single et Heather McAfee

Copies of this publication may be purchased by contacting the following organizations:

Residents of Canada (other than Ontario)
Canadian Centre on Substance Abuse
75 Albert Street, Suite 300
Ottawa, Ontario K1P 5E7
Telephone: (613) 235-4048
Fax: (613) 235-8101

Residents of Ontario
Marketing
Addiction Research Foundation
33 Russell Street
Toronto, Ontario M5S 2S1
Telephone: (416) 595-6059 (Toronto)
1-800-661-1111 (outside Toronto)

Pour se procurer la présente publication, s'adresser aux organismes suivants :

Résidants du Canada (sauf de l'Ontario)
Centre canadien de lutte contre
l'alcoolisme et les toxicomanies
75, rue Albert, Bureau 300
Ottawa (Ontario) K1P 5E7
Téléphone : (613) 235-4048
Fax : (613) 235-8101

Résidants de l'Ontario
Marketing
Fondation de la recherche
sur la toxicomanie
33, rue Russell
Toronto (Ontario) M5S 2S1
Téléphone : (416) 595-6059
de l'extérieur de Toronto : 1-800-661-1111

We gratefully acknowledge the financial assistance from

Health Canada and Solicitor General Canada

for the printing of this publication

Nous tenons à remercier Santé Canada et Solliciteur Général Canada

dont l'aide financière nous a permis de couvrir

les frais d'impression de la publication

Canadian Profile 1997

1 Introduction
The organization of the report is presented, along with the methodological caveats and population data.

2 Alcohol
Alcohol consumption continues to decline: 72.3% of Canadians report drinking in 1994 compared to 79% in 1990.

3 Tobacco
According to the February 1995 Survey on Smoking in Canada, 30% of Canadians over 15 smoke cigarettes. Rates of use are highest among adults between 20 and 24 (37%) and lowest over 65 (14%).

4 Drugs
More Canadians used illicit drugs in 1994 than in 1993: cannabis increased from 4.2% to 7.4%; cocaine went from 0.3% to 0.7%. In 1993, Canadian police forces seized 144,548 kg of cannabis, 4,515 kg of cocaine and 94 kg of heroin.

5 Indigenous Canadians
Indigenous men are more likely to abuse alcohol while Indigenous women tend to abuse drugs alone. Thirty per cent of men and 16% of women (Inuit and Dene) used cannabis in the past year.

6 Street Youth
Drugs are used by street youth to cope with the effects of a violent home life and the day-to-day hardship of living on the street

7 AIDS
About 11,529 Canadians have developed AIDS since 1977; of these, 8,199 have died.

8 Fetal Alcohol Syndrome
In 1992/93 18 cases of suspected fetal alcohol syndrome were reported and 74 babies were treated for noxious influences transmitted by the placenta or breast milk; 250 pregnant women were treated for drug dependence.

9 Public attitudes
Most Canadians consider government action on drugs to be of high importance, and the majority favour current alcohol controls.

10 Economic aspects
The average Canadian spends $462 on alcoholic beverages each year and more than $10.4 billion were spent on alcohol. Government revenue from tobacco taxes declined by $896.5 million in 1993/94.

11 The Law
Drug offenders remain subject to the provisions of the Narcotic Control Act and the Food and Drugs Act.

12 Crime
In 1993, there were 56,811 drug-related offences, 63% of which involved cannabis and 22% involved cocaine. Two thirds of offences reported under provincial statutes were liquor act offences.

Profil canadien 1997

 # Acknowledgments

 # Remerciements

This report is a collaborative effort by many persons in the Canadian Centre on Substance Abuse (CCSA), the Addiction Research Foundation (ARF) and elsewhere. Mr. Robin Dupuis of the Medical Services Branch of the Alcohol and Community Funded Programs planned and funded the chapter on Aboriginal substance use. Minh Van Truong, Gary Timoshenko and Theresa Williams of ARF, and Norma Turner of the CCSA helped compile the statistics and produce the tables and graphs presented in the report. Paul Prechner, John Wagner and Mark Whelan of Commerce Press Inc., and Heather McAfee of the Canadian Centre on Substance Abuse collaborated on the production of the report. Margy Chan of ARF and Richard Garlick of the CCSA helped manage the project. The support of Robin Room, Vice President of Research and Development at ARF, and Jacques LeCavalier, CEO of the CCSA, is also gratefully acknowledged.

Previous reports in this series

Statistics on Alcohol and Drug Use in Canada and Other Countries, Data Available by August 1982 (Toronto: Addiction Research Foundation, 1983). Out-of-print.

Statistics on Alcohol and Drug Use in Canada and Other Countries - Volume I: Statistics on Alcohol Use, Data Available by September 1984 (Toronto: Addiction Research Foundation, 1985). Out-of-print.

Statistics on Alcohol and Drug Use in Canada and Other Countries - Volume II: Statistics on Drug Use, Data Available by September 1984 (Toronto: Addiction Research Foundation, 1985). Out-of-print.

Statistics on Alcohol and Drug Use in Canada and Other Countries - Volume I: Statistics on Alcohol Use, Data Available by 1988 (Toronto: Addiction Research Foundation 1989). Out-of-print.

Nous rendons hommage à tous ceux et celles du Centre canadien de lutte contre l'alcoolisme et les toxicomanies (CCLAT), de la Fondation de la recherche sur la toxicomanie (ARF) et d'autres organismes qui ont rendu la présente publication possible. Nous exprimons notre profonde gratitude à M. Robin Dupuis, de la section Toxicomanie et Programmes subventionnés par la communauté de la Direction générale des services médicaux, du ministère fédéral de la Santé, qui a veillé à la planification et au financement du chapitre consacré à la consommation des drogues chez les Autochtones. Nous remercions tout spécialement Minh Van Truong, Gary Timoshenko et Theresa Williams de la Fondation, ainsi que Norma Turner du Centre, qui ont contribué à la compilation des données statistiques et à la production des tableaux et graphiques, de même que Paul Prechner, John Wagner et Mark Whelan de Commerce Press Inc. et Heather McAfee du Centre qui ont collaboré à l'édition. Margy Chan de l'ARF et Richard Garlick du CCLAT ont pour leur part contribué avec brio à la gestion du projet. Nous remercions enfin de leur précieux soutien Robin Room, vice-président de la recherche et du développement à la Fondation, et Jacques LeCavalier, directeur général du Centre.

Rapports déjà parus dans la même collection

Statistics on Alcohol and Drug Use in Canada and Other Countries, Data Available by August 1982} (Toronto : Fondation de la recherche sur la toxicomanie, 1983). Epuisé.

Statistics on Alcohol and Drug Use in Canada and Other Countries - Volume I : Statistics on Alcohol Use, Data Available by September 1984} (Toronto : Fondation de la recherche sur la toxicomanie, 1985). Epuisé.

Statistics on Alcohol and Drug Use in Canada and Other Countries - Volume II: Statistics on Drug Use Data Available by 1988 (Toronto: Addiction Research Foundation 1989). Out-of-print

Canadian Profile, Alcohol and Other Drug Statistics, 1992 (Toronto: Addiction Research Foundation 1992).

Canadian Profile Alcohol, Tobacco and Other Drugs, 1994 (Ottawa: Canadian Centre on Substance Abuse, 1994).

Canadian Profile Alcohol, Tobacco and Other Drugs, 1995 (Ottawa: Canadian Centre on Substance Abuse, 1995).

Statistics on Alcohol and Drug Use in Canada and Other Countries - Volume II : Statistics on Drug Use, Data Available by September 1984) (Toronto : Fondation de la recherche sur la toxicomanie, 1985). Epuisé.

Statistics on Alcohol and Drug Use in Canada and Other Countries - Volume I : Statistics on Alcohol Use, Data Available by 1988) (Toronto : Fondation de la recherche sur la toxicomanie 1989). Epuisé.

Statistics on Alcohol and Drug Use in Canada and Other Countries - Volume II : Statistics on Drug Use Data Available by 1988) (Toronto : Fondation de la recherche sur la toxicomanie 1989). Epuisé.

Canadian Profile, Alcohol and Other Drug Statistics, 1992) (Toronto : Fondation de la recherche sur la toxicomanie 1992).

Profil canadien : l'alcool, le tabac et les autres drogues, 1994) (Ottawa : Centre canadien de lutte contre l'alcoolisme et les toxicomanies, 1994).

Profil canadien : l'alcool, le tabac et les autres drogues, 1995) (Ottawa : Centre canadien de lutte contre l'alcoolisme et les toxicomanies, 1995).

1 Introduction

1 Introduction

Tables

Tableaux

Introduction

by Diane McKenzie, Canadian Centre on Substance Abuse; Bob Williams, Addiction Research Foundation and Eric Single, Canadian Centre on Substance Abuse

Purpose and structure of the report

The following report presents the most current statistics on alcohol, tobacco and other psychoactive substances in Canada. This is the third edition in an ongoing collaboration between the Canadian Centre on Substance Abuse and the Addiction Research Foundation of Ontario. As with previous national profiles (ARF, 1986; 1988; 1990; 1992; CCSA/ARF, 1994; 1995), the aim is to summarize recent trends in drug use and related problems. The report is intended for researchers, programmers, law enforcement officials, policy makers and the media.

Each edition of the Canadian Profile draws on a variety of sources to describe patterns of drug use and problems each year. These sources include surveys, sales data and statistics on law enforcement and the health care system (morbidity and mortality data). As new issues arise, information systems become more complex, and new data is available, these sources will be included. The 1995 volume had four separate chapters on Natives, street youth, AIDS and steroids. For 1997, the Native chapter is expanded, written by a prominent Aboriginal researcher, Kim Scott and a new chapter on Fetal Alcohol Syndrome is included. New information on mortality, morbidity and economic costs associated with the misuse of alcohol, tobacco and illicit drugs is included (Single et al., 1996). Since no significant new information is available on steroids, the topic has been eliminated.

Not every edition will have new data for all subject areas. The data in Chapter 6 on street youth is repeated from the last edition of the Canadian Profile. In this case

Introduction

par Diane McKenzie, Centre canadien de lutte contre l'alcoolisme et les toxicomanies; Bob Williams, Fondation de la recherche sur la toxicomanie; Eric Single, Centre canadien de lutte contre l'alcoolisme et les toxicomanies

But et structure du rapport

Le présent rapport s'appuie sur les plus récentes statistiques de l'usage de l'alcool, du tabac et des autres substances psychotropes au Canada. Il s'agit en fait de la troisième édition, fruit d'un projet mixte permanent du Centre canadien de lutte contre l'alcoolisme et les toxicomanies et de la Fondation de la recherche sur la toxicomanie de l'Ontario. Comme les précédents rapports de la même collectioni publiés par les deux organismes (ARF, 1986; 1988; 1990; 1992; CCLAT/ ARF, 1994; 1995), il trace essentiellement le profil national des récentes tendances observées concernant la consommation des drogues et les problèmes connexes. Il s'adresse aux chercheurs, aux responsables de programmes, aux agents chargés de l'exécution des lois, aux décideurs, et aux médias.

L'information sur les habitudes de consommation de drogues et les problèmes connexes que nous livre chaque édition de *Profil canadien* provient de plusieurs sources, à savoir, diverses enquêtes, les données sur les ventes, les statistiques de la criminalité, ainsi que les données (morbidité et mortalité) des régimes de soins de santé. On ne cesse par ailleurs de raffiner les systèmes de données au fur et à mesure que surgissent de nouveaux éléments d'étude, de manière à obtenir une information toujours plus complète, ce dont nous tûcherons de tenir compte dans nos rapports. L'édition de 1995 comportait quatre chapitres distincts sur les Autochtones, les jeunes de la rue, le sida et les stéroïdes. Celle de 1997 présente un chapitre augmenté sur les Autochtones, rédigé par

there have been no new studies about street youth that focus on substance abuse since the 1992 Toronto and Halifax studies. The Solicitor General's Office prepared reports on runaways and street youth in Ottawa and Saskatoon that focus on service-related issues rather than substance abuse *per se*.

Each chapter is introduced by the annual highlights, followed by an analysis that is based on statistical tables compiled from national reporting systems available across the country. As indicated in the Table of Contents, aggregate statistical information has been compiled on:

- Alcohol consumption, patterns of drinking and problems associated with alcohol use

- Tobacco consumption, trends in smoking and tobacco-related morbidity and mortality

- Licit and illicit drug use, drug seizures, diverted pharmaceuticals and drug-related crime, morbidity and mortality

- Aboriginal people

- Street youth

- AIDS and intravenous drug use

- Public attitudes

- Economic aspects of alcohol, tobacco and other psychoactive substances

- The law regarding substance use and abuse

- Crime

The information presented in this report is organized by topic. This format helps identifies gaps in the report and alerts the reader when different sources of data give conflicting views of reality. From 1988 to 1993 social surveys indicated that cocaine was on the decline while enforcement agencies and health data indicated an increase in cocaine-related problems. This conflict was probably due to the fact that although the number of casual, occasional users declined, the number of heavy users did not. Many heavy users would not be captured by traditional survey methods.

l'éminent chercheur autochtone Kim Scott, et un nouveau chapitre consacré au syndrome d'alcoolisme foetal. Elle comporte en outre de nouvelles données sur la mortalité, la morbidité et les coûts économiques liés à l'abus de l'alcool, du tabac et des drogues illicites (Single et coll, 1996). Aucune nouvelle information d'importance n'ayant été relevée sur les stéroïdes, ce sujet a été mis de côté.

Les différentes éditions ne présentent pas nécessairement de nouvelles données sur tous les secteurs d'étude. C'est le cas notamment du Chapitre 6 sur les jeunes de la rue, qui est repris de la plus récente édition, puisqu'aucune nouvelle étude sur l'abus de drogue dans ce secteur de la population n'a été réalisée depuis les études menées à Toronto et à Halifax en 1992. Des rapports sur les fugueurs et les jeunes de la rue à Ottawa et à Saskatoon ont été publiés par le Cabinet du Solliciteur général, mais ils portaient essentiellement sur les services offerts plutôt que sur l'abus de drogues comme tel.

Chaque chapitre débute par un exposé des points saillants de l'année, lequel est suivi par une analyse fondée sur des tableaux statistiques établis à partir des divers systèmes nationaux d'enregistrement des données. Tel qu'il apparaît à la Table des matières, des données statistiques globales ont été regroupées selon les thèmes suivants :

- Consommation d'alcool, profils de consommation, problèmes reliés à l'usage d'alcool.

- Usage du tabac, tendances du tabagisme, morbidité et mortalité reliées au tabac

- Usage de drogues licites et illicites, saisies de drogues, détournement de produits pharmaceutiques et crimes reliés à la drogue, morbidité et mortalité

- Peuples autochtones

- Jeunes de la rue

- Sida et toxicomanie par injection

Other circumstances contribute to this picture. The purity of street drugs was very high (heroin and cocaine) at this time and resulted in many drug-overdose deaths (and related morbidity) across the country. As a result, police and front-line treatment workers felt that cocaine created more serious problems than that depicted by surveys. Such situations justify using a variety of information sources to obtain a balanced view of psychoactive drug use in Canada today.

Some methodological caveats

The data presented in this report are subject to a number of caveats. First, the data are limited to reporting systems maintained by treatment, law enforcement and government regulatory agencies, supplemented by available national surveys and special studies. There are little or no data available on many important aspects of alcohol and other drug use. Information is not available on a national basis about weekly drinking patterns. This gap is mainly due to weaknesses in national survey questions that measure aspects of drinking behaviour. Similarly, information is very limited about dose, patterns of use and the method of administration for illicit drugs. The measures used in surveys to gather information about patterns of use (alcohol, licit and illicit drugs) are still unsophisticated and preclude precise statements about consumption.

Each data source has various strengths and weaknesses. For most topics described in this report, there is no single source that gives a complete picture of the problem. Treatment data often represents the availability of treatment rather than the true incidence or prevalence of a disease. A further limitation of treatment data is that health statistics are reported on hospital separations rather than admissions. A "separation" can refer to patients who leave the hospital alive or dead. As a result, there can be an overlap between mortality and morbidity data. There are also discrepancies among officially collected statistics on drug-related mortality. In 1993, Statistics Canada reported 546 drug-related deaths for Canada as a whole

- Opinions publiques

- Aspects économiques de l'alcool, du tabac et des autres substances psychotropes

- La loi régissant l'usage et l'abus des substances

- La criminalité

Nous avons choisi d'organiser l'information par thème, ce qui permet de relever plus facilement les lacunes du rapport et d'attirer l'attention du lecteur sur les différentes perceptions de la réalité exprimées à travers les diverses sources de données. De 1988 à 1993, par exemple, les enquêtes sociales révélaient un recul de l'usage de la cocaïne, tandis que les corps policiers et les données sur la santé indiquaient une croissance des problèmes liés à son usage, contradiction sans doute attribuable au fait que le nombre des consommateurs occasionnels diminuait, contrairement à celui des gros consommateurs. Un nombre important des gros consommateurs échappent aux méthodes d'enquêtes traditionnelles. D'autres facteurs peuvent aussi expliquer la divergence des interprétations, notamment le fait que les drogues de la rue (héroïne et cocaïne) étaient alors d'une très grande puret et que leur consommation ait ainsi entraîné de nombreux décès par surdose (plus les cas de morbidité connexes) à travers le pays, ce qui a fait croire aux policiers et aux intervenants en traitement de première ligne que les problèmes associés à la cocaïne créaient des problèmes plus graves que ne le décrivaient les enquêtes. De telles situations illustrent bien la nécessité de puiser à plusieurs sources si l'on veut obtenir un tableau réaliste de la consommation des psychotropes au Canada.

Mises en garde concernant la méthodologie utilisée

Les données du présent rapport obligent à quelques mises en garde. Soulignons en premier lieu qu'elles proviennent exclusivement des syst èmes d'enregistrement alimentés par les services de traitement, les agents chargés de l'exécution des lois et les organismes gouvernementaux de réglementation,

while the Coroner's Office in British Columbia reported 342 drug deaths for that province alone. In that year, drug deaths were also high in Toronto, Montreal, Ottawa and Halifax, suggesting that national mortality statistics may underestimate drug deaths across the country.

Enforcement data are also influenced by factors other than the incidence of alcohol- or drug-related crime. The discretionary powers of police determine if charges are laid when alcohol and drugs are involved in criminal events. Epidemiological surveys often exclude groups that suffer the most from substance abuse, such as street youth, the homeless, Natives and intravenous drug users. Respondents also tend to under report how much they drink and what drugs they use. Even sales data on legal drugs are not without problems. Not all alcohol sold is consumed, due to spoilage, breakage and spilling. Although alcohol sales are the best indicator of aggregate alcohol consumption, there are many sources of unrecorded consumption that under-estimate true consumption. These sources include homemade or brew-on-premise alcoholic beverages, illegally produced alcohol, illegally imported alcohol, and the legal importation of small quantities of duty-free alcohol for personal use. Therefore, wherever possible, a variety of sources are used to describe the extent and nature of substance use and abuse.

Another issue is the comparability of data among provinces and/or regions. Different definitions or interpretations affect the quality of information in reporting systems. Often, it must be assumed that differences between provinces or regions are not significant, when it is not certain whether this is true. The conversion factors for alcohol provide a national estimate of alcohol consumption because they account for the trend toward lower-alcohol content within each major type of beverage (beer, wine and spirits). The extent to which these conversion factors represent the alcohol content of beer, wine and spirits for each province is not clear because detailed information is not available. It is assumed that the overall alcohol content

auxquels s'ajoutent les résultats des enquêtes nationales et des études spéciales disponibles. Il n'existe que très peu de données, parfois même aucune, sur de multiples aspects majeurs de l'usage de l'alcool et des autres drogues. On ne dispose non plus d'aucune donne nationale sur les profils de la consommation hebdomadaire. Ce manque s'explique surtout par certaines lacunes dans les questions d'enquête nationale servant à mesurer les divers aspects des habitudes de consommation. Cette limitation touche également les doses, les profils de consommation et les modes d'administration des drogues illicites. Les mesures utilisées aujourd'hui dans le cadre des enquêtes pour rassembler l'information sur les profils de consommation (alcool, drogues licites et illicites) étant toujours peu sophistiquées, il est impossible de tirer des conclusions précises quant à la consommation.

Quant aux sources de données, toutes ont leurs points forts et leurs points faibles, et pour la majorité des sujets étudiés dans le présent rapport, aucune ne permet d'obtenir un tableau complet de la situation. Ainsi, les données sur le traitement constituent souvent un indicateur de la disponibilité des services plutôt que de la fréquence réelle d'une maladie. Elles sont aussi limitées du fait que les statistiques sur la santé sont déclarées à partir des départs des hôpitaux plutôt que des admissions. Or, les «départs» comprennent aussi bien les patients qui quittent vivants que ceux qui quittent décédés, ce qui peut entraîner des chevauchements entre les données sur la mortalité et celles sur la morbidité. On note également des divergences dans les statistiques officielles sur la mortalité reliée à la drogue. En 1993, Statistique Canada a déclaré 546 décès de cette catégorie pour l'ensemble du Canada alors que le Bureau des coroners de la Colombie-Britannique en a déclaré 342 pour cette seule province. Leur nombre était aussi très élevé dans les villes de Toronto, Montréal, Ottawa et Halifax, ce qui laisse croire que l'estimation de ces décès dans les statistiques nationales sur la mortalité est peut-être inférieure à la réalité.

Les données concernant les activités policières sont pour leur part influencées par des facteurs autres que le

Population statistics

for each type of alcohol is approximately the same for Canada as a whole.

Most of the information in this report consists of numbers and/or percentages on aspects of substance use and abuse. For selected tables, rates per 100,000 people are also presented to allow comparisons between provinces or to other countries. For certain purposes, the rate is based on adults over 15 years, which is often used as an international standard.

Although we presented the numbers as rates per unit of population for the most important variables, some readers may prefer to base their statistics on something other than the total population. Therefore, in the following tables, population information is provided to allow the numbers in this report to be converted to a variety of rates. Table 1.1 presents the population figures by age and gender for all of Canada from 1984 to 1994. Table 1.2 presents the population total and by gender for each province from 1984 to 1994. Table 1.3 presents the population age 15 or older for Canada and the provinces from 1984 to 1994.

The population estimates have been revised based on Statistics Canada's *Revised Intercensal Population and Family Estimates, July 1, 1971-1991* and *Annual Demographic Statistics, 1994*. Unlike previous population estimates, the new figures incorporate net census undercoverage. The net undercoverage is an estimate of people who were not enumerated and non-permanent residents such as refugees, student visa holders, foreign workers, persons holding a Minister's permit and their dependents. As a result of this adjustment, most of the population estimates are higher and this has subsequently resulted in slightly lower rates. In 1991, the "net undercoverage" increased the Canadian population by 791,000 people (an undercoverage rate of about 3%). The tables with rates for earlier years were adjusted to include the new population estimates. Therefore these rates are different from those in earlier editions.

taux de la criminalité reliée à l'alcool ou aux drogues. Les agents de police ont le pouvoir discrétionnaire de déterminer s'il convient de porter accusation dans le cas des activités criminelles impliquant alcool et drogues. Quant aux enquêtes épidémiologiques, elles excluent souvent les groupes les plus atteints par l'abus d'intoxicants, notamment les jeunes de la rue, les sans abri, les Autochtones, et les toxicomanes par injection. Les répondants aux enquêtes hésitent pour leur part à déclarer leur consommation réelle d'alcool et les drogues qu'ils consomment. Les données sur les ventes des drogues illicites posent aussi des difficultés. Par exemple, l'alcool vendu n'est pas toujours consommé, soit parce qu'il s'est détérioré, qu'il a été renversé ou que son contenant a été brisé. Même si les ventes d'alcool constituent le meilleur indicateur de la consommation globale, il existe plusieurs sources de consommation non déclarées, ce qui fausse la consommation réelle. On pense notamment aux boissons alcooliques maison ou brassées sur les lieux d'achat, aux alcools produits ou importés illégalement, ainsi qu'à l'importation légale hors taxe de petites quantités pour consommation personnelle. Pour brosser un tableau le plus juste possible de l'usage et de l'abus d'intoxicants, il convient donc, dans la mesure du possible, de puiser les données à plusieurs sources.

Nous attirons en outre l'attention sur la non-comparabilité des données entre les provinces et/ou les régions. Les différentes définitions ou interprétations en usage influencent la qualité de l'information fournie par les systèmes d'enregistrement des données. Il faut souvent supposer que les écarts entre les provinces ou les régions sont négligeables, même si rien ne le confirme. Puisqu'ils tiennent compte de la tendance à consommer des produits à plus faible teneur en alcool pour chaque grand groupe de boissons (bières, vins, spiritueux), les facteurs de conversion de l'alcool fournissent une estimation plus juste de la consommation de l'alcool à l'échelle nationale. Mais comme il n'existe aucune information détaille, il est impossible de savoir avec certitude dans quelle mesure ces facteurs de conversion représentent la teneur en alcool de la bière, du vin et des spiritueux dans chaque province. Il faut donc supposer

References

Addiction Research Foundation (ARF), *Statistics on Alcohol and Drug Use in Canada and Other Countries*, Toronto: Addiction Research Foundation, 1983.

Addiction Research Foundation (ARF), *Statistics on Alcohol and Drug Use in Canada and Other Countries, Vols. 1 and 2*, Toronto: Addiction Research Foundation, 1985.

Addiction Research Foundation (ARF), *Statistics on Alcohol and Drug Use in Canada and Other Countries, Vols. 1 and 2*, Toronto: Addiction Research Foundation, 1989.

Addiction Research Foundation (ARF), *Canadian Profile 1992: Alcohol and Other Drugs, Toronto: Addiction Research Foundation, 1992.*

Canadian Centre on Substance Abuse (CCSA) and Addiction Research Foundation (ARF), *Canadian Profile: Alcohol, Tobacco and Other Drugs*, 1994, Ottawa: Canadian Centre on Substance Abuse, 1994.

Canadian Centre on Substance Abuse (CCSA) and Addiction Research Foundation (ARF), *Canadian Profile: Alcohol, Tobacco and Other Drugs, 1995*, Ottawa: Canadian Centre on Substance Abuse, 1995.

Single, E., L. Robson, J. Rehm, et X. Xie. *The Costs of Substance Abuse in Canada*, Ottawa: Canadian Centre on Substance Abuse, 1996.

Statistics Canada, *Revised Intercensal Population and Family Estimates, July 1, 1971-1991*, Ottawa: Statistics Canada, Catalogue Number 91-537, July 1994.

Statistics Canada, *Annual Demographic Statistics*, 1993 Ottawa: Statistics Canada, Catalogue Number 91-213, March 1994.

que la teneur générale en alcool de ces produits dans chaque province est à peu près la même que pour l'ensemble du Canada.

Statistiques démographiques

Le présent rapport consiste principalement en une série de tableaux et figures composés de multiples nombres et pourcentages établis au regard des divers aspects de l'usage et de l'abus des intoxicants. Certains tableaux affichent aussi les taux par 100 000 habitants de manière à permettre les comparaisons entre les provinces ou avec les autres pays. Aux fins de diverses applications, les taux sont établis à partir de la population des 15 ans et plus, souvent utilisée comme norme internationale.

Les nombres sont fournis en taux par tranche de population dans le cas des plus importantes variables, mais sachant que certains lecteurs peuvent préférer appuyer leurs statistiques sur des éléments autres que la population globale, nous avons présenté l'information démographique des tableaux suivants de manière à permettre leur conversion selon divers taux. Ainsi, le Tableau 1.1 donne les chiffres de la population selon l'âge et le sexe, pour tout le Canada, de 1984 à 1994; le Tableau 1.2, la population globale selon le sexe, pour chaque province, de 1984 à 1994; et le Tableau 1.3, la population des 15 ans et plus pour le Canada et les provinces, de 1984 à 1994.

Les estimations démographiques ont été entièrement révisées en fonction des plus récentes données de Statistique Canada telles qu'elles ont été publiées dans *Estimations intercensitaires révisées de la population et des familles au 1er juillet)*, période de *1971 à 1991*, et dans *Statistiques démographiques annuelles, 1994.* Contrairement aux estimations antérieures, les nouveaux chiffres tiennent compte du sous-dénombrement net du recensement. On entend par sous-dénombrement net le nombre estimatif des personnes non recensées et des résidants temporaires tels les réfugiés, les étudiants détenteurs de visas, les travailleurs étrangers, les détenteurs d'un permis

ministériel et les personnes à leur charge. Dans l'ensemble, cet ajustement donne lieu à des estimations démographiques supérieures à ce qu'elles n'étaient et, par ricochet, à des taux légèrement inférieurs. Ainsi en 1991, on a ajouté 791 000 personnes à la population canadienne, ce qui correspondait à un «sous-dénombrement net» d'environ 3 %. Les taux des tableaux établis pour les années antérieures ont donc été révisés en fonction des nouvelles estimations démographiques. Ces taux diffèrent donc de ceux présents dans les éditions précédentes.

Ouvrages de référence

Fondation de la recherche sur la toxicomanie (ARF), *Statistics on Alcohol and Drug Use in Canada and Other Countries}*, Toronto : Fondation de la recherche sur la toxicomanie, 1983

Fondation de la recherche sur la toxicomanie (ARF), *Statistics on Alcohol and Drug Use in Canada and Other Countries}, Vol. 1 et 2*, Toronto : Fondation de la recherche sur la toxicomanie, 1985.

Fondation de la recherche sur la toxicomanie (ARF), *Statistics on Alcohol and Drug Use in Canada and Other Countries*, Vol. 1 et 2, Toronto : Fondation de la recherche sur la toxicomanie, 1989.

Fondation de la recherche sur la toxicomanie (ARF), *Profil canadien 1992 : L'alcool et les autres drogues}*, Toronto : Fondation de la recherche sur la toxicomanie, 1992.

Centre canadien de lutte contre l'alcoolisme et les toxicomanies (CCLAT) et Fondation de la recherche sur la toxicomanie (ARF), *Profil canadien : L'alcool, le tabac et les autres drogues, 1994*, Ottawa : Centre canadien de lutte contre l'alcoolisme et les toxicomanies,

Centre canadien de lutte contre l'alcoolisme et les toxicomanies (CCLAT) et Fondation de la recherche sur la toxicomanie (ARF), *Profil canadien : L'alcool, le tabac et les autres drogues, 1995*, Ottawa : Centre canadien de lutte contre l'alcoolisme et les toxicomanies,

Single, E., L. Robson, X Xie, et J. Rehm, *The Costs of Substance Abuse in Canada*, Ottawa : Centre canadien de lutte contre l'alcoolisme et les toxicomanies, 1996.

Statistique Canada, *Statistiques démographiques annuelles, 1993*, Ottawa : Statistique Canada, Cat. no 91-213, mars 1994.

Statistique Canada, *Estimations intercensitaires révisées sur la population et les familles au 1er juillet, 1971-1991}*, Ottawa : Statistique Canada, Cat. no , juillet 1994.

TABLE 1.1　　　　　　　　　　　　　　　　　　　　　　　　　**TABLEAU 1.1**

Population by age and gender, Canada, 1985 to 1994　　　　　Population selon l'âge et le sexe, Canada, 1985 à 1994

AGE	1985	1986	1987	1988	1989	1990	1991	1992	1993	1994
				MALE (IN THOUSANDS)/HOMMES (MILLIERS)						
0- 4	949.9	945.5	952.5	958.1	972.0	989.7	1,000.3	1,015.3	1,031.3	1027.6
5- 9	934.1	941.7	953.4	967.9	982.8	992.9	998.2	1,002.8	1,006.0	1008.5
10-14	943.6	929.1	930.9	939.4	955.8	969.0	980.5	992.6	1,005.5	1015
15-19	1,042.3	1,025.2	1,007.6	997.5	991.2	989.0	985.1	986.0	990.8	1005
20-24	1,290.0	1,266.9	1,223.5	1,165.0	1,122.7	1,089.0	1,067.7	1,056.3	1,046.1	1042.3
25-29	1,240.6	1,264.6	1,289.2	1,308.0	1,329.6	1,322.7	1,282.2	1,238.9	1,188.6	1163.5
30-34	1,119.4	1,148.4	1,186.1	1,219.6	1,258.4	1,285.8	1,312.0	1,322.7	1,329.6	1357.7
35-39	1,019.7	1,046.8	1,057.8	1,078.5	1,113.5	1,146.6	1,173.5	1,204.6	1,236.0	1280
40-44	813.2	849.2	905.2	950.2	996.4	1,040.4	1,077.0	1,083.7	1,095.1	1127.7
45-49	660.9	675.7	702.3	737.8	773.3	807.6	844.1	903.1	950.7	1001.6
50-54	629.2	626.0	623.9	627.2	640.2	654.0	673.2	698.1	729.5	764.9
55-59	600.0	607.4	613.3	617.1	618.5	617.7	618.2	614.9	617.0	630.7
60-64	530.1	537.0	544.0	554.0	561.4	570.3	578.6	586.9	591.5	596.1
65-69	406.2	420.8	440.3	458.5	477.6	488.4	497.9	502.9	510.7	518.5
70-74	322.2	328.2	332.9	334.4	337.0	348.2	364.3	382.9	400.2	416.8
75-79	206.1	212.9	221.0	229.9	239.6	249.1	255.6	259.7	261.9	264
80-84	113.6	117.1	121.6	125.8	130.6	136.0	142.2	148.9	156.3	163.4
85-89	47.7	49.4	52.4	55.2	58.2	60.6	62.2	64.5	67.8	70.1
90+	20.9	21.0	21.5	21.8	22.6	23.7	25.5	26.8	28.4	29.6
Total	12,889.9	13,012.9	13,179.6	13,346.0	13,581.4	13,780.7	13,938.1	14,091.6	14,242.8	14482.9
				FEMALE (IN THOUSANDS)/FEMMES (MILLIERS)						
0- 4	900.2	899.2	909.4	916.3	929.1	944.9	952.9	966.0	980.4	977.8
5- 9	886.4	892.2	902.7	917.2	933.5	946.3	954.7	959.3	961.9	966.4
10-14	900.4	888.9	891.6	897.5	910.2	920.6	932.5	943.8	957.5	969.4
15-19	985.8	970.2	958.0	952.2	949.2	946.6	940.9	941.6	944.9	957.3
20-24	1,233.6	1,207.1	1,164.5	1,114.7	1,084.6	1,057.4	1,041.3	1,027.6	1,014.6	1015.2
25-29	1,217.2	1,231.4	1,247.6	1,264.8	1,286.9	1,283.1	1,246.5	1,205.7	1,158.0	1141.3
30-34	1,117.2	1,147.5	1,179.8	1,207.1	1,238.0	1,263.0	1,285.9	1,294.2	1,300.9	1324.4
35-39	997.8	1,027.1	1,042.1	1,068.9	1,107.0	1,144.2	1,171.2	1,203.4	1,231.8	1268.1
40-44	786.8	823.4	881.6	927.6	975.8	1,022.5	1,061.8	1,072.3	1,091.9	1127.9
45-49	646.4	662.4	688.2	723.1	758.3	792.3	830.0	889.6	937.7	990
50-54	622.6	621.2	619.7	621.3	633.3	646.6	666.7	692.2	725.4	761.2
55-59	621.2	623.7	626.1	625.8	624.0	621.4	620.2	618.9	622.3	637.8
60-64	598.8	603.7	605.8	608.9	608.9	610.3	611.6	615.3	617.1	618.3
65-69	485.7	506.5	529.9	550.9	571.4	580.4	586.7	586.6	588.7	588.5
70-74	411.0	420.9	429.3	432.4	436.9	450.3	469.7	493.0	514.7	534.5
75-79	295.0	305.9	317.9	330.0	344.3	357.9	366.6	374.1	378.7	382.8
80-84	190.2	197.7	206.6	214.4	222.6	230.5	240.1	250.6	262.2	274.5
85-89	101.7	105.6	110.0	114.8	120.4	125.6	130.2	136.5	143.7	148.6
90+	53.9	56.2	59.0	60.9	63.4	66.3	70.0	73.3	77.7	81.1
Total	13,051.8	13,190.9	13,370.1	13,548.8	13,797.9	14,009.9	14,179.5	14,344.0	14,510.2	14765.2

Population by age and gender, Canada, 1985 to 1994   Population selon l'âge et le sexe, Canada, 1985 à 1994

AGE	1985	1986	1987	1988	1989	1990	1991	1992	1993	1994
					TOTAL (IN THOUSANDS)/TOTAL (MILLIERS)					
0- 4	1,850.1	1,844.7	1,861.9	1,874.4	1,901.1	1,934.6	1,953.2	1,981.3	2,011.7	2,005.4
5- 9	1,820.5	1,833.9	1,856.1	1,885.1	1,916.3	1,939.2	1,952.9	1,962.1	1,967.9	1,974.9
10-14	1,844.0	1,818.0	1,822.5	1,836.9	1,866.0	1,889.6	1,913.0	1,936.4	1,963.0	1,984.4
15-19	2,028.1	1,995.4	1,965.6	1,949.7	1,940.4	1,935.6	1,926.0	1,927.6	1,935.7	1,962.3
20-24	2,523.6	2,474.0	2,388.0	2,279.7	2,207.3	2,146.4	2,109.0	2,083.9	2,060.7	2,057.5
25-29	2,457.8	2,496.0	2,536.8	2,572.8	2,616.5	2,605.8	2,528.7	2,444.6	2,346.6	2,304.8
30-34	2,236.6	2,295.9	2,365.9	2,426.7	2,496.4	2,548.8	2,597.9	2,616.9	2,630.5	2,682.1
35-39	2,017.5	2,073.9	2,099.9	2,147.4	2,220.5	2,290.8	2,344.7	2,408.0	2,467.8	2,548.1
40-44	1,600.0	1,672.6	1,786.8	1,877.8	1,972.2	2,062.9	2,138.8	2,156.0	2,187.0	2,255.6
45-49	1,307.3	1,338.1	1,390.5	1,460.9	1,531.6	1,599.9	1,674.1	1,792.7	1,888.4	1,991.6
50-54	1,251.8	1,247.2	1,243.6	1,248.5	1,273.5	1,300.6	1,339.9	1,390.3	1,454.9	1,526.1
55-59	1,221.2	1,231.1	1,239.4	1,242.9	1,242.5	1,239.1	1,238.4	1,233.8	1,239.3	1,268.5
60-64	1,128.9	1,140.7	1,149.8	1,162.9	1,170.3	1,180.6	1,190.2	1,202.2	1,208.6	1,214.4
65-69	891.9	927.3	970.2	1,009.4	1,049.0	1,068.8	1,084.6	1,089.5	1,099.4	1,107.0
70-74	733.2	749.1	762.2	766.8	773.9	798.5	834.0	875.9	914.9	951.3
75-79	501.1	518.8	538.9	559.9	583.9	607.0	622.2	633.8	640.6	646.8
80-84	303.8	314.8	328.2	340.2	353.2	366.5	382.3	399.5	418.5	437.9
85-89	149.4	155.0	162.4	170.0	178.6	186.2	192.4	201.0	211.5	218.7
90+	74.8	77.2	80.5	82.7	86.0	90.0	95.5	100.1	106.1	110.7
Total	25,941.7	26,203.8	26,549.7	26,894.8	27,379.3	27,790.6	28,117.6	28,435.6	28,753.0	29,248.1

Sources: Statistics Canada, *Revised Intercensal Population and Family Estimates, July 1, 1971-1991* (Ottawa: Statistics Canada, Catalogue 91-537 Occasional, July 1994); Statistics Canada, *Annual Demographic Statistics, 1993*, and *1994* (Ottawa: Statistics Canada, Catalogue No. 91- 213 Annual, March 1994 and March 1995 respectively).

Statistique Canada, *Estimations intercensitaires révisées de la population et des familles au 1er juillet, 1971-1991* (Ottawa: Statistique Canada, Catalogue no 91-537, hors série, juillet 1994); Statistique Canada, *Statistiques démographiques annuelles, 1993* et *1994* (Ottawa: Statistique Canada, Catalogue no 91-213, annuel, mars 1994 et mars 1995, respectivement).

TABLE 1.2

TABLEAU 1.2

Population by gender, Canada and provinces, 1985 to 1994

Population selon le sexe, Canada et provinces, 1985 à 1994

PROVINCE	1985	1986	1987	1988	1989	1990	1991	1992	1993	1994
MALE (IN THOUSANDS)/HOMMES (MILLIERS)										
Nfld./T.-N.	291.8	290.0	289.3	289.1	289.7	290.5	291.0	291.5	291.4	292.6
P.E.I./I.-P.-É.	63.8	64.2	64.2	64.5	64.8	64.9	64.7	64.4	65.0	66.4
N.S./N.-É.	440.6	442.7	444.4	445.9	448.7	451.1	453.5	454.2	454.9	462.4
N.B./N.-B.	361.2	361.8	363.0	364.1	366.4	368.7	371.3	371.4	372.2	376.0
Que./Qué.	3,304.2	3,324.2	3,358.7	3,384.4	3,426.5	3,461.1	3,489.8	3,524.1	3,551.4	3,586.9
Ont./Ont.	4,619.4	4,690.4	4,791.6	4,888.7	5,018.9	5,111.3	5,173.7	5,242.9	5,309.1	5,395.1
Man./Man.	537.5	542.4	545.8	548.0	548.9	550.1	552.7	551.9	552.8	561.0
Sask./Sask.	515.9	517.4	518.7	515.9	511.0	504.5	502.1	500.0	498.6	505.9
Alta./Alb.	1,222.8	1,233.0	1,234.8	1,244.0	1,264.2	1,289.8	1,311.2	1,326.7	1,341.3	1,365.8
B.C./C.-B.	1,490.6	1,504.3	1,526.2	1,557.7	1,597.8	1,642.9	1,681.0	1,716.1	1,756.6	1,821.6
Yukon/Yukon	13.0	13.1	13.7	14.1	14.4	14.7	15.2	15.7	16.5	15.7
N.W.T./T.N.-O.	29.1	29.3	29.4	29.6	30.2	31.1	32.0	32.6	33.0	33.5
Canada	**12,889.9**	**13,012.9**	**13,179.6**	**13,346.0**	**13,581.4**	**13,780.7**	**13,938.1**	**14,091.6**	**14,242.8**	**14,482.9**
FEMALE (IN THOUSANDS)/FEMMES (MILLIERS)										
Nfld./T.-N.	289.1	288.0	287.3	287.1	287.7	288.4	289.0	289.6	289.7	289.8
P.E.I./I.-P.-É.	64.3	64.7	64.8	65.3	65.8	66.1	66.1	65.9	66.5	68.1
N.S./N.-É.	447.2	449.4	451.9	454.3	458.0	461.4	464.7	466.6	468.1	474.3
N.B./N.-B.	364.9	365.9	367.5	369.0	371.6	374.3	377.3	377.7	378.7	383.2
Que./Qué.	3,386.1	3,409.6	3,447.2	3,476.0	3,521.5	3,559.5	3,591.4	3,626.6	3,657.4	3,694.3
Ont./Ont.	4,715.0	4,786.7	4,893.2	4,995.7	5,132.1	5,230.1	5,297.5	5,366.9	5,437.2	5,532.7
Man./Man.	547.0	551.6	554.7	556.7	557.3	558.3	560.6	561.2	563.1	570.0
Sask./Sask.	513.0	515.5	517.7	515.8	511.9	506.4	504.9	504.5	504.5	510.2
Alta./Alb.	1,188.3	1,205.7	1,208.7	1,219.0	1,240.1	1,266.6	1,289.1	1,305.7	1,321.0	1,350.5
B.C./C.-B.	1,499.4	1,516.1	1,538.4	1,570.5	1,611.4	1,657.2	1,695.9	1,735.2	1,778.5	1,846.7
Yukon/Yukon	11.6	11.7	12.3	12.7	13.0	13.3	13.9	14.5	15.5	14.4
N.W.T./T.N.-O.	26.0	26.1	26.3	26.7	27.3	28.3	29.2	29.7	29.9	30.9
Canada	**13,051.8**	**13,190.9**	**13,370.1**	**13,548.8**	**13,797.9**	**14,009.9**	**14,179.5**	**14,344.0**	**14,510.2**	**14,765.2**
TOTAL (IN THOUSANDS)/TOTAL (MILLIERS)										
Nfld./T.-N.	580.9	578.0	576.6	576.2	577.4	578.9	580.0	581.1	581.1	582.4
P.E.I./I.-P.-É.	128.1	128.9	129.0	129.8	130.6	131.0	130.8	130.3	131.5	134.5
N.S./N.-É.	887.8	892.1	896.3	900.2	906.7	912.5	918.2	920.8	923.0	936.7
N.B./N.-B.	726.1	727.7	730.5	733.1	738.0	743.0	748.6	749.1	750.9	759.2
Que./Qué.	6,690.3	6,733.8	6,805.9	6,860.4	6,948.0	7,020.6	7,081.2	7,150.7	7,208.8	7,281.2
Ont./Ont.	9,334.4	9,477.1	9,684.8	9,884.4	10,151.0	10,341.4	10,471.2	10,609.8	10,746.3	10,927.8
Man./Man.	1,084.5	1,094.0	1,100.5	1,104.7	1,106.2	1,108.4	1,113.3	1,113.1	1,115.9	1,131.0
Sask./Sask.	1,028.9	1,032.9	1,036.4	1,031.7	1,022.9	1,010.9	1,007.0	1,004.5	1,003.1	1,016.1
Alta./Alb.	2,411.1	2,438.7	2,443.5	2,463.0	2,504.3	2,556.4	2,600.3	2,632.4	2,662.3	2,716.3
B.C./C.-B.	2,990.0	3,020.4	3,064.6	3,128.2	3,209.2	3,300.1	3,376.9	3,451.3	3,535.1	3,668.3
Yukon/Yukon	24.6	24.8	26.0	26.8	27.4	28.0	29.1	30.2	32.0	30.1
N.W.T./T.N.-O.	55.1	55.4	55.7	56.3	57.5	59.4	61.2	62.3	62.9	64.4
Canada	**25,941.7**	**26,203.8**	**26,549.7**	**26,894.8**	**27,379.3**	**27,790.6**	**28,117.6**	**28,435.6**	**28,753.0**	**29,248.1**

Sources: Statistics Canada, *Revised Intercensal Population and Family Estimates, July 1, 1971-1991* (Ottawa: Statistics Canada, Catalogue 91-537 Occasional, July 1994); Statistics Canada, *Annual Demographic Statistics, 1993* and *1994* (Ottawa: Statistics Canada, Catalogue No. 91-213 Annual, March 1994 and 1995 respectively).

Statistique Canada, *Estimations intercensitaires révisées de la population et des familles au 1er juillet, 1971-1991* (Ottawa : Statistique Canada, Catalogue no 91-537, hors série, juillet 1994); Statistique Canada, *Statistiques démographiques annuelles, 1993 et 1994 (Ottawa : Statistique Canada, Catalogue no 91-213, annuel, mars 1994 et 1995 respectivement).*

TABLE 1.3 | **TABLEAU 1.3**

Population age 15 or older by gender, Canada and provinces, 1985 to 1994

Population des 15 ans et plus, selon le sexe, Canada et provinces, 1985 à 1994

AGE	1985	1986	1987	1988	1989	1990	1991	1992	1993	1994
MALE (IN THOUSANDS)/HOMMES (MILLIERS)										
Nfld./T.-N.	213.8	214.5	216.1	217.9	220.4	222.9	225.5	227.0	227.9	231.6
P.E.I./I.-P.-É.	48.5	49.0	49.1	49.4	49.6	49.8	49.7	49.5	50.1	51.4
N.S./N.-É.	342.3	346.0	348.3	350.4	353.3	355.7	358.4	359.2	360.0	367.8
N.B./N.-B.	276.2	278.4	280.7	283.0	285.9	288.6	291.9	293.1	294.5	299.3
Que./Qué.	2,601.6	2,626.3	2,658.6	2,681.5	2,717.8	2,747.3	2,771.7	2,801.4	2,825.2	2,864.5
Ont./Ont.	3,637.1	3,707.5	3,792.2	3,868.6	3,971.5	4,041.2	4,088.3	4,138.4	4,184.1	4,264.9
Man./Man.	414.5	420.0	422.4	424.2	424.9	425.8	428.1	426.8	427.0	435.2
Sask./Sask.	388.9	390.4	391.3	389.4	385.6	380.7	379.3	377.7	376.9	384.9
Alta./Alb.	931.0	941.0	941.9	948.4	962.4	981.2	998.1	1,010.7	1,023.3	1,045.7
B.C./C.-B.	1,178.5	1,193.3	1,211.6	1,236.4	1,267.7	1,303.4	1,334.8	1,362.9	1,396.2	1,451.7
Yukon/Yukon	9.8	9.9	10.4	10.7	10.9	11.1	11.5	11.9	12.5	12.0
N.W.T./T.N.-O.	20.0	20.3	20.4	20.5	20.9	21.4	21.9	22.3	22.6	495.1
Canada	**10,062.3**	**10,196.6**	**10,342.7**	**10,480.6**	**10,670.8**	**10,829.1**	**10,959.2**	**11,081.0**	**11,200.1**	**11,431.9**
FEMALE (IN THOUSANDS)/FEMMES (MILLIERS)										
Nfld./T.-N.	214.7	215.9	217.5	219.2	221.5	223.6	225.8	227.4	228.6	231.2
P.E.I./I.-P.-É.	49.9	50.4	50.5	50.9	51.3	51.6	51.7	51.6	52.2	53.9
N.S./N.-É.	353.0	356.6	359.9	362.9	366.8	370.0	373.4	375.4	377.1	383.4
N.B./N.-B.	283.9	286.6	289.4	291.8	295.0	298.1	301.7	303.1	304.8	309.7
Que./Qué.	2,720.5	2,747.1	2,781.0	2,807.0	2,846.6	2,879.4	2,906.6	2,938.0	2,965.1	3,004.5
Ont./Ont.	3,783.0	3,852.5	3,939.9	4,022.4	4,134.2	4,211.3	4,263.9	4,315.9	4,367.0	4,454.3
Man./Man.	429.5	434.5	437.1	438.8	439.2	439.9	442.0	442.1	443.3	450.5
Sask./Sask.	391.1	393.6	395.2	394.4	391.7	388.0	387.8	387.9	388.4	394.1
Alta./Alb.	910.9	926.8	929.9	938.1	953.6	973.8	991.6	1,005.4	1,018.6	1,046.0
B.C./C.-B.	1,202.4	1,220.4	1,238.9	1,264.6	1,296.9	1,333.3	1,365.2	1,397.4	1,433.7	1,492.2
Yukon/Yukon	8.6	8.8	9.2	9.5	9.8	10.0	10.5	11.0	11.8	10.9
N.W.T./T.N.-O.	17.4	17.5	17.7	18.0	18.3	18.9	19.4	19.7	19.7	500.0
Canada	**10,364.9**	**10,510.6**	**10,666.3**	**10,817.7**	**11,025.0**	**11,198.1**	**11,339.4**	**11,474.9**	**11,610.4**	**11,851.6**
TOTAL (IN THOUSANDS)/TOTAL (MILLIERS)										
Nfld./T.-N.	428.5	430.4	433.6	437.1	441.9	446.5	451.3	454.4	456.5	462.8
P.E.I./I.-P.-É.	98.4	99.4	99.6	100.3	100.9	101.4	101.4	101.1	102.3	105.3
N.S./N.-É.	695.3	702.6	708.2	713.3	720.1	725.7	731.8	734.6	737.1	751.2
N.B./N.-B.	560.1	565.0	570.1	574.8	580.9	586.7	593.6	596.2	599.3	609.0
Que./Qué.	5,322.1	5,373.4	5,439.6	5,488.5	5,564.4	5,626.7	5,678.3	5,739.4	5,790.3	5,869.0
Ont./Ont.	7,420.1	7,560.0	7,732.1	7,891.0	8,105.7	8,252.5	8,352.2	8,454.3	8,551.1	8,719.2
Man./Man.	844.0	854.5	859.5	863.0	864.1	865.7	870.1	868.9	870.3	885.7
Sask./Sask.	780.0	784.0	786.5	783.8	777.3	768.7	767.1	765.6	765.3	779.0
Alta./Alb.	1,841.9	1,867.8	1,871.8	1,886.5	1,916.0	1,955.0	1,989.7	2,016.1	2,041.9	2,091.7
B.C./C.-B.	2,380.9	2,413.7	2,450.5	2,501.0	2,564.6	2,636.7	2,700.0	2,760.3	2,829.9	2,943.9
Yukon/Yukon	18.4	18.7	19.6	20.2	20.7	21.1	22.0	22.9	24.3	22.9
N.W.T./T.N.-O.	37.4	37.8	38.1	38.5	39.2	40.3	41.3	42.0	42.3	995.1
Canada	**20,427.2**	**20,707.2**	**21,009.0**	**21,298.3**	**21,695.8**	**22,027.2**	**22,298.6**	**22,555.9**	**22,810.5**	**23,283.5**

Source: Statistics Canada, *Revised Intercensal Population and Family Estimates, July 1, 1971-1991* (Ottawa: Statistics Canada, Catalogue 91-537 Occasional, July 1994); Statistics Canada, *Annual Demographic Statistics, 1993* and *1994* (Ottawa: Statistics Canada, Catalogue No. 91-213 Annual, March 1994 and March 1995, respectively).

Statistique Canada, *Estimations intercensitaires révisées de la population et des familles au 1er juillet, 1971-1991*, (Ottawa : Statistique Canada, Catalogue no 91-537, hors série, juillet 1994); Statistique Canada, *Statistiques démographiques annuelles, 1993 et 1994* (Ottawa : Statistique Canada, Catalogue no 91-213, annuel, mars 1994 et mars 1995 respectivement).

2 The Use and Abuse of Alcohol in Canada

Figures

Tables

2 L'usage et l'abus de l'acool au Canada

Figures

Tableaux

Highlights

★ Alcohol consumption continues to decline: 72.3% of Canadians report drinking in 1994 compared to 79% in 1990. The average adult drank the equivalent of 7.58 litres of absolute alcohol in 1992/93, a decline of 5% from the previous year. Young adults, males and those with higher incomes drink more than other Canadians.

★ According to the 1993 General Social Survey, nearly one in 10 adult Canadians (9.2%) said they have problems with their drinking. The most common problems affect physical health (5.1%) and financial position (4.7%). Almost half of Canadians (43.9%) say they have had problems from other people's drinking, such as being disturbed by loud parties (23.8%), being insulted or humiliated (20.9%) and having a serious argument (15.6%).

★ There were 6,701 deaths and 86,076 hospitalizations attributed to alcohol in 1992. Motor vehicle accidents accounted for the largest number of alcohol related deaths while accidental falls and alcohol dependence syndrome accounted for the largest number of alcohol-related hospitalizations

★ Impaired driving is a major cause of death; among fatally injured drivers, 45% had some alcohol in their blood and 38% were over the legal limit of .08% Blood Alcohol Concentration.

Points saillants

★ La consommation d'alcool continue de régresser, 72,3 % des Canadiens ayant déclaré en consommer en 1994 contre 79 % en 1990. L'adulte moyen a consommé l'équivalent de 7,58 litres d'alcool alsolu en 1992-1993, un recul de 5 % sur l'année précédente. Les jeunes adultes, les hommes et les personnes disposant d'un revenu supérieur consomment davantage que les autres Canadiens.

★ Selon l'Enquête sociale générale de 1993, près de un adulte sur 10 (9,2 %) a déclaré avoir des problèmes de consommation. Les problèmes les plus courants ont des répercussions sur la santé physique (5,1 %) et la situation financière (4,7 %). Près de la moitié des Canadiens (43,9 %) affirment avoir déjà souffert de la consommation des autres, soit en raison de fêtes trop bruyantes (23,8 %), d'insultes ou d'humiliations (20,9 %) ou de graves disputes (15,6 %).

★ En 1992 on a imputé 6 701 décès et 86 076 hospitalisations imputables à l'alcool, la majeure partie des décès ont été provoqués par des accidents routiers, tandis que la majorité des hospitalisations ont été attribuées aux chutes accidentelles et à l'alcoolisme.

★ La conduite avec facultés affaiblies représente l'une des principales causes de décès; parmi les conducteurs mortellement blessés, 45 % affichaient une alcoolémie, dont 38 % un taux supérieur à la limite légale de 0,08 %.

Alcohol

by Diane McKenzie and Eric Single, Canadian Centre on Substance Abuse

Drinking Trends

Alcohol consumption continues to decline across Canada. According to various national surveys, the proportion of Canadians who drink declined in the past decade. About 80% of the population drank in 1979, 81% in 1985, 78% in 1989, 79% in 1991, 74% in 1993, and 72% in 1994 (Table 2.1). Of the 9,189 respondents in the 1994 Canadian Alcohol and Drug Survey, 72.3% were current drinkers, 13.5% were former drinkers and 12.8% never had alcohol (Table 2.2). Men were more likely than women to be current drinkers (78.1% versus 66.7%), and the proportion who said they drank ranged from 84% among 20 to 24-year-olds to 46% among individuals over 75 (Table 2.2). More people in Alberta (76.4%) and British Columbia (75.6%) said they drink than in other parts of the country (i.e., 67.2% in Prince Edward Island). A higher proportion of drinkers have higher incomes, post-secondary education and are employed (Table 2.3).

SOURCES OF INFORMATION: Information about how much Canadians drink, and the problems they experience, is available from several sources. Sales reports from provincial monopoly boards give information about the type of alcohol Canadians drink and the quantities they consume annually. These data are compiled and reported by Statistics Canada in an annual report entitled *The Control and Sale of Alcoholic Beverages in Canada.* Although sales statistics are the most reliable source of information available, they are limited, because they do not include products such as homemade wine and beer, assisted "homemade" alcohol in commercial establishments, illegal production, illegal imports or legal imports of small amounts for personal use. Special studies estimate the extent to which sales data reflect overall drinking. In 1978, an

L'alcool

par Diane McKenzie et Eric Single, Centre canadien de lutte contre l'alcoolisme et les toxicomanies

Tendances de consommation

La consommation d'alcool continue de régresser dans tout le Canada. Selon les diverses enquêtes nationales, le pourcentage des Canadiens consommateurs d'alcool a régressé au cours des dix dernières années. Quelque 80 % de la population en ont consomé en 1979, 81 % en 1985, 78 % en 1989, 79 % en 1991, 74 % en 1993, et 72 % en 1994 (Tableau 2.1). Sur les 9 189 répondants de l'Enquête canadienne sur l'alcool et les autres drogues de 1994, 72,3 % ont déclaré être buveurs, 13,5 % anciens buveurs et 12,8 % n'avoir jamais bu (Tableau 2.2). La catégorie des buveurs actuels comportait un plus grand nombre d'hommes que de femmes (78,1 % contre 66,7 %), leur pourcentage passant de 84 % chez les 20 à 24 ans à 46 % chez les plus de 75 ans (Tableau 2.2). Plus de gens ont affirmé consommer de l'alcool en Alberta (76,4 %) et en Colombie-Britannique (75,6 %) que dans les autres régions du pays (p. ex., 67,2 % en Ile-du-Prince-Edouard). Ce sont les personnes qui disposent d'un revenu supérieur, d'un niveau d'instruction postsecondaire et d'un emploi qui comptent le plus haut taux de buveurs (Tableau 2.3).

SOURCES D'INFORMATION : L'information sur la quantité d'alcool consommé par les Canadiens et les problèmes qu'ils rencontrent provient de plusieurs sources. Par exemple, les rapports de ventes des régies provinciales monopolistes nous renseignent sur le genre d'alcool et les quantités annuelles que consomment les Canadiens. Ces données sont rassemblées et publiées par Statistique Canada dans le rapport annuel intitulé, *Le contrôle et la vente des boissons alcooliques au Canada.* Bien que les statistiques sur les ventes constituent actuellement la source d'information la plus fiable, elles

Ontario study indicated that sales figures underestimate true consumption by 6% to 7% (Single and Giesbrecht, 1979).

Another source of error is the formula used to convert the alcohol content of beer, wine and spirits to absolute alcohol. These formulas must change regularly to reflect variations in the alcohol content of alcoholic beverages sold in the Canadian marketplace. The conversion factors used in this report are based on the alcohol content of products sold in 1991 as recommended by industry representatives. The conversion factors are 36.9% for spirits, 4.9% for beer and 11.7% for wine.

The most serious limitation of sales data is that they do not document the individual characteristics of drinkers. General population surveys give information on the sociodemographic characteristics of people who drink and those who abstain. Surveys account for only a small amount of alcohol sold (Pernanen, 1974). For example, the number of drinks per week reported by drinkers in the Canadian Alcohol and Drug Survey of 1994, was 3.9. This is less than one half (8.6 drinks per week per capita) the average number of drinks indicated by sales data for 1992/93 (Table 2.7). This discrepancy occurs because the heaviest drinkers tend to be under-represented in survey samples. Heavy drinkers who are captured in surveys are more likely than light drinkers to under-report their drinking (Pernanen, 1974). Therefore, surveys are not used to estimate the total amount of alcohol consumed in a population.

LEVEL OF DRINKING: According to sales data, Canadians drank almost 2 billion litres of beer, 229 million litres of wine and 129 million litres of spirits in 1992/93 (Table 2.4). This amounts to 7.58 litres of absolute alcohol per adult. The average Canadian drank about 8.6 standard drinks per week in 1992/93 (Table 2.7). Beer accounted for 56.5% of all alcohol consumed while spirits accounted for 27.8% and wine 15.7% (Table 2.5).

sont limitées en ce sens qu'elles ne tiennent pas compte des produits tels les vins et bières de fabrication maison, de fabrication artisanale assistée dans des établissements commerciaux, de fabrication illégale, d'importation illégale, ou les produits légalement importés mais en faibles quantités pour consommation personnelle. Des études spéciales évaluent dans quelle mesure les données des ventes reflètent la consommation globale. Selon une étude ontarienne menée en 1978, la consommation réelle dépassait de 6 à 7 % celle obtenue par les chiffres des ventes (Single et Giesbrecht, 1979).

Comme autre source d'erreur, notons les formules utilisées pour convertir la teneur en alcool de la bière, du vin et des spiritueux en alcool absolu. Ces formules doivent régulièrement être mises à jour de manière à tenir compte des différentes teneurs en alcool des boissons alcooliques vendues sur le marché canadien. Les facteurs de conversion utilisés dans le présent rapport sont fondés sur la teneur en alcool des produits vendus en 1991 recommandée par les représentants de l'industrie. Les facteurs de conversion ont ainsi été établis à 36,9 % pour les spiritueux, à 4,9 % pour la bière et à 11,7 % pour le vin.

La plus grave limitation de ces données découle du fait qu'elles ne documentent pas les caractéristiques individuelles des consommateurs d'alcool. Les enquêtes générales sur la population nous dévoilent les caractéristiques sociodémographiques des personnes qui consomment et de celles qui s'en abstiennent. Mais dans l'ensemble, les enquêtes ne révèlent qu'une infime partie de l'alcool vendu (Pernanen, 1974). Par exemple, le nombre de consommations par semaine déclaré par les buveurs dans l'Enquête canadienne sur l'alcool et les autres drogues de 1994 s'établissait à 3,9. C'est là moins de la moitié (8,6 consommations par semaine par habitant) du nombre moyen des consommations indiqué par les chiffres des ventes en 1992-1993 (Tableau 2.7). Cet écart s'explique du fait que les plus gros buveurs sont généralement sous-représentés dans les échantillons d'enquête et que les gros buveurs qui participent sont plus susceptibles que les buveurs légers de déclarer une consommation inférieure à la réalité (Pernanen, 1974).

In 1992/93, Yukon Territory (14.4 litres per adult), the Northwest Territories (9.6 litres) and British Columbia (9.4 litres) had the highest levels of drinking while New Brunswick (6.2 litres), Saskatchewan (7.1 litres) and Quebec (7.1 litres) had the lowest levels (Figure 2.1). Tourism may account for the exceptionally high alcohol sales in the Yukon. The market share of beer, wine and spirits also varies from province to province. For example, a higher percentage of beer is consumed in Quebec (64.3%) and New Brunswick (61%) and a higher percentage of wine is sold in Quebec (21%) and British Columbia (20%). A higher percentage of spirits are sold in the Northwest Territories (43%) and Saskatchewan (42%) than other provinces.

The per adult sales figure of 7.6 litres of absolute alcohol for 1992/93 represents a decline of 5% from the previous year (Table 2.6). Alcohol sales steadily declined from 10.9 litres (per adult) in 1981/82 to 7.6 litres in 1992/93 (Figure 2.2). There is no obvious trend in the market share of beer, wine and spirits. Beer sales improved in recent years while spirits sales declined. A trend toward more wine and less beer in the 1950s and 1960s has not continued.

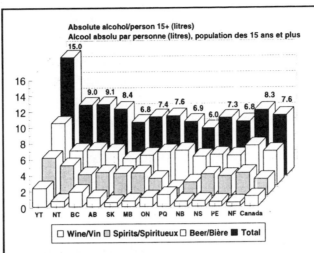

Figure 2.1　Consumption of beer, wine, spirits and total alcohol, Canada and provinces, 1992-93

Figure 2.1　Consommation de la bière, du vin et des spiritueux, et de l'alcool dans son ensemble, Canada et provinces, 1992-1993

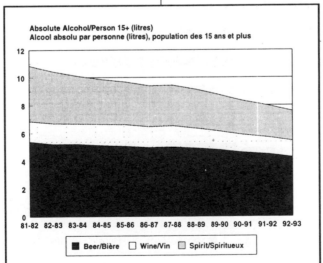

Figure 2.2　Consumption of beer, wine, spirits and total alcohol from 1981/82 to 1992/93

Figure 2.2　Consommation de la bière, du vin, des spiritueux, et de l'alcool dans son ensemble, de 1981-1982 à 1992-1993

Par conséquent, on ne se sert pas des données d'enquête pour évaluer la quantité globale d'alcool consommé par une population.

NIVEAU DE CONSOMMATION : Selon les données des ventes, les Canadiens ont bu près de 2 milliards de litres de bière, 229 millions de litres de vin et 129 millions de litres de spiritueux en 1992-1993 (Tableau 2.4), ce qui représente 7,58 litres d'alcool pur par adulte. Cette même année, le Canadien moyen a pris quelque 8,6 consommations standard par semaine (Tableau 2.7). La bière a représenté 56,5 % de tout l'alcool consommé, les spiritueux 27,8 % et le vin 15,7 % (Tableau 2.5).

En 1992-1993, les taux de consommation globale les plus élevés revenaient au Yukon (14,4 litres par adulte), aux Territoires du Nord-Ouest (9,6 litres) et à la Colombie-Britannique (9,4 litres), et les plus bas au Nouveau-Brunswick (6,2 litres), à la Saskatchewan (7,1 litres) et au Québec (7,1 litres) (Figure 2,1). On croit que le volume exceptionnellement élevé des ventes enregistré au Yukon pourrait être imputable au tourisme. La part du marché de la bière, du vin et des spiritueux varie d'une province à l'autre, celle de la bière étant plus élevée au Québec (64,3 %) et au Nouveau-Brunswick (61 %), celle du

Characteristics of high-volume drinkers

According to the 1993 General Social Survey, the portrait of the heavy drinker is that of a well-to-do young male (Table 2.8). Men drink more than twice as much as women (5.9 drinks/wk. for men versus 2.3 drinks for women) and have twice as many heavy drinking occasions as women (19.4% compared with 8.4% for women). Drinking levels are highest among young adults (18-24 years old), men and single people. These individuals are most likely to have five or more drinks on an occasion.

A higher income is related to how much a person drinks while a higher education is related to drinking but not to how much a person drinks. For example, university graduates are more likely to drink, but they tend to drink less when they do. People looking for work drink the most. Students drink less overall, but they tend to have five or more drinks on an occasion (63%). There is no clear relationship between community size and level of drinking or number of heavy drinking occasions.

The 1989 National Alcohol and Drug Survey asked questions about where people drink. Canadians were asked how often they spent a quiet evening at home, going to a bar, visiting friends, as well as how often and how much they drink when they engage in these activities. These questions are used to estimate how much drinking occurs in different settings. Figure 2.3 indicates that most drinking is done in private settings, such as during a quiet evening at home (18%),

vin au Québec (21 %) et en Colombie-Britannique (20 %), et celle des spiritueux dans les Territoires du Nord-Ouest (43 %) et en Saskatchewan (42 %).

En 1992-1993, la vente d'alcool pur par adulte s'est établie à 7,6 litres, soit 5 % de moins que l'année précédente (Tableau 2,6). Les ventes de boissons alcooliques ont constamment régressé, passant de 10,9 litres (par adulte) en 1981-1982 à 7,6 litres en 1992-1993 (Figure 2.2). Il n'existe aucune tendance nette quant à la part du marché de la bière, du vin et des spiritueux. Les ventes de bière ont augmenté au cours des récentes années tandis que celles des spiritueux ont diminué. La tendance à consommer plus de vin et moins de bière observée durant les années 50 et 60 ne s'est pas maintenue.

Caractéristiques des gros buveurs

Selon l'Enquête sociale générale de 1993, l'image du gros consommateur correspond à celle du jeune homme bourgeois aisé (Tableau 2.8). Les hommes consomment deux fois plus que les femmes (5,9 consommations par semaine contre 2,3 chez les femmes) et ont au moins deux fois plus d'occasions que les femmes de consommer de fortes quantités (19,4 % contre 8,4 %). Les jeunes adultes (18 à 24 ans), les hommes et les célibataires affichent les taux de consommation les plus élevés et sont plus nombreux à boire cinq consommations ou plus par occasion.

Pendant que le revenu supérieur d'une personne influera sur la quantité d'alcool qu'elle consommera, son niveau d'instruction supérieur influera lui sur la consommation mais

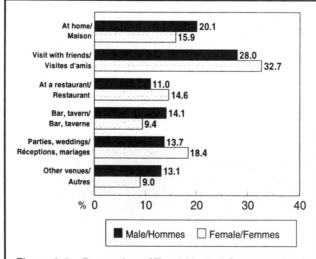

Figure 2.3　Proportion of Total Alcohol Consumption in Different Settings, Males and Females, Canada, 1989

Figure 2.3　Proportion de la consommation globale d'alcool selon les différents contextes, hommes et femmes, Canada, 1989

going to a party or other social gathering (16%), having friends visit (16%) or visiting others (15%). Drinking in licensed establishments account for one quarter of all consumption (12% in bars or taverns and 13% in restaurants). Other drinking is done during outdoor activities (5%), sports activities (2%), at a club or meeting (2%) and when attending a concert or sports event (1%). Drinking locations are strongly related to the characteristics of the drinkers and how much they drink (Figure 2.3). Heavy drinking and drinking problems are associated with drinking in bars and taverns.

Alcohol Problems

PERSONAL DRINKING PROBLEMS: Respondents in the 1993 General Social Survey were asked if their drinking affected their social life, physical health, happiness, home life or marriage, work, or finances. The proportion of drinkers in each demographic group with problems, the average number of problems reported, and the proportion of people reporting each problem, are shown in Table 2.9. One in ten (9.2%) drinkers suffered at least one problem as a result of their drinking. The most common problems relate to physical health (5.1%) and financial position (4.7%).

Men are more likely to have drinking problems (11.9% versus 6.2% of women), especially around finances (6.7% versus 2.5% of women), work or school (2.0% versus 0.8% of women), home life and marriage (2.4% versus 1.1% for women) and physical health (6.7% versus 3.2% for women). Young people between the ages of 15 and 24 have the most difficulties, with problems declining after age 19. Since individuals who are single or divorced tend to drink more, they are also more likely to have alcohol-related problems (16.9% and 11.0) than married (5.9%) or widowed (5.6%) people.

Canadians with the lowest incomes (17.9%) are more likely to have drinking problems than those with the highest incomes (7.9%), especially money difficulties. Students and those looking for work

non sur la quantité. Par exemple, les diplômés universitaires sont plus nombreux à consommer de l'alcool que les autres, mais ils ont par contre tendance à consommer de moins grandes quantités à la fois. Ce sont les personnes qui cherchent un emploi qui consomment le plus. Dans l'ensemble, les étudiants consomment moins, mais ils sont plus nombreux à prendre au moins cinq consommations par occasion (63 %). Il n'existe aucun lien évident entre la taille de la collectivité et le niveau de consommation ou le nombre des occasions de forte consommation.

L'Enquête nationale sur l'alcool et les autres drogues de 1989 nous renseigne sur les lieux de consommation. On avait alors demandé aux participants combien souvent ils passaient une soirée tranquille à la maison, fréquentaient les bars, ou visitaient les amis, et combien souvent et quelles quantités d'alcool consommaient-ils lors de ces activités. De telles questions servent à évaluer dans quelle mesure les gens consomment dans différents contextes. Or à ce propos, la Figure 2.3 indique que l'on consomme surtout dans des contextes intimes, notamment lors de soirées tranquilles à la maison (18 %), de réceptions ou d'autres rencontres sociales (16 %), de visites d'amis (16 %) ou à d'autres personnes (15 %). L'alcool consommé dans les débits de boisson représente un quart de la consommation globale (12 % dans les bars ou tavernes et 13 % dans les restaurants). Le reste de la consommation est répartie entre les activités de plein air (5 %), les activités sportives (2 %), les rencontres à un club ou à une réunion (2 %) et les concerts ou les événements sportifs (1 %). Les lieux de consommation dépendent étroitement des caractéristiques des buveurs et des quantités consommées (Figure 2.3). Par exemple, on associe généralement les consommations élevées et les problèmes de consommation aux bars et aux tavernes.

Problèmes d'alcool

PROBLÈMES DE CONSOMMATION PERSONNELLE : Lors de l'Enquête sociale générale de 1993, les répondants devaient déclarer si leur consommation d'alcool avait eu des effets négatifs sur leur vie sociale, leur santé

(16.9%) are most likely have drinking problems while homemakers (4.7%), the retired (5.2%) and professionals (5.8%) have the least problems. Residents of the Atlantic provinces are the most likely to have drinking problems (13.0%) while Ontarians are the least likely to have such a problem (7.5%).

PROBLEMS WITH OTHERS' DRINKING: The 1993 General Social Survey also asked Canadians if they had problems because of someone else's drinking. The proportion of people with any of 10 difficulties and the average number of problems experienced for several demographic categories, is shown in Table 2.10.

Almost half of all Canadians (43.9%) said they had problems because of other people's drinking. The most common complaints were being disturbed by loud parties (23.8%), being insulted or humiliated by someone (20.9%), and having a serious argument (15.6%) as a result of someone's drinking.

Men (45.5%) are just as likely as women (42.5%) to have problems because of someone else's drinking behaviour. Men are more likely to be involved in an impaired driving incident or an accident, while women are more likely to have family or marital problems. For age, young people between age 15 and 17 (43.4%) and between 20 and 24 (66%) have difficulties in each category. After age 24, problems decline, to a low of 12.4% among those over 75. Family and marriage problems peak among those aged 25-34.

Problems from others' drinking are experienced most by single or divorced people (55.6% and 58.8%, respectively) and least by the widowed (19.4%). Separated or divorced people have more family or marriage problems (19.5%) or broken friendships (13.9%) than others.

Individuals with lower incomes had more personal problems (having an argument; broken friendships; family or marriage problems; being a passenger with an impaired driver; being assaulted; financial problems). The proportion of people who experienced these problems declined with higher incomes.

physique, leur bonheur, leur vie familiale ou conjugale, leur travail ou leur situation financière. Le Tableau 2.9 indique le taux des buveurs de chaque catégorie démographique ayant déclaré un problème, le nombre moyen des problèmes déclarés, et le taux des répondants ayant déclaré chaque problème cité. Un buveur sur 10 (9,2 %) avait éprouvé au moins un problème à cause de sa consommation. Les problèmes les plus souvent mentionnés concernaient la santé physique (5,1 %) et la situation financière (4,7 %).

Ce sont surtout les hommes qui éprouvent des problèmes (11,9 % contre 6,2 % chez les femmes) et ce, principalement au chapitre des finances (6,7 % contre 2,5 % chez les femmes), du travail ou des études (2,0 % contre 0,8 %), de la vie familiale ou conjugale (2,4 % contre 1,1 %) et de la santé physique (6,7 % contre 3,2 %). Ce sont les 15 à 24 ans qui en ont le plus grand nombre, mais celui-ci diminue après l'âge de 19 ans. Les célibataires ou les divorcés ayant tendance à consommer davantage, ils sont plus nombreux à éprouver des problèmes d'alcool (16,9 % et 11,0) que les personnes mariées (5,9 %) ou veuves (5,6 %).

Les Canadiens aux revenus les plus faibles (17,9 %) sont plus susceptibles que ceux jouissant des revenus les plus élevés (7,9 %) d'éprouver des problèmes, principalement d'ordre financier. Les étudiants et ceux qui cherchent un emploi sont les plus nombreux à déclarer un problème de consommation (16,9 %), tandis que les personnes au foyer (4,7 %), les retraités (5,2 %) et les professionnels (5,8 %) sont les moins nombreux. Les Maritimes comptent le plus grand nombre de citoyens touchés par des problèmes d'alcool (13,0 %) et l'Ontario, le plus petit nombre (7,5 %).

PROBLÈMES LIÉS À LA CONSOMMATION DES AUTRES : Lors de l'Enquête sociale générale de 1993, les répondants devaient déclarer s'ils avaient souffert de la consommation d'alcool d'une autre personne. Le Tableau 2.10 donne le pourcentage de ceux qui ont déclaré l'une ou l'autre des 10 difficultés mentionnées et le nombre moyen des problèmes déclarés selon diverses catégories démographiques. Dans l'ensemble, près de la moitié des

More than half (55.1%) of those with some post-secondary education had problems from someone else's drinking, while 35.1% with less than secondary education experienced these problems.

Semi-professional workers (53.7%), students (53.7%), those looking for work (52.0%) and unskilled workers (51.8%) were most likely to report problems with others' drinking. Those who are retired were least likely to report such problems (21.4%).

Residents of British Columbia (57.8%) were most likely to have problems with others' drinking, while those in Quebec (39.6%) were least likely to experience them. However, residents of the Prairie provinces were most likely to be a passenger with an impaired driver (10.8%) and Quebeckers were most likely to have financial problems because of another's drinking (2.9%). Rural residents were less likely to have a problem with others' drinking, but they had more problems when they did experience difficulties.

MORBIDITY: The estimated prevalence of alcoholism in Canada was 488,500 or 1,700 per 100,000 population in 1991 (Table 2.11). These estimates are calculated from the number of cirrhosis deaths each year using the Jellinek formula, based on estimates of the proportion of cirrhosis deaths attributed to alcoholism. These estimates give a crude assessment of how many Canadians are dependent on alcohol. The calculations are based on outdated formulas and should be interpreted with caution.

A study of the economic costs of substance abuse in Canada (Single et al., 1996) generated new estimates of morbidity and mortality attributable to the use of alcohol. Using aetiologic fractions by age, gender and province for 40 causes of disease and death partly or fully attributable to alcohol, the number of deaths, years of potential life lost, hospitalizations and hospitalization days attributable to alcohol, tobacco and illicit drugs are estimated.

The establishment of the most appropriate attributable factors for alcohol and other drug-related

Canadiens (43,9 %) ont affirmé avoir souffert de la consommation des autres. Ils ont le plus souvent déclaré le fait d'avoir été ennuyés par des fêtes bruyantes (23,8 %), insultés ou humiliés (20,9 %) et avoir eu une grave dispute (15,6 %).

Les hommes (45,5 %) et les femmes (42,5 %) sont aussi nombreux les uns que les autres à déclarer des problèmes dus à la consommation d'une autre personne. Les hommes sont plus nombreux à déclarer un incident ou un accident relié à la conduite en état d'ébriété, et les femmes, des problèmes familiaux ou conjugaux. Quant à l'âge, on constate que les jeunes de 15 à 17 ans (43,4 %) et de 20 à 24 ans (66 %) éprouvent des difficultés indépendamment de la catégorie. Après 24 ans, le taux des répondants ayant des problèmes diminuent pour tomber à 12,4 % seulement chez les plus de 75 ans. Les difficultés familiales et conjugales visent surtout les 25 à 34 ans.

Les groupes les plus touchés par la consommation des autres sont les personnes célibataires ou divorcées (55,6 % et 58,8 % respectivement) et les moins touchées, les personnes veuves (19,4 %). Les personnes séparées ou divorcées déclarent plus de problèmes familiaux ou conjugaux (19,5 %) ou des ruptures d'amitiés (13,9 %) que les autres.

Les répondants à plus faible revenu ont déclaré un plus grand nombre de problèmes (disputes; ruptures d'amitiés; difficultés familiales ou conjugales; passagers dans un véhicule conduit par une personne en état d'ébriété; victimes d'agressions; problèmes financiers). Le pourcentage des répondants ayant déclaré de tels problèmes diminue au fur et à mesure qu'augmente le revenu.

Plus de la moitié (55,1 %) des répondants ayant fait des études postsecondaires avaient éprouvé des problèmes dus à la consommation d'alcool d'une autre personne, contre seulement 35,1 % chez ceux n'ayant pas fait leur secondaire.

Les travailleurs semi-professionnels (53,7 %), les étudiants (53,7 %), les personnes en quête d'un emploi (52,0 %) et les travailleurs non spécialisés (51,8 %)

illnesses and social problems is based on a detailed literature reviews for each consequence. In the economic cost study, the most complete and recent reviews of the appropriate aetiologic fractions for alcohol, tobacco and illicit drugs (Single et al., 1996) are used to identify substance-related disorders and studies bearing upon the aetiologic fractions. The aetiologic fractions are tailored to the Canadian situation by taking differences in prevalence into account and making adjustments where indicated by Canadian studies and a special analysis of coroner reports (Rehm et al, 1996). Where there is sufficient information, separate aetiologic fractions are estimated for substance-related morbidity and mortality. It should also be noted that the cost study uses gross rather than net aetiologic fractions for those disorders where the use of substance has both adverse and beneficial effects on health—the deaths and hospitalizations prevented by the use of psychoactive substances is, however, computed and reported (Single et al., 1996).

Table 2.12 presents the resulting number of hospital separations and hospital days which may be attributed to alcohol use in 1992 by cause and gender. It is estimated that there were 86,076 hospital separations (56,474 for men and 29,602 for women) due to alcohol in 1992. The number of alcohol-related hospital days is estimated at 1,149,106 (755,205 for men and 393,902 for women). The greatest number of alcohol-related hospital separations are for accidental falls (16,901), alcohol dependence syndrome (14,316) and motor vehicle accidents (11,154). The greatest number of hospital days were for accidental falls (308,224 days), indicating the debilitating nature of many such injuries. The 86,076 hospitalizations due to alcohol constitute 2% of all hospitalizations, and the 1.15 million days of hospitalization due to alcohol represent 3% of the total days spent in hospital for any cause.

Table 2.13 presents the number of hospitalizations and hospitalization days attributed to alcohol in each province. The estimates are presented in terms of both

étaient plus nombreux que les autres à déclarer des problèmes dus à la consommation des autres, tandis que les retraités étaient les moins nombreux (21,4 %).

C'est en Colombie-Britannique que la consommation d'alcool des autres affecte le plus grand nombre de gens (57,8 %), et au Québec le moins grand nombre (39,6 %). Les répondants des Prairies sont plus nombreux à déclarer avoir été passagers dans un véhicule conduit par un conducteur en état d'ébriété (10,8 %) et les Québécois à avoir des problèmes financiers dus à la consommation d'une autre personne (2,9 %). Les résidants des régions rurales étaient moins nombreux à déclarer un problème dû à la consommation de quelqu'un d'autre, mais ceux à le faire déclaraient un plus grand nombre de problèmes que ceux des autres régions.

MORBIDITÉ : En 1991, la prévalence estimative de l'alcoolisme au Canada s'établissait à 488 500 personnes, soit à 1 700 habitants par tranche de 100 000 (Tableau 2.11). Ces estimations sont calculées à partir du nombre des décès par cirrhose enregistrés chaque année, selon la formule Jellinek, qui s'appuie sur des estimations de la proportion des décès par cirrhose imputable à l'alcoolisme. Elles donnent une évaluation approximative du nombre de Canadiens dépendants de l'alcool. Mais vu la désuétude des formules de calcul, il convient d'interpréter les estimations avec réserve.

Une étude des coûts économiques de l'abus des drogues au Canada (Single et coll., 1996) fournit de nouvelles estimations de la morbidité et de la mortalité attribuables à la consommation de l'alcool. Cette étude considère quarante causes de maladie et de décès attribuables en totalité ou en partie à l'alcool, le nombre de décès, les années de vie potentielle perdues, le nombre et les jours d'hospitalisation attribuables à l'alcool, au tabac et aux drogues illicites en se fondant sur les fractions étiologiques du risque selon l'âge, le sexe et la province.

Les facteurs de risque les plus pertinents aux maladies et aux problèmes sociaux reliés à l'alcool et aux autres drogues sont déterminés à partir d'une analyse

the number of cases and rates per unit of population. It may be seen that overall rates of alcohol attributable morbidity are highest in Prince Edward Island (489 hospitalizations per 100,000 population) and lowest in New Brunswick (178 hospitalizations per 100,000 population). The highest rate of hospitalization days, however, is in British Columbia (5,583 hospital days per 100,000 population).

MORTALITY: Table 2.14 presents the estimated number of deaths and years of potential life lost attributable to alcohol in Canada in 1992 by cause and by gender. It is estimated that 6,701 Canadians lost their lives as a result of alcohol consumption in 1992. The largest number of alcohol-related deaths stem from impaired driving accidents. It is estimated that 1,021 Canadian men and 456 women died in motor vehicle accidents in 1992 as the result of drinking. Alcoholic liver cirrhosis accounted for 960 deaths and there were 918 alcohol-related suicides.

Furthermore, the findings regarding years of life lost indicate that many of these deaths involved relatively young persons. Due to the high incidence of alcohol-related accidental deaths and suicides, the number of potential years of life lost is relatively high at 186,257 (134,495 years for mean and 51,762 for women). This represents 27.8 years lost per alcohol-related death. Motor vehicle deaths represent 22% of all alcohol-related deaths and 33% of productive life years lost, indicating the relatively young age of alcohol-related traffic fatalities.

The estimated 6,701 deaths due to alcohol represent 3% of total mortality in Canada for 1992. The 186,257 years of potential life lost due to alcohol represents 6% of the total years of potential life lost due to any cause.

Table 2.15 presents the number and rates of death and years of potential life lost due to alcohol for each of the provinces. It can be seen that the lowest rates of death due to alcohol was in Newfoundland (15 per 100,000 population). There was relatively little variation between the other provinces, with alcohol-related mortality rates ranging from 27 per 100,000 in

détaillée de la documentation concernant chacune des conséquences. Dans cette étude des coûts économiques, on s'est servi de l'analyse la plus complète et la plus récente des fractions étiologiques du risque pertinents à l'alcool, au tabac et aux drogues illicites (Single et coll.,1996) pour identifier les troubles reliés aux drogues et les études qui ont une portée sur les fractions étiologiques du risque. On y adapte ces dernières au contexte canadien, en tenant compte des écarts de prévalence et en apportant les correctifs exigés selon que l'indiquent les études canadiennes et une analyse particulière des rapports des médecins légistes (Rehm et coll., 1996). Lorsque l'information relevée est suffisante, on calcule plusieurs fractions étiologiques du risque en fonction de la morbidité et de la mortalité reliées aux drogues. Il importe cependant de signaler, en ce qui concerne les maladies, que l'étude des coûts économiques utilise des fractions étiologiques brutes plutît que nettes, lorsque la consommation des drogues a des effets tant négatifs que positifs sur la santé les décès et les hospitalisations évités par la consommation de substances psychotropes sont cependant calculés et relevés (Single et coll., 1996).

Le Tableau 2.12 présente les résultats en termes de départs des hôpitaux et de jours d'hospitalisation attribuables à la consommation d'alcool en 1992, selon la cause et le sexe. Le nombre de ces départs est évalué à 86 076 (56 474 chez les hommes contre 29 602 chez les femmes) et celui des jours d'hospitalisations à 1 149 106 (755 205 chez les hommes contre 393 902 chez les femmes). Le plus grand nombre de départs est dû aux chutes accidentelles (16 901), puis au syndrome de dépendance d'alcool (14 316), et aux accidents de véhicules automobiles (11 154). Le plus grand nombre de jours d'hospitalisation est attribuable aux chutes accidentelles (308 224 jours), ce qui indique l'effet affaiblissant de bon nombre des blessures causées par ce genre d'accident. Les 86 076 hospitalisations dues à l'alcool représentent 2 % de toutes les hospitalisations et les 1,15 million de jours d'hospitalisation due à l'alcool, 3 % du nombre total, indépendamment de la cause.

British Columbia to 23 in Ontario, Quebec and New Brunswick.

MORTALITY AND MORBIDITY PREVENTED BY ALCOHOL USE: The economic cost study (Single et al., 1996) also found that alcohol prevented 7,401 deaths in 1992 (5,162 males and 2,239 females). This includes deaths due to ischaemic heart disease (4,205 deaths prevented), stroke (2,965 deaths prevented), heart failure and ill-defined heart conditions (183 deaths prevented), and from various other causes(47 deaths prevented). Thus the number of deaths averted by the use of alcohol is greater than the number of deaths caused by alcohol use. However, alcohol-related mortality frequently involves young adults while the benefits of low level consumption to preventing heart disease generally involves preventing the loss of life among older adults. Thus, the years of potential life lost due to alcohol (186,257) is more than twice as large as the number of years of potential life saved by the beneficial effects of alcohol (88,656). With regard to morbidity, while alcohol accounts for approximately 86,000 hospitalizations in 1992, it is estimated that 45,414 hospitalizations (31,270 for males and 14,114 for females) were prevented by low level alcohol use in the same year. These were mainly due to the benefits of drinking to ischaemic heart disease (18,705), stroke (16,138), cholelithiasis (7,722), and heart conditions (2,312). Therefore, the number of hospitalizations caused by alcohol far outnumbers the number prevented by alcohol use.

FATAL ACCIDENTS: Motor vehicle injuries and fatalities are almost the only national data available on alcohol-related trauma. The contribution of alcohol to other types of trauma such as boating accidents, fires and assaults is not recorded. In 1993, 46% of fatally injured drivers had some alcohol in their blood, 39% were over the legal limit of 0.8% Blood Alcohol Concentration (BAC) and 30% were over .15% BAC (Table 2.20). Since 1991, the proportion of fatally injured drivers with BAC levels over the legal limit has increased, following a decade of decline. The proportion of drivers who are impaired is high among drivers between 20 and

Le Tableau 2.13 présente le nombre et les jours d'hospitalisation attribuables à l'alcool dans chaque province. Les estimations y sont données selon le nombre de cas et le pourcentage par tranche de la population. On y observe ainsi que les pourcentage globaux de morbidité attribuables à l'alcool sont les plus élevés à l'Ile-du-Prince-Edouard (489 hospitalisations par tranche de 100 000) et les plus bas au Nouveau-Brunswick (178 hospitalisations par 100 000). Le taux le plus élevé des jours d'hospitalisation revient cependant à la Colombie-Britannique (5 583 jours par 100 000 habitants).

MORTALITÉ : Le Tableau 2.14 présente le nombre estimatif des décès et des années de vie potentielle perdues attribuables à l'alcool au Canada en 1992 selon la cause et le sexe. On estime que 6 701 Canadiens sont décédés par suite de la consommation d'alcool en 1992, l'alcool au volant étant la principale cause. En fait, 1 021 Canadiens et 456 Canadiennes ont été tués dans des accidents automobiles causés par la consommation d'alcool. La cirrhose alcoolique du foie a pour sa part causé 960 décès et le suicide relié à l'alcool, 918.

Selon les résultats concernant les années de vie potentielle perdues, bon nombre de ces décès visaient de jeunes personnes. Vu le taux élevé de l'incidence des décès accidentels et des suicides reliés à l'alcool, le nombre des années de vie potentielle perdues, soit 186 257, est aussi relativement élevé (134 495 années chez les hommes contre 51 762 chez les femmes). Ces chiffres traduisent une perte de 27,8 années par décès relié à l'alcool. Les accidents de véhicules automobiles représentent 22 % de tous les décès reliés à l'alcool et 33 % des années de vie productive perdues, révélant ainsi l'âge relativement jeune des victimes de la route associées à la consommation d'alcool.

Les 6 701 décès estimatifs dus à l'alcool constituent 3 % de toutes les mortalités au Canada en 1992. Les 186 257 années de vie potentielle perdues en raison de l'alcool représentent 6 % du nombre total des années de vie potentielle perdues indépendamment de la cause.

25 (46.2%) and 26 and 35 (47.6%) (Table 2.21). Regionally, Prince Edward Island (60%) and Newfoundland (56.3%) have the highest proportion of fatally injured drivers who are impaired and Alberta (26.8%) has the lowest proportion.

In the 1993 General Social Survey, one in eight (12.9%) adults said that in the past year, they had driven after having two or more drinks (Table 2.22). Impaired driving was high among males, especially those between age 18 and 45 and with high incomes (Table 2.22). Quebeckers (19.4%) were the most likely to drive after drinking compared with the Prairies (13.4%), British Columbia (13.1%), the Atlantic provinces (10.7%) and Ontario (9.2).

References

Association of Canadian Distillers, personal communication, 1993

Brewers Association of Canada, personal communication, 1993

Canadian Wine Institute, personal communication, 1993

Pernanen, K., 1974. "Validity of survey data on alcohol use" in: R.J. Gibbins, et al (eds.), *Research Advances in Alcohol and Other Drug Problems, Vol. 1* (New York: Wiley and Sons).

Single, E. and Giesbrecht, N., 1979. "The 16% solution and other mysteries concerning the accuracy of alcohol consumption estimates based on sales data" *British Journal of Addictions* 74: 165-179.

Single, E., L. Robson, J. Rehm, et X. Xie. *The Costs of Substance Abuse in Canada*, Ottawa: Canadian Centre on Substance Abuse, 1996.

Le Tableau 2.15 présente le nombre et le taux des décès et des années de vie potentielle perdues à cause de l'alcool pour chaque province. Le taux des décès attribuables à l'alcool le plus bas revient à Terre-Neuve (15 par 100 000 habitants). On constate par ailleurs un écart assez léger entre les autres provinces, en ce qui concerne les taux de mortalité reliés à l'alcool, lesquels vont de 27 par 100 000 habitants en Colombie-Britannique à 23 en Ontario, au Québec et au Nouveau-Brunswick.

MORTALITÉ ET MORBIDITÉ ÉVITÉES PAR LA CONSOMMATION D'ALCOOL : L'étude des coûts économiques (Single et coll., 1996) a en outre établi que la consommation d'alcool avait permis d'éviter 7 401 décès en 1992 (5 162 chez les hommes contre 2 239 chez les femmes). Cela comprend les décès dus à la cardiopathie ischémique (4 205 décès évités), aux accidents cérébro-vasculaires (2 965 décès évités), aux insuffisances cardiaques et aux cardiopathies mal définies (183 décès évités), ainsi qu'ê d'autres causes diverses (47 décès évités). Ainsi la consommation d'alcool a permis d'éviter un plus grand nombre de décès qu'elle n'en a provoqués. Cependant, la mortalité reliée à l'alcool vise souvent de jeunes adultes tandis que les avantages d'une faible consommation d'alcool en vue de prévenir les maladies cardiaques sauve généralement la vie d'adultes plus âgés. Par conséquent, les années de vie potentielle perdues reliées à l'alcool (186 257) sont deux fois plus importantes que celles sauvées par les effets bénéfiques de l'alcool (88 656). En ce qui concerne la morbidité en 1992, bien que l'alcool ait causé quelque 86 000 cas d'hospitalisation, on estime que 45 414 cas (31 270 chez les hommes contre 14 114 chez les femmes) ont été évités grâce aux effets bénéfiques d'une faible consommation d'alcool notamment pour les victimes de cardiopathie ischémique (18 705), d'accidents cérébro-vasculaires (16 138), de cholélithiase (7 722), et de cardiopathies diverses (2 312). Par conséquent, le nombre des hospitalisations causées par la consommation d'alcool dépasse de loin celui des hospitalisations évitées par une telle consommation.

Accidents mortels

Les blessures et les décès dus aux accidents de la route constituent à peu près les seules données nationales disponibles sur les accidents reliés à l'alcool. La part de l'alcool dans les autres genres d'accidents, tels les accidents de navigation, les feux et les agressions n'est pas enregistrée. En 1993, 46 % des conducteurs mortellement blessés présentaient des traces d'alcool dans le sang, dont 39 % une alcoolémie excédant la limite légale de 0,08 % et 30 %, une alcoolémie supérieure à 0,15 % (Tableau 2.20). On note que depuis 1991, après une période de régression de dix ans, la proportion des conducteurs mortellement blessés présentant une alcoolémie supérieure à la limite officielle augmente. Le taux des conducteurs en état d'ébriété est élevé chez les 20 à 25 ans (46,2 %) et les 26 à 35 ans (47,6 %) (Tableau 2.21). A l'échelle régionale, c'est à l'Ile-du-Prince-Edouard (60 %) et à Terre-Neuve (56,3 %) que l'on retrouve les plus hauts taux de conducteurs mortellement blessés en état d'ébriété, et en Alberta (26,8 %), le plus bas.

Lors de l'Enquête sociale générale de 1993, un adulte sur huit (12,9 %) a déclaré avoir conduite un véhicule après avoir pris deux consommations ou plus (Tableau 2.22). Un tel comportement est fréquent chez les hommes, surtout chez les 18 à 45 ans et ceux ayant un revenu élevé (Tableau 2.22). Les plus nombreux à prendre le volant après avoir consommé de l'alcool étaient les Québécois (19,4 % contre 13,4 % dans les Prairies, 13,1 % en Colombie-Britannique, 10,7 % dans les Maritimes et 9,2 % en Ontario).

Références

Association canadienne des distillateurs, communication personnelle, 1993.

Association des brasseurs du Canada, communication personnelle, 1993.

Institut canadien du vin, communication personnelle, 1993.

Pernanen, K., *Validity of survey data on alcool use*. In R.J. Gibbins et coll. (éd.), Research Advances in Alcohol and Other Drug Problems, Vol. 1 (New York: Wiley and Sons, 1974).

Single, E. et Giesbrecht, N., 1979. "The 16% solution and other mysteries concerning the accuracy of alcohol consumption estimates based on sales data" *British Journal of Addictions 74: 165-179.*

Single, E., L. Robson, J. Rehm, et X. Xie. *The Costs of Substance Abuse in Canada*, Ottawa: Centre canadien de lutte contre l'alcoolisme et les toxicomanies, 1996.

TABLE 2.1   **TABLEAU 2.1**

Proportion reporting the consumption of alcohol in the past year among those age 15 or older, Canada, 1979 to 1994

Taux des 15 ans et plus ayant déclaré avoir consommé de l'alcool l'année précédente, Canada, 1979 à 1994

YEAR/ ANNEE	SURVEY/ENQUETE	NON-DRINKERS/NON-BUVEURS		CURRENT DRINKERS[2]/ BUVEURS ACTUELS[2]
		NEVER/ JAMAIS BU	FORMER[1]/ ANCIENS BUVEURS[1]	
1978-79	Canada Health Survey/ Enquête Santé Canada	11.5 %	3.7 %	84.0 %
1985	Health Promotion Survey/ Enquête Promotion de la santé	7.7	10.4	81.4
1985	General Social Survey/ Enquête sociale générale	13.0	6.0	81.0
1989	National Alcohol and Other Drugs Survey/ Enquête nationale sur l'alcool et les autres drogues	6.6	15.7	77.7
1990	Health Promotion Survey/ Enquête Promotion de la santé	8.0	11.0	81.0
1991	General Social Survey/ Enquête sociale générale	9.0	12.0	79.0
1993	General Social Survey/ Enquête sociale générale	7.7	18.0	74.4
1994	Canadian Alcohol and Other Drugs survey/ Enquête canadienne sur l'alcool et les autres drogues	12.8	13.5	72.3

[1] A former drinker is anyone who used to drink alcohol but has had no alcoholic drinks in the last 12 months./Est considéré ancien buveur quiconque avait l'habitude de consommer de l'alcool et qui n'a consommé aucune boisson alcoolique durant les 12 derniers mois.

[2] In Canada Health Survey, Canada's Health Promotion Survey, and General Social Survey, current drinker is anyone who drinks alcoholic beverages at once a month. In the National Alcohol and Other Drugs Survey, current drinker is anyone who consumed alcohol in the 12 months preceding the survey. Aux fins de l'Enquête Santé Canada, de l'Enquête Promotion de la santé, et de l'Enquête sociale générale,est considéré buveur quiconque consomme des boissons alcooliques au moins une fois par mois. Aux fins de l'Enquête nationale sur l'alcool et les autres drogues, est considéré buveur quiconque a consommé de l'alcool durant les 12 mois précédents.

Source: Health and Welfare Canada, *The Health of Canadians - Report of the Canada Health Survey* (Ottawa: Health and Welfare Canada and Statistics Canada, Catalogue 82-538E, June 1981); Health and Welfare Canada, *Canada's Health Promotion Survey* (Ottawa: Health and Welfare, 1988); Statistics Canada, *General Social Survey Analysis Series, Health and Social Support, 1985* (Ottawa: Statistics Canada, Catalogue 11-612E, No. 1, December 1987); *Health and Welfare Canada, National Alcohol and Other Drugs Survey* (Ottawa: Health and Welfare Canada, 1990); *Health and Welfare, Canada's Health Promotion Survey 1990 - Technical Report* (Ottawa: Health and Welfare Canada, 1993); Statistics Canada, Millar, W. "A Trend to a Healthier Lifestyle" in *Canadian Social Trends, No.24 - Spring 1992* (Ottawa: Statistics Canada, Catalogue 11-008, 1992); Statistics Canada, *General Social Survey*, analysis prepared by Eric Single, Joan Brewster, Patricia MacNeil and Jeffrey Hatcher (Ottawa: Canadian Centre on Substance Abuse, 1994); Canadian Alcohol and Other Drugs Survey data obtained from the Canadian Centre for Health Information, Statistics Canada.

Santé et Bien-Etre Canada, *La santé des Canadiens, Rapport de l'Enquête Santé Canada* (Ottawa : Santé et Bien-être Canada et Statistique Canada, Catalogue n° 82-538F, juin 1981; Santé et Bien-être Canada, *Enquête Promotion de la santé* (Ottawa: Santé et Bien-être Canada, 1988); Statistique Canada, *Enquête sociale générale, Série analytique, Santé et aide du milieu* (Ottawa: Statistique Canada, Catalogue n° 11-612F, n° 1, décembre 1987); Santé et Bien-Etre Canada, *Enquête nationale sur l'alcool et les autres drogues* (Ottawa : Santé et Bien-être Canada, 1990). Santé et Bien-être Canada, *Enquête Promotion de la santé 1990 - Rapport technique* (Ottawa : Santé et Bien-être Canada, 1993); Statistique Canada, Millar, W. «Vers de meilleures habitudes de vie» in Tendances sociales, n° 24, printemps 1992 (Ottawa : Statistique Canada, Catalogue n° 11-008, 1992); Statistique Canada, Enquête sociale générale, analyse de Eric Single, Joan Brewster, Patricia MacNeil et Jeffrey Hatcher. (Ottawa : Centre canadien de lutte contre l'alcoolisme et les toxicomanies, 1994); Données de l'Enquête canadienne sur l'alcool et les autre drogues, obtenues du Centre canadien d'information sur la santé, Statistique Canada.

TABLE 2.2

TABLEAU 2.2

Type of drinker by age, gender and marital status among those age 15 or older, Canada, 1994

Genres de buveurs selon l'âge, le sexe et l'état matrimonial, population des 15 ans et plus, Canada, 1994

VARIABLE	DRINKING STATUS/GENRES DE BUVEURS		
	NEVER/ JAMAIS BU	FORMER[1]/ ANCIENS BUVEURS[1]	CURRENT DRINKERS[2]/ BUVEURS ACTUELS[2]
Gender/Sexe:			
Male/Hommes	8.9 %	11.2 %	78.1 %
Female/Femmes	16.7	15.6	66.7
Total 15+/Total des 15+	**12.8**	**13.5**	**72.3**
Age/Age:			
5-17	21.8	12.8	65
18-19	11.5	9.0	79.6
20-24	8.0	7.1	83.9
25-34	8.6	10.4	79.9
35-44	9.2	11.7	77.7
45-54	10.8	14.7	73
55-64	16.7	16.8	64.3
65-74	21.6	21.2	54.8
75+	28.4	24.0	46.2
Marital Status/Etat matrimonial:			
Single/Célibataire	12.3	10.6	76.5
Married or cohabiting/Marié ou conjoint de fait	11.3	13.9	73.4
Widowed, divorced or separated/ Veuf, divorcé ou séparé	20.3	17.7	61.0

[1] A former drinker is anyone who used to drink alcohol but has had n° alcoholic drink in the past 12 months. Est considéré ancien buveur quiconque avait l'habitude de consommer de l'alcool et qui n'a consommé aucune boisson alcoolique durant les 12 derniers mois.

[2] Respondents who have consumed at least one drink of alcohol in the past 12 months. Participants ayant pris au moins une consommation alcoolique durant les 12 derniers mois.

Source: Data obtained from the Canadian Centre for Health Information, Statistics Canada

Données obtenues du Centre canadien d'information sur la santé, Statistique Canada.

TABLE 2.3

TABLEAU 2.3

Type of drinker by income, education, employment status, and region, among those age 15 or older, Canada, 1994

Genres de buveurs selon le revenu, le niveau d'instruction, la situation d'emploi, et la région, population des 15 ans et plus, Canada, 1994

VARIABLE	DRINKING STATUS/GENRES DE BUVEURS		
	NEVER/ JAMAIS BU	FORMER[1]/ ANCIENS BUVEURS[1]	CURRENT DRINKERS[2]/ BUVEURS ACTUELS[2]
Income/Revenu :			
Lowest/Inférieur	17.3 %	18.3 %	64.4 %
Lower middle/Inférieur à moyen	19.1	15.9	64.3
Middle/Moyen	10.4	15.2	74.3
Upper middle/Moyen à supérieur	6.8	10.8	82.4
Highest/Supérieur	5.0	8.8	86.1
Education/Niveau d'instruction :			
Completed university/Diplôme universitaire	1.3	1.4	12.9
Some post-secondary/Postsecondaire partiel	2.6	3.0	22.4
Secondary/Secondaire	2.6	3.0	17.9
Less than secondary/Moins que le secondaire	4.8	5.2	15.7
Employment/Situation d'emploi :			
Professional/Professionnel	6.5	9.5	84.0
White Collar/Cols blancs	8.5	10.4	81.0
Blue Collar/Cols bleus	7.1	9.8	83.1
Unemployed/Chômeurs	15.6	13.1	71.2
Student/Aux études	18.0	10.3	71.6
Retired/A la retraite	20.7	22.1	56.3
Homemaker/Au foyer	18.8	21.7	59.3
Other/Autre	15.0	22.5	62.5
Region/Région :			
Nfld./T.-N.	17.0	11.5	71.4
P.E.I./Î.-P.-E.	16.9	16.8	67.2
N.S./N.-É.	14.3	13.5	72.1
N.B./N.-B.	15.6	16.4	67.8
Que./Québec	11.0	11.0	73.9
Ont./Ont.	14.3	13.1	69.4
Man./Man.	10.4	15.6	73.6
Sask./Sask.	8.5	18.2	73.0
Alta./Alb.	9.7	13.7	76.4
B.C./C.-B.	7.0	16.8	75.6

[1] A former drinker is anyone who used to drink alcohol but has had n° alcoholic drink in the past 12 months./Est considéré ancien buveur quiconque avait l'habitude de consommer de l'alcool et qui n'a consommé aucune boisson alcoolique durant les 12 derniers mois.

[2] Respondents who have consumed at least one drink of alcohol in the past 12 months./Participants ayant consommé au moins une boisson alcoolique durant les 12 derniers mois.

Source: Data obtained from the Canadian Centre for Health Information, Statistics Canada

Données obtenues du Centre canadien d'information sur la santé, Statistique Canada.

| TABLE 2.4 | TABLEAU 2.4 |

Sales of beverage alcohol and volume of absolute alcohol per person age 15 or older, Canada and provinces, 1988-1989 to 1992-1993

Ventes des boissons alcooliques et volume d'alcool[1] absolu par personne, population des 15 ans et plus, Canada et provinces, 1988-1989 à 1992-1993

PROVINCE	BEVERAGE ALCOHOL (x000 litres)/ BOISSONS ALCOOLIQUES (milliers de litres)			ABSOLUTE ALCOHOL[1]/PERSON 15+ (litres) ALCOOL ABSOLU[1] PAR PERSONNE, 15+ (litres)			
	BEER/ BIERE	WINE/ VIN	SPIRITS/ SPIRITUEUX	BEER/ BIERE	WINE/ VIN	SPIRITS/ SPIRITUEUX	TOTAL/ TOTAL
1988/89							
Nfld./T.-N.	52,302	1,613	3,917	5.91	0.44	3.35	9.70
P.E.I./I.-P.-E.	8,618	559	780	4.24	0.66	2.91	7.82
N.S./N.-É.	62,474	5,364	6,352	4.33	0.90	3.33	8.55
N.B./N.-B.	47,841	3,468	3,128	4.11	0.72	2.04	6.87
Que./Québec	554,336	80,840	21,299	4.99	1.76	1.45	8.20
Ont./Ont.	836,569	84,741	67,227	5.24	1.28	3.19	9.70
Man./Man.	79,595	6,109	7,504	4.56	0.84	3.25	8.65
Sask./Sask.	63,681	4,381	7,001	4.01	0.67	3.34	8.02
Alta./Alb.	173,028	21,002	19,445	4.53	1.33	3.86	9.71
B.C./C.-B.	233,169	47,218	21,516	4.61	2.25	3.22	10.07
Yukon/Yukon	3,569	330	285	8.73	1.95	5.28	15.95
N.W.T./T.N.-O.	4,271	272	516	5.48	0.84	5.01	11.34
Canada	**2,119,453**	**255,897**	**158,970**	**4.92**	**1.43**	**2.79**	**9.14**
1989/90							
Nfld./T.-N.	49,834	1,586	3,983	5.55	0.42	3.35	9.32
P.E.I./I.-P.-E.	8,461	596	771	4.13	0.70	2.84	7.66
N.S./N.-É.	62,313	5,119	6,233	4.26	0.84	3.22	8.31
N.B./N.-B.	47,708	3,480	3,039	4.04	0.71	1.94	6.69
Que./Québec	553,539	78,589	19,749	4.89	1.67	1.32	7.88
Ont./Ont.	829,824	80,051	63,866	5.04	1.17	2.93	9.13
Man./Man.	74,476	5,761	7,250	4.24	0.79	3.12	8.15
Sask./Sask.	57,955	4,089	6,641	3.67	0.62	3.17	7.46
Alta./Alb.	172,837	20,080	18,875	4.44	1.24	3.66	9.34
B.C./C.-B.	246,930	46,143	21,163	4.74	2.12	3.07	9.93
Yukon/Yukon	3,617	336	268	8.60	1.92	4.81	15.32
N.W.T./T.N.-O.	4,087	257	533	5.13	0.77	5.05	10.96
Canada	**2,111,581**	**246,087**	**152,371**	**4.79**	**1.34**	**2.61**	**8.74**
1990/91							
Nfld./T.-N.	48,904	1,543	3,936	5.37	0.40	3.25	9.02
P.E.I./I.-P.-E.	8,310	561	732	4.02	0.65	2.66	7.33
N.S./N.-É.	59,492	4,667	5,762	4.02	0.75	2.93	7.70
N.B./N.-B.	46,473	3,422	2,943	3.88	0.68	1.85	6.41
Que./Québec	540,195	72,764	17,759	4.70	1.51	1.16	7.38
Ont./Ont.	813,304	79,166	59,700	4.83	1.12	2.67	8.62
Man./Man.	70,946	5,586	6,908	4.02	0.75	2.94	7.72
Sask./Sask.	54,766	3,896	6,461	3.49	0.59	3.10	7.19
Alta./Alb.	177,230	19,452	18,209	4.44	1.16	3.44	9.04
B.C./C.-B.	254,756	45,880	20,640	4.73	2.04	2.89	9.66
Yukon/Yukon	3,581	335	261	8.32	1.86	4.56	14.74
N.W.T./T.N.-O.	3,968	251	493	4.82	0.73	4.51	10.07
Canada	**2,081,925**	**237,523**	**143,804**	**4.63**	**1.26**	**2.41**	**8.30**

TABLE 2.4 (concluded)   **TABLEAU 2.4** (fin)

Sales of beverage alcohol and volume of absolute alcohol per person age 15 or older, Canada and provinces, 1988-1989 to 1992-1993

Ventes des boissons alcooliques et volume d'alcool[1] absolu par personne, population des 15 ans et plus, Canada et provinces, 1988-1989 à 1992-1993

PROVINCE	BEVERAGE ALCOHOL (x000 litres)/ BOISSONS ALCOOLIQUES (milliers de litres)			ABSOLUTE ALCOHOL[1]/PERSON 15+ (litres) ALCOOL ABSOLU[1] PAR PERSONNE, 15+ (litres)			
	BEER/ BIERE	WINE/ VIN	SPIRITS/ SPIRITUEUX	BEER/ BIERE	WINE/ VIN	SPIRITS/ SPIRITUEUX	TOTAL/ TOTAL
1991/92							
Nfld./T.-N.	47,755	1,732	3,649	5.19	0.45	2.98	8.62
P.E.I./Î.-P.-E.	7,825	512	694	3.78	0.59	2.53	6.90
N.S./N.-É.	58,995	4,784	5,645	3.95	0.76	2.85	7.56
N.B./N.-B.	45,696	3,332	2,765	3.77	0.66	1.72	6.15
Que./Québec	524,102	70,430	16,723	4.52	1.45	1.09	7.06
Ont./Ont.	788,218	78,442	55,389	4.62	1.10	2.45	8.17
Man./Man.	70,674	5,296	6,912	3.98	0.71	2.93	7.62
Sask./Sask.	55,204	3,592	6,214	3.53	0.55	2.99	7.06
Alta./Alb.	182,104	19,549	17,384	4.48	1.15	3.22	8.86
B.C./C.-B.	256,761	42,963	20,716	4.66	1.86	2.83	9.35
Yukon/Yukon	3,687	373	249	8.21	1.98	4.18	14.37
N.W.T./T.N.-O.	3,928	245	478	4.66	0.69	4.27	9.63
Canada	**2,044,949**	**231,250**	**136,818**	**4.49**	**1.21**	**2.26**	**7.97**
1992/93							
Nfld./T.-N.	46,323	1,686	3,508	5.00	0.43	2.85	8.28
P.E.I./Î.-P.-E.	7,789	488	680	3.78	0.56	2.48	6.82
N.S./N.-É.	58,431	4,451	5,404	3.90	0.71	2.71	7.32
N.B./N.-B.	44,599	3,275	2,756	3.67	0.64	1.71	6.01
Que./Québec	515,994	70,544	15,704	4.41	1.44	1.01	6.85
Ont./Ont.	738,902	77,417	50,565	4.28	1.07	2.21	7.56
Man./Man.	67,851	5,289	6,808	3.83	0.71	2.89	7.43
Sask./Sask.	53,112	3,409	5,917	3.40	0.52	2.85	6.77
Alta./Alb.	177,388	19,245	16,391	4.31	1.12	3.00	8.43
B.C./C.-B.	255,216	42,442	20,369	4.53	1.80	2.72	9.05
Yukon/Yukon	3,687	442	300	7.89	2.26	4.83	14.98
N.W.T./T.N.-O.	3,797	248	437	4.43	0.69	3.84	8.96
Canada	**1,973,089**	**228,936**	**128,839**	**4.29**	**1.19**	**2.11**	**7.58**

[1] For notes on conversion factors please see discussion prior to tables/Pour les notes sur les facteurs de conversion, voir l'exposé précédant les tableaux.

Source: Statistics Canada, *The Control and Sale of Alcoholic Beverages in Canada - Fiscal Year Ended March 31, 1993* (Ottawa: Statistics Canada, Catalogue No. 63-202, 1994).

Statistique Canada, *Le contrôle et la vente des boissons alcooliques au Canada - Exercice financier clos le 31 mars 1993* (Ottawa: Statistique Canada, Catalogue n° 63-202, 1994).

TABLE 2.5

TABLEAU 2.5

Percentage contribution of major beverage types of total alcohol[1] sales, Canada and provinces, 1983/84 to 1992/93

Ventilation en pourcentage des ventes globales d'alcool[1] selon les principales catégories de boissons alcooliques, Canada et provinces, 1983-1984 à 1992-1993

PROVINCE	1983/84	1984/85	1985/86	1986/87	1987/88	1988/89	1989/90	1990/91	1991/92	1992/93
					BEER/BIERE					
Nfld./T.-N.	59.0	61.4	52.3	60.5	60.7	60.9	59.5	59.5	60.2	60.3
P.E.I./Î.-P.-E.	52.1	53.5	53.8	54.0	54.3	54.3	53.8	54.8	54.8	55.3
N.S./N.-É.	49.4	51.6	51.9	50.6	51.9	50.6	51.2	52.2	52.2	53.2
N.B./N.-B.	58.7	60.0	59.9	59.1	60.2	59.9	60.4	60.5	61.4	60.9
Que./Québec	60.5	60.4	60.1	61.1	61.0	60.9	62.1	63.7	64.1	64.3
Ont./Ont.	52.2	52.0	53.9	53.7	53.6	54.0	55.2	56.0	56.6	56.6
Man./Man.	50.8	52.4	49.7	51.8	51.7	52.7	52.1	52.0	52.2	51.5
Sask./Sask.	46.2	48.4	47.2	47.5	47.3	50.0	49.1	48.6	49.9	50.2
Alta./Alb.	42.0	43.3	42.3	44.6	45.6	46.6	47.5	49.1	50.6	51.2
B.C./C.-B.	42.4	43.3	42.9	44.0	44.3	45.7	47.7	49.0	49.8	50.0
Yukon/Yukon	48.5	50.8	51.8	52.2	55.1	54.7	56.1	56.4	57.1	52.7
N.W.T./T.N.-O.	44.9	45.4	46.2	49.2	48.7	48.3	46.8	47.9	48.4	49.4
Canada	**51.7**	**52.1**	**52.3**	**53.0**	**53.3**	**53.8**	**54.8**	**55.8**	**56.4**	**56.5**
					WINE/VIN					
Nfld./T.-N.	4.8	4.8	6.0	5.0	5.0	4.5	4.5	4.5	5.2	5.2
P.E.I./Î.-P.-E.	8.1	7.6	8.3	9.0	8.6	8.5	9.1	8.8	8.6	8.3
N.S./N.-É.	10.1	10.5	10.6	11.1	12.1	10.5	10.1	9.8	10.1	9.7
N.B./N.-B.	8.7	9.1	9.2	9.7	9.8	10.5	10.6	10.6	10.7	10.7
Que./Québec	17.2	18.3	19.9	20.1	20.8	21.4	21.2	20.5	20.6	21.0
Ont./Ont.	13.5	14.2	14.1	13.9	13.9	13.2	12.8	13.0	13.4	14.2
Man./Man.	10.5	10.4	11.3	11.5	10.5	9.7	9.7	9.8	9.3	9.6
Sask./Sask.	8.8	9.1	9.7	9.3	9.5	8.3	8.3	8.3	7.8	7.7
Alta./Alb.	13.2	13.7	14.8	13.9	13.9	13.7	13.3	12.9	13.0	13.3
B.C./C.-B.	20.5	21.4	22.3	22.1	23.1	22.3	21.4	21.1	19.9	19.9
Yukon/Yukon	14.0	14.0	14.4	13.7	12.1	12.2	12.5	12.6	13.8	15.1
N.W.T./T.N.-O.	8.1	8.5	8.0	7.7	7.6	7.4	7.1	7.2	7.2	7.7
Canada	**14.6**	**15.3**	**15.9**	**15.7**	**16.0**	**15.7**	**15.3**	**15.2**	**15.2**	**15.7**
					SPIRITS/SPIRITUEUX					
Nfld./T.-N.	36.2	33.8	41.7	34.5	34.3	34.6	35.9	36.0	34.6	34.4
P.E.I./Î.-P.-E.	39.9	38.8	37.9	37.0	37.1	37.2	37.1	36.4	36.6	36.4
N.S./N.-É.	40.5	37.9	37.5	38.3	36.0	38.9	38.7	38.1	37.6	37.1
N.B./N.-B.	32.6	30.8	30.9	31.2	30.0	29.7	29.0	28.9	28.0	28.4
Que./Québec	22.2	21.3	20.0	18.8	18.2	17.7	16.7	15.8	15.4	14.7
Ont./Ont.	34.2	33.8	32.1	32.4	32.5	32.8	32.1	31.0	30.0	29.2
Man./Man.	38.7	37.1	39.0	36.6	37.8	37.6	38.3	38.2	38.5	38.9
Sask./Sask.	45.1	42.5	43.2	43.2	43.2	41.7	42.5	43.2	42.3	42.1
Alta./Alb.	44.7	43.0	43.0	41.5	40.5	39.7	39.2	38.0	36.4	35.6
B.C./C.-B.	37.1	35.3	34.8	34.0	32.6	32.0	30.9	29.9	30.3	30.1
Yukon/Yukon	37.5	35.3	33.8	34.1	32.8	33.1	31.4	31.0	29.1	32.3
N.W.T./T.N.-O.	47.0	46.1	45.8	43.1	43.6	44.2	46.1	44.8	44.4	42.8
Canada	**33.8**	**32.6**	**31.8**	**31.3**	**30.7**	**30.6**	**29.9**	**29.0**	**28.4**	**27.8**

[1] For notes on conversion factors please see discussion prior to tables/Pour les notes sur les facteurs de conversion, voir l'exposé précédant les tableaux.

Source: Statistics Canada, *The Control and Sale of Alcoholic Beverages in Canada - Fiscal Year Ended March 31, 1993* (Ottawa: Statistics Canada, Catalogue No. 63-202, 1994).

Statistique Canada, *Le contrôle et la vente des boissons alcooliques au Canada - Exercice financier clos le 31 mars 1993* (Ottawa: Statistique Canada, Catalogue n° 63-202, 1994).

TABLE 2.6

TABLEAU 2.6

Sales of alcoholic beverages[1] in litres of absolute alcohol per person age 15 or older, Canada and provinces, 1978-1979 to 1992-1993

Ventes des boissons alcooliques[1] en litres d'alcool absolu par personne, population des 15 ans et plus, Canada et provinces, 1978-1979 à 1992-1993

PROVINCE	1978/79	1979/80	1980/81	1981/82	1982/83	1983/84	1984/85	1985/86
Nfld./T.-N.	10.75	11.12	10.67	10.39	10.39	9.91	9.78	8.75
P.E.I./I.-P.-E.	11.39	10.50	10.22	9.15	9.35	8.83	8.76	8.44
N.S./N.-É.	10.50	10.25	10.10	9.87	9.64	9.28	9.15	8.91
N.B./N.-B.	9.37	9.21	9.05	8.67	8.58	8.03	7.84	7.61
Que./Québec	10.28	9.56	9.77	9.50	8.92	8.92	8.77	8.58
Ont./Ont.	11.54	11.23	11.14	11.01	10.73	10.38	10.10	10.05
Man./Man.	10.72	10.87	11.14	10.96	10.56	10.06	10.10	9.72
Sask./Sask.	10.28	10.10	10.13	9.80	9.75	9.47	9.16	8.86
Alta./Alb.	13.27	13.07	10.23	13.21	12.46	11.62	11.12	11.14
B.C./C.-B.	12.77	12.98	12.75	12.84	12.22	11.59	11.36	10.93
Yukon/Yukon	19.75	19.99	21.69	20.32	18.16	17.24	17.38	16.50
N.W.T./T.N.-O.	13.46	12.56	12.95	13.17	13.11	12.73	12.75	12.02
Canada	**11.28**	**10.99**	**10.74**	**10.86**	**10.44**	**10.09**	**9.86**	**9.68**

PROVINCE	1986/87	1987/88	1988/89	1989/90	1990/91	1991/92	1992/93	
Nfld./T.-N.	9.47	9.70	9.70	9.32	9.02	8.62	8.28	
P.E.I./I.-P.-E.	8.07	7.90	7.82	7.66	7.33	6.90	6.82	
N.S./N.-É.	8.71	8.50	8.55	8.31	7.70	7.56	7.32	
N.B./N.-B.	7.26	7.12	6.87	6.69	6.41	6.15	6.01	
Que./Québec	8.16	8.34	8.20	7.88	7.38	7.06	6.85	
Ont./Ont.	9.88	10.07	9.70	9.13	8.62	8.17	7.56	
Man./Man.	9.18	9.04	8.65	8.15	7.72	7.62	7.43	
Sask./Sask.	8.46	8.24	8.02	7.46	7.19	7.06	6.77	
Alta./Alb.	10.47	10.00	9.71	9.34	9.04	8.86	8.43	
B.C./C.-B.	10.96	10.66	10.07	9.93	9.66	9.35	9.05	
Yukon/Yukon	16.87	16.58	15.95	15.32	14.74	14.37	14.98	
N.W.T./T.N.-O.	11.22	11.24	11.34	10.96	10.07	9.63	8.96	
Canada	**9.41**	**9.43**	**9.14**	**8.74**	**8.30**	**7.97**	**7.58**	

[1] For notes on conversion factors please see discussion prior to tables./Pour une discussion des facteurs de conversion, veuillez voir le texte avant les tableaux.

Source: Statistics Canada, *The Control and Sale of Alcoholic Beverages in Canada 1980, 1981, 1982, 1983, 1984, 1985, 1986, 1992*, and *1993* (Ottawa: Statistics Canada, Catalogue No. 63-202, 1982, 1983, 1984, 1985, 1986, 1987, 1989, 1993 and 1994 respectively). Additional data was obtained from the Public Institutions Division, Statistics Canada.

Statistique Canada, *Le contrôle et la vente des boissons alcooliques au Canada, 1980, 1981, 1982, 1983, 1984, 1985, 1986, 1992 et 1993.* (Ottawa : Statistique Canada, Catalogue n° 63-202, 1982, 1983, 1984, 1985, 1986, 1987, 1989, 1993, et 1994 respectivement). Des données supplémentaires ont été obtenues de la Division des institutions publiques, Statistique Canada.

TABLE 2.7   **TABLEAU 2.7**

Sales of alcoholic beverages[1], in drinks[2] per week per person age 15 or older, Canada and provinces, 1978/79 to 1992/93

Ventes des boissons alcooliques[1] selon le nombre de consommations[2] hebdomadaires par personne, population des 15 ans et plus, Canada et provinces, 1978-1979 à 1992-1993

PROVINCE	1978/79	1979/80	1980/81	1981/82	1982/83	1983/84	1984/85	1985/86
Nfld./T.-N.	12.2	12.6	12.1	11.8	11.8	11.2	11.1	9.9
P.E.I./Î.-P.-É.	12.9	11.9	11.6	10.4	10.6	10.0	9.9	9.6
N.S./N.-É.	11.9	11.6	11.4	11.2	10.9	10.5	10.4	10.1
N.B./N.-B.	10.6	10.4	10.2	9.8	9.7	9.1	8.9	8.6
Que./Québec	11.6	10.8	11.0	10.8	10.1	10.1	9.9	9.7
Ont./Ont.	13.1	12.7	12.6	12.5	12.1	11.7	11.4	11.4
Man./Man.	12.1	12.3	12.6	12.4	12.0	11.4	11.4	11.0
Sask./Sask.	11.6	11.4	11.5	11.1	11.0	10.7	10.4	10.0
Alta./Alb.	15.0	14.8	11.6	14.9	14.1	13.1	12.6	12.
B.C./C.-B.	14.4	14.7	14.4	14.5	13.8	13.1	12.9	12.4
Yukon/Yukon	22.3	22.6	24.5	23.0	20.5	19.5	19.7	18.7
N.W.T./T.N.-O.	15.2	14.2	14.6	14.9	14.8	14.4	14.4	13.6
Canada	**12.8**	**12.4**	**12.1**	**12.3**	**11.8**	**11.4**	**11.2**	**10.9**

PROVINCE	1986/87	1987/88	1988/89	1989/90	1990/91	1991/92	1992/93	
Nfld./T.-N.	10.7	11.0	11.0	10.5	10.2	9.7	9.4	
P.E.I./Î.-P.-É.	9.1	8.9	8.8	8.7	8.3	7.8	7.7	
N.S./N.-É.	9.9	9.6	9.7	9.4	8.7	8.6	8.3	
N.B./N.-B.	8.2	8.1	7.8	7.6	7.3	7.0	6.8	
Que./Québec	9.2	9.4	9.3	8.9	8.4	8.0	7.8	
Ont./Ont.	11.2	11.4	11.0	10.3	9.8	9.2	8.6	
Man./Man.	10.4	10.2	9.8	9.2	8.7	8.6	8.4	
Sask./Sask.	9.6	9.3	9.1	8.4	8.1	8.0	7.7	
Alta./Alb.	11.8	11.3	11.0	10.6	10.2	10.0	9.5	
B.C./C.-B.	12.4	12.1	11.4	11.2	10.9	10.6	10.2	
Yukon/Yukon	19.1	18.8	18.0	17.3	16.7	16.3	16.9	
N.W.T./T.N.-O.	12.7	12.7	12.8	12.4	11.4	10.9	10.1	
Canada	**10.6**	**10.7**	**10.3**	**9.9**	**9.4**	**9.0**	**8.6**	

[1] For notes on conversion factors please see discussion prior to tables./Pour une discussion des facteurs de conversion, veuillez voir le texte avant les tableaux.

[2] One drink = 1.7 cl (0.6 oz) of absolute alcohol./Un verre=1.7 cl (0,6) d'alcool absolu.

Source: Statistics Canada, *The Control and Sale of Alcoholic Beverages in Canada 1980, 1981, 1982, 1983, 1984, 1985, 1986, 1992*, and *1993* (Ottawa: Statistics Canada, Catalogue No. 63-202, 1982, 1983, 1984, 1985, 1986, 1987, 1989, 1993 and 1993 respectively). Additional data was obtained from the Public Institutions Division, Statistics Canada.

Statistique Canada, *Le contrôle et la vente des boissons alcooliques au Canada, 1980, 1981, 1982, 1983, 1984, 1985, 1986, 1992 et 1993.* (Ottawa : Statistique Canada, Catalogue n° 63-202, 1982, 1983, 1984, 1985, 1986, 1987, 1989, 1993, et 1994 respectivement). Des données supplémentaires ont été obtenues de la Division des institutions publiques, Statistique Canada.

TABLE 2.8   **TABLEAU 2.8**

Level of drinking and heavy drinking occasions among current drinkers by gender, age, marital status, income, education, employment status and level, region and community size, Canada, 1993

Niveau de consommation et occasions de forte consommation chez les buveurs de 15 ans et plus, selon le sexe, l'âge, l'état matrimonial, le revenu, le niveau d'instruction, la situation d'emploi, la région et la taille de la collectivité, Canada, 1993

VARIABLE	LEVEL AND HEAVY DRINKING OCCASIONS AMONG CURRENT DRINKERS/NIVEAU ET OCCASIONS DE FORTE CONSOMMATION			
	DRINKS PER WEEK[1]/ CONSOMMATIONS PAR SEMAINE[1]	% ANY HEAVY OCCASION[2]/ OCCASIONS DE FORTE CONSOMMATION[2] (%)	MEAN NUMBER OF HEAVY OCCASION[3]/ OCCASIONS DE FORTE CONSOMMATION (moyenne)[3]	SAMPLE SIZE/ TAILLE DE L'ÉCHANTILLON
Gender/Sexe :				
Total 15+/Total des 15+	4.2	46.2	15.7	10,385
Male/Hommes	5.9	58.0	19.4	4,789
Female/Femmes	2.3	33.1	8.4	5,596
Age/Age :				
15-17	2.4	56.2	12.2	383
18-19	5.0	76.9	17.2	300
20-24	5.2	68.8	19.2	805
25-34	4.3	57.4	14.5	2,500
35-44	3.7	46.5	15.2	2,222
45-54	4.5	36.3	16.2	1,416
55-64	4.5	25.9	13.9	1,118
65-74	3.6	16.7	19.2	985
5+	3.8	9.8	4.5	656
Marital Status/Etat matrimonial :				
Single/Célibataire	5.0	63.4	18.6	2,733
Married or cohabitating/Marié ou conjoint de fait	3.9	41.0	13.4	5,735
Divorced or separated/Divorcé ou séparé	4.6	43.5	18.1	924
Widowed/Veuf	2.7	14.9	6.8	923
Income/Revenu :				
Lowest/Inférieur	3.5	49.3	16.0	666
Lower middle/Inférieur à moyen	3.9	39.1	20.8	941
Middle/Moyen	4.0	44.1	16.7	2,317
Upper middle/Moyen à supérieur	4.1	47.6	14.9	2,841
Highest/Supérieur	4.8	53.4	13.0	1,014
Education/Niveau d'instruction :				
Completed university/Diplôme universitaire	4.0	44.1	12.7	3,753
Some post secondary/ Postsecondaire partiel	4.5	52.7	19.6	1,573
Secondary/Secondaire	4.0	49.1	14.0	1,617
Less than secondary/Moins que le secondaire	4.6	43.7	18.6	3,023

TABLE 2.8 (concluded)

TABLEAU 2.8 (fin)

Level of drinking and heavy drinking occasions among current drinkers by gender, age, marital status, income, education, employment status and level, region and community size, Canada, 1993

Niveau de consommation et occasions de forte consommation chez les buveurs de 15 ans et plus, selon le sexe, l'âge, l'état matrimonial, le revenu, le niveau d'instruction, la situation d'emploi, la région et la taille de la collectivité, Canada, 1993

VARIABLE	LEVEL AND HEAVY DRINKING OCCASIONS AMONG CURRENT DRINKERS/NIVEAU ET OCCASIONS DE FORTE CONSOMMATION			
	DRINKS PER WEEK[1]/ CONSOMMATIONS PAR SEMAINE[1]	% ANY HEAVY OCCASION[2]/ OCCASIONS DE FORTE CONSOMMATION[2] (%)	MEAN NUMBER OF HEAVY OCCASION[3]/ OCCASIONS DE FORTE CONSOMMATION (moyenne)[3]	SAMPLE SIZE/ TAILLE DE L'ÉCHANTILLON
Employment/Situation d'emploi :				
Professional/Professionnel	3.5	40.1	9.5	738
Semi-professional/ Semi-professionnel	4.2	49.9	14.2	1,093
Supervisor/Surveillant	4.9	53.5	16.4	278
Skilled/Farmer/ Spécialisé/agriculteur	4.6	56.1	15.2	1,119
Semi-Skilled/ Semi-spécialisé	4.7	54.9	18.1	1,100
Unskilled/Non spécialisé	5.0	54.6	17.4	1,036
Other Working/Autre	3.9	44.0 *	21.4	75
Looking For Work/ En quête d'un emploi	5.9	54.2	22.6	413
Student/Aux études	3.8	63.1	13.4	1,020
Homemaker/Au foyer	2.2	22.8	10.3	1,537
Retired/A la retraite	4.2	17.8	16.4	1,382
Other/Autre	8.1	40.6	56.4	230
Region/Région :				
Atlantic/Atlantique	4.1	53.0	16.7	2,118
Quebec/Québec	4.5	45.4	17.5	1,949
Ontario/Ontario	4.4	44.0	16.7	2,268
Prairies/Prairies	3.5	50.0	14.2	2,680
B.C./C.-B.	3.9	45.0	10.2	1,370
Community size/Taille de la collectivité :				
>1,000,000	4.3	43.0	15.1	2,467
500,000-999,999	4.1	46.8	17.5	1,781
100,000-499,999	4.2	47.0	13.5	1,815
<100,000	4.2	46.4	15.2	1,572
Rural/Rurale	4.2	49.7	16.8	2,750

*Data should be interpreted with caution due to sampling variability./Interpréter avec prudence en raison de la variabilité de l'échantillonnage.

[1] Mean number of drinks per week for current drinkers only./Nombre moyen de consommations par semaine, chez les buveurs actuels seulement.

[2] Percentage of current drinkers reporting consumption of five or more drinks on at least one occasion in the past year./Taux des buveurs ayant déclaré avoir pris cinq consommations ou plus lors d'une même occasion l'année précédente.

[3] Mean number of occasions in the past year on which five or more drinks were consumed, among those reporting at least one occasion./Nombre moyen d'occasions au cours desquelles les buveurs ayant déclaré au moins une occasion, l'année précédente, ont alors pris cinq consommations ou plus.

Source: Statistics Canada, *General Social Survey*, analysis prepared by Eric Single, Joan Brewster, Patricia MacNeil and Jeffrey Hatcher (Ottawa: Canadian Centre on Substance Abuse, 1994).

Statistique Canada, *Enquête sociale générale*, analyse de Eric Single, Joan Brewster, Patricia MacNeil et Jeffrey Hatcher (Ottawa : Centre canadien de lutte contre l'alcoolisme et les toxicomanies, 1994).

TABLE 2.9   **TABLEAU 2.9**

Occurrence of alcohol-related problems in the past 12 months by gender, age, marital status, income, education, employment status and level, region and community size, Canada, 1993

Fréquence, chez les buveurs actuels, des problèmes reliés à l'alcool durant les 12 derniers mois, selon le sexe, l'âge, l'état matrimonial, le revenu, le niveau d'instruction, la situation d'emploi, la région et la taille de la collectivité, Canada, 1993

VARIABLE	% WITH ANY PROBLEM[1]/ BUVEURS AVEC PROBLEMES[1] (%)	MEAN # AMONG THOSE WITH ANY PROBLEMS (N[2])/ NOMBRE MOYEN DE PROBLEMES[2] SOCIALE	% OR CURRENT DRINKERS REPORTING INDIVIDUAL PROBLEMS[3]/ BUVEURS AYANT DECLARE DES PROBLEMES SPECIFIQUES (%)					
			FRIENDS, SOCIAL LIFE/ AMIS, VIE SOCIALE	PHYSICAL HEALTH/ SANTE PHYSIQUE	HAPPI-NESS/ BIEN-ETRE	HOME LIFE, MARRIAGE/ VIE FAMILIALE, VIE CONJUGALE	WORK,/ SCHOOL/ TRAVAIL, ETUDES	FINANCES/ FINANCES
Overall/Population globale:	9.2 %	1.9	(750)	2.1 %	5.1 %	2.7 %	1.8 %	1.4 %	4.7 %
Gender/Sexe :									
Male/Hommes	11.0	2.0	(482)	2.7	6.7	3.2	2.4	2.0	6.7
Female/Femmes	6.2	1.8	(268)	1.5	3.2	2.1	1.1	0.8	2.5
Age:									
15-17	15.3	1.9	(36)	5.8	5.1	2.13*	3.5*	2.0*	9.2
18-19	21.5	1.7	(59)	3.7*	7.4	4.1*	3.8*	3.9*	14.1
20-24	17.0	1.7	(130)	3.4	6.7	3.9	1.4*	2.4	11.2
25-34	9.9	2.1	(227)	2.4	6.1	3.0	2.1	2.1	4.6
35-44	8.0	2.0	(169)	1.6	5.1	2.9	1.6	1.1	3.8
45-54	5.8	2.2	(66)	1.4	3.9	2.1	2.2	1.0*	2.3
55-64	6.5	1.9	(41)	1.5*	5.0	2.3	1.4*	0.4*	1.6*
65-74	3.6*	1.8	(20)	1.0*	1.8*	1.1*	0.5*	0.2*	2.0*
75+	1.7*	1.0	(2)	0.2*	1.4*	0.0*	0.0*	0.0*	0.0*
Marital Status/Etat matrimonial :									
Single/Célibataire	16.9	1.9	(392)	3.7	7.7	4.3	2.4	3.0	10.6
Married or cohabiting/ Marié ou conjoint de fait	5.9	1.9	(262)	1.3	3.8	1.8	1.5	0.8	2.1
Divorced or separated/ Divorcé ou séparé	11.0	2.4	(76)	3.6	7.9	4.9	2.8*	1.3*	5.8
Widowed/Veuf	5.6*	2.0	(17)	1.4*	2.3*	2.0	0.7*	1.2*	3.7*
Income/Revenu :									
Lowest/Inférieur	17.6	2.3	(75)	4.7	10.8	5.8	4.9	4.7	10.0
Lower middle/ Intérieur à moyen	9.1	1.7	(65)	1.2	4.4	2.8	1.5	1.8	4.4
Middle/Moyen	9.7	2.1	(182)	2.4	4.9	3.5	2.4	1.6	5.7
Upper middle/ Moyen à supérieur	8.1	1.7	(217)	1.4	4.8	1.9	1.2	0.7	3.7
Highest/Supérieur	7.9	1.8	(67)	1.6	4.8	2.0	1.3	1.0	3.3

TABLE 2.9 (continued)   **TABLEAU 2.9** (suite)

Occurrence of alcohol-related problems in the past 12 months by gender, age, marital status, income, education, employment status and level, region and community size, Canada, 1993

Fréquence, chez les buveurs actuels, des problèmes reliés à l'alcool durant les 12 derniers mois, selon le sexe, l'âge, l'état matrimonial, le revenu, le niveau d'instruction, la situation d'emploi, la région et la taille de la collectivité, Canada, 1993

VARIABLE	% WITH ANY PROBLEM[1]/ BUVEURS AVEC PROBLEMES[1] (%)	MEAN # AMONG THOSE WITH ANY PROBLEMS (N[2])/ NOMBRE MOYEN DE PROBLEMES[2] SOCIALE	% OR CURRENT DRINKERS REPORTING INDIVIDUAL PROBLEMS[3]/ BUVEURS AYANT DECLARE DES PROBLEMES SPECIFIQUES (%)					
			FRIENDS, SOCIAL LIFE/ AMIS, VIE SOCIALE	PHYSICAL HEALTH/ SANTE PHYSIQUE	HAPPI-NESS/ BIEN-ETRE	HOME LIFE, MARRIAGE/ VIE FAMILIALE, VIE CONJUGALE	WORK,/ SCHOOL/ TRAVAIL, ETUDES	FINANCES/ FINANCES
Education/Niveau d'instruction :								
Completed university/ Diplôme universitaire	7.6 %	1.9	(255)	1.7 %	5.1 %	2.4 %	1.3 %	1.0 %	3.0 %
Some post-secondary/ Postsecondaire partiel	12.0	1.7	(173)	1.6	5.7	1.9	1.6	2.3	6.9
Secondary/Secondaire	7.0	1.9	(99)	1.9	3.6	2.1	0.8	1.3	3.8
Less than secondary/ Moins que le secondaire	11.5	2.2	(220)	3.3	5.7	4.3	3.4	1.7	6.6
Employment/Situation d'emploi:								
Professional/ Professionnel	5.8	1.4	(45)	0.9	3.9	1.4	0.1	0.5	1.6
Semi-professional/ Semi-professionnel	8.4	1.6	(81)	1.3	5.6	1.8	1.6	0.6	2.7
Supervisor/Surveillant	7.3*	1.9	(23)	2.3	3.9	2.2	2.1	0.8	2.2
Skilled/Farmer/ Spécialisé/agriculteur	7.6	1.9	(90)	1.4	4.9	1.8	1.0	1.2	4.0
Semi-Skilled/ Semi-spécialisé	10.5	2.0	(97)	2.2	5.8	3.2	2.0	1.6	6.3
Unskilled/Non spécialisé	9.9	2.0	(100)	2.4	4.0	3.2	2.4	1.3	5.9
Other Working/Autre	1.4*	3.5	(2)	1.2	1.2	1.2	1.4	0.0	0.0
Looking For Work/ En quête d'un emploi	16.9	2.3	(54)	4.1	9.0	7.0	4.3	4.7	9.9
Student/Aux études	16.9	1.8	(143)	4.0	6.4	3.5	3.0	3.5	10.2
Homemaker/ Au foyer	4.7	2.5	(54)	1.6	3.3	2.6	1.1	1.1	2.3
Retired/A la retraite	5.2	2.0	(34)	1.5	3.8	1.8	1.2	0.3	1.8
Other/Autre	18.5*	2.7	(22)	5.3	16.0	8.5	5.8	2.0	10.8

TABLE 2.9 (concluded)   **TABLEAU 2.9** (fin)

Occurence of alcohol-related problems in the past 12 months by gender, age, marital status, income, education, employment status and level, region and community size, Canada, 1993

Fréquence, chez les buveurs actuels, des problèmes reliés à l'alcool durant les 12 derniers mois, selon le sexe, l'âge, l'état matrimonial, le revenu, le niveau d'instruction, la situation d'emploi, la région et la taille de la collectivité, Canada, 1993

VARIABLE	% WITH ANY PROBLEM[1]/ BUVEURS AVEC PROBLEMES[1] (%)	MEAN # AMONG THOSE WITH ANY PROBLEMS (N[2])/ NOMBRE MOYEN DE PROBLEMES[2] SOCIALE	% OR CURRENT DRINKERS REPORTING INDIVIDUAL PROBLEMS[3]/ BUVEURS AYANT DECLARE DES PROBLEMES SPECIFIQUES (%)					
			FRIENDS, SOCIAL LIFE/ AMIS, VIE SOCIALE	PHYSICAL HEALTH/ SANTE PHYSIQUE	HAPPI-NESS/ BIEN-ETRE	HOME LIFE, MARRIAGE/ VIE FAMILIALE, VIE CONJUGALE	WORK,/ SCHOOL/ TRAVAIL, ETUDES	FINANCES/ FINANCES
Region/Région :								
Atlantic/Atlantique	13.0 %	2.0	(187)	2.9 %	7.1 %	4.4 %	2.2 %	1.9 %	6.9 %
Québec	10.2	2.0	(142)	2.0	5.9	3.3	2.1	1.1	5.8
Ontario	7.5	1.9	(130)	1.9	3.8	2.0	1.4	1.6	3.7
Prairies	10.2	1.9	(211)	2.7	5.6	2.5	1.9	1.6	4.9
B.C./C.-B.	8.7	1.9	(80)	1.7	5.3	2.7	2.0	1.1	3.6
Community size/Taille de la collectivité :								
> 1,000,000	8.1	1.9	(144)	1.5	4.9	2.3	1.4	1.3	4.3
500,000-999,999	9.2	2.0	(144)	2.7	5.1	2.4	1.8	1.6	4.9
100,000-499,999	9.0	2.0	(147)	1.6	5.7	3.3	1.8	1.6	4.1
< 100,000	9.2	1.6	(111)	1.8	4.1	2.1	1.1	0.9	4.6
Rural/Rurale	10.8	2.1	(204)	3.0	5.4	3.5	2.7	1.7	5.6

*Data should be interpreted with caution due to sampling variability./Interpréter avec prudence en raison de la variabilité de l'échantillonnage.

[1] Percentage of current drinkers reporting any of the named problems due to drinking (not including drinking and driving)./Pourcentage des buveurs actuels ayant déclaré l'un des problèmes reliés à l'alcool susmentionnés (exclut l'alcool au volant).

[2] Mean number of problems reported by those reporting at least one problem due to drinking and the number of respondents (reporting any problem) contributing to this mean./Nombre moyen des problèmes des participants qui ont déclaré au moins un problème relié à l'alcool et nombre de ces participants.

[3] Percentage of current drinkers reporting each of the individual problems./Pourcentage des buveurs ayant déclaré chacun des problèmes mentionnés.

Source: Statistics Canada, General Social Survey, analysis prepared by Eric Single, Joan Brewster, Patricia MacNeil and Jeffrey Hatcher (Ottawa: Canadian Centre on Substance Abuse, 1994).

Statistique Canada, *Enquête sociale générale*, analyse de Eric Single, Joan Brewster, Patricia MacNeil et Jeffrey Hatcher (Ottawa: Centre canadien de lutte contre l'alcoolisme et les toxicomanies, 1994).

TABLE 2.10   **TABLEAU 2.10**

Problems experienced in the past twelve months as a result of others' drinking by gender, age, marital status, income, education, employment status and level, region and community size, among those age 15 or older, Canada, 1993

Problèmes éprouvés au cours des 12 derniers mois par suite de la concommation d'alcool d'une autre personne, selon le genre, l'âge, l'état matrimonial, le revenu, le niveau d'instruction, la situation d'emploi, la région et la taille de la collectivité, population des 15 ans et plus, Canada, 1993

VARIABLE	% WITH ANY PROBLEM[1]/ BUVEURS AVEC PROBLEMES[1] (%)	MEAN # AMONG THOSE WITH ANY PROBLEMS (N²)/ NOMBRE MOYEN DE PROBLEMES[2]		% OF CURRENT DRINKERS REPORTING INDIVIDUAL PROBLEMS[3] BUVEURS AYANT DECLARE DES PROBLEMES SPECIFIQUES[3] (%)									
				INSULT/ INSULTE	ARGUE/ ARGU- MENT	BREAK FRIEND/ RUPTURE D'AMITIE	FAMILY MARRIAGE/ FAMILLE ET MARIAGE	DRINK & DRIVE/ ALCOOL AU VOLANT	MV ACCIDENT/ ACCIDENT DE LA ROUTE	VANDALS/ VANDA- LISME	ASSAULT/ VOIES DE FAIT	LOUD PARTIES/ FETES BRUYANTES	MONEY/ FINAN- CES
Overall/Population globale :	43.9 %	2.2	(4,443)	20.9 %	15.6 %	7.1 %	9.3 %	8.5 %	0.8 %	2.1 %	5.6 %	23.8 %	1.8%
Gender/Sexe :													
Male/Hommes	45.5	2.0	(2,127)	21.3	15.3	6.7	6.4	9.6	1.0	2.3	6.6	23.2	1.4
Female/Femmes	42.5	2.3	(2,316)	20.5	16.0	7.5	12.1	7.5	0.5	1.9	4.7	24.3	2.2
Age/Age :													
15-17	43.4	2.2	(186)	19.6	19.0	6.2	7.1	9.8	1.6	2.9	9.3	19.6	1.4
18-19	59.5	2.5	(192)	36.6	31.1	8.4	11.3	15.5	1.5	4.2	16.7	22	2.1
20-24	66.0	2.5	(536)	36.6	31.5	10.2	11.1	20.3	2	3.6	16	30.8	2.3
25-34	54.2	2.2	(1,358)	26.4	21.6	8.1	13.6	11.5	1.1	2.6	5.8	28.2	1.8
35-44	49.4	2.2	(1,064)	23.0	16.0	9.1	11.4	8.3	0.5	2.4	5.2	28.8	2.7
45-54	38.5	2.0	(547)	17.8	10.6	6.8	7.4	5.8	0.4	1.6	2.7	24	1.5
55-64	21.1	1.8	(325)	12.8	5.9	5.4	6.9	3.2	0.5	1.2	2.1	17.9	1.5
65-74	18.3	1.6	(169)	5.3	3.0	3.1	3.3	0.9	0.1	0.1	0.6	11.9	1.1
75+	12.4	1.3	(66)	2.5	1.7 *	0.4	1.1	0.5	0	0.4	0.9	8.2	0.9
Marital Status/Etat matrimonial :													
Single/Célibataire	55.6	2.4	(1,542)	29.9	25	9.1	9.6	14.6	1.5	2.9	11.5	25.6	2.1
Married or cohabiting/ Marié ou conjoint de fait	39.9	2.0	(2,213)	17.3	11.8	5.9	8.8	6.1	0.5	1.7	3	23.4	1.3
Divorced or separated/ Divorcé ou séparé	58.8	2.7	(522)	33.8	24.8	13.9	19.5	13.3	0.8	3.7	10.7	30.7	6.9
Widowed/Veuf	19.4	1.9	(158)	6.0	4.5	3.9	3.7	1.6	0.4	1	1.5	12.1	1.3
Income/Revenu :													
Lowest/Inférieur	46.1	2.7	(307)	23.5	18.7	12.2	13.4	13.8	1	3.1	9	25	4.5
Lower middle/Inférieur à moyen	42.5	2.6	(409)	23.2	18.6	8.9	11.9	7.8	0.7	2.8	7.7	22.7	4.2
Middle/Moyen	43.4	2.2	(1,017)	21.4	14.9	7.1	9.7	8.6	1	2	5.2	24.3	2
Upper middle/Moyen à supérieur	47.5	2.1	(1,358)	21.8	16.4	7.1	9.9	8	0.7	2.3	4.8	26.4	1.1
Highest/ Supérieur	46.7	2.0	(491)	23.1	15.2	6.1	9.1	8.6	0.8	1.7	5	28.1	0.8

TABLE 2.10 (continued)   **TABLEAU 2.10** (suite)

Problems experienced in the past twelve months as a result of others' drinking by gender, age, marital status, income, education, employment status and level, region and community size, among those age 15 or older, Canada, 1993

Problèmes éprouvés au cours des 12 derniers mois par suite de la concommation d'alcool d'une autre personne, selon le genre, l'âge, l'état matrimonial, le revenu, le niveau d'instruction, la situation d'emploi, la région et la taille de la collectivité, population des 15 ans et plus, Canada, 1993

VARIABLE	% WITH ANY PROBLEM[1]/ BUVEURS AVEC PROBLEMES[1] (%)	MEAN # AMONG THOSE WITH ANY PROBLEMS (N[2])/ NOMBRE MOYEN DE PROBLEMES[2]	% OF CURRENT DRINKERS REPORTING INDIVIDUAL PROBLEMS[3] BUVEURS AYANT DECLARE DES PROBLEMES SPECIFIQUES[3] (%)									
			INSULT/ INSULTE	ARGUE/ ARGU- MENT	BREAK FRIEND/ RUPTURE D'AMITIE	FAMILY MARRIAGE/ FAMILLE ET MARIAGE	DRINK & DRIVE/ ALCOOL AU VOLANT	MV ACCIDENT/ ACCIDENT DE LA ROUTE	VANDALS/ VANDA- LISME	ASSAULT/ VOIES DE FAIT	LOUD PARTIES/ FETES BRUYANTES	MONEY/ FINAN- CES
Education/Niveau d'instruction :												
Completed university Diplôme universitaire 48.7 %	2.1	(1,823)	22.0 %	14.7 %	6.5 %	9.4 %	8.5 %	0.7 %	2.2 %	4.6 %	29.4 %	1.7 %
Some post-secondary/Postsecon- daire partiel 55.1	2.4	(889)	28.4	23.2	9.6	11.9	13.4	0.9	2.6	9.5	28.3	2.1
Secondary/ Secondaire 39.8	2.2	(676)	19.2	14.8	6.3	9.1	7.7	0.6	2.1	4.6	20.3	1.3
Less than secondary/Moins que le secondaire 35.1	2.3	(1,035)	17.0	13.4	7	8.2	6.4	0.8	1.8	5.5	16.8	2.2
Employment/Situation d'emploi :												
Professional/ Professionnel 46.9	1.9	(350)	19.8	12.9	5.8	11.1	7.2	0.1	1.5	2.6	29.3	0.8
Semi-professional/Semi- professionnel 53.7	2.1	(594)	24.8	17	7.8	8.8	9.9	0.6	2.6	5.5	32.7	1.1
Supervisor/ Surveillant 42.8	2.0	(126)	17.8	14.2	6.5	8.8	7.1	0.2	2.5	3.3	23	2.8
Skilled/Farmer/Spécialisé/ agriculteur 46.8	2.2	(543)	24.2	15.7	7.4	11.5	8.9	0.9	2.3	5	23.5	1.9
Semi-skilled/Semi- spécialisé 47.7	2.1	(533)	22.6	19.9	6.2	9.2	9.2	1.5	1.9	6.8	22.5	1.6
Unskilled/Non spécialisé 51.8	2.2	(526)	26.9	18.2	9.5	10.3	10.7	1.0	1.8	6.9	26.4	1.5
Other working/ Autre 36.5	2.1	(29*)	17.2	8.9	9.4	4.9	5.1	0.0	2.4	2.5	25.8	0.0
Looking for work/En quête d'un emploi 52.0	2.8	(222)	28.9	25.3	12.1	12.5	16.5	1.3	3.5	9.8	25.7	6.5
Student/Aux études 53.7	2.3	(598)	27.0	23.5	7.6	9.1	13.3	1.2	3.1	11.3	26.2	2.1
Homemaker/Au foyer 33.5	2.4	(535)	15.9	11.5	6.9	11.3	5.5	0.6	2.1	4.2	19.6	2.6
Retired/A la retraite 21.4	1.6	(263)	6.1	3.6	3.5	3.5	1.9	0.1	0.2	0.6	13.8	0.8
Other/Autre 49.5	2.6	(103)	28.3	20.5	10	11.2	8.5	0.6	3.6	10.7	28.7	1.6
Region/Région :												
Atlantic/ Atlantique 42.3	2.2	(853)	23.9	16.2	5.8	8.5	8.5	0.6	1.8	7	19.7	1.4
Quebec/Québec 39.6	2.4	(759)	19.1	16.4	9.2	10	9.1	0.9	3	6.4	18.8	2.9
Ontario/Ontario 42.2	2.0	(947)	19.0	14	6.6	8.6	7.1	0.8	1.6	4.5	22.4	1.3
Prairies/Prairies 45.3	2.2	(1,153)	22.5	16.5	6.6	9.2	10.8	0.8	2	5.7	23.5	1.9
B.C./C.-B. 57.8	2.1	(731)	26.4	17.2	5.8	11.2	8.1	0.4	2.2	6.4	31.8	1.4

TABLE 2.10 (concluded)

TABLEAU 2.10 (fin)

Problems experienced in the past twelve months as a result of others' drinking by gender, age, marital status, income, education, employment status and level, region and community size, among those age 15 or older, Canada, 1993

Problèmes éprouvés au cours des 12 derniers mois par suite de la concommation d'alcool d'une autre personne, selon le genre, l'âge, l'état matrimonial, le revenu, le niveau d'instruction, la situation d'emploi, la région et la taille de la collectivité, population des 15 ans et plus, Canada, 1993

VARIABLE	% WITH ANY PROBLEM[1]/ BUVEURS AVEC PROBLEMES[1] (%)	MEAN # AMONG THOSE WITH ANY PROBLEMS (N[2])/ NOMBRE MOYEN DE PROBLEMES[2]	% OF CURRENT DRINKERS REPORTING INDIVIDUAL PROBLEMS[3] BUVEURS AYANT DECLARE DES PROBLEMES SPECIFIQUES[3] (%)									
				INSULT/ INSULTE	ARGUE/ ARGU-MENT	BREAK FRIEND/ RUPTURE D'AMITIE	FAMILY MARRIAGE/ FAMILLE ET MARIAGE	DRINK & DRIVE/ ALCOOL AU VOLANT	MV ACCIDENT/ ACCIDENT DE LA ROUTE	VANDALS/ VANDA-LISME	ASSAULT/ VOIES DE FAIT	LOUD PARTIES/ FETES BRUYANTES	MONEY/ FINAN-CES
Community Size/Taille de la collectivité :													
>1,000,000	45.0 %	2.1	(1,107)	19.7 %	14.8 %	7.2 %	8.8 %	7.8 %	0.8 %	2.3 %	5 %	25.4 %	1.9 %
>500,000 <1,000,000	43.8	2.2	(771)	20.7	16.3	7.4	8.6	8.6	0.9	1.7	6.2	25	1.8
>100,000 <500,000	46.2	2.2	(818)	22.6	16.8	6.7	10.6	8.3	0.7	2	5.4	25.4	1.6
<100,000	46.7	2.2	(709)	23.1	17.3	6.4	8.5	8.3	0.6	2.8	6.4	26.6	1.4
Rural/Rurale	39.3	2.3	(1,038)	20.1	14.4	7.5	10.3	9.7	0.8	1.7	5.6	17.8	2.2

[1] Percentage of respondents reporting any of the named problems in the past twelve months as a result of someone else's drinking./Pourcentage des buveurs actuels ayant déclaré avoir éprouvé l'un des problèmes mentionnés par suite de la consommation d'alcool d'une autre personne.

[2] Mean number of problems reported by those reporting at least one problem as a result of someone else's drinking, and the number of respondents (those reporting any problem) contributing to the mean./Nombre moyen des problèmes des participants qui ont déclaré au moins un problème relié à la consommation d'alcool d'une autre personne, et nombre de ces participants.

[3] Percentage of respondents reporting having experienced each of the individual problems in the past twelve months as a result of someone else drinking. The actual questions asked were:/Pourcentage des participants ayant déclaré avoir éprouvé chacun des problèmes mentionnés à cause de la consommation d'alcool d'une autre personne. On leur avait posé les questions suivantes:

During the past 12 months, have you ever .../Au cours des 12 derniers mois, avez-vous ...

(a) been insulted or humiliated by someone who had been drinking?/été insulté ou humilié par quelqu'un qui avait bu?

(b) had serious arguments or quarrels as a result of someone else's drinking?/eu un grave argument ou une dispute parce que quelqu'un avait bu?

(c) had friendships break up as a result of someone else's drinking?/subi une rupture d'amitié parce quelqu'un avait bu?

(d) had family problems or marriage difficulties due to someone else's drinking/éprouvé des problèmes familiaux ou conjugaux parce que quelqu'un avait bu?

(e) been a passenger with a driver who had too much to drink?/été passager dans un véhicule dont le conducteur avait trop bu?

(f) been in a motor vehicle accident because of someone else's drinking?/été impliqué dans un accident de la route parce que quelqu'un avait bu?

(g) had your property vandalized by someone who had been drinking?/eu votre propriété vandalisée par quelqu'un qui avait bu?

(h) been pushed, hit or assaulted by someone who had been drinking? /été poussé, frappé ou agressé par quelqu'un qui avait bu?

(i) been disturbed by loud parties or the behaviour of people drinking?/été incommodé par des fêtes bruyantes ou le comportement de personnes qui avaient bu?

(j) had financial trouble because of someone else's drinking?/éprouvé des difficultés financières parce que quelqu'un avait bu?

Source: Statistics Canada, *General Social Survey*, analysis prepared by Eric Single, Joan Brewster, Patricia MacNeil and Jeffrey Hatcher. (Ottawa: Canadian Centre on Substance Abuse, 1994).

Statistique Canada, *Enquête sociale générale*, analyse de Eric Single, Joan Brewster, Patricia MacNeil et Jeffrey Hatcher. (Ottawa: Centre canadien de lutte contre l'alcoolisme et les toxicomanies, 1994).

TABLE 2.11　　　　　　　　　　　　　　　　　　　　　**TABLEAU 2.11**

Estimated prevalence of alcoholism and rates per 100,000 population, Canada and provinces, 1974 to 1991

Fréquence estimative de l'alcoolisme et taux par 100 000 habitants, Canada et provinces, 1974 à 1991

Year/ Année	Nfld./ T.-N.	P.E.I./ I.-P.-E.	N.S./ N.É.	N.B./ N.-B.	Que./ Québec	Ont./ Ont.	Man./ Man.	Sask./ Sask.	Alta./ Alb.	B.C./ C.-B.	Canada[2,3]
NUMBER OF ALCOHOLICS[1]/NOMBRE D'ALCOOLIQUES[1]											
1974	4,100	1,700	13,900	11,100	165,400	226,800	24,000	16,100	33,600	88,000	**584,800**
1975	3,200	1,800	14,200	11,100	172,700	230,300	24,500	17,900	37,300	93,700	**606,700**
1976	3,900	1,700	14,100	12,300	176,700	235,900	23,100	17,500	41,300	91,900	**618,400**
1977	5,900	1,500	13,500	13,400	176,100	235,100	22,300	17,100	43,900	94,200	**622,900**
1978	6,600	1,500	13,400	13,500	168,900	228,600	24,000	16,800	46,200	100,200	**619,700**
1979	6,100	1,800	13,700	12,800	155,200	222,400	24,900	16,400	49,000	103,000	**605,300**
1980	6,000	1,700	12,700	11,900	150,900	221,000	24,400	17,200	51,400	104,400	**601,600**
1981	5,300	1,600	11,800	11,400	148,700	218,500	24,900	16,900	52,300	98,700	**589,900**
1982	5,000	1,400	12,600	10,700	137,500	206,700	24,500	17,200	50,800	85,300	**551,600**
1983	5,200	1,100	13,400	10,200	130,900	197,700	22,600	19,600	48,600	71,400	**520,500**
1984	4,700	1,100	12,800	9,900	130,900	194,700	21,600	20,300	44,300	62,400	**502,800**
1985	4,900	1,800	12,300	9,500	129,300	193,600	21,900	19,200	38,400	62,700	**493,600**
1986	5,800	2,400	12,000	10,100	128,000	193,500	21,000	18,100	35,800	63,500	**490,100**
1987	5,900	2,400	11,800	10,400	127,800	191,300	19,100	16,800	35,300	59,300	**480,000**
1988	5,700	2,300	11,900	8,800	126,700	195,100	20,300	15,400	34,900	55,700	**476,800**
1989	6,700	1,700	12,000	7,600	127,400	201,800	21,800	14,300	36,600	55,800	**486,100**
1990	7,800	800	12,300	8,400	127,900	200,400	19,100	14,500	40,100	58,700	**490,700**
1991	7,200	1,000	13,200	10,600	124,700	196,900	17,000	16,100	39,600	61,800	**488,500**
ALCOHOLICS[1] PER 100,000 POPULATION/ NOMBRE D'ALCOOLIQUES[1] PAR 100 000 HABITANTS											
1974	700	1,500	1,700	1,700	2,600	2,800	2,400	1,800	1,900	3,600	**2,600**
1975	600	1,500	1,700	1,600	2,700	2,800	2,400	1,900	2,100	3,700	**2,600**
1976	700	1,400	1,700	1,800	2,800	2,800	2,200	1,900	2,200	3,600	**2,600**
1977	1,000	1,200	1,600	1,900	2,700	2,800	2,100	1,800	2,200	3,600	**2,600**
1978	1,200	1,200	1,600	1,900	2,600	2,700	2,300	1,800	2,300	3,800	**2,600**
1979	1,100	1,500	1,600	1,800	2,400	2,600	2,400	1,700	2,300	3,900	**2,500**
1980	1,000	1,400	1,500	1,700	2,300	2,500	2,400	1,800	2,300	3,800	**2,400**
1981	900	1,300	1,400	1,600	2,300	2,500	2,400	1,700	2,300	3,500	**2,400**
1982	900	1,100	1,500	1,500	2,100	2,300	2,300	1,700	2,100	3,000	**2,200**
1983	900	900	1,500	1,400	2,000	2,200	2,100	2,000	2,000	2,400	**2,000**
1984	800	900	1,500	1,400	2,000	2,100	2,000	2,000	1,800	2,100	**2,000**
1985	800	1,400	1,400	1,300	1,900	2,100	2,000	1,900	1,600	2,100	**1,900**
1986	1,000	1,900	1,300	1,400	1,900	2,000	1,900	1,800	1,500	2,100	**1,900**
1987	1,000	1,900	1,300	1,400	1,900	2,000	1,700	1,600	1,400	1,900	**1,800**
1988	1,000	1,800	1,300	1,200	1,800	2,000	1,800	1,500	1,400	1,800	**1,800**
1989	1,200	1,300	1,300	1,000	1,800	2,000	2,000	1,400	1,500	1,700	**1,800**
1990	1,300	600	1,300	1,100	1,800	1,900	1,700	1,400	1,600	1,800	**1,800**
1991	1,200	800	1,400	1,400	1,800	1,900	1,500	1,600	1,500	1,800	**1,700**

TABLE 2.11 (concluded)　　　　　　　　　**TABLEAU 2.11** (fin)

Estimated prevalence of alcoholism and rates per 100,000 population, Canada and provinces, 1974 to 1991

Fréquence estimative de l'alcoolisme et taux par 100 000 habitants, Canada et provinces, 1974 à 1991

Year/ Année	Nfld./ T.-N.	P.E.I./ I.-P.-E.	N.S./ N.É.	N.B./ N.-B.	Que./ Québec	Ont./ Ont.	Man./ Man.	Sask./ Sask.	Alta./ Alb.	B.C./ C.-B.	Canada[2,3]
	ALCOHOLICS[1] PER 100,000 POPULATION AGED 20 AND OLDER/ TAUX D'ALCOOLIQUES[1] PAR 100 000 HABITANTS, 20 ANS ET PLUS										
1974	1,400	2,400	2,800	2,800	4,200	4,300	3,700	2,900	3,100	5,500	**4,100**
1975	1,000	2,500	2,800	2,700	4,300	4,300	3,700	3,100	3,300	5,700	**4,100**
1976	1,200	2,300	2,700	2,900	4,200	4,300	3,500	3,000	3,500	5,400	**4,100**
1977	1,900	2,000	2,500	3,100	4,200	4,200	3,300	2,900	3,600	5,400	**4,000**
1978	2,000	2,000	2,500	3,100	3,900	4,000	3,500	2,800	3,600	5,600	**3,900**
1979	1,800	2,300	2,500	2,900	3,600	3,800	3,600	2,600	3,600	5,600	**3,700**
1980	1,800	2,100	2,300	2,600	3,400	3,700	3,500	2,700	3,600	5,500	**3,600**
1981	1,500	2,000	2,100	2,500	3,300	3,600	3,500	2,600	3,400	5,000	**3,500**
1982	1,400	1,700	2,200	2,300	3,000	3,300	3,400	2,600	3,200	4,200	**3,200**
1983	1,500	1,300	2,300	2,100	2,800	3,100	3,100	2,900	3,000	3,400	**2,900**
1984	1,300	1,300	2,100	2,000	2,800	3,000	2,900	3,000	2,700	2,900	**2,800**
1985	1,300	2,100	2,000	1,900	2,700	2,900	2,900	2,800	2,300	2,900	**2,700**
1986	1,600	2,700	1,900	2,000	2,600	2,800	2,700	2,600	2,100	2,900	**2,600**
1987	1,600	2,700	1,900	2,000	2,600	2,700	2,500	2,400	2,100	2,700	**2,500**
1988	1,500	2,600	1,900	1,700	2,500	2,700	2,600	2,200	2,000	2,400	**2,500**
1989	1,700	1,900	1,800	1,500	2,500	2,700	2,800	2,000	2,100	2,400	**2,500**
1990	2,000	900	1,900	1,600	2,500	2,700	2,400	2,100	2,300	2,400	**2,400**
1991	1,800	1,100	2,000	2,000	2,400	2,600	2,200	2,300	2,200	2,500	**2,400**

[1] Estimated using the Jellinek formula with proportion of liver cirrhosis deaths due to alcoholism equal to 0.37 and rate of death from liver cirrhosis among all alcoholics equal to 16.53 per 10,000./Estimation fondée sur la formule Jellinek selon laquelle la proportion de tous les décès par cirrhose du foie imputable à l'alcoolisme est de 0,37 et le taux des décès par cirrhose du foie chez tous les alcooliques, de 16,53 par 10 000.

[2] Excludes Yukon and Northwest Territories./Exclut le Territoire du Yukon et les Territoires du Nord-Ouest.

[3] Due to rounding, the components may not add up to the total/Vu l'arrondissement des chiffres, leur total peut différer de celui indique.

Sources: For 1973 to 1981, Statistics Canada, *Causes of Death: Provinces by Sex and Canada by Sex and Age* (Ottawa: Statistics Canada, Catalogue No. 84- 203, from 1974 to 1982); for 1982 to 1986, Statistics Canada, *Causes of Deaths - Vital Statistics Vol. IV, 1982 1983, 1984, 1985, 1986,* (Ottawa: Statistics Canada, Catalogue No. 84-203, 1984, 1985, 1986, 1987, and 1988 respectively); Statistics Canada, *Health Reports Supplement, Vol. 1, No. 1, 1989 - Causes of Death, 1987* (Ottawa: Statistics Canada, Catalogue No. 82 -0003S, 1989); Statistics Canada, *Health Reports, Supplement No. 11, 1990, Vol. 2, No. 1 - Causes of Deaths, 1988* (Ottawa: Statistics Canada, Catalogue No. 82-003S, 1990); Statistics Canada, *Health Reports Supplementary No. 11, 1991, Volume 3, No.1 - Causes of Death, 1989* (Ottawa: Statistics Canada, Catalogue No. 82-003S, 1991); Statistics Canada, *Causes Death 1990* (Ottawa: Statistics Canada Catalogue No. 82-003S, 1992); Statistics Canada, *Causes of Death 1991,* and *1992* (Ottawa: Statistics Canada, Catalogue No. 84-208, 1993 and 1994 respectively).

Pour 1973 à 1981, Statistique Canada, *Causes de décès : provinces, selon le sexe, et Canada, selon le sexe et l'âge,* éditions annuelles de 1974 à 1982. (Ottawa : Statistique Canada, Catalogue n° 84-203); pour 1982 à 1986, Statistique Canada, *Causes de décès,* Statistiques de l'état civil, Volume IV, éditions annuelles de 1982 à 1986 (Ottawa : Statistique Canada, Catalogue n° 84-203, 1984, 1985, 1986, 1987, et 1988 respectivement); Statistique Canada, *Cause de décès, 1987,* Rapports sur la santé, supplément, Volume 1, n° 1, 1989 (Ottawa : Statistique Canada, Catalogue n° 82-0003S, 1989); Statistique Canada, *Causes de décès, 1988,* Rapports sur la santé, supplément n° 11, 1990, Volume 2, n° 1 (Ottawa : Statistique Canada, Catalogue n° 82-0003S, 1990); Statistique Canada, *Causes de décès, 1989,* Rapports sur la santé, supplément n° 11, 1991, Volume 3, n° 1 (Ottawa : Statistique Canada, Catalogue n° 82-0003S, 1991); Statistique Canada, *Causes de décès, 1990* (Ottawa : Statistique Canada, Catalogue n° 82-0003S, 1992); Statistique Canada, *Causes de décès, 1991 et 1992* (Ottawa: Statistique Canada, Catalogue n° 84-208, 1993 et 1994 respectivement).

TABLE 2.12

TABLEAU 2.12

Hospital separations and days of hospitalization attributed to alcohol by gender and cause, Canada, 1992

Départs des hôpitaux et jours d'hospitalisation attribués à l'alcool, selon le sexe et la cause, 1992

DISEASE/MALADIE	ICD-9 code(s) Code(s) CIM-9	HOSPITAL SEPARATIONS / DEPART DES HOPITAUX			DAYS OF HOSPITALIZATION/ JOURS D'HOSPITALISATION		
		MALE/ HOMMES	FEMALE/ FEMMES	TOTAL/ TOTAL	MALE/ HOMMES	FEMALE/ FEMMES	TOTAL/ TOTAL
Lip and oropharangyeal Cancer/ Tumeur des lèvres et de l'oropharynx	140-141, 143- 146, 148-149, 230.0	756	164	919	12,093	2,951	15,045
Oesophageal Cancer/ Tumeur de l'oesophage	150, 230.1	696	146	842	11,682	3,192	14,874
Liver Cancer/Tumeur du foie	155, 230.8	316	94	410	4,096	1,858	5,953
Laryngeal Cancer/Tumeur du larynx	161, 231.0	722	108	830	12,071	1,770	13,841
Breast cancer/Tumeur du sein	174, 233.0	0	898	898	0	8,970	8,970
Alcoholic psychosis/ psychoses alcoolique	291	4,144	1,225	5,369	122,559	36,897	159,456
Alcohol dependence syndrome/ Syndrome d'alcoolomanie	303	10,670	3,646	14,316	112,394	38,693	151,087
Alcohol abuse/Abus d'alcool	305.0	1,966	1,163	3,129	6,323	2,912	9,235
Epilepsy/Epilepsie		655	569	1,224	7,497	6,698	14,195
Alcoholic polyneuropathy/ Polyneuropathie alcoolique	357.5	41	13	54	838	564	1,402
Hypertension/Hypertension	401-405	329	134	462	2,894	1,259	4,153
Alcoholic cardiomyopathy/ Cardiomyopathie alcoolique	425.5	205	17	222	1,945	145	2,090
Cardiac dysrhythmias/ Arythmie cardiaque	427.0. 427.2, 427.3	2,984	1,620	4,604	16,114	10,257	26,371
Heart failure & ill-defined condition/ Insuffisance cardiaque et maladie cardiaque mal définie	428-429	359	211	570	5,142	3,940	9,082
Stroke/Accident cérébro-vasculaire	430-438	900	74	973	36,566	3,357	39,923
Oesophageal varices/ Varices oesophagiennes	456.0-456.2	254	96	350	2,190	902	3,091
Gastro-oesophag. lac.-haemorrhage/ Syndrome de Mallory-Weiss	530.7	218	97	315	1,013	427	1,441
Alcoholic gastritis/Gastrite alcoolique	535.5	1,500	553	2,053	5,740	2,225	7,965
Alcoholic liver cirrhosis/ Cirrhose alcoolique du foie	571.0- 571.3	3,750	1,470	5,220	56,182	22,008	78,190
Pancreatitis/Pancréatite	577.0-577.1	2,371	1,599	3,969	24,422	18,055	42,477
Pregnancy complications/ Complications de la grossesse	634	0	382	382	0	529	529
Psoriasis/Psoriasis	696.1	134	90	224	2,245	1,757	4,002
Neonatal conditions/Affections néonatales	760.7, 761.8	24	25	49	757	1,080	1,837
Excess blood alcohol/Alcoolémie	790.3	0	1	1	0	1	1
Alcohol toxicity/Toxicité due à l'alcool	980.0 or E860.0- E860.2	392	242	634	1,007	553	1,560
Mediolegal blood exam alcohol driver/Examen sanguin médico-légal alc./cond.	V70.4	0	1	1	0	1	1

TABLE 2.12 (concluded)

TABLEAU 2.12 (fin)

Hospital separations and days of hospitalization
attributed to alcohol by gender and cause, Canada, 1992

Départs des hôpitaux et jours d'hospitalisation attribués à
l'alcool, selon le sexe et la cause, 1992

DISEASE/MALADIE	ICD-9 code(s) Code(s) CIM-9	HOSPITAL SEPARATIONS / DEPART DES HOPITAUX			DAYS OF HOSPITALIZATION/ JOURS D'HOSPITALISATION		
		MALE/ HOMMES	FEMALE/ FEMMES	TOTAL/ TOTAL	MALE/ HOMMES	FEMALE/ FEMMES	TOTAL/ TOTAL
Motor vehicle accidents/ Accidents de la route	E810-819, E820-825	7,192	3,969	11,154	87,760	47,157	134,917
Other road vehicle accidents/Autres accidents de véhicules routiers	E826-829	455	221	676	1,939	987	2,926
Water transport accident/ Accidents de transport par eau	E830-839	67	26	92	474	186	661
Air-space transport accident/ Accidents de transport aérien ou de vol spatial	E840-845	30	8	38	350	74	425
Accidental falls/Chutes accidentelles	E880-888	9,290	7,611	16,901	165,408	142,816	308,224
Accidents by fire and flames/ Accidents provoqués par le feu	E890-E899	95	34	128	1,951	848	2,799
Accidental excessive cold/Accidents provoqués par le froid excessif	E901	97	31	128	1,896	305	2,201
Accidental drowning/ Noyades Accidentelles	E910	39	13	52	407	73	480
Aspiration vomitus/Aspiration d'aliments régurgités	E911	94	73	167	3,052	1,606	4,658
Accidents with objects/machines/ Accidents causés par des objets et des machines	E917, E918, E919-920	831	180	1,011	4,444	3,631	8,075
Accidents with firearm missle/ Accidents causés par des projectiles d'armes à feu	E922	74	9	82	640	87	727
Suicide, self-inflicted injury/ Suicides et automutilations	E950-959	2,319	2,053	4,372	21,732	17,724	39,456
Victim, assault/Victime, agression	E960-966, E968-969	2,475	700	3,175	18,600	7,060	25,660
Victim, child battering/ Victime, enfant maltraité	E967	39	37	76	781	345	1,126
Total/Total		56,474	29,602	86,076	755,205	393,902	1,149,106
Rate per 100,000 population/ Taux par 100 000 habitants		401	206	303	5,359	2,746	4,041
Alcohol-attributed total as % of all causes/Pourcentage global des cas reliés à l'alcool par rapport à la totalité des cas indépendamment de la cause		1.55	0.81	2.36	1.83	0.95	2.78

Source: Single et al., 1996, Table 1.

Single et coll., 1996, Tableau 1.

TABLE 2.13

TABLEAU 2.13

Number and rates of hospitalization and hospitalization days attributed to alcohol by province, Canada, 1992

Nombre et taux des hospitalisations et des jours d'hospitalisation attribués à l'alcool, selon la province, Canada, 1992

PROVINCE PROVINCE	NUMBER/ NOMBRE		RATES PER 100,00 POPULATION/ PAR 100 000 HABITANTS	
	HOSPITALIZATIONS/ HOSPITALISATIONS	HOSPITAL DAYS/ JOURS D'HOSPITALISATION	HOSPITALIZATIONS/ HOSPITALISATIONS	HOSPITAL DAYS/ JOURS D'HOSPITALISATION
Nfld./T.-N.	1,568	16,020	270	2,757
P.E.I./I.-P.-E.	636	3,859	489	2,968
N.S./N.-É.	2,950	28,431	320	3,088
N.B./N.-B.	1,336	15,878	178	2,120
Que./Québec	17,778	387,359	249	5,417
Ont./Ont.	29,180	335,034	275	3,158
Man./Man.	3,975	47,159	357	4,237
Sask./Sask.	4,936	43,048	491	4,286
Alta./Alb.	9,990	80,976	380	3,076
B.C./C.-B.	13,710	192,678	397	5,583

Source: Single et al., 1996, Table 10.

Single et coll., 1996, Tableau 10.

TABLE 2.14　　　　　　　　　　　　**TABLEAU 2.14**

Deaths and potential years of life lost attributed to alcohol[1] by gender and cause, Canada, 1992

Décès et années de vie potentielle perdues attribués à l'alcool, selon le sexe et la cause, Canada, 1992

DISEASE/MALADIE	ICD-9 code(s) Code(s) CIM-9	MORTALITY / MORTALITÉ			POTENTIAL YEARS OF LIFE LOST[1]/ ANNÉES DE VIE POTENTIELLE PERDUES		
		MALE/ HOMMES	FEMALE/ FEMMES	TOTAL/ TOTAL	MALE/ HOMMES	FEMALE/ FEMMES	TOTAL/ TOTAL
Lip and oropharangyeal Cancer/ Tumeur des lèvres et de l'oropharynx	140-141, 143-146, 148-149, 173	38	3	41	756	164	919
Oesophageal Cancer/ Tumeur de l'oesophage	150, 230.1	304	65	370	4,431	1,095	5,529
Liver Cancer/Tumeur du foie	155, 230.8	171	63	234	2,620	1,100	3,720
Laryngeal Cancer/Tumeur du larynx	161, 231.0	170	17	186	2,535	302	2,837
Breast cancer/Tumeur du sein	174, 233,0	0	189	189	0	4,204	4,204
Alcoholic psychosis/ psychoses alcoolique	291	46	6	52	641	134	774
Alcohol dependence syndrome/ Syndrome d'alcoolomanie	303	416	117	533	8,093	2,766	10,859
Alcohol abuse/Abus d'alcool	305.0	70	21	91	2,228	685	2,913
Epilepsy/Epilepsie	345	21	17	37	662	518	1,177
Alcoholic polyneuropathy/ Polyneuropathie alcoolique	357.5	0	0	0	0	0	0
Hypertension/Hypertension	401-405	23	7	30	278	81	360
Alcoholic cardiomyopathy/ Cardiomyopathie alcoolique	425.5	69	4	73	1,238	67	1,305
Cardiac dysrhythmias/ Arythmie cardiaque	427.0. 427.2, 427.0. 427.2, 427.3	56	48	103	493	441	934
Heart failure & ill-defined condition/ Insuffisance cardiaque et maladie cardiaque mal définie	428-429	8	5	12	90	43	133
Stroke/Accident cérébro-vasculaire	430-438	142	12	153	1,555	192	1,747
Oesophageal varices/ Varices oesophagiennes	456.0-456.2	5	1	6	75	16	91
Gastro-oesophag. lac.-haemorrhage/ Syndrome de Mallory-Weiss	530.7	3	0	4	37	7	43
Alcoholic gastritis/Gastrite alcoolique	535.5	18	5	23	413	149	562
Alcoholic liver cirrhosis/ Cirrhose alcoolique du foie	571.0-'571.3	719	241	960	14,652	6,425	21,077
Pancreatitis/Pancréatite	577.0-577.1	40	34	74	697	545	1,242
Pregnancy complications/ Complications de la grossesse	634	0	0	0	0	1	1
Psoriasis/Psoriasis	6961	0	0	0	0	0	0
Neonatal conditions/Affections néonatales	760.7, 761.8	0	0	0	1	0	1
Excess blood alcohol/Alcoolémie	7903	0	0	0	0	0	0
Alcohol toxicity/Toxicité due à l'alcool	980.0 or E860.0- 980.0 or E860.0-E860.2	47	9	56	1,685	339	2,024
Mediolegal blood exam alcohol driver/Examen sanguin médico-légal alc./cond.	V70.4	0	0	0	0	0	0

TABLE 2.14 (concluded)

TABLEAU 2.14 (fin)

Deaths and potential years of life lost attributed to alcohol[1] by gender and cause, Canada, 1992

Décès et années de vie potentielle perdues attribués à l'alcool, selon le sexe et la cause, Canada, 1992

DISEASE/MALADIE	ICD-9 code(s) Code(s) CIM-9	MORTALITY / MORTALITÉ			POTENTIAL YEARS OF LIFE LOST[1]/ ANNÉES DE VIE POTENTIELLE PERDUES		
		MALE/ HOMMES	FEMALE/ FEMMES	TOTAL/ TOTAL	MALE/ HOMMES	FEMALE/ FEMMES	TOTAL/ TOTAL
Motor vehicle accidents/ Accidents de la route	E810-819, E810-819, E820-825	1,021	456	1,477	41,920	18,990	60,910
Other road vehicle accidents/Autres accidents de véhicules routiers	E826-829	2	1	3	67	36	102
Water transport accident/ Accidents de transport par eau	E830-839	33	3	36	1,288	152	1,440
Air-space transport accident/ Accidents de transport aérien ou de vol spatial	E840-845	10	1	11	377	31	408
Accidental falls/Chutes accidentelles	E880-888	233	175	408	3,723	2,094	5,817
Accidents by fire and flames/ Accidents provoqués par le feu	E890-E899	82	41	123	3,187	1,771	4,958
Accidental excessive cold/Accidents provoqués par le froid excessif	E901	13	4	17	380	100	480
Accidental drowning/ Noyades Accidentelles	E910	69	13	83	2,795	486	3,280
Aspiration vomitus/Aspiration d'aliments régurgités	E911	25	20	45	514	323	837
Accidents with objects/machines/ Accidents causés par des objets et des machines	E917, E918, E919-920	8	1	9	261	26	287
Accidents with firearm missle/ Accidents causés par des projectiles d'armes à feu	E922	13	1	13	560	31	591
Suicide, self-inflicted injury/ Suicides et automutilations	E950-959	788	131	918	29,634	5,391	35,025
Victim, assault/Victime, agression	E960-966, E960-966, E968-969	107	52	160	4,387	2,500	6,887
Victim, child battering/ Victime, enfant maltraité	E967	1	0	1	59	13	71
Total/Total		4,904	1,796	6,701	134,495	51,762	186,257
Rate per 100,000 population/ Taux par 100 000 habitants		34.80	12.50	23.60	954	361	655
Alcohol-attributed total as % of all causes/Pourcentage global des cas reliés à l'alcool par rapport à la totalité des cas indépendamment de la cause		2.50	0.91	3.41	4.37	1.68	6.05

[1]Potential years of life lost refers to the difference between age of death and the life expectancy of a person of the same age and gender as the deceased.

[1]Les années de vie potentielle correspondent à l'écart entre l'âge de la personne décédée et l'espérance de vie d'une personne du même âge et du même sexe

Source: Single et al., 1996, Table 1

Single et coll., 1996, Tableau 1

TABLE 2.15   **TABLEAU 2.15**

Number and rates of death and years of potential life lost attributable to alcohol by province,Canada, 1992

Nombre et taux des décès et des années de vie potentielle perdues attribuables à l'alcool, selon la province, Canada, 1992

Province Province	POPULATION (1,000s)/ POPULATION/ (en milliers)	NUMBER/ NOMBRE		RATES PER 100,000 PAR 100 000 HABITANTS	
		Deaths/ Décès	Years of Life Lost/ Années de vie perdues	Deaths/ Décès	Years of Life Lost/ Années de vie perdues
Nfld./T.-N.	581.1	89	2,544	15	438
P.E.I./I.P.É.	130.3	33	865	25	664
N.S./N.-É.	920.8	222	6,061	24	658
N.B./N.-B.	749.1	169	4,922	23	657
Que./Québec	7,150.7	1,637	46,684	23	653
Ont./Ont.	10,609.8	2,392	61,750	23	582
Man./Man.	1,113.1	276	7,732	25	695
Sask./Sask.	1,004.5	255	7,371	25	734
Alta./Alb.	2,632.4	666	20,765	25	789
B.C./C.-B.	3,451.3	929	26,309	27	762

Source: Single et al., 1996, Table 10.

Single et coll., 1996, Tableau 10.

TABLE 2.16   **TABLEAU 2.16**

Alcohol use among fatally[1] injured drivers[2] in seven provinces[3], 1979 to 1993

Consommation d'alcool chez les conducteurs mortellement blessés, sept provinces, 1979 à 1993

| YEAR/ ANNEE | NUMBER OF/ NOMBRE | | DRIVER TESTED GROUPED BY BAC (MG%)/ CONDUCTEURS TESTES, SELON L'ALCOOLEMIE (mg %) | | | |
	DRIVERS/ CONDUCTEURS	DRIVERS TESTED/ CONDUCTEURS TESTES	0	1-80	81-150	>150
1979	1,426	1,190 83.5 %	497 41.8 %	131 11.0 %	165 13.9 %	397 33.4 %
1980	1,423	1,136 79.8	455 40.1	129 11.4	161 14.2	391 34.4
1981	1,549	1,326 85.6	504 38.0	132 10.0	212 16.0	478 36.0
1982	1,312	1,098 83.7	432 39.3	117 10.7	162 14.8	387 35.2
1983	1,345	1,193 88.7	502 42.1	120 10.1	135 11.3	436 36.5
1984	1,207	1,079 89.4	470 43.6	112 10.4	148 13.7	349 32.3
1985	1,269	1,146 90.3	551 48.1	120 10.5	136 11.9	339 29.6
1986	1,277	1,177 92.2	561 47.7	89 7.6	132 11.2	395 33.6
1987	1,413	1,257 89.0	623 49.6	104 8.3	131 10.4	399 31.7
1988	1,333	1,225 91.9	629 51.3	125 10.2	116 9.5	355 29.0
1989	1,423	1,301 91.4	734 56.4	99 7.6	134 10.3	334 25.7
1990	1,239	1,162 93.8	665 57.2	85 7.3	98 8.4	314 27.0
1991	1,180	1,082 91.7	580 53.6	78 7.2	101 9.3	323 29.9
1992	1,123	1,024 91.2	530 51.8	73 7.1	107 10.4	314 30.7
1993	1,233	1,113 90.3	604 54.3	81 7.3	100 9.0	328 29.5

[1] Includes only drivers that died *within 6 hours* of their accidents, as a result figures should not be compared to data in Table 2.12./Inclut seulement les conducteurs décédés dans les six heures suivant l'accident. Ces données ne sont donc pas comparables à celles du Tableau 2.12.

[2] Includes drivers of automobiles, non-articulated trucks/vans, motorcycles, tractor trailers and buses. Excluded are operators of snowmobiles, other off-road vehicles, and bicycles./Inclut les conducteurs d'automobiles, de camions et fourgons, de motocyclettes, de semi-remorques, et autobus. Exclut les conducteurs de motoneiges, d'autres véhicules non routiers, et de bicyclettes.

[3] Includes data for the original seven provinces that have been participating in this system since 1973: Prince Edward Island, New Brunswick, Ontario, Manitoba, Saskatchewan, Alberta, and British Columbia./Inclut les données des sept provinces qui participent à ce système de déclaration depuis 1973 : Ile-du-Prince-Edouard, Nouveau-Brunswick, Ontario, Manitoba, Saskatchewan, Alberta, Colombie-Britannique.

Source: The Traffic Injury Research Foundation of Canada, *Alcohol Use Among Drivers and Pedestrians Fatally Injured In Motor Vehicle Accidents: Canada, 1993* (Ottawa: The Traffic Injury Research Foundation of Canada, 1995).

Fondation de recherches sur les blessures de la route au Canada, *L'usage d'alcool chez les personnes mortellement blessées dans des accidents de la route au Canada, 1993* (Ottawa: Fondation de recherches sur les blessures de la route au Canada, 1995).

TABLE 2.17

TABLEAU 2.17

Distribution of blood alcohol concentration (BAC) among fatally[1] injured drivers[2], Canada, 1993

Ventilation de l'alcoolémie chez les conducteurs mortellement[1] blessés[2], Canada, 1993

PROVINCE	NUMBER OF/ NOMBRE		DRIVER TESTED GROUPED BY BAC (MG%)/ CONDUCTEURS TESTES, SELON L'ALCOOLEMIE (mg %)				
	DRIVERS/ CONDUCTEURS	DRIVERS TESTED/ CONDUCTEURS TESTES	0	1-48	50-80	81-150	>150
Nfld./T.-N.	25	16	5	2	0	1	8
		64.0 %	31.3 %	12.5 %	0.0 %	6.3 %	50.0 %
P.E.I./I.-P.-É.	11	10	4	0.0	0.0	1	5
		90.9	40.0	0.0	0.0	10.0	50.0
N.S./N.-É.	60	43	22	0.0	0.0	4	17
		71.7	51.2	0.0	0.0	9.3	39.5
N.B./N.-B.	83	68	31	3	1	11	22
		81.9	45.6	4.4	1.5	16.2	32.4
Que./Québec	496	404	237	16	8	49	94
		81.5	58.7	4.0	2.0	12.1	23.3
Ont./Ont.	711	543	299	27	18	40	159
		76.4	55.1	5.0	3.3	7.4	29.3
Man./Man	68	56	29	4	3	7	13
		82.4	51.8	7.1	5.4	12.5	23.2
Sask./Sask.	90	85	51	4	3	7	20
		94.4	60.0	4.7	3.5	8.2	23.5
Alta./Alb.	216	198	129	10	6	11	42
		91.7	65.2	5.1	3.0	5.6	21.2
B.C./C.-B.	271	247	116	7	3	31	90
		91.1	47.0	2.8	1.2	12.6	36.4
Yukon/Yukon	5	3	1	0	0	0	2
		60.0	33.3	0.0	0.0	0.0	66.7
N.W.T./T.N.-O.	2	1	1	0	0	0	0
		50.0	100.0	0.0	0.0	0.0	0.0
Canada	**2,038**	**1,674**	**925**	**73**	**42**	**162**	**472**
		82.1	**55.3**	**4.4**	**2.5**	**9.7**	**28.2**

TABLE 2.17 (concluded)

TABLEAU 2.17 (fin)

Distribution of blood alcohol concentration (BAC) among fatally[1] injured drivers[2], Canada, 1993

Ventilation de l'alcoolémie chez les conducteurs mortellement[1] blessés[2], Canada, 1993

PROVINCE	NUMBER OF/ NOMBRE		DRIVER TESTED GROUPED BY BAC (MG%)/ CONDUCTEURS TESTES, SELON L'ALCOOLEMIE (mg %)				
	DRIVERS/ CONDUCTEURS	DRIVERS TESTED/ CONDUCTEURS TESTES	0	1-48	50-80	81-150	> 150
< 16	9	6 66.7 %	6 100.0 %	0 0.0 %	0 0.0 %	0 0.0 %	0 0.0 %
16-17	74	56 75.7	39 69.6	2 3.6	3 5.4	6 10.7	6 10.7
18-19	114	96 84.2	57 59.4	3 3.1	3 3.1	10 10.4	23 24.0
20-25	357	307 86.0	144 46.9	11 3.6	16 5.2	49 16.0	87 28.3
26-35	461	416 90.2	190 45.7	18 4.3	7 1.7	51 12.3	150 36.1
36-45	353	309 87.5	157 50.8	10 3.2	5 1.6	22 7.1	115 37.2
46-55	257	207 80.5	135 65.2	13 6.3	2 1.0	10 4.8	47 22.7
> 55	413	277 67.1	197 71.1	16 5.8	6 2.2	14 5.1	44 15.9
Total	**2,038**	**1,674 82.1**	**925 55.3**	**73 4.4**	**42 2.5**	**162 9.7**	**472 28.2**

[1] Includes drivers dying *within 12 months* as a result of injuries sustained in a collision involving a motor vehicle, as result these figures should not be compared to the data in Table 2.16./Inclut les conducteurs décédés par suite de blessures subies dans un accident de la route moins de 12 mois après l'accident. Ces données ne sont pas comparables à celles du Tableau 2.16.

[2] Includes drivers of automobiles, non-articulated trucks/vans, motorcycles, tractor trailers and buses. Excluded are operators of snowmobiles, other off-road vehicles, and bicycles./Inclut les conducteurs d'automobiles, de camions et fourgons, de motocyclettes, de semi-remorques, et d'autobus. Exclut les conducteurs de motoneiges, d'autres véhicules non routiers, et de bicyclettes.

Source: The Traffic Injury Research Foundation of Canada, *Alcohol Use Among Drivers and Pedestrians Fatally Injured In Motor Vehicle Accidents: Canada, 1993* (Ottawa: The Traffic Injury Research Foundation of Canada, 1995).

Fondation de recherches sur les blessures de la route au Canada, *L'usage d'alcool chez les personnes mortellement blessées dans des accidents de la route au Canada, 1993* (Ottawa: Fondation de recherches sur les blessures de la route au Canada, 1995).

TABLE 2.18

TABLEAU 2.18

Frequency of driving after drinking by gender, age, marital status, income, education, employment status and level, region and community size, among current drinkers, Canada, 1993

Fréquence de la conduite avec facultés affaiblies, selon le sexe, l'âge, l'état matrimonial, le revenu, le niveau d'instruction, la situation d'emploi, la région et la taille de la collectivité, buveurs actuels, Canada, 1993

VARIABLE	% DRINKING & DRIVING CONDUCTEURS AVEC FACULTÉS AFFAIBLIES (%)
Overall/Population globale :	12.9 %
Gender/Sexe	
Male/Hommes	18.3
Female/Femmes	6.1
Age/Age:	
15-17 yrs	7.8
18-19 yrs	15.6
20-24 yrs	14.3
25-34 yrs	16.0
35-44 yrs	14.0
45-54 yrs	12.5
55-64 yrs	8.9
65-74 yrs	5.2
75+ YRS	1.1
Marital Status/Etat matrimonial:	
Single/Célibataire	15.7
Married or cohabiting/ Marié ou conjoint de fait	11.8
Divorced or separated/ Divorcé ou séparé	16.0
Widowed/Veuf	6.4
Income/Revenu:	
Lowest/Inférieur	12.0
Lower middle/ Inférieur à moyen	8.2
Middle/Moyen	11.9
Upper middle/ Moyen à supérieur	13.8
Highest/Supérieur	17.0
Community Size/Taille de la collectivité :	
> 1,000,000	11.5
> 500,000, < 1,000,000	11.9
> 100,000, < 500,000	11.5
< 100,000	14.2
Rural/Rurale	15.6

VARIABLE	% DRINKING & DRIVING CONDUCTEURS AVEC FACULTÉS AFFAIBLIES (%)
Education/Niveau d'instruction :	
Completed university/ Diplôme universitaire	12.9 %
Some post-secondary/ Postsecondaire partiel	12.7
Secondary/Secondaire	14.4
Less than secondary/ Moins que le secondaire	11.8
Employment/Situation d'emploi :	
Professional/Professionnel	11.2
Semi-professional/ Semi-professionnel	15.7
Supervisor/Surveillant	17.7
Skilled/Farmer/ Spécialisé/agriculteur	18.2
Semi-Skilled/Semi-spécialisé	15.5
Unskilled/Non spécialisé	14.4
Other working/Autres	17.3
Looking for work/En quête d'emploi	15.6
Student/Aux études	10.2
Homemaker/Au foyer	4.9
Retired/A la retraite	5.7
Other/Autre	10.8
Region/Région :	
Atlantic/Atlantique	10.7
Québec	19.4
Ontario	9.2
Prairies	13.4
B.C./C.-B.	13.1

[1] Percentage of current drinkers and drivers who, at least once in the past year, drove after having consumed two or more drinks in the previous hour./ Pourcentage des buveurs actuels et des conducteurs qui ont conduit au moins une fois l'année précédente après avoir consommé deux verres ou plus durant l'heure qui précédait.

Source: Statistics Canada General Social Survey, 1993. Analysis by: E. Single, J. Brewster, P. MacNeil and J. Hatcher, *Alcohol and Drug Use: Results of the General Social Survey, 1993*, Ottawa: Canadian Centre on Substance Abuse).

Statistique Canada, *Enquête sociale générale*, analyse de Eric Single, Joan Brewster, Patricia MacNeil et Feffrey Hatcher (Ottawa: Centre canadien de lutte contre l'alcoolisme et les toxicomanies, 1994).

3 Tobacco

3 Le tabac

Figures

Tables

Figures

Tableaux

Highlights

★ According to the February 1995 survey on smoking in Canada, 27% of Canadians over 15 smoke cigarettes. Rates of use are highest among those 20 to 24 (37%) and lowest for adults over 65 (14%).

★ About 29% of youth between 18 and 19 are current smokers (22% are daily smokers and only 7% are non-daily smokers) according to the 1994 youth smoking survey.

★ In 1994, tobacco sales in Canada increased 10.1% from the previous year. The average Canadian age 15 and over smoked 2,315 cigarettes in 1994 up from 2,103 cigarettes in 1993. This works out to 20.5 cigarettes per day per person.

★ Approximately 33,500 deaths, more than 200,000 hospitalizations and more than 3 million hospitalization days were attributed to smoking in 1992. The highest rates of tobacco attributable death or hospitalization are in Nova Scotia, and the lowest rates in Alberta. However, the highest rates of hospitalization days due to smoking are in New Brunswick and Québec.

Points saillants

★ Selon l'enquàte nationale de février 1995 sur le tabagisme, 27% des 15 ans et plus fument la cigarette. Les taux d'usage les plus élevés s'appliquent aux 20 à 24 ans (37%) et les plus bas, les plus de 65 ans (14%).

★ Quelque 29% des 18 et 19 ans fument (22% quotidiennement et 7% occasionnellement), selon l'enquête de 1994 sur le tabagisme chez les jeunes.

★ En 1994, les ventes de tabac au Canada ont excédé de 10,1% celles de 1993. Le Canadien moyen de 15 ans et plus a alors fumé 2 315 cigarettes contre 2 103 l'année précédente, ce qui équivaut à 20,5 cigarettes par personne par jour.

★ En 1992, on a imputé au tabagisme quelque 33 500 décès, plus de 200 000 hospitalisations et plus de trois millions de jours d'hospitalisation. Les taux de décès et d'hospitalisation les plus élevés revenaient à la Nouvelle-Ecosse et les plus bas, à l'Alberta. Par contre, les taux des jours d'hospitalisation les plus élevés revenaient au Nouveau-Brunswick et au Québec.

Tobacco

by Minh Van Truong and Gary Timoshenko, Addiction Research Foundation, and Diane McKenzie and Eric Single, Canadian Centre on Substance Abuse

Sources of Data

Information about smoking and related problems is drawn from a variety of sources. Distribution reports from agricultural sources, manufacturers and customs

Le tabac

par Minh Van Truong et Gary Timoshenko, de la Fondation de la recherche sur la toxicomanie, et Diane McKenzie et Eric Single, du Centre canadien de lutte contre l'alcoolisme et les toxicomanies

Sources des données

L'information sur le tabagisme et les problèmes connexes provient de plusieurs sources. Les estimations

provide the most reliable estimate of tobacco consumption. These data are compiled by Statistics Canada in a monthly report titled *Production and Disposition of Tobacco Products.* Manufacturer's data provide the most accurate estimate of total annual tobacco consumption.

Estimates of tobacco production are limited and do not include unrecorded sources of consumption such as imported tobacco, cross border shopping, illicit production and illegal importation. The consumption of tobacco products obtained through unrecorded sources increased substantially in 1991 with the introduction of the Federal Goods and Services Tax (GST) and a 3-cents-per-cigarette federal tax. These tax changes led to a protest by Canadian consumers who increasingly purchased tobacco products in the United States (Kaiserman, 1992). For example, it is estimated that 6.4 billion cigarettes were illegally brought into Canada in 1991, about 11% of the total market (Stamler, 1992).

Just as different conversion factors are used to calculate the amount of alcohol sold in Canada, estimates of tobacco sales involve similar calculations. Tobacco products are categorized as cigarettes, fine-cut tobacco, cigars, pipe tobacco and smokeless tobacco. The conversion factors used by Statistics Canada for calculating "pieces" of tobacco are 0.865 g (1 cigarette) for manufactured cigarettes, 0.77 g (1 cigarette) for fine-cut tobacco and 3.72 g (1 cigar) for cigars (Kaiserman, 1992).

The problems and size of the illegal tobacco market continued to grow through 1993. As indicated by data in Table 10.10, exports of Canadian cigarettes increased dramatically during the early 90's and a large proportion of these products ultimately found their way illegally back into Canada. In an effort to eliminate the illegal tobacco market the federal government introduced the anti-tobacco smuggling initiative in early 1994. While the most obvious impact was to lower the federal taxes on tobacco products this was only one component of the overall initiative. In addition to the tax changes, the federal government also announced the Tobacco

les plus fiables sur la consommation du tabac nous proviennent des rapports de distribution fournis par les sources agricoles, les rapports des manufacturiers et de la douane. Statistique Canada publie ces données dans le rapport mensuel Production et disposition des produits du tabac. Ce sont les manufacturiers qui nous offrent l'estimation la plus juste de la consommation annuelle globale du tabac.

Les estimations de la production de tabac sont limitées et font exclusion des sources non consignées de consommation, par exemple le tabac importé, les achats outre-frontière, la production illicite et l'importation illégale. La consommation des produits du tabac obtenue par les sources non consignées a sensiblement augmenté en 1991 avec l'introduction de la taxe fédérale sur les produits et services (TPS) et d'une seconde taxe fédérale de 3 cents par cigarette. Cette majoration des taxes a soulevé un tollé de protestations chez les consommateurs canadiens, qui ont réagi en achetant de plus en plus de produits de tabac aux Etats- Unis (Kaisermann, 1992). On estime ainsi que 6,4 milliards de cigarettes sont entrées illégalement au Canada en 1991, représentant quelque 11% du marché global.

Tout comme l'estimation des ventes d'alcool, celle des ventes de tabac repose aussi sur divers facteurs de conversion. Les produits du tabac se divisent en plusieurs catégories : cigarettes, tabac fine coupe, cigares, tabac à pipe et tabac à priser ou à chiquer.

Aussi, Statistique Canada calcule les unités de tabac au moyen des facteurs de conversion suivants : 0,865 g (1 cigarette) pour les cigarettes usinées; 0,77 g (1 cigarette) pour le tabac fine coupe;

3,72 g (1 cigare) pour les cigares (Kaisermann, 1992).

Les problèmes et la taille du marché illégal du tabac ont continué de croître en 1993. Comme le montre le Tableau 10.10, les exportations de cigarettes canadiennes ont considérablement augmenté au début des années 90, et une bonne part de ces dernières ont plus tard été réintroduites illégalement au pays.

Demand Reduction Strategy, a three year program to fund legislative changes, research and public education. As part of this strategy, legislative changes have been made to increase the legal smoking age and substantially increase the penalties associated with tobacco sales to minors. During 1994/95 a number of national surveys are also being conducted as part of the strategy to monitor the impact of the tobacco tax reductions and other initiatives. Subsequent to the federal actions several provinces also lowered their provincial tax rates (most notably Quebec and Ontario). Cigarette tax rates can be found in Table 10.9.

In comparison to what we know about the individual patterns of alcohol use and characteristics of drinkers, information about tobacco consumption is seriously limited. General population surveys provide information on the number and socio-demographic characteristics of abstainers, former smokers and current smokers. Little information, however, is available about the quantity/frequency/patterns of use that allow us to measure the overall effect of individual consumption patterns. These measurement issues also make it difficult to examine the correlates of heavy consumption and the behaviours for hard-core smokers — individuals who do not respond to the usual smoking prevention programs.

Consumption trends and patterns of smoking

The patterns and levels of smoking have changed substantially in Canada since the mid-1960s. The proportion of Canadians who reported smoking in various national surveys decreased steadily in the past 30 years, from 50% in 1965, to 44% in 1975, to 40% in 1981, to 32% in 1989 and to 27% in 1995 (Table 3.1). In 1995, there were about 6.1 million smokers (includes both daily and non-daily smokers) among persons age 15 or older in Canada. Although the proportion of the population who smoke has dropped almost 50% since 1965, there have been little change since 1990. The number of cigarettes consumed per adult declined almost as much over the same period.

Dans le but de contrecarrer le marché illégal du tabac, le gouvernement fédéral a lancé, en 1994, une opération anti-contrebande. Il a, d'une part, abaissé les taxes fédérales sur les produits du tabac et, d'autre part, annoncé la Stratégie de réduction de la demande du tabac, programme triennal pour le financement des modifications législatives, de même que des travaux de recherche et la sensibilisation du public. C'est dans cette optique que le Parlement a par la suite haussé l'âge légal de fumer et augmenté sensiblement les amendes pour vente de tabac aux mineurs. En 1994-1995, plusieurs enquêtes nationales ont aussi été effectuées dans le cadre d'une stratégie visant à vérifier l'impact des réductions de taxe sur le tabac et des autres initiatives. Plusieurs provinces ont emboîté le pas, en abaissant de leur côté les taxes provinciales (principalement le Québec et l'Ontario). Les taux des taxes sur les cigarettes paraissent au Tableau 10.9.

Comparativement à ce que nous savons sur les profils individuels de la consommation d'alcool et les caractéristiques des buveurs, nos connaissances sur l'usage du tabac sont plutôt limitées. Les enquêtes sur l'ensemble de la population nous fournissent bien de l'information quant au nombre et aux caractéristiques sociodémographiques des abstinents, des anciens fumeurs et des fumeurs, mais nous ne disposons que de peu de données sur la quantité, la fréquence et les profils de l'usage, éléments qui permettent de mesurer les répercussions générales des habitudes de consommation individuelle. Il est donc difficile d'examiner les corrélats des consommations élevées et des comportements des fumeurs invétérés, c'est-à-dire ceux qui ne répondent pas aux programmes antitabac traditionnels.

Tendances et profils de la consommation du tabac

Les profils et les niveaux de l'usage du tabac ont sensiblement évolué depuis le milieu des années 60. La proportion des fumeurs a régulièrement diminué au cours des trente dernières années, passant de 50% en 1965 à 44% en 1975, à 40% en 1981, à 32% en 1989,

Canadian alcohol and other drugs survey 1994

Of those who responded to the Canadian alcohol and other drugs survey, 27% said they were current smokers, 26% were former smokers and 46% were non-smokers (Table 3.2). Men were slightly more likely to be current smokers than women (28% vs. 26%), and men were more likely to be former smokers than women (29% vs. 24%). The proportion of respondents who are smokers is highest among 18 to 19 year olds (37%) and lowest for those over 65 (8%). In terms of marital status, single, married, widowed/divorced/separated were equally likely to be current smokers (31.8%, 31.8% and 29.7%, respectively).

Individuals with low socio-economic status (low income, lower level of education, and low literacy skills) have much higher rates of smoking (Table 3.3). For example, smoking prevalence among the lowest income group is 42.6%, compared to 21.0% among those with the highest income. When looking at employment status, the unemployed have the highest smoking prevalence (45.1%) while professionals have the lowest (21.0%).

The proportion of the population who smoke varies across the provinces. Quebec (33.6%), Newfoundland (32.4%), New Brunswick (32.3%), Nova Scotia (31.0%), Prince Edward Island (30%), and Manitoba (27.3%) were all above the national rate. On the other hand, Ontario (22.4%), B.C. (25.0%), Saskatchewan (25.8%) and Alberta were below the national rate.

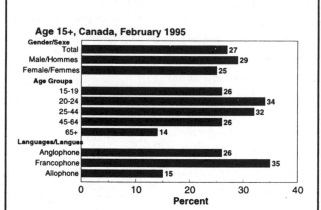

Figure 3.1: Smoking Status by gender, age, and home language among those age 15 or older, Canada, February 1995

Figure 3.1: Catégories de fumeurs selon le sexe, l'âge et la langue parlée à la maison, population des 15 ans et plus, Canada, février 1995

et à 27% en 1995 (Tableau 3.1). En 1995, on a dénombré quelque 6,1 millions de fumeurs (fumeurs quotidiens et occasionnels) chez les 15 ans et plus. La proportion de la population qui fume est tombée de près de la moitié depuis 1965, mais est demeurée à peu près inchangée depuis 1990. Le nombre de cigarettes fumées par adulte a diminué de presque autant sur la même période.

L'Enquête nationale sur l'alcool et les autres drogues (1994)

Parmi les répondants à l'Enquête nationale sur l'alcool et les autres drogues, 27% ont déclaré être fumeurs; 26% anciens fumeurs; et 46% non-fumeurs (Tableau 3.2). Les hommes étaient un peu plus nombreux que les femmes à fumer (28% contre 26%) et plus nombreux aussi à être d'anciens fumeurs (29% contre 24%).

Ce sont les répondants de 18 à 19 ans (37%) qui comptent la plus forte proportion de fumeurs et les plus de 65 ans (8%), la plus faible. Quant à l'état matrimonial, les répondants étaient tous aussi susceptibles d'etre fumeurs, indépendamment qu'ils soient célibataires, mariés, ou veufs, divorcés ou séparés (31,8%, 31,8% et 29,7% respectivement).

Les personnes de bas statut socio-économique (faible revenu, faible niveau d'instruction, et bas niveau d'alphabétisme) présentent des taux de tabagisme beaucoup plus élevés que les autres (Tableau 3.3). La prévalence du tabagisme chez les sujets de faible revenu se situe par exemple à 42,6% comparativement à 21% chez ceux ayant le revenu le plus élevé. Sur le plan

Survey on Smoking in Canada, February 1995

This survey indicates the proportion of current smokers is 27.4%, almost the same as the previous survey. However, the survey contains the component of current smokers (daily and non-daily), the component of former smokers (daily and non-daily) and the component of non-smokers (experimental and abstainers). Table 3.4 shows 23.2% are daily smokers, 4.2% are non-daily smokers, 27.1% are former daily smokers, 4.7% are former non-daily, 14.1% are experimental and 26.7% are abstainers. This table also contains smoking status by gender, age, home language, and income level.

Francophones both inside and outside Quebec have a relatively high prevalence of smoking. There are 6.8 millions Canadian who report french as their home language, representing 25% of the population as a whole. Survey shows that francophones are more likely to smoke than anglophones: 35.5% of francophones are current vs. 25.6% of anglophones. Allophones have a much lower prevalence of smoking than francophones or anglophones. Only 15.4% of allophones are current smokers.

On the average, smokers consume about 15 cigarettes per day (daily smokers have 18 while non-daily have 2 cigarettes per day) (Table 3.4). Men are heavier smokers than women. Men smokers consume 17 cigarettes per day, while women smokers consume 13 cigarettes per day. Among age and gender groups, the heaviest smokers are men age 45 to 64, having 19 cigarettes per day. Young female adult, on the other hand, are the lightest smokers group, consuming seven cigarettes per day. Anglophones smoke almost the same amount of cigarettes as francophone (15 cigarettes per day).

travail, ce sont les sans emploi qui affichent la plus forte prévalence (45,1%) et les professionnels, la plus faible (21,0%).

La proportion de la population qui fume varie d'une province à l'autre. Le Québec (33,6%), Terre-Neuve (32,4%), le Nouveau- Brunswick (32,3%), la Nouvelle-Ecosse (31%), l'Ile-du-Prince-Edouard (30%), et le Manitoba (27,3%) présentaient toutes des taux supérieurs au taux national, tandis que l'Ontario (22,4 %), la Colombie-Britannique (25%), la Saskatchewan (25,8%) et l'Alberta avaient un taux inférieur.

Enquête nationale sur le tabagisme, février 1995

Cette enquête établit le taux des fumeurs actuels à 27,4%, soit à peu près le même que lors de l'enquête précédente. Cette enquête comportait trois grandes catégories : les fumeurs actuels (quotidiens et occasionnels), les anciens fumeurs (quotidiens et occasionnels), et les non-fumeurs (à titre expérimental et abstinents). Le Tableau 3.4 indique 23,2% de fumeurs quotidiens, 4,2% de fumeurs occasionnels, 27,1% d'anciens fumeurs quotidiens, 4,7% d'anciens fumeurs occasionnels, 14,1% de fumeurs expérimentaux et 26,7 % d'abstinents. Ce tableau montre également les catégories de fumeurs selon le sexe, l'âge, la langue parlée à la maison, et le niveau de revenu.

Or les francophones, tant du Québec que de l'extérieur, affichent un taux de prévalence du tabagisme relativement élevé. On note que 6,8 millions de Canadiens ont déclaré le franáais comme langue parlée à la maison, soit 25% de l'échantillon étudié. L'enquête révèle que les francophones sont plus nombreux à fumer que les anglophones : 35,5% de fumeurs francophones contre 25,6% chez les anglophones. Le taux de prévalence du tabagisme est nettement plus bas chez les allophones que chez les francophones ou les anglophones. Seulement 15,4% des allophones sont fumeurs.

Youth Smoking Survey 1994

In 1994, there were more than 3.9 million Canadian youth between 10 and 19 (Table 3.6). Youth in general are the highest risk group for starting tobacco use. The risk of starting to smoke climbs steadily between 10 and 19. About 29,000 youths ages 10 to 12 are current smokers, representing 2.5% of its population. This number increases significantly as young people grow older. For example, 227,000 youths ages 18 to 19 are current smokers, representing 29% of its population. Figure 3.2 shows the smoking prevalence among youth by age and gender.

Traditionally, men are more likely to smoke than women. However, young females are more likely to be current smokers than young males (15.6% and 14.9%, respectively). Girls, particularly between 13 and 17, are significantly more likely to be current smokers than boys (14.4% of females and 12.4% of males for ages 13 to 14; 21.9% of females and 17.7% of males for ages 15 to 17). Provincially speaking, Newfoundland and Quebec have the highest prevalence for this age group than any other provinces (18.7% and 18.4% respectively). Saskatchewan, on the other hand, has the lowest smoking prevalence in the country.

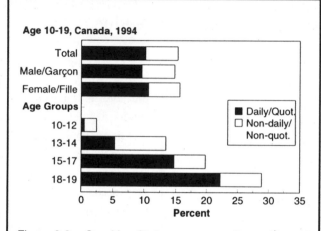

Figure 3.2: Smoking Status among youth age 10 to 19 by age and gender, Canada, 1994

Figure 3.2: Catégories de fumeurs chez les 10 à 19 ans, selon l'âge et le sexe, Canada, 1994

Consumption of domestically sold cigarettes and tobacco

Sales data indicate that Canadians consumed approximately 52.8 billion cigarettes in 1994, down 9.2% from the previous year (Table 3.6). Since 1980, tobacco consumption has decreased at an annual average

Les fumeurs consomment en moyenne quelque 15 cigarettes par jour (les fumeurs quotidiens 18 et les occasionnels 2) (Tableau 3.4).

Les hommes fument davantage que les femmes, soit 17 et 13 cigarettes par jour respectivement. Les plus gros fumeurs, selon l'âge et le sexe, sont les hommes de 45 à 64 ans, avec 19 cigarettes par jour. Les jeunes femmes adultes sont de leur côté celles qui fument le moins, avec 7 cigarettes par jour. Les anglophonesfument presque autant de cigarettes par jour que les francophones (15 cigarettes).

Enquête sur le tabagisme chez les jeunes, 1994

En 1994, le Canada comptait plus de 3,9 millions de jeunes âgés entre 10 et 19 ans (Tableau 3.6). C'est normalement vers cet âge que l'on risque le plus de commencer à fumer. Ce risque croât constamment entre 10 et 19 ans. Quelque 29 000 jeunes de 10 à 12 ans sont fumeurs, soit 2,5% de l'ensemble des jeunes. Leur nombre augmente sensiblement au fur et à mesure qu'ils vieillissent. On dénombre ainsi 227 000 fumeurs chez les 18 et 19 ans, soit 29% de l'ensemble des jeunes. La Figure 3.2 indique la prévalence du tabagisme chez les jeunes selon l'âge et le sexe.

On compte normalement plus de fumeurs chez les hommes que les femmes, mais c'est le cas inverse chez les jeunes, oó le nombre des fumeuses excède celui des fumeurs (15,6% et 14,9% respectivement). Les jeunes filles, surtout entre 13 et 17 ans, sont considérablement plus nombreuses que les jeunes garáons à fumer (14,4 % contre 12,4% chez les 13 et 14 ans; 21,9% contre

rate of 1.8%. In 1994, Canadians consumed an average of 2,315 cigarettes per person over 15 years (approximately 6.3 cigarettes per day). About 20 cigarettes per smoker are consumed per day, costing the average Canadian smoker anywhere from an estimated $864 per year in Quebec to $2,132 in Newfoundland. Manufactured cigarettes account for about 85% of total tobacco consumption while fine-cut tobacco accounts for 14%. Cigars, pipe tobacco and smokeless tobacco account for less than 2% of all sales.

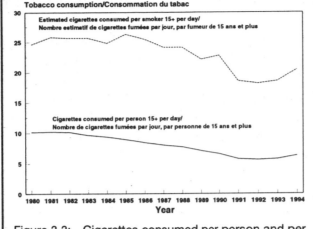

Figure 3.3:   Cigarettes consumed per person and per smoker, per day, Canada, 1980 to 1994

Figure 3.3:   Nombre de cigarettes fumées par personne et par fumeur, par jour, Canada, 1980 à 1994

17,7% chez les 15 à 17). Sur le plan régional, les taux de prévalence chez les jeunes de cet âge sont nettement plus élevés à Terre-Neuve et au Québec (18,7% et 18,4% respectivement) que dans les autres provinces. Le taux le plus bas au pays revient à la Saskatchewan.

Consommation des cigarettes et du tabac vendus sur le marché canadien

Tobacco-related mortality and morbidity

Estimates of tobacco-attributable deaths and hospitalizations are available for 1992 from a recent study of the economic costs of substance abuse in Canada (Single et al., 1996). These estimates are based on the application of aetiologic fractions of the proportion of disease and death attributable to tobacco for 31 causes of disease and death to the number of cases of death or hospitalization for each of these causes in each age, gender and province. The aetiologic fractions are based on estimates of the relative risk of smoking combined with data on province, age and

Selon les données des ventes, les Canadiens ont fumé quelque 52,8 milliards de cigarettes en 1994, soit 9,2 % de moins que l'année précédente (Tableau 3.6). Depuis 1980, la consommation du tabac a régressé en moyenne de 1,8% par année. En 1994, les 15 ans et plus ont fumé une moyenne de 2 315 cigarettes chacun (environ 6,3 cigarettes par jour). Les fumeurs fument environ 20 cigarettes chacun par jour, pour un coût moyen allant de 864 $ par année au Québec à 2 132 $ par année à Terre-Neuve. Les cigarettes fabriquées représentent quelque 85% de la consommation globale de tabac et le tabac fine coupe, 14%. Les cigares, le tabac à pipe, et le tabac à priser ou à chiquer composent moins de 2% de toutes les ventes.

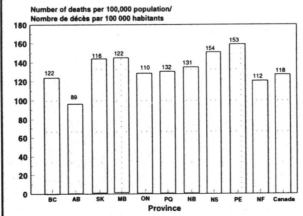

Figure 3.4:   Rates of death per 100,000 population indirectly due to Smoking, Canada and Provinces, 1992.

Figure 3.4:   Taux de décès par 100 000 habitants indirectement reliés au tabagisme, Canada et provinces, 1992

---

gender specific prevalence of current and former smoking (Single et al., 1996). The relative risk estimates are based on pooled estimates from large scale epidemiological studies in meta-analyses of 31 causes of death or disease attributable to smoking.

There were an estimated 33,498 deaths attributed to tobacco in 1992 (Table 3.7). The largest number of tobacco-related deaths (11,704) stem from lung cancer, representing 35% of all such deaths. Tobacco-related ischaemic heart disease accounts for 6,762 deaths and chronic obstructive pulmonary disease (COPD) accounts for 5,816 deaths. More than two thirds (69%) of those who die from tobacco-related causes in Canada are men.

As seen in Table 3.8, tobacco-attributable mortality is highest in Nova Scotia (154 deaths per 100,000) and Prince Edward Island (153 per 100,000). Alberta, on the other hand, has the lowest rate of mortality due to smoking (89 deaths per 100,000 population). Ontario (110 per 100,000), Newfoundland (112 per 100,000) and Saskatchewan (116 per 100,000) also have relatively low tobacco mortality rates, while Québec (132 per 100,000) and New Brunswick (131 per 100,000) are above the national average.

There were 208,095 hospital separations due to tobacco use in Canada in 1992 (Table 3.9). The largest number were for ischaemic heart disease (37,648 hospital separations for men and 14,363 for women). There were more than 3 million hospital days (3,024,265) resulting from tobacco-related causes. The largest contributors to the number of tobacco-related hospital days were COPD (630,282 days or 21% of the total due to tobacco), stroke (570,289 days or 19%), ischaemic heart disease (450,795 days or 15%) and lung cancer (423,239 days or 14%).

Provincial differences in hospitalizations and hospitalization days due to tobacco use (Table 3.10) generally reflect the mortality pattern, with the highest rate of tobacco attributable hospitalizations per capita in Nova Scotia (1,079 per 100,000 population) and the lowest per capita rate in Alberta (636 per 100,000). However, the highest rates of hospital days due to

Mortalité et morbidité reliées au tabac

Les estimations des décès et des hospitalisations imputables au tabac en 1992 sont tirées d'une récente étude sur les coûts économiques de l'abus des drogues au Canada (Single et coll., 1996). Ces estimations sont établies à partir des fractions étiologiques obtenues quant à la proportion des maladies et des décès imputables au tabac dans le cas de 31 causes de maladies et de décès par rapport au nombre de décès ou d'hospitalisations enregistrés pour chacune de ces causes, selon l'âge, le sexe et la province. Le calcul des fractions étiologiques s'appuie sur le risque estimatif associé au tabagisme et sur la prévalence spécifique à la province, à la tranche d'âge et au sexe s'appliquant aux fumeurs actuels et aux anciens fumeurs (Single et coll., 1996). Les estimations du risque relatif sont pour leur part établies d'après les estimations regroupées des études épidémiologiques à grande échelle effectuées dans le cadre des méta-analyses de 31 causes de décès ou de maladies imputables au tabagisme.

En 1992, le nombre estimatif des décès imputables au tabac s'élevait à 33 498 (Tableau 3.7). La majorité de ces décès (11 704 ou 35%) découlent du cancer du poumon. Les cardiopathies ischémiques dues au tabac sont responsables de 6 762 décès et les maladies pulmonaires obstructives chroniques, de 5 816 décès. Plus des deux tiers (69%) des Canadiens qui décèdent de causes imputables au tabac sont des hommes.

Comme l'indique le Tableau 3.8, c'est en Nouvelle-Ecosse et à l'Ile-du-Prince-Edouard que l'on enregistre la plus forte mortalité due au tabac, avec 154 et 153 décès par 100 000 habitants respectivement. C'est en Alberta que ce type de mortalité est le plus faible, avec 89 décès par 100 000 habitants, puis en Ontario (110 par 100 000), à Terre-Neuve (112 par 100 000) et en Saskatchewan (116 par 100 000), tandis que le Québec (132 par 100 000) et le Nouveau-Brunswick (131 par 100 000) affichent pour leur part des taux supérieurs à la moyenne nationale.

tobacco-related illnesses are in New Brunswick (13,493 days per 100,000 population) and in Quäbec (13,225 per 100,000).

The estimated 33,498 deaths due to tobacco represent 17% of total mortality in Canada for 1992. The 495,640 years of potential life lost due to tobacco represents 16% of the total years of potential life lost due to any cause, the 208,095 hospitalizations due to tobacco constitute 6% of all hospitalizations, and the 3.0 million days of hospitalization due to tobacco represent 7% of all hospital days for any cause.

References

Health and Welfare Canada, Stephens, T. and Fowler Graham D., editors *Canada's Health Promotion Survey 1990: Technical Report*, (Ottawa: Ministry of Supply and Services Canada, 1993)

Kaisermann, M.J. Tobacco Production, Sales and Consumption in Canada, 1991. *Chronic Diseases in Canada* 13, 4 (1992): 68-71.

Stamler, R.T. Contraband Tobacco Estimate - June 30, 1992.

Single, E., L. Robson, X Xie, and J. Rehm, *The Costs of Substance Abuse in Canada*, Ottawa, Canadian Centre on Substance Abuse, 1996.

Stamler, R.T. Contraband Tobacco Estimate - June 30, 1992.

En 1992, on a dénombré 208 095 départs des hôpitaux dus au tabac (Tableau 3.9). La majeure partie de ces départs étaient associés à des cardiopathies ischémiques (37 648 chez les hommes contre 14 363 chez les femmes). On a par ailleurs relié plus de 3 millions de jours d'hospitalisation (3 024 265) au tabagisme, dont les principales causes sont les maladies pulmonaires obstructives chroniques (630 282 jours ou 21%), les accidents cérébro- vasculaires (570 289 jours ou 19%), les cardiopathies ischémiques (450 795 jours ou 15%), et le cancer du poumon (423 239 jours ou 14 %).

Les écarts provinciaux observés quant aux nombres des hospitalisations et aux jours d'hospitalisation dus au tabac (Tableau 3.10) suivent généralement le profil de la mortalité, avec le taux d'hospitalisation le plus élevé par habitant imputable au tabac revenant à la Nouvelle-Ecosse (1 079 par 100 000 habitants) et le plus faible, à l'Alberta (636 par 100 000). Par contre, c'est au Nouveau-Brunswick et au Québec que l'on a enregistré les taux les plus élevés en ce qui concerne les jours d'hospitalisation dus aux maladies associées au tabac, avec 13 493 jours et 13 225 jours par 100 000 habitants respectivement.

Les 33 498 décès que l'on estime être imputables au tabac constituent 17% de l'ensemble de la mortalité au Canada en 1992.

Quant aux 495 640 années de vie potentielle perdues associées au tabac, elles représentent 16% de l'ensemble des années de vie potentielle perdues abstraction faite de la cause, tandis que les 208 095 hospitalisations dues au tabac comptent pour 6% de l'ensemble des hospitalisations, et les trois millions de jours d'hospitalisation, pour 7% de tous les jours d'hospitalisation, indépendamment de la cause.

Ouvrages de référence

Santé Canada, Stephens, T. et D. Fowler-Graham, éd., enquête *Promotion de la santé 1990 : rapport technique*, (Ottawa : Approvisionnements et Services Canada, 1993)

Kaisermann, M.J. Tobacco Production, Sales and Consumption in Canada, 1991. *Chronic Diseases in Canada*, vol. 13, no 4, 1992, p. 68-71.

Single, E., L. Robson, X. Xie et J. Rehm, *The Costs of Substance Abuse in Canada*, Ottawa, Centre canadien de lutte contre l'alcoolisme et les toxicomanies, 1996.

Stamler, R.T. *Contraband Tobacco Estimate* - June 30, 1992.

TABLE 3.1	TABLEAU 3.1

Adjusted prevalence of current[1] cigarette smokers, age 15 or older, Canada, 1965 to 1995

Prévalence ajustée des fumeurs actuels[1] de cigarettes, population des 15 ans et plus, Canada, 1965 à 1995

YEAR/ ANNEE	SMOKERS/ FUMEURS	SOURCE/ SOURCE
1965	49.5%	Labour Force Survey supplement, adjusted/ Enquête sur la population active, supplément, données ajustées
1970	46.5	Labour Force Survey supplement, adjusted/ Enquête sur la population active, supplément, données ajustées
1974	45.5	Labour Force Survey supplement, adjusted/ Enquête sur la population active, supplément, données ajustées
1975	44.5	Labour Force Survey supplement, adjusted/ Enquête sur la population active, supplément, données ajustées
1977	43.0	Labour Force Survey supplement, adjusted/ Enquête sur la population active, supplément, données ajustées
1978	40.5	Canada Health Survey self-completed questionnaire/ Enquête Santé Canada, questionaire rempli sans intermédiaire
1979	41.0	Labour Force Survey supplement, adjusted/ Enquête sur la population active, supplément, données ajustées
1981	39.5	Labour Force Survey supplement, non-proxy only/ Enquête sur la population active, supplément, données ajustées
1983	37.5	Labour Force Survey supplement, non-proxy only/ Enquête sur la population active, supplément, données ajustées
1985	34.0	General Social Survey Telephone Interview/ Enquête sociale générale, interview téléphonique
1986	33.0	Labour Force Survey supplement, non-proxy only/ Enquête sur la population active, supplément, données ajustées
1988	32.0	Campbell Survey on Well-being in Canada/ Enquête Campbell sur le bien-être au Canada
1989	32.0	National Alcohol and Other Drugs Survey/ Enquête nationale sur l'alcool et les autres drogues
1990	29.0	Health Promotion Suvey/Enquête promotion de la santé
1991	31.0	General Social Survey Telephone Interview/ Enquête sociale générale, interview téléphonique
1994	31.0	Survey on Smoking in Canada/ Enquête sur le tabagisme au Canada
1994	27.0	Canadian Alcohol and Other Drugs survey/ Enquête Canada sur l'alcool et les autres drogues
Feb. 1995	27.4	Survey on Smoking in Canada/ Enquête sur le tabagisme au Canada

| TABLE 3.1 (concluded) | TABLEAU 3.1 (fin) |

Adjusted prevalence of current[1] cigarette smokers, age 15 or older, Canada, 1965 to 1995

Prévalence ajustée des fumeurs actuels[1] de cigarettes, population des 15 ans et plus, Canada, 1965 à 1995

[1] Current cigarette smokers are regular (daily) smokers plus occasional smokers./Incluent les fumeurs quotidiens et les fumeurs occasionnels.

Note: Estimates for 1981, 1983, and 1986 are based on non-proxy data only from the labour Force Survey supplements (The Smoking Habits of Canadians series). Estimates from this source prior to 1981 have been adjusted to account for proxy data, since it was not possible to identify the proxy responses and remove them from the estimate. The adjustment is based on making systematic comparisons for individual age and sex groups between two estimates: (a) those based on self-reports only from the 1981-86 Labour Force Survey supplements, and (b) those based on all data (self- and proxy reports) from these same sources. The average discrepancy for these three years, for individual age and sex groups, was calculated and applied to the published estimates for the Labour Force survey supplements of 1965 through 1979. For further details on this adjustment, see: Stephens T. A Critical Review of Canadian Survey Data on Tobacco Use, Attitudes and Knowledge. Ottawa: Tobacco Programs Unit, 1988. No adjustments were made to the published data from the other sources as these were all based exclusively on self-reports.

Note: Les estimations pour les années 1981, 1983, et 1986 sont exclusivement basées sur les données fournies directement et provenant des suppléments de l'Enquête sur la population active (Collection Les habitudes des Canadiens à l'égard du tabac). Les estimations d'avant 1981 tirées de cette source ont été ajustées de façon. à tenir compte des données fournies par un intermédiaire, puisqu'il était impossible de repérer ces données et de les soustraire de l'estimations. L'ajustement est fonction des comparasons systématiques établies entre deux estimations pour chaque groupe selon l'âge et le sexe: a) les estimations basées uniquement sur les autodéclarations des suppléments de l'Enquête sur la population active de 1981 à 1986, et b) les estimations basées sur toutes les données, fournies directement et par intermédiaire, de ces mêmes sources. L'écart moyen observé durant ces trois ans, pour les groupes individuels d'âge et de sexe, a été évalué et pris en compte dans les estimations des suppléments de l'Enquête sur la population active de 1965 à 1979. Pour de plus amples renseignements sur cet ajustement, consulter A Critical Review of Canadian Survey, de T. Stephens. Aucun ajustement n'a été apporté aux données publiées provenant d'autres sources, puisqu'elles ont été tirées exclusivement d'autodéclarations.

Source: Health and Welfare Canada, *Canadians and Smoking: An Update* (Ottawa: Health and Welfare Canada, Health Services and Promotion Branch, 1991); Data obtained from the Canadian Centre for Health Information, Statistics Canada.

Santé et Bien-être Canada, Les Canadiens et le tabagisme: Mise à jour (Ottawa: Santé et Bien-être Canada, Direction de la promotion des services de santé, 1991); Données obtenues du Centre canadien d'information sur la santé, Statistique Canada.

TABLE 3.2   **TABLEAU 3.2**

Smoking status by age, gender, and marital status, among those aged 15 or older, Canada, 1994

Catégories de fumeurs selon l'âge, le sexe, et l'état matrimonial, population des 15 ans et plus, Canada, 1994

	SMOKING STATUS (%)/ CATÉGORIES DE FUMEURS (%)		
	NEVER/ JAMAIS FUME	FORMER/ ANCIENS	CURRENT/ ACTUELS
Total 15+	**45.5%**	**26.3%**	**27.0%**
Male/Hommes	41.3	28.7	28.4
Female/Femme	49.6	23.9	25.6
Age/Age:			
15-17	62.6	10.4	26.7
18-19	51.6	11.3	37.0
20-24	52.4	12.4	34.3
25-34	48.3	19.9	30.7
35-44	40.7	28.2	29.7
45-54	39.7	32.4	26.2
55-64	39.3	37.0	21.8
65-74	43.1	36.5	18.6
75+	55.2	36.0	8.2
Marital Status/ Etat matrimonial:			
Single/Célibataire	52.5	15.1	31.8
Married/Marié	52.5	15.1	31.8
Widowed/Divorced/Separated/ Veuf/Divorcé/Séparé	40.7	28.9	29.7

Source: Data obtained from the Canadian Centre for Health Information, Statistics Canada.

Données obtenues du Centre canadien d'information sur la santé, Statistique Canada.

TABLE 3.3

TABLEAU 3.3

Smoking status by income, education, employment, and province, among those aged 15 or older, Canada, 1994

Catégories de fumeurs selon le revenu, le niveau d'instruction, la situation d'emploi, et la province, population des 15 ans et plus, Canada, 1994

	SMOKING STATUS (%)/ CATÉGORIES DE FUMEURS (%)		
	NEVER/ JAMAIS FUME	FORMER/ ANCIENS	CURRENT/ ACTUELS
Income/Revenu :			
Lowest/Inférieur	40.1	17.3	42.6
Lower middle/Inférieur à moyen	41.6	26.9	31.5
Middle/Moyen	40.6	28.7	30.5
Upper middle/Moyen à supérieur	43.4	29.1	27.5
Highest/Supérieur	47.4	31.6	21.0
Education/Niveau d'instruction :			
Completed university/ Diplôme universitaire	9.1	4.3	2.3
Some post-secondary/ Postsecondaire partiel	12.9	7.8	7.4
Secondary/Secondaire	10.1	6.3	7.1
Less than secondary/ Moins que le secondaire	10.1	6.7	9.0
Employment/Situation d'emploi :			
Professional/Professionnel	49.3	29.7	21.0
White Collar/Col blanc	40.4	27.0	32.5
Blue Collar/Col bleu	34.5	27.7	37.4
Unemployed/Sans emploi	37.9	17.0	45.1
Student/Aux études	61.3	12.3	26.4
Retired/A la retraite	44.6	37.3	17.8
Homemaker/Au foyer	46.7	27.5	25.9
Other/Autre	45.2	27.3	27.5
Province			
Nfld./T.-N.	37.1%	30.4%	32.4%
P.E.I./I.-P.-E	38.3	31.3	30.3
N.S./N.-É.	39.4	29.4	31.0
N.B./N.-B.	40.3	27.4	32.3
Que./Québec	37.5	28.8	33.6
Ont./Ont.	52.2	22.4	22.4
Man./Man.	45.8	26.8	27.3
Sask./Sask.	43.8	30.2	25.8
Alta./Alb.	46.0	27.5	26.3
B.C./C.-B.	45.9	28.7	25.0

Source: Data obtained from the Canadian Centre for Health Information, Statistics Canada.

Données obtenues du Centre canadien d'information sur la santé, Statistique Canada.

TABLE 3.4   **TABLEAU 3.4**

Smoking status by age, gender, language, and income among those aged 15 or older, Canada, February 1995

Catégories de fumeurs selon l'âge, le sexe, et la langue et le/revenu population des 15 ans et plus, Canada, Février 1995

| | POP. EST. (000's)/ POP. EST. (MILLIERS) | SMOKING STATUS (%)/ CATÉGORIES DE FUMEURS (%) | | | | | | AMOUNT SMOKED/ CIG. FUMEES | |
| | | CURRENT SMOKERS[3]/ FUMEURS ACTUELS[3] | | FORMER SMOKERS[2]/ ANCIENS FUMEURS[2] | | NON-SMOKERS[1]/ JAMAIS FUME[1] | | Daily/ Quoti-dienne | Non-daily Non-quoti-dienne |
		Daily/ Quot.	Non-daily Non-quot.	Daily/ Quot.	Non-daily Non-quot.	Experimental/ titre d'essai	Abstainer/ jamais fumé	Ave. cigarettes/day/ Moyenne/Jour	
Total 15+	**22,765**	**23.2%**	**4.2%**	**27.1%**	**4.7%**	**14.1%**	**26.7%**	**17.7**	**2.0**
Male/Hommes	11,180	25.0	4.4	30.6	5.5	15.2	19.2	19.6	2.3
Female/Femmes	11,585	21.5	4.0	23.6	3.9	13.0	34.0	15.6	1.6
Age/Age:									
15-19	**1,936**	**18.4**	**7.3***	**7.0***	**3.1***	**18.2**	**46.0**	**11.4**	**1.6**
Male/Hommes	993	18.4	6.7*	6.9*	#	18.6	46.4	12.9	2.1
Female/Femmes	943	18.4	8.0*	7.1*	#	17.7	45.7	9.9	1.1
20-24	**2,036**	**26.0**	**8.0***	**12.3**	**3.2***	**18.1**	**32.4**	**14.9**	**1.7**
Male/Hommes	1,023	27.4	9.1*	11.3*	#	19.1	29.9	16.3	1.9
Female/Femmes	1,013	24.5	7.0*	13.3*	#	17.1*	34.9	13.3	1.4
25-44	**9,703**	**27.4**	**4.1**	**24.6**	**3.8**	**14.6**	**25.5**	**18.0**	**2.1**
Male/Hommes	4,875	28.4	4.4	27.0	3.7	16.8	19.7	17.1	2.3
Female/Femmes	4,829	26.4	3.9	22.1	3.8	12.5	31.4	14.6	1.8
45-64	**5,915**	**22.9**	**3.1**	**37.3**	**6.3**	**12.2**	**18.3**	**20.5**	**2.3**
Male/Hommes	2,938	26.2	3.2*	39.1	9.5	13.8	8.2	21.4	2.7
Female/Femmes	2,978	19.5	3.0*	35.5	3.2*	10.6	28.2	14.5	1.9
65+	**3,174**	**12.4**	**2.0***	**37.5**	**6.3**	**11.0**	**30.9**	**15.6**	**2.0**
Male/Hommes	1,352	12.9	#	57.5	7.0*	7.2*	13.3	16.2	2.7*
Female/Femmes	1,822	11.9	#	22.7	5.7*	13.7	43.9	15.1	1.6
Language/Langue									
Anglophone/Anglophones/	**16,043**	**21.6**	**4.0**	**28.5**	**4.9**	**13.7**	**27.4**	**17.9**	**1.8**
Male/Hommes	7,836	23.6	4.2	32.3	6.1	14.9	19.0	20.2	2.2
Female/Femmes	8,207	19.8	3.7	24.9	3.8	12.4	35.4	15.3	1.3
/Francophone/Francophones	**5,153**	**30.8**	**4.6**	**25.4**	**3.4**	**15.1**	**20.4**	**17.6**	**2.6**
Male/Hommes	2,492	31.7	3.5*	28.0	3.0*	15.1	17.6	18.9	2.9
Female/Femmes	2,661	30.0	4.7*	23.0	3.7*	15.6	23.0	16.4	2.2
Allophone/Allophones	**1,291**	**10.7***	**4.7***	**16.8**	**6.9***	**16.0**	**44.9**	**12.2**	**1.5**
Male/Hommes	710	13.8*	#	23.0	#	20.9	28.2	13.1	#
Female/Femmes	581	#	#	#	#	9.9*	65.6	#	#
Income/Revenu:									
Lowest/ Inférieur	**5,352**	**28.1**	**4.2**	**25.5**	**5.1**	**10.3**	**26.8**	**17.2**	**2.4**
Male/Hommes	2,253	30.1	4.7*	28.6	6.9*	11.2	18.4	18.4	2.4
Female/Femmes	3,095	26.5	3.9*	23.2	3.9*	9.6	32.9	16.2	2.5
Lower middle/Intérieur à moyen	**6,530**	**24.5**	**4.0**	**29.5**	**3.4**	**14.3**	**24.3**	**18.4**	**2.0**
Male/Hommes	3,163	25.2	4.9*	35.4	4.3*	14.3	16.0	19.5	2.6
Female/Femmes	3,367	23.9	3.2*	23.9	2.5*	14.3	32.1	17.3	1.2
Middle/Moyen	**4,971**	**20.3**	**4.5**	**31.1**	**3.6**	**16.8**	**23.7**	**17.5**	**1.6**
Male/Hommes	2,790	24.6	3.8*	33.2	3.3*	18.6	16.6	19.3	2.0
Female/Femmes	2,181	14.9	5.4*	28.4	4.1*	14.5	32.7	13.6	1.3
Upper middle/Moyen à supérieur	**2,638**	**18.8**	**4.2***	**26.9**	**4.3***	**17.6**	**28.1**	**20.0**	**1.7**
Male/Hommes	1,583	22.2	5.0*	26.3	#	17.4	24.5	22.1	2.0
Female/Femmes	1,055	13.7*	#	27.8	#	17.9	34.4	14.8	#

TABLE 3.4 (concluded)   **TABLEAU 3.4 (fin)**

Smoking status by age, gender, language, and income among those aged 15 or older, Canada, February 1995

Catégories de fumeurs selon l'âge, le sexe, et la langue et le revenu, population des 15 ans et plus, Canada, février 1995

Note/ - Data not available.
Nota: - Données non disponible
       * High sampling variability.
       * Grande variabilité de l'echantillonage.
       # Data suppressed
       # Données supprimées

[1] **NON SMOKERS** - Presently does not smoke cigarettes and has smoked fewer than 100 in lifetime.

[1] **NON FUMEURS** --Personnes ne fumant pas actuellement et ayant déjà fumé moins d'une centaine de fois.

[2] **FORMER SMOKER** - Presently does not smoke cigarettes and has smoked at least 100 in lifetime.

[2] **ANCIENS FUMEURS** -- Personnes ne fumant pas actuellement et ayant déjà fumé au moins une centaine de fois.

[3] **CURRENT SMOKER** - presently smokes cigarettes either daily or non-daily./

[3] **FUMEURS ACTUELS** -- Personnes fumant actuellement, soit quotidiennement, soit non quotidiennement.

Source: Health Canada, Survey on Smoling in Canada, cycle 4 (Ottawa: Health Canada, February 1995).

Santé Canada, Enquête sur le tabagisme au Canada,4 cycle (Ottawa : Santé Canada, février 1995)

TABLE 3.5

TABLEAU 3.5

Smoking status and the amount smoked by age and province among youth age 10 to 19, Canada, 1994

Catégories de fumeurs et nombre de cigarettes fumées, selon l'âge et la province population des 10 à 19 ans, Canada, 1994

	Pop. Est. ('000s)/ Pop. est. (milliers)	CURRENT SMOKERS/ FUMEURS ACTUELS			FORMER SMOKERS[2]/ ANCIENS FUMEURS[2]	NEVER SMOKERS[1]/ PERSONNE N'AYANT JAMAIS FUME[1]		
		Total/ Total	Daily smoker/ Fumeurs	Non-daily smoker/ Fumeurs occ.		Began smoking/ Débu-tants	Past-experimental/ Ex-fumeurs, essai	Lifetime abstainer/ Abstinents
AGE/AGE								
Total 10-19	**3,881**	**15.2%**	**10.2%**	**5.1%**	**1.5%**	**6.7%**	**11.7%**	**64.9%**
Male/Hommes	1,986	14.9	9.6	5.2	1.5	5.8	12.0	65.8
Female/Femmes	1,896	15.6	10.7	4.9	1.4	7.7	11.4	63.9
10-12	**1,166**	**2.5**	**0.5**	**2.0 ***	**--**	**4.4**	**6.1**	**86.6**
Male/Hommes	596	2.7 *	--	2.2 *	--	4.4	7.1	85.4
Female/Femmes	571	2.3 *	--	1.7 *	--	4.4	5.1	87.9
13-14	**783**	**13.4**	**5.3**	**8.1**	**0.7 ***	**11.7**	**14.8**	**59.4**
Male/Hommes	401	12.4	5.4 *	7.0	--	9.1	14.8	62.7
Female/Femmes	382	14.4	5.2 *	9.2	--	14.5	14.7	55.8
15-17	**1,149**	**19.8**	**14.7**	**5.1**	**2.2**	**6.5**	**13.8**	**57.6**
Male/Hommes	589	17.7	12.6	5.1	2.5 *	5.2	13.8	60.8
Female/Femmes	560	21.9	16.9	5.1	2.0 *	8.0	13.8	54.3
18-19	**783**	**29.0**	**22.2**	**6.7**	**2.7 ***	**5.6**	**14.0**	**48.7**
Male/Hommes	400	31.0	22.8	8.2	2.1 *	5.5 *	14.1	47.3 *
Female/Femmes	383	26.8	21.7	5.1 *	3.2 *	5.7 *	14.0	50.2
PROVINCE/PROVINCE								
Nfld./T.-N.	93	18.7%	13.5%	5.2%	2.5%	6.7%	12.7%	59.5%
P.E.I./I.-P.-E	20	15.3	11.1	4.1	--	7.1	10.3	65.6
N.S./N.-É.	126	15.1	10.3	4.8	--	6.3	11.2	66.3
N.B./N.-B.	107	16.2	11.5	4.6	--	6.0	12.0	64.3
Que./Québec	966	18.4	12.1	6.3	1.8	8.0	13.9	57.8
Ont./Ont.	1,415	13.1	8.7	4.4		6.1	10.1	69.3
Man./Man.	150	15.3	10.0	5.3	1.6	9.1	11.8	62.2
Sask./Sask.	148	11.9	7.9	4.0	--	8.8	12.9	65.4
Alta./Alb.	387	14.9	10.3	4.7	--	5.8	11.5	66.5
B.C./C.-B.	470	15.2	10.0	5.2	1.4	5.4	11.9	66.0

TABLE 3.5 (concluded)

TABLEAU 3.5 (fin)

Smoking status and the amount smoked by age and province among youth age 10 to 19, Canada, 1994

Catégories de fumeurs et nombre de cigarettes fumées, selon l'âge et la province population des 10 à 19 ans, Canada, 1994

*Data should be interpreted with caution due to sampling variability./Interpréter avec prudence en raison de la variabilité de l'échantillonnage.

--Data suppressed due to high sampling variability./Données supprimées en raison de la grande variabilité de l'échantillonnage.

[1] Never smoker - has smoked fewer than 100 cigarettes in his/her lifetime, and includes the following:/Personnes n'ayant jamais fumé -- Personnes ayant déjà fumé au plus 100 cigarettes; elles comprennent les groupes suivants

- Beginning smoker - a never smoker who has smoked between 1 and 99 cigarettes in his/her lifetime and has smoked in the past 30 days./Fumeurs débutants -- personnes ayant déjà fumé entre 1 et 99 cigarettes au cours de leur existence et ayant fumé durant les 30 jours précédents.
- Past experienter - a never smoker who has smoked between 1 and 99 cigarettes in his/her lifetime and has NOT smoked in the past 30 days./Ex-fumeurs, essai -- personnes ayant déjà fumé entre 1 et 99 cigarettes au cours de leur existence et n'ayant PAS fumé durant les 30 jours précédents.
- Lifetime abstainer - a never smoker who has smoked less than one whole cigarettes in his/her lifetime./Abstinents -- personnes ayant déjà fumé moins d'une cigarette au cours de leur existence.

[2] Former smoker - smoked 100 or more cigarettes in his/her lifetime and has not smoked at all during the past 30 days/Anciens fumeurs -- personnes ayant déjà fumé 100 cigarettes ou plus et n'ayant pas fumé durant les 30 jours précédents.

[3] Current smoker - has smoked at least 100 cigarettes in his/her lifetime, and includes the following:/Fumeur actuel - a fumé au moins 100 cigarettes au cours de son existence et comprend les catégories suivantes:

- Current daily - a current smoker who has smoked at least one cigarette per day for each of the 30 days preceeding the survey. fumeurs quotidiens -- personnes ayant fumé au moins une cigarette par jour durant les 30 jours précédents
- Current non-daily - a current smoker who has smoked at least one cigarette per day for each of the 30 days, but has not smoked every day./fumeurs non quotidiens -- personnes ayant fumé au moins une cigarette par jour mais pas à chacun des 30 jours précédents.

Source: Health Canada, *1994 youth smoking survey* (Ottawa: Health Canada, Cycle 4, 1995).

Santé Canada, *1994 Enquête sur le tabagisme auprès des jeunes* 4 cycle, 1995).

TABLE 3.6
TABLEAU 3.6

Consumption of domestically sold cigarettes and tobacco, Canada, 1980 to 1994

Consommation de cigarettes et de tabac vendus au pays, Canada, 1980 à 1994

YEAR/ ANNEE	CIGARETTES (MILLIONS)/ CIGARETTES (MILLIONS)	CIGARETTES PER PERSON 15+/ CIGARETTES PAR PERSONNE DE 15+	CIGARETTES PER DAY PER PERSON 15+/ CIGARETTES PAR JOUR PAR PERSONNE DE 15+	ESTIMATED CIGARETTES PER SMOKER[1] 15+/ CIGARETTES PAR JOUR PAR FUMEUR DE 15+
1980	70,085	3,687	10.10	24.64
1981	72,159	3,728	10.21	25.86
1982	72,818	3,703	10.14	25.68
1983	70,010	3,514	9.63	25.67
1984	68,621	3,401	9.32	24.85
1985	66,642	3,262	8.94	26.29
1986	63,544	3,069	8.41	25.48
1987	61,135	2,910	7.97	24.16
1988	60,058	2,820	7.73	24.14
1989	56,190	2,590	7.10	22.17
1990	53,154	2,413	6.61	22.80
1991	46,781	2,098	5.75	18.54
1992	46,288	2,052	5.62	18.14
1993	47,962	2,103	5.76	18.58
1994	52,807	2,315	6.34	20.46

[1] Estimated based on smoking population as presented in Table 3.1./Estimation fondée sur la population des fumeurs indiquée au Tableau 3.1.

Source: Kaiserman, M.J. *Tobacco Production, Sales and Consumption in Canada, 1991* in Chronic Diseases in Canada, Volume 13, No. 4pp. 68-71. Statistics Canada, *Production and Distribution of Tobacco Products 1980-94* (Ottawa: Statistics Canada, Catalogue No. 32-022 monthly); Statistics Canada, *Revised Intercensal Population and Family Estimates, July 1, 1971-1991* (Ottawa: Statistique Canada, Catalogue No. 91-537 Occasional, July 1994); Statistics Canada, *Annual Demographic Statistics, 1993* and *1994* (Ottawa: Statistique Canada, Catalogue No. 91-213 Annual, March 1994 and March 1995 respectively). Data for 1992 and 1993 have been estimated using the procedure described by Kaiserman.

Kaiserman, M.J. «Tobacco Production, Sales and Consumption in Canada, 1991» in *Chronic Diseases in Canada 1992, Volume 13, n° 4, p. 68-71; Statistique Canada, Production et distribution des produits du tabac 1980 à 1994* (Ottawa: Statistique Canada, Catalogue no 32-022, mensuel); Statistique Canada, Estimations intercensitaires révisées de la population et des familles au 1er juillet, 1971-1991, (Ottawa : Statistique Canada, Catalogue no 91-537, hors série, juillet 1994); Statistique Canada, *Statistiques démographiques annuelles, 1993 et 1994* (Ottawa : Statistique Canada, Catalogue no 91-213, annuel, mars 1994 et mars 1995).
Les estimations pour 1992 et 1993 ont été établies selon la formule Kaiserman.

TABLE 3.7　　　　　　　　　　　　　　　　　　　　　**TABLEAU 3.7**

Deaths and years of potential life lost attributed to tobacco by gender and cause, Canada, 1992

Décès et années de vie potentielle perdues imputables au tabac, selon le sexe et la cause, Canada, 1992

Disease/Maladie	ICD-9 Code(s) Code(s) CIM-9	Deaths / Décès			Years of Potential Life Lost/ Années de vie potentielle perdues		
		Male/ Hommes	Female/ Femmes	Total/ Total	Male/ Hommes	Female/ Femmes	Total/ Total
Lip and oropharangyeal Cancer/ /Tumeur des lèvres et de l'oropharynx	140-141, 143-146, 148-149, 230.0	/319	107	426	5,453	2,032	7,485
Oesophageal Cancer/ Tumeur de l'oesophage	150,230.1	412	117	529	6,073	2,041	8,114
Stomach cancer/Cancer de l'estomac	151,230.2	160	67	227	2,339	1,251	3,589
Anal cancer/Cancer de l'anus	154.2-154.3, 230.5 -230.6	7	5	12	123	82	205
Pancreatic cancer/Cancer du pancréas	157,230.9	284	192	476	4,352	3,429	7,781
Laryngeal Cancer/Tumeur du larynx	161, 231.0	290	39	329	4,329	720	5,050
Lung cancer/Cancer du poumon	162,231.2	8,255	3,449	11,704	117,917	67,986	185,903
Lung cancer (spousal ETS)/ Cancer du poumon (conjoint; FTA)	162,231.2	24	77	101	337	1,469	1,805
Cervical cancer/Cancer du col de l'utérus	180,233.1	0	72	72	0	2,094	2,094
Vulvar cancer/Cancer de la vulve	1844	0	17	17	0	232	232
Penile cancer/Cancer du pénis	187.1-187.4	7	0	7	89	0	89
Bladder cancer/Cancer de la vessie	188,233.7	320	87	407	3,675	1,259	4,934
Renal cancer/Cancer du rein	189.0-189.2	226	89	316	3,450	1,633	5,083
Tobacco abuse/Dépendance à l'égard du tabac	3051	11	6	17	168	86	254
Ischaemic heart disease/ Cardiopathies ischémiques	410-414	4,876	1,886	6,762	78,914	29,123	108,037
Pulmonary circulatory disease/ Affections du système circulatoire pulmonaire	415.0,416-417	63	53	116	1,012	1,204	2,217
Cardian dysrhythmias/ Dysrythmie du monocarde	427	262	143	404	4,422	2,424	6,846
Heart failure & ill-defined condition/ Insuffisance cardiaque et maladie cardiaque mal définie	428-429	321	206	527	3,923	2,534	6,457
Stroke/Accident cérébro-vasculaire	430-438	1,156	951	2,107	15,530	15,327	30,857
Arterial disease/Maladies artérielles	440-448	1,128	596	1,724	12,022	6,670	18,693
Pneumonia and influenza/ Pneumonie et grippe	480-487	608	322	930	5,677	3,562	9,240
COPD/Maladies pulmonaires obstructives chroniques	490-492,496	3,998	1,817	5,816	38,377	23,237	61,614

TABLE 3.7 (concluded)   ## TABLEAU 3.7 (fin)

Deaths and years of potential life lost attributed to tobacco by gender and cause, Canada, 1992

Décès et années de vie potentielle perdues imputables au tabac, selon le sexe et la cause, Canada, 1992

Disease/Maladie	ICD-9 Code(s) Code(s) CIM-9	Deaths / Décès			Years of Potential Life Lost/ Années De Vie Potentielle Perdues		
		Male/ Hommes	Female/ Femmes	Total/ Total	Male/ Hommes	Female/ Femmes	Total/ Total
Ulcers/Ulcères	531-534	147	74	221	1,767	960	2,728
Chrohn's disease/Maladie de Crohn	555	8	9	17	149	171	320
Ulcerative colitis/Colites	556	4	3	7	47	40	87
Pregnancy complications/ Complications de la grossesse	633-634,640-641, 656.5,658.1-658.2	0	0	0	0	15	15
Stillbirth/Mortinaissance	740-759,760-779	53	40	93	3,954	3,236	7,191
Sudden infant death syndrome/ Syndrome de la mort subite chez le nourrisson	7980	49	39	88	3,628	3,176	6,804
Accidents by fire and flames/ Accidents provoqués par le feu	E890-E899	32	16	48	1,232	685	1,917
Total/Total		23,018	10,480	33,498	318,960	176,679	495,640
Rate per 100,000 population/ Taux par 100 000 habitants		163	73	118	2,263	1,232	1,743
Tobacco-attributed deaths as % of total mortality from any cause/Décès imputés au tabac en pourcentage de la mortalité totale, indépendamment de la cause		11.71	5.33	17.05	10.36	5.74	16.09

Source: E. Single, L. Robson, X. Xie and J. Relm, *The Costs of Substance Abuse in Canada*, Ottawa: Canadian Centre on Substance Abuse, 1996.

E. Single, L. Robson, X. Xie et J. Rehm, *The Costs of Substance Abuse in Canada*, Ottawa : Centre canadien de lutte contre l'alcoolisme et les toxicomanies, 1996.

TABLE 3.8　　　　　　　　　　　　　　　　　　　　**TABLEAU 3.8**

Number and rates of death and years of potential life lost attributed to tobacco, Canadian provinces, 1992　　　Nombre et taux des décès et des années de vie potentielle perdues imputés au tabac, selon la province, 1992

Province/ Province	Deaths Due to Tobacco/ Décès imputés au tabac		Potential Years of Life Lost Due to Alcohol/ Années de vie potentielle Perdues imputées au tabac	
	Number/ Nombre	Rates per 100,00 Population/ Taux par 100 000 habitants Habitants	Number/ Nombre	Rates per 100,00 Population/ Taux par 100 000 Habitants
Nfld./T.-N.	648	112	9,650	1,661
P.E.I./I.-P.-E.	199	153	2,991	2,301
N.S./N.-É.	1,417	154	20,312	2,206
N.B./N.-B.	979	131	14,260	1,904
Que./Québec	9,457	132	144,725	2,024
Ont./Ont.	11,647	110	171,421	1,616
Man./Man.	1,362	122	18,756	1,685
Sask./Sask.	1,165	116	15,628	1,556
Alta./Alb.	2,344	89	35,531	1,350
B.C./C.-B.	4,202	122	59,784	1,732

Source: E. Single, L. Robson, X. Xie and J. Relm, *The Costs of Substance Abuse in Canada*, Ottawa: Canadian Centre on Substance Abuse, 1996.

E. Single, L. Robson, X. Xie et J. Rehm, *The Costs of Substance Abuse in Canada*, Ottawa : Centre canadien de lutte contre l'alcoolisme et les toxicomanies, 1996

TABLE 3.9

TABLEAU 3.9

Hospital separations and hospitalization days attributed to tobacco by gender and cause, Canada, 1992

Départs des hôpitaux et jours d'hospitalisation imputés au tabac selon le sexe et la cause, Canada, 1992

Disease/Maladie	ICD-9 Code(S) Code(s) CIM-9	Hospital Separations/ Départs des hôpitaux			Hospital Days/ Jours d'hospitalisation		
		Male/ Hommes	Female/ Femmes	Total/ Total	Male/ Hommes	Female/ Femmes	Total/ Total
Lip and oropharangyeal Cancer/ /Tumeur des lèvres et de l'oropharynx	140-141, 143-146, 148-149, 230.0	1,403	465	1,868	22,397	8,268	30,665
Oesophageal Cancer/ Tumeur de l'oesophage	150, 230.1	945	262	1,208	15,821	5,707	21,529
Stomach cancer/Cancer de l'estomac	151,230.2	406	150	556	6,966	3,028	9,994
Anal cancer/Cancer de l'anus	154.2-154.3, 230.5-230.6	60	80	141	641	1,422	2,064
Pancreatic cancer/Cancer du pancréas	157,230.9	515	352	866	8,943	7,232	16,174
Laryngeal Cancer/Tumeur du larynx	161,231.0	1,232	256	1,488	20,557	4,190	24,747
Lung cancer/Cancer du poumon	1162,231.2	17,290	7,734	25,024	285,511	137,728	423,239
Lung cancer (spousal ETS)/ Cancer du poumon (conjoint; FTA)	162,231.2	49	170	219	819	3,068	3,887
Cervical cancer/Cancer du col de l'utérus	180,233.1	0	1,118	1,118	0	8,627	8,627
Vulvar cancer/Cancer de la vulve	1844	0	145	145	0	2,303	2,303
Penile cancer/Cancer du pénis	187.1-187.4	48	0	48	544	0	544
Bladder cancer/Cancer de la vessie	188,233.7	3,821	874	4,698	33,307	8,386	41,693
Renal cancer/Cancer du rein	189.0-189.2	885	417	1,301	14,235	6,472	20,707
Tobacco abuse/Dépendance à l'égard du tabac	305.1	10	9	19	88	52	140
Ischaemic heart disease/ Cardiopathies ischémiques	410-414	37,648	14,363	52,011	302,584	148,211	450,795
Pulmonary circulatory disease/ Affections du système circulatoire pulmonaire	415.0,416-417	356	357	713	5,219	7,653	12,872
Cardian dysrhythmias/ Dysrythmie du monocarde	427	5,895	4,130	10,023	33,385	25,865	59,250
Heart failure & ill-defined condition/ Insuffisance cardiaque et maladie cardiaque mal définie	428-429	6,598	4,235	10,833	83,642	74,674	158,316
Stroke/Accident cérébro-vasculaire	30-438	8,389	5,508	13,897	313,352	256,937	570,289
Arterial disease/Maladies artérielles	440-448	8,594	3,534	12,129	152,758	88,167	240,925
Pneumonia and influenza/ Pneumonie et grippe	480-487	5,709	3,487	9,196	78,343	48,952	127,294
COPD/Maladies pulmonaires obstructives chroniques	490-492,496	22,595	14,277	36,872	381,254	249,028	630,282

TABLE 3.9 (concluded)　　　　　　　　　　　　　　　　**TABLEAU 3.9** (fin)

Hospital separations and hospitalization days attributed to tobacco by gender and cause, Canada, 1992

Départs des hôpitaux et jours d'hospitalisation imputés au tabac selon le sexe et la cause, Canada, 1992

DISEASE/MALADIE	ICD-9 code(s) Code(s) CIM-9	DEATHS / DÉCÈS			YEARS OF POTENTIAL LIFE LOST/ ANNÉES DE VIE POTENTIELLE PERDUES		
		MALE/ HOMMES	FEMALE/ FEMMES	TOTAL/ TOTAL	MALE/ HOMMES	FEMALE/ FEMMES	TOTAL/ TOTAL
Ulcers/Ulcères	531-534	147	74	221	1,767	960	2,728
Chrohn's disease/Maladie de Crohn	555	1,095	2,231	3,326	12,859	24,839	37,698
Ulcerative colitis/Colites	556	351	239	590	4,683	2,896	7,579
Pregnancy complications/ Complications de la grossesse	633-634,640-641, 656.5, 658.1-658.2	0	8,280	8,280	0	31,561	31,561
Neonatal conditions/Affections périnatales	760.1,761.4&.8, 762.0-&.1,764-765	354	287	641	7,355	6,008	13,363
Sudden infant death syndrome/ Syndrome de la mort subite chez le nourrisson	7980	7	5	11	8	5	13
Chemotherapy/Chémotherapie	V07.3,V58.1, V66.2	1,234	1,719	2,953	5,488	5,157	10,645
Accidents by fire and flames/ Accidents provoqués par le feu	E890-E899	37	13	50	754	328	1,082
Total/Total		**130,724**	**77,371**	**208,095**	**1,833,024**	**1,191,241**	**3,024,265**
Rate per 100,000 population/ Taux par 100 000 habitants		928	539	732	13,008	8,305	10,635
Tobacco-attributed hospitalizations as % of total mortality from any cause/Hospitalisations imputés au tabac en pourcentage de la mortalité totale, indépendamment de la cause		3.58	2.12	5.71	4.43	2.88	7.31

Source: E. Single, L. Robson, X. Xie and J. Relm, *The Costs of Substance Abuse in Canada*, Ottawa: Canadian Centre on Substance Abuse, 1996.

E. Single, L. Robson, X. Xie et J. Rehm, *The Costs of Substance Abuse in Canada*, Ottawa : Centre canadien de lutte contre l'alcoolisme et les toxicomanies, 1996.

TABLE 3.10

TABLEAU 3.10

Hospital separations and hospitalization days attributed to tobacco by cause, Canadian provinces, 1992

Départs des hôpitaux et jours d'hospitalisation imputés au tabac, selon la cause et la province, 1992

Province/ Province	Hospital Separations / Due to Tobacco/ Départs des hôpitaux imputés au tabac		Hospital Days Tobacco Due to Tobacco/ Jours d'hospitalisation imputées au tabac	
	Number/ Nombre	Rates Per 100,000 Population/ Taux par 100 000 habitants Habitants	Number/ Nombre	Rates Per 100,000 Population/ taux par 100 000 Habitants
Nfld./T.-N.	4,664	803	54,404	9,362
P.E.I./Î.-P.-E.	1,138	875	12,243	9,418
N.S./N.-É.	9,932	1,079	106,416	11,554
N.B./N.-B.	7,688	1,026	101,078	13,493
Que./Québec.	52,735	737	945,656	13,225
Ont./Ont.	69,319	653	1,007,646	9,497
Man./Man.	8,576	770	115,329	10,361
Sask./Sask.	9,817	977	113,544	11,304
Alta./Alb.	16,738	636	171,228	6,505
B.C./C.-B.	25,123	728	376,545	10,910

Source: E. Single, L. Robson, W. Xie and J. Rehm, *The Cost of Substance Abuse in Canada*, Ottawa: Canadian Centre on Substance Abuse, 1996.

E. Single, L. Robson, X. Xie et J. Rehm, *The Costs of Substance Abuse in Canada*, Ottawa : Centre canadien de lutte contre l'alcoolisme et les toxicomanies, 1996.

4 Licit and Illicit Drugs

4 Les drogues licites et illicites

Figures

Tables

Figures

Tableaux

Highlights

★ The 1994 *Canadian Alcohol and Drug Survey* indicates that 13.1% of Canadians use opiate narcotics, 4.3% use tranqillizers, 4.5% use sleeping pills and 3.0% use antidepressants.

★ In 1995, the number of prescriptions written for psychotherapeutic drugs increased by 7.1% and prescriptions for analgesics increased by 3.0% over the previous year.

★ Illicit drug use increased substantially across the country from 1993 to 1994. Use of cannabis increased from 4.2% to 7.4%, cocaine increased from 0.3% to 0.7%, and LSD, speed or heroin increased from 0.3% in 1993 to 1.1% in 1994.

★ In 1993, Canadian police forces seized 144,548 kg of cannabis, 4,515 kg of cocaine and 94 kg of heroin. Cannabis seizures represent a 25% increase over the previous year. There were 1,115 thefts and other losses involving narcotics and controlled drugs; 1,592 prescription forgeries were detected.

★ In 1991 and 1992, more than half of the people accused of homicide used a substance of some kind at the time of the incident. About 4% of all homicide victims were on drugs; one in ten had both alcohol and drugs in their systems. According to Juristat, 51 people are known to be killed in drug disputes.

★ In 1992, there were 732 deaths (641 males and 91 females) in Canada attributable to illicit drugs. This includes 308 suicides, 104 opiate poisonings, 68 cocaine poisonings and 61 AIDS deaths due to intravenous drug use. The highest risk of death due to illicit drugs is in British Columbia and the lowest in Newfoundland.

★ There were 7,095 hospitalizations and 58,571 hospitalizations days attributable to illicit drugs in Canada in 1992.

Points saillants

★ Selon l'Enquête canadienne sur l'alcool et les drogues de 1994, 13,1 % de la population consomme des narcotiques, 4,3 % des tranquillisants, 4,5 % des somnifères, et 3,0 % des antidépresseurs.

★ En 1995, le nombre des ordonnances émises a augmenté de 7.1 % dans le cas des drogues psychothérapeutiques et de 3 % dans celui des analgésiques, par rapport à l'année précédente.

★ En 1994, la consommation des drogues illicites a considérablement augmenté dans tout le pays, par rapport à 1993, celle du cannabis passant de 4,2 % à 7,4 %, celle de la cocaïne de 0,3 % à 0,7 %, et celle du LSD, du speed ou de l'héroïne de 0,3 % à 1,1 %.

★ En 1993, les forces policières canadiennes ont saisi 144 548 kg de cannabis, 4 515 kg de cocaïne et 94 kg d'héroïne. Les saisies de cannabis représentent une hausse de 25 % sur l'année précédente. On a relevé 1 115 vols et autres pertes de narcotiques et de drogues contrôlées et détecté 1 592 ordonnances falsifiées.

★ Il a été établi qu'en 1991 et 1992, plus de la moitié des personnes accusées d'homicide avaient consommé une substance intoxicante. Environ 4 % des victimes d'homicide étaient sous l'effet de la drogue; dans un cas sur dix, l'organisme portait des traces d'alcool et de drogue. Selon Juristat, au moins 51 personnes ont été tuées dans des querelles de drogues.

★ En 1992, le Canada a enregistré 732 décès (641 hommes et 91 femmes) imputables aux drogues illicites. Ce chiffre comprend 308 suicides, 104 empoisonnements par opiacés, 68 empoisonnements cocaïniques et 61 décès de sidéens contaminés par intraveineuses. Le taux de décès le plus élevé dû aux drogues illicites revient à la Colombie- Britannique et le plus bas à Terre-Neuve.

★ Le Canada a enregistré 7 095 hospitalisations et 58 571 jours d'hospitalisation imputables aux drogues illicites en 1992.

Licit and Illicit Drugs

by Diane McKenzie and Eric Single, Canadian Centre on Substance Abuse

Overview

In past years, there has been ongoing pressure to treat licit and illicit drugs separately in this volume. Several issues associated with the realities of drug reporting systems and harms to society defy the logic of this approach. For example, the medical profession's practice of merging the diagnostic classifications for licit and illicit drug problems complicates efforts to divide the information base. Another reality is that the diversion of licit drugs onto illicit markets plays a critical role in drug-related deaths across the country. Studies of drug deaths in Vancouver and Toronto emphasize this interaction (British Columbia, 1994; Metro Toronto Research Group on Drug Use [MTRGDU], 1995). This chapter adopts the position that licit and illicit drug use should be analyzed for their interconnecting elements.

Unlike alcohol, the use of licit and illicit drugs in Canada is not well documented, a situation that affects what we know about them, and the adequacy of policies to address the consequences of their use. Sales of prescription drugs are not monitored on a national basis and information about illicit drugs is limited to reports of drug seizures, enforcement activities and surveys. This information base is limited in quality and scope. The relationship between licit and illicit drug use is a puzzle to be pieced together with caution.

Licit Drugs

SOURCES OF INFORMATION: The patterns of licit drug use and associated problems are difficult to describe. Information about prescription drugs is available from industry-based services (e.g. IMS) that supply market information and analysis to Canada's health and

Les drogues licites et illicites

par Diane McKenzie et Eric Single, Centre de lutte contre l'alcoolisme et les toxicomanies

Àperçu

Au cours des récentes années, nous avons été maintes fois pressés de traiter séparément, dans la présente collection, les drogues licites et les drogues illicites. Toutefois, les réalités des systèmes de déclaration des drogues et de leurs méfaits sur la société sont telles qu'il est pour l'instant inconcevable de procéder ainsi. Par exemple, le fait que le corps médical n'établisse aucune distinction de classification entre les diagnostics associés aux drogues licites et ceux associés aux drogues illicites décourage toute initiative visant à diviser la base d'information. Une autre difficulté découle du fait que le détournement des drogues licites vers les marchés illicites occupe une place majeure dans les décès reliés à la drogue au pays. Des études de ces décès à Vancouver et à Toronto insistent sur cette interaction (Colombie-Britannique, 1994; Metro Toronto Research Group on Drug Use [MTRGDU], 1995). Nous avons donc jugé à-propos, dans le présent chapitre, d'analyser la consommation des drogues licites et illicites en fonction de leurs éléments interrelationnels.

Contrairement à l'alcool, la consommation des drogues licites et illicites au Canada demeure mal documentée, situation qui affecte nos connaissances à leur sujet ainsi que la pertinence des politiques adoptées pour contrer leurs méfaits. Les ventes des drogues d'ordonnance ne sont pas contrôlées sur une base nationale, et l'information disponible sur les drogues illicites provient strictement des rapports des saisies de drogues, des activités policières et des enquêtes. La qualité et la valeur de cette base d'information sont limitées. Le lien entre la consommation des drogues

pharmaceutical industries. Surveys, another source of information about drug-related behaviour, are limited because "use" is measured in ways that do not quantify safe and hazardous behaviour.

The following information about licit drugs is based on five sources: (1) the 1994 Canadian Alcohol and Drug Survey, (2) market survey research by IMS, (3) Bureau of Drug Surveillance diversion statistics, (4) hospital separations, from the Canadian Centre for Health Information, and (5) causes of death, from Statistics Canada.

PATTERNS OF USE: Use of licit drugs, such as sleeping pills, increased between 1993 and 1994 (Figure 4.1). The 1994 Canadian Alcohol and Drug Survey documented use of five categories of licit prescription drugs over the past year: sleeping pills, tranquillizers, diet pills and stimulants, antidepressants, and narcotic pain relievers (Health Canada, 1995). Licit drug use tends to decrease with higher education and income (Table 4.1). tranquillizers, sleeping pills and antidepressants are used by lower income groups and the less educated. People with higher education or income tend to use more prescription narcotics and aspirin. There are no clear occupational trends.

Codeine, Demerol and Morphine: Overall, 13.1% of adult Canadians used an opiate narcotic (e.g. codeine, Demerol, and morphine) in the year before answering the Canadian Alcohol and Drug Survey (Table 4.1). Use of these drugs was highest among those 18 to 19 (15.5%) and lowest between age 55 and 64 (10.8%). Codeine, Demerol and morphine were more likely to be used by people who are divorced or separated (15%), and least

licites et des drogues illicites se présente un peu à la manière d'un puzzle dont il convient de rassembler les pièces avec beaucoup d'attention.

Les drogues licites

SOURCES D'INFORMATION : Expliquer les profils de la consommation des drogues licites et des problèmes connexes constitue une tâche complexe. L'information sur les drogues d'ordonnance provient des services de l'industrie (notamment IMS) chargés de fournir données et analyses de marché aux secteurs des services de santé et des produits pharmaceutiques. Les enquêtes, autre source d'information sur les comportements liés à la drogue, sont limitées puisque leurs mesures de la consommation ne permettent pas d'établir la frontière entre les comportements sécuritaires et dangereux.

L'information sur les drogues licites présentée ci-après s'appuie sur cinq sources, à savoir : l'Enquête canadienne sur l'alcool et les drogues de 1994; les études de marché d'IMS; les statistiques du Bureau de la surveillance des médicaments sur le détournement des produits pharmaceutiques; les départs des hôpitaux, du Centre canadien d'information sur la santé; et les causes de décès, de Statistique Canada.

PROFILS DE CONSOMMATION : En 1994, la consommation des drogues licites, telles les somnifères, a excédé celle de 1993 (Figure 4.1). L'Enquête canadienne sur l'alcool et les drogues de 1994 a documenté la consommation de cinq catégories de drogues d'ordonnance licites au cours de la récente année :somnifères, tranquillisants, amphétamines et

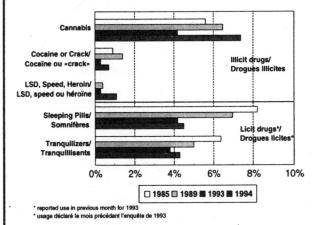

Figure 4.1:   Proportion reporting use of selected drugs in the past year, age 15 and over, Canada, 1985, 1990, 1993 and 1994.

Figure 4.1:   Proportion de ceux qui ont déclaré avoir utilisé certaines drogues l'année précédente, population des 15 ans et plus, Canada, 1985, 1990, 1993 et 1994.

likely to be used by those who are married (12.8). Use was highest among those with the lowest income (16.4%). Women (14.1%) were more likely to use these drugs than men (12%). Regionally, opiate narcotics were most likely to be used in British Columbia (21.2%) and least likely to be used in Quebec (6.8%).

Tranquillizers, Sleeping Pills and Antidepressants: Use of tranquillizers (4.3%), sleeping pills (4.5%) and antidepressants (3.0%) is low in Canada (Table 4.1). They tend to be used more as people age. For example, the elderly (over 75) had the highest levels of use (8.8% for tranquillizers and 11.4% for sleeping pills). Antidepressants were used more often by individuals between 45 and 64 (3.9%). Women tended to use these drugs (5.3% for tranqillizers; 5.4% for sleeping pills; 4.2% for antidepressants) more frequently than men (3.4% for tranquillizers; 3.7% for sleeping pills; 1.7% for antidepressants).

The proportion of Canadians who used tranquillizers, sleeping pills and antidepressants decreases as income increases. tranquillizers (6.3%) and sleeping pills (8.0%) were used most by those in the low income categories and antidepressants were used most by those in the low (3.8%) and lower middle groups (3.9%).

Regional patterns of use differ across the country for these drugs. For example, tranquillizers were used most in Quebec (6.8%) and least in Alberta (3.0%). Sleeping pills were most popular in Prince Edward Island (6.1%) and least popular in Newfoundland (2.7%). Antidepressants were used most in Nova Scotia (4.1%) and least in Ontario (1.8%).

Diet Pills: Diet pills were used by less than 1% of the Canadian population (0.9%) (Table 4.1). Young people between 15 and 17 (1.7%) and 20 and 24 (2.2%), single (1.6%), with low incomes (1.2%), white collar workers (1.4%), students (1.4%) and the unemployed (1.3%) tended to use them more than others. Regionally, diet pills were more popular in New Brunswick (1.4%) and Alberta (1.4%).

stimulants, antidépresseurs, et analgésiques narcotiques (Santé Canada, 1995). La consommation de ces drogues tend à diminuer au fur et à mesure qu'augmentent le niveau d'instruction et le revenu (Tableau 4.1). Les tranquillisants, les somnifères et les antidépresseurs sont consommés par les groupes les moins nantis et les moins instruits, tandis que les plus instruits ou les mieux nantis consomment surtout des narcotiques d'ordonnance et de l'aspirine. On ne constate aucune tendance clairement rattachée à la profession.

Codéine, Demerol et morphine : Dans l'ensemble, 13,1 % des Canadiens adultes ont utilisé un narcotique (-à-d., codéine, Demerol, et morphine) l'année précédant l'Enquête canadienne sur l'alcool et les drogues (Tableau 4.1). La plus forte consommation de ces drogues vise les 18 et 19 ans (15,5 %) et la plus basse, les 55 à 64 ans (10,8 %). La codéine, le Demerol et la morphine sont surtout utilisés par les personnes divorcées ou séparées (15 %), et le moins utilisés par les personnes mariées (12,8 %). Le taux de consommation le plus élevé revenait au groupe de plus faible revenu (16,4 %). Les femmes (14,1 %) étaient plus nombreuses que les hommes (12 %) à utiliser ces produits. Sur le plan régional, c'est en Colombie-Britannique que l'on utilise le plus de narcotiques (21,2 %) et au Québec le moins (6,8 %).

Tranquillisants, somnifères et antidépresseurs : Les Canadiens utilisent peu de tranquillisants (4,3 %), de somnifères (4,5 %) et d'antidépresseurs (3,0 %) (Tableau 4.1). Mais ils tendent à en consommer davantage avec l'âge. Ainsi, ce sont les plus âgés (plus de 75 ans) qui ont enregistré les taux de consommation les plus élevés (tranquillisants, 8,8 % et somnifères, 11,4 %). Les antidépresseurs sont surtout consommés par les 45 à 64 ans (3,9 %). Les femmes sont plus nombreuses à en consommer que les hommes (tranquillisants, 5,3 % contre 3,4 %; somnifères, 5,4 % contre 3,7 %; antidépresseurs, 4,2 % contre 1,7 %).

La proportion des Canadiens qui utilisent des tranquillisants, des somnifères et des antidépresseurs diminue au fur et à mesure que les revenus augmentent.

Steroids and Solvents: Less than 0.5% of Canadians over age 15 are currently using steroids or have ever tried them in the past (Health Canada, 1995). Solvents were used by less than 0.1% of adult Canadians in the year before answering the *Canadian Alcohol and Drug Survey* (Table 4.2). Young people between 15 and 17 were the main consumers. Regionally, solvents were used by more people in Quebec (0.2%), Ontario (0.1%) and Alberta (0.1%). These estimates may be low because people who use solvents are not usually captured in telephone surveys.

LEVEL OF CONSUMPTION: In the 12-month period ending July, 1995, about 226.8 million prescriptions were dispensed throughout Canadian retail pharmacies, rising almost 4% over the previous year (IMS, 1995). The top three therapeutic classes of drug prescriptions were cardiovascular drugs, accounting for 12.7% (28.5 million prescriptions) of all prescriptions, followed by systemic anti-infective drugs (12.3% or 28.1 million prescriptions) and psychotherapeutic drugs (7.1% or 22.6 million prescriptions) (IMS, 1995).

A complete documentation is available for 1993/94. Of the top 10 therapeutic classes of drug prescriptions, cardiovascular drugs also lead the list, accounting for 12.7% of all prescriptions, followed by systemic anti-infective drugs (12.1%), psychotherapeutic drugs (9.7%), analgesics (8.6%), hormone drugs (7.5%), bronchial therapy drugs (5.1%), anti-spasmodics (4.8%), anti-arthritics (4.5%), contraceptives (4.1%) and diuretics (4.0%) (Figure 4.2). These 10 therapeutic classes accounted for 73.1% of all prescriptions written in 1993/94 and 65.5% of total drug sales (Therriault, 1994). In 1993/94, the number of prescriptions

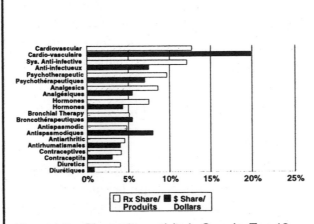

Figure 4.2:   Dispensing activity in Canada: Top 10 therapeutic classes of licit drugs in 1994

Figure 4.2:   Emission des ordonnances au Canada : les 10 grandes classes de drogues licites thérapeutiques, 1994

Ce sont les groupes à faible revenu qui consomment le plus de tranquillisants (6,3 %) et de somnifères (8,0 %), tandis que ceux de revenu le plus bas (3,8 %) et de revenu faible à moyen (3,9 %) consomment le plus d'antidépresseurs.

Les tendances régionales de consommation de ces drogues varient à travers le pays. Par exemple, c'est au Québec (6,8 %) que l'on utilise le plus de tranquillisants et en Alberta (3,0 %) le moins. Le plus grand usage des somnifères revient à l'Ile-du-Prince-Edouard (6,1 %) et le plus faible à Terre-Neuve (2,7 %). Les antidépresseurs sont surtout utilisés en Nouvelle-Ecosse (4,1 %) et le moins utilisés en Ontario (1,8 %).

Amphétamines : Moins de 1 % de la population canadienne (0,9 %) utilise des amphétamines (Tableau 4.1). Ces produits attirent surtout les jeunes de 15 à 17 ans (1,7 %) et de 20 à 24 ans (2,2 %), les célibataires (1,6 %), les personnes de faible revenu (1,2 %), les cols blancs (1,4 %), les étudiants (1,4 %) et les sans emploi (1,3 %). Sur le plan régional, les plus hauts taux d'utilisateurs vont au Nouveau-Brunswick (1,4 %) et à l'Alberta (1,4 %).

Stéroïdes et solvants : Moins de 0,5 % des Canadiens de plus de 15 ans utilisent actuellement des stéroïdes ou en ont déjà fait l'essai (Santé Canada, 1995). Moins de 0,1 % des répondants adultes avaient utilisé des solvants l'année précédant l'Enquête canadienne sur l'alcool et les drogues (Tableau 4.2). Les principaux consommateurs étaient les 15 à 17 ans. Plus de gens en ont fait usage au Québec (0,2 %), en Ontario (0,1 %) et en Alberta (0,1 %) qu'ailleurs. Ces estimations peuvent être inférieures à la réalité puisque les personnes qui consomment des solvants ne sont pas saisies normalement.

dispensed increased slightly over the previous year (1.4%) with hormones (+6.0%), systemic anti-infectives (+4.3%), bronchial therapy drugs (+4.3%), anti-spasmodics (+4.1%) and psychotherapeutic drugs (+4.0%) increasing more than others.

Illicit Drugs

SOURCES OF INFORMATION: Information about the medical and scientific use of psychoactive drugs is maintained by the Bureau of Drug Surveillance (Clark, 1992). The Bureau of Drug Surveillance functions under two legislative instruments, the *Narcotic Control Act* (NCA) and the *Food and Drugs Act* (FDA) (Clark, 1992). Under the *Narcotics Control Act*, drugs defined pharmacologically as narcotics (e.g. opium, codeine, morphine, heroine, pentazocine [Talwin], methadone, cocaine and its derivatives, cannabis and its derivatives [e.g. marijuana and hashish] and phencyclidine [PCP]) are monitored and regulated. Under the *Food and Drugs Act*, drugs are categorized as "controlled" and "restricted" drugs. Controlled drugs include stimulants such as amphetamines, methulphenidate (Ritalin), and diet prescription drugs, depressants such as the barbiturates and methaqualone and some analgesics such as butorphanol and nalbuphine. Restricted drugs are those considered to have no known medical use, such as LSD (Clark, 1992). The supply of psychoactive drugs is monitored to make sure that drugs are available for medical and scientific purposes, but to control their illegal use (Clark, 1992). The Bureau of Drug Surveillance also monitors information about drug seizures and related criminal activity. Another source, Juristat, monitors alcohol and drug involvement in crimes handled by police enforcement units across the country.

PATTERNS OF USE: Many Canadians admit using illicit drugs (Figure 4.2). Almost one in four adult Canadians, or 5,500,000 people have used an illegal substance. The most widely used illicit drug is cannabis (marijuana or hashish), used by about 5,320,000 (23.1%) adult Canadians sometime in their lives. About 875,000

TAUX D'UTILISATION : Durant la période des douze mois prenant fin en juillet 1995, quelque 226,8 millions d'ordonnances ont été remplies dans les pharmacies de détail à travers le Canada, soit près de 4 % de plus que l'année précédente (IMS, 1995). Les trois principales catégories de drogues thérapeutiques prescrites comprenaient dans l'ordre les cardio-vasculaires, soit 12,7 % (ou 28,5 millions) de toutes les ordonnances émises, les anti-infectueux (12,3 % ou 28,1 millions) et les psychothérapeutiques (7,1 % ou 22,6 millions) (IMS, 1995).

Il existe une documentation complète pour 1993-1994. Parmi les dix grandes catégories de drogues d'ordonnance thérapeutiques, ce sont aussi les cardio-vasculaires qui se sont classées en tête de liste, représentant 12,7 % de toutes les ordonnances, suivies par les anti-infectueux (12,1 %), les psychothérapeutiques (9,7 %), les analgésiques (8,6 %), les hormones (7,5 %), les bronchothérapeutiques (5,1 %), les antispasmodiques (4,8 %), les antiarthritiques (4,5 %), les contraceptifs (4,1 %), et les diurétiques (4,0 %) (Figure 4.2). En 1993-1994, ces dix classes de drogues ont représenté 73,1 % de toutes les ordonnances émises et 65,5 % des ventes de drogues globales (Therriault, 1994). La même année, le nombre des ordonnances a dépassé de 1,4 % celui de l'année précédente, les hormones (+6,0 %), les anti-infectueux (+4,3 %), les bronchothérapeutiques (+4,3 %), les antispasmodiques (+4,1 %), et les psychothérapeutiques (+4,0 %) ayant augmenté davantage que les autres.

Drogues illicites

SOURCES D'INFORMATION : L'information sur l'usage médical et scientifique des psychotropes est tenue à jour par le Bureau de surveillance des médicaments (Clark, 1992), lequel est exploité conformément à deux instruments législatifs, la Loi sur les stupéfiants et la Loi sur les aliments et drogues (Clark, 1992). En vertu de la Loi sur les stupéfiants, les drogues définies comme stupéfiants sur le plan pharmaceutique (c.-à-d. opium, codéine, morphine, héroïne, pentazocine [Talwin],

people (3.8%) say they have used cocaine or crack, 1,200,000 have used LSD (5.2 %), 485,000 people (2.1%) have used amphetamines (speed) and 115,000 people have used heroin (0.5%) in their lifetime. Although the annual use of all drugs declined over the past five years, there is evidence that Canadians used substantially more of some drugs in 1994 than in the past (Table 4.3).

Cannabis: The proportion of Canadians who said they used cannabis increased dramatically from 4.2% in 1993 to 7.4% in 1994 (Table 4.3). People under age 44, especially young adults, used more cannabis in 1994 than in the previous year. For example, individuals between 15 and 19 (10.3% in 1993 to 24.2% in 1994) and between 20 and 24 (9.7% in 1993 to 19.3% in 1994) used more cannabis in the past year (Table 4.5 and Table 4.6 respectively).

Regionally, the trend toward higher levels of cannabis use spread across the country (Table 4.5 and Table 4.6). The greatest changes were in British Columbia (6.0% in 1993 to 11.6% in 1994), Manitoba (3.3% in 1993 to 9.1% in 1994) and Alberta (3.7% in 1993 to 8.4% in 1994). The exception to this pattern was in Newfoundland (3.4% in 1993 and 3.8% in 1994) and Prince Edward Island (5.4% in 1993 to 5.6% in 1994), where the use of cannabis was stable.

Cocaine: The proportion of Canadians who used cocaine in the past year increased from 0.3% in 1993 to 0.7% in 1994 (Table 4.3). Young people under age 34 used more cocaine than in the past (Table 4.5 and Table 4.6). Regionally, cocaine use increased in Quebec (from 0.6% in 1993 to 1.2% in 1994), Alberta (from 0.1% in 1993 to 1.3% in 1994) and British Columbia (from 0.8% in 1993 to 1.2% in 1994), but stabilized in Newfoundland, Ontario and New Brunswick (Table 4.5 and Table 4.6).

LSD, Speed and Heroin: The proportion of the Canadians who used LSD, speed or heroin in the past year also increased between 1993 (0.3%) and 1994 (1.1%) (Table 4.3). Substantially more young people between 15 and 19 (from 1.7% in 1993 to 7.0% in

méthadone, cocaïne et dérivés, cannabis et dérivés [c.-à-d. marijuana et hachisch] et phencyclidine [PCP]) sont contrôlées et réglementées. La Loi sur les aliments et drogues établit deux catégories de drogues, les drogues «contrôlées»et les drogues «restreintes». Les premières incluent les stimulants tels les amphétamines, le méthulphénidate (Ritalin), et les amaigrisseurs sur ordonnance, les dépresseurs tels les barbituriques et la méthaqualone ainsi que certains analgésiques tels le butorphanol et la nalbuphine. Les drogues restreintes sont celles que l'on considère n'avoir aucun usage médical, tels le LSD (Clark, 1992). On surveille l'approvisionnement en psychotropes afin de garantir leur disponibilité aux fins médicales et scientifiques, mais aussi pour surveiller leur usage illégal (Clark, 1992). Le Bureau de surveillance des médicaments tient également à jour l'information sur les saisies de drogues et l'activité criminelle connexe. Une autre source d'information, Juristat, surveille le rôle de l'alcool et des autres drogues dans les crimes traités par les forces policières à travers le pays.

PROFILS D'UTILISATION : De nombreux Canadiens admettent consommer des drogues illicites (Figure 4.2). Près de un adulte sur quatre, soit au total cinq millions deux cent milles personnes, a déjà consommé une substance illicite. La plus populaire est le cannabis (marijuana ou haschich); quelque 5 320 000 adultes (23,1 %) ont déclaré en avoir déjà consommé. Environ 875 000 personnes (3,8 %) ont déjà consommé au moins à une reprise de la cocaïne ou du crack;, 1 200 000 (5,2 %) du LSD; 485 000 (2,1 %) des amphétamines (speed); et 115 000 (0,5 %) de l'héroïne. Même si la consommation annuelle de toutes les drogues a régressé au cours des cinq dernières années, les faits démontrent que les Canadiens ont consommé considérablement plus de certaines drogues en 1994 que dans le passé (Tableau 4.3).

Cannabis : La proportion de la population qui a déclaré avoir consommé du cannabis a fortement augmenté, passant de 4,2 % en 1993 à 7,4 % en 1994 (Tableau 4.3). Cette consommation accrue du cannabis vise principalement les moins de 44 ans, surtout les

1994) and 20 and 24 (from 1.0% in 1993 to 2.8% in 1994) reported using them (Table 4.5 and Table 4.6). Although few Canadians use these drugs, the highest proportion was in New Brunswick (1.8%), Quebec (1.6%) and B.C. (1.6%). Prince Edward Island was the only province in 1994 with no reported use of LSD, speed or heroin (Table 4.5 and Table 4.6).

SUPPLY OF ILLICIT DRUGS: The use of illicit drugs in the general population may be linked to the overall availability of drugs in society (U.N., 1994). Changes in the availability of particular drugs may be connected to home production, trafficking, diversion or control. The seizure statistics reported below are indirect indicators of trafficking as reported by the Bureau of Drug Surveillance. Because of the low statistical coverage of drug-related activities, the patterns reported below may reflect changes in reporting or recording procedures, enforcement activities or actual trafficking. Although incomplete information is available for 1994, the following analysis is based on 1993 data.[1]

Cannabis: Canadian police forces seized 144,548 kg of cannabis in 1993, a 25.6% increase over 1992 (115,081 kg) (Table 4.7). About 106,365 kg of marijuana, 36,688 kg of hash and 1,495 kg of hash oil were seized in 1993. Regionally, marijuana was seized in all areas of the country, most notably in Quebec (37,672 kg), British Columbia (29,187 kg), Alberta (22,381 kg) and Ontario (13,413 kg). Substantial quantities were also seized in Nova Scotia (1,461 kg) and Saskatchewan (999 kg). The main centres in terms of quantity of marijuna seized were Montreal, Trois Rivières, Sherbrooke and Ottawa-Hull in Quebec; Toronto, London and St. Catharines in Ontario, and Calgary and Vancouver in Western Canada.

In 1993, there were major seizures of hash in Quebec (36,273 kg) and Ontario (293 kg), and hash oil

---

[1]It is estimated that only 70% of all seizures have been reported for 1994.

jeunes adultes de 15 à 19 ans (10,3 % en 1993 contre 24,2 % en 1994) et de 20 à 24 ans (9,7 % en 1993 contre 19,3 % en 1994) (Tableau 4.5 et Tableau 4.6 respectivement).

Cette tendance à la hausse de la consommation du cannabis est perceptible dans toutes les régions du pays (Tableau 4.5 et Tableau 4.6). Les plus fortes hausses ont marqué la Colombie-Britannique (6,0 % en 1993, 11,6 % en 1994), le Manitoba (3,3 % en 1993, 9,1 % en 1994) et l'Alberta (3,7 % en 1993, 8,4 % en 1994), et les moins fortes, Terre-Neuve (3,4 % en 1993, 3,8 % en 1994) et l'Ile-du-Prince-Edouard (5,4 % en 1993, 5,6 % en 1994), où la consommation est restée stable.

Cocaïne : La proportion des Canadiens qui ont consommé de la cocaïne a aussi augmenté, passant de 0,3 % en 1993 à 0,7 % en 1994 (Tableau 4.3). Les moins de 34 ans en ont consommé davantage que dans le passé (Tableau 4.5 et Tableau 4.6). L'usage de ce produit s'est accru au Québec (0,6 % en 1993, 1,2 % en 1994), en Alberta (0,1 % en 1993, 1,3 % en 1994) et en Colombie-Britannique (0,8 % en 1993, 1,2 % en 1994), mais s'est stabilisé à Terre-Neuve, en Ontario et au Nouveau-Brunswick (Tableau 4.5 et Tableau 4.6).

LSD, speed et héroïne : La proportion des Canadiens qui ont utilisé du LSD, du speed ou de l'héroïne est passée de 0,3 % en 1993 à 1,1 % en 1994 (Tableau 4.3). Un nombre sensiblement plus important de jeunes de 15 à 19 ans (1,7 % en 1993, 7,0 % en 1994) et de 20 à 24 ans (1,0 % en 1993, 2,8 % en 1994) ont déclaré ces produits (Tableau 4.5 et Tableau 4.6). Les consommateurs de ces drogues sont peu nombreux. On les retrouve surtout au Nouveau-Brunswick (1,8 %), au Québec (1,6 %) et en Colombie-Britannique (1,6 %). Seule l'Ile-du-Prince-Edouard n'a compté aucune déclaration de ces produits en 1994 (Tableau 4.5 et Tableau 4.6).

APPROVISIONNEMENT DES DROGUES ILLICITES : La consommation des drogues illicites par la population en général peut découler de leur disponibilité dans la société (ONU, 1994). La disponibilité de

in Ontario (1,373 kg) (Table 4.7). The majority of activity was in Montreal (36,078 kg) and Toronto (141 kg) (Table 4.8). For hash oil, Toronto (335.3 kg) and Montreal (102.5 kg) were the centres of activity (Table 4.8).

Although the overall quantity of cannabis seized by enforcement units increased by one quarter in 1993, the total *number* of seizures declined (30,229 in 1993 from 32,630 in 1992). This change was due to fewer seizures of marijuana across the country (19,761 in 1993 from 24,392 in 1992) (Table 4.7).

In 1992, the highest level of THC for marijuana was 12%, and the average level was 3.1%. For hashish, the highest level was 15% and the average was 6.3%. For liquid hashish, the highest level was 35%, and the average was 12%.

Cocaine: Overall, the amount of cocaine seized by Canadian police forces declined by about 15% in 1993 (4,354.8 kg) as compared with 1992 (5,302 kg) (Table 4.7). Regionally, the most seizures were in Quebec (4,354.8 kg), Ontario (91.4 kg), British Columbia (29.45 kg) and Nova Scotia (24.7 kg) (Table 4.7). Montreal (2,903.8 kg), Toronto (57.4 kg), Halifax (24.2 kg) and Vancouver (22.6 kg) were centres for the drug trade in 1993 (Table 4.8).

Heroin: The amount of heroin seized by police enforcement agencies stabilized between 1993 (94.57 kg) and 1992 (92.3 kg) (Table 4.7). Regionally, seizures occurred almost exclusively in Ontario (47.8 kg) and British Columbia (26.27 kg). The most activity was in Toronto (45 kg), and Vancouver (25.27 kg).

Chemical Drugs: Less hallucinogens and pharmaceuticals were seized in 1993 than in the recent past (Table 4.7). For example, hallucinogens were available in all parts of Canada in 1993, especially in Quebec (17.3 kg), Ontario (5.3 kg), Alberta (4.6 kg) and British Columbia (4.27 kg). The largest quantities were seized in Quebec, especially in Trois-Rivières (5.24 kg), Quebec City (3.4 kg), and Montreal (2.68 kg). Seizures were also made in Toronto (3.47 kg) and Edmonton (2.58 kg) (Table 4.8). As compared to 1992 (546.2 kg),

certaines drogues peut varier selon leur production locale, leur trafic, leur détournement et leur contrôle. Les statistiques sur les saisies de drogues présentées ci-après sont des indicateurs indirects de leur trafic, telles qu'elles sont relevées par le Bureau de la surveillance des médicaments. Etant donné qu'il existe peu de statistiques sur les activités reliées à la drogue, les profils exposés ci-après peuvent refléter les changements survenus dans les procédures de déclaration ou d'enregistrement, les activités policières ou le trafic réel. L'information disponible pour 1994 est incomplète, mais l'analyse suivante s'appuie sur les données de 1993.[1]

Cannabis : En 1993, les forces policières canadiennes ont saisi 144 548 kg de cannabis, soit 25,6 % de plus qu'en 1992 (115,081 kg) (Tableau 4.7). Elles ont aussi saisi quelque 106 365 kg de marijuana, 36 688 kg de haschich et 1 495 kg de haschich liquide. La marijuana a été saisie dans toutes les régions du pays, surtout au Québec (37 672 kg), dont plus particulièrement à Montréal, Trois-Rivières, Sherbrooke et Hull (Tableau 4.8), en Colombie-Britannique (29 187 kg), en Alberta (22 381 kg) soit surtout à Calgary, et en Ontario (13 413 kg). D'importantes quantités ont également été saisies en Nouvelle-Ecosse (1 461 kg) et en Saskatchewan (999 kg). Les principaux centres, pour ce qui est des quantités de drogues saisies, étaient Montréal, Trois Rivières, Sherbrooke et Hull, au Québec; Ottawa, Toronto, London et St. Catharines, en Ontario; Calgary et Vancouver, dans l'ouest du Canada.

En 1993, on a procédé à d'importantes saisies de haschich au Québec (36 273 kg) et en Ontario (293 kg), ainsi que de haschich liquide en Ontario (1 373 kg) (Tableau 4.7). Elles ont surtout touché Montréal (36 078 kg) et Toronto (141 kg) (Tableau 4.8). Pour ce qui est du haschich liquide, le centre de l'activité se situait à Toronto (335,3 kg) et à Montréal (102,5 kg) (Tableau 4.8).

_____

[1]On estimé que 70% seulement des saisies de 1994 ont été déclarées.

very few pharmaceuticals were seized in 1993 (7.3 kg). The centre of activity was in Montreal (3.6 kg).

The RCMP provides information on representative street prices of illegal drugs at successive stages of trafficking (see Table 10.13). In 1992, the street price was estimated to be $35 to $50 for 0.1 gram of injectable (5% to 6%) heroin, $70 to $200 for 1 gram of 60% pure cocaine hydrochloride, $10 to $50 for 1 gram of Lebanese hashish, and $30 to $50 for 1 gram of Jamaican hashish.

Diversion of Licit Drugs to Illicit Markets

SOURCES OF INFORMATION: Licit drug diversion is defined as any illegal manoeuvre to secure drugs from the accepted distribution system (Clark, 1992; Archer, 1984). Diversion occurs at the international, national, regional or local level of the drug production and distribution systems. International/national drug diversion involves large scale criminal activity. Other sources of clandestine production involve illegal laboratories of "look-alike" drugs sold on the illicit market as prescription drugs. Losses in transit by legitimate drug manufacturers account for a small proportion of diversion activity.

At the local level, pharmacies are subject to thefts, such as break and entry, grab thefts, armed robberies and pilfering by staff (Clark, 1992). Thefts against drug wholesalers, such as manufacturers, account for less diversion in Canada because of their small numbers and because they are less accessible.

Another source of diversion at the local level is physicians (Clark, 1992). Physicians are only permitted to prescribe specially monitored drugs "to a person if that person is a patient and if the drug is required for the condition being treated" (Clark, 1992). Physicians are involved in diversion when they prescribe for themselves, are tricked by patients into supporting their addictions, or are involved in overt criminal activity for monetary gain (Clark, 1992; Wesson, 1990). Patients

La quantité globale de cannabis saisie par les forces policières a augmenté du quart en 1993, mais le nombre total des saisies a de son côté régressé (30 229 en 1993 contre 32 630 en 1992). Ce recul s'explique par un moins grand nombre de saisies de marijuana à l'échelle nationale (19 761 en 1993 contre 24 392 en 1992) (Tableau 4.7).

En 1992, le niveau de THC le plus élevé de la marijuana s'établissait à 12 %, alors que le niveau moyen était de 3,1 %. Le niveau le plus élevé enregistré pour le haschich atteignait 15 % et le niveau moyen, 6,3 %, niveaux qui se situaient à 35 % et à 12 % respectivement dans le cas du haschich liquide.

Cocaïne : Dans l'ensemble, la quantité de cocaïne saisie par les forces policières canadiennes a diminué d'environ 15 % en 1993 (4 354,8 kg) par rapport à 1992 (5 302 kg) (Tableau 4.7). Sur le plan régional, les plus importantes saisies ont eu lieu au Québec (4 354,8 kg), en Ontario (91,4 kg), en Colombie-Britannique (29,45 kg) et en Nouvelle-Écosse (24,7 kg) (Tableau 4.7). Les centres de trafic en 1993 ont été Montréal (2 903,8 kg), Toronto (57,4 kg), Halifax (24,2 kg) et Vancouver (22,6 kg) (Tableau 4.8).

Héroïne : La quantité d'héroïne saisie par les forces policières en 1993 (94,57 kg) a peu bougé par rapport à 1992 (92,3 kg) (Tableau 4.7). Dans les régions, les saisies ont presque exclusivement touché l'Ontario (47,8 kg) et la Colombie-Britannique (26,27 kg). Le plus gros de l'activité s'est déroulé à Toronto (45 kg) et à Vancouver (25,27 kg).

Drogues chimiques : On a saisi moins d'hallucinogènes et de produits pharmaceutiques en 1993 qu'au cours des années précédentes (Tableau 4.7). Cette même année, les hallucinogènes étaient disponibles dans toutes les régions du pays, surtout au Québec (17,3 kg), en Ontario (5,3 kg), en Alberta (4,6 kg), et en Colombie-Britannique (4,27 kg). C'est au Québec que l'on a saisi les quantités les plus importantes, plus précisément à Trois-Rivières (5,24 kg), à Québec (3,4 kg), et à Montréal (2,68 kg). Des saisies ont aussi été effectuées à Toronto (3,47 kg) et à

become involved in diversion when they obtain drugs illegally from physicians for personal use or for resale on the illicit market (Clark, 1992). These patients engage in double-doctoring, multiple or multi-doctoring or doctor shopping by visiting more than one physician to obtain enough drugs to meet a drug dependency or to sell.

Information about the diversion of prescription drugs to the illegal market comes from three sources. Estimates are made of the amount of prescription drugs available on the illicit market, based on information from Canadian Triplicate Prescription Programs in Alberta, Saskatchewan, Manitoba and British Columbia. Seizures of diverted licit pharmaceutical drugs and precursor chemicals by police agencies are another source. The third source involves estimates of non-medical use of prescription drugs. In Canada, all information about the diversion of licit drugs to illegal markets is problematic (Clark, 1992).

SUPPLY OF DIVERTED LICIT DRUGS: In 1993, there were 1,115 reported thefts and other losses involving narcotics and controlled drugs (Table 12.23). More than half (61%) of these thefts were from pharmacies, almost one third (33.1%) were from hospitals and 4.5% were from licensed dealers (Figure 4.3). The largest quantity of stolen narcotic drugs were methadone powder (983.2 gm), codeine tablets (535,798 tabs) and liquid (224,179 ml), hydrocodone liquid (307,507 ml), meperidine tablets (54,309 tabs), morphine tablets (94,309 tabs) and powder (77,600 gm), oxycodone tablets (223,872 tabs) and cocaine powder (80.000 gm).

The largest quantities of stolen controlled drugs for 1993 were methylphenidate tablets (45,246 tabs), phentermine capsules (14,240 caps),

Edmonton (2,58 kg) (Tableau 4.8). Par rapport à 1992 (546,2 kg), très peu de produits pharmaceutiques ont été saisis en 1993 (7,3 kg). Le centre névralgique se situait à Montréal (3,6 kg).

La GRC fournit de l'information sur les prix de la rue des drogues illicites à différentes étapes de leur trafic (voir le Tableau 10.13). En 1992, on estime qu'il en coûtait dans la rue de 35 $ à 50 $ pour se procurer 0,1 gramme d'héroïne injectable (taux de pureté établi à 5 % ou 6 %), de 70 $ à 200 $ pour 1 gramme de chlorydrate de cocaïne d'une pureté de 60 %, de 10 $ à 50 $ pour 1 gramme de haschich libanais, et de 30 $ à 50 $ pour 1 gramme de haschich jamaïcain.

Détournement des drogues licites vers les marchés illicites

SOURCES D'INFORMATION : Le détournement des drogues licites désigne toute action illégale visant à obtenir des drogues à partir du réseau officiel de distribution (Clark, 1992; Archer, 1984). Il se produit au niveau international, national, régional ou local des réseaux de production et de distribution. Le détournement international ou national suppose nécessairement une activité criminelle à large échelle. D'autres sources de production clandestine nécessite la participation de laboratoires illégaux qui fabriquent des drogues d'imitation par la suite vendues illégalement comme des drogues d'ordonnance. Les pertes de médicaments en transit par les fabricants légitimes ne représentent qu'une faible proportion de l'activité de détournement.

Au niveau local, les pharmacies sont victimes de vols, notamment les vols par effraction, les vols à l'arraché, les vols à main armée et le chapardage par

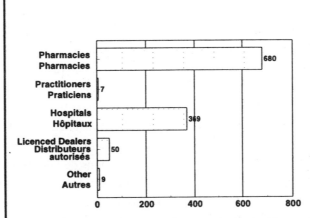

Figure 4.3:   Drug Diversion: Source of reported losses, 1993

Figure 4.3:   Détournement des drogues : Sources des pertes déclarées, 1993

barbiturate tablets (136,118 tabs), and powder (25.00 gm) (Table 12.24). Regionally, the greatest proportion of thefts were in Ontario (47.5%), followed by Quebec (17.2%), Alberta (14.1%), and British Columbia (9.1%) (Table 12.23).

Prescription forgeries also fall under drug diversion. In 1993, 1,827 prescription forgeries were detected across the country: 1,592 for narcotic drugs and 235 for controlled drugs (Table 12.25). This change represents a 16% decline from the previous year. The largest number of forgeries for narcotic drugs were for codeine (782), oxycodone (345) and meperidine (119). The largest number of prescription forgeries for controlled drugs were for secobarbital (54), methylphenidate (38), oxymetholone (38) and testosterone (38).

Drug-Related Problems

Drugs and Crime: "Drug crime" implies the involvement of illicit substances as defined by law, such as cannabis and cocaine (Wolff and Reingold, 1994). It involves activities such as possession and supply offences. Violence in the drug trade and crime that support drug habits (e.g. prostitution, theft) are other dimensions. Another facet is where drug use facilitates crime and victimization (Wolff and Reingold, 1994). The relationship between drug use and crime is based on information analyzed by Juristat.

Reported drug crime in Canada not only reflects drug use by Canadians, but police enforcement activity and reporting procedures. The number of police-reported incidents involving possession crimes declined from 58,838 incidents in 1981 to 33,037 in 1992 (Figure 4.4). Supply offences, on the other hand, increased and represent a growing proportion of drug-related crimes. For example, between 1977 and 1992, trafficking incidents increased from 10,816 to 19,539, importation incidents increased from 397 to 1,073 and cultivation incidents from 595 to 2,841. These crimes made up 18% of total drug incidents in 1977, but by 1992, this proportion more than doubled to 42% (Wolff and Reingold, 1994).

le personnel (Clark, 1992). Les vols commis contre les grossistes pharmaceutiques, tels les fabricants, constituent un pourcentage minime de l'activité de détournement au Canada, en raison du petit nombre et de la moins grande accessibilité de ces derniers.

Une autre source de détournement au niveau local concerne les médecins (Clark, 1992). En effet, ces derniers ont le droit de prescrire des *drogues contrôlées* à leurs patients uniquement et cela seulement lorsque l'état du patient l'exige (Clark, 1992). Les médecins commettent des actes de détournement lorsqu'ils libellent des ordonnances à leur propre nom, qu'ils sont amenés par la ruse des patients à entretenir la toxicomanie de ces derniers, ou qu'ils participent à des actes criminels manifestes dans le but d'un gain monétaire (Clark, 1992; Wesson, 1990). Les patients participent pour leur part au détournement lorsqu'ils obtiennent des drogues illégalement de leurs médecins, soit pour usage personnel, soit pour revente sur le marché illicite (Clark, 1992). Ces patients consultent plusieurs médecins dans le but d'obtenir suffisamment de drogues pour entretenir leur toxicomanie ou pour les revendre.

L'information sur le détournement des drogues d'ordonnance vers les marchés illicites provient de trois sources. Les estimations des quantités de drogues d'ordonnance disponibles sur le marché illicite sont calculées à partir des données fournies par les programmes d'émission des ordonnances en trois exemplaires (Canadian Triplicate Prescription Programs) adoptés par l'Alberta, la Saskatchewan, le Manitoba et la Colombie-Britannique. Les saisies de médicaments licites et de produits chimiques précurseurs effectuées par les services de police constituent une deuxième source d'information. Les estimations de l'usage non médical des drogues d'ordonnance composent la troisième. Au Canada, toute l'information sur le détournement des drogues licites vers les marchés illicites pose problème (Clark, 1992).

Approvisionnement en drogues licites détournées : En 1993, on a déclaré 1 115 vols et autres pertes de

A shift in enforcement activity is responsible for the downward trend in possession offences and a move to more serious drugs (Wolff and Reingold, 1994). Ninety-three percent of incidents involved cannabis in 1977 compared to 69% in 1992; the proportion of cocaine-related activity increased from 1% of possession incidents in 1977 to 18% in 1989. Trafficking in cocaine made up 37% of trafficking incidents in 1992 compared to 4% in 1977,

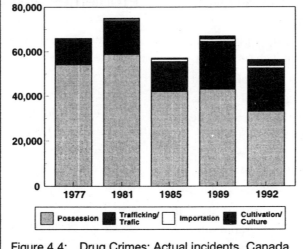

Figure 4.4:   Drug Crimes: Actual incidents, Canada 1977 to 1992

Figure 4.4:   Narco-criminalité : Nombre réel de cas, Canada, 1977 à 1992

while trafficking incidents involving cannabis declined from 69% to 40% (Wolff and Reingold, 1994).

Drugs and homicide: The illegal drug trade promotes violence in disputes or as a disciplinary measure (Wolff, and Reingold, 1994). In 1991 and 1992, 51 people in Canada are known to have been killed in connection with drug disputes, accounting for 3% of all people murdered during that time (Revised Homicide Survey, 1991). More than half (52.3%) of all those accused of homicide were known to have used a substance at the time of the incident. Of these individuals, 3.9% used drugs and 14% used both drugs and alcohol (Wolff and Reingold, 1994). Of the total number of homicide victims (n=1,487) in Canada for 1991 and 1992, 4% were on drugs at the time of the incident and 9.3% had both alcohol and drugs in their systems (Wolff and Reingold, 1994).

Drugs and robbery: In 1992, 31% of those accused of personal robbery and 40% of those accused of commercial robbery were on a substance during the incident (Wolff, and Reingold, 1994). The level of injury to victims of personal robbery was greater when the perpetrator was on drugs of some kind. Among known cases, 77% of those robbed by someone on drugs were physically injured, compared to 33% where drugs

narcotiques et de drogues contrôlées (Tableau 12.23). Plus de la moitié (61 %) de ces vols concernaient des pharmacies; près du tiers (33,1 %), des hôpitaux, et 4,5 % des revendeurs autorisés (Figure 4.3). Les plus gros vols de narcotiques visaient la poudre de méthadone (983,2 g), les comprimés de codéine (535 798) et la codéine liquide (224 179 ml), l'hydrocodone liquide (307 507 ml), les comprimés de mépéridine (54 309),les comprimés de morphine (94 309) de même que la poudre (77 600 g), ainsi que les comprimés d'oxycodone (223 872) et la poudre de cocaïne (80 000 g).

En 1993, les plus grosses quantités de drogues contrôlées qui ont été volées visaient les comprimés de méthylphénidate (45 246), les capsules de phentermine (14 240), les comprimés de barbituriques (136 118) de même que la poudre (25 g) (Tableau 12.24). Sur le plan régional, la majorité des vols ont été commis, dans l'ordre, en Ontario (47,5 %), au Québec (17,2 %), en Alberta (14,1 %), et en Colombie-Britannique (9,1 %) (Tableau 12.23).

Les ordonnances falsifiées constituent un autre aspect du détournement des drogues. En 1993, on a relevé dans tout le pays 1 827 ordonnances falsifiées, dont 1 592 pour des narcotiques et 235 pour des drogues contrôlées (Tableau 12.25). C'est là un recul de 16 % par rapport à l'année précédente. Les falsifications pour narcotiques concernaient principalement la codéine (782), l'oxycodone (345) et la mépéridine (119). Celles établies pour les drogues contrôlées visaient surtout le sécobarbital (54), le méthylphénidate (38), l'oxymétholone (38) et le testostérone (38).

were not involved. Fifty-eight percent had a minor injury and 19% were seriously injured.

MORTALITY: The number of deaths and potential years of life lost[1] attributable to the use of illicit drugs have been calculated in the recent study of the costs of substance abuse in Canada (Single et al., 1996). As seen in Table 4.9, it is estimated that there were 732 deaths due to the use of illicit drugs in Canada in 1992, representing approximately 0.4% of total mortality. The vast majority (87%) of these deaths involve males. Suicide accounts for 42% of illicit drug-related deaths, while opiate poisoning and cocaine poisoning account for 14% and 9%, respectively. AIDS acquired through the use of illicit drugs accounts for 61 deaths (8% of all illicit drug-related deaths).

Mortality due to illicit drug use may be relatively infrequent compared with alcohol and tobacco-related mortality, but illicit drug death tends to involve younger victims. The 732 illicit drug-related deaths result in 31,147 potential years of life lost, representing 42.6 years per death and about 1% of total years of life lost due to any cause in Canada in 1992.

There is considerable provincial variation in death rates due to illicit drugs (Table 4.10). The greatest number of deaths per capita occur in British Columbia (4.7 per 100,000 population). Alberta (3.1) and Québec (2.8) also have illicit drug mortality rates which are above the national average. The lowest rate of death due to illicit drugs is in Newfoundland (1.0 per l00,000). There is relatively little variation among the other provinces, which range from 1.5 in New Brunswick to 2.0 in Saskatchewan and Ontario. Somewhat surprisingly, illicit drug mortality in Ontario is close to the national average despite the concentration of drug users in metropolitan Toronto.

MORBIDITY: There were 7,095 hospital separations (0.2% of all hospitalizations) and 58,571 hospital days

---

[1]Potential years of life lost equals the difference between age of death and life expectancy for a person of the same age and gender as the victim

Problèmes associés à la drogue

DROGUES ET CRIMINALITÉ : La narco-criminalité suppose la présence de substances illicites telles qu'elles sont définies par la loi, notamment le cannabis et la cocaïne (Wolff et Reingold, 1994). Elle concerne les crimes tels la possession et l'approvisionnement. La violence marquant le commerce de la drogue et les activités criminelles permettant d'entretenir la toxicomanie (notamment la prostitution et le vol) constituent aussides aspects de la narco-criminalité. Une autre dimension porte celle-là sur le rôle que joue la consommation de drogues dans la participation aux activités criminelles et dans la victimisation (Wolff et Reingold, 1994). Le lien établi entre la consommation de drogues et la criminalité s'appuie sur l'information analysée par Juristat.

Au Canada, les crimes déclarés en matière de drogue ne reflètent pas seulement la consommation qui en est faite par les Canadiens, mais aussi l'activité policière et les procédures de déclaration. Le nombre des cas de possession déclarés par la police a diminué, passant de 58 838 en 1981 à 33 037 en 1992 (Figure 4.4). Celui des cas d'approvisionnement a par contre augmenté et représente une part croissante de la narco-criminalité. Ainsi, de 1977 à 1992, les infractions concernant le trafic sont passées de 10 816 à 19 539; l'importation, de 397 à 1 073; la culture, de 595 à 2 841. En 1977, ces infractions représentaient jusqu'à 18 % de tous les cas reliés à la drogue, taux qui a plus que doublé en 1992 pour atteindre 42 % (Wolff et Reingold, 1994).

La modification de l'activité policière a entraîné une tendance à la baisse des délits de possession en même temps qu'une tendance à consommer des drogues plus dures (Wolff et Reingold, 1994). En 1977, 99 % des infractions concernaient le cannabis contre 69 % en 1992; le taux des activités reliées à la possession de la cocaïne en 1977 est passé de 1 % à 18 % en 1989. En 1992, le trafic de ce produit représentait 37 % des cas de trafic contre 4 % en 1977, tandis que les cas de trafic

of all hospital days) as a result of illicit drug use in 1992 (Table 4.11). Drug psychosis (1,207 or 17%), assaults (1,184 or 17%) and cocaine abuse (1,151 or 16%) account for about one half of all illicit drug-related hospital separations. The greatest proportion of hospital days due to illicit drugs is for drug psychosis (13,183 days or 22%), cocaine abuse (9,044 days or 15%) and assault (8,508 days or 14%).

The provincial differences in potential years of life lost, hospitalizations and hospital days generally reflect the same patterns as the mortality rates (Table 4.12), with the highest rate of hospitalizations attributed to illicit drugs in British Columbia (39 per 100,000) and the lowest rate in Newfoundland (15 per 100,000). However, Newfoundland has a relatively high rate of hospital days related to illicit drug use even though the mortality and hospitalization rates in that province are relatively low.

References

British Columbia, 1994. Task Force into Illicit Narcotic Overdose Deaths into Illicit Narcotic Overdose Deaths in British Columbia. Ministry of Attorney General.

Health Canada, 1995. Canada's Alcohol and Other Drug Survey. Ottawa: Ministry of Supply and Services.

IMS Canada, 1995. The Pharmacy Practice 200: An exclusive IMS Canada Ranking of the top 200 Prescription drugs of 1995. Pharmacy Practice 11 (10): 81-92.

Metro Toronto Research Group on Drug Use, 1995. Drug Use in Metropolitan Toronto. Toronto.

Single et al., 1996. *The Costs of Substance Abuse in Canada*, Ottawa: Canadian Centre on Substance Abuse.

Statistics Canada, 1991. Preliminary Crime Statistics - 1991. Catalogue #85-002.

UN International Drug Control Programme, 1994. "Present Status of Knowledge on the Illicit Drug Industry: Discussion paper", ACC Sub-Committee on Drug Control, Vienna, September 5-7.

impliquant le cannabis ont eux régressé de 69 % à 40 % (Wolff et Reingold, 1994).

Drogues et homicides : Le commerce illégal de la drogue favorise le recours à la violence dans les querelles ou comme mesure disciplinaire (Wolff et Reingold, 1994). En 1991 et 1992, 51 personnes au Canada ont été tuées dans des querelles reliés à la drogue, soit 3 % de toutes les personnes assassinées durant cette période (Enquête révisée sur les homicides, 1991). Plus de la moitié (52,3 %) des personnes accusées d'homicide avaient consommé une substance intoxicante au moment du drame; 3,9 % des drogues et 14 %, des drogues et de l'alcool (Wolfram et Reingold, 1994). Sur la totalité des victimes d'homicide (1 487) relevées au Canada en 1991 et 1992, 4 % étaient sous l'influence d'un intoxicant au moment du drame et 9,3 % portaient des traces d'alcool et de drogue dans leur organisme (Wolfram et Reingold, 1994).

Drogues et vols qualifiés : En 1992, 31 % des personnes accusées de vols personnels et 40 % de celles accusées de vols commerciaux avaient commis leur crime alors qu'elles étaient sous l'influence d'un intoxicant (Wolfram et Reingold, 1994). Les blessures causées aux victimes de vols personnels étaient plus graves lorsque l'auteur était sous l'influence d'une substance intoxicante. Sur l'ensemble des cas connus, 77 % des personnes qui ont été volées par une personne intoxiquée ont été blessées, contre 33 % seulement en l'absence de toute drogue, dont 58 % légèrement et 19 % gravement.

MORTALITÉ : Le nombre des décès et des années de vie potentielle perdues[1] imputables à la consommation des drogues illicites a été calculé lors de la récente étude des coûts économiques de l'abus des drogues au Canada (Single et coll., 1996). Comme l'indique le Tableau 4.9,

---

[1]Les années de vie potentielle perdues correspondent à l'écart qui existe entre l'âge du décès et les années de vie potentielle d'une personne du même âge et du même sexe que la victime.

Wolff, L. and Reingold, B., 1994. "Drug Use and Crime", Juristat Service Bulletin vol. 14 (6).

on estime que 732 décès ont été causés par la consommation des drogues illicites au Canada en 1992, soit quelque 0,4 % de la mortalité globale. La vaste majorité (87 %) des personnes ainsi décédées sont des hommes.

Quarante-deux pour cent des décès associés aux drogues illicites sont attribuables au suicide et 14 % et 9 % respectivement aux empoisonnements par opiacés et cocaïne. Le sida contracté par intraveineuses a causé 61 décès (8 % de tous les décès associés aux drogues illicites).

Comparativement à l'alcool et au tabac, les drogues illicites causent relativement moins de décès, mais les victimes sont par contre plus jeunes. En 1992, les 732 décès associés aux drogues illicites au Canada ont provoqué la perte de 31 147 années de vie potentielle, soit 42,6 années par décès et 1 % environ de l'ensemble des années de vie potentielle perdues, toutes causes confondues.

L'écart entre les taux de décès dus aux drogues illicites varie considérablement d'une province à l'autre (Tableau 4.10). Le plus grand nombre de décès par habitant revient à la Colombie-Britannique (4,7 par 100 000 habitants). Les taux excèdent également la moyenne nationale dans les provinces de l'Alberta (3,1) et du Québec (2,8). Terre-Neuve a enregistré le taux le plus faible (1,0 par 100 000 habitants). L'écart entre les autres provinces varie peu, les taux allant de 1,5 au Nouveau-Brunswick à 2,0 en Saskatchewan et en Ontario. Fait étonnant, la mortalité due aux drogues illicites en Ontario reste près de la moyenne nationale malgré une concentration de toxicomanes dans l'agglomération urbaine de Toronto.

MORBIDITÉ : En 1992, on a dénombré 7 095 départs des hôpitaux (0,2 % de toutes les hospitalisations) et 58 571 jours d'hospitalisation (0,1 % de tous les jours d'hospitalisation) imputables à la consommation des drogues illicites (Tableau 4.11). La moitié environ de ces départs découlent de psychoses toxicomaniaques (1 207 départs ou 17 %), d'agressions (1 184 ou 17 %), et d'abus de cocaïne (1 151 ou 16 %). Quant aux jours

d'hospitalisation, ils découlent en majeure partie des psychoses toxicomaniaques (13 183 jours ou 22 %), des abus de cocaïne (9 044 jours ou 15 %), et des agressions (8 508 ou 14 %).

Les écarts provinciaux marquant les années de vie potentielle perdues, les hospitalisations et les jours d'hospitalisation reflètent généralement les màmes tendances que les taux de mortalité (Tableau 4.12), le taux des hospitalisations le plus élevé associés aux drogues illicites revenant à la Colombie-Britannique (39 par 100 000 habitants), et le plus bas à Terre-Neuve (15 par 100 000 habitants). Terre-Neuve accuse toutefois un taux relativement élevé de jours d'hospitalisation, malgré des taux de mortalité et d'hospitalisation relativement faibles.

Ouvrages de référence

Colombie-Britannique, 1994. Task Force into Illicit Narcotic Overdose Deaths into Illicit Narcotic Overdose Deaths in Colombie-Britannique. Ministry of Attorney General.

Santé Canada, 1995. Enquête canadienne sur l'alcool et les autres drogues. Ottawa : Approvisionnements et Services.

IMS Canada, 1995. *The Pharmacy Practice 200: An exclusive IMS Canada Ranking of the top 200 Prescription drugs of 1995*. Pharmacy Practice, vol. 11, no 10, p. 81-92.

Metro Toronto Research Group on Drug Use, 1995. Drug Use in Metropolitan Toronto. Toronto.

Single, E., L. Robson, X. Xie, J. Rehm, 1996. *The Costs of Substance Abuse in Canada*, Ottawa, Centre canadien de lutte contre l'alcoolisme et les toxicomanies.

Statistique Canada, 1991. Statistiques préliminaires sur la criminalité, 1991. Cat. no 85-002.

Programme international de contrôle des drogues des Nations Unies, 1994. Present Status of Knowledge on the Illicit Drug Industry: Discussion paper, Sous-comité *ACC* du contrôle des drogues, Vienne, 5-7 septembre.

Wolff, L. et B. Reingold, 1994. *Drug Use and Crime*, Bulletin

TABLE 4.1　　　　　　　　　　　　　　　　　　　　　**TABLEAU 4.1**

Use of non-prescription and prescription drugs in the past year by selected characteristics among those age 15 or older, Canada, 1994

Usage de médicaments prescrits et non prescrits l'année précédente, selon certaines caractéristiques, population des 15 ans et plus, Canada, 1994

VARIABLE	% OF RESPONDENTS USING DRUG IN PAST YEAR/ TAUX DES REPONDANTS AYANT UTILISE DES MEDICAMENTS L'ANNEE PRECEDENTE					
	TRANQUILLIZERS/ TRANQUIL- LISANTS	DIET PILLS/ AMPHE- TAMINES	ANTI- DEPRESSANTS/ ANTI- DEPRESSEURS	CODEINE DEMEROL/ CODEINE DEMEROL	SLEEPING PILLS/ SOMNIFERES	ANY 5 LICIT DRUGS/ UNE DES 5 DROGUES
Total 15+	4.3 %	0.9 %	3.0 %	13.1 %	4.5 %	20.8 %
Male/Hommes	3.4	0.7	1.7	12.0	3.7	17.7
Female/Femmes	5.3	1.0	4.2	14.1	5.4	23.9
Age/Age:						
15-17	1.1	1.7	1.2	12.3	2.3	15.0
18-19	0.7	1.6	1.5	15.5	1.9	19.8
20-24	1.7	2.2	1.2	14.6	3.7	20.3
25-34	2.5	0.6	2.6	13.3	3.4	18.4
35-44	3.3	0.8	3.5	14.6	3.7	21.1
45-54	5.5	0.5	3.9	11.7	4.0	19.8
55-64	7.7	0.4	3.9	10.8	5.7	21.3
65-74	8.3	0.7	3.4	11.6	8.1	25.8
75+	8.8	0.6	2.6	14.7	11.4	30.7
Marital Status/Etat Matrimonial:						
Single/Célibataire	2.7	1.6	2	13.1	3.9	19.2
Married/Marié	4.4	0.6	2.8	12.8	4.2	20.1
Divorced, separated or windowed/ Divorcé, séparé ou veuf	7.7	0.6	5.9	15	7.9	28.3
Income/Revenu:						
Very low/Très faible	6.3	0.8	2.4	16.4	5.9	27.5
Low/Faible	5.8	1.2	3.8	13.4	8.0	25.2
Lower middle/Faible à moyen	4.8	0.4	3.9	14.1	4.5	22.6
Upper middle/Moyen à supérieur	3.1	0.6	3.2	15.4	3.9	21.9
High/Supérieur	4.0	0.9	2.9	15.3	4.6	22.9

TABLE 4.1 (concluded)

TABLEAU 4.1 (fin)

Use of non-prescription and prescription drugs in the past year by selected characteristics among those age 15 or older, Canada, 1994

Usage de médicaments prescrits et non prescrits l'année précédente, selon certaines caractéristiques, population des 15 ans et plus, Canada, 1994

VARIABLE	% OF RESPONDENTS USING DRUG IN PAST YEAR/ TAUX DES REPONDANTS AYANT UTILISE DES DROGUES LICITES L'ANNEE PRECEDENTE					
	TRANQUILLIZERS/ TRANQUI- LISANTS	DIET PILLS/ AMPHE- TAMINES	ANTI- DEPRESSANTS/ ANTI- DEPRESSEURS	CODEINE DEMEROL/ CODEINE DEMEROL	SLEEPING PILLS/ SOMNIFERES	ANY 5 LICIT DRUGS/ CINQ DROGUES LICITES
Employment/Situation d'emploi:						
Professional/Professionnel	2.8 %	0.4 %	3.0 %	13.6 %	3.8 %	19.5 %
White Collar/Col blanc	3.4	1.4	2.8	12.5	3.7	19.4
Blue Collar/Col bleu	2.6	0.6	2.2	15.1	2.9	19.4
Unemployed/Sans emploi	5.6	1.3	4.6	12.1	3.7	22.5
Student/Aux études	1.5	1.4	1.2	11.6	2.8	16.2
Retired/A la retraite	8.4	0.4	3.3	13.4	8.4	27.0
Homemaker/Au foyer	8.1	0.9	5.0	14.1	6.3	25.1
Other/Autre	11.4	0.7	10.6	25.3	9.0	39.8
Province						
Nfld./T.-N.	4.1	0.7	2.0	12.7	2.7	18.0
P.E.I./I.-P.-E.	3.4	1.0	3.6	16.8	6.1	25.0
N.S./N.-E.	3.8	1.2	4.1	12.9	4.5	21.8
N.B./N.-B.	5.5	1.4	3.1	13.6	5.1	23.3
Que./Québec.	6.8	0.7	3.7	6.8	5.8	18.5
Ont./Ont.	3.3	0.7	1.8	12.6	3.5	17.9
Man./Man.	3.3	0.9	3.6	18.2	5.4	26.4
Sask./Sask.	3.4	1.2	3.5	14.4	3.5	21.4
Alta./Alb..	3.0	1.4	3.7	18.3	4.5	25.6
B.C./C.-B.	4.0	0.9	3.9	21.2	5.3	28.4

Source: Data obtained from the Canadian Centre for Health Information, Statistics Canada.

Données obtenues du Centre canadien d'information sur la santé, Statistique Canada.

TABLE 4.2

TABLEAU 4.2

Solvent use in Canada, 1994

Usage des solvants au Canada, 1994

VARIABLE	LIFETIME USE/ USAGE AE JOUR	USE IN THE PAST YEAR/ USAGE, ANNEE PRECEDENTE
Total 15+	0.8 %	0.1 %
Male/Hommes	1.2	0.2
Female/Femmes	0.3	0.0
Age/Age:		
15-17	1.7	1.3
18-19	0.5	—
20-24	1.6	—
25-34	0.9	0.0
35-44	1.1	0.1
45-54	0.3	—
55-64	0.3	—
65-74	—	—
75+	—	—
Marital Status/Etat Matrimonial:		
Single/Celibataire	1.4	0.3
Married/Marié	0.6	0.0
Divorced, separated or windowed/ Divorcé, séparé ou veuf	0.4	—
Province		
Nfld./T.-N.	0.2	—
P.E.I./I.-P.-E.	0.9	—
N.S./N.-E.	0.7	—
N.B./N.-B.	1.2	—
Que./Québec.	1.4	0.2
Ont./Ont.	0.2	0.1
Man./Man.	0.5	—
Sask./Sask.	0.7	—
Alta./Alb..	1.2	0.1
B.C./C.-B.	0.9	—

* Moderate sampling variability; read with caution./Variabilité moyenne de l'échantillonnage; interpréter avec prudence.

Source: Data obtained from the Canadian Centre for Health Information, Statistics Canada.

Données obtenues du Centre canadien d'information sur la santé, Statistique Canada.

TABLE 4.3　　　　　　　　　　　　　　　　　**TABLEAU 4.3**

Proportion reporting use of selected drugs in the past year by gender, age 15 or older, Canada 1985, 1989, 1990, 1993, and 1994

Proportion de ceux qui ont déclaré avoir utilisé certaines drogues l'année précédente, selon le sexe, population des 15 ans et plus, Canada, 1985, 1989, 1990, 1993 et 1994

YEAR/ ANNEE	SURVEY/ENQUETE	GENDER/SEXE		
		MALE/ HOMMES	FEMALE/ FEMMES	TOTAL
CANNABIS/CANNABIS:				
1985	Health Promotion Survey/ Enquête promotion de la santé	6.9 %	4.3 %	5.6 %
1989	National Alcohol and Drug Survey/ Enquête nationale sur l'alcool et les autres drogues	8.9	4.1	6.5
1990	Health Promotion Survey/ Enquête promotion de la santé	7	3	5
1993	General Social Survey/Enquête sociale générale	5.9	2.5	4.2
1994	Canadian Alcohol and Drug Survey/Enquête canadienne sur la consommation de l'alcool et des autres drogues drogues	10.1	5.1	7.4
COCAINE/COCAINE:				
1985	Health Promotion Survey/ Enquête promotion de la santé	1.3	0.6 *	0.9
1989	National Alcohol and Drug Survey/ Enquête nationale sur l'alcool et les autres drogues	2 *	0.8 *	1.4 *
1990	Health Promotion Survey/ Enquête promotion de la santé	1	1 *	—
1993	General Social Survey/Enquête sociale générale	0.4	0.2	0.3
1994	Canadian Alcohol and Drug Survey/Enquête canadienne sur la consommation de l'alcool et des autres drogues	0.8	0.5	0.7
LSD, SPEED OR HEROIN/LSD, SPEED OU HEROINE:				
1989	National Alcohol and Drug Survey/Enquête nationale Enquête nationale sur l'alcool et les autres drogues	0.5 *	—	0.4 *
1993	General Social Survey/Enquête sociale générale	0.4 *	0.2 *	0.3 *
1994	Canadian Alcohol and Drug Survey/Enquête canadienne sur la consommation de l'alcool et des autres drogues	1.5	0.7	1.1

*Moderate sampling variability; read with caution/Variabilité moyenne de l'échantillonnage; interpréter avec prudence.

— Data suppressed due to high sampling variability/Données supprimées en raison de la grande variabilité de l'échantillonnage.

Source: Data obtained from the Canadian Centre for Health Information, Statistics Canada, 1995. Health and Welfare Canada, McNeil, P., *Horizons*. (Ottawa: Ministry of Supply and Services, Canada, 1994). Health and Welfare Canada, Stephens, T., Fowler-Graham, D., Editors, *Canada's Health Promotion Survey 1990: Technical Report* (Ottawa: Ministry of Supply and Services Canada, 1993). Health and Welfare Canada, Eliany, M., Giesbrecht N., Nelson, M., Wellman, B., and Wortley, S., *Alcohol and Other Drug Use by Canadians: A National Alcohol and Other Drugs Survey (1989): Technical Report* (Ottawa: Ministry of Supply and Services Canada, 1992) Health and Welfare Canada, Rootman, I., Warren, R., Stephens, T., and Peters, L., Editors, *Canada's Health Promotion Survey 1985: Technical Report* (Ottawa: Ministry of Supply and Services Canada, 1993).

Données obtenues du Centre canadien d'information sur la santé, Statistique Canada, 1995. Santé et Bien-être Canada, McNeil, P., *Horizons* (Ottawa, Approvisionnements et Services Canada, 1994). Santé et Bien-être Canada, Stephens, T. et D. Fowler-Graham, éditeurs, *Enquête Promotion de la santé 1990 : Rapport technique* (Ottawa : Approvisionnements et Services Canada, 1993). Santé et Bien-être Canada, Eliany, M., N. Giesbrecht, M. Nelson, B. Wellman, et S. Wortley, éditeurs, *L'usage de l'alcool et des autres drogues par les Canadiens : Une enquête nationale sur l'alcool et les autres drogues (1989) - Rapport technique* (Ottawa : Approvisionnements et Services Canada, 1992). Santé et Bien-être Canada, Rootman, I., R. Warren, T. Stephens, et L. Peters, éditeurs, *Enquête Promotion de la santé 1985 : Rapport technique* (Ottawa : Approvisionnements et Services Canada, 1993).

TABLE 4.4   **TABLEAU 4.4**

Lifetime use of illicit drugs by selected characteristics among those 15 or older, Canada, 1994

Répondants ayant déjà utilisé des drogues illicites, selon certaines caractéristiques, population des 15 ans et plus, Canada, 1994

VARIABLE	% OF RESPONDENTS USING DRUG IN LIFETIME/ TAUX DES REPONDANTS AYANT DÉJÀ UTILISE DES			
	CANNABIS/ CANNABIS	COCAINE/ COCAINE	LSD, SPEED, HEROIN/ LSD, SPEED, HEROINE	USE OF ANY 5 ILLEGAL DRUGS/ UNE DES CINQ DROGUES LICITES
Total 15+	23.1 %	3.8 %	5.9 %	23.9 %
Male/Hommes	27.7	4.9	8.1	28.5
Female/Femmes	18.7	2.7	3.6	19.4
Age/Age:				
15-17	28.8	1.8	10.7	30.4
18-19	32.7	3.2	11.5	32.9
20-24	36.5	4.9	11.7	37.7
25-34	37.0	7.6	7.7	38.2
35-44	32.1	5.9	8.4	32.9
45-54	14.4	1.6	2.5	14.8
55-64	3.2	0.6	0.7	3.7
65-74	0.9	0.1	0.1	0.9
75+	0.4	0.1	—	0.5
Marital Status/Etat Matrimonial:				
Single/Celibataire	35.5	34.5	5.7	10.7
Married/Marié	20.2	19.6	2.9	3.9
Divorced, separated or windowed/ Divorcé, séparé ou veuf	16.4	15.7	3.7	4.2
Province				
Nfld./T.-N.	16.3	1.0	1.9	16.3
P.E.I./I.-P.-E.	18.6	2.0	3.0	18.6
N.S./N.-E.	25.1	1.8	4.1	25.5
N.B./N.-B.	21.7	1.9	6.5	22.3
Que./Québec.	24.7	4.9	6.0	25.3
Ont./Ont.	16.6	2.0	4.1	17.5
Man./Man.	25.2	2.5	5.6	25.8
Sask./Sask.	22.0	2.6	5.6	22.2
Alta./Alb.	29.4	5.2	7.9	30.1
B.C./C.-B.	35.4	8.1	10.4	36.6

Source: Data obtained from the Canadian Centre for Health Information, Statistics Canada.

Données obtenues du Centre canadien d'information sur la santé, Statistique Canada.

| TABLE 4.5 | TABLEAU 4.5 |

Use of illicit drugs in the past year by selected characteristics among those 15 or older, Canada, 1994

Usage des drogues illicites l'année précédente, selon certaines caractéristiques, population des 15 ans et plus, Canada, 1994

VARIABLE	% OF RESPONDENTS USING DRUG IN LIFETIME/ TAUX DES REPONDANTS AYANT DÉJÀ UTILISE DES			
	CANNABIS/ CANNABIS	COCAINE/ COCAINE	LSD, SPEED, HEROIN/ LSD, SPEED, HEROINE	USE OF ANY 5 ILLEGAL DRUGS/ UNE DESCINQ DROGUES LICITES
Total 15+	7.4%	0.7 %	1.1 %	7.7 %
Male/Hommes	10	0.8	1.5	10.1
Female/Femmes	4.9	0.5	0.7	5.1
Age/Age:				
15-17	25.4	1.3	8.3	25.7
18-19	23.0	1.9	5.6	24.1
20-24	19.3	1.4	2.8	19.8
25-34	9.6	1.0	0.6	9.9
35-44	5.8	0.8	0.2	5.9
45-54	1.4	0.1	—	1.5
55-64	0.7	0.1	—	0.8
65-74	0.2	—	—	0.2
75+	—	—	—	—
Marital Status/Etat Matrimonial:				
Single/Celibataire	18.1	1.6	3.7	18.7
Married/Marié	3.3	3.3	0.3	0.1
Divorced, separated or windowed/ Divorcé, séparé ou veuf	3.7	0.4	0.1	3.8
Province				
Nfld./T.-N.	3.8	0.1	0.3	3.8
P.E.I./I.-P.-E.	5.6	0.5	—	6.1
N.S./N.-E.	8.0	0.0	0.7	8.1
N.B./N.-B.	6.2	—	1.8	6.2
Que./Québec.	8.6	1.2	1.6	9.0
Ont./Ont.	5.1	0.1	0.5	5.1
Man./Man.	9.1	0.3	0.9	9.1
Sask./Sask.	6.6	0.6	1.0	6.9
Alta./Alb.	8.4	1.3	1.3	8.8
B.C./C.-B.	11.6	1.2	1.6	11.8

Source: Data obtained from the Canadian Centre for Health Information, Statistics Canada.

Données obtenues du Centre canadien d'informationsur la santé, Statistique Canada.

TABLE 4.6

TABLEAU 4.6

Use of illicit drugs in the past year by selected characteristics among those age 15 or older, Canada, 1993

Usage des drogues illicites l'année précédente, selon certaines caractéristiques, population des 15 ans et plus, Canada, 1993

VARIABLE	% USING/ % USAGERS		FREQUENCY OF CANNABIS USE (% OF USERS)/ FREQUENCE D'UTILISATION DU CANNABIS (% DES USAGERS)				
	CANNABIS/ CANNABIS	COCAINE/ COCAINE	SPEED, LSD OR HEROIN/ SPEED, LSD OU HEROINE	LESS THAN ONCE A MONTH/ MOINS D'UNE FOIS PAR MOIS	1-3 TIMES PER MONTH/ 1-3 FOIS PAR MOIS	ONCE PER WEEK/ UNE FOIS PAR SEMAINE	MORE THAN ONCE A WEEK/ PLUS D'UNE FOIS PAR SEMAINE
Total 15+	4.2 %	0.3 %	0.3 %	55.8 %	24.3 %	7.3 %	2.5 %
Male/Hommes	5.9	0.4	0.4	48.4	26.9	8.4	1.6
Female/Femmes	2.5	0.2	0.2	62.8	18.4	4.9	3.4
Age/Age:							
15-17	7.1	0.0*	2.0	67.5*	26.1*	2.7	3.7*
18-19	13.4	1.8*	1.4	48.7*	23.9*	3.5	23.8*
20-24	9.7	1.0*	1.0	53.4	24.8	8.4	13.4*
25-34	7.4	0.6	0.2	47.6	27.8	8.2	16.1
35-44	2.9	0.1*	0.0	57.6	17.7	7.1	17.6
45-54	1.1	0.0*	0.0	55.5	17.7	7.1	17.6
55-64	0.3	0.0*	0.1	100.0	0.0	0.0	0.0
65-74	0.1	0.0*	0.0	0.0	0.0	0.0	100.0
75+	0.0	0.0*	0.0	—	—	—	—
Marital Status/Etat Matrimonial:							
Single/Celibataire	9.4	1.0	1.0	56.1	21.1	6.5	16.4
Married or cohabiting/Marié ou conjoint de fait	2.3	0.1	0.0	46.8	29.2	8.5	15.2
Divorced or separated/ Divorcé ou séparé	3.8	0.0*	0.1	57.0	28.9	8.9	5.3
Widowed/Veuf	0.1	0.0*	0.0	100.0	0.0	0.0	0.0
Income/Revenu:							
Lowest/Inférieur	5.2	0.5	0.4	46.2	34.6	14.1	5.0
Lower middle/Inférieur à moyen	2.9	0.4*	0.3*	48.9*	—	11.3*	7.4*
Middle/Moyen	4.6	0.4*	0.3*	46.2	21.9	11.2*	20.7
Upper Middle/Moyen à supérieur	4.4	0.2*	0.1*	57.7	22.0	5.1*	15.2
Highest/Supérieur	4.2	0.4*	0.3*	51.2	27.3	8.4*	13.1*
Education/Niveau d'instruction:							
Completed university/ Diplôme universitaire	3.8	0.1*	0.1*	57.8	19.3	8.3*	14.3
Some post -secondary/ Post-secondaire partiel	7.7	1.0	0.8*	44.1	31.3	6.4*	18.2
Secondary/ Secondaire	2.9	0.1*	0.3*	64.4	18.3	8.1*	9.1*
Less than secondary/Moins que le secondaire	3.5	0.3*	0.4*	51.3	25.2	6.6*	16.9

TABLE 4.6 (concluded)　　　　　　　　　　**TABLEAU 4.6 (fin)**

Use of illicit drugs in the past year by selected characteristics among those age 15 or older, Canada, 1993

Usage des drogues illicites l'année précédente, selon certaines caractéristiques, population des 15 ans et plus, Canada, 1993

VARIABLE	% USING/ % USAGERS		FREQUENCY OF CANNABIS USE (% OF USERS)/ FREQUENCE D'UTILISATION DU CANNABIS (% DES USAGERS)				
	CANNABIS/ CANNABIS	COCAINE/ COCAINE	SPEED, LSD OR HEROIN/ SPEED, LSD OU HEROINE	LESS THAN ONCE A MONTH/ MOINS D'UNE FOIS PAR MOIS	1-3 TIMES PER MONTH/ 1-3 FOIS PAR MOIS	ONCE PER WEEK/ UNE FOIS PAR SEMAINE	MORE THAN ONCE A WEEK/ PLUS D'UNE FOIS PAR SEMAINE
Employment/Situation d'emploi:							
Professional/ Professionnel	2.3%	0.0%*	0.1%*	55.0%*	16.0%*	23.6%*	5.4%*
Semi-professional/ Semi-professionnel	4.8	0.4*	0.2*	65.1	16.8*	5.0*	12.2*
Supervisor/Surveillant	3.8*	0.1*	0.0*	66.2*	25.8*	1.3*	6.7*
Skilled, farmer/Spécialisé, agriculteur	4.9	0.2*	0.0	47.8	24.2*	4.9*	23.1*
Semi-skilled/ Semi-spécialisé	5.4	0.8*	0.3*	46.7	27.6	14.1*	11.7*
Unskilled/ Non spécialisé	4.5	0.5*	0.2*	49.4	20.3*	3.3*	26.9*
Other working/Autre	1.9*	0.0*	0.0*	70.2*	0.0*	29.8*	0.0*
Looking for work/Enquête d'un emploi	7.0	0.2*	0.1*	41.2*	32.6*	6.5*	19.8*
Student/Aux études	9.0	0.9*	1.7	57.5	27.3	4.3*	10.9*
Homemaker/Au foyer	1.3	0.0*	0.0*	41.9*	21.5*	4.1*	32.5*
Retired/A la retraite	0.2*	0.0*	0.0*	100.0*	0.0*	0.0*	0.0*
Other/Autre	6.1*	0.0*	0.3*	45.0*	23.9*	25.5*	5.7*
Region/Région:							
Atlantic/Atlantique	4.2	0.2*	0.4*	51.2	19.9*	16.0*	11.6*
Quebec/Québec	4.7	0.6	0.3*	53.3	26.1	2.8*	18.9
Ontario	3.6	0.1*	0.1*	58.1	23.3	9.0*	9.6*
Prairies	3.3	0.0*	0.4*	44.1	29.2	3.2*	23.5*
B.C./C.-B.	6.0	0.8*	0.6*	49.7	21.6	10.3*	18.4*
Community size/Taille de la collectivité:							
> 1,000,000	5.0	0.4*	0.3*	57.4	20.7	5.6*	16.3
500,000-999,999	4.8	0.2*	0.3*	57.0	19.6	4.9*	18.6
100,000-499,999	3.9	0.3*	0.4*	49.4	26.5	12.1*	12.0*
< 100,000	2.9	0.5*	0.1*	51.5	42.6	5.3*	0.5*
Rural/Rurale	3.5	0.3*	0.4*	43.0	25.1	10.2*	21.0

*Moderate sampling variability; read with caution/Variabilité moyenne de l'échantillonnage; interpréter avec prudence.

Source: Statistics Canada, *General Social Survey*, analysis prepared by Eric Single, Joan Brewster, Patricia MacNeil and Jeffrey Hatcher (Ottawa: Canadian Centre on Substance Abuse, 1994).

Statistique Canada, *Enquête sociale générale*, analyse de Eric Single, Joan Brewster, Patricia MacNeil et Jeffrey Hatcher. (Ottawa : Centre canadien de lutte contre l'alcoolisme et les toxicomanies, 1994).

TABLE 4.7   **TABLEAU 4.7**

Number and quantity of drug exhibits seized by drug type
and province/territory, Canada, 1990 to 1994

Drogues saisies et quantités, et nombre de pièces
justificatives, selon le genre de drogue, la province
ou le territoire, Canada, 1990 à 1994

PROVINCE	NUMBER/NOMBRE					QUANTITY (kg)/QUANTITE (kg)				
	1990	1991	1992	1993	1994	1990	1991	1992	1993	1994
MARIJUANA/MARIHUANA										
Nfld/T.-N.	73	109	239	145	89	43	89	64	64	151
P.E.I./I.-P.-E.	15	26	49	21	16	28	4,437	136	58	58
N.S./N.-E.	299	360	600	420	362	390	517	2,263	1,461	706
N.B./N.-B.	203	273	354	249	270	116	364	1,214	778	832
Que./Québec.	1,212	2,040	3,196	3,703	4,006	24,047	30,012	37,919	37,672	46,046
Ont./Ont.	4,074	4,894	7,014	5,381	4,946	5,051	10,803	21,046	13,413	23,386
Man./Man.	593	808	998	893	781	342	295	796	294	408
Sask./Sask.	509	616	832	517	386	364	225	481	999	259
Alta./Alb.	1,263	2,344	2,533	1,224	906	1,689	2,445	2,700	22,381	1,533
B.C./C.-B.	6,238	7,733	8,366	7,005	6,989	10,584	19,174	33,861	29,187	23,571
Yukon/Yukon	91	134	126	121	129	19	78	74	39	8
N.W.T./T.-N.-O.	56	84	85	82	69	2	11	3	20	9
Canada	**14,626**	**19,421**	**24,392**	**19,761**	**18,949**	**42,674**	**68,449**	**100,559**	**106,365**	**96,964**
HASH/HASCHICH										
Nfld/T.-N.	404	242	178	289	230	24.8	8.7	7.0	28.4	28.0
P.E.I./I.-P.-E.	91	44	37	57	19	7.0	12.6	2.0	1.0	0.1
N.S./N.-E.	854	502	327	321	329	70,332.2	9,251.3	19.9	32.4	8.3
N.B./N.-B.	711	456	348	276	203	32.8	15.1	16.4	15.0	15.8
Que./Québec.	4,288	3,929	3,540	4,518	4,351	22,589.6	51,408.6	2,953.6	36,273.3	36,141.7
Ont./Ont.	7,733	3,385	1,992	2,357	2,079	658.4	5,093.4	352.1	292.8	167.2
Man./Man.	936	452	130	240	94	134.8	32.3	1.8	4.7	2.8
Sask./Sask.	524	136	107	180	74	17.2	5.1	1.0	1.5	1.4
Alta./Alb.	3,348	1,055	518	463	134	133.4	23.7	16.9	17.0	8.8
B.C./C.-B.	2,346	569	583	418	180	45.5	10.8	11,546.7	15.8	1.2
Yukon/Yukon	56	21	11	13	4	0.7	0.4	0.2	0.4	0.0
N.W.T./T.-N.-O.	198	119	116	99	73	4.7	5.5	1.6	5.8	1.5
Canada	**21,489**	**10,910**	**7,887**	**9,231**	**7,770**	**93,981.2**	**65,867.6**	**14,919.0**	**36,688.1**	**36,376.8**
HASH OIL & T.H.C./HASCHICH LIQUIDE ET THC										
Nfld/T.-N.	69	61	102	88	121	0.3	0.9	1.1	7.3	1.7
P.E.I./I.-P.-E.	3	1	3	-	1	0.1	0.0	0.0	-	0.0
N.S./N.-E.	25	23	39	37	50	0.2	0.5	0.9	1.3	0.2
N.B./N.-B.	19	11	20	8	11	1.0	0.1	4.6	0.3	0.0
Que./Québec.	48	80	56	95	96	15.8	20.5	23.9	109.2	28.9
Ont./Ont.	979	680	748	786	924	62.3	95.1	399.5	1,373.4	475.3
Man./Man.	69	34	31	20	26	4.0	1.1	0.8	0.2	0.1
Sask./Sask.	88	57	31	49	57	0.6	0.6	0.3	0.3	0.3
Alta./Alb.	137	88	66	56	32	1.6	1.8	2.9	0.2	0.1
B.C./C.-B.	83	77	93	95	75	17.1	1.7	1.2	2.7	0.7
Yukon/Yukon	4	7	8	1	3	0.1	0.0	0.1	-	0.0
N.W.T./T.-N.-O.	-	-	2	2	2	-	-	0.0	0.0	0.0
Canada	**1,524**	**1,119**	**1,199**	**1,237**	**1,398**	**102.8**	**122.3**	**435.3**	**1,494.8**	**507.3**

TABLE 4.7 (continued)   **TABLEAU 4.7** (suite)

Number and quantity of drug exhibits seized by drug type and province/territory, Canada, 1990 to 1994

Drogues saisies et quantités, et nombre de pièces justificatives, selon le genre de drogue, la province ou le territoire, Canada, 1990 à 1994

PROVINCE	NUMBER/NOMBRE					QUANTITY (kg)/QUANTITE (kg)				
	1990	1991	1992	1993	1994	1990	1991	1992	1993	1994
HEROIN/HEROINE										
Nfld/T.-N.	-	1	-	-	-	-	0.002	-	-	-
P.E.I./I.-P.-E.	-	-	-	-	-	-	-	-	-	-
N.S./N.-E.	-	-	1	3	-	-	-	0.077	3.412	-
N.B./N.-B.	2	3	1	-	-	0.005	0.064	-	-	-
Que./Québec.	181	202	241	204	161	26.946	29.897	29.912	12.377	3.516
Ont./Ont.	236	255	281	274	231	19.289	65.377	36.393	47.847	53.981
Man./Man.	-	1	5	8	1	-	0.003	0.001	4.633	2.958
Sask./Sask.	4	2	5	5	2	0.002	0.056	0.001	0.006	0.030
Alta./Alb.	8	12	2	2	1	0.051	0.043	0.010	0.023	0.132
B.C./C.-B.	365	404	422	608	550	10.419	23.800	25.897	26.272	1.645
Yukon/Yukon	-	-	-	-	-	-	-	-	-	-
N.W.T./T.-N.-O.	-	-	-	-	-	-	-	-	-	-
Canada	**796**	**880**	**958**	**1,104**	**946**	**56.712**	**119.242**	**92.291**	**94.570**	**62.262**
HALLUCINOGENS/HALLUCINOGENES										
Nfld/T.-N.	15	33	26	28	20	0.195	0.073	0.519	0.051	0.150
P.E.I./I.-P.-E.	13	11	13	11	7	0.015	0.131	0.415	0.456	0.570
N.S./N.-E.	71	47	31	32	31	0.270	0.092	0.199	0.018	0.020
N.B./N.-B.	68	71	39	65	31	0.269	0.644	0.403	1.086	0.010
Que./Québec.	492	670	1,010	1,108	987	86.649	11.957	23.448	17.323	45.231
Ont./Ont.	474	394	418	318	301	17.585	4.431	5.618	5.278	14.142
Man./Man.	85	84	65	41	43	2.966	0.653	0.265	0.044	1.476
Sask./Sask.	52	48	33	43	24	3.266	6.195	0.856	0.136	0.438
Alta./Alb.	235	183	142	109	65	4.764	65.904	1.449	4.586	0.554
B.C./C.-B.	395	350	392	406	294	7.471	13.210	8.114	4.271	7.048
Yukon/Yukon	3	13	15	4	3	0.003	0.585	0.390	0.027	0.005
N.W.T./T.-N.-O.	3	3	5	10	4	0.011	0.005	0.300	0.056	0.050
Canada	**1,906**	**1,907**	**2,189**	**2,175**	**1,810**	**123.464**	**103.880**	**41.976**	**33.332**	**69.694**
COCAINE/COCAINE										
Nfld/T.-N.	10	27	13	16	6	0.90	0.99	1.13	0.37	0.27
P.E.I./I.-P.-E.	6	7	4	5	2	0.14	0.00	0.24	0.03	0.00
N.S./N.-E.	91	199	249	186	230	5.05	2.97	65.24	24.73	751.06
N.B./N.-B.	83	104	48	55	35	1.41	4.23	2.08	0.83	5420.61
Que./Québec.	3,772	5,294	5,164	4,840	4,300	310.34	1487.22	4906.82	4354.80	1773.74
Ont./Ont.	3,289	3,386	3,641	3,011	2,621	144.81	151.66	231.90	91.43	321.25
Man./Man.	149	175	133	133	87	3.49	13.06	2.61	4.38	4.01
Sask./Sask.	36	36	29	19	15	0.37	0.85	4.32	0.12	0.13
Alta./Alb.	585	589	470	466	168	12.24	13.52	20.60	7.76	8.10
B.C./C.-B.	1,648	2,016	2,196	1,966	1,844	31.58	25.38	66.72	29.45	82.02
Yukon/Yukon	15	13	25	15	2	0.14	0.02	0.72	0.86	0.04
N.W.T./T.-N.-O.	5	19	12	7	15	0.17	0.29	0.30	0.76	0.06
Canada	9,689	11,865	11,984	10,719	9,325	510.61	1700.18	5302.67	4515.52	8361.29

TABLE 4.7 (concluded)   **TABLEAU 4.7** (fin)

Number and quantity of drug exhibits seized by drug type and province/territory, Canada, 1990 to 1994

Drogues saisies et quantités, et nombre de pièces justificatives, selon le genre de drogue, la province ou le territoire, Canada, 1990 à 1994

PROVINCE	NUMBER/NOMBRE					QUANTITY (kg)/QUANTITE (kg)				
	1990	1991	1992	1993	1994	1990	1991	1992	1993	1994
PHARMACEUTICALS/MEDICAMENTS										
Nfld/T.-N.	7	4	-	1	4	0.007	0.022	-	-	0.002
P.E.I./I.-P.-E.	-	-	-	-	-	-	-	-	-	-
N.S./N.-E.	7	11	6	7	3	0.003	0.020	0.001	0.008	0.001
N.B./N.-B.	13	10	5	6	3	0.011	0.002	0.003	0.198	0.006
Que./Québec.	76	39	115	103	109	0.631	522.302	2.444	3.813	1.170
Ont./Ont.	252	207	239	201	169	1.952	1.593	9.288	1.254	2.579
Man./Man.	86	59	63	72	15	0.162	0.063	5.761	0.226	0.703
Sask./Sask.	96	79	77	47	32	0.170	0.060	0.069	0.351	0.046
Alta./Alb.	304	330	202	216	64	0.574	0.564	0.228	0.475	0.309
B.C./C.-B.	221	288	217	136	113	1.709	24.539	0.811	0.954	0.942
Yukon/Yukon	7	1	2	1	-	0.001	0.030	0.011	-	-
N.W.T./T.-N.-O.	2	1	1	-	-	0.001	0.001	-	-	-
Canada	**1,071**	**1,029**	**927**	**790**	**512**	**5.221**	**549.196**	**18.616**	**7.279**	**5.758**
OTHERS/AUTRES										
Nfld/T.-N.	-	-	-	1	-	-	-	-	-	-
P.E.I./I.-P.-E.	-	-	-	-	-	-	-	-	-	-
N.S./N.-E.	1	-	1	1	-	0.003	-	0.004	-	-
N.B./N.-B.	1	1	1	1	-	-	-	-	-	-
Que./Québec.	6	5	4	6	4	3.654	0.118	0.013	0.061	0.067
Ont./Ont.	13	17	32	43	39	0.214	0.729	1.845	1.222	16.904
Man./Man.	6	1	-	-	3	0.021	-	-	-	0.003
Sask./Sask.	2	4	1	-	2	0.007	1.849	0.001	-	0.005
Alta./Alb.	9	14	4	14	10	1.094	0.337	0.108	1.441	0.083
B.C./C.-B.	42	41	42	39	53	3.048	1.770	1.981	2.138	0.424
Yukon/Yukon	-	-	1	3	-	-	-	-	0.004	-
N.W.T./T.-N.-O.	-	-	-	-	-	-	-	-	-	-
Canada	**80**	**83**	**86**	**108**	**111**	**8.041**	**4.803**	**3.952**	**4.866**	**17.486**

Source: Health Canada, Bureau of Drug Surveillance, Health Protection Branch.

Santé Canada, Bureau de la surveillance des médicaments, Direction de la protection de la santé.

TABLE 4.8

TABLEAU 4.8

Number and quantity of drug exhibits seized by drug type, metropolitian areas, Canada, 1990 to 1994

Drogues saisies et quantités, et nombre de pièces justificatives, selon le genre de drogue, principaux centres urbains, du Canada, 1990 à 1994

| | MARIJUANA/MARIHUANA | | | | | | | | | |
| | NUMBER/NOMBRE | | | | | QUANTITY (KG)/QUANTITE (KG) | | | | |
CITY/VILLE	1990	1991	1992	1993	1994	1990	1991	1992	1993	1994
St. John's	18	33	71	58	28	13	72	45	19	18
Halifax-Dartmouth	51	70	172	102	73	10	31	409	146	46
Saint John	21	42	51	16	23	12	30	51	58	29
Chicoutimi-Jonquière	13	14	42	55	52	1	1	103	96	1,976
Québec	58	87	148	164	110	26	39	806	588	740
Trois-Rivières	45	58	115	153	205	281	2,351	1,518	3,570	8,695
Sherbrooke	47	121	158	248	336	3,638	1,135	1,239	6,843	5,951
Montreal	374	896	1,144	1,440	1,539	10,729	2,034	1,634	5,091	2,329
Ottawa-Hull	150	175	268	230	262	97	705	247	1,333	3,313
Oshawa	165	227	298	267	182	340	233	125	46	10
Toronto	1,345	1,525	2,324	1,872	1,834	500	1,516	3,699	1,726	2,285
St. Catharines	261	206	253	101	45	482	289	958	750	171
Hamilton	405	473	628	398	425	849	265	821	339	605
Kitchener	111	195	407	267	302	41	145	618	128	445
London	154	189	264	281	241	215	801	1,710	830	197
Windsor	90	197	199	105	58	14	91	32	128	65
Sudbury	17	31	71	13	1	4	135	541	15	0
Thunder Bay	85	90	189	164	170	99	36	111	65	21
Winnipeg	350	451	520	396	369	163	120	522	77	74
Regina	81	85	137	79	45	20	61	59	484	77
Saskatoon	131	184	187	45	11	79	45	25	97	56
Calgary	278	549	525	236	66	167	707	1,142	20,454	72
Edmonton	322	648	667	159	99	58	75	77	349	1,123
Vancouver	2,679	3,558	4,018	3,759	3,998	1,763	3,072	6,610	7,091	12,464
Victoria	452	465	530	488	539	723	211	827	764	1,369
Rest of Canada/ Reste du Canada	6,923	8,852	11,006	8,665	7,936	22,350	54,251	76,629	55,277	54,832
Total	**14,626**	**19,421**	**24,392**	**19,761**	**18,949**	**42,674**	**68,451**	**100,559**	**106,365**	**96,964**

TABLE 4.8 (continued)　　　　　　　　　　　　　　　　**TABLEAU 4.8** (suite)

Number and quantity of drug exhibits seized by drug type, metropolitian areas, Canada, 1990 to 1994

Drogues saisies et quantités, et nombre de pièces justificatives, selon le genre de drogue, principaux centres urbains, du Canada, 1990 à 1994

| | HASH/HASCHICH | | | | | | | | | |
| | NUMBER/NOMBRE | | | | | QUANTITY (KG)/QUANTITE (KG) | | | | |
CITY/VILLE	1990	1991	1992	1993	1994	1990	1991	1992	1993	1994
St. John's	98	75	53	112	92	19	3	4	24	24
Halifax-Dartmouth	374	221	181	140	158	30	9,229	11	14	5
Saint John	92	103	73	25	35	3	7	3	6	3
Chicoutimi-Jonquière	93	101	68	120	124	5	6	3	2	6
Québec	255	318	331	386	317	21	9	46	14	12
Trois-Rivières	166	125	127	124	180	2	6	3	32	3
Sherbrooke	92	55	54	68	124	1	0	2	7	4
Montreal	1,827	2,025	1,672	2,090	2,016	10,154	50,994	2,257	36,078	36,058
Ottawa-Hull	689	438	400	427	504	19	233	8	12	15
Oshawa	409	197	118	135	103	6	2	1	2	1
Toronto	2,951	1,115	743	935	831	414	4,713	300	231	141
St. Catharines	133	81	24	12	4	3	3	2	1	0
Hamilton	582	341	107	112	111	30	7	2	3	1
Kitchener	358	147	100	127	123	7	2	5	1	2
London	205	118	81	87	106	7	9	2	3	0
Windsor	55	48	19	9	4	13	1	2	1	0
Sudbury	176	82	34	15	7	35	5	1	1	0
Thunder Bay	143	20	29	31	46	2	1	1	13	2
Winnipeg	634	309	69	121	40	129	29	1	3	2
Regina	95	31	23	39	30	1	1	0	1	0
Saskatoon	110	30	15	13	1	4	0	0	0	0
Calgary	767	227	57	40	11	21	5	5	2	8
Edmonton	1,418	418	232	113	19	83	13	9	8	0
Vancouver	1,469	323	329	223	100	28	3	6,539	9	1
Victoria	233	67	80	61	18	4	1	4	0	0
Rest of Canada/ Reste du Canada	8,067	3,895	2,868	3,666	2,666	82,938	584	5,709	220	88
Total	**21,491**	**10,910**	**7,887**	**9,231**	**7,770**	**93,981**	**65,868**	**14,919**	**36,688**	**36,377**

TABLE 4.8 (continued)   **TABLEAU 4.8** (suite)

Number and quantity of drug exhibits seized by drug type, metropolitian areas, Canada, 1990 to 1994

Drogues saisies et quantités, et nombre de pièces justificatives, selon le genre de drogue, principaux centres urbains, du Canada, 1990 à 1994

| CITY/VILLE | HASH OIL/HASCHICH LIQUIDE | | | | | | | | | |
| | NUMBER/NOMBRE | | | | | QUANTITY (KG)/QUANTITE (KG) | | | | |
	1990	1991	1992	1993	1994	1990	1991	1992	1993	1994
St. John's	2	4	3	0	0	0.010	0.019	0.023	0.000	0
Halifax-Dartmouth	3	3	11	7	6	0.106	0.207	0.704	0.722	0.023
Saint John	2	3	2	0	0	0.135	0.006	0.001	0.000	0
Chicoutimi-Jonquière	3	1	1	3	3	0.087	0.001	0.000	0.006	1.113
Québec	2	1	3	8	4	0.009	0.005	0.144	0.021	0.26
Trois-Rivières	3	2	2	6	2	0.009	0.004	0.068	0.094	0.029
Sherbrooke	3	6	4	8	14	0.064	0.156	0.042	0.354	0.034
Montreal	15	23	24	35	29	0.125	0.615	1.591	102.504	5.901
Ottawa-Hull	9	6	4	3	10	0.219	0.009	0.006	5.737	0.86
Oshawa	253	127	134	156	153	7.441	1.757	4.749	3.588	1.67
Toronto	94	84	143	118	99	42.657	72.791	363.833	335.251	268.19
St. Catharines	13	13	9	4	2	0.099	0.174	0.810	0.008	0.006
Hamilton	55	52	111	49	65	2.626	0.510	21.517	4.228	0.277
Kitchener	24	50	64	41	95	0.607	0.948	0.883	0.391	0.867
London	138	68	29	59	89	1.315	0.381	5.039	5.131	1.430
Windsor	8	3	4	2	0	0.046	0.043	0.007	0.008	0
Sudbury	20	21	13	13	4	0.490	0.944	0.644	0.058	0.424
Thunder Bay	10	18	8	31	77	0.030	0.263	0.021	0.148	2.568
Winnipeg	41	16	17	10	9	3.824	1.011	0.675	0.380	0.044
Regina	30	21	9	19	21	0.290	0.073	0.009	0.087	0.267
Saskatoon	17	9	6	1	1	0.055	0.318	0.037	0.000	0
Calgary	9	4	2	2	1	0.175	0.019	0.169	0.006	0.017
Edmonton	35	11	8	2	3	0.491	0.707	0.101	0.020	0.029
Vancouver	27	22	46	51	38	0.060	1.415	0.870	2.307	0.487
Victoria	5	4	4	3	3	0.269	0.014	0.140	0.086	0.003
Rest of Canada/ Reste du Canada	703	547	538	606	670	41.565	39.877	33.184	1034.068	222.729
Total	**1,524**	**1,119**	**1,199**	**1,237**	**1,398**	**102.8**	**122.27**	**435.3**	**1,495**	**507.228**

TABLE 4.8 (continued)   **TABLEAU 4.8** (suite)

Number and quantity of drug exhibits seized by drug type, metropolitian areas, Canada, 1990 to 1994

Drogues saisies et quantités, et nombre de pièces justificatives, selon le genre de drogue, principaux centres urbains, du Canada, 1990 à 1994

	HEROIN/HEROINE									
	NUMBER/NOMBRE					QUANTITY (KG)/QUANTITE (KG)				
CITY/VILLE	1990	1991	1992	1993	1994	1990	1991	1992	1993	1994
St. John's	0	1	0	0	0	0.000	0.002	0.000	0.000	0
Halifax-Dartmouth	0	0	1	1	0	0.000	0.000	0.077	3.412	0
Saint John	0	0	0	0	0	0.000	0.000	0.000	0.000	0
Chicoutimi-Jonquière	0	0	0	1	0	0.000	0.000	0.000	0.002	0
Québec	0	1	0	1	2	0.000	0.000	0.000	0.005	0.016
Trois-Rivières	0	0	0	0	0	0.000	0.000	0.000	0.000	0
Sherbrooke	0	2	0	6	1	0.000	0.004	0.000	0.012	0.001
Montreal	162	189	227	182	154	10.321	7.100	15.171	7.987	3.495
Ottawa-Hull	6	1	4	2	1	0.609	0.001	3.846	0.100	0.001
Oshawa	0	0	3	2	0	0.000	0.000	0.128	0.004	0
Toronto	215	213	243	246	200	18.627	62.030	32.232	45.173	50.53
St. Catharines	5	20	4	2	3	0.006	0.009	0.029	0.003	0.041
Hamilton	5	1	5	3	3	0.026	0.000	0.112	0.002	0
Kitchener	4	11	9	3	1	0.019	0.005	0.010	0.029	0
London	0	1	1	0	0	0.000	0.001	0.001	0.000	0
Windsor	0	0	1	0	3	0.000	0.000	0.004	0.000	0.007
Sudbury	0	0	0	0	0	0.000	0.000	0.000	0.000	0
Thunder Bay	0	1	0	0	0	0.000	0.004	0.000	0.000	0
Winnipeg	0	0	5	8	1	0.000	0.000	0.001	4.633	2.958
Regina	0	2	4	0	1	0.000	0.056	0.001	0.001	0.03
Saskatoon	4	0	0	2	0	0.002	0.000	0.000	0.005	0
Calgary	6	5	1	0	1	0.051	0.013	0.003	0.000	0.132
Edmonton	1	7	1	2	0	0.001	0.030	0.007	0.023	0
Vancouver	342	350	346	425	416	10.296	23.667	25.532	25.279	1.222
Victoria	5	18	16	84	53	0.034	0.023	0.017	0.586	0.291
Rest of Canada/ Reste du Canada	41	57	87	132	106	16.720	26.297	15.119	7.316	3.539
Total	**796**	**880**	**958**	**1,102**	**946**	**56.712**	**119.242**	**92.290**	**94.572**	**62.263**

TABLE 4.8 (continued)	TABLEAU 4.8 (suite)

Number and quantity of drug exhibits seized by drug type, metropolitian areas, Canada, 1990 to 1994

Drogues saisies et quantités, et nombre de pièces justificatives, selon le genre de drogue, principaux centres urbains, du Canada, 1990 à 1994

CITY/VILLE	HALLUCINOGENS/HALLUCINOGENES									
	NUMBER/NOMBRE					QUANTITY (KG)/QUANTITE (KG)				
	1990	1991	1992	1993	1994	1990	1991	1992	1993	1994
St. John's	2	5	5	6	2	0.000	0.000	0.008	0.011	0.003
Halifax-Dartmouth	29	10	9	11	13	0.053	0.025	0.001	0.003	0.003
Saint John	11	9	11	11	8	0	0.004	0.000	0.016	0
Chicoutimi-Jonquière	17	15	36	43	34	0.18	0.048	0.334	0.432	3.941
Québec	107	176	269	289	214	2.234	3.205	9.886	3.387	2.082
Trois-Rivières	53	63	83	90	64	1.755	1.468	0.507	5.239	9.717
Sherbrooke	8	14	14	20	53	0.654	0.072	0.305	0.024	4.465
Montreal	160	233	340	322	333	78.429	2.241	9.369	2.680	10.371
Ottawa-Hull	25	29	32	23	34	3.467	1.091	0.348	1.390	0.288
Oshawa	29	31	22	22	17	0.036	0.229	0.375	0.037	0.024
Toronto	130	91	98	66	77	9.193	0.857	0.653	3.471	12.314
St. Catharines	13	8	6	3	6	0.065	0.009	0.006	0.029	0.141
Hamilton	58	29	70	15	6	1.327	0.119	1.399	0.018	0.051
Kitchener	15	31	33	21	21	0.168	0.740	0.505	0.162	0.039
London	16	6	21	20	21	0.256	0.050	0.498	0.241	0.1
Windsor	4	8	11	15	2	0.133	0.013	0.034	0.000	0
Sudbury	30	12	7	4	0	0.000	0.087	0.011	0.017	0
Thunder Bay	26	13	20	7	21	0.162	0.093	0.068	0.004	0.082
Winnipeg	66	48	41	19	23	2.054	0.523	0.180	0.023	1.098
Regina	9	6	5	7	4	0.096	0.698	0.011	0.007	0.001
Saskatoon	19	16	9	7	5	2.453	5.216	0.098	0.016	0.007
Calgary	52	28	21	28	10	0.422	8.378	0.291	0.175	0.036
Edmonton	76	63	41	22	6	1.403	0.402	0.388	2.577	0.050
Vancouver	201	141	198	173	171	2.677	1.957	4.471	1.808	2.787
Victoria	28	38	33	64	34	0.125	0.100	0.723	0.110	0.526
Rest of Canada/ Reste du Canada	722	784	754	867	631	16.123	76.253	11.663	11.310	21.570
Total	1,906	1,907	2,189	2,175	1,810	123.47	103.88	42.13	33.19	69.70

TABLE 4.8 (continued)   **TABLEAU 4.8** (suite)

Number and quantity of drug exhibits seized by drug type, metropolitian areas, Canada, 1990 to 1994

Drogues saisies et quantités, et nombre de pièces justificatives, selon le genre de drogue, principaux centres urbains, du Canada, 1990 à 1994

	COCAINE/COCAINE									
	NUMBER/NOMBRE					QUANTITY (KG)/QUANTITE (KG)				
CITY/VILLE	1990	1991	1992	1993	1994	1990	1991	1992	1993	1994
St. John's	4	15	3	9	2	0.85	0.92	0.57	0.35	0.07
Halifax-Dartmouth	69	168	225	160	215	4.62	2.81	2.76	24.15	750.95
Saint John	9	27	5	4	1	0.08	2.00	0.16	0.21	0.00
Chicoutimi-Jonquière	128	165	54	73	33	1.15	2.19	0.64	1.84	0.77
Québec	246	464	471	253	237	12.34	15.46	9.24	5.92	3.20
Trois-Rivières	141	180	183	168	207	2.93	1.02	3920.48	3.05	2.36
Sherbrooke	82	67	79	62	85	0.93	1.17	0.62	0.65	0.43
Montreal	1,944	3,135	3,079	2,985	2,838	252.72	592.42	350.14	2903.81	1742.70
Ottawa-Hull	384	330	371	293	280	10.48	4.77	8.83	10.79	7.76
Oshawa	62	101	87	78	141	0.45	1.06	0.98	0.29	0.30
Toronto	2,294	2,306	2,455	1,987	1,540	115.24	130.41	196.43	57.35	303.72
St. Catharines	103	58	52	28	18	5.27	3.92	1.03	10.63	0.44
Hamilton	119	150	162	219	188	3.72	2.55	2.48	1.37	3.31
Kitchener	54	79	210	207	194	0.64	0.99	0.89	1.34	0.74
London	29	31	70	62	158	1.27	0.55	4.41	0.46	0.68
Windsor	29	95	55	39	19	0.63	0.55	0.36	0.31	0.11
Sudbury	28	70	21	7	0	1.30	1.03	0.08	0.07	0.00
Thunder Bay	22	31	62	47	38	0.47	1.49	7.12	2.03	0.84
Winnipeg	132	144	123	115	71	3.29	12.84	2.53	3.26	3.29
Regina	14	17	5	5	1	0.07	0.38	0.08	0.08	0.00
Saskatoon	15	9	11	6	2	0.28	0.10	0.47	0.02	0.00
Calgary	153	117	92	47	20	2.26	3.07	7.57	2.30	0.20
Edmonton	351	329	261	307	91	8.70	8.68	8.64	3.99	6.80
Vancouver	1,239	1,521	1,738	1,494	1,371	27.29	19.42	58.74	22.61	73.72
Victoria	108	149	114	168	180	0.79	3.18	2.12	2.78	2.21
Rest of Canada/ Reste du Canada	1,930	2,107	1,996	1,896	1,395	52.84	887.22	715.31	1455.88	5456.72
Total	9,689	11,865	11,984	10,719	9,325	510.6	1,700.2	5,302.7	4,515.5	8,361.3

TABLE 4.8 (continued)

TABLEAU 4.8 (suite)

Number and quantity of drug exhibits seized by drug type, metropolitian areas, Canada, 1990 to 1994

Drogues saisies et quantités, et nombre de pièces justificatives, selon le genre de drogue, principaux centres urbains, du Canada, 1990 à 1994

CITY/VILLE	PHARMACEUTICALS/MEDICAMENTS									
	NUMBER/NOMBRE					QUANTITY (KG)/QUANTITE (KG)				
	1990	1991	1992	1993	1994	1990	1991	1992	1993	1994
St. John's	1	3	0	1	0	0.000	0.021	0.000	0.000	0
Halifax-Dartmouth	2	4	3	3	1	0.000	0.017	0.000	0.005	0
Saint John	0	3	0	2	0	0.000	0.002	0.000	0.000	0
Chicoutimi-Jonquière	3	1	5	1	3	0.002	0.012	0.632	0.000	0.001
Québec	2	6	5	6	16	0.006	0.017	0.022	0.017	0.048
Trois-Rivières	14	1	8	0	1	0.033	0.000	0.401	0.000	0
Sherbrooke	0	0	2	2	7	0.000	0.000	0.000	0.001	0.103
Montreal	33	26	66	58	52	0.102	522.258	1.328	3.616	0.863
Ottawa-Hull	23	13	16	27	4	0.108	0.266	7.492	0.053	0.011
Oshawa	9	10	19	8	5	0.002	0.011	0.427	0.010	0.063
Toronto	125	66	110	67	61	1.050	0.960	1.084	0.737	0.705
St. Catharines	12	23	12	7	2	0.010	0.063	0.145	0.050	0.001
Hamilton	22	18	10	13	7	0.111	0.074	0.060	0.068	0.06
Kitchener	11	13	10	2	11	0.079	0.002	0.004	0.000	0.381
London	0	3	10	18	19	0.000	0.002	0.014	0.141	0.014
Windsor	3	10	9	15	4	0.001	0.004	0.015	0.007	0.001
Sudbury	0	2	3	0	0	0.000	0.001	0.009	0.000	0
Thunder Bay	5	5	4	4	6	0.004	0.012	0.001	0.004	0.120
Winnipeg	74	48	58	67	8	0.142	0.032	5.754	0.164	0.080
Regina	31	21	35	26	21	0.027	0.060	0.030	0.344	0.010
Saskatoon	46	48	29	10	2	0.102	0.037	0.020	0.004	0.000
Calgary	53	23	12	31	7	0.074	0.146	0.023	0.207	0.245
Edmonton	238	267	169	161	30	0.478	0.365	0.196	0.209	0.047
Vancouver	141	212	153	71	70	1.602	24.449	0.707	0.696	0.828
Victoria	32	15	13	10	10	0.049	0.011	0.014	0.010	0.023
Rest of Canada/ Reste du Canada	191	188	166	180	165	1.239	0.418	0.238	0.823	2.152
Total	**1,071**	**1,029**	**871**	**634**	**634**	**5.22**	**549.24**	**18.62**	**7.17**	**5.76**

TABLE 4.8 (concluded)　　　　　　　　　　　　　　　　**TABLEAU 4.8** (fin)

Number and quantity of drug exhibits seized by drug type, metropolitian areas, Canada, 1990 to 1994

Drogues saisies et quantités, et nombre de pièces justificatives, selon le genre de drogue, principaux centres urbains, du Canada, 1990 à 1994

	OTHER/AUTRES									
	NUMBER/NOMBRE					QUANTITY (KG)/QUANTITE (KG)				
CITY/VILLE	1990	1991	1992	1993	1994	1990	1991	1992	1993	1994
St. John's	0	0	0	0	0	0.000	0.000	0.000	0.000	0
Halifax-Dartmouth	1	0	0	0	0	0.003	0.000	0.000	0.000	0
Saint John	0	0	0	0	0	0.000	0.000	0.000	0.000	0
Chicoutimi-Jonquière	0	0	0	0	0	0.000	0.000	0.000	0.000	0
Québec	0	0	0	0	0	0.000	0.000	0.000	0.000	0
Trois-Rivières	0	0	0	0	0	0.000	0.000	0.000	0.000	0
Sherbrooke	0	0	0	0	0	0.000	0.000	0.000	0.000	0
Montreal	5	1	4	4	3	3.654	0.001	0.013	0.049	0.049
Ottawa-Hull	0	2	0	1	2	0.000	0.012	0.000	0.275	2.696
Oshawa	0	0	0	0	0	0.000	0.000	0.000	0.000	0
Toronto	4	4	5	15	14	0.151	0.641	1.461	0.558	2.105
St. Catharines	2	0	4	1	0	0.006	0.000	0.011	0.015	0
Hamilton	0	0	2	2	2	0.000	0.000	0.030	0.006	0.004
Kitchener	0	0	3	1	0	0.000	0.000	0.219	0.002	0
London	0	1	2	4	3	0.000	0.019	0.012	0.018	0.003
Windsor	2	1	0	1	3	0.003	0.000	0.000	0.064	0.048
Sudbury	0	0	0	0	0	0.000	0.000	0.000	0.000	0
Thunder Bay	0	0	0	1	0	0.000	0.000	0.000	0.000	0
Winnipeg	0	1	0	0	0	0.000	0.000	0.000	0.000	0
Regina	0	3	0	0	0	0.000	1.849	0.000	0.000	0
Saskatoon	1	1	0	0	1	0.006	0.001	0.000	0.000	0
Calgary	0	2	0	0	1	0.000	0.003	0.000	0.000	0.002
Edmonton	5	11	4	13	4	1.026	0.333	0.108	1.440	0.050
Vancouver	34	39	36	36	46	2.760	1.767	1.974	1.935	0.414
Victoria	6	0	0	0	0	0.003	0.000	0.000	0.000	0.000
Rest of Canada/ Reste du Canada	20	17	25	29	32	0.429	0.179	0.123	0.502	12.115
Total	**80**	**83**	**82**	**91**	**634**	**8.041**	**4.805**	**3.951**	**4.864**	**17.486**

Source: Health Canada, Bureau of Drug Surveillance, Health Protection Branch.

Santé Canada, Bureau de la surveillance des médicaments, Direction de la protection de la santé.

TABLE 4.9   **TABLEAU 4.9**

Deaths and years of potential life lost attributed to illicit drugs by gender and cause, Canada, 1992

Décès et années de vie potentielle perdues, attribués aux drogues illicites, selon le sexe et la cause, Canada, 1992

Disease/Maladie	ICD-9 Code(s) Code(s) CIM-9	Deaths / Décès			Years of Potential Life Lost/ Années de vie potentielle perdues		
		Male/ Hommes	Female/ Femmes	Total/ Total	Male/ Hommes	Female/ Femmes	Total/ Total
AIDS/Sida	042-044	52	9	61	1,965	401	2,366
Viral hepatitis B/ Hépatite B	070.2-070.3	5	0	5	191	10	201
Viral Hepatitis non-A,-B/ Hépatite autre que A, B	070.4-070.5	23	11	34	89	75	164
Drug pychoses/Psychose due à la drogue	292	0	0	0	0	0	0
Opioid dependence/abuse/ Dépendance et abus, opiacés	304.0,304.7,305.5	28	0	28	1,139	0	1,139
Cocaine dependence/abuse/ Dépendance et abus, cocaïne	304.2,305.6	7	3	10	301	150	451
Cannabis dependence/abuse/ Dépendance et abus, cannabis	304.3,305.2	0	0	0	0	0	0
Amphetamine dependence/abuse/ Dépendance et abus, d'amphetamines	304.3,305.2	0	1	1	0	45	45
Hallucinogen dependence/abuse/ Dépendance et abus, hallucinogènes	304.4,205.7	0	0	0	0	0	0
Infective endocarditis/ Endocardite infectueuse	421	1	0	1	47	22	68
Pregnancy complications/Suites de grossesse	640-641,648.3, 656.5	0	0	0	0	3	3
Neonatal conditions/Conditions néonatales	760.7,762.0-762.1, 764-765,779.5	3	3	6	252	219	471
Opiate poisoning/ Empoisonnements par opiacés	E850.0,E850.1, E935.1	82	22	104	2,987	875	3,861
Cocaine poisoning/ Empoisonnements par cocaïne	E855.2	59	9	68	2,548	460	3,008
Psychotropic poisoning/ Empoisonnements par psychotropes	E854.2,E854.2	1	0	1	40	0	40
Motor vehicle accidents/ Accidents routiers	E810-E819	31	0	31	1,486	0	1,486
Suicide, self-inflicted injury/ Suicides, blessures auto-infligées	E950-E959	292	16	308	12,868	796	13,664
Victim, assault/Victimes, agressions	E960-E969	44	4	48	1,917	220	2,137
Injuring rec'd during legal intervention/Blessures causées durant intervention légale	E970-E978	1	0	1	65	0	65
Poisoning, intent undetermined/ Empoisonnements, intention non précisée	E980	34	24	57	1,226	888	2,113

TABLE 4.9 (concluded)   **TABLEAU 4.9** (fin)

Deaths and years of potential life lost attributed to illicit drugs by gender and cause, Canada, 1992

Décès et années de vie potentielle perdues, attribués aux drogues illicites, selon le sexe et la cause, Canada, 1992

Disease/Maladie	ICD-9 Code(s) Code(s) CIM-9	Deaths / Décès			Years of Potential Life Lost/ Années de vie potentielle perdues		
		Male/ Hommes	Female/ Femmes	Total/ Total	Male/ Hommes	Female/ Femmes	Total/ Total
Total/Total		**641**	**91**	**732**	**27,044**	**4,103**	**31,147**
Rate per 100,000 population/ Taux par 100 000 habitants		4.55	0.64	2.57	192	29	1.10
Illicit drugs attributed deaths as % of total mortality from any cause/aux des décès imputés aux drogues illicites par rapport à l'ensemble de la mortalité, toutes causes confondues		0.33	0.05	0.37	0.88	0.13	1.01

Source: E. Single, L. Robson, W. Xie and J. Rehm, *The Cost of Substance Abuse in Canada*, Ottawa: Canadian Centre on Substance Abuse,1996.

Single, E., L. Robson, X. Xie et J. Rehm, *The Costs of Substance Abuse in Canada*, Ottawa, Centre canadien de lutte contre l'alcoolisme et les toxicomanies, 1996.

TABLE 4.10

TABLEAU 4.10

Number and rates of death and years of potential life lost attributed to illicit drugs, Canadian provinces, 1992

Nombre et taux des décès et des années de vie potentielle perdues imputés aux drogues illicites, selon la province, 1992

Province/ Province	Deaths Due to Illicit Drugs/ Décès imputés aux drogues illicitess		Potential Years of Life Lost Due to Illicit Drugs/ Années de vie potentielle Perdues imputées aux drogues illicites	
	Number/ Nombre	Rates per 100,00 Population/ Taux par 100 000 habitants Habitants	Number/ Nombre	Rates per 100,00 Population/ Taux par 100 000 Habitants
Nfld./T.-N.	6	1.0	261	45
P.E.I./I.-P.-E.	3	2.3	99	76
N.S./N.-É.	15	1.6	663	72
N.B./N.-B.	11	1.5	517	69
Que./Québec	198	2.8	8,568	120
Ont./Ont.	211	2.0	9,184	87
Man./Man.	21	1.9	951	85
Sask./Sask.	20	2.0	855	85
Alta./Alb.	82	3.1	3,439	133
B.C./C.-B.	163	4.70	6,658	193

Source: E. Single, L. Robson, W. Xie and J. Rehm, *The Cost of Substance Abuse in Canada*, Ottawa: Canadian Centre on Substance Abuse, 1996.

Single, E., L. Robson, X. Xie et J. Rehm, *The Costs of Substance Abuse in Canada*, Ottawa, Centre canadien de lutte contre l'alcoolisme et les toxicomanies, 1996.}

TABLE 4.11   **TABLEAU 4.11**

Hospital separations and hospitalization days attributed to illicit drugs by gender and cause, Canada, 1992

Départs des hôpitaux et jours d'hospitalisation imputés aux drogues illicites selon le sexe et la cause, Canada, 1992

Disease/Maladie	ICD-9 Code(S) Code(s) CIM-9	Hospital Separations/ Départs des hôpitaux			Hospital Days/ Jours d'hospitalisation		
		Male/ Hommes	Female/ Femmes	Total/ Total	Male/ Hommes	Female/ Femmes	Total/ Total
AIDS/Sida	042-044	136	36	172	2360	730	3091
Viral hepatitis B/ Hépatite B	070.2-070.3	65	34	100	444	264	708
Viral hepatitis B/ Hépatite B	070.4-070.5	23	11	34	89	75	164
Viral Hepatitis non-A,-B/	070.4-070.5	23	11	34	89	75	164
Drug pychoses/Psychose due à la drogue	292	679	528	1207	7146	6037	13183
Opioid dependence/abuse/ Dépendance et abus, opiacés	304.0,304.7, 305.5	379	306	685	2615	2802	5417
Cocaine dependence/abuse/ Dépendance et abus, cocaïne	304.2,305.6	746	405	1151	6011	3033	9044
Cannabis dependence/abuse/ Dépendance et abus, cannabis	304.3,305.2	118	36	154	1304	502	1806
Amphetamine dependence/abuse/ Dépendance et abus, d'amphetamines	304.4,205.7	25	22	47	286	319	605
Hallucinogen dependence/abuse/ Dépendance et abus, hallucinogènes	304.5,205.3	103	22	125	692	80	772
Infective endocarditis/ Endocardite infectueuse	421	16	12	28	336	242	578
Pregnancy complications/Suites de grossesse	640-641,648.3, 656.5	0	649	649	0	2,762	2,762
Neonatal conditions/Conditions néonatales	760.7,762.0-762.1, 764-765,779.5	74	67	141	1464	1433	2897
Opiate poisoning/ Empoisonnements par opiacés	965.0	235	261	496	819	1018	1837
Cocaine poisoning/ Empoisonnements par cocaïne	968.5	130	62	192	272	177	449
Psychotropic poisoning/ Empoisonnements par psychotropes	969.6-969.9	211	228	439	1305	1888	3193
Motor vehicle accidents/ Accidents routiers	E810-E819	286	0	286	3523	0	3523
Suicide, self-inflicted injury/ Suicides, blessures auto-infligées	E950-E959	286	0	286	3,523	0	3,523
Victim, assault/Victimes, agressions	E960-E969	1113	71	1184	7835	672	8508
Injuring rec'd during legal intervention/Blessures causées durant intervention légale	E970-E978	5	0	5	33	0	33
Poisoning, intent undetermined/ Empoisonnements, intention non précisée	E980						

TABLE 4.11 (concluded)   **TABLEAU 4.11** (fin)

Hospital separations and hospitalization days attributed to illicit drugs by gender and cause, Canada, 1992

Départs des hôpitaux et jours d'hospitalisation imputés aux drogues illicites selon le sexe et la cause, Canada, 1992

Disease/Maladie	ICD-9 Code(S) Code(s) CIM-9	Hospital Separations/ Départs des hôpitaux			Hospital Days/ Jours d'hospitalisation		
		Male/ Hommes	Female/ Femmes	Total/ Total	Male/ Hommes	Female/ Femmes	Total/ Total
Total/Total		**4,345**	**2,750**	**7,095**	**36,536**	**22,035**	**58,571**
Rate per 100,000 population/ Taux par 100 000 habitants		30.80	19.20	25.00	259	154	206
Illicit drugs attributed deaths as % of total mortality from any cause/aux des décès imputés aux drogues illicites par rapport à l'ensemble de la mortalité, toutes causes confondues		0.12	0.08	0.19	0.09	0.05	0.14

Source: E. Single, L. Robson, W. Xie and J. Rehm, *The Cost of Substance Abuse in Canada*, Ottawa: Canadian Centre on Substance Abuse, 1996.

Single, E., L. Robson, X. Xie et J. Rehm, *The Costs of Substance Abuse in Canada*, Ottawa, Centre canadien de lutte contre l'alcoolisme et les toxicomanies, 1996.

TABLE 4.12   **TABLEAU 4.12**

Hospital separations and hospitalization days attributed to illicit drugs, Canada provinces, 1992

Départs des hôpitaux et jours d'hospitalisation imputés aux drogues illicites, selon le sexe et la cause, Canada,

Province/ Province	Hospital Separations Due to Illicit Drugs/ Départs des hôpitaux imputés aux drogues illicites		Hospitalization Days Due to Illicit Drugs/ Jours d'hospitalisation imputés aux drogues illicites	
	Number/ Nombre	Rates per 100,00 Population/ Taux par 100 000 habitants Habitants	Number/ Nombre	Rates per 100,00 Population/ Taux par 100 000 Habitants
Nfld./T.-N.	86	15	1,464	252
P.E.I./I.-P.-E.	23	18	202	155
N.S./N.-E.	190	21	1,835	199
N.B./N.-B.	88	12	583	78
Que./Québec	1,624	23	19,410	271
Ont./Ont.	2,524	24	18,164	171
Man./Man.	273	25	1,926	173
Sask./Sask.	255	25	1,453	145
Alta./Alb..	867	33	6,848	260
B.C./C.-B.	1,363	39	7,983	231

Source: E. Single, L. Robson, W. Xie and J. Rehm, *The Costs of Substance Abuse in Canada*, Ottawa: Canadian Centre on Substance Abuse, 1996.

Single, E., L. Robson, X. Xie et J. Rehm, *The Costs of Substance Abuse in Canada*, Ottawa, Centre canadien de lutte contre l'alcoolisme et les toxicomanies, 1996.}

5 Indigenous Canadians

5 Populations autochtones

Figures

Figures

Tables

Tableaux

Highlights

★ Native youths are at two to six times greater risk for every alcohol-related problems than their counterparts in other segments of the Canadian population.

★ Saskatchewan Indian children (0 to14 years) have a suicide rate that is much higher than their national or provincial counterparts (27.5 times greater than Canadian children generally and 33.6 times greater than children in Saskatchewan generally).

★ Indigenous men may be more likely to abuse alcohol while Indigenous women tend to abuse drugs alone.

★ 30% of men and 16% of women (Inuit and Dene) used cannabis in the last year.

★ The Treatment Activity Reporting System (TARS) shows that narcotics are the second most popular drug among Indigenous adults seeking treatment.

★ The majority of Aboriginal Canadians smoke; half of those who smoke, do so daily.

★ One in five Native youth have used solvents. One third of all users are under 15 and more than half began to use solvents before they were 11 years old.

Points saillants

★ Les jeunes Autochtones sont de deux à six fois plus nombreux à éprouver des problèmes reliés à l'alcool que leurs homologues des autres segments de la population canadienne.

★ Le taux de suicide est beaucoup plus élevé chez les enfants indiens de la Saskatchewan (0 à 14 ans) que chez les jeunes du même âge dans l'ensemble du pays ou de la province (27,5 fois plus élevé que pour l'ensemble des enfants canadiens et 33,6 fois plus élevé que pour l'ensemble des enfants de la Saskatchewan).

★ Les hommes autochtones tendent à faire abus d'alcool tandis que les femmes autochtones font plutôt abus de drogue seulement.

★ L'an dernier, 30 % des hommes et 16 % des femmes (Inuit et Dénés) ont consommé du cannabis.

★ Selon le Système de rapports sur les activités de traitement (SRAT), les stupéfiants viennent au deuxième rang des drogues les plus populaires chez les Autochtones adultes qui se font traiter.

★ La majorité des Canadiens autochtones fument, dont la moitié quotidiennement.

★ Un jeune Autochtone sur cinq a déjà utilisé des solvants. Un tiers de ces consommateurs ont moins de 15 ans, et plus de la moitié ont commencé à en consommer avant l'âge de 11 ans.

Indigenous Canadians

by Kim Scott, Kishk Anaquot Health Research and Program Development

INTRODUCTION: It would be foolhardy for the reader to digest this information without some qualification of its limitations and some recommendations for its improvement. Furthermore, while this is meant to be an exclusively Canadian profile, this distinction is not useful for researchers or Indigenous groups because the similarity of circumstance north and south of the border warrants attention to American data. With respect to Canada, a sizable portion of Indigenous peoples, namely the Métis, are excluded from most data bases. Also, unless otherwise specified, this information *cannot* be generalized to the off-reserve (including the urban) context, where we know the majority of Canadian Indigenous peoples live.

While some argue that the health of Indigenous peoples is similar whether they reside in the city or rural settlements, others suggest that those who live in the city may be slightly better off than their rural counterparts.[1] But the debate has never been settled conclusively.

The social indicators from which Indigenous substance abuse and its consequences are inferred is collected primarily by the federal government (i.e. Medical Services Branch, Health Canada), whose collection methods vary considerably among regions, and from provincial systems. This makes national normative data unavailable. Where survey research is available, the construct validity and reliability of the instruments used is rarely discussed. In addition, the response burden of the litany of surveys and questionnaires in recent years has tainted most data with apathy or majority non-participation.

The differences between western and Indigenous sciences, together with other cultural barriers,

Populations autochtones

par Kim Scott, Kishk Anaquot Health Research and Program Development

INTRODUCTION : Il serait téméraire de la part du lecteur que de vouloir assimiler toute l'information ici présentée sans en connaître les limitations et les possibilités. Aussi convient-il, à ce propos, de préciser que bien qu'il s'agisse d'un profil exclusivement canadien, cette distinction perd tout sens pour les chercheurs ou les groupes autochtones, puisque la similarité des contextes de chaque côté de la frontière canado-américaine justifierait que l'on s'attarde aux données américaines. Quant aux bases de données canadiennes, la plupart font exclusion d'un segment fort important des peuples indigènes, les Métis. En outre, sauf indication contraire, on *ne peut pas* généraliser cette information pour l'appliquer aux contextes hors réserve (urbains compris), où vivent, comme nous le savons, la majorité des populations autochtones au Canada.

Pendant que certains soutiennent que l'état de santé des populations autochtones est semblable indépendamment qu'elles habitent la ville ou la campagne, d'autres suggèrent que celui des populations urbaines est peut-être un peu mieux que celles des régions rurales.[1] Mais la question n'a jamais été entièrement élucidée.

Les indicateurs sociaux servant à analyser la toxicomanie et ses effets chez les Autochtones sont normalement recueillis par le gouvernement fédéral (c.-à-d. la Direction des services médicaux, Santé Canada), dont les méthodes de collecte varient considérablement d'une région et d'une province à l'autre. Il y a donc absence de données normatives nationales. Et là où l'on effectue des enquêtes, rarement se penche-t-on sur la validité conceptuelle et sur la fiabilité des outils utilisés. Mentionnons en outre que le fardeau de réponse imposé par la kyrielle de sondages et de questionnaires administrés ces dernières années a eu

complicate communications, data collection and interpretation. Scattered groups are extremely heterogeneous in community structure and, even within communities, many people recognized as "Indian" are of various racial and ethnic origins. Urban Indigenous populations are either not identified or do not participate in Canadian polls such as the National Alcohol and Drug Survey.

Still, from crude and indirect assessment, some patterns are clear. The following profile attempts to supplement previous CCSA and federal works (to which we refer the reader for further information), although some information is replicated. It will highlight what is known about abuse in the Indigenous community and, to the extent possible, illustrate differences between Indians on- and off-reserve, Métis and Inuit communities.

DETERMINING PREVALENCE: Generally, substance use is inferred from social indicators analysis and by most indicators, it is clear that the Indigenous community is at a relatively greater risk for abuse-related physical consequences than their general counterparts.[2] Traditional formulae that extrapolate the prevalence of alcoholism from liver cirrhosis rates are not appropriate for the Indigenous population because the life span is not long enough. Similarly, the marginalization of Indigenous groups has made them difficult to capture in Canadian data bases and no studies have examined alcohol-related diagnoses and discharge rates for Canadian Indigenous groups. Therefore, the most indicative records are violent death rates, which bear strong statistical correlations with substance abuse.[3,4]

Medical Services Branch (MSB), responsible for Indian and Inuit health services, reports that the leading causes of death for their service population, in hierarchical order, were injury and poisoning (including suicides) and circulatory system diseases, with the exception of the Atlantic and Ontario regions, where death due to circulatory system diseases was more prevalent than death due to injury and poisoning. These are fairly stable patterns in the mortality data for this group.[2,5]

pour effet de teinter la plupart des données d'une certaine apathie ou d'entraîner un taux élevé de non participation.

Par ailleurs, ajoutées aux autres divergences culturelles, les différences entre les sciences occidentales et autochtones viennent compliquer encore davantage les communications, la collecte et l'interprétation des données. La structure communautaire des groupes éparpillés est extrêmement hétérogène, et il arrive qu'au sein même de certaines collectivités, de nombreux sujets reconnus comme «Indiens» soient d'origines raciales et ethniques différentes. Les populations autochtones urbaines ne sont pas relevées comme telles ou ne participent pas aux sondages canadiens tels l'Enquête nationale sur l'alcool et les autres drogues.

Il est néanmoins, à partir d'une évaluation brute et indirecte, de dégager clairement certaines tendances. Ainsi, le profil fourni ci-après vise à compléter les travaux antérieurs du CCLAT et de l'administration fédérale sur le sujet (auxquels nous renvoyons le lecteur pour de plus amples informations), malgré que certaines données soient purement répétitives. Ce profil souligne ce que l'on sait déjà de la toxicomanie en milieu autochtone et illustre, dans la mesure du possible, les écarts existant entre les Indiens des réserves et de l'extérieur, les Métis et les Inuit.

CALCUL DE L'INCIDENCE : En règle générale, on infère de l'usage des drogues en se fondant sur les indicateurs sociaux, et la majorité de ceux-ci indiquent clairement que les populations autochtones risquent beaucoup plus que les autres de souffrir des conséquences physiques de l'abus de ces produits.[2] Mais les formules habituellement utilisées pour mesurer l'alcoolisme, qui s'appuient sur les cas de cirrhose du foie, ne conviennent pas à la durée de vie des populations autochtones. Dans un même ordre d'idée, la marginalisation des groupes autochtones a rendu leur capture par les bases de données difficiles, et aucune étude ne s'est penchée sur les diagnostics et les taux de départ reliés à l'alcool les concernant. Par conséquent, les données les plus révélatrices sont les taux de mort violente, qui

Indigenous patterns of violent death show a clear and consistently elevated risk. In some cases, the rate is three and four times greater than national norms, with young people accounting for much of the variation between groups. When broken down by region and sex, it is clear that rates of violent death escalate with westward and northern movement, and that males account for much of the elevated risk of violent mortality.[6]

Suicide has always featured prominently as an indicator of social distress and is a subset of the violent death category, which also has strong statistical associations with addiction.[4] While some studies have found that violent death rates increase from south to north,[7,8] suicide patterns in British Columbia differ somewhat, with interior groups being at greatest risk.[9] In fact, Cooper et al (1992) found that suicide rates for those off-reserve (16/100,000) closely paralleled that of British Columbians generally, whereas those on-reserve had a dramatically elevated risk (37/100,000). Another important finding is the apparent structural difference between on-reserve communities with high suicide rates and those with low suicide rates:

"on average, people living in areas with high suicide rates had lower levels of education; lived in households with larger numbers of occupants; had more children living at home; included more single parents and fewer elders, and had lower incomes, generated by a smaller proportion of the population" (page 21).[9]

The same comparison was attempted with non-Indigenous areas with high and low suicide rates, but

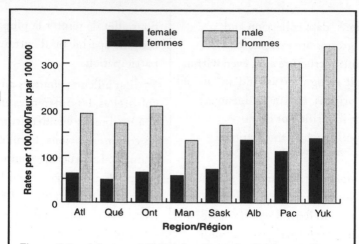

Figure 5.1:   Injury and Poisoning Rates by Region and Gender (5 Year Average 1988-1992)
Note: reproduced from Bobet, E.; Mustard, C.: Unpublished presentation to Focus Group on Suicide, June 24-25, 1995, Health Programs Analysis, Medical Services Branch.

Figure 5.1   Taux des blessures et des empoisonnements selon la région et le sexe (moyenne sur 5 années, 1988-1992) Nota : Tiré de E. Bobet et C. Mustard. Exposé non publié présenté à un groupe de discussions dirigées, les 24 et 25 juin 1995, Analyse des programmes de santé, Direction des services médicaux.

présentent de fortes corrélations statistiques avec l'abus des drogues.[3,4]

La Direction des services médicaux (DSM), chargée des services de santé auprès des Indiens et des Inuit, estime que les principales causes de décès chez les populations qu'elle dessert sont, dans l'ordre, les blessures et les empoisonnements (suicides compris) ainsi que les maladies de l'appareil circulatoire, sauf dans les régions de l'Atlantique et de l'Ontario, où les décès imputables à ces dernières étaient plus nombreux que ceux causés par les blessures et les empoisonnements. Il s'agit là de tendances relativement stables dans les données sur la mortalité concernant ce groupe.[2,5]

Les profils autochtones de mort violente indiquent régulièrement un risque particulièrement élevé. Dans certains cas, le taux excède même de trois ou quatre fois les normes nationales, et la plupart des écarts entre les groupes sont attribuables aux jeunes. Lorsque l'on procède à une ventilation selon la région et le sexe, il est clair que les taux de mort violente augmentent au fur et à mesure que l'on se déplace vers les régions de l'ouest et du nord et qu'ils visent principalement les hommes.[6]

Le suicide a toujours constitué un important indicateur de détresse sociale et compose un sous-ensemble de la catégorie des morts violentes, laquelle comporte également d'étroites corrélations statistiques avec la toxicomanie.[4] Or bien que certaines études aient démontré que les taux de mort violente vont croissant du sud au nord,[7,8] les profils de suicide établis pour la Colombie-Britannique indiquent pour leur part que les

this yielded more similarities than differences: the authors conclude that non-Indigenous suicide rates are "apparently not predictable on the basis of the characteristics examined" (page 21).[9]

Unlike death rates from injury and poisoning, which seem to escalate from east to west and south to north, suicide rates from Medical Services Branch (Indian and Inuit groups) indicate that men seem at greatest risk in Atlantic, Alberta, Pacific and Yukon regions, while women seem at greatest risk in Pacific, Alberta and Ontario regions.

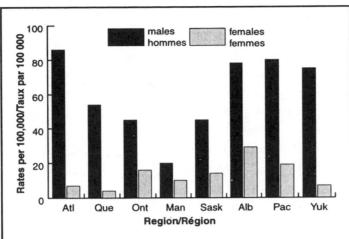

Figure 5.2:　Suicide Rates by Region and Gender 5 Year Average 1988-1992
Note: reproduced from Bobet, E.; Mustard, C.: Unpublished presentation to Focus Group on Suicide, June 24-25, 1995, Health Programs Analysis, Medical Services Branch
Figure 5.2　Taux des suicides selon la région et le sexe (moyenne sur 5 années, 1988-1992)
Nota : Tiré de E. Bobet, et C. Mustard. Exposé non publié présenté à un groupe de discussions dirigées sur le suicide, les 24 et 25 juin 1995, Analyse des programmes de santé, Direction des services médicaux.

Although suicide has received much attention as an indicator of social distress, accidental death rates are sometimes twice the suicide rate.[10] In a five-year trend analysis of unnatural death rates in Alberta, Indigenous risk was four to five times the general rate.[10] Such a pattern of dramatically escalated risk has also been documented in Saskatchewan and British Columbia.[7,11] Interestingly, the Saskatchewan study noted that northern groups fared far worse than the less isolated regions.

GENDER DIFFERENCES: When we infer substance abuse from social indicators analysis, there are some apparent differences between the sexes. With respect to death due to injury and poisoning, there is a wide and fairly stable discrepancy between the sexes in Indian and Inuit groups, with men being much more likely than women to die violently.[2,5] These data suggest a couple of things about gender differences in addiction. The first conclusion we might draw is that women do not suffer

groupes les plus à risque sont ceux de l'intérieur.[9] En fait, le collectif Cooper (1992) a constaté que les taux de suicide des populations vivant hors réserve (16:100 000) suivaient étroitement ceux de la Colombie-Britannique en général, tandis que ceux des populations vivant sur les réserves étaient considérablement plus élevés (37:100 000). Fait important, on a découvert au sujet des réserves qu'il existait une nette différence structurelle entre les groupes ayant des taux de suicide élevés et ceux ayant des taux peu élevés :

«En règle générale, les répondants provenant d'endroits marqués par de hauts taux de suicide possédaient un niveau d'instruction inférieur; vivaient dans des foyers comptant un plus grand nombre d'occupants; comptaient davantage d'enfants au foyer; comprenaient plus de chefs de familles monoparentales et moins d'aînés, et disposaient de revenus inférieurs, produits par une plus petite proportion de la population» (page 21).[9]

On a tenté de procéder à une comparaison similaire en ce qui concerne les régions non autochtones présentant des taux de suicide élevés et faibles, mais les résultats ont donné plus de similarités que d'écarts. Il serait donc impossible, selon les auteurs, de prévoir les taux de suicide chez les non Autochtones en se fondant sur les seules caractéristiques examinées (page 21).[9]

Contrairement à ce que l'on a observé au regard des taux de décès dus aux blessures et aux empoisonnements, qui vont croissant d'est en ouest et du sud au nord, les taux de suicide (Indiens et Inuit)

from addiction to the same extent that men do. It is clear, after all, that they do not die as frequently from violent or accidental means. The second conclusion we could draw is that they may be suffering to the same extent but they suffer quite differently. In other words, the physical consequences of their addictions is not fatal as frequently as it is for their male counterparts. This conclusion is supported by the fact that usually the sexes of Indigenous groups are more similar to each other than they are to Canadians generally when we look at opportunities for social reinforcement of substance use and adolescent use patterns.[12,13,14] Examination of gender-specific abuse-related diagnoses and discharge rates might shed a conservative light on which conclusion is valid.[15]

When we look strictly at within-group gender differences, there is some evidence to suggest, at least in Maritime provinces, that Indigenous men are more likely to abuse alcohol, while Indigenous women tend to abuse drugs alone.[16] The Yukon Alcohol and Drug Survey suggested that Indigenous women were more likely to have irregular/infrequent drinking patterns than their male counterparts, and men were almost three times more likely than women to declare themselves heavy frequent drinkers. The comparison between the sexes is depicted in Figure 5.3.[17]

With respect to tobacco use, only slight gender difference were noted in Smoking Among Aboriginal People in Canada (1991), including older women being more likely to have never smoked daily (women 27%, men 18%) and women 65+ being less likely to be current smokers (women 28%,

fournis par la Direction des services médicaux indiquent que les hommes seraient plus vulnérables dans les régions de l'Atlantique, de l'Alberta, du Pacifique et du Yukon, et les femmes, dans les régions du Pacifique, de l'Alberta et de l'Ontario.

On s'est déjà beaucoup attardé au suicide comme indicateur de détresse sociale, mais il convient de souligner que les taux de mort accidentelle sont parfois deux fois plus élevés que les taux de suicide.[10] Selon une analyse tendancielle des taux de mort naturelle en Alberta, portant sur cinq années, les Autochtones sont de quatre à cinq fois plus vulnérables que l'ensemble de la population.[10] Un risque aussi élevé a également été documenté en Saskatchewan et en Colombie-Britannique.[7,11] En Saskatchewan, l'étude a démontré que les groupes du nord étaient considérablement plus à risque que ceux des régions moins isolées.

ÉCARTS ENTRE LES SEXES : L'analyse des indicateurs sociaux nous apprend que le phénomène de la toxicomanie présente des écarts évidents entre les sexes. Dans le cas des décès dus aux blessures et aux empoisonnements, on note ainsi un écart important et relativement stable entre les sexes chez les Indiens et les Inuit, les hommes étant beaucoup plus nombreux que les femmes à décéder de mort violente.[2,5] Ces observations laissent croire, d'une part, que les femmes ne souffrent pas de la toxicomanie dans une mesure aussi grande que les hommes; de fait, elles ne sont pas aussi nombreuses à décéder de mort violente ou accidentelle et, d'autre part, qu'elles en souffrent peut-être autant, mais d'une façon probablement fort différente. En d'autres termes, les

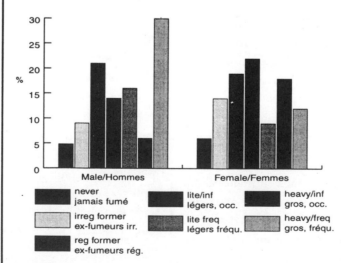

Figure 5.3:　Analytic Drinker Category by Sex, Yukon, Indigenous Respondents

Figure 5.3　Catégorie analytique des buveurs selon le sexe, répondants autochtones, Yukon.

men 38%). When broken down by age and gender, there were slight differences in consumption patterns in the 45+ age group. Women in the 45 to 64 age category were more likely to be light consumers (1 to 10 cigarettes daily, women 30%, men 17%), whereas men in the same age category were more likely to be heavy smokers (26+ cigarettes/day, men 13%, women 6%).[18]

Examination of gender specific issues in addiction would be incomplete without some profile of FAS (Fetal Alcohol Syndrome) prevalence. Much controversy surrounds the estimation of FAS incidence and prevalence in Indigenous communities. Bray and Anderson (1989) claim that failure to control for higher fertility rates and increased span of childbearing years account for much of the inflated rates currently published.[19] Burd and Moffat (1994) believe that some of this inflation can be accounted for by screening procedures and diagnostic criteria, neither of which is always detailed in the literature. Methodologically, they recommend that investigators:

a)   be blind to maternal alcohol ingestion

b)   select communities where rates may be low

c)   engage in longitudinal cohort studies

d)   review death certificates whenever possible[20]

By most published accounts, rates of FAS incidence are indeed higher than average among Indigenous Canadians, although much fluctuation occurs in American data. Conservative estimates of FAS/FAE (Fetal Alcohol Effect) incidence in general samples yielded 1 to 3 per 1000:[21] American studies show an Indian FAS incidence ranging from 1.4 to 9.8 per 1000.[22] A Canadian study discovered an FAS/FAE rate of 25 per 1000 children (0 to 16 years) among Indigenous northwestern BC populations (Métis and Indian) and a rate of 46 per 1000 among Yukon Indigenous groups. The rate for general Canadian populations in both regions was 0.4 per 1000.[23]

While there is argument that the epidemiological methods of these Canadian studies are questionable, Indian women recognize "that the full potential of

conséquences physiques de leur toxicomanie ne sont pas aussi fatales que chez leurs homologues masculins. Cette conclusion est appuyée par le fait que, lorsque nous examinons l'influence de la société sur l'abus des drogues et les profils de consommation des adolescents, les profils des femmes et des hommes se rapprochent davantage entre les divers groupes autochtones qu'avec ceux des Canadiens en général.[12,13,14] Un examen des diagnostics associés à l'abus selon le sexe et des taux de départ des hôpitaux pourrait nous fournir une certaine idée de la conclusion à tirer.[15]

Lorsque l'on s'arrête aux écarts entre les sexes à l'intérieur d'un même groupe, il ressort, du moins dans le cas des Maritimes, que les hommes autochtones sont plus nombreux que les femmes à boire avec excès, mais que les femmes autochtones sont par contre plus nombreuses à consommer des drogues uniquement.[16] Selon l'enquête du Yukon sur l'alcool et les autres drogues, la consommation d'alcool chez les femmes autochtones serait plus irrégulière et moins fréquente que chez les hommes, mais ces derniers seraient près de trois fois plus nombreux à se déclarer gros et fréquents buveurs. La Figure 5.3 présente une comparaison entre les deux sexes.[17]

En ce qui concerne la consommation du tabac, seul un léger écart entre les sexes a été noté dans le rapport de 1991 sur le tabagisme au sein des populations autochtones du Canada, qui tient notamment compte du fait que les femmes plus âgées sont plus nombreuses à n'avoir jamais fumé quotidiennement (27 % contre 18 % chez les hommes) et que les femmes de 65 ans et plus sont aussi plus nombreuses à ne pas fumer (28 % contre 38 % chez les hommes). La ventilation des données selon l'âge et le sexe révèle de légers écarts dans les profils de consommation des 45 ans et plus. On compte plus de fumeuses légères chez les femmes de 45 à 64 ans (1 à 10 cigarettes par jour, 30 % contre 17 % chez les hommes), mais plus de gros fumeurs chez les hommes de la même catégorie d'âge (au moins 26 cigarettes par jour, 13 % contre 6 % chez les femmes).[18]

Aucun examen de la toxicomanie effectué en fonction du sexe ne peut être considéré complet sans un

Indian people may be jeopardized as the result of a race of people weakened by fetal alcohol syndrome".[24] Therefore, while exact prevalence cannot be nailed down which isolates how many Indigenous women might be considered alcoholic or how many might give birth to a child with FAS or FAE, we can infer that substance abuse results in severe and debilitating consequences at rates above North American females generally in some regions.

CHILDREN: Beyond what effects children may endure as a result of FAS/FAE, rarely do addiction profiles take into account the special substance use patterns of children (those under age 12 years). While much attention has been focused upon adolescent substance use, the only literature that describes the use patterns of children focuses on substance-specific use (e.g. smoke-less tobacco and solvents). Still, one of the most disquieting epidemiological facts about addiction in the Indigenous community is the alarming rate of substance use in this age group. Although children are most likely to abuse tobacco (including smokeless products), alcohol, cannabis and solvents, age at use onset has been shown to be substantially younger than general North American children for a variety of substances[25,26,27,28,29,30] and children are entering Canadian Indigenous treatment facilities at younger ages,[31,32,33] primarily in central and western provinces. Fiddler (1985) discovered a suicide rate of Saskatchewan Indian children (0 to 14 years) phenomenally higher than their national or provincial counterparts (27.5 times greater than Canadian children generally and 33.6 times greater than children in Saskatchewan generally).[7] In the most recent profile of addictions patterns of Indigenous peoples in urban centres, 67% of participating Friendship Centres reported that children were consuming alcohol and sniffing solvents during school hours, after school, on the streets and in their homes, sometimes with their families.[34]

ALCOHOL USE: Apart from self report survey data, the Post Censal Aboriginal Peoples Survey (APS) and that collected at Indigenous treatment centres, very little exists that directly describes alcohol use in Indigenous

profil de l'incidence du SAF (Syndrome d'alcoolisme foetal). L'estimation de l'incidence et de la prévalence du FAS dans les collectivités autochtones demeure fort controversée. Selon Bray et Anderson (1989), les taux exagérément élevés actuellement publiés sont dus au fait que l'on ne tient pas compte des taux de fertilité plus élevés et de la plus longue durée de la période d'enfantement.[19] Quant à Burd et Moffat (1994), ils imputent une partie de cette inflation aux méthodes de sélection et aux critères de diagnostic, qui ne sont toujours pas exposés dans la documentation. Sur le plan de la méthodologie, ils recommandent que les chercheurs :

a)   ignorent l'ingestion d'alcool par la mère

b)   sélectionnent des collectivités où les taux peuvent être bas

c)   réalisent des études longitudinales des cohortes

d)   examinent les certificats de décès chaque fois que cela est possible.[20]

La majorité des rapports parus sur le sujet indiquent que les taux d'incidence du SAF sont effectivement supérieurs à la moyenne chez les Autochtones du Canada, bien qu'une importante fluctuation marque les données américaines. Des estimations modérées de l'incidence du SAF et des EAF (effets de l'alcoolisme foetal) effectuées à partir des échantillons de l'ensemble de la population ont donné un rapport de 1 à 3 sur 1 000,[21] tandis que des études américaines ont conclu que l'incidence du SAF chez les Indiens varie entre 1,4 et 9,8 sur 1 000 habitants.[22] Enfin, une étude canadienne a établi le taux de SAF/EAF à 25 par 1 000 enfants (0 à 16 ans) chez les Autochtones du nord-ouest de la Colombie-Britannique (Métis et Indiens) et à 46 sur 1 000 chez les groupes autochtones du Yukon. Le taux observé pour l'ensemble des populations canadiennes dans les deux régions était de 0,4 sur 1 000.[23]

Même si l'on met en doute les méthodes épidémiologiques utilisées lors des études canadiennes, les femmes indiennes reconnaissent «que la capacité du peuple Indien à se réaliser pleinement se trouve menacée par l'affaiblissement de la race, associé au syndrome

communities. The Northwest Territories (NWT) Health Promotion Survey provides some information about Inuit and Dene who have been grouped together for these analyses.[12] Responses to questions about alcohol consumption revealed a clearly greater polarization in drinking patterns among this northern Indigenous group; i.e. there were more abstainers and more heavy drinkers.

In the Yukon Alcohol and Drug Survey, in which respondents were broken down by ethnicity and drinker category, the following patterns resulted:[17] Congruent with the NWT Health Promotion Survey data, a greater polarization in drinking patterns of Indigenous groups is noted, and is maintained when broken down by sex. However, when drinker categories were broken down by ethnicity and age, it became clear that groups over age 20 account for the greater polarization in drinking patterns. Canadian adolescents in general were slightly more

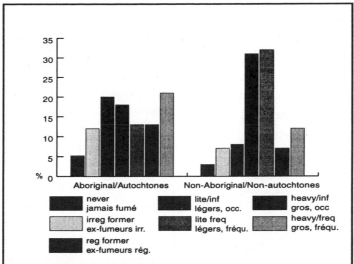

Figure 5.4:   Analytic Drinker Category by Ethnicity Yukon- All Respondents
Figure 5.4   Catégorie analytique des buveurs selon l'ethnicité, Yukon, tous les répondants

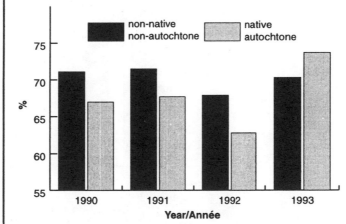

Figure 5.5:   Comparison of Alcohol of Use between Indian/ Métis and non-Indigenous groups
Note: This information reproduced from: Gfellner, B. M.: Hundelby, J. D., 1995. Patterns of Drug Use Among Native and White Adolescents: 1990-1993, Canadian Journal of Public Health, March-April, 95-97.
Figure 5.5   Comparaison de la consommation d'alcool entre les groupes Indiens et Métis et les groupes non autochtones
Nota : Information tirée de Gfellner, B. M. et J.D. Hundelby, 1995. Patterns of Drug Use Among Native and White Adolescents: 1990-1993, Revue canadienne de santé publique, mars-avril, p.95-97.

d'alcoolisme foetal».[24] Par conséquent, bien que l'on ne puisse pas déterminer avec exactitude la prévalence et prévoir le nombre potentiel des femmes autochtones alcooliques ou de celles qui risquent de donner naissance à un enfant victime du SAF ou des EAF, il est clair que l'abus de drogue entraîne davantage de conséquences graves et débilitantes dans certaines régions que pour l'ensemble des femmes nord-américaines.

LES ENFANTS : Mis à part les éventuelles répercussions du SAF et des EAF sur les enfants, il est rare que les profils de toxicomanie tiennent compte des caractéristiques particulières de la consommation de drogue chez les moins de 12 ans. Cette consommation chez les adolescents a certes reçu beaucoup d'attention, mais dans le cas des enfants, la seule documentation qui décrive les tendances de consommation porte sur des drogues spécifiques (notamment, le tabac à priser ou à chiquer et les solvants). Pourtant, le taux alarmant de la consommation de

polarized in drinking patterns than their Indigenous counterparts in the Yukon sample.

When examining adolescent alcohol use patterns in greater detail, some regional variations were noted. In a Manitoba sample, it appears that Indian and Métis adolescents off-reserve are similar to their non-Indigenous counterparts, whereas greater differences were noted between general Canadian samples when compared to Indian adolescents on-reserve in Quebec. These differences may be explained by the fact that the Indigenous group of comparison differs by residence, or the fact that the general Canadian group of comparison is geographically similar to the Indigenous group in the Manitoba sample.

When examining adolescent alcohol use patterns in greater detail, some regional variations were noted. In a Manitoba sample, it appears that Indian and Métis adolescents off-reserve are similar to their non-Indigenous counterparts, whereas greater differences were noted between general Canadian samples when compared to Indian adolescents on-reserve in Quebec. These differences may be explained by the fact that the Indigenous group of comparison differs by residence, or the fact that the general Canadian group of comparison is geographically similar to the Indigenous group in the Manitoba sample.

The most recent survey of alcohol consumption patterns among Indigenous

drogue dans ce groupe d'âge constitue l'un des faits épidémiologiques les plus troublants qui soient concernant la toxicomanie en milieu autochtone. Les enfants consomment normalement le tabac (tabac sans fumée compris), l'alcool, le cannabis et les solvants, mais dans le cas de plusieurs drogues,[25,26,27,28,29,30] ils commencent à consommer à un âge sensiblement plus jeune que leurs homologues d'Amérique du Nord et, au Canada, leur admission dans les établissements de traitement autochtones se fait aussi à un plus jeune âge,[31,32,33] surtout dans les provinces du centre et de l'ouest. Fiddler (1985) a découvert que les enfants indiens (0 à 14 ans) de la Saskatchewan présentaient un taux de suicide *tragiquement élevé* par rapport aux moyennes nationale et provinciale établies pour les enfants du même groupe d'âge (27,5 fois plus élevé que la moyenne nationale et 33,6 fois plus élevé que la moyenne de la Saskatchewan).[7] Dans le dernier profil des habitudes toxicomaniaques dressé au regard des populations autochtones vivant en centre urbain, 67% des Centres d'amitié participant ont déclaré que les enfants consommaient de l'alcool et reniflaient des solvants durant les heures de classe, après la classe, dans la rue et à la maison, et parfois avec la famille.[34]

CONSOMMATION D'ALCOOL : Sauf les faits auto-déclarés par les participants aux enquêtes, les données de l'enquête postcensitaire tenue auprès des peuples

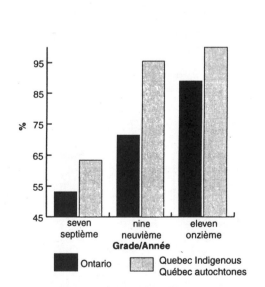

Figure 5.6:   Comparison of alcohol use between Indian and Non-Indigenous Adolescents
Note: This information reproduced from Scott, K. A., 1986. Self Evaluation: It's relationship to substance use in native adolescents, Unpublished Master's thesis, Health Studies Department, University of Waterloo.

Figure 5.6   Comparaison de la consommation d'alcool entre les adolescents indiens et non autochtones
Nota : Information tirée de Scott, K. A., 1986. Self Evaluation: Its relationship to substance use in native adolescents, thèse de maîtrise non publiée, Health Studies Department, University of Waterloo.

peoples is reported in the Language, Health and Social Issues subset of the Aboriginal Peoples Survey, 1991. Fortunately, these data allow us to compare between Indigenous groups, namely Indians on and off reserve, Inuit and Métis. Recall the clearly greater polarization in drinking patterns of previous data sets, where abstention and heavy drinking was greater in Indigenous groups than in general Canadian populations. When we look at abstention by Aboriginal identity, the Inuit have a significantly higher abstinence rate than either Indian or Métis groups.

This may suggest that the greater polarization pattern is more evident in the North. These patterns by Indigenous grouping lend greater evidence to the notion that there is something significant about community. When questioned about whether or not they perceived alcohol abuse as a problem in their community, Indian groups on- and off-reserve were more likely to perceive alcohol abuse as a problem in their community than either Métis or Inuit groups. Inuit, on the other hand, were most likely to believe that alcohol abuse is not a problem.[35]

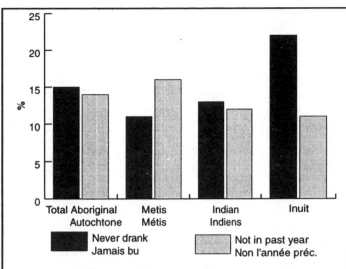

Figure 5.7:   Rate of Alcohol Abstinence by Aboriginal Identity

Figure 5.7   Taux d'abstinents selon le groupe autochtone.

autochtones (EAPA), ainsi que les données fournies par les centres de traitement autochtones, il existe très peu de données décrivant immédiatement la consommation de l'alcool dans les collectivités autochtones. L'enquête des Territoires du Nord-Ouest sur la promotion de la santé nous renseigne en partie sur les Inuit et les Dénés qui ont été regroupés aux fins de ces analyses.[12] Les réponses des participants aux questions sur la consommation de l'alcool ont en effet révélé une polarisation nettement plus importante des habitudes de consommation chez ces groupes autochtones du nord, lesquels comptent plus d'abstinents et plus de gros buveurs.

Par ailleurs, l'enquête du Yukon sur l'alcool et les autres drogues, pour laquelle on avait ventilé les répondants selon l'ethnicité et la catégorie de buveurs, a permis de dégager les tendances suivantes[17]: à l'instar de l'enquête des Territoires du Nord-Ouest sur la promotion de la santé, elle révèle une plus grande polarisation des habitudes de consommation d'alcool chez les groupes autochtones, et ce, indépendamment du sexe. La ventilation selon l'ethnicité et l'âge a

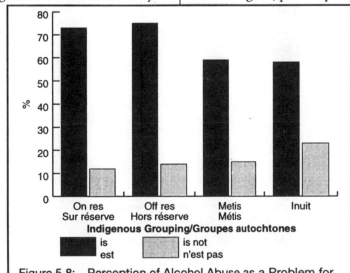

Figure 5.8:   Perception of Alcohol Abuse as a Problem for Various Indigenous Groups

Figure 5.8   Perception de l'abus d'alcool comme étant un problème, selon le groupe autochtone

DRUG USE: Much of the direct assessment of drug use patterns is done with Indigenous adolescents. The adult data available from the NWT Health Promotion Survey reveals that 30% of Indigenous men and 16% of Indigenous women (Inuit and Dene) claimed to have used cannabis in the last year. The Treatment Activity Reporting System (TARS) shows that narcotics are consistently the second most popular drug in the adult institutionalized group.[31,32,33] The most recent Canadian data available about drug use among Indigenous adolescents (limited to Indian and Métis residents off-reserve) was conducted in a Manitoba non-metropolitan city.[36] Interestingly, the rate of marijuana use is three times greater for Indigenous adolescents. Rates of use were also consistently and significantly higher in the Indigenous group for non-medical tranquilizers, LSD and other hallucinogens. Higher rates of use were also noted for crack, cocaine, PCP, stimulants, speed, heroin and barbiturates in the Indigenous group. These differ somewhat from a comparison of Indian adolescents on-reserve and general Canadian adolescents in that rates of depressant, hallucinogen and stimulant use were lower in the Indian group across all age levels, while rates of cocaine and solvent use were higher in the lower grades in the general Canadian sample. However, consistently higher rates of cannabis use were noted in the Quebec Indian sample across all grade levels.[13]

TOBACCO USE: From the NWT Health Promotion Survey, it is clear that the overwhelming majority of Indigenous (Inuit and Dene) men and women currently smoke cigarettes (women 72%, men 71%), and many claimed to smoke

toutefois permis d'attribuer la majeure partie de cette polarisation aux plus de 20 ans. Dans l'ensemble, les adolescents canadiens accusaient une polarisation légèrement plus importante que leurs homologues autochtones de l'échantillon yukonais.

Un examen plus poussé des habitudes de consommation d'alcool des adolescents a fait ressortir plusieurs écarts régionaux. On a ainsi constaté, dans un échantillon du Manitoba, que les adolescents indiens et métis vivant hors réserve se rapprochaient sensiblement de leurs homologues non autochtones par leurs habitudes, mais que des écarts plus marqués séparaient les sujets des échantillons canadiens en général des adolescents indiens vivant sur les réserves au Québec. Ces écarts sont potentiellement attribuables au fait que le groupe autochtone de comparaison diffère par son lieu d'habitation, ou au fait que les caractéristiques géographiques du groupe canadien général de comparaison s'apparentent à celles du groupe autochtone de l'échantillon du Manitoba.

Les résultats de l'enquête la plus récente sur les habitudes de consommation d'alcool chez les peuples autochtones paraissent dans le sous-ensemble «questions de langue, de santé et de société» (Language, Health and Social Issues) de l'enquête de 1991 sur les peuples autochtones. Heureusement, ces données permettent de comparer entre eux les groupes autochtones, nommément les Indiens des réserves et de l'extérieur, les Inuit et les Métis. Elles confirment en outre la polarisation nettement plus grande des habitudes de consommation déjà observée lors d'études antérieures, c'est-à-dire que les groupes

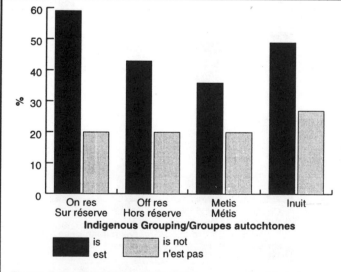

Figure 5.9:   Perception of Drug Abuse as a Problem for Various Indigenous Groups

Figure 5.9   Perception de l'abus de drogue comme étant un problème, selon le groupe autochtone

regularly (women 57%, men 59%).[12] A national survey of Indian and Inuit women revealed that 78% of Inuit women smoke before pregnancy, 76% during pregnancy and 75% in the first month postpartum. Fifty four percent of Indian women smoked during pregnancy and just under half (49%) smoked before and after pregnancy.[37]

Figures 5.10 and 5.11 illustrate that Indigenous adolescents show consistently higher rates of tobacco use even when broken down by grade.[36,13]

The most recent and comprehensive information on the smoking patterns of Indigenous Canadians is based on data collected in the Aboriginal Peoples Survey, which has been analyzed and compiled in Smoking Among Aboriginal People in Canada, 1991.[54] From this report, we know that the majority (57%) of those age 15+ currently smoke. Daily smokers (46%) are almost twice as prevalent as in the general Canadian population (26%). Like alcohol patterns, smoking is highest among those ages 20 to 44. The vast majority (65%) of 20 to 24-year-olds currently smoke and more than half (53%) claim to be daily smokers. While very few differences were noted between the sexes,

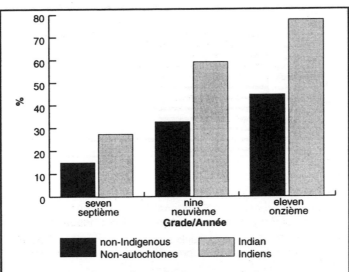

Figure 5.10:   Comparison of tobacco use between non-indigenous and Indian adolescents (1983-86)

Figure 5.10   Comparaison de la consommation du tabac entre les adolescents non autochtones et les adolescents indiens, 1983-1986

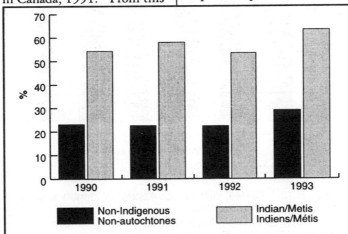

Figure 5.11:   Comparison of tobacco use between Indian/ Métis and non-Indigenous Adolescents (Manitoba, 1990-1993)

Figure 5.11   Comparaison de la consommation du tabac entre les adolescents indiens et métis et les adolescents non autochtones, Manitoba, 1990-1993

autochtones comptent plus d'abstinents et de gros buveurs que la population canadienne en général. Lorsque l'on s'arrête à l'abstention selon le groupe autochtone, on constate que les Inuit présentent un taux d'abstinents considérablement plus élevé que les Indiens ou les Métis.

Ces résultats laissent croire à une plus grande polarisation dans les régions du Nord. Les profils de consommation observés selon le groupe autochtone tendent à confirmer l'influence de la communauté. A la question de savoir s'ils croyaient que l'abus d'alcool constituait un problème au sein de leur communauté, les Indiens des réserves et de l'extérieur étaient plus nombreux à le croire que les Métis ou les Inuit. Ces derniers étaient cependant plus nombreux à croire que l'abus d'alcool n'était pas un problème.[35]

ABUS DE DROGUE : L'évaluation directe des habitudes d'abus de drogue est pour une bonne part réalisée auprès des adolescents. Les données sur les adultes tirées de l'enquête des Territoires du Nord-Ouest sur la promotion de la santé révèlent que 30 % des hommes autochtones et 16 % des femmes autochtones (Inuit et

smoking did decrease with increased education and income. Regional variations were also apparent.[38]

In addition to the wide variability in the percentage of current smokers (includes daily and occasional) by region, there seem to be different smoking patterns between regions. Aboriginal peoples from the Maritime provinces have the highest daily consumption rate, while those residing in Saskatchewan, British Columbia and the Northwest Territories have relatively low daily consumption rates. Therefore, while northern groups may have the greatest number of current smokers, they are likely to smoke less on a daily basis than those in other regions.

Regardless of age, the Inuit were much more likely to be current smokers than either Indian or Métis groups (See Figure 5.13). Few gender differences were noted within Aboriginal groups, but Métis consumption patterns on a daily basis were much higher than for Indians or Inuit.

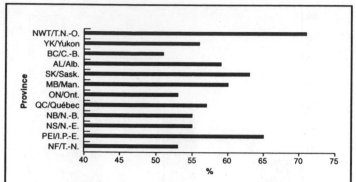

Figure 5.12:   Current smokers by region (age 15+ APS, 1991)
Note: reproduced from Stephens, T.: Smoking Among Aboriginal People in Canada, 1991, Health Canada, 1994.

Figure 5.12   Fumeurs actuels selon la région, population des 15 ans et plus, Enquête auprès des peuples autochtones, 1991
Nota : Tirée de Stephens, T., 1994. Le tabagisme chez les peuples autochtones au Canada, 1991, Santé Canada.

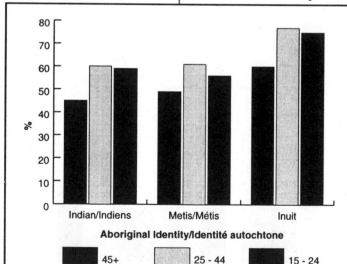

Figure 5.13:   Current smokers by Aboriginal identity and age group (Age 15+, APS, 1991)
Note: reproduced from Stephens, T.: Smoking Among Aboriginal People in Canada, 1991, Health Canada, 1994.

Figure 5.13   Fumeurs actuels selon le groupe autochtone et la tranche d'âge, population des 15 ans et plus, Enquête auprès des peuples autochtones, 1991
Nota : Tirée de Stephens, T., 1994. Le tabagisme chez les peuples autochtones au Canada, 1991, Santé Canada.

Dénés) ont déclaré avoir consommé du cannabis l'année précédente. Le Système de rapports des activités de traitement (SRAT) indique que les stupéfiants se classent régulièrement au deuxième rang des drogues les plus populaires parmi les adultes en établissement.[31,32,33] Les plus récentes données canadiennes disponibles sur la consommation de drogue chez les adolescents autochtones (limitées aux Indiens et aux Métis vivant hors réserve) ont été recueillies dans une ville non métropolitaine du Manitoba.[36] Or il est intéressant de noter que le taux de consommation de la marijuana y est trois fois plus élevée chez les adolescents autochtones. De plus, ces jeunes affichaient régulièrement des taux de consommation nettement plus élevés pour les analgésiques non médicaux, le LSD et d'autres hallucinogènes. Le groupe autochtone a aussi enregistré une plus forte consommation de crack, de cocaïne, de PCP, de stimulants, de speed, d'héroïne et de barbituriques. Ces résultats s'éloignent légèrement d'une comparaison antérieure

SOLVENT USE: In a recent national consultation with Indigenous youth and service providers representing Indian, Métis and Inuit groups, the following profile of the solvent abuser emerged:

a) Age at use onset is roughly 9 to 10, but some start sniffing as early as age five; age at use onset seems to be steadily decreasing.

b) Boys are more likely than girls to abuse but more girls are abusing now than ever before.

c) Solvent-abusing youth come from dysfunctional families with a history of addiction.

d) Abusers are often from isolated communities, suffer poorer grades or drop out of school.

e) Unemployment, illiteracy, poor housing and history of physical/emotional/sexual abuse are associated with their sniffing.[39]

Most children (49.3%) in a First Nations and Inuit community youth solvent survey began sniffing when they were age 4 to 11. Compared to the overall average, a much higher percentage of children began to use solvents at this age in Alberta (79.4%), Saskatchewan (64.8%) and the Yukon (81.3%). The familial and social factors related to their sniffing included alcohol and drug abuse in the home (67.2%), family conflict (65.3%), unemployment (51.7%), malnutrition or neglect (43.5%), financial hardship in the home (42.3%) and physical abuse (31.3%).[40]

In a recent multi-year Manitoba survey of Indian and Métis adolescents, glue sniffing

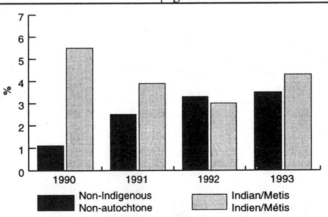

Figure 5.14: Comparison of glue use by Indian/Métis and Non-Indigenous Adolescents (Manitoba, 1990-1993)
Note: Figure 5.s 14 and 15 reproduced from Gfellner, B. M.; Hundelby, J. D.: Patterns of Drug Use Among Native and White Adolescents: 1990-1993, Canadian Journal of Public Health, March-April 1995, Vol. 86, No. 2, 95-97.

Figure 5.14   Comparaison de la consommation de colle entre les adolescents indiens et métis et les adolescents non autochtones, Manitoba, 1990-1993
Nota : Les Figures 5.14 et 5.15 sont tirées de Gfellner, B. M. et J.D. Hundelby: Patterns of Drug Use Among Native and White Adolescents: 1990-1993, Revue canadienne de santé publique, mars-avril 1995, vol. 86, no 2, p. 95-97.

des adolescents indiens vivant sur les réserves et des adolescents canadiens en général, qui indiquait des taux inférieurs de consommation des dépresseurs, des hallucinogènes et des stimulants dans le groupe indien, tous âge confondus, et des taux de consommation supérieurs de cocaïne et de solvants dans les tranches d'âge inférieures des Canadiens en général. Cependant, des taux régulièrement plus élevés de consommation de cannabis ont été observés pour le groupe des Indiens du Québec, et ce pour toutes les tranches d'âge.[13]

CONSOMMATION DE TABAC : Selon l'enquête des Territoires du Nord-Ouest sur la promotion de la santé, il est clair que la très grande majorité des Autochtones (Inuit et Dénés) hommes et femmes fument la cigarette (femmes 72 %, hommes 71 %) et que bon nombre d'entre eux fument régulièrement (femmes 57 %, hommes 59 %).[12] Une enquête nationale menée auprès des femmes indiennes et inuit a révélé que 78 % des femmes inuit fumaient avant la grossesse, 76 % durant la grossesse, et 75 % dans le premier mois suivant la grossesse. Chez les femmes indiennes, 54 % fumaient durant la grossesse et tout près de la moitié (49 %) fumaient avant et après la grossesse.[37]

Les Figures 5.10 et 5.11 révèlent des taux de consommation de tabac régulièrement plus élevés chez les adolescents autochtones, même lorsque ventilés selon le niveau d'étude.[36,13]

L'information la plus récente et la plus complète dont nous disposons sur les habitudes de tabagisme des Autochtones au Canada provient des données de l'Enquête

was higher in the Indian/ Métis group with the exception of 1992 data; however, solvent use was consistently higher in the Indian/Métis group for all years.[36]

INDIGENOUS TREAT-MENT CENTRE ACTIVITY: The Treatment Activity Reporting System (TARS) yields the most recent, systematic data on the institutionalized chemically dependent person. In hierarchical order, national TARS data reveal that alcohol and narcotics are consistently the most widely abused substances, with alcohol at least twice as likely to be the abused substance of choice.[31,32,33] In recent TARS data sets, there is an increasing trend of narcotics and prescription drug abuse; however, this trend must be viewed with caution as there has been confusion about where cannabis has been classified. Based on the national client profile, roughly 45% of people seeking treatment are female, up from previous TARS data where roughly 41% were female. By age, the distribution of females and males in treatment is depicted in Figure 5.16.[33]

Consistently, the bulk of treatment participants is found in the 25 to 34 age category, with a slightly greater proportion of men in the older age categories. Interestingly, there has been a slight narrowing of the discrepancy

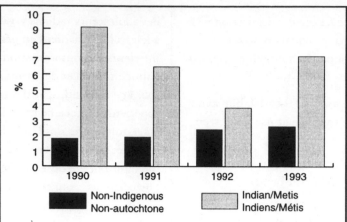

Figure 5.15:   Comparison of solvent use by Indian/Métis and non-Indigenous Adolescents (Manitoba, 1990-1993)

Figure 5.15   Comparaison de l'usage de solvants entre les adolescents indiens et métis et les adolescents non autochtones, Manitoba, 1990-1993

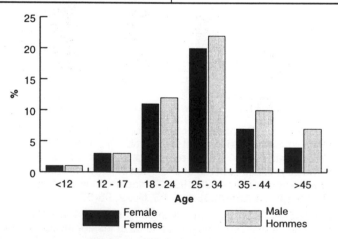

Figure 5.16:   Treatment Participation by Age and Gender April 1994 to March 1995.

Figure 5.16   Participation aux traitements, selon l'âge et le sexe, avril 1994 à mars 1995

auprès des peuples autochtones, dont les résultats d'analyse ont été présentés dans le rapport intitulé, *Le tabagisme chez les peuples autochtones au Canada,* 1991.[54] Ce rapport nous apprend que la majorité (57 %) des 15 ans et plus fument. Les fumeurs quotidiens (46 %) sont presque deux fois plus nombreux que dans l'ensemble de la population canadienne (26%). Comme dans le cas de l'alcool, ce sont les 20 à 44 ans qui fument le plus. La vaste majorité (65 %) des 20 à 24 ans fument régulièrement, et plus de la moitié (53 %) affirment fumer quotidiennement. Peu d'écarts ont été observés entre les sexes, mais plus le niveau d'instruction et le revenu sont élevés, moins on fume. Des variations régionales sont également évidentes.[38]

En plus de la grande variabilité relevée quant au taux des fumeurs actuels (fumeurs quotidiens et occasionnels) selon la région, un écart semble marquer les habitudes de tabagisme selon la région. Les populations autochtones des Maritimes présentent les taux de consommation quotidienne les plus élevés, tandis que celles de la Saskatchewan, de la Colombie-Britannique et des Territoires du Nord-Ouest ont des taux relativement bas. Ainsi, les groupes du nord comptent plus de fumeurs actuels que dans

between the sexes in treatment participation in older age groups over time. Previous TARS data reveal a pattern where males greatly outnumber females.[31,32] This may reflect several important gender-specific trends. One theory is that treatment centres are now becoming female-friendly institutions or that the attitudinal barriers to seeking treatment have been removed or reduced

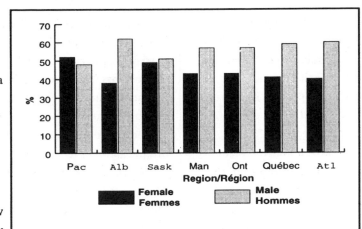

Figure 5.17:   Percentage Sex Distribution of Treatment Participation by Region, April 1994-March 1995

Figure 5.17   Taux de participation aux traitements, selon le sexe et la région, avril 1994-mars 1995

for women. The second theory is, of course, that more women than ever before need treatment. When broken down by region in Figure 5.17, it also becomes obvious that with a westward movement, the discrepancy between the sexes in treatment participation narrows.[33]

The stark exception in this TARS data set is the difference between the sexes in Alberta, a pattern not obvious in previous data sets.

ADDRESSING THE PROBLEM: Just for a moment let's move away from identifying the problem and look at the factors that seem to offer protection. Communities with clear proscriptive norms about alcohol and drug abuse fare better than those without them.[40] The O'Chiese guidelines for community sobriety[41] strongly recommend addiction free community leadership as a good first start. It is obvious that some Indigenous leaders recognize this modeling role and are even participating in treatment as a group.[42] Recreation, be it sports or hobbies, offers protection from an abusing lifestyle.[13,43] Strong cultures, families and the value of spirituality have all been shown to be associated with drug free life.[13,43,44] And lastly, the opportunity to participate in meaningful work reduces the risk of addiction.[44]

les autres régions, mais moins de fumeurs quotidiens.

Tous âges confondus, les Inuit comptent beaucoup plus de fumeurs actuels que les Indiens ou les Métis (voir Figure 5.13). Peu d'écarts existent entre les groupes des deux sexes, mais les Métis sont plus nombreux que les Indiens ou les Inuit à fumer quotidiennement.

CONSOMMATION DE SOLVANTS : Lors d'un sondage national effectué récemment auprès des jeunes Autochtones et des fournisseurs de services représentant les populations indiennes, métis et inuit, on a dégagé le profil suivant des consommateurs excessifs de solvants :

a)   Les jeunes commencent à consommer vers 9 ou 10 ans, mais certains commencent à renifler dès l'âge de 5 ans; l'âge des premières consommations semblent diminuer régulièrement.

b)   Les garçons sont plus nombreux que les filles à faire excès de solvants, mais ces dernières sont plus nombreuses que jamais.

c)   Les jeunes qui font abus de solvants proviennent de familles dysfonctionnelles déjà marquées par la toxicomanie.

d)   Les consommateurs de solvants viennent souvent de collectivités isolées, ont de piètres résultats scolaires ou sont des décrocheurs scolaires.

e)   Sont associés aux cas de renifflage, le chômage, l'analphabétisme, les mauvaises conditions de logement et les antécédents d'abus physique, affectif et sexuel.[39]

Une enquête sur la consommation de solvants par les jeunes des communautés Inuit et des Premières nations a révélé que la majorité des participants (49,3 %)

Several targets have been identified in the primary prevention of abuse-related problems, including the person, community and specific substances.[45] Families must be included in future prevention frameworks because they are recognized as an important and integral part of treatment intervention,[46] and as the single best predictor of success in continuing recovery.[47] Consistently, what seem to work best are treatment interventions that emphasize strengthening from the inside out (where communities direct the healing process and tap into internal and external resources as necessary) and the essential balance between physical, mental, emotional and spiritual elements.[48,49]

RECOMMENDATIONS FOR FUTURE RESEARCH: Although this chapter replicates some information previously published in Indigenous addiction profiles,[50,51] it is an attempt to shed new light and review more recent literature, comparing it, where appropriate, to historical trends. Despite the limitations of the data presented here and in previous reviews, more detailed epidemiological scrutiny is hard to justify (except perhaps for the Métis, where little health information exists). Without argument, there is a socially and physically devastating addictions problem in some Indigenous communities. The important and operative questions remain, "which ones and why?" For national program and policy development purposes, some fundamentals are clear. Indigenous children are at great risk not only for substance abuse but also — most alarmingly — for its violent consequences. Tobacco, alcohol, cannabis and solvents are the most commonly abused substances, and substance abuse is greatest where people suffer from poverty, isolation, low self-image, weak family structure and dysfunctional dynamics, as well as personal histories of physical, sexual and emotional abuse.[52,53]

Addiction in a community context shows some curious patterns unlike those found in general Canadian populations. Consistently, there is a greater polarization of alcohol consumption between individuals within communities where the same structural conditions exist. Certainly worth pursuing as part of our endeavour to

avaient commencé à renifler entre 4 et 11 ans. Comparativement à la moyenne globale, un taux nettement plus élevé d'enfants ont commencé à utiliser des solvants à cet âge en Alberta (79,4 %), en Saskatchewan (64,8 %) et au Yukon (81,3 %). Parmi les facteurs familiaux et sociaux associés à leur consommation de solvants, notons l'abus d'alcool et de drogue au foyer (67,2 %), les conflits familiaux (65,3 %), le chômage (51,7 %), la malnutrition ou la négligence (43,5 %), les problèmes financiers du foyer (42,3 %) et l'agression physique (31,3 %).[40]

Selon une récente enquête pluriannuelle menée auprès des adolescents au Manitoba, le reniflage de la colle était plus courant dans le groupe Indien-Métis sauf en 1992, mais l'usage de solvants était régulièrement plus important dans ce même groupe indépendamment de l'année d'étude.[36]

CENTRES DE TRAITEMENT AUTOCHTONES : Le Système de rapports des activités de traitement (SRAT) fournit les données les plus actuelles sur les toxicomanes traités en établissement. Or ces données nationales révèlent que les substances dont on fait toujours le plus grand abus sont, dans l'ordre, l'alcool et les stupéfiants, l'alcool étant préféré au moins une fois sur deux.[31,32,33] De récents ensembles de données du SRAT démontrent un abus croissant de l'abus des stupéfiants et des drogues sur ordonnance; il convient cependant d'interpréter cette tendance avec réserve puisqu'il y a eu confusion quant à la classification du cannabis. Le profil national des clients des centres de traitement fixe à 45 % environ le pourcentage des femmes clientes, alors que des données antérieures du SRAT l'établissent plutôt à 41 %. La Figure 5.16 présente la population en traitement selon le sexe et le groupe d'âge.[33]

Comme toujours, la majorité des toxicomanes en traitement ont entre 25 et 34 ans, les hommes étant légèrement plus nombreux dans les catégories d'âge plus avancé. Il est intéressant de noter qu'au fil du temps, les proportions de patients hommes et femmes se sont sensiblement rapprochées dans les groupes plus âgés. Selon des données antérieures du SRAT, le nombre des

solve the problem is to figure out why individuals who endure fundamentally the same conditions do not succumb to the addictions.

Lastly, but perhaps most importantly, there are also extreme differences in addiction patterns between regions and communities and possibly between various Indigenous groupings. In those communities where there is widespread addiction, there is evidence to suggest that community characteristics,[52] socioeconomic and lifestyle factors[54] contribute substantially to substance use and its consequences. More specifically, future research should illuminate:

1. What are the structural differences between communities that are relatively free of addiction problems and those that are devastated by them?

2. What are the differences in substance use patterns between Indigenous and Canadian groups when socio-economic factors are controlled?

3. What are the familial and psychological differences between heavy drinkers and abstainers in the same milieu?

4. What are the correlates of non-use among Indian, Inuit and Métis groups and how can these be promoted in the context of familial and community development?

Future research efforts would be infinitely more practical if they were solution-oriented, by initiating creative action to arrest the problem with rigorous evaluation, and then modifying this action to be portable. In any case, addictions research must bear maximum relevance to the situation of Indian, Inuit and Métis groups, and this can only be achieved in partnership with them, where they are in control, centering and developing the research endeavour to suit their circumstance. Success stories certainly do exist wherever self-help groups have evolved, but their progress and development is largely unknown outside local environments. As part of the future research efforts, these stories need to be told.

hommes dépasse de loin celui des femmes.[31,32] Cette situation indique peut-être d'importantes tendances spécifiques au sexe. Selon une première hypothèse, les centres de traitement se feraient plus conviviaux à l'égard des femmes ou les préjugés envers les femmes désireuses de se faire traiter auraient disparu ou diminué. Une seconde hypothèse prétend, bien sûr, que plus de femmes que jamais ont besoin d'être traitées. Mais lorsque l'on examine la ventilation par région telle qu'elle est présentée à la Figure 5.17, il devient aussi évident que l'écart entre les taux de participation des hommes et des femmes rétrécit au fur et à mesure que l'on progresse vers l'ouest.[33]

L'exception qui ressort le plus de cet ensemble de données du SRAT est l'écart marquant les deux sexes en Alberta, tendance absente dans les précédents ensembles.

CORRECTION DU PROBLÈME : Oublions un instant le problème même pour nous pencher sur les facteurs susceptibles d'offrir une protection. Les communautés qui prônent des règles de conduite bien définies sur l'abus d'alcool et de drogue obtiennent des résultats nettement meilleurs que les autres.[40] Les lignes directrices de la communauté O'Chiese sur la sobriété de ses membres[41] incitent en tout premier lieu ses dirigeants à s'abstenir de toute toxicomanie. Il est clair que certains chefs autochtones acceptent ce rôle modèle et s'inscrivent même à des traitements en groupe.[42] Les loisirs, qu'il s'agisse de sports ou de passe-temps, constituent une certaine muraille contre les modes de vie abusifs.[13,43] Les cultures et les familles fortes sont tous des facteurs associés à une vie exempte de drogue.[13,43,44] Le bonheur d'accomplir un travail utile réduit également le risque de toxicomanie.[44]

Les mesures de prévention primaire ont permis de cerner plusieurs objectifs en ce qui concerne les problèmes associés à la consommation excessive, notamment la personne, la communauté et les substances spécifiques.[45] Il importe d'intégrer aux futures démarches de prévention la famille, puisque celle-ci tient un rôle majeur et fait partie intégrante de l'intervention de traitement[46] et constitue enfin le

CONCLUSIONS: Indigenous children are at substantially greater risk for substance use and its violent consequences than Canadian children generally. Proportionately more adults participated in treatment in the western provinces, with the bulk being age 25 to 34. Indian and Inuit groups are at greater risk of abuse-related mortality, especially in the 15 to 35 age group, when compared with their North American counterpart. And, although the Indigenous woman's risk of abuse-related death is substantially lower than her male counterpart's, much data suggest that she is more like him than other females in substance use patterns.

There is a greater polarization in alcohol consumption patterns among individuals within communities and significant variation among communities. Social support norms seem related consistently to use across sex and age groups. But for much of the research cited here the artifacts of acculturation and socio-economic status have not been controlled. We know that culture, family and distribution of wealth play a significant role in healing and protection from addiction, but resolving the dilemma requires particular attention and sensitivity to group needs of Métis, Inuit and Indians — what makes them resilient and, most importantly, what are the structural changes which are necessary concomitants to the community quest to heal?

meilleur gage de succès de la réadaptation du toxicomane à long terme.[47] Les interventions de traitement qui semblent le mieux porter fruit sont toujours celles qui favorisent le renforcement de la personne, axé sur le développement intérieur (c'est le cas des collectivités qui dirigent le processus de guérison de leurs membres et qui puisent dans les ressources internes et extérieures selon les besoins) et l'harmonisation du physique, du mental, de l'affectif et du spirituel.[48,49]

RECOMMANDATIONS POUR LA RECHERCHE FUTURE : Le présent chapitre reprend, il est vrai, de l'information déjà parue dans des profils antérieurs de la toxicomanie chez les Autochtones,[50,51] mais il vise à apporter un *éclairage* nouveau, à examiner des données plus récentes et les comparer, au besoin, aux tendances antérieures. Les données fournies dans cet ouvrage et la documentation antérieure comportent des limitations, mais il demeure néanmoins difficile de justifier un examen épidémiologique plus détaillé (sauf peut-être pour les Métis, au regard desquels on possède peu d'information sur la santé). Il existe indiscutablement un problème de toxicomanie socialement et physiquement dévastateur au sein de certaines communautés autochtones. Or la question majeure et fonctionnelle qu'il convient de se poser est de savoir «lesquelles et pourquoi». Pour ce qui est du développement de programmes et de politiques de portée nationale, certains principes de base ressortent clairement. Les enfants autochtones sont extrêmement vulnérables, non seulement à la toxicomanie mais aussi, de façon plus alarmante, à ses terribles conséquences. Le tabac, l'alcool, le cannabis et les solvants sont les substances qui entraînent le plus d'excès de consommation, et la consommation excessive est à son plus fort là où l'on souffre de pauvreté, d'isolement, d'un manque d'estime, de structures familiales fragiles, de dynamiques dysfonctionnelles, ainsi que d'antécédents personnels en matière d'abus physiques, sexuels et émotifs.[52,53]

La toxicomanie au sein des collectivités revêt des aspects quelque peu différents de ceux observés au sujet des populations canadiennes en général. La polarisation de la consommation d'alcool est toujours plus marquée

References

[1] Canada, Department of the Secretary of State, Social trends Analysis Directorate for the Native Citizens Directorate, *Canada's Off-Reserve Aboriginal Population: A Statistical Overview*, 1991.

[2] Health and Welfare Canada, *Health Status of Canadian Indians and Inuit*, 1990.

[3] Jarvis, G.K. and Boldt, M., "Death Styles Among Canada's Indians", *Social Science and Medicine*, 16, 1345-1352.

[4] Health Canada. *Suicide in Canada. Update of the Report of the Task Force on Suicide in Canada*, 1994.

[5] Health and Welfare, Canada. Demographics and Statistical Division, Medical Services Branch: *Indian and Inuit of Canada, Health Status Indicators 1974-1983*, December 1986, page B104.

[6] Bobet, E and Mustard, C. 1995. Unpublished presentation to Focus Group on Suicide, June 24-25, 1995, Health Programs Analysis, Medical Services Branch.

[7] Fiddler, S. 1985. Federation of Saskatchewan Indian Nations: *Suicides, Violent and Accidental Deaths Among Treaty Indians In Saskatchewan; Analysis and Recommendations for Change.*

[8] Bagley, C., Wood, M. and Khumar, H. "Suicide and careless death in young males: Ecological study of an Aboriginal population in Canada", *Canadian Journal of Community Mental Health* vol. 9, Issue 1: 127-142.

[9] Cooper, M., Corrado, R., Karlberg, A.M. and Adams, L.P., 1992. "Aboriginal Suicide in British Columbia: An Overview". *Canada's Mental Health*, September, 19-23.

[10] Arnup, M.E. and Butt, J.C., 1992. Office of Chief Medical Examiner, Alberta Attorney General, Submission to the Royal Commission on Aboriginal Peoples.

[11] Jelik, W., 1982. *Indian Healing: Shamanic Ceremonialism in the Pacific North West Today.* Hancock House, British Columbia.

entre les collectivités présentant des conditions structurelles semblables. Il est sûrement utile, si nous devons trouver une solution au problème, de poursuivre notre recherche afin de saisir pourquoi des sujets qui vivent en principe dans des conditions semblables ne succombent pas tous à la toxicomanie.

Soulignons enfin, et c'est peut-être là le point le plus important, qu'il existe aussi des écarts considérables dans les profils de la toxicomanie, selon la région et la collectivité, et potentiellement selon le groupe autochtone. Dans les collectivités fortement touchées par la toxicomanie, les faits tendent à démontrer que les caractéristiques de la collectivité,[52] les facteurs socio-économiques et le mode de vie[54] contribuent de façon significative à la consommation de drogue et à ses conséquences. La recherche future devrait donc en particulier s'efforcer de répondre aux questions suivantes :

1. Quelles sont les différences structurelles entre les collectivités qui sont relativement exemptes de problèmes de toxicomanie et celles qui sont absolument dévastées par ces problèmes?

2. Quelles sont les différences entre les profils de consommation de drogue des groupes autochtones et ceux des groupes canadiens lorsque les facteurs socio-économiques sont sous contrôle?

3. Quelles sont les différences familiales et psychologiques entre les gros consommateurs d'alcool et les abstinents d'un même milieu?

4. Quelles sont les corrélatifs de l'abstinence chez les Indiens, les Inuit et les Métis et comment peut-on les mettre en valeur dans le contexte du développement familial et communautaire?

Il serait *infiniment* plus utile à l'avenir d'axer la recherche sur la découverte de solutions, et de tenter ainsi, par une évaluation rigoureuse, de cerner le problème, puis de prendre des initiatives originales en vue de résoudre le problème en prenant soin d'assurer que les solutions trouvées soient transférables d'une collectivité à une autre. Quoiqu'il en soit, il importe de

[12] Health and Welfare Canada, 1989. Health Promotion in the Northwest Territories, Ottawa, Ministry of National Health and Welfare, 1989.

[13] Scott, K.A., 1986. Self-Evaluation: Its relationship to substance use in native adolescents. Unpublished Master's thesis, Health Studies Department, University of Waterloo.

[14] Gfellner, B.M. and Hundelby, J.D., 1995. "Patterns of Drug Use Among Native and White Adolescents: 1990-1993". *Canadian Journal of Public Health*, March-April, 95-97.

[15] Unfortunately these statistics are not available in an ethnic specific way from provincial health care systems and they are not routinely collected from federally operated hospitals which service Indigenous groups.

[16] Whitehead Research Consultants Ltd., 1985. *Assessment of National Needs Through Regional Needs Assessment Studies*, National Native Alcohol and Drug Abuse Program, Indian and Inuit Health Services, Medical Services Branch, Health Canada.

[17] Yukon Government, 1991. The Executive Council Office, Bureau of Statistics, *Yukon Alcohol and Drug Survey: Fall 1990*, volume 1, Technical Report.

[18] Stephens, T., 1994. *Smoking Among Aboriginal People in Canada, 1991*, Health Canada.

[19] Bray, D.L. and Anderson, P.D. "Appraisal of the Epidemiology of Fetal Alcohol Syndrome Among Canadian Native People", *Canadian Journal of Public Health*, 80: 42-45.

[20] Burd, L. and Moffat, M.E.K. *Epidemiology of Fetal Alcohol Syndrome in American Indians, Alaskan Natives, and Canadian Aboriginal Peoples: A Review of the Literature, Public Health Reports*, September-October, Vol. 109 (5): 688-693.

[21] Rosett, H.L., 1980. *Fetal Alcohol Syndrome. Alcoholism Update*, Vol. 1,8.

[22] McTimoney, D.C., Savoy, R.C. and Van Gall, M.A., 1989. Your Child, Our Future! Fetal Alcohol Syndrome Education Package and Resource Kit, March.

veiller à ce que la recherche sur la toxicomanie tienne pleinement compte de la situation réelle des Indiens, des Inuit et des Métis. Seul un partenariat avec ces derniers, là où ils détiennent le contrôle, et qui permette de diriger et de développer les recherches en fonction du contexte pourra garantir un tel résultat. Certes, des résultats heureux ont été obtenus grâce aux groupes d'entraide là où ils existent, mais les réalisations et l'essor de ces groupes sont presque totalement ignorés à l'extérieur de leurs milieux d'action. Or il faudra bien, dans le cadre des futurs travaux de recherche, faire connaître ces réalisations.

CONCLUSIONS : Les enfants autochtones sont considérablement plus vulnérables à l'usage de la drogue et à ses terribles conséquences que l'ensemble des enfants canadiens. On dénombre proportionnellement un plus grand nombre d'adultes ayant suivi un traitement dans les provinces de l'ouest, dont la majorité avaient entre 25 et 34 ans. Les Indiens et les Inuit, surtout les 15 à 35 ans, courent un plus grand risque que leurs homologues de l'Amérique du Nord de décéder d'une cause associée à un abus de drogue. Et bien que ce même risque soit nettement plus bas chez la femme autochtone que chez l'homme autochtone, de nombreuses données suggèrent qu'elle se rapproche davantage de l'homme autochtone que des autres femmes en matière de consommation de drogue.

Il existe une plus grande polarisation dans les habitudes de consommation d'alcool chez les membres des collectivités ainsi qu'une importante variation entre les collectivités. Les normes d'appui social semblent constamment reliées à la consommation chez les deux sexes et dans toutes les catégories d'âge. Mais dans une bonne partie des recherches ici mentionnées, les effets de l'acculturation et de la situation socio-économique n'ont pas été vérifiés. Nous savons que la culture, la famille et la répartition de la richesse occupent une place importante dans la guérison du toxicomane et la protection contre la toxicomanie, mais si l'on veut résoudre le dilemme, il convient de se montrer tout particulièrement attentif et sensible aux besoins des Métis, des Inuit et des Indiens, c'est-à-dire à ce qui les

[23] Asante, K.O. and Melms-Matzke, J., 1985. *Report on the Survey of Children with Chronic Handicaps and Fetal Alcohol Syndrome in the Yukon and Northwest British Columbia.*

[24] Van Bibber, M, 1993. Press release issued at the Fetal Alcohol Syndrome Symposium, Proceedings of the National Symposium on Fetal Alcohol Syndrome. Winnipeg, Manitoba, March, page 2.

[25] Scott, K.A., 1986. Self-Evaluation: Its relationship to substance use in native adolescents. Unpublished Master's thesis, Health Studies Department, University of Waterloo.

[26] Okwumbabua, J.O. and Duryea, E.J. "Age of Onset, Periods of Risk and Patterns of Progression in Drug Use Among American Indian High School Students". *International Journal of Addictions*, 22 (12): 1269-1276.

[27] Oetting, E.R., Swaim, R.C., Edwards, R.W. and Beauvais, F., 1989. "Indian and Anglo Adolescent Alcohol and Emotional Distress: Pat Models", *American Journal of Drug and Alcohol Abuse*, 15 (2): 153-172.

[28] Hoover, J., McDermott, R. And Hartsfield, T., 1990. "The Prevalence of Smokeless Tobacco Use in Native Children in Northern Saskatchewan, Canada", *Canadian Journal of Public Health*, 81: 350-352.

[29] Bruerd, B., 1990. "Smokeless Tobacco Use Among Native American School Children", *Public Health Reports*, 105 (2): 196-201.

[30] Christensen, R. "Health Problems Among Alaskan Eskimo Infants and Young Children", *Arctic Medical Research* 49: 63-67.

[31] National Native Alcohol and Drug Abuse Program, 1991. *Treatment Activity Reporting Systems (TARS).* Quarterly report. Apr-Sept.

[32] National Native Alcohol and Drug Abuse Program, 1989. *Treatment Activity Reporting Systems (TARS).* Quarterly report. Apr.-June.

[33] National Native Alcohol and Drug Abuse Program, 1995. *Treatment Activity Reporting Systems (TARS).* Quarterly report. Apr- 94-March 95.

rend résistants, et de façon plus urgente encore, aux changements structurels nécessaires à la recherche collective d'une guérison.

Ouvrages de référence

[1] Canada, Ministère du Secrétariat d'Etat (1991). Direction de l'analyse des tendances sociales pour le compte de la Direction des citoyens autochtones, La population autochtone du Canada vivant hors réserve : Survol statistique.

[2] Santé et Bien-Etre Canada (1990). L'état de santé des Indiens et des Inuit du Canada.

[3] Jarvis, G.K. et M. Boldt. «Death Styles Among Canada's Indians», Social Science and Medicine, no 16, p. 1345-1352.

[4] Santé Canada (1994), Le suicide au Canada. Mise à jour du Rapport du groupe de travail sur le suicide au Canada.

[5] Santé et Bien-Etre Canada (1986). Division des services démographiques et statistiques, Direction générale des services médicaux, Indiens et Inuit du Canada : indicateurs de l'état de santé, 1974-1983, décembre, p. B104.

[6] Bobet, E. et C. Mustard (1995). Communication non publiée présentée à un groupe de discussions dirigées sur le suicide, 24-25 juin, Analyse des programmes de santé, Direction générale des services médicaux.

[7] Fiddler, S. (1985). Federation of Saskatchewan Indian Nations : Suicides, Violent and Accidental Deaths Among Treaty Indians In Saskatchewan; Analysis and Recommendations for Change.

[8] Bagley, C., M. Wood et H. Khumar. «Suicide and careless death in young males: Ecological study of an Aboriginal population in Canada», Canadian Journal of Community Mental Health, vol. 9, numéro 1, p. 127-142.

[9] Cooper, M., R. Corrado, A.M. Karlberg et L.P. Adams (1992). «Aboriginal Suicide in British Columbia: An Overview». Canada's Mental Health, septembre, p. 19-23.

[34] David, D., 1993. *Aboriginal Peoples in Urban Centres, Report of the National Roundtable on Aboriginal Urban Issues*, Royal Commission on Aboriginal Peoples, page 68.

[35] Statistics Canada, 1993. *Language, Tradition, health, Lifestyle and Social Issues*, 1991 Aboriginal Peoples Survey, June.

[36] Gfellner, B.M. and Hundleby, J.D. 1990-1993. *Patterns of Drug Use Among Native and White Adolescents*, pp. 95-97, p. 96.

[37] Langer, N., 1995. *National Database on Breast feeding Among Indian and Inuit Women: Survey of Infant feeding practices from birth to six months*, Unpublished report. Medical Services Branch, Health and Welfare Canada, April 1990, as cited in Health Canada: *Smoking and Pregnancy: A Woman's Dilemma.*

[38] Health Canada: Stephens, T., 1994. *Smoking Among Aboriginal People in Canada*, 1991. Minister of Supply and Services, Canada.

[39] Health Canada, Addiction and Community Funded Programs, Medical Services Branch, 1993. *The Truth Health: Notes from a National consultation with youth and service providers on Aboriginal solvent use*, page 2.

[40] National Association of Friendship Centres (NAFC), 1985. *Urban Research Project, Phase 1 & 11, Alcohol, Drug and Solvent Abuse*, July.

[41] Howarth, D.J., Stiffarm, D.W. and Webster, K. *Sharing, Caring and Consequences: A study of Sobriety and Healing at Alkali Lake reserve*, Health Canada, Ottawa.

[42] Government of Canada, 1995. *Towards Holistic Wellness: The Aboriginal People*, Report of the Standing Committee on Health, July, page 35.

[43] Longclaws, L., Games, E., Grieve, L. and Durnoff, R. "Alcohol and drug use among the Brokenhead Ojibwa", *Journal of Studies on Alcohol*, 41, 21-36.

[44] May, P.H., 1982. "Substance abuse and American Indians: Prevalence and susceptibly", *International Journal of the Addictions*, 17: 1185-1209.

[10] Arnup, M.E. et J.C. Butt (1992). Cabinet du médecin légiste en chef, Procureur général de l'Alberta, Présentation à la Commission royale sur les peuples autochtones.

[11] Jelik, W. (1982). Indian Healing: Shamanic Ceremonialism in the Pacific North West Today. Hancock House, Colombie-Britannique.

[12] Santé et Bien-être Canada (1989). Promotion de la santé dans les Territoires du Nord-Ouest, Ministère de la Santé et du Bien-être social, Ottawa.

[13] Scott, K.A. (1986). Self-Evaluation: Its relationship to substance use in native adolescents. Thèse de maîtrise non publiée, Health Studies Department, University of Waterloo.

[14] Gfellner, B.M. et J.D. Hundelby, 1995. «Patterns of Drug Use Among Native and White Adolescents: 1990-1993». Revue canadienne de santé publique, mars-avril, p. 95-97.

[15] Malheureusement, ces statistiques ne sont pas établies selon l'ethnie par les systèmes de santé provinciaux, et elles ne sont pas régulièrement recueillies des hôpitaux de compétence fédérale desservant les populations autochtones.

[16] Whitehead Research Consultants Ltd. (1985). Assessment of National Needs Through Regional Needs Assessment Studies, Programme national de lutte contre l'abus de l'alcool et des drogues chez les Autochtones, Services de santé des Indiens et des Inuit, Direction générale des services médicaux, Santé Canada.

[17] Gouvernement du Yukon (1991). The Executive Council Office, Bureau of Statistics, Yukon Alcohol and Drug Survey: Fall 1990, volume 1, Technical Report.

[18] Stephens, T. (1994). Le tabagisme chez lesAutochtones du Canada, 1991, Santé Canada.

[19] Bray, D.L. et P.D. Anderson. «Appraisal of the Epidemiology of Fetal Alcohol Syndrome Among Canadian Native People», Revue canadienne de santé publique, 80, p. 42-45.

[45] Health Canada, Addictions and Community Funded Programs, Medical Services Branch, Prevention Framework for First Nations Communities.

[46] National Association of Treatment Directors, 1989. *In the Spirit of the Family, Native Alcohol and Drug Counselor's Family Systems treatment Intervention Handbook*, February.

[47] Canada, Government of, House of Commons, Standing Committee on Health, 1995. *Towards Holistic Wellness: The Aboriginal Peoples*, Issue No. 31. July.

[48] Rowe, W. And Lieber, J., 1994. *Round Lake Treatment Centre: The Next Generation: Solvent Abuse Community Intervention Resource Project. A Demonstration Project to Test a Community Based Solvent Abuse Intervention Model.*

[49] McTimoney, D.C. and van Gaal, M.A. *Your Sobriety! Our Future: A Spiritual Model of Recovery*, Oromacto, New Brunswick Eel Ground Reserve.

[50] Scott, K.A., 1994. "Substance Use Among Indigenous Canadians" in McKenzie, D. (Ed.), *Aboriginal Substance Use: Research Issues.* Proceeds of a Joint Research Advisory Meeting. Canadian Centre on Substance Abuse and National Native Alcohol and Drug Abuse Program.

[51] McKenzie, D., 1995. "Aboriginal People" In: *Canadian Centre on Substance Abuse/Addiction Research Foundation (ed.) Canadian Profile* 1995, pp. 205-225.

[52] Cooper, M., Corado, R., Karlberg, A.M. and Peletier Adams, L., 1992. "Aboriginal Suicide in British Columbia: An Overview", *Canada's Mental Health*, September.

[53] Oettig, E.R., Beauvais, F., Edwards, R., Waters, M., Velard, and Goldstein, G., 1982. *Drug Use Among Native American Youth: Summary of Findings.* Ft. Collins, Colorado: Rocky Mountain Behavioural Science Institute.

[54] Wallace, J. and Bachman, J., 1991. "Explaining racial/ethnic differences in adolescent use: The impact of background and lifestyle", *Social Problems*, 38 (3): 333-357.

[20] Burd, L. et M.E.K. Moffat. Epidemiology of Fetal Alcohol Syndrome in American Indians, Alaskan Natives, and Canadian Aboriginal People: A Review of the Literature, Public Health Reports, septembre-octobre, Vol. 109, no 5, p. 688-693.

[21] Rosett, H.L. (1980). Fetal Alcohol Syndrome. Alcoholism Update, Vol. 1, no 8.

[22] McTimoney, D.C., R.C. Savoy et M.A. van Gall (1989). Your Child, Our Future! Fetal Alcohol Syndrome Education Package and Resource Kit, mars.

[23] Asante, K.O. et J. Melms-Matzke (1985). Report on the Survey of Children with Chronic Handicaps and Fetal Alcohol Syndrome in the Yukon and Northwest British Columbia.

[24] Van Bibber, M. (1993). Communiqué de presse diffusé lors du Colloque sur le syndrome d'alcoolisme foetal, Actes du Colloque national sur le syndrome foetal, Winnipeg (Manitoba), mars, p. 2.

[25] Scott, K.A. (1986). Self-Evaluation: Its relationship to substance use in native adolescents. Thèse de maîtrise non publiée, Health Studies Department, University of Waterloo.

[26] Okwumbabua, J.O. et E.J. Duryea. «Age of Onset, Periods of Risk and Patterns of Progression in Drug Use Among American Indian High School Students». International Journal of Addictions, vol. 22, no 12, p. 1269-1276.

[27] Oetting, E.R., R.C. Swaim, R.W. Edwards et F. Beauvais (1989). «Indian and Anglo Adolescent Alcohol and Emotional Distress: Pat Models», American Journal of Drug and Alcohol Abuse, vol. 15, no 2, p. 153-172.

[28] Hoover, J., R. McDermott et T. Hartsfield (1990). «The Prevalence of Smokeless Tobacco Use in Native Children in Northern Saskatchewan, Canada», Revue canadienne de santé publique, no 81, p. 350-352.

[29] Bruerd, B. (1990). «Smokeless Tobacco Use Among Native American School Children», Public Health Reports, vol. 105, no 2, p. 196-201.

[30] Christensen, R. «Health Problems Among Alaskan Eskimo Infants and Young Children», Arctic Medical Research, no 49, p. 63-67.

[31] Programme national de lutte contre l'abus de l'alcool et des drogues chez les Autochtones (1991). Système de rapports des activités de traitement (SRAT), rapport trimestriel, avril-septembre.

[32] Programme national de lutte contre l'abus de l'alcool et des drogues chez les Autochtones (1989). Système de rapports des activités de traitement (SRAT), rapport trimestriel, avril-juin.

[33] Programme national de lutte contre l'abus de l'alcool et des drogues chez les Autochtones (1995). Système de rapports des activités de traitement (SRAT), rapport trimestriel, avril 1994-mars 1995.

[34] David, D. (1993). Aboriginal Peoples in Urban Centres, Report of the National Roundtable on Aboriginal Urban Issues, Commission royale sur les peuples autochtones, p. 68.

[35] Statistique Canada (1993). Langues, traditions, santé, habitudes de vie et préoccupations sociales, Enquête auprès des peuples autochtones (EAPA) 1991, juin.

[36] Gfellner, B.M. et J.D. Hundelby, 1995. «Patterns of Drug Use Among Native and White Adolescents: 1990-1993». Revue canadienne de santé publique, mars-avril, p. 95-97.

[37] Langer, N. (1995). Base national de données sur l'allaitement maternel chez les Indiennes et les Inuit : sondage sur les pratiques d'alimentation des nourrissons de la naissance à six mois; rapport inédit. Direction générale des services médicaux, Santé et Bien-être Canada, avril 1990, tel que cité dans Santé Canada: Le tabagisme pendant la grossesse : Un choix difficile.

[38] Santé Canada, Stephens, T. (1994). Le tabagisme chez les peuples autochtones du Canada, 1991. Ministère des Approvisionnements et Services Canada.

[39] Santé Canada, Toxicomanie et programmes subventionnés par les communautés, Direction générale des services médicaux (1993), The Truth Health: Notes from a National consultation with youth and service providers on Aboriginal solvent use, p. 2.

[40] Association nationale des centres d'amitié (ANCA) (1985). Urban Research Project, Phase 1 & 11, Alcohol, Drug and Solvent Abuse, juillet.

[41] Howarth, D.J., C.W. Stiffarm et K. Webster, Sharing, Caring and Consequences: A study of Sobriety and Healing at Alkali Lake reserve, Santé Canada, Ottawa.

[42] Gouvernement du Canada (1995). Vers le mieux-être holistique : les peuples autochtones, Quatrième rapport du Comité permanent de la santé, juillet.

[43] Longclaws, L., E. Games, L. Grieve et R. Durnoff. «Alcohol and drug use among the Brokenhead Ojibwa», Journal of Studies on Alcohol, no 41, p. 21-36.

[44] May, P.H. (1982). «Substance abuse and American Indians: Prevalence and susceptibility», International Journal of Addictions, no 17, p. 1185-1209.

[45] Santé Canada, Toxicomanie et programmes subventionnés par les communautés, Direction générale des services médicaux, Cadre de prévention pour les communautés des premières nations.

[46] National Association of Treatment Directors (1989). In the Spirit of the Family, Native Alcohol and Drug Counsellor's Family Systems Treatment Intervention Handbook, février.

[47] Gouvernement du Canada, Chambre des communes, Comité permanent de la santé (1995). Vers le mieux-être holistique : les peuples autochtones, no 31, juillet.

[48] Rowe, W. et J. Lieber (1994). Round Lake Treatment Centre: The Next Generation: Solvent Abuse Community Intervention Resource Project. A Demonstration Project to Test a Community Based Solvent Abuse Intervention Model.

[49] McTimoney, D.C. et M.A. van Gaal. Your Sobriety! Our Future: A Spiritual Model of Recovery, Oromacto, Réserve Eel Ground du Nouveau-Brunswick.

[50] Scott, K.A. (1994). «Substance Use Among Indigenous Canadians» dans McKenzie, D. (éd.), Aboriginal Substance Use: Research Issues. Actes d'une consultation mixte de recherche. Centre canadien de lutte contre l'alcoolisme et les toxicomanies et le Programme national de lutte contre l'abus de l'alcool et des drogues chez les Autochtones.

[51] McKenzie, D. (1995). «Populations autochtones» dans Profil canadien 1995, Centre canadien de lutte contre l'alcoolisme et les toxicomanies et la Fondation de la recherche sur la toxicomanie (éd.), p. 205-223.

[52] Cooper M., R. Corado, A.M. Karlberg et Adams L. Peletier (1992). «Le suicide chez les Autochtones de la Colombie-Britannique : survol», Santé mentale au Canada, vol. 40, no 3, septembre, p.20-25.

[53] Oetting, E.R., F. Beauvais, R. Edwards, M. Waters, Velard et G. Goldstein (1982). Drug Use Among Native American Youth: Summary of Findings. Ft. Collins, Colorado : Rocky Mountain Behavioural Science Institute.

[54] Wallace J. et J. Bachman (1991). «Explaining racial/ethnic differences in adolescent use: The impact of background and lifestyle», Social Problems, vol. 38, no 3, p. 333-357.

TABLE 5.1

TABLEAU 5.1

Percentage of Indian/Metis and non-Indigenous students who have used drugs in the previous year, Canada, 1990 to 1993

Taux des étudiants indiens et métis et des étudiants non autochtones ayant consommé des drogues l'année précédente.

Substance/Drogue	Group/Groupe	1990	1991	1992	1993
Marijuana/Marijuana	White/Non-autochtone	10.3%	9.8%	7.8%	10.4%
	Native/Autochtone	38.8*	38.7*	29.7	36.9*
Barbiturates (NM)/ Barbituriques (NM)	White/Non-autochtone	2.8	3.1	2.4	2.6
	Native/Autochtone	7.3*	6.5*	3.8	7.2*
Barbiturates (M)/ Barbituriques (M)	White/Non-autochtone	8.8	7.4	6.1	5.1
	Native/Autochtone	11.6	7.8	8.1	12.2*
Heroin/Heroïne	White/Non-autochtone	0.7	1.4	1.2	2.1
	Native/Autochtone	1.8	1.7	2.1	5.5*
Speed/Speed	White/Non-autochtone	3.2	3.7	3.0	3.3
	Native/Autochtone	7.8*	6.1	3.8	9.8*
Stimulants (NM)/Stimulants (NM)	White/Non-autochtone	5.3	5.6	4.8	5.5
	Native/Autochtone	11.5*	10.9*	4.2	8.5
Stimulants (M)/Stimulants (M)	White/Non-autochtone	4.0	4.9	3.6	4.3
	Native/Autochtone	10.2*	7.0	6.0	7.2*
Tranquillizers (NM)/ Tranquillisants (NM)	White/Non-autochtone	1.8	1.8	1.3	1.9
	Native/Autochtone	7.8*	5.2*	3.4*	4.2*
Tranquillizers (M)/ Tranquillisants (M)	White/Non-autochtone	4.4	3.0	2.0	2.3
	Native/Autochtone	6.1	2.6	3.4	3.8
LSD/LSD	White/Non-autochtone	3.4	3.3	3.3	4.7
	Native/Autochtone	15.7*	11.3*	12.7*	14.4*
PCP/PCP	White/Non-autochtone	0.5	1.1	1.3	2.0
	Native/Autochtone	2.4*	3.0*	1.7	5.1*
Other Hallucinogens/ Autres hallucinogènes	White/Non-autochtone	3.9	3.6	3.4	4.5
	Native/Autochtone	10.2*	8.3*	8.1*	9.4*
Cocaine/Cocaïne	White/Non-autochtone	1.1	2.3	2.0	2.6
	Native/Autochtone	4.9*	3.5	6.4*	4.7
Crack/Crack	White/Non-autochtone	1.8	2.7	2.8	3.4
	Native/Autochtone	4.2*	4.8	5.6*	8.1

NM - Non-Medical/Non médicaux   M - Medical/médicaux

Source: This table has been reproduced from Gfellner, B. M.; Hundleby, J. D.; *Patterns of Drug Use Among Native and White Adolescents: 1990-1993*, Canadian Journal of Public Health, March-April, 1995, page 96.

Tableau tiré de Gfeliner, B.M. et J.D. Hundleby; *Patterns of Drug Use Among Native and While Adolescents: 1990–1993*, Revue canadienne de santé publique, mars-avril 1996, p.96

TABLE 5.2

TABLEAU 5.2

Percentage drug use among students by grade, non-Indigenous 1983/Native 1986, Canada

Pourcentage de la consommation de drogues chez les élèves non-autochtones (1983) et les élèves autochtones (1986), selon la classe.

Type of Drug/ Drogue	Group/ Groupe	Grade 7/ 7e année	Grade 9/ 9e année	Grade 11/ 11e année
Cannabis/Cannabis	White/Non autochtone	5.2%	68.2%	42.1%
	Native/Autochtone	9.1	25.1	66.6
Cocaine/Cocaïne	White/Non autochtone	2.8	4.6	5.0
	Native/Autochtone	0.0	4.5	33.3
Depressants/Depresseurs	White/Non autochtone	3.5	13.3	18.7
	Native/Autochtone	0.0	0.0	0.0
Hallucinogens/Hallucinogènes	White/Non autochtone	2.9	15.9	28.0
	Native/Autochtone	0.0	9.1	22.2
Stimulants/Stimulants	White/Non autochtone	4.4	22.3	34.4
	Native/Autochtone	0.0	9.0	0.0

Source: Source: This table has been reproduced from Scott, K. A.: Unpublished Master's thesis, Health Studies Department, University of Waterloo, 1986

Tableau tiré de Scott, K.A: Thèse de doctorat non-publiée, Health Studies Department, University of Waterloo, 1986 - Département des études

6 Street Youth

6 Les jeunes de la rue

Highlights

★ Although illicit drug use is high for street youth, there is evidence of decline.

★ Between 1990 and 1992, a smaller proportion of Toronto street youth report using cannabis, LSD, cocaine, tranquilizers, speed, heroin and "Ice".

★ Drugs are used by street youth to cope with the effects of a violent home life and the day-to-day hardship of living on the street. Drug use is also part of street life because drugs are easy to obtain.

Points saillants

★ La consommation de drogues illicites chez les jeunes de la rue est élevée, mais accuse néanmoins un recul.

★ Entre 1990 et 1992, moins de jeunes de la rue à Toronto ont déclaré faire usage de cannabis, de LSD, de cocaïne, de tranquilisants, de speed, d'héroïne et du produit «ice».

★ Les jeunes de la rue adoptent la drogue afin de surmonter les blessures laissées par la violence familiale et les épreuves quotidiennes inhérentes à leur mode de vie. Ils l'adoptent aussi en raison de sa facilité d'accès.

Street Youth

by Diane McKenzie, Canadian Centre on Substance Abuse

Overview

Street kids are heavy users of illicit drugs. Street youth, often referred to as "runaways" or "throwaways," are defined by two factors — their age and their absence from home without a parent's permission for 24 hours or more (Radford et al., 1989).

"Throwaway" youths are those who have been overtly rejected by their parents (Radford et al., 1989). There are no reliable estimates of the size of the street youth population in Canada because of the transitory nature of these young people. The size and composition of the group is constantly changing (Zdanowicz et al, 1993); as many as 150,000 street youths move through Canadian cities every year (Covenant House, 1988).

Several studies indicate that Canadian adolescents turn to the street to escape situations of physical, emotional and sexual abuse or neglect in the home (Radford et al., 1989; Smart et al., 1992; Anderson, 1992). The lifestyles of street youth involve many high-risk behaviours (Radford et al., 1989; Smart et al., 1992;

Les jeunes de la rue

par Diane McKenzie, Centre canadien de lutte contre l'alcoolisme et les toxicomanies

Vue d'ensemble

Les jeunes de la rue sont de gros consommateurs de drogues illicites. Souvent considérés comme des fugueurs ou des rebuts de la société, les jeunes de la rue sont définis par deux facteurs : leur âge et leur absence du foyer pendant vingt-quatre heures ou plus sans la permission d'un parent (Radford et coll., 1989).

Les «rebuts de la société» sont ceux ouvertement rejetés par les parents (Radford et coll., 1989). Vu leur situation transitoire, il n'existe aucune estimation fiable de leur nombre à travers le pays. La taille et la composition du groupe varient continuellement (Zdanowicz et coll., 1993). Chaque année, au moins 150 000 jeunes de la rue se déplacent entre les grands centres urbains (Covenant House, 1988).

Selon diverses études, ils choisissent la rue dans le but d'échapper à des situations d'abus physique, émotif ou sexuel ou encore de négligence au foyer (Radford et

---

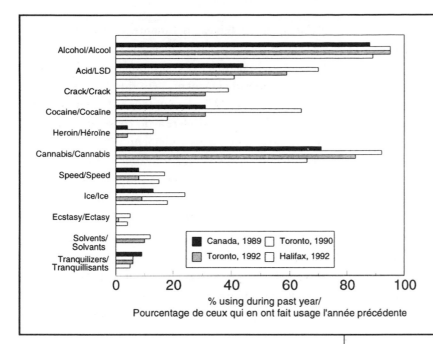

Figure 6.1   Alcohol and Drug Use Among Street Youth across Canada

Figure 6.1   Consommation d'alcool et de drogue chez les jeunes de la rue au Canada

Anderson, 1992). HIV infection is a particularly serious risk because of drug use and needle sharing, unsafe sex practices, lack of resources and opportunity to maintain proper hygiene.

Patterns of Drug Use

Studies show that street youth in each city have different patterns of drug use. Radford et al.'s (1989) national study indicated that two-thirds of all street youth used drugs and/or alcohol weekly or daily. Only a small proportion abstained from all substances. The most popular substances are alcohol, cannabis, LSD and cocaine (Radford et al., 1989; Smart et al., 1990; 1992; Anderson, 1992). Although use of illicit drugs is very high in this population, there is evidence that overall use is declining.

ALCOHOL: Although the majority of street youth across Canada use alcohol, research indicates that a substantial proportion does not. Table 6.1 indicates that in 1989, about 88% of Radford et al.'s national sample of street youth drank alcohol, but 12% abstained; 9% reported drinking daily. In 1992, about the same proportion of Halifax street youth said they used alcohol

coll., 1989; Smart et coll., 1992; Anderson, 1992). Leur vie dans la rue suppose de nombreux comportements à haut risque (Radford et coll., 1989; Smart et coll., 1992; Anderson, 1992). Leur usage de la drogue, leur partage des seringues, leurs rapports sexuels non protégés, leur manque de ressources et leur difficulté à pratiquer une bonne hygiène, les rendent extrêmement vulnérables au VIH.

Profils de consommation des drogues

La consommation de drogue chez les jeunes de la rue varie d'une ville à l'autre. D'après l'étude nationale menée par le collectif Radford en 1989, les deux tiers de ces jeunes consommaient de la drogue et/ou de l'alcool à toutes les semaines ou à tous les jours. Une faible proportion seulement s'abstenaient de toute substance. Les produits les plus populaires sont l'alcool, le cannabis, le LSD et la cocaïne (Radford et coll., 1989; Smart et coll., 1990; 1992; Anderson, 1992). La consommation des drogues illicites demeure très élevée au sein de cette population, mais on constate néanmoins un recul de la consommation générale.

L'ALCOOL : La majorité des jeunes de la rue consomment de l'alcool, mais un nombre important s'en

in the past year, but a much lower proportion used alcohol daily (5%). The proportion of youth who use alcohol is higher in Toronto, with about 95% using alcohol in the past year, and 6% using every day (Figure 6.1).

CANNABIS: In 1989, the national study of street youth indicated that 71% of those interviewed used cannabis in the past year (Table 6.2) and 24% used it almost daily (Radford et al., 1989) (Table 6.3). In 1992, about two thirds of Halifax street youth (66%) used cannabis in the past year; 27% of those who used cannabis, used daily (Anderson et al., 1992). Toronto street youth reported more cannabis use than other cities, with 83% using in the past year (Smart et al., 1992). The proportion of daily users (15%) of cannabis remained stable between 1990 and 1992 in the Toronto sample.

COCAINE AND CRACK: In 1989, about 31% of Canada's street youth used cocaine in the past year and 4% used it on a daily basis. In 1992, 18% of Halifax street youth used cocaine, with 4% using it daily. One in eight reported using crack, with 4% doing so daily. In Toronto, 31% used cocaine in the past year, and 3% used it daily. Thirty-one percent used crack in the past year and 5% used crack daily.

LSD AND OTHER HALLUCINOGENS: In 1989, 44% of Canadian street youth used LSD in the past year and 4% used it daily. Fifty-nine percent of the Toronto group used LSD in the past year. The proportion who used LSD daily was 1%. "Ice" and "Ecstasy" are other drugs currently being used on the street in Toronto, Halifax and other major centres across the country. The majority of street youth use inhalants, including industrial purpose glue, paint thinner and other solvents because they are inexpensive and easily attainable.

On average, the most frequently used drugs are cannabis (92 times in the past year), crack (68 times) and cocaine (49 times) (Smart et al., 1992).

The age of initiation into drug use differs according to the nature of the drug. On average, street youth began

abstiennent. Le Tableau 6.1 montre que, en 1989, 88 % de l'échantillon des jeunes de la rue constitué pour l'étude nationale précitée consommaient de l'alcool, dont 9 % quotidiennement, mais que 12 % s'en abstenaient. En 1992, un taux tout aussi élevé de ces jeunes, à Halifax, ont déclaré avoir consommé de l'alcool l'année précédente, mais seulement 5 % quotidiennement. Ces taux sont toutefois nettement supérieurs à ceux observés pour Toronto, où 95 % environ avaient consommé de l'alcool l'année précédente, dont 6 % à tous les jours (Figure 6.1).

LE CANNABIS : En 1989, 71 % des participants à une étude nationale des jeunes de la rue avaient consommé du cannabis l'année précédente (Tableau 6.2), dont 24 % presque quotidiennement (Radford et coll., 1989) (Tableau 6.3). En 1992, à Halifax, quelque 66 % des jeunes de la rue en avaient aussi consommé l'année précédente, dont 27 % quotidiennement (Anderson et coll., 1992). A Toronto, l'usage déclaré de cannabis était supérieur à ceux des autres villes, 83 % en ayant consommé l'année précédente (Smart et coll., 1992). Le taux des consommateurs quotidiens de cannabis s'y est par contre maintenu à 15 % entre 1990 et 1992.

LA COCAÏNE ET LE CRACK : En 1989, quelque 31 % des jeunes de la rue au Canada avaient consommé de la cocaïne l'année précédente, dont 4 % quotidiennement. En 1992, ces taux à Halifax s'établissaient à 18 % et à 4 % respectivement. Un jeune sur huit y avait déclaré faire usage de crack, dont 4 % à tous les jours. A Toronto, les taux atteignaient 31 % et 3 % respectivement pour la cocaïne, et 31 % et 5 % pour le crack.

LE LSD ET LES AUTRES HALLUCINOGÈNES : En 1989, 44 % des jeunes de la rue au Canada avaient utilisé du LSD l'année précédente, dont 4 % quotidiennement. A Toronto, ces taux étaient de 59 % et de 1 % respectivement. Les jeunes de la rue de Toronto, Halifax et des autres grands centres du pays consomment aussi régulièrement les produits «ice» et «ecstasy». La majorité utilisent par ailleurs des inhalants, dont la colle industrielle, les diluants à peinture et d'autres solvants, en raison de leur bas prix et de leur facilité d'accès.

using cannabis at 13 years old and LSD at 15 years old. Most other drugs were first used at 16 years old, except for crack and heroin, where first use occurs at 18.

INJECTION DRUG USE: Injection drug use and the practice of sharing needles place street youth at great risk of HIV infection. In 1989, 12% of the national sample of street youth admitted injecting drugs such as talwin, and ritalin, speed, cocaine and heroin and almost half of those shared needles (Radford et al., 1989). In Toronto, 28% injected drugs at some point in their lifetime and 4% shared needles during the past year (Smart et al., 1992).

DECLINING DRUG USE: There is evidence of declining levels of drug use among street youth in the Toronto studies conducted by the Addiction Research Foundation (Smart et al., 1992). Between 1990 and 1992, fewer street youth used cannabis (from 92% to 83%), LSD (from 70% to 59%), cocaine (from 64% to 31%), tranquilizers (59% to 29%), speed (from 24% to 9%), heroin (from 13% to 4%) and "Ice" (from 5% to 1%) (Figure 6.2). Overall, the number of drugs used at the same time also declined between 1990 and 1992 in this group. There was a decrease in the proportion of individuals using five or more drugs (from 38% to 22%) and an increase in the number that only used one or two drugs (from 15% to 36%).

Substance-related Problems

The 1992 Toronto study (Smart et. al., 1992) examined the drug-related problems of street youth (Table 6.4). About half of those surveyed said they had

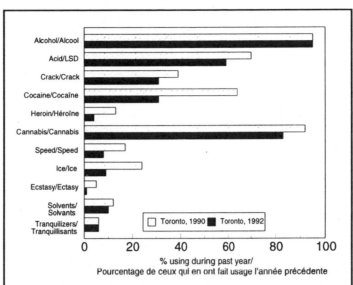

Figure 6.2   Declines in drug use Among Toronto Street Youth, 1990, 1992.

Figure 6.2   Baisse de l'usage de la drogue chez les jeunes de la rue à Toronto, 1990, 1992.

En règle générale, on consomme surtout le cannabis (92 fois l'année précédente), le crack (68 fois) et la cocaïne (49 fois) (Smart et coll., 1992).

L'âge d'initiation varie selon la nature du produit. Le jeune de la rue commence normalement à consommer le cannabis à 13 ans et le LSD, à 15 ans. Il essaie la plupart des autres drogues à 16 ans, sauf le crack et l'héroïne, dont il tente généralement l'expérience à 18 ans.

LA CONSOMMATION DE DROGUE PAR INJECTION : La prise de drogue par injection et le partage des seringues font du jeune de la rue une proie facile du VIH. En 1989, 12 % des participants à l'étude nationale ont admis s'injecter des drogues telles le Talwin, le Ritalin, le speed, la cocaïne, et l'héroïne, et près de 50 %, partager les seringues (Radford et coll., 1989). A Toronto, 28 % avaient fait l'expérience de l'injection et 4 % avaient partagé les seringues l'année précédente (Smart et coll., 1992).

BAISSE DE L'USAGE DE LA DROGUE : Selon des études effectuées par la Fondation de la recherche sur la toxicomanie, l'usage de la drogue chez les jeunes de la rue à Toronto régresse (Smart et coll., 1992). Entre 1990 et 1992, l'usage du cannabis est passé de 92 % à 83 %; celui du LSD, de 70 % à 59 %; de la cocaïne, de 64 % à 31 %; des tranquilisants, de 59 % à 29 %; du speed, de 24 % à 9 %; de l'héroïne, de 13 % à 4 %; et du produit «ice», de 5 % à 1 %. (Figure 6.2). L'usage simultané de plusieurs drogues a aussi accusé une diminution générale durant la même période. La proportion des jeunes utilisant cinq drogues ou plus est tombée de 38 % à 22 %, alors que celle des jeunes

flash-backs or blackouts, one quarter found they were not able to stop using drugs when they wanted to stop. About 40% were concerned about their drug use and 35% said they wanted to use drugs less often. More street youth were arrested for drug-related offenses (from 26% to 34%), had medical problems (from 19% to 22%), sought help (from 21% to 30%) and received medical attention (13% to 21%) in 1992 than in 1990 (Smart et al., 1992).

The Toronto sample reported being more heavily involved in illegal activities than for Halifax (Smart et al., 1992; Anderson, 1992). About 27% of the Toronto group and 15% of the Halifax group participated in break and enter offenses (Table 6.5). About 43% of Toronto street youth compared to 16% of the Halifax sample sold drugs; 23% and 14% participated in robbery or robbery with violence respectively. About 10% of the Toronto and Halifax samples were prostitutes. The Toronto group reported substantial involvement of alcohol or drugs in their illegal activities: 28% in break and enter, 65% in prostitution, 48% in selling drugs and 51% in robbery with violence.

Street youth use drugs to cope with the effects of a violent home life and the day-to-day hardship of living on the street. Drugs are also part of street life because they are easy to get. Drug use helps them cope or escape their situation, particularly if they turn to prostitution or pushing drugs for their livelihood.

utilisant une ou deux drogues seulement a légèrement augmenté, passant de 15 % à 36 %.

Les problèmes reliés à la drogue

L'étude de 1992 réalisée sur les jeunes de la rue à Toronto (Smart et coll., 1992) a notamment porté sur les problèmes reliés à la drogue (Tableau 6.4). La moitié environ des participants à cette enquête ont déclaré avoir fait l'expérience de flash-back ou d'évanouissements, et le quart, ne pas être capables d'abandonner la drogue comme ils le voulaient. Quelque 40 % s'inquiétaient de leur consommation, et 35 % souhaitaient la réduire. Si l'on compare les chiffres de 1992 à ceux de 1990, on constate pour la première année qu'un plus grand nombre de jeunes ont été arrêtés pour infractions reliées à la drogue (26 % contre 34 %), ont éprouvé des problèmes médicaux (19 % contre 22 %), ont demandé de l'aide (21 % contre 30 %) et ont reçu des soins médicaux (13 % contre 21 %) (Smart et coll., 1992).

L'étude a par ailleurs démontré que les jeunes de Toronto participaient davantage aux activités illégales que ceux de Halifax (Smart et coll., 1992; Anderson, 1992). Dans les deux villes, 27 % et 15 % respectivement avaient pris part à des vols par effraction (Tableau 6.5); 43 % et 16 % vendaient de la drogue; 23 % et 14 % avaient participé à des vols ou à des vols qualifiés, Quelque 10 % dans les deux villes se prostituaient. A Toronto, l'alcool ou la drogue représentait une part importante de leurs activités illégales, soit 28 % en ce qui concernait les vols par effraction; 65 %, la prostitution; 48 %, la vente de drogue; et 51 %, les vols qualifiés.

Les jeunes adoptent la drogue afin de surmonter les blessures laissées par la violence familiale et les épreuves quotidiennes inhérentes à leur mode de vie. Ils l'adoptent aussi en raison de sa facilité d'accès. Elle les aide à affronter ou à oublier leur situation, surtout s'ils se prostituent ou vendent eux-mêmes de la drogue pour survivre.

References

Anderson, J. 1992. *A Study of "Out-of-the Mainstream" Youth in Halifax, Nova Scotia*, Ottawa: Health Promotion Directorate, Health Canada.

Covenant House, 1988. (Information Brochure). 70 Gerrard Street East, Toronto, Ontario.

Radford, J.L., King, A.J. and Warren, W.K. 1989. *Street Youth and AIDS*. Ottawa: Health and Welfare Canada.

Smart, R.G., Adlaf, E.M. Porterfield, K.M. and Canale, M.D. 1990. *Drugs, Youth and the Street*. Toronto: Addiction Research Foundation.

Smart, R.G., Adlaf, E.M, Walsh, G.W. and Zdanowicz, Y.M. 1992. *Drifting and Doing; Changes in Drug Use Among Toronto Street Youth, 1990-1992*. Toronto: Addiction Research Foundation.

Zdanowicz, Y.M., Adlaf, E.M. and Smart, R.G. 1993. *Views from the Street*. Toronto: Addiction Research Foundation.

Ouvrages de référence

Anderson, J. 1992. *Etude sur les jeunes marginaux à Halifax (Nouvelle-Ecosse)*. Ottawa : Direction de la promotion de la santé, Santé Canada.

Covenant House, 1988. (Brochure d'information). 70 est, rue Gerrard, Toronto (Ontario).

Radford, J.L., A.J. King, et W.K. Warren, 1989. *Les jeunes des rues face au sida*. Ottawa : Santé et Bien-être Canada.

Smart, R.G., E.M. Adlaf, K.M. Porterfield, et M.D. Canale, 1990. *Drugs, Youth and the Street*. Toronto : Fondation de la recherche sur la toxicomanie.

Smart, R.G., E.M. Adlaf, G.W. Walsh, et Y.M. Zdanowicz, 1992. *Drifting and Doing; Changes in Drug Use Among Toronto Street Youth, 1990-1992*. Toronto : Fondation de la recherche sur la toxicomanie.

Zdanowicz, Y.M., E.M. Adlaf, et R.G. Smart, 1993. *Views from the Street*. Toronto : Fondation de la recherche sur la toxicomanie.

TABLE 6.1

TABLEAU 6.1

Frequency of alcohol use among street youth, 1989, 1990 and 1992

Fréquence de la consommation d'alcool chez les jeunes de la rue, 1989, 1990, et 1992

	CANADA RADFORD ET AL./ RADFORD ET COLL.	TORONTO SMART ET AL./ SMART ET COLL.		HALIFAX ANDERSON
	1989 (N=712)	1990 (N=145)	1992 (N=217)	1992 (N=201)
Never/Jamais bu	12 %	5 %	5 %	11 %
< 1 month/<1 fois par mois	19	23	22	11
Once a month/1 fois par mois	10	3	4	11
2-3 times per month/2 à 3 fois par mois	14	16	19	20
Once a week/1 fois par semaine	14	13	9	8
2-3 times per week/2 à 3 fois par semaine	22	24	22	25
4-6 times per week/4 à 6 fois par semaine	n.a.	10	13	9
Every day/Tous les jours	9	6	6	5

Source: Radford, J.L., King, A.J. and Warren, W.K., *Street Youth and AIDS* (Ottawa: Health and Welfare Canada, 1989); Smart, R.G., Adlaf, E.M., Porterfield, K.M. and Canale, M.D., *Drugs, Youth and the Street* (Toronto: Addiction Research Foundation, 1990); Smart, R.G., Adlaf, E.M. Walsh, G.W. and Zdanowicz, Y.M., *Drifting and Doing: Changes in Drug Use Among Toronto Street Youth, 1990-1992* (Toronto: Addiction Research Foundation, 1992); Anderson, J., *A study of "Out-of-the Mainstream" Youth in Halifax, Nova Scotia* (Ottawa: Health and Welfare Canada, Health Promotion Directorate, 1992).

Radford, J.L., A.J. King, et W.K. Warren, *Les jeunes des rues face au sida* (Ottawa : Santé et Bien-être Canada, 1989); Smart, R.G., E.M. Adlaf, K.M. Porterfield, et M.D. Canale, *Drugs, Youth and the Street* (Toronto : Fondation de la recherche sur la toxicomanie, 1990); Smart, R.G., E.M. Adlaf, G.W. Walsh, et Y.M. Zdanowicz, *Drifting and Doing: Changes in Drug Use Among Toronto Street Youth, 1990-1992* (Toronto : Fondation de la recherche sur la toxicomanie, 1992); Anderson, J., *Etude sur les jeunes marginaux à Halifax, Nouvelle-Ecosse* (Ottawa : Santé et Bien-être Canada, Direction de la Promotion de la santé, 1992).

| TABLE 6.2 | TABLEAU 6.2 |

Drugs used in the past year by street youth, 1989, 1990 and 1992

Drogues utilisées par les jeunes de la rue l'année précédente, 1989, 1990, et 1992

TYPE OF DRUG/ GENRES DE DROGUES	CANADA RADFORD ET AL./ RADFORD ET COLL.	TORONTO SMART ET AL./ SMART ET COLL.		HALIFAX ANDERSON
	1989 (N=712)	1990 (N=145)	1992 (N=217)	1992 (N=201)
Acid/LSD	44 %	70 %	59 %	41 %
Crack/Crack	n.a.	39	31	12
Cocaine/Cocaïne	31	64	31	18
Heroin/Héroïne	4	13	4	n.a.
Cannabis/Cannabis	71	92	83	66
Solvents/Solvants	8	17	8	15
Speed/Speed	13	24	9	18
Tranquilizers/Tranquillisants	9	6	6	5
Ice/Ice	n.a.	5	1	4
Ecstasy/Ecstasy	n.a.	12	10	n.a.

Source: Radford, J.L., King, A.J. and Warren, W.K., *Street Youth and AIDS* (Ottawa: Health and Welfare Canada, 1989); Smart, R.G., Adlaf, E.M., Porterfield, K.M. and Canale, M.D., *Drugs, Youth and the Street* (Toronto: Addiction Research Foundation, 1990); Smart, R.G., Adlaf, E.M. Walsh, G.W. and Zdanowicz, Y.M., *Drifting and Doing: Changes in Drug Use Among Toronto Street Youth, 1990-1992* (Toronto: Addiction Research Foundation, 1992); Anderson, J., *A study of "Out-of-the Mainstream" Youth in Halifax, Nova Scotia* (Ottawa: Health and Welfare Canada, Health Promotion Directorate, 1992).

Radford, J.L., A.J. King, et W.K. Warren, *Les jeunes des rues face au sida* (Ottawa : Santé et Bien-être Canada, 1989); Smart, R.G., E.M. Adlaf, K.M. Porterfield, et M.D. Canale, *Drugs, Youth and the Street* (Toronto : Fondation de la recherche sur la toxicomanie, 1990); Smart, R.G., E.M. Adlaf, G.W. Walsh, et Y.M. Zdanowicz, *Drifting and Doing: Changes in Drug Use Among Toronto Street Youth, 1990-1992* (Toronto : Fondation de la recherche sur la toxicomanie, 1992); Anderson, J., *Etude sur les jeunes marginaux à Halifax, Nouvelle-Ecosse* (Ottawa : Santé et Bien-être Canada, Direction de la Promotion de la santé, 1992).

TABLE 6.3

TABLEAU 6.3

Drugs used daily by street youth, 1989, 1990 and 1992

Drogues utilisées quotidiennement par les jeunes de la rue, 1989, 1990, et 1992

TYPE OF DRUG/ GENRES DE DROGUES	CANADA RADFORD ET AL./ RADFORD ET COLL.	TORONTO SMART ET AL./ SMART ET COLL.		HALIFAX ANDERSON
	1989 (N=712)	1990 (N=145)	1992 (N=217)	1992 (N=201)
Acid/LSD	4 %	3 %	1 %	2 %
Crack/Crack	n.a.	6	5	4
Cocaine/Cocaïne	4	6	3	5
Cannabis/Cannabis	24	16	15	18
Solvents/Solvants	2	n.a.	2	n.a.
Speed/Speed	1	0	1	1
Tranquillizers/Tranquillisants	1	2	0	1

Source: Smart, R.G., Adlaf, E.M., Porterfield, K.M. and Canale, M.D., *Drugs, Youth and the Street* (Toronto: Addiction Research Foundation, 1990); Smart, R.G., Adlaf, E.M. Walsh, G.W. and Zdanowicz, Y.M., *Drifting and Doing; Changes in Drug Use Among Toronto Street Youth, 1990-1992* (Toronto: Addiction Research Foundation, 1992).

Smart, R.G., E.M. Adlaf, K.M. Porterfield, et M.D. Canale, *Drugs, Youth and the Street* (Toronto : Fondation de la recherche sur la toxicomanie, 1990); Smart, R.G., E.M. Adlaf, G.W. Walsh, et Y.M. Zdanowicz, *Drifting and Doing: Changes in Drug Use Among Toronto Street Youth, 1990-1992* (Toronto : Fondation de la recherche sur la toxicomanie, 1992).

TABLE 6.4

TABLEAU 6.4

Drug problems reported by street youth during the past year, 1990 and 1992

Problèmes reliés à la drogue déclarés par les jeunes de la rue l'année précédente, 1990 et 1992

DRUG PROBLEMS/ PROBLEMES RELIES A LA DROGUE	TORONTO, SMART ET AL./TORONTO, SMART ET COLL.	
	1990 (N=145)	1992 (N=48)
Had blackouts or flashbacks/ Evanouissements, «flash-back»	54 %	48 %
Concerned about drug use/ Inquiétudes associées à l'usage	45	40
Unable to stop when desired/ Impossibilité d'abandonner malgré le désir	43	25
Desire to use less/Désir de diminuer	38	35
Drug-related arrest/Arrestations	26	34
Sought help/Demandes d'aide	21	30
Medical problems/Problèmes médicaux	19	22
Received medical attention/ Ont reçu des soins médicaux	13	21

Source: Smart, R.G., Adlaf, E.M., Porterfield, K.M. and Canale, M.D., *Drugs, Youth and the Street* (Toronto: Addiction Research Foundation, 1990); Smart, R.G., Adlaf, E.M. Walsh, G.W. and Zdanowicz, Y.M., *Drifting and Doing; Changes in Drug Use Among Toronto Street Youth, 1990-1992* (Toronto: Addiction Research Foundation, 1992).

Smart, R.G., E.M. Adlaf, K.M. Porterfield, et M.D. Canale, *Drugs, Youth and the Street* (Toronto : Fondation de la recherche sur la toxicomanie, 1990); Smart, R.G., E.M. Adlaf, G.W. Walsh, et Y.M. Zdanowicz, *Drifting and Doing: Changes in Drug Use Among Toronto Street Youth, 1990-1992* (Toronto : Fondation de la recherche sur la toxicomanie, 1992).

TABLE 6.5

TABLEAU 6.5

Criminal involvement among street youth, 1990 and 1992

Participation des jeunes de la rue aux activités criminelles, 1990 et 1992

PERCENTAGE WHO USED ALCOHOL OR DRUGS OFTEN OR ALWAYS DURING EACH EVENT/ POURCENTAGE DE CEUX QUI ONT SOUVENT OU TOUJOURS PRIS DE L'ALCOOL OU DE LA DROGUE DURANT CHAQUE ACTIVITE			
	TORONTO SMART ET AL./SMART ET COL.		HALIFAX ANDERSON
	1990 (N=145)	1992 (N=217)	1992 (N=201)
Break and enter/Entrées par effraction	27 %	28 %	15 %
Prostitution/Prostitution	10	65	10
Selling drugs/Ventes de drogues	43	48	16
Robbery or with violence/Vol ou vol avec violence	23	51	14

Source: Smart, R.G., Adlaf, E.M., Porterfield, K.M. and Canale, M.D., *Drugs, Youth and the Street* (Toronto: Addiction Research Foundation, 1990); Smart, R.G., Adlaf, E.M. Walsh, G.W. and Zdanowicz, Y.M., *Drifting and Doing; Changes in Drug Use Among Toronto Street Youth, 1990-1992* (Toronto: Addiction Research Foundation, 1992).

Smart, R.G., E.M. Adlaf, K.M. Porterfield, et M.D. Canale, *Drugs, Youth and the Street* (Toronto : Fondation de la recherche sur la toxicomanie, 1990); Smart, R.G., E.M. Adlaf, G.W. Walsh, et Y.M. Zdanowicz, *Drifting and Doing: Changes in Drug Use Among Toronto Street Youth, 1990-1992* (Toronto : Fondation de la recherche sur la toxicomanie, 1992).

7 AIDS and Drug Use

Figures

Tables

7 Le SIDA et l'usage de la drogue

Figures

Tableaux

Highlights

★ About 11,529 Canadians have developed AIDS since 1977; of these, 8,199 have died.

★ HIV prevalence rates among injection drug users in Montreal, Quebec and Ottawa are already very high.

★ HIV incidence rates in some Canadian cities are amongst the highest in North America.

★ More than one percent of inmates of federal correctional institutions have HIV or AIDS. In some institutions, as many as five percent of the inmate population are HIV-positive. Few measures are in place to check the spread of HIV in prisons.

AIDS and Drug Use

by Diane Riley and Diane McKenzie, Canadian Centre on Substance Abuse

Overview

Drug use puts an individual at risk for infection with Human Immunodeficiency Virus (HIV) and other pathogens such as hepatitis. Injection drug use poses direct risk of infection through sharing of contaminated drug equipment. Non-injection drug use, including alcohol use, poses indirect risks of infection in that it can increase the likelihood of unsafe sexual and drug-injecting practices (see Riley, MacKenzie, Hankins et al., 1995, for an overview). This chapter focuses on the relationship between HIV and injection drug use, because there is little information about the relationship between HIV and non-injection drug use.

Points saillants

★ Depuis 1977, 11 529 Canadiens environ ont développé le sida, dont 8 199 sont décédés.

★ Les taux de prévalence du VIH parmi les consommateurs de drogue par injection à Montréal, Québec et Ottawa sont déjà très élevés.

★ Les taux d'incidence du VIH dans certaines villes canadiennes sont parmi les plus élevés en Amérique du Nord.

★ Plus de 1 % des détenus dans les établissements pénitenciers fédéraux sont porteurs du VIH ou ont développé le sida. Dans certains établissements, près de 5 % de la population des détenus sont séropositifs. Peu de mesures ont été mises en place pour vérifier la propagation du VIH dans les prisons.

Le sida et l'usage de la drogue

par Diane Riley et Diane McKenzie, Centre canadien de lutte contre l'alcoolisme et les toxicomanies

Vue d'ensemble

Toute personne qui consomme de la drogue s'expose au danger d'être contaminée par le virus de l'immunodéficience humaine (VIH) et d'autres agents pathogènes tels celui de l'hépatite. Celle qui a recours à l'injection s'expose immédiatement au danger d'infection s'il y a partage de matériel contaminé. L'usage de drogue par voie autre que l'injection, y compris la consommation d'alcool, pose des risques indirects en ce sens qu'il peut accroître la possibilité de rapports sexuels et d'injections de drogue non

Sources of Information

Information about AIDS, HIV, hepatitis, injecting behaviour and related high risk behaviour is limited. Two sources are used to track changing infection patterns in the Canadian population: Health and Welfare Canada's Quarterly Surveillance update on AIDS is the main source of information for following new AIDS cases and deaths across the country. Surveys of user populations in cities and of inmates of correctional facilities help monitor the spread of HIV and AIDS in high risk populations.

AIDS and Injection Drug Use

Only a small proportion of drug users inject drugs, but those who do are particularly at risk of infection by HIV and hepatitis. Globally, injection drug use is a primary risk factor for the transmission of the HIV. In Canada, injection drug use is second only to homosexual/bisexual activity as a means of HIV transmission in men, and second only to heterosexual acquisition in women. Transmission occurs when blood is transferred from one person to another by sharing unclean needles, syringes or other drug paraphernalia.

In 1991, it was estimated that approximately 100,000 injection drug users in Canada were at risk for HIV infection through sharing needles and syringes (Addiction Research Foundation [ARF], 1991). These individuals are concentrated, for the most part, in the metropolitan areas of Montreal, Toronto and Vancouver, but there are injection drug users in most urban and rural areas of Canada.

Traditionally, heroin has been the main drug administered by injection in Canada; Talwin and Ritalin have also been popular injectables at various times in different parts of the country. Over the last several years, cocaine has been used increasingly by injection drug users, either on its own or in combination with heroin. There is also increasing non-medical use of anabolic steroids by athletes, dancers and the general male population throughout Canada.

sécuritaires (voir Riley, MacKenzie, Hankins et coll. 1995, pour un aperçu général). Le présent chapitre porte essentiellement sur le lien entre le VIH et la prise de drogue par injection puisqu'il existe encore peu de données sur le lien éventuel entre ce virus et l'usage de drogue par des voies autres que l'injection.

Sources d'information

Il existe peu d'information sur le sida, le VIH, l'hépatite, l'administration de drogue par injection et le comportement à haut risque que l'on y associe. Deux sources permettent à ce jour de suivre l'évolution des profils d'infection au sein de la population canadienne : le bulletin trimestriel de surveillance du sida (Quarterly Surveillance update) de Santé Canada est la principale source permettant de suivre les nouveaux cas et décès de sida au pays. Les enquêtes auprès des populations de consommateurs de drogue dans les villes et des détenus dans les établissements pénitentiers aident à vérifier la propagation du VIH et du sida au sein des populations les plus vulnérables.

Le sida et la prise de drogue par injection

Seule une petite proportion d'usagers de drogue ont recours à l'injection, mais ceux qui le font sont tout particulièrement vulnérables au VIH et au virus de l'hépatite. Sur le plan mondial, la toxicomanie par voie d'injection constitue l'un des premiers facteurs de transmission du VIH. Au Canada, elle vient en deuxième place, tout de suite après l'activité homosexuelle et bisexuelle chez les hommes, et tout de suite après l'activité hétérosexuelle chez les femmes. Le virus se transmet par voie sanguine lors du partage d'aiguilles, de seringues ou d'autre matériel souillés.

En 1991, au Canada, on avait évalué à quelque 100 000 le nombre des toxicomanes pratiquant l'injection qui couraient le danger d'être infectés par le VIH à cause du partage d'aiguilles et de seringues contaminées (Fondation de la recherche sur la

In Canada, as in other countries, the heterosexual transmission of HIV infection is fueled by the spread of infection among injection drug users. HIV infection spreads from injection drug users to their sexual partners. About one-third of injection drug users are female. It is estimated that at least 40% of injection drug users are in relationships with non-users. There is also a risk that babies will be infected through perinatal transmission of the virus.

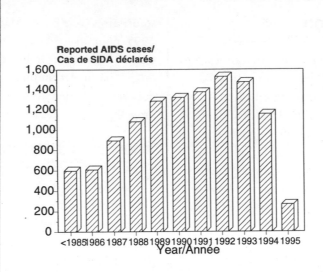

**Reported AIDS cases/
Cas de SIDA déclarés**

Year/Année

Figure 7.1   Reported number of AIDS cases, Canada 1977 to 1995

Figure 7.1   Nombre déclaré des cas de sida, Canada, 1977 à 1995

toxicomanie [ARF], 1991). On les retrouve surtout dans les grandes agglomérations de Montréal, Toronto et Vancouver, mais ils sont néanmoins présents dans la plupart des régions urbaines et rurales du pays.

L'héroïne représente depuis toujours la principale drogue administrée par injection au Canada; le Talwin et le Ritalin ont aussi été populaires à diverses périodes, dans différentes régions du pays. Depuis quelques années, la cocaïne se prend de plus en plus souvent par injection, seule ou en association avec l'héroïne. On constate également un usage non médical croissant de stéroïdes anabolisants chez les athlètes, les danseurs et la population mâle en général dans tout le pays.

About 11,529 Canadians have developed AIDS since 1977 (Table 7.1). Of these, 8,199 have died (Health Canada, 1995). Between 1985 and 1992, the number of AIDS cases increased dramatically (Figure 7.1). The number of new cases increased between 1987 and 1988 and has remained high (ranging from 892 in 1987 to 1,529 in 1992) (Table 7.2).

The majority of AIDS cases occur among those between age 20 and 49, proportionately as follows: 30 to 39 (44.0%), 40 to 49 (26.5%) and 20 to 29 (17.8%) (Table 7.3). About 41.5% of AIDS cases occur in Ontario, 29.7% in Quebec, 17.6% in British Columbia and 6.4% in Alberta. AIDS-related mortality follows a similar regional pattern. To date, the vast majority of deaths due to AIDS-related causes have occurred in Ontario (n=3,969) and Quebec (n=2,084).

Compared to New York and Milan, where HIV infection prevalence levels among injection drug users are more than 50%, HIV rates among Canadian injection drug users are low to moderate. However, by comparison with a number of European and Australian

Au Canada comme ailleurs, la transmission du VIH chez les hétérosexuels se trouve accélérée par la propagation du virus chez les toxicomanes adeptes de l'injection, puisque ces derniers contaminent leurs partenaires sexuels. On estime que le tiers environ des toxicomanes par injection sont des femmes, dont au moins 40 % ont des rapports sexuels avec des non-usagers. Il y a aussi danger que les nouveau-nés soient contaminés durant la période périnatale.

Depuis 1977, 11 529 Canadiens environ ont développé le sida (Tableau 7.1), dont 8 199 sont décédés (Santé Canada, 1995). Entre 1985 et 1992, le nombre des cas de sida a considérablement augmenté (Figure 7.1), celui des nouveaux cas s'étant accru entre 1987 et 1988 pour demeurer élevé par la suite (892 en 1987 contre 1 529 en 1992) (Tableau 7.2).

cities, where, in many cases, infection rates remain below 5%, rates in some Canadian regions are already high. For example, in British Columbia, prevalence increased from 3% to 6% between 1992 and 1995 (Figure 7.2) (BC Ministry of Health, 1995). In Toronto, a 1994 survey of injection drug users reported a seropositivity rate of 7.6%[1] compared to a rate of 4.8% in 1992/93 (Millson, personal communication, 1994). In Montreal, rates range between 10% and 22%, depending on the testing site (Bruneau, Cloutier, Hankins, Morisette, personal communications, 1995). In Quebec and Ottawa, prevalence rates are about 10 percent (Health Canada, 1995).

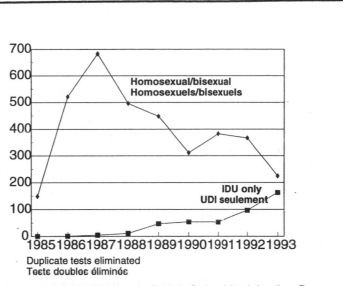

Figure 7.2   HIV Testing in British Columbia: Injection Drug Users, 1985 to 1995.

Figure 7.2   Dépistage du VIH en Colombie-Britannique : Consommateurs de drogue par injection. 1985 à 1995

The incidence rates of HIV among injection drug users in some Canadian cities are now very high. Montreal and Vancouver have incidence rates of more than 5% (Health Canada, 1995), amongst the highest in North America.

Clearly, both prevalence and incidence rates of HIV infection among injection drug users are already high in a number of Canadian cities. Intensive prevention efforts are needed immediately (Riley, MacKenzie, Hankins et al., 1995). Experts from around the world indicate that once levels of infection among injection drug users reach 10%, the epidemic can become explosive (Hankins, 1993). A comprehensive harm reduction approach to AIDS and drug use is required to keep rates of HIV

---

[1] Rate includes gay and bisexual respondents.

Les plus touchés par le sida sont les 20 à 49 ans, dans les proportions suivantes : 30 à 39 ans (44,0 %); 40 à 49 (26,5 %); 20 à 29 (17,8 %) (Tableau 7.3). L'Ontario compte quelque 41,5 % des cas de sida; le Québec, 29,7 %; la Colombie-Britannique, 17,6 %; et l'Alberta, 6,4 %. La mortalité reliée au sida obéit à un profil régional similaire. A ce jour, la grande majorité des décès reliés au sida sont survenus en Ontario (n=3 969) et au Québec (n=2 084).

Par comparaison avec New York et Milan, où les taux de prévalence d'infection au VIH chez les toxicomanes pratiquant l'injection atteignent plus de 50 %, les taux enregistrés au Canada sont de faibles à modérés. Mais si l'on établit toutefois des comparaisons avec certaines villes européennes et australiennes (où les taux d'infection demeurent souvent en-deçà de 5 %), les taux de certaines régions canadiennes sont déjà élevés. En Colombie-Britannique, par exemple, la prévalence est passée de 3 % à 6 % entre 1992 et 1995 (Figures 7.2 et 7.3) (Ministère de la Santé de la Colombie-Britannique, 1995). A Toronto, une enquête menée auprès des toxicomanes par injection en 1994 a révélé un taux de séropositivité de 7,6 %[1] comparativement à 4,8 % en 1992-1993 (Millson, communication personnelle, 1994). A Montréal, les taux varient entre 10 % et 22 %, selon le lieu de dépistage (Bruneau, Cloutier, Hankins, Morissette, communications

---

[1] Ce taux inclut les participants homosexuels et bisexuels.

infection low in Canada. Such an approach would involve ready availability of clean syringes, access to flexible and liberal methadone programs and an end to the marginalization and criminalization of drug users (Riley, 1993, 1994).

Correctional Institutions

Rates among injection drug users in correctional institutions reflect the levels of infection in the drug injecting community outside the institution. For example, among inmates who inject drugs in Provincial prisons in Quebec, 8% of men and 13% of women are HIV positive (Hankins et al., 1991, 1994).

Studies of Federal jails in B.C. and Ontario found that about 1% of the inmates tested were infected with HIV, about 10 times the rate in the general public (Calzavara, 1993; Rothon, 1993). The highest rates of infection were among prisoners with a history of injection drug use (2.1% for B.C.; 3.8% for Ontario).

As of August 1995, 152 inmates were known to have HIV or AIDS in federal prisons in Canada (CSC, 1995). This represents more than 1% of federal inmates. In some institutions, especially in Quebec, close to 5% of inmates are HIV-positive (Jurgens, 1995).

There is now evidence of the rapid spread of hepatitis B and C in prisons. Between January and August, 1995, 223 new cases of active hepatitis C and 22 new cases of hepatitis B were reported in federal prisons in Canada (CSC, 1995). These data suggest that there is potential for the rapid spread of HIV in prisons.

Three studies in Canadian prisons found hepatitis C seroprevalence rates of between 28% and 40% (Jurgens, 1995). Hepatitis C is usually spread by either blood transfusion or sharing of contaminated drug paraphernalia. Sexual transmission of hepatitis C is a less common form of transmission. Among inmates of correctional institutions, hepatitis C-positivity is a probable marker of injection drug use. These data suggest that there is a very marked potential for a rise in HIV rates.

personnelles, 1995). A Québec et à Ottawa, les taux de prévalence sont de 10 % environ (Santé Canada, 1995).

Dans plusieurs villes canadiennes, les taux actuels de séropositivité chez les toxicomanes par injection sont très élevés. Les taux d'incidence relevés à Montréal et à Vancouver excèdent 5 % (Santé Canada, 1995), ce qui les place parmi les plus élevés en Amérique du Nord.

De toute évidence, les taux de prévalence et d'incidence de l'infection au VIH chez les consommateurs de drogue par injection sont déjà très élevés dans certaines villes canadiennes. Une action intensive de prévention doit être engagée sans plus tarder (Riley, MacKenzie, Hankins et coll. 1995). Des experts de différents pays estiment que lorsque que les niveaux d'infection chez cette population atteindront 10 %, l'épidémie risquera alors de devenir explosive (Hankins, 1993). Il convient donc, face au sida et à la drogue, d'adopter une approche globale de réduction des méfaits si l'on veut maintenir la séropositivité à un bas niveau au Canada. Une telle approche suppose l'accessibilité immédiate à des seringues stériles, l'accès à des programmes souples et libéraux de distribution de la méthadone, et la fin de la marginalisation et de la criminalisation des usagers de drogue (Riley, 1993, 1994).

Milieu carcéral

Les taux d'infection chez les usagers de drogues par injection dans les établissements correctionnels reflètent les niveaux d'infection observés pour ce genre de toxicomanes à l'extérieur des établissements. Dans les prisons provinciales du Québec, par exemple, 8 % des hommes et 13 % des femmes ayant recours à l'injection sont séropositifs (Hankins et coll., 1991, 1994).

Des études des pénitenciers fédéraux en Colombie-Britannique et en Ontario ont révélé que 1 % environ des détenus testés étaient séropositifs, soit dix fois plus environ que dans la population en général (Calzavara, 1993; Rothon, 1993). Ceux qui ont déjà fait l'usage de drogue par injection sont les plus nombreux à être infectés (2,1 % en C.-B.; 3,8 % en Ontario).

Many individuals report sharing injection equipment for the first time in prison; others first use drugs and first inject drugs in prison. There are few measures in place to check the spread of HIV in institutions (ECAP, 1994; Jurgens, 1995; Riley, 1992).

References

Addiction Research Foundation, 1991. *Prevention Strategies: Injection Drug Users and AIDS.* Best Advice report from the Addiction Research Foundation of Ontario.

Calzavara, L., 1993. *Results from an anonymous unlinked HIV seroprevalence study of inmates in Ontario.* Paper presented at the BC AIDS Conference, Vancouver, October.

Correctional Service Canada, 1995. Health Care Services, Ottawa, August.

Expert Committee on AIDS and Prisons (ECAP), 1994. *HIV/AIDS in Prisons: Final Report*, Correctional Service of Canada, Ottawa.

Hankins, C.A., Gendron, S., Handley, M., Rouah F., O'Shaughnesssy, M., 1991. "HIV-1 infection among incarcerated men — Quebec", *Canada Diseases Weekly Report*, 17-43, 233-235.

Hankins, C.A., Gendron, S., Handley, M.A., Richard, C., Lai Tung, M.T., O'Shaughnessy, M., 1994. "HIV and women in prison: Assessment of risk factors using a non-nominal methodology", *American Journal of Public Health*, 84 (10), 1637-1640.

Hankins, C.A., 1993. Introduction, Principles and recommendations on HIV infection and injection drug use, Working Group on HIV Infection and Injection Drug Use of the National Advisory Committee on AIDS.

Health Canada, 1995. Division of HIV/AIDS Epidemiology, Laboratory Centre for Disease Control.

Jurgens, R., 1995. *HIV/AIDS in prisons: A discussion paper.* Canadian AIDS Society, Montreal, November.

Au mois d'août 1995, les prisons fédérales du Canada comptaient 152 détenus séropositifs ou sidéens (SCC, 1995). Cela représente plus de 1 % des détenus fédéraux. Dans certains établissements, surtout au Québec, près de 5 % des détenus sont porteurs du VIH (Jurgens, 1995).

Les faits indiquent maintenant propagation rapide de l'hépatite B et C dans les prisons. Entre janvier et août 1995, 223 nouveaux cas d'hépatite active C et 22 nouveaux cas d'hépatite B ont été signalés dans les prisons fédérales du Canada (SCC, 1995). Ces chiffres tendent à démontrer qu'il pourrait y avoir propagation rapide du VIH dans les prisons.

Trois études effectuées dans les prisons canadiennes ont établi les taux de séroprévalence de l'hépatite C entre 28 % et 40 % (Jurgens, 1995). L'hépatite C est normalement transmise, soit par les transfusions sanguines, soit par le partage de matériel souillé servant à la consommation de drogue. La transmission de l'hépatite C par voie sexuelle est moins courante. Chez les détenus, la positivité à l'hépatite C est un marqueur probable de la consommation de drogue par injection. Ces données suggèrent une très forte probabilité de la croissance de la séropositivité.

De nombreux individus affirment avoir partagé leur matériel d'injection pour la première fois en prison; d'autres y être devenus des consommateurs de drogue, et d'autres encore à y avoir pratiqué l'injection. Il existe peu de moyens en place pour contrôler l'ampleur de la propagation du VIH en milieu carcéral (CESP, 1994; Jurgens, 1995; Riley, 1992).

Ouvrages de référence

Calzavara, L., 1993. Results from an anonymous unlinked HIV seroprevalence study of inmates in Ontario. Communication présentée à la Conférence de la Colombie-Britannique sur le sida, Vancouver, octobre.

Comité d'experts sur le SIDA et les prisons (CESP) (1994), Le VIH/SIDA en milieu carcéral : Rapport final, Service correctionnel du Canada, Ottawa.

Millson, P.C., 1994. University of Toronto, personal communication.

Riley, D.M., 1992. *Drug Use in Prisons: A Harm Reduction Approach.* Canadian Centre on Substance Abuse, Ottawa.

Riley, D.M., 1993. *The Policy and Practice of Harm Reduction*, Canadian Centre on Substance Abuse. Ottawa.

Riley, D.M., 1994. *The Harm Reduction Model: Pragmatic Approaches to Drug Use from the Area between Intolerance and Neglect.* Canadian Centre on Substance Abuse, Ottawa.

Riley, D.M, MacKenzie, B., Hankins, C., et al., 1995. *Second National Workshop on HIV, Alcohol, and Other Drug Use, Proceedings*, Ottawa, Canadian Centre on Substance Abuse.

Rothon, D., 1993. *Results from the HIV prevalence study of inmates in BC prisons.* Paper presented at the B.C. AIDS Conference, Vancouver, October.

Fondation de la recherche sur la toxicomanie (1991), Prévention du SIDA chez les usagers de drogues injectées. Série de rapports Best Advice de la Fondation de la recherche sur la toxicomanie de l'Ontario.

Hankins, C.A., S. Gendron, M. Handley, F. Rouah, M. O'Shaughnessy, (1991). HIV-1 infection among incarcerated men - Québec. Canada Diseases Weekly Report, 17-43, 233-235.

Hankins, C.A., S. Gendron, M.A. Handley, C. Richard, M.T. Lai Tung, M. O'Shaughnessy, (1994), HIV and women in prison: Assessment of risk factors using a non-nominal methodology. American Journal of Public Health, 84(10), 1637-1640.

Hankins, C.A. (1993), Introduction, Principles and Recommendations on HIV Infection and Injection Drug Use, Working Group on HIV Infection and Injection Drug Use of the National Advisory Committee on AIDS.

Jurgens, R. (1995), HIV/AIDS in prisons: A discussion paper. Société canadienne du sida, Montréal, novembre.

Millson, P.C. (1994), University of Toronto, communication personnelle.

Riley, D.M. (1992), Drug Use in Prisons: A Harm Reduction Approach. Centre canadien de lutte contre l'alcoolisme et les toxicomanies, Ottawa.

Riley, D.M. (1993), The Policy and Practice of Harm Reduction, Centre canadien de lutte contre l'alcoolisme et les toxicomanies, Ottawa.

Riley, D.M. (1994), Le modèle de réduction des méfaits: Une approche pragmatique sur l'utilisation des drogues aux confins entre l'intolérance et l'apathie. Centre canadien de lutte contre l'alcoolisme et les toxicomanies, Ottawa.

Riley, D.M., B. MacKenzie, C. Hankins, et coll. (1995), Deuxième Atelier national sur le VIH, l'alcool et les autres drogues, Actes, Centre canadien de lutte contre l'alcoolisme et les toxicomanies, Ottawa.

Rothon, D. (1993), Results from the HIV prevalence study of inmates in BC prisons. Communication présentée à la Conférence de la Colombie-Britannique sur le sida, Vancouver, octobre.

Santé Canada (1995), Division de l'épidémiologie VIH/SIDA, Laboratoire de lutte contre la maladie.

Service correctionnel du Canada (1995), Service de santé, Ottawa, août.

TABLE 7.1

TABLEAU 7.1

Number of AIDS cases by risk factors and gender, Canada, 1977 to June 30, 1995

Nombre de cas de sida, selon le facteur de risque, Canada, 1977 au 30 Juin 1995

RISK FACTORS/ FACTEURS DE RISQUE	NUMBER OF CASES/ NOMBRE DE CAS			NUMBER OF KNOWN DEATHS/ NOMBRE DE DÉCÈS CONNUS		
	MALE/ HOMMES	FEMALE/ FEMMES	TOTAL/ Total	MALE/ HOMMES	FEMALE/ FEMMES	TOTAL/ TOTAL
PEDIATRIC CASES/ENFANTS:						
Perinatal transmission/ Transmission périnatale	40	47	87	n.a.	n.a.	n.a.
Recipient of blood/Receveur de sang	7	2	9	n.a.	n.a.	n.a.
Recipient of clotting factor/ Receveur de facteurs de coagulation	10	0	10	n.a.	n.a.	n.a.
No identified risk/ Aucun facteur de risque identifié	5	4	9	n.a.	n.a.	n.a.
Total	**62**	**53**	**115**	**39**	**36**	**75**
ADULTS/ADULTES:						
Homosexual or bisexual activity/ Activité homosexuelle ou bisexuelle	8,810	0	8,810	6,389	0	6,389
Injection drug use/ Usage de drogues par intraveineuse	274	98	372	167	54	221
Both of the above/ Les deux facteurs précédent	463	0	463	304	0	304
Recipient of blood/Receveur de sang	121	87	208	94	66	160
Recipient of clotting factor/ Receveur de facteurs de coagulation	202	10	212	163	8	171
HETEROSEXUAL ACTIVITY/ACTIVITE HETEROSEXUELLE:						
Origin in pattern-II Country[1]/ Provenant d'un pays de modèle II[1]	288	161	449	169	104	273
Sexual contact with person at risk[2]/Contact sexuel avec une personne à risque[2]	310	242	552	211	156	367
Occupational exposure/Exposition au travail	1	1	2	0	1	1
No identified risk factors/ Aucun facteur de risque identifié	411	50	461	284	29	313
Total	**10,880**	**649**	**11,529**	**7,781**	**418**	**8,199**

[1] Pattern-II countries are defined by WHO as countries where the predominant means of transmission is heterosexual contact./Les pays de modèle II sont définis par l'OMS comme les pays ayant un taux important d'infection à VIH, ou le mode prédominant de transmission est le contact hétérosexuel.

[2] Persons reporting heterosexual activity with person(s) at risk of HIV infection/Personnes ayant déclaré des rapports hétérosexuels avec une ou plusieurs personnes à risque d'être infectées par le VIH.

Source: Health and Welfare Canada, *Quarterly Surveillance Update: AIDS in Canada* (Ottawa: Health and Welfare Canada, HIV/AIDS Division, August, 1995).

Santé et Bien-être Canada, *Mise à jour de surveillance : le sida au Canada* (Ottawa : Santé et Bien-être Canada, Division du VIH/SIDA, august 1995).

TABLE 7.2

TABLEAU 7.2

Number of AIDS cases by risk factors and year of diagnosis, Canada, 1977 to June 30, 1995

Nombre de cas de SIDA selon le facteur de risque et l'année du diagnostic, Canada, 1977 au juin 1995

RISK FACTORS/FACTEURS DE RISQUE	YEAR OF DIAGNOSIS/ANNEE DE DIAGNOSTIC								
	< 1989	1989	1990	1991	1992	1993	1994	1995	Total
PEDIATRIC CASES/ENFANTS:									
Males/Garçons	24	7	4	5	11	5	6	0	**62**
Females/Filles	25	4	5	4	4	6	5	0	**53**
Total	**49**	**11**	**9**	**9**	**15**	**11**	**11**	**0**	115
ADULTS/ADULTES:									
Males/Hommes	3,018	1,203	1,253	1,290	1,427	1,379	1,060	250	**10,880**
Females/Femmes	174	70	58	76	87	84	83	17	**49**
Total	**3,192**	**1,273**	**1,311**	**1,366**	**1,514**	**1,463**	**1,143**	**267**	11,529
NUMBER OF CASES/NOMBRE DE CAS:									
Males/Hommes	3,042	1,210	1,257	1,295	1,438	1,384	1,066	250	**10,942**
Females/Femmes	199	74	63	80	91	90	88	17	**702**
Total	**3,241**	**1,284**	**1,320**	**1,375**	**1,529**	**1,474**	**1,154**	**267**	11,644
NUMBER OF KNOWN DEATHS[1]/ NOMBRE DE DECES CONNUS[1]	1,698	739	808	953	1,143	1,208	780	803	8,274
PEDIATRIC CASES/ENFANTS:									
Perinatal transmission/ Transmission périnatale	42	8	6	8	11	7	5	0	**87**
Recipient of blood/Receveur de sang	6	0	0	0	1	1	1	0	**9**
Recipient of clotting factor/ Receveur de facteur de coagulation	1	3	3	0	2	0	1	0	**10**
No identified risk/ Aucum facteur de risque identifié	0	0	0	1	1	3	4	0	**9**
ADULTS/ADULTES:									
Homosexual or bisexual activity/ Activité homosexuelle ou bisexuelle	2,544	1,001	1,019	1,033	1,129	1,072	823	189	**8,810**
Injection drug use/ Usage de drogues intraveineuse	36	26	32	54	66	71	69	18	**372**
Both of the above/Les deux qui précèdent	106	47	52	52	71	64	58	13	**463**
Heterosexual activity/Activité hétérosexuelle:									
Origin in pattern-II Country[2]/ Origine d'un pays de modèle II[2]	169	41	43	43	48	65	31	9	**449**
Sexual contact with person at risk[3]/ Contact sexuel avec une personne à risque[3]	95	54	48	64	80	104	95	12	**552**
Occupational exposure[4]/ Exposition professionelle[4]	0	0	1	0	0	0	1	0	**2**
Recipient of blood/Receveur de sang	98	28	15	18	23	14	8	4	**208**
Recipient of clotting factor/ Receveur de facteurs de coagulation	60	29	34	29	27	14	15	4	**212**
No identified risk factors/ Aucun facteur de risque identifié	84	47	67	73	70	59	43	18	**461**

TABLE 7.2 (concluded)   **TABLEAU 7.2** (fin)

Number of AIDS cases by risk factors and year of diagnosis, Canada, 1977 to June 30, 1995

Nombre de cas de SIDA selon le facteur de risque et l'année du diagnostic, Canada, 1977 au juin 1995

*The total number of known deaths included 142 deaths which the dates were unknown.

[1] Pattern-II countries are defined by WHO as countries where the predominant means of transmission is heterosexual contact./Les pays de modèle II sont définis par l'OMS comme les pays ayant un taux important d'infection à VIH, ou le mode prédiminant de transmission est le contact hétérosexuel.

[2] Persons reporting heterosexual activity with person(s) at risk of HIV infection./Personnes ayant déclaré des rapports hétérosexuels avec une ou plusieurs personnes à risque d'être infectées par le VIH.

[3] Full information regarding this laboratory accident can be found in the CCDR, Vol. 18-13, July 17, 1992./Des renseignements détaillés concernant cet accident de laboratoire sont disponibles dans le RMTC, vol.18-13, du 17 juillet 1992.

Source: Health and Welfare Canada, *Quarterly Surveillance Update: AIDS in Canada* (Ottawa: Health and Welfare Canada, Division of HIV/AIDS, August, 1995).

Santé et Bien-être Canada, *Mise à jour de surveillance : le sida au Canada* (Ottawa : Santé et Bien-être Canada, Division du VIH/SIDA, august 1995).

TABLE 7.3

TABLEAU 7.3

Number of AIDS cases reported by province and age, Canada, 1977 to June 30, 1995

Nombre de cas de sida déclarés, selon la province et l'âge, Canada, 1977 au 30 juin 1995

PROVINCE[1]	NUMBER OF CASES/ NOMBRE DE CAS			% DISTRIBUTION/ % VENTILATION			KNOWN DEATHS/ DÉCÈS CONNUS
	MALE/ HOMMES	FEMALE/ FEMMES	TOTAL/ Total	MALE/ HOMMES	FEMALE/ FEMMES	TOTAL/ Total	
Nfld./T.-N.	38	9	47	0.3	1.3	0.4	35
P.E.I./I.-P.-E.	8	1	9	0.1	0.1	0.1	8
N.S./N.-E.	172	16	188	1.6	2.3	1.6	128
N.B./N.-B.	81	9	90	0.7	1.3	0.8	48
Que./Québec	3,116	343	3,459	28.5	48.9	29.7	2,084
Ont./Ont.	4,620	214	4,834	42.2	30.5	41.5	3,969
Man./Man.	118	4	122	1.1	0.6	1.0	95
Sask./Sask.	81	11	92	0.7	1.6	0.8	67
Alta./Alb.	705	36	741	6.4	5.1	6.4	291
B.C./C.-B.	1,994	58	2,052	18.2	8.3	17.6	1,544
Yukon/Yukon	2	0	2	..	0.0	..	1
N.W.T./T.N.-O.	7	1	8	0.1	0.1	0.1	4
Canada	**10,942**	**702**	**11,644**	**100.0**	**100.0**	**100.0**	**8,274**
AGE/AGE							
PEDIATRIC CASES/ENFANTS:							
< 1	23	32	55	0.2	4.6	0.5	n.a.
1-4	17	19	36	0.2	2.7	0.3	n.a.
5-9	9	1	10	0.1	0.1	0.1	n.a.
10-14	13	1	14	0.1	0.1	0.1	n.a.
Subtotal/Sous-Total	**62**	**53**	**115**	**0.6**	**7.5**	**1.0**	**72**
ADULTS/ADULTES:							
15-19	35	3	38	0.3	0.4	0.3	24
20-29	1,873	195	2,068	17.1	27.8	17.8	1,258
30-39	4,869	250	5,119	44.5	35.6	44.0	3,056
40-49	2,989	92	3,081	27.3	13.1	26.5	1,943
50+	1,114	109	1,223	10.2	15.5	10.5	830
Subtotal/Sous-Total	**10,880**	**649**	**11,529**	**99.4**	**92.5**	**99.0**	**7,111**
Total	**10,942**	**702**	**11,644**	**100.0**	**100.0**	**100.0**	**7,183**

[1] Cases are attributed to the province where onset of illness occured./Les cas sont imputés â la province de résidence â l'installation de la maladie.

Source: Health and Welfare Canada, *Quarterly Surveillance Update: AIDS in Canada* (Ottawa: Health and Welfare Canada, HIV/AIDS Division, August, 1995).

Santé et Bien-être Canada, *Mise à jour de surveillance : le sida au Canada* (Ottawa : Santé et Bien-être Canada, Division du VIH/SIDA, august 1995).

TABLE 7.4

TABLEAU 7.4

Number of disease occurences among cases reported with AIDS, Canada, 1977 to June 30, 1995

Nombre d'affections[1] chez les cas de sida déclarés, Canada, 1977 au 30 juin 1995

ALL DISEASE OCCURENCES[1]/ TOUTES LES AFFECTIONS	NUMBER OF CASES/ NOMBRE DE CAS			NUMBER OF KNOWN DEATHS/ NOMBRE DE DÉCÈS CONNUS		
	MALE/ HOMMES	FEMALE/ FEMMES	TOTAL/ Total	MALE/ HOMMES	FEMALE/ FEMMES	TOTAL/ TOTAL
PEDIATRIC CASES/ENFANTS:						
Candidiasis/Candidiase	n.a.	n.a.	21	n.a.	n.a.	12
Crypto	n.a.	n.a.	13	n.a.	n.a.	13
CMV/MCV	n.a.	n.a.	26	n.a.	n.a.	21
Dementia	n.a.	n.a.	36	n.a.	n.a.	23
Herpes	n.a.	n.a.	5	n.a.	n.a.	3
Other opportunistic infections/ Autre infections opportunistes	n.a.	n.a.	9	n.a.	n.a.	6
PCP/PPC	n.a.	n.a.	37	n.a.	n.a.	29
HIV Wasting Syndrome/ Syndrome d'émaciation à VIH	n.a.	n.a.	16	n.a.	n.a.	11
Bact. Infect	n.a.	n.a.	7	n.a.	n.a.	3
LIP/PLI	n.a.	n.a.	17	n.a.	n.a.	9
Total[1]	**n.a.**	**n.a.**	**187**	**n.a.**	**n.a.**	**130**
ADULTS/ADULTES:						
KS/SK	2,394	18	2,412	1,787	15	1,802
PCP/PPC	5,646	301	5,947	4,146	211	4,357
Candidiasis/Candidiase	1,992	197	2,189	1,410	118	1,528
HIV wasting syndrome/ Syndrome d'émaciation à VIH	1,217	76	1,293	1,017	57	1,074
CMV	1,217	72	1,289	1,013	53	1,066
Dementia	757	40	797	659	32	691
Herpes	559	58	617	438	39	477
Mycobact/Extp	1,349	73	1,422	1,144	48	1,192
Non-Hodgkin's lymphoma/ Lymphomes (Non-Hodgkinien)	572	22	594	474	18	492
Toxo. Brain	551	57	608	436	42	478
Other opportunistic infections/ Autre infections opportunistes	1,091	57	1,148	876	41	917
Pulmonary tuberculosis/ Tuberculose pulmonaire	47	9	56	13	3	16
Invasive cervical cancer/ Cancer invasif du col utérin	0	2	2	0	0	0
Total[1]	**17,392**	**982**	**18,374**	**13,413**	**677**	**14,090**

[1] Since some cases report more than 1 disease, the total number of diseases is greater than the total number of cases./Puisque plus d'une infection sont parfois déclarées par cas, le total des infections est supérieur au total des cas.

Source: Health and Welfare Canada, *Quarterly Surveillance Update: AIDS in Canada* (Ottawa: Health and Welfare Canada, HIV/AIDS Division, August, 1995).

Santé et Bien-être Canada, *Mise à jour de surveillance : le sida au Canada* (Ottawa : Santé et Bien-être Canada, Division du VIH/SIDA, august 1995).

8 Fetal Alcohol Syndrome

Tables

8 Le syndrome d'alcoolisme foetal

Tableaux

Highlights

★ Fetal alcohol syndrome (FAS) involves growth deficiencies, central nervous system problems and a characteristic face with short eye openings, a thin upper lip and a flattened groove in the middle of the upper lip. FAS can occur depending on how much the mother drinks when she's pregnant and the characteristics of the mother or fetus. Binge drinking is the pattern associated with FAS.

★ In 1992/93, 18 pregnant women across Canada were diagnosed as damaging the fetus because of their drinking, and 74 babies were treated because of "noxious influences transmitted via the placenta or breast milk".

★ In 1992/93, 250 pregnant women were treated for drug dependence. Thirty per cent were between age 20 and 24 and more than half were between 25 and 34. Only 10 cases of suspected damage to the fetus were reported. Approximately 72 cases of drug withdrawal syndrome in the new-born and 18 cases of suspected damage to the fetus were reported.

★ About 0.33 cases of FAS occur in every 1,000 births in western countries; about 100 children are born in Canada each year with FAS. The incidence of FAS in some Native communities is much higher than other parts of Canada

Points saillants

★ Le syndrome d'alcoolisme foetal (SAF) concerne les inhibitions de croissance, les troubles du système nerveux central et un faciès caractérisé par une petite ouverture des yeux, une lèvre supérieure mince, et un sillon aplati au milieu de la lèvre supérieure. L'apparition du SAF est fonction de la quantité d'alcool consommé par la mère durant la grossesse, ainsi que des caractéristiques de la mère ou du foetus. On associe normalement le SAF avec les beuveries fréquentes.

★ En 1992-1993, dans tout le Canada, on a relevé seulement 18 femmes enceintes ayant reçu un diagnostic de préjudices au foetus dus à la consommation d'alcool, alors que 74 bébés ont été traités pour «influences nocives transmises par le placenta ou le lait maternel».

★ En 1992-1993, 250 femmes enceintes ont été traitées pour dépendance aux drogues. Trente pour cent avaient entre 20 et 24 ans et plus de la moitié entre 25 et 34 ans. Seulement 10 cas de préjudices potentiels au foetus ont été déclarés. Quelque 72 cas de syndrome de sevrage de drogue chez les nouveau-nés et 18 cas de préjudices possibles au foetus ont été déclarés.

★ On établit le nombre de cas de SAF à 0,33 par 1 000 naissances dans les pays occidentaux. Au Canada, une centaine d'enfants naîtraient victimes du SAF chaque année. L'incidence du SAF dans certaines communautés autochtones est nettement plus élevée qu'ailleurs au Canada.

Fetal Alcohol Syndrome

by Diane McKenzie, Canadian Centre on Substance Abuse

Terminology

The effect of alcohol on the fetus was first described in 1973 (Jones and Smith, 1973). Since that time, more than 5,000 articles have been published on the topic (Abel and Sokol, 1990). Studies show that drinking during pregnancy can result in a variety of alcohol-related birth defects known as the fetal alcohol syndrome (FAS). This syndrome is defined by growth deficiencies (prenatal and/or postnatal growth retardation with weight and/or length below the 10th percentile), central nervous system involvement (including neurological abnormalities, developmental delays, behavioural dysfunction, intellectual impairment, and skull or brain malformations) and a characteristic face (with short palpebral fissures [eye openings], a thin upper lip and an elongated, flattened philtrum [the groove in the middle of the upper lip]) (U.S. Department of Health and Human Services, 1991). When some, but not all of these abnormalities are found and prenatal alcohol use is a possible cause, the term fetal alcohol effects (FAE) is used. FAS and FAE are life-long disorders (Ashley, 1994).

The occurrence of FAS and FAE depends on how much the mother drinks during pregnancy, in combination with other factors (Ashley, 1994). These factors relate to the use of alcohol and the characteristics of the mother or fetus. For example, the frequency and quantity of alcohol consumed during pregnancy, the stage of fetal development at the time of its exposure, the nutritional status of the mother, use of other drugs, the genetic background of the mother and fetus and the mother's state of health affect the development of FAS (Michaelis and Michaelis, 1994). The age, weight,

Le syndrome d'alcoolisme foetal

par Diane McKenzie, Centre canadien de lutte contre l'alcoolisme et les toxicomanies

Terminologie

L'effet de l'alcool sur le foetus a été décrit pour la première fois en 1973 (Jones et Smith, 1973). Depuis, plus de 5 000 articles ont été publiés sur le sujet (Abel et Sokol, 1990). Des études démontrent que la consommation d'alcool durant la grossesse peut entraîner diverses malformations congénitales appelées «syndrome d'alcoolisme foetal (SAF)». Ce syndrome se traduit par des inhibitions de croissance (retard de croissance prénatal et/ou postnatal donnant un poids et/ou une longueur au dessous du 10e percentile), des troubles du système nerveux central (comprenant des anomalies neurologiques, des retards de développement, un comportement dysfonctionnel, un affaiblissement intellectuel, des malformations crâniennes ou cérébrales), ainsi qu'un faciès particulier (courtes fentes palpébrales [ouvertures des yeux], une lèvre supérieure mince et un enfoncement allongé et aplati de la lèvre supérieure [le sillon de la lèvre supérieure]) (U.S. Department of Health and Human Services, 1991). Lorsque certaines de ces anomalies seulement sont présentes et que la consommation prénatale d'alcool constitue une cause possible, on parle alors des effets de l'alcoolisme foetal (EAF). Le SAF et les EAF sont des troubles permanents (Ashley, 1994).

L'apparition du SAF et des EAF dépendra dans quelle mesure la mère aura bu durant la grossesse, en association avec d'autres facteurs (Ashley, 1994). Ces facteurs concernent la consommation d'alcool et les caractéristiques de la mère ou du foetus. Par exemple, la fréquence des consommations et la quantité d'alcool consommé durant la grossesse, le stade de développement du foetus au moment de son exposition, l'état nutritionnel de la mère, la consommation d'autres drogues, le bagage génétique de la mère et du foetus et

number of children and smoking habits of the mother are important as well. Binge drinking is the pattern associated with FAS. Some racial groups or subgroups may be more susceptible to the adverse effects of alcohol because of differences in the way alcohol is metabolized (May, 1991; Ashley, 1994). The primary metabolic product of alcohol, acetaldehyde, may be responsible for some FAS effects (Michaelis and Michaelis, 1994).

The Effect of Alcohol During Stages of Fetal Development

The consumption of large quantities of alcohol during two stages of human development can lead to FAS. The first stage is the *embryonic period* (up to eight weeks of gestation) and the second stage is the *fetal period* (from eight weeks to delivery). During the embryonic period, abnormalities can be produced by different drugs that enter the blood stream directly or are taken in the mother's diet. Chemical agents that lead to malformation in the fetus are called teratogens. Teratogens act selectively on certain organs. The effect depends on the timing of the exposure, how much of the chemical is taken by the mother (dose) and the sensitivity of each developing organ to the chemical (Larsson, 1973; Michaelis and Michaelis, 1994). Exposure to alcohol during the embryonic stage lead to malformations of the head and face (Michaelis and Michaelis, 1994). These are the most common abnormalities seen in FAS. The effects of exposure in the fetal stage include growth retardation and neurological defects (Scialli, 1992; Coles, 1994). (See Table 8.1 for a list of the life long effects of FAS.)

INCIDENCE: The formal diagnosis of FAS and FAE is difficult; only a small proportion of affected mothers and babies are accounted for in official statistics.[1] For example, in 1992/93 only 18 pregnant women across Canada were diagnosed as damaging the fetus because

---

[1] Little and associates (1990) found a 100 percent failure rate to diagnose FAS at birth in a large teaching hospital.

l'état de santé de la mère influencent tous le développement du SAF (Michaelis et Michaelis, 1994). L'âge, le poids, le nombre d'enfants et le tabagisme de la mère sont aussi importants. On associe les beuveries fréquentes au SAF. Certains groupes ou sous-groupes ethniques peuvent s'avérer plus vulnérables que d'autres aux effets nocifs de l'alcool, selon leur métabolisme de l'alcool (May, 1991; Ashley, 1994). Le principal produit métabolique de l'alcool, l'acétaldéhyde, peut engendrer certains effets du SAF (Michaelis et Michaelis, 1994).

L'effet de l'alcool durant les stades de développement du foetus

La consommation d'importantes quantités d'alcool durant deux stades précis du développement peut induire le SAF. Le premier est la période embryonnaire (jusqu'à la huitième semaine du développement dans l'utérus) et le deuxième, la période foetale (de la huitième semaine du développement à l'accouchement). Durant la période embryonnaire, la pénétration directe de drogues dans le circuit sanguin ou leur introduction par l'alimentation de la mère peut provoquer des anomalies. Les agents chimiques susceptibles de provoquer des monstruosités chez le foetus sont appelés les tératogènes. Ces agents agissent sélectivement sur certains organes. Leur effet variera selon le moment de l'exposition, la dose chimique absorbée par la mère et la sensibilité de chaque organe en développement au produit chimique en cause (Larsson, 1973; Michaelis et Michaelis, 1994). L'exposition à l'alcool durant le stade embryonnaire entraîne des malformations de la tête et du faciès (Michaelis et Michaelis, 1994), soit les anomalies les plus communes observées chez les victimes du SAF. L'exposition durant le stade foetal entraînera notamment un retard de croissance et des anomalies neurologiques (Scialli, 1992; Coles, 1994). (Pour une liste des effets permanents du SAF, voir le Tableau 8.1.)

L'INCIDENCE : Poser un diagnostic formel de SAF et de EAF n'est pas facile; seule une petite proportion des mères et des bébés affectés sont inclus dans les statistiques officielles.[1] Ainsi en 1992-1993, dans tout le Canada, on a relevé seulement 18 femmes enceintes ayant reçu un diagnostic de préjudices au foetus dus à la consommation d'alcool (Tableau 8.2). En outre, 74

of their drinking (Table 8.2). In addition, 74 babies were treated in hospital because of "noxious influences transmitted by the placenta or breast milk".

More is known about the effects of drugs on mothers and their unborn babies. In 1992/93, 250 pregnant women were treated for drug dependence (Table 8.2). One third of these women were between age 20 and 24 and one half were between 25 and 34. Only 10 cases of suspected damage to the fetus and 72 cases of drug withdrawal syndrome in the new-born were reported.

There are no national data on the rate of occurrence of FAS and FAE in Canada (Ashley, 1994). Conservative estimates are that 0.33 cases of FAS occur in every 1,000 births in western countries (Abel and Sokol, 1991). This estimate means that approximately 100 children are born in Canada each year with FAS (Ashley, 1994) and approximately 1,200 cases occur in the United States (Abel and Sokol, 1991). In some remote, rural communities and some Aboriginal communities, the incidence of FAS is much higher than for Canada as a whole (Standing Committee on Health and Welfare, 1992). The incidence of FAE is about three times higher than the full FAS (House of Commons, 1991).

Although few studies exist, the incidence of FAS in some Aboriginal communities is much higher than in other parts of Canada (Scott, 1994). Despite the methodological weaknesses of these studies, Robinson et al. (1987) found a rate of 190 FAS/FAE cases in 1,000 children. Two thirds of the affected children were mentally retarded. Wong estimated that FAS occurred in 4.7/1,000 births of Native children, compared with 0.25/1,000 births in the general population, including Natives (Abel and Sokol, 1991). Asante and Nelms-Matzke found an FAS/FAE rate of 25/1,000 children (age 0 to 16) among Native groups in Northwestern British Columbia (Métis and Indian) and 46/1,000 among those in the Yukon, as compared to 0.4/1,000 for other groups in both regions (Asante and Nelms-Matzke, 1985).

American studies show Native FAS incidence ranging from 1.4/1,000 to 9.8/1,000 (McTimoney et

bébés ont été traités dans les hôpitaux pour «influences nocives transmises par le placenta ou le lait maternel».

On connaît mieux cependant les effets des drogues sur les mères et leurs enfants à naître. En 1992-1993, 250 femmes enceintes ont été traitées pour dépendance aux drogues (Tableau 8.2). Un tiers de ces femmes avaient entre 20 et 24 ans et une moitié entre 25 et 34 ans. Seulement 10 cas de préjudices potentiels au foetus et 72 cas de syndrome de sevrage de drogue chez les nouveau-nés ont été déclarés.

Il n'existe aucune donnée nationale sur le taux d'incidence du SAF et des EAF au Canada (Ashley, 1994). Selon des estimations conservatrices, on établit le nombre de cas de SAF à 0,33 par 1 000 naissances dans les pays occidentaux (Abel et Sokol, 1991). Il naîtrait ainsi chaque année au Canada quelque 100 enfants victimes du SAF (Ashley, 1994) et quelque 1 200 aux Etats-Unis (Abel et Sokol, 1991). L'incidence du SAF de certaines communautés rurales isolées et de certaines communautés autochtones est supérieure à l'incidence nationale (Comité permanent de la santé et du bien-être social, 1992). L'incidence des EAF est environ trois fois plus grande que celle du SAF (Chambre des communes, 1991).

Peu d'études ont été effectuées, mais il est déjà permis d'affirmer que l'ncidence du SAF est beaucoup plus grande dans certaines communautés autochtones qu'ailleurs au Canada (Scott, 1994). Malgré les faiblesses méthodologiques de ces études, le collectif Robinson (1987) a établi l'incidence du SAF et des EAF à 190 cas par 1 000 enfants. Il a été constaté que les deux tiers des enfants atteints étaient mentalement retardés. Wong a évalué la manifestation du SAF à 4,7 naissances autochtones sur 1 000, contre 0,25 sur 1 000 pour la population en général, les Autochtones compris (Abel et Sokol, 1991). Asante et Nelms-Matzke ont pour leur part conclu à un taux (SAF et EAF) de 25 sur 1 000 enfants (de 0 à 16 ans) chez les Autochtones du nord-

---

[1] Le collectif Little (1990) a constaté un taux d'échec de 100 % en ce qui concerne la capacité de diagnostiquer le SAF à la naissance, dans un important hôpital universitaire.

al., 1989; Scott, 1994). High FAS rates (5.1/1,000) have been reported in Alaskan Native populations as well (Christensen, 1990). The differences in incidence may be due to alcohol abuse in women of child-bearing years, variations in how alcohol is metabolized, drinking patterns or dietary deficiencies in communities (Asante, 1981).

Several characteristics have been identified in communities that indicate a high or low risk of alcohol problems, including FAS and FAE. For example, some Native communities have much higher rates of FAS and FAE than others because of the predominant drinking norms (Ashley, 1994; May, et al., 1987). FAS and FAE rates should change over time in these communities, fluctuating with the level and pattern of drinking. Tribal affiliation is another factor that influences drinking norms in ways similar to other cultures. Drinking norms vary greatly by community and by subgroups. Communities that are less socially integrated, where drinking habits differ in each subgroup, have higher levels of FAS/FAE among their children (Ashley, 1994).

METHODOLOGICAL ISSUES: Findings on fetal alcohol syndrome are far from conclusive. The methodological problems of these studies may distort estimates of FAS incidence. For example, in catchment area studies, FAS is diagnosed during the neonatal period, when characteristics like the facial features, central nervous system involvement and mental retardation are difficult to identify and do not emerge until children are older. Retrospective studies over-sample groups in which FAS is expected to occur more often. FAS may be overestimated if the health data come from organizations that charge for the information (i.e., insurance companies). Prospective studies may underestimate the incidence of FAS because women who are at greatest risk for FAS babies do not receive prenatal care.

There are other, more basic weaknesses in FAS studies, particularly for high risk populations. Studies of minority groups may be severely biased (Abel and Sokol, 1991). For example, two of the most common

ouest de la Colombie-Britannique (Métis et Indiens) et de 46 sur 1 000 chez ceux du Yukon, comparativement à 0,4 sur 1 000 chez les autres groupes des deux régions (Asante et Nelms-Matzke, 1985).

Selon des études américaines, l'incidence du SAF chez les Autochtones varie entre 1,4 à 9,8 sur 1 000 (McTimoney et coll., 1989; Scott, 1994). Des taux élevés du SAF (5,1 sur 1 000) ont aussi été déclarés chez les populations autochtones de l'Alaska (Christensen, 1990). Les écarts observés peuvent s'expliquer par les divers degrés de l'abus d'alcool chez les femmes durant l'âge de fécondité, les variations marquant le métabolisme de l'alcool, les habitudes de consommation et les carences alimentaires dans les diverses communautés (Asante, 1981).

Les communautés qui présentent des risques élevés ou peu élevés de problèmes d'alcool, SAF et EAF compris, présentent plusieurs particularités. Par exemple, certaines communautés autochtones ayant une propension marquée à consommer de l'alcool affichent des taux du SAF et de EAF beaucoup plus élevés que les autres (Ashley, 1994; May et coll., 1987). Ces taux devraient évoluer avec les années, en même temps que le niveau et le profil de consommation. L'affiliation tribale influence également les normes de consommation, tout comme dans le cas des autres cultures. Ces normes varient considérablement selon la communauté et le sous-groupe. Les communautés moins intégrées sur le plan social, dont les habitudes de consommation diffèrent dans chaque sous-groupe, comptent davantage de victimes du SAF et des EAF que les autres (Ashley, 1994).

QUESTIONS DE MÉTHODOLOGIE : L'information rassemblée sur le syndrome d'alcoolisme foetal est loin d'être définitive. En raison de lacunes méthodologiques, les études menées à ce jour risquent de donner lieu à des estimations erronées de l'incidence du SAF. Par exemple, dans les études fondées sur un bassin de collecte des données, le SAF est diagnostiqué durant la période néonatale, alors que les caractéristiques comme les traits faciaux, le comportement du système nerveux central et le retard mental sont difficiles à percevoir et n'apparaissent pas avant que l'enfant soit plus âgé. Les études rétrospectives ont tendance à tirer leurs

facial features associated with FAS — the short eyefolds and the flat philtrum — occur normally among Aboriginals and blacks. The potential cultural bias in these studies brings into question the findings of studies that found inordinately high incidence of FAS in these populations. Inaccurate diagnoses of FAS can lead to overestimating the effects of small amounts of alcohol taken during pregnancy, creating unnecessary panic in no-risk groups.

CONCLUSIONS: Children who meet the criteria for FAS are born only to mothers who drink large amounts of alcohol during pregnancy. Other risk factors are not well understood, e.g. women who drink heavily during pregnancy are often poor, undernourished, depressed and abused. These problems are present among heavy drinking populations generally.

The reasons for drinking during pregnancy are based not only on personal beliefs, but also on a complex mix of socio-environmental factors and other reinforcing factors. These factors include the drinking patterns of friends or family and the situations that lead to heavy drinking.

échantillons parmi les groupes dans lesquels on prévoit que le SAF se produira plus souvent. L'incidence du SAF peut aussi être surestimée lorsque les données sur la santé sont fournies par des organismes qui exigent le paiement d'un droit (c.-à-d. les compagnies d'assurance). Quant aux études prospectives, elles risquent de sous-évaluer l'incidence, puisque les femmes les plus susceptibles de donner naissance à des enfants victimes du SAF ne reçoivent pas de soins prénataux.

Les études sur le SAF présentent d'autres lacunes encore plus fondamentales, principalement en ce qui concerne les populations les plus vulnérables. Des études des groupes minoritaires peuvent s'avérer gravement faussées (Abel et Sokol, 1991). Par exemple, deux des caractéristiques faciales les plus courantes associées au SAF, la petite ouverture des yeux et le sillon aplati de la lèvre supérieure, apparaissent normalement chez les Autochtones et chez les Noirs. Or vu ces traits ethniques particuliers, il convient de s'interroger sur l'incidence démesurément élevée du SAF chez ces populations, telle que l'établissent certaines études. Des diagnostics erronés du SAF peuvent donner lieu à une surestimation des effets associés à la consommation de petites quantités d'alcool durant la grossesse et créer une panique injustifiée chez les groupes non à risque.

CONCLUSIONS : Les enfants correctement diagnostiqués victimes du SAF sont nés seulement de mères ayant consommé de fortes quantités d'alcool durant la grossesse. On saisit mal encore les autres facteurs de risque. Par exemple, les femmes qui boivent beaucoup durant la grossesse sont souvent pauvres, dénutries, déprimées et victimes d'abus. Ces problèmes sont normalement présents chez les populations qui consomment beaucoup.

Les raisons de boire durant la grossesse reposent non seulement sur des convictions personnelles, mais aussi sur une combinaison complexe de facteurs socio-environnementaux et d'autres facteurs de renforcement, dont entre autres les habitudes de consommation des amis ou de la famille et les situations qui mènent à une forte consommation.

References

Abel, E.L. and Sokol, R.J., 1990. "Is Occasional Light Drinking During Pregnancy Harmful?" in: Engs, R.N. (ed.). *Controversies in the Addictions Field: Volume 1.* Dubuque, Iowa: Kendall/Hunt Publishing Company.

Abel, E.L. and Sokol, R.J., 1991. "A Revised Conservative Estimate of the Incidence of FAS and its Economic Impact." *Alcoholism: Clinical and Experimental Research* 15 (3): 514-524.

Asante, K.O. and Nelms-Matzke, J., 1985. *Report on The Survey of Children with Chronic Handicaps and Fetal Alcohol Syndrome in the Yukon and Northwest British Columbia.*

Ashley, M.J., 1994. "Alcohol-related birth defects" in: McKenzie, D., *Aboriginal Substance Abuse: Research Issues.* Ottawa: Canadian Centre on Substance Abuse.

Bray, D.L. and Anderson, P.D., 1989. "Appraisal of the Epidemiology of Fetal Alcohol Syndrome Among Canadian Native People", *Canadian Journal of Public Health* 80: 42-45.

Canadian Centre on Substance Abuse., 1992. *Statement on Fetal Alcohol Effects.* Ottawa: Canadian Centre on Substance Abuse.

Carmichael Olson, H., Burgess, D.M. and Streissguth, A.P., 1992. "Fetal Alcohol Syndrome (FAS) and Fetal Alcohol Effects (FAE): A Life Span View, with Implications for Early Intervention" in: *Zero to Three. National Centre for Clinical Infant Programs* 13 (1): 24-29.

Christensen, R., 1990. "Health Problems Among Alaskan Eskimo Infants and Young Children", *Arctic Medical Research* 49:63-67.

Coles, C., 1994. "Critical Periods for Prenatal Alcohol Exposure: Evidence from animal and human studies", *Alcohol Health and Research World* 18 (1): 22-29.

Ouvrages de référence

Abel, E.L. et R.J. Sokol (1990). «Is Occasional Light Drinking During Pregnancy Harmful?» in Engs, R.N. (éd.). *Controversies in the Addictions Field: Volume 1.* Dubuque, Iowa : Kendall/Hunt Publishing Company.

Abel, E.L. et R.J. Sokol (1991). «A Revised Conservative Estimate of the Incidence of FAS and its Economic Impact.» *Alcoholism: Clinical and Experimental Research,* vol. 15, n° 3, p. 514-524.

Asante, K.O. et J. Nelms-Matzke (1985). *Report on The Survey of Children with Chronic Handicaps and Fetal Alcohol Syndrome in the Yukon and Northwest British Columbia.*

Ashley, M.J. (1994). «Alcohol-related birth defects» dans McKenzie, D., *Aboriginal Substance Abuse: Research Issues.* Ottawa : Centre canadien de lutte contre l'alcoolisme et les toxicomanies.

Bray, D.L. et P.D. Anderson (1989). «Appraisal of the Epidemiology of Fetal Alcohol Syndrome Among Canadian Native People», *Revue canadienne de santé publique,* n° 80. p. 42-45.

Centre canadien de lutte contre l'alcoolisme et les toxicomanies (1992). *Statement on Fetal Alcohol Effects.* Ottawa : Centre canadien de lutte contre l'alcoolisme et les toxicomanies.

Carmichael Olson, H., D.M. Burgess et A.P. Streissguth (1992). «Fetal Alcohol Syndrome (FAS) and Fetal Alcohol Effects (FAE): A Life Span View, with Implications for Early Intervention» dans *Zero to Three. National Centre for Clinical Infant Programs,* vol. 13, n° 1, p. 24-29.

Christensen, R. (1990). «Health Problems Among Alaskan Eskimo Infants and Young Children», *Arctic Medical Research,* n° 49, p. 63-67.

Coles, C. (1994) «Critical Periods for Prenatal Alcohol Exposure: Evidence from animal and human studies», *Alcohol Health and Research World,* vol. 18, n° 1, p. 22-29.

Government of Canada., 1992. *Fetal Alcohol Syndrome: From Awareness to Prevention*, Government Response to the Fifth Report of the Standing Committee of the House of Commons on Health and Welfare, Social Affairs, Seniors, and the Status of Women. Ottawa, Canada.

Issue No. 10, Minutes of Proceedings and Evidence of the Standing Committee on Health and Welfare, Social Affairs, Seniors and the Status of Women, June 11, 1992. *Fifth Report to the House: Foetal Alcohol Syndrome: A Preventable Tragedy*, Third Session of the Thirty-fourth Parliament, 1991-92. Ottawa, Canada.

Jones, K.L. and Smith, D.W., 1973. "Recognition of fetal alcohol syndrome in early infancy", *Lancet* 2: 999-1001.

Larsson, K.S., 1973. Contributions of teratology to fetal pharmacology. In: Bores, L., (ed.) *Fetal Pharmacology*, New York: Raven Press.

May, P.A., 1991. "Fetal alcohol effects among North American Indians. Evidence and implications for society", *Alcohol Health and Research World* 15: 239-248.

McTimoney, D.C., Savoy, R.C. and van Gaal, M.A., 1989. Your Child, Our Future! Fetal Alcohol Syndrome Education Package and Resource Kit.

Michaelis, E.K. and Michaelis, M.L., 1994. "Cellular and Molecular Bases of Alcohol's Teratogenic Effects", *Alcohol Health and Research World* 18 (1): 17-21.

Robinson, G.C., Conry, J.L. and Conry, R.F., 1987. "Clinical profile and prevalence of fetal alcohol syndrome in an isolated community in British Columbia", *Canadian Medical Association Journal* 137: 203-207.

Scialli, A.R., 1994. *A Clinical Guide to Reproductive and Developmental Toxicology*, Boca Raton, Fl.: CRC Press, 1992.

Scott, K. A., 1994. "Substance Use Among Indigenous Canadians" in: McKenzie, D., *Aboriginal Substance Abuse: Research Issues*, Ottawa: Canadian Centre on Substance Abuse.

Gouvernement du Canada (1992). *Le syndrome d'alcoolisme foetal : De la sensibilisation à la prévention*, Réponse du gouvernement au cinquième rapport du Comité permanent de la Chambre des communes de la santé et du bien-être social, des affaires sociales, du troisième âge et de la condition féminine, Ottawa, Canada.

Question n° 10, Procès-verbaux et Témoignages du Comité permanent de la santé et du bien-être social, des affaires sociales, du troisième âge et de la condition féminine, 11 juin 1992. *Cinquième rapport à la Chambre des communes, Le syndrome d'alcoolisme foetal : Une tragédie évitable*, Troisième session de la 34ᴇ Législature, 1991-1992, Ottawa, Canada.

Jones, K.L. et D.W. Smith (1973). «Recognition of fetal alcohol syndrome in early infancy», *Lancet*, n° 2, p. 999-1001.

Larsson, K.S. (1973), Contributions of teratology to fetal pharmacology, in Bores, L., (éd.) *Fetal Pharmacology*, New York : Raven Press.

May, P.A. (1991). «Fetal alcohol effects among North American Indians. Evidence and implications for society», *Alcohol Health and Research World*, 15, p. 239-248.

McTimoney, D.C., R.C. Savoy et M.A. van Gaal (1989). Your Child, Our Future! Fetal Alcohol Syndrome Education Package and Resource Kit.

Michaelis, E.K. et M.L. Michaelis (1994). «Cellular and Molecular Bases of Alcohol's Teratogenic Effects», *Alcohol Health and Research World*, vol. 18, n° 1, p. 17-21.

Robinson, G.C., J.L. Conry, et R.F. Conry (1987). «Clinical profile and prevalence of fetal alcohol syndrome in an isolated community in British Columbia», *Canadian Medical Association Journal*, n° 137, p. 203-207.

Scialli, A.R. (1994). *A Clinical Guide to Reproductive and Developmental Toxicology*, Boca Raton, Fl. : CRC Press, 1992.

Standing Committee on Health and Welfare, 1992. Social Affairs, Seniors and the Status of Women, *Foetal Alcohol Syndrome: A Preventable Tragedy*, Ottawa, Canada.

Steissguth, A.P., Aase, J. M., Clarren, S.K., Randels, S.P., LaDue, R.A., and Smith, D.F., 1991. "Fetal alcohol syndrome in adolescents and adults", *Journal of the American Medical Association* 265: 1961-1967.

U.S. Department of Health and Human Services, 1991. National Institute on Alcohol Abuse and Alcoholism. "Fetal Alcohol Syndrome", *Alcohol Alert* No. 13. Rockville, MD.

Young, T.J., 1991. "Native American Drinking: A Neglected Subject of Study and Research", *Journal of Drug Education* 21 (1): 65-72.

Scott, K. A. (1994). «Substance Use Among Indigenous Canadians» in McKenzie, D., *Aboriginal Substance Abuse: Research Issues*, Ottawa : Centre canadien de lutte contre l'alcoolisme et les toxicomanies.

Comité permanent de la santé et du bien-être social, des affaires sociales, du troisième âge et de la condition féminine (1992), *Le syndrome d'alcoolisme foetal : Une tragédie évitable*, Ottawa, Canada.

Steissguth, A.P., J.M. Aase, S.K. Clarren, S.P. Randels, R.A. LaDue, et D.F. Smith (1991). «Fetal alcohol syndrome in adolescents and adults», *Journal of the American Medical Association*, n° 265, p. 1961-1967.

U.S. Department of Health and Human Services (1991). National Institute on Alcohol Abuse and Alcoholism. «Fetal Alcohol Syndrome», *Alcohol Alert* n° 13. Rockville, MD.

Young, T.J. (1991). «Native American Drinking: A Neglected Subject of Study and Research», *Journal of Drug Education*, vol. 21, n° 1, p. 65-72.

Table 8.1 - Characteristics of FAS Children

(Carmichael Olsen et al., 1992).

Infants:

- small for height and weight
- jittery
- weak suck
- hyper-excitability
- fitful sleeping
- low muscle tone
- irritable
- poor adjustment to stimulation in their environment
- FAS should be considered when infants are diagnosed as "failure to thrive" since growth deficiency and problems in sucking are characteristic of both diagnostic classifications

Pre-school:

- short and thin
- butterfly-like movements
- hyperactive
- over-sensitive to the touch or other stimulation
- attention deficits
- fine motor difficulties
- developmental delays
- eye problems
- congenital anomalies

Table 8.1 - Caractéristiques des enfants victimes du SAF

(Carmichael Olsen et coll., 1992).

Première enfance :

- petit de taille et de poids
- agitation des membres
- difficulté de téter
- hyperexcitabilité
- sommeil agité
- faible tonicité
- irritabilité
- piètre adaptation aux stimuli de l'environnement
- Il conviendrait de considérer le SAF comme cause potentielle lorsqu'il y a diagnostic de «déficience du développement», puisque la déficience du développement et les difficultés de téter sont caractéristiques des deux classifications diagnostiques.

Enfance préscolaire :

- petit et maigre
- mouvements agités
- hyperactivité
- hypersensibilité au toucher ou à d'autres stimuli
- trouble déficitaire de l'attention
- troubles de la motricité fine
- retards du développement
- troubles oculaires
- anomalies congénitales

Middle Childhood:

- hyperactive
- highly distractible
- impulsive
- memory problems
- affectionate and interested in those around them
- lack social skills to make friends
- problems predicting the consequences of their behaviour
- developmental deficits leading to academic problems
- tend toward concrete thinking, interfering with learning abstract concepts required in subjects such as math

Adolescent and Adult Development:

- after puberty, the facial features and growth deficiency become less marked
- remain short and have small head size
- adults may have an average IQ in the mildly mentally retarded range
- range of functioning — from severe retardation to normal intelligence
- attention deficits
- poor judgement
- impulsiveness
- problems become obstacles to employment and stable living
- at risk for depression and alcohol abuse

Enfance intermédiaire :

- hyperactive
- grande distractibilité
- impulsivité
- déficience de la mémoire
- affectuosité et intérêt envers les personnes de l'entourage
- manque de sociabilité
- difficultés à prévoir les conséquences de leurs actes
- troubles développementaux menant à des difficultés scolaires
- difficulté à passer de la «pensée concrète» à la «pensée formelle», nécessaire à l'apprentissage notamment de disciplines telles les mathématiques

Passage à l'âge de l'adolescence et à l'âge adulte :

- après la puberté, les caractéristiques faciales et la déficience du développement s'atténuent
- le sujet reste petit et a une tête de petite taille
- les adultes ont parfois un quotient intellectuel correspondant à celui d'un déficient mental léger
- fonctionnement   arriération sévère à intelligence normale
- déficience de l'attention
- piètre jugement
- impulsivité
- les troubles et déficiences deviennent des obstacles à l'emploi et à une vie stable
- vulnérable à la dépression et à l'alcoolomanie

TABLE 8.2

TABLEAU 8.2

Alcohol and drug-related morbidity for mother and fetus, by diagnosis and gender, Canada, 1990-91 to 1992-93

Morbidité reliée à l'alcool et à la drogue, chez la mère et le foetus, selon le diagnostic et le sexe, Canada, 1990-1991 à 1992-1993

MORBIDITY/MORBIDITE	Male/Hommes			Female/Femmes			Total		
	1990-91	1991-92	1992-93	1990-91	1991-92	1992-93	1990-91	1991-92	1992-93
DRUG DEPENDENCE **DEPENDANCE A LA DROGUE**			COMPLICATIONS OF PREGNANCY, CHILDBIRTH AND THE PUERPERIUM:/ COMPLICATIONS DE LA GROSSESSE, DE LA ACCOUCHEMENT ET DU PUERPERIUM :						
Age/Âge									
15-19				26	20	21	26	20	21
20-24				57	59	87	57	59	87
25-34				92	110	124	92	110	124
35-44				16	8	18	16	8	18
Total				191	197	250	191	197	250
Province									
Nfld./T.-N.				2	-	1	2	-	1
N.S./N.-É.				3	3	4	3	3	4
N.B./N.-B.				2	1	1	2	1	1
Que./Québec				60	78	83	60	78	83
Ont./Ont.				44	37	45	44	37	45
Man./Man.				10	6	4	10	6	4
Sask./Sask.				4	12	7	4	12	7
Alta./Alb.				10	10	16	10	10	16
B.C./C.-B.				56	50	89	56	50	89
			SUSPECTED DAMAGE TO THE FETUS FROM DRUGS/ LESION FOETALE PRESUMEE DUE A LES DROGUES						
Age/Âge									
15-19				-	-	2	-	-	2
20-24				5	4	-	5	4	-
25-34				13	17	6	13	17	6
35-44				6	1	2	6	1	2
Total				24	22	10	24	22	10
Province									
N.B./N.-B.				-	-	1	-	-	1
Que./Qué.				15	12	4	15	12	4
Ont./Ont.				4	7	2	4	7	2
Man./Man.				1	-	-	1	-	-
Sask./Sask.				-	-	1	-	-	1
Alta./Alb.				1	2	1	1	2	1
B.C./C.-B.				3	1	1	3	1	1

TABLE 8.2 (continued)　　　　　　　　　　　　　　**TABLEAU 8.2** (suite)

Alcohol and drug-related morbidity for mother and fetus, by diagnosis and gender, Canada, 1990-91 to 1992-93

Morbidité reliée à l'alcool et à la drogue, chez la mère et le foetus, selon le diagnostic et le sexe, Canada, 1990-1991 à 1992-1993

MORBIDITY/MORBIDITE	Male/Hommes			Female/Femmes			Total		
	1990-91	1991-92	1992-93	1990-91	1991-92	1992-93	1990-91	1991-92	1992-93
DRUG DEPENDENCE / **DEPENDANCE A LA DROGUE**	CONDITIONS ORIGINATING IN THE PERINATAL PERIOD: DRUG WITHDRAWAL SYNDROME IN NEWBORN/ CERTAINES CONDITIONS D'ORIGINE PERINATALE : SYNDROME DE SEVRAGE DE LA DROGUE CHEZ LE NOUVEAU NE								
Age/Âge									
Less than 15/Moins de 15 ans	25	40	40	28	39	32	53	79	72
Province									
P.E.I./I.-P.-É.		1	-	-	-	-	-	1	-
N.S./N.-É.		1		-	-	-	-	1	-
N.B./N.-B.			1	-	1	1	-	1	2
Que./Québec		2	1	-	2	1	-	4	2
Ont./Ont.	3	3	2	1	3		4	6	2
Man./Man.		1	1	-	-	-	-	1	1
Sask./Sask.	3	3	2	-	1	-	3	4	2
Alta./Alb.		1		-	1	-	-	2	-
B.C./C.-B.	19	28	33	27	31	30	46	59	63
ALCOHOL / **ALCOOL**	SUSPECTED DAMAGE TO THE FETUS FROM MATERNAL ALCOHOL ADDICTION, LISTERIOSIS OR TOXOPLASMOSIS/ LESION FOETALE PRESUMEE DUE A L'ALCOOLISME, A UNE LISTERIOSE OU A UNE TAXOPLASMOSE CHEZ LA MERE								
Age/Âge									
15-19				1	2	2	1	2	2
20-24				6	3	4	6	3	4
25-34				12	6	11	12	6	11
35-44				2		1	2		1
Total				21	11	18	21	11	18
Province									
Nfld./T.-N.				1	-	-	1	-	-
N.S./N.-É.				-	1	1	-	1	1
N.B./N.-B.				3	1	1	3	1	1
Que./Qué.				6	4	-	6	4	-
Ont./Ont.				5	2	6	5	2	6
Man./Man.				-	-	3	-	-	3
Sask./Sask.				1	-	-	1	-	-
Alta./Alb.				4	-	6	4	-	6
B.C./C.-B.				1	3	1	1	3	1

TABLE 8.2 (concluded)

TABLEAU 8.2 (fin)

Alcohol and drug-related morbidity for mother and fetus, by diagnosis and gender, Canada, 1990-91 to 1992-93

Morbidité reliée à l'alcool et à la drogue, chez la mère et le foetus, selon le diagnostic et le sexe, Canada, 1990-1991 à 1992-1993

MORBIDITY/MORBIDITE	Male/Hommes			Female/Femmes			Total		
	1990-91	1991-92	1992-93	1990-91	1991-92	1992-93	1990-91	1991-92	1992-93
	NOXIOUS INFLUENCES TRANSMITTED VIA PLACENTA OR BREAST MILK/ INFLUENCES NOCIVES TRANSMISES PAR LE PLACENTA OU LE LAIT MATERNEL								
Age/Âge									
Less than 15/Moins de 15 ans	38	50	30	45	49	44	83	99	74
Province									
N.S./N.-É.				-	-	1	-	-	1
N.B./N.-B.				-	-	1	-	-	1
Que./Qué.				-	4	2	-	4	2
Ont./Ont.	4	7	2	5	1	3	9	8	5
Sask./Sask.	4	2	1	1	1	-	5	3	1
Alta./Alb.	2	3	3	1	2	6	3	5	9
B.C./C.-B.	28	38	24	38	41	31	66	79	55

Source: Data were obtained from the Canadian Centre for Health Information, Statistics Canada.

Données obtenues du Centre canadien d'information sur la santé, Statistique canada

9 Public Attitudes Towards Drug Use

9 Attitudes de la population concernant l'usage de la drogue

Highlights

★ In 1994, although the majority of Canadians favoured government controls on the sale of alcohol, support for additional intervention was less on some issues.

★ Canadians supported increases in prevention programs (74.4%), server intervention programs (75.5%), and treatment programs (64.6%).

★ 66.8% of Canadians oppose selling alcohol in convenience stores and 69.5% favour placing warning labels on alcoholic beverage containers.

★ 66.6% believe that beer and liquor store hours should stay the same and 45% believe that alcohol taxes should remain the same.

★ 27% think possession of cannabis should not be against the law and 67% think possession of small amounts should not have jail sentences.

★ 71% of smokers between 12 and 19 think smoking helps people relax and 31% think it helps people stay slim.

Points saillants

★ En 1994, la majorité des Canadiens ont appuyé les contrôles gouvernementaux sur la vente des boissons alcooliques, mais se sont montrés moins favorables à de nouvelles interventions possibles touchant d'autres aspects du dossier.

★ Les Canadiens approuvent l'élargissement des programmes de prévention (74,4 %), des programmes d'intervention des serveurs (75,5 %), et des programmes de traitement (64,6 %).

★ des Canadiens s'opposent à la vente de l'alcool dans les dépanneurs, et 69,5 % appuient l'inscription d'une mise en garde sur les contenants des boissons alcooliques.

★ croient que les magasins de bières et de liqueurs devraient garder les mêmes heures d'ouverture et 45 %, que l'on ne devrait pas modifier les taxes sur l'alcool.

★ 27 % croient qu'il faudrait légaliser la possession du cannabis et 67 %, que la possession de petites quantités ne devrait pas entraîner de peines d'emprisonnement.

★ 71 % des fumeurs de 12 à 19 ans croient que fumer favorise la détente et 31 %, que cela aide à rester mince.

Public Attitudes Towards Drug Use

by Diane McKenzie, Canadian Centre on Substance Abuse

Sources of Information

Surveys monitor changes in people's values, their views of government policies and their ideas about the benefits/harms of health practices. These changes are often used by government to guide decisions about alcohol, tobacco and other drugs. This section is based on the 1994 Canadian Alcohol and Drug Survey, the 1990 Health Promotion survey and the 1989 National Alcohol and Other Drugs Survey.[1]

Perceived health benefits

The 1990 Health Promotion Survey asked Canadians about whether certain health-related activities would improve their health and well-being. Four in five smokers (81%) felt they would benefit if they quit smoking and 16% of current drinkers felt they would benefit from drinking less (Table 9.1). Older Canadians were less likely to see a benefit from using less tobacco, alcohol or other drugs. Male drinkers were twice as likely as female drinkers to feel they would benefit from less drinking.

Importance of government action

The 1990 Health Promotion Survey also asked Canadians to rate (on a scale of 1 to 10) the importance of government intervention in certain health problems

---

[1] Only current smokers were asked about "Stop smoking" and current drinkers about "Reduce drinking". Current smokers represent 29% of the population while 81% of Canadians were current drinkers.

Attitudes de la population concernant l'usage de la drogue

par Diane McKenzie, Centre canadien de lutte contre l'alcoolisme et les toxicomanies

Sources d'information

Les enquêtes permettent de suivre l'évolution des citoyens, en ce qui touche notamment leurs valeurs, leurs perceptions des politiques gouvernementales et leurs opinions quant aux avantages et aux dangers des pratiques sanitaires. Dans leurs décisions sur l'alcool, le tabac et les autres drogues, les gouvernements tiennent compte de l'évolution observée. Le présent chapitre s'appuie sur l'Enquête canadienne sur l'alcool et les drogues de 1994, l'Enquête Promotion de la santé de 1990, et l'Enquête nationale sur l'alcool et les autres drogues de 1989.[1]

Avantages perçus pour la santé

A la question posée aux participants à l'Enquête Promotion de la santé de 1990, à savoir s'ils pouvaient, par certaines mesures sanitaires, améliorer leur santé et leur bien-être en général, 81 % des fumeurs, soit quatre sur cinq, ont répondu qu'ils auraient intérêt à cesser de fumer et 16 % des buveurs, à moins consommer (Tableau 9.1). Les plus âgés ont moins tendance que les autres à voir l'avantage de diminuer leur usage du tabac,

---

[1] Seuls les fumeurs et les buveurs ont eu à répondre respectivement aux questions posées sur le fait de «cesser de fumer» et de «réduire sa consommation d'alcool». Les fumeurs représentent 29 % de la population canadienne et les buveurs, 81 %.

(Table 9.2). The results reported reflect the percentage of Canadians who rated each action at a level of 7 or higher. Drug use (79%) is regarded as the most important substance-related topic for governments to address. AIDS (78%), alcohol problems (63%) and smoking (53%) were also a high priority. Women were more likely than men to regard government action as important. Younger Canadians were more concerned with AIDS, while older people thought drug abuse was more serious (Figure 9.1)

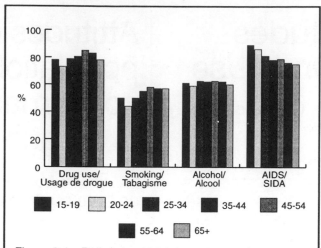

Figure 9.1   Belief about high importance of government action on selected health topics by age, Canada, 1990.

Figure 9.1   Opinion sur l'urgence d'une action gouvernementale face à certaines questions de santé, selon l'âge, Canada, 1990.

Canadians in Atlantic Canada showed more support for government intervention than other parts of the country. Government action had less support moving across Canada from east to west. There were no noticeable differences across income and education groups.

Opinions on alcohol and drug policy

According to the 1994 Canadian Alcohol and Drug Survey, there was widespread support for alcohol and drug prevention and control measures (Health Canada, 1995) (Table 9.3). The majority of Canadians supported increases in prevention programs (74.4%), strategies that prevent serving alcohol to intoxicated people (75.5%), and treatment programs (64.4%).

Two thirds of Canadians felt alcohol should not be sold in convenience stores (66.8%) and favoured placing warning labels on alcoholic beverage containers (69.5%). A similar proportion thought beer and liquor store hours should stay the same (66.6%). Over half of Canadians thought the drinking age (54.7%) and alcohol taxes (44.8%) should not change.

usage du tabac, de l'alcool ou des autres drogues. Les hommes sont deux fois plus nombreux que les femmes à croire au bienfait de réduire leur consommation d'alcool.

L'urgence d'une action gouvernementale

Lors de la même enquête, on avait aussi demandé aux participants de coter, sur une échelle de 1 à 10, l'urgence d'une action gouvernementale face à certaines questions de santé (Tableau 9.2). Les résultats présentés reflètent le taux des Canadiens qui ont attribué une cote 7 ou supérieure aux différentes questions. De celles reliées à l'abus des substances, ils ont classé comme étant les plus urgentes l'abus de drogue (79 %), puis le sida l'urgence d'une action gouvernementale face à certaines questions de santé (Tableau 9.2). Les résultats présentés reflètent le taux des Canadiens qui ont attribué une cote 7 ou supérieure aux différentes questions. De celles reliées à l'abus des substances, ils ont classé comme étant les plus urgentes l'abus de drogue (79 %), puis le sida (78 %), l'alcool (63 %), et le tabagisme (53 %). Les femmes sont plus nombreuses que les hommes à souhaiter une action gouvernementale. Les plus jeunes se préoccupent surtout du sida, et les plus âgés, de la drogue (Figure 9.1).

Les habitants des Maritimes accordent plus d'importance à l'action gouvernementale que ceux des autres régions du pays. En fait, cette importance diminue au fur et à mesure que l'on traverse le pays vers l'ouest. Aucun écart évident n'est observable entre les différents groupes de revenu et de niveau d'instruction.

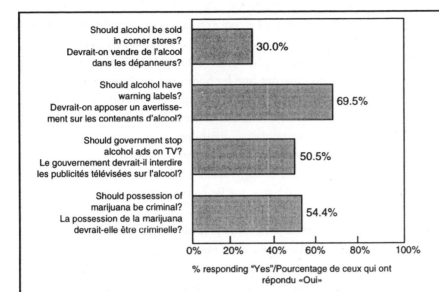

Figure 9.2   Public opinion concerning government policy relating to alcohol and drug use, age 15 and over, Canada, 1994, 1989.

Figure 9.2   Opinion publique sur la politique gouvernementale concernant l'usage de l'alcool et des drogues, population des 15 ans et plus, Canada, 1994, 1989.

Most Canadians wanted the government to increase health promotion and treatment activities. Canadians who favoured more restrictive alcohol policies and government funding for prevention and treatment tended to be female and older (Table 9.3). Women were more likely to support a higher drinking age, shorter hours of sale, more government counter-advertising. They also supported more server intervention programs, higher taxes and warning labels on alcoholic beverage containers. Older people favoured a higher drinking age, shorter hours of sale and higher taxes. They tended to be against the sale of alcohol in convenience stores. Young people under 19 years of age supported increases in alcohol prevention activities and warning labels.

Canadians showed less support for prevention and control measures in 1994 than they did in 1989 (Health Canada, 1995). For example, support for more government counter-advertising declined from 61% to 49% (Table 9.4). Support for increases in prevention programs (-6.6%), server intervention programs (-6.6%) and treatment programs (-9.5%) also declined. Fewer Canadians supported warning labels (-4.9%) and government counter-advertising (-12.3%) in 1994 than in 1989.

In the 1994 Canadian Alcohol and Drug Survey, people were asked about their opinion on the legal status

Opinions sur les politiques concernant l'alcool et les drogues

Selon l'Enquête canadienne sur l'alcool et les drogues de 1994, la population approuve généralement les mesures de prévention et de contrôle en matière d'alcool et de drogues (Santé Canada, 1995) (Tableau 9.3). La majorité des Canadiens appuient l'élargissement des programmes de prévention (74,4 %), des stratégies visant à éviter de servir les personnes déjà ivres (75,5 %), ainsi que des programmes de traitement (64,4 %).

Deux tiers des Canadiens estiment qu'il faudrait interdire la vente de l'alcool dans les dépanneurs (66,8 %) et souhaitent l'apposition d'une mise en garde sur les contenants de boissons alcooliques (69,5 %). Ils sont tout aussi nombreux à croire que les magasins de bières et de liqueurs devraient conserver les mêmes heures d'ouverture (66,6 %). Plus de la moitié favorisent le statut quo concernant l'âge de boire (54,7 %) et les taxes sur l'alcool (44,8 %).

La plupart des Canadiens souhaiteraient que le gouvernement intensifie les activités de promotion de la santé et de traitement. Ceux qui voudraient voir le gouvernement adopter des politiques plus restrictives

of marijuana (Health Canada, 1995). Over one quarter (27%) of Canadians thought possession of marijuana should be legal (Table 9.5). An additional 42% felt possession should be illegal, but have a fine or non-jail sentence as a penalty. About 17% thought possession of small quantities of marijuana should have a jail sentence.

Males were more likely than females to believe that the possession of small amounts of cannabis should be legal (33.4% and 20.8% respectively) (Table 9.5). They were also less likely than females to favour potential jail sentences for cannabis possession (14.7% and 18.9%). Support for jail sentences for possession declines with age. Young people (under 45) were more likely to support the policy that possession of cannabis should be legal than older Canadians. About one quarter of Canadians over 55 express no opinion about the legal status of cannabis possession.

The greatest support for legalizing possession of cannabis is in British Columbia (36.9%), Quebec (28.9%) and Alberta (28.2%) (Table 9.5). The least support for this policy was in Newfoundland (16.3%). By contrast, the greatest support for maintaining the illegal status of cannabis possession without a jail sentence was in Saskatchewan (52.9%), Prince Edward Island (47.8%) and Manitoba (47.2%). In 1989, over half (54%) of Canadians said possession of marijuana should be a criminal offence and 35% said possession should be legal.

Opinions on smoking

The 1995 Health Canada Survey on Smoking asked questions about people's beliefs and attitudes about smoking. The results indicated that one in three Canadians believed a long-term history of smoking can lead to health damage (Table 9.6). Half of Canadians thought smoking was relaxing (52.7%) and one in three thought smokers could quit anytime (35.2). Most people thought smoking was addictive (96.8%) and that the health of long-time smokers would improve (91.3%) if they quit. Men and women held similar

concernant l'alcool et financer les activités de prévention et de traitement sont en général des femmes et les personnes plus âgées (Tableau 9.3). Les femmes sont plus nombreuses que les hommes à souhaiter que l'on repousse l'âge de boire, que l'on écourte les heures d'ouverture, et que le gouvernement fasse davantage de contre-publicité. Elles approuvent aussi la multiplication des programmes d'intervention des serveurs, la majoration des taxes et l'apposition d'une mise en garde sur les contenants des boissons alcooliques. Les plus âgés souhaiteraient que l'on reporte l'âge de boire, que l'on réduire les heures d'ouverture et que l'on majore les taxes. Ils désapprouvent en général la vente de l'alcool dans les dépanneurs. Quant aux moins de 19 ans, ils appuient un plus grand nombre d'activités de prévention contre l'alcool et l'inscription de mises en garde sur les contenants.

En 1994, les Canadiens n'ont pas appuyé les mesures de prévention et de contrôle avec autant de ferveur qu'ils ne l'avaient fait en 1989 (Santé Canada, 1995). Ainsi, l'appui favorisant une plus grande contre-publicité gouvernementale est tombé de 61 % à 49 % (Tableau 9.4), tandis que celui des programmes de prévention a reculé de 6,6 %, des programmes d'intervention des serveurs, de 6,6 % et des programmes de traitement, de 9,5 %. Les Canadiens sont aussi moins nombreux en 1994 qu'en 1989 à appuyer l'apposition d'une mise en garde sur les contenants (-4,9 %) et la contre-publicité gouvernementale (-12,3 %).

Lors de l'Enquête canadienne sur l'alcool et les drogues de 1994, on a demandé aux participants leur opinion sur le statut légal de la marijuana (Santé Canada, 1995). Plus du quart (27 %) ont répondu qu'il faudrait légaliser sa possession (Tableau 9.5). Un additionnel 42 % considérait que sa possession devrait être illégale, mais entraîner une amende plutôt qu'une peine d'emprisonnement. Quelque 17 % estimaient cependant que la possession de petites quantités méritait une peine d'emprisonnement.

Les hommes étaient plus nombreux que les femmes à souhaiter la légalité de posséder de petites quantités de cannabis (33,4 % contre 20,8 %) (Tableau 9.5). Ils

opinions on most issues; men (56.8%) were more likely to think smoking was relaxing than women (48.8%).

According to the 1994 Youth Smoking Survey, most teenagers think tobacco is addictive, harms the health of non-smokers and that having even an occasional cigarette endangers health (Table 9.7). Young people age 10 to 14 (47%) are less likely to think health will improve if smoking stops than those 15 to 19 (69%).

The majority of teenage smokers believe smoking helps people relax (71%). One in three believe smoking reduces boredom (37%), that it is nicer to date people who don't smoke (36%) and smoking helps people stay slim (31%). Most teenagers who never smoked prefer to date people who don't smoke (77%). Teenagers do not think smoking is "cool".

References

Health and Welfare Canada, Stephens T., Fowler-Graham D., editors, *Canada's Health Promotion Survey 1990; Technical Report* (Ottawa: Ministry of Supply and Services Canada, 1993).

Health and Welfare Canada, Eliany M., Giesbrecht N., Nelson M., Wellman B and Wortley S., editors *National Alcohol and Other Drugs Survey (1989); Highlights Report* (Ottawa: Ministry of Supply and Government Services, 1990).

Health Canada, 1995. *Canada's Alcohol and Other Drugs Survey. Preview.* Minister of Supply and Services, 1995, Catalogue No. H39-338/1995E. ISBN 0-662-23876-1.

Health Canada, 1995. *Survey on Smoking in Canada, cycle 4.* (Ottawa: Health Canada, February, 1995).

Health Canada, 1995. *1994 Youth Smoking Survey* (Ottawa: Health Canada).

étaient moins nombreux à appuyer l'emprisonnement pour la possession de cannabis (14,7 % contre 18,9 %). La tendance à appuyer un tel emprisonnement diminue avec l'âge. Ainsi, les moins de 45 ans étaient plus susceptibles que les plus âgés d'appuyer une éventuelle légalisation de la possession de cannabis. Environ un quart des plus de 55 ans n'ont exprimé aucune opinion quant au statut légal de sa possession.

C'est en Colombie-Britannique que l'on retrouve le plus de défenseurs de la légalisation de la possession du cannabis (36,9 %), puis au Québec (28,9 %) et en Alberta (28,2 %) (Tableau 9.5) et à Terre-Neuve le moins grand nombre (16,3 %). Par contre, c'est en Saskatchewan (52,9 %), à l'Ile-du-Prince- Edouard (47,8 %) et au Manitoba (47,2 %) que le maintien du statut illégal de la possession de la marijuana, mais sans peine d'emprisonnement, trouve le plus grand appui. En 1989, plus de la moitié (54 %) des Canadiens ont déclaré que la possession de la marijuana devait être considérée comme une infraction pénale et 35 %, comme étant légale.

Opinions sur le tabagisme

Selon l'Enquête sur le tabagisme réalisée par Santé Canada en 1995, dans le cadre de laquelle on avait posé aux participants quelques questions sur leurs croyances et attitudes concernant le tabagisme, un Canadien sur trois croit que l'habitude de fumer peut à long terme nuire à la santé (Tableau 9.6), la moitié, que fumer procure la détente (52,7 %) et un tiers, que les fumeurs peuvent cesser de fumer comme ils le désirent (35,2 %). La moitié considèrent que fumer crée une dépendance (96,8 %) et que les fumeurs de longue date auraient une meilleure santé (91,3 %) s'ils cessaient. Les opinions des hommes et des femmes sur ces questions sont analogues, les hommes (56,8 %) étant cependant plus nombreux à croire que fumer procure une détente (48,8 %).

Selon l'Enquête sur le tabagisme chez les jeunes de 1994, la majorité des adolescents estiment que le tabac crée une dépendance, qu'il est nocif pour la santé des

non-fumeurs et que fumer même occasionnellement est dangereux pour la santé (Tableau 9.7). Les jeunes de 10 à 14 ans (47 %) sont moins nombreux que les 15 à 19 ans (69 %) à accepter que celui ou celle qui cesse de fumer aura une meilleure santé.

La majorité des fumeurs adolescents croient que fumer aide à se détendre (71 %). Un sur trois considèrent que fumer tue l'ennui (37 %), qu'il est plus agréable de sortir avec des personnes qui ne fument pas (36 %) et que fumer aide à rester mince (31 %). La plupart des adolescents qui n'ont jamais fumé préfèrent sortir avec des personnes qui ne fument pas (77 %). Les adolescents ne croient pas que fumer est «cool».

Ouvrages de référence

1. Santé et Bien-être Canada, T. Stephens, D. Fowler Graham, éditeurs. Enquête Promotion de la Santé (1990) : Rapport technique (Ottawa : Approvisionnements et Services Canada, 1993).

2. Santé et Bien-être Canada, M. Eliany, N. Giesbrecht, M. Nelson, B. Wellman et S. Wortley, éditeurs. Enquête nationale sur l'alcool et les autres drogues (1989) : Points saillants Report (Ottawa : Approvisionnements et Services Canada, 1990).

3. Santé Canada. Enquête canadienne sur l'alcool et les autres drogues (1995). Aperçu préliminaire. (Ottawa : Approvisionnements et Services Canada, 1995). Cat. no H39 338/1995F. ISBN 0 662 23876.

4. Santé Canada, 1995. Enquête sur le tabagisme au Canada, cycle 4. (Ottawa : Santé Canada, février 1995).

5. Santé Canada, 1995. Enquête sur le tabagisme chez les jeunes (1994). (Ottawa : Santé Canada).

TABLE 9.1   **TABLEAU 9.1**

Belief that particular actions would help Canadians to improve their health and well-being, by age, gender, province, income, and education, age 15 or older, Canada 1990

Opinions quant à la capacité de certaines mesures d'améliorer la santé et le bien-être des Canadiens, selon l'âge, le sexe, la province, le revenu, et le niveau d'instruction, population des 15 ans et plus, Canada, 1990

	STOP SMOKING[1]/ CESSER DE FUMER[1]	REDUCE DRINKING[1]/ CONSOMMER MOINS D'ALCOOL[1]	REDUCE DRUG USE/UTILISER MOINS DE DROGUE	POP. EST. (000's)/ POP. EST. (milliers)
AGE AND GENDER/AGE ET SEXE:				
Total 15+	81%	16%	9%	20,643
Male/Hommes	79	21	9	10,097
Female/Femmes	82	10	8	10,546
15-19	84	24	16	1,842
Male/Hommes	81	29	16	944
Female/Femmes	88	19	16	899
20-24	82	23	13	1,976
Male/Hommes	78	29	16	1,002
Female/Femmes	86	17	11	973
25-34	85	19	9	4,718
Male/Hommes	83	25	10	2,345
Female/Femmes	88	12	8	2,373
35-44	84	13	6	4,142
Male/Hommes	86	17	7	2,055
Female/Femmes	82	7	5*	2,087
45-54	83	14	8	2,808
Male/Hommes	80	17	7*	1,403
Female/Femmes	86	10	8	1,405
55-64	71	11	7	2,339
Male/Hommes	71	15	8*	1,143
Female/Femmes	71	6*	5*	1,197
65+	57	7*	7	1,818
Male/Hommes	54	9*	6*	1,205
Female/Femmes	61	—	8	1,613

TABLE 9.1 (concluded)   **TABLEAU 9.1** (fin)

Belief that particular actions would help Canadians to improve their health and well-being, by age, gender, province, income, and education, age 15 or older, Canada 1990

Opinions quant à la capacité de certaines mesures d'améliorer la santé et le bien-être des Canadiens, selon l'âge, le sexe, la province, le revenu, et le niveau d'instruction, population des 15 ans et plus, Canada, 1990

	STOP SMOKING[1]/ CESSER DE FUMER[1]	REDUCE DRINKING[1]/ CONSOMMER MOINS D'ALCOOL[1]	REDUCE DRUG USE/UTILISER MOINS DE DROGUE	POP. EST. (000's)/ POP. EST. (milliers)
PROVINCE:				
Nfld./T.-N.	84%	18%	14%	434
P.E.I/I.-P.-E.	80	16	8	99
N.S./N.-E.	84	16	8	697
N.B./N.-B.	81	16	7	560
Que./Qué.	79	15	8	5,313
Ont./Ont.	82	15	9	7,636
Man./Man.	78	15	11	834
Sask./Sask.	77	20	10	743
Alta./Alb.	82	17	10	1,862
B.C./C.-B.	81	16	8	2,464
INCOME ADEQUACY/REVENU:				
Very poor/Très faible	69%	15%*	14%	912
Other poor/Assez faible	75	15	10	1,466
Lower middle/ Moyennement faible	79	16	9	5,008
Upper middle/ Moyennement élevé	85	16	8	7,442
Rich/Supérieur	85	15	5	3,014
Unknown/Inconnu	74	15	11	2,801
EDUCATION LEVEL/NIVEAU D'INSTRUCTION:				
Elementary/Primaire	78%	16%	11%	6,859
Secondary/Secondaire	84	16	8	7,801
College/Collégial	85	15	8	2,544
University/Universitaire	79	13	6	2,947

*Moderate sampling variability; read with caution/Variabilité moyenne de l'échantillonnage; interpréter avec prudence.

— Data suppressed due to high sampling variability./Données supprimées en raison de la grande variabilité de l'échantillonnage.

[1] The results apply to only to current smokers for "Stop Smoking" and current drinkers for "Reduce Drinking"./S'applique exclusivement aux fumeurs ou buveurs actuels, selon le cas.

Source: Health and Welfare Canada, Stephens T., Fowler-Graham D., editors. *Canada's Health Promotion Survey 1990: Technical Report* (Ottawa: Ministry of Supply and Services Canada, 1993).

Santé et Bien-être Canada, Stephens T., D. Fowler-Graham, éditeurs. *Enquête Promotion de la santé 1990 :Rapport technique* (Ottawa :Approvisionnements et Services Canada, 1993).

TABLE 9.2

TABLEAU 9.2

Belief about high importance (rating 7-10 out of 10) of government action on selected health topics, by age, gender, province, income and education, age 15 or older, Canada 1990

Opinions sur l'urgence (cotée de 7 à 10 sur 10) d'une action gouvernementale face à certaines questions de santé, selon l'âge, le sexe, la province, le revenu et le niveau d'instruction, population des 15 ans et plus, Canada, 1990

	DRUG USE/ USAGE DE DROGUE	SMOKING/ TABAGISME	ALCOHOL PROBLEMS/ PROBLEMES D'ALCOOL	AIDS/ SIDA	POP. EST. (000's)/ POP. EST. (milliers)
AGE AND GENDER/AGE ET SEXE:					
Total 15+	79%	53%	63%	78%	20,643
Male/Hommes	75	48	55	74	10,097
Female/Femmes	84	57	71	82	10,546
15-19	77	50	61	89	1,842
Male/Hommes	72	44	53	87	944
Female/Femmes	82	57	69	91	899
20-24	72	44	59	85	1,976
Male/Hommes	62	39	49	81	1,002
Female/Femmes	82	50	70	89	973
25-34	78	50	65	81	4,718
Male/Hommes	74	46	56	75	2,345
Female/Femmes	83	54	73	87	2,373
35-44	81	54	64	77	4,142
Male/Hommes	75	49	56	70	2,055
Female/Femmes	86	58	72	83	2,087
45-54	85	58	65	78	2,808
Male/Hommes	82	53	57	75	1,403
Female/Femmes	88	63	74	82	1,405
55-64	83	56	64	71	2,339
Male/Hommes	81	56	58	70	1,143
Female/Femmes	85	57	69	73	1,197
65+	77	56	60	69	1,818
Male/Hommes	73	52	52	65	1,205
Female/Femmes	81	60	66	72	1,613

TABLE 9.2 (concluded)   **TABLEAU 9.2 (fin)**

Belief about high importance (rating 7-10 out of 10) of government action on selected health topics, by age, gender, province, income and education, age 15 or older, Canada 1990

Opinions sur l'urgence (cotée de 7 à 10 sur 10) d'une action gouvernementale face à certaines questions de santé, selon l'âge, le sexe, la province, le revenu et le niveau d'instruction, population des 15 ans et plus, Canada, 1990

	DRUG USE/ USAGE DE DROGUE	SMOKING/ TABAGISME	ALCOHOL PROBLEMS/ PROBLEMES D'ALCOOL	AIDS/ SIDA	POP. EST. (000's)/ POP. EST. (milliers)
PROVINCE:					
Nfld./T.-N.	86%	63%	72%	88%	434
P.E.I/I.-P.-E.	81	55	67	80	99
N.S./N.-E.	82	56	64	83	697
N.B./N.-B.	85	62	69	84	560
Que./Qué.	80	58	68	77	5,313
Ont./Ont.	80	50	60	79	7,636
Man./Man.	73	47	56	74	834
Sask./Sask.	78	46	60	73	743
Alta./Alb.	76	48	62	79	1,862
B.C./C.-B.	77	53	63	78	2,464
INCOME ADEQUACY/REVENU:					
Very poor/Très faible	76%	53%	65%	80%	912
Other poor/Assez faible	78	53	66	75	1,466
Lower middle/ Moyennement faible	84	57	69	84	5,008
Upper middle/ Moyennement élevé	83	53	64	81	7,442
Rich/Supérieur	81	54	62	79	3,014
Unknown/Inconnu	63	42	50	86	2,801
EDUCATION LEVEL/NIVEAU D'INSTRUCTION:					
Elementary/Primaire	80%	54%	65%	79%	6,859
Secondary/Secondaire	81	52	65	82	7,801
College/Collègial	84	57	65	80	2,544
University/Universitaire	79	57	60	76	2,947

*Moderate sampling variability; read with caution/Variabilité moyenne de l'échantillonnage; interpréter avec prudence.

— Data suppressed due to high sampling variability./Données supprimées en raison de la grande variabilité de l'échantillonnage.

Source: Health and Welfare Canada, Stephens T., Fowler-Graham D., editors. *Canada's Health Promotion Survey 1990: Technical Report* (Ottawa: Ministry of Supply and Services Canada, 1993).

Santé et Bien-être Canada, Stephens T., D. Fowler-Graham, éditeurs. *Enquête Promotion de la santé 1990 :Rapport technique* (Ottawa :Approvisionnements et Services Canada, 1993).

TABLE 9.3

TABLEAU 9.3

Public opinion on alcohol issues by gender, age, and province, Canada, 1994

Opinion publique sur les questions liées à l'alcool, selon le sexe, l'âge et la province, Canada, 1994

Variables	Favours higher drinking age/ En faveur d'une hausse de l'âge pour boire	Favours fewer store hours/ En faveur d'heures de vente raccourcies	Favours more ads against drinking/ En faveur de plus de publicité contre l'alcool	Favours more alcohol prevention/ En faveur de plus de prévention	Favours more to prevent drunks served/ En faveur de plus de prévention contre le service des personnes ivres
Total	38.3%	16.0%	48.8%	74.4%	75.5%
Gender/Sexe					
Male/Hommes	33.3	12.4	42.2	71.3	72.1
Female/Femmes	43.2	19.5	55.2	77.4	78.8
Age					
15-17	10.9%	12.6%	46.3%	66.1%	66.2%
18-19	14.8	10.0	40.8	75.7	71.4
20-24	24.1	9.6	51.9	80.5	77.0
25-34	35.6	12.5	53.0	78.4	78.3
35-44	41.7	16.2	51.6	77.0	77.9
45-54	46.0	18.4	49.3	74.2	78.0
55-64	46.1	18.9	43.4	69.7	71.5
65-74	47.2	20.8	42.8	69.7	72.4
75+	49.0	27.5	42.0	62.6	69.0
Province					
Nfld./T.-N.	42.8%	17.3%	57.2%	84.9%	83.9%
P.E.I./I.-P.-E.	33.5	15.4	56.2	83.8	82.5
N.S./N.-E.	36.7	12.7	52.2	81.9	82.8
N.B./N.-B.	34.5	19.6	55.3	79.4	76.3
Que./Qué.	37.2	16.0	53.1	75.3	76.5
Ont./Ont.	37.4	11.2	44.5	69.3	69.0
Man./Man.	45.9	18.6	45.8	76.5	82.1
Sask./Sask.	39.0	17.0	46.0	76.4	79.2
Alta./Alb..	46.8	33.0	46.6	76.7	82.3
B.C./C.-B.	35.5	17.0	52.3	80.2	81.4

TABLE 9.3 (concluded)

TABLEAU 9.3 (fin)

Public opinion on alcohol issues by gender, age, and province, Canada, 1994

Opinion publique sur les questions liées à l'alcool, selon le sexe, l'âge et la province, Canada, 1994

Variables	Favours more alcohol treatment/ En faveur de plus de traitement	Favours higher alcohol taxes/ En faveur d'une hausse des taxes	Favours alcohol warning labels/ En faveur des mises en garde sur l'alcool	Against alcohol in corner stores/ Contre la vente d'alcool dans les dépanneurs
Total	64.6%	25.4%	69.5%	66.8
Gender/Sexe				
Male/Hommes	59.7	20.8	63.8	57.1
Female/Femmes	69.3	29.8	75.1	76.2
Age				
15-17	68.4%	22.6%	76.9%	62.5%
18-19	72.7	19.1	68.1	69.1
20-24	68.6	21.4	66.6	67.3
25-34	66.1	21.6	68.6	65.7
35-44	65.3	26.9	67.8	66.3
45-54	66.1	28.8	68.3	64.6
55-64	60.8	26.1	70.5	64.2
65-74	57.7	26.7	74.7	72.6
75+	54.2	34.8	70.6	77.4
Province				
Nfld./T.-N.	76.6%	31.3%	87.4%	64.4%
P.E.I./Î.-P.-É.	60.3	22.5	78.1	77.0
N.S./N.-É.	69.7	24.0	79.9	72.5
N.B./N.-B.	69.7	27.1	83.6	60.7
Que./Qué.	65.7	21.7	68.3	52.3
Ont./Ont.	62.1	23.0	65.5	69.1
Man./Man.	66.0	28.6	69.9	85.3
Sask./Sask.	62.8	34.4	75.3	78.7
Alta./Alb..	59.0	31.6	71.2	75.5
B.C./C.-B.	69.4	31.0	72.5	74.3

Source: Data obtained from the Canadian Centre for Health Information, Statistics Canada.

Données obtenues du Centre canadien d'information sur la santé, Statistique Canada.

TABLE 9.4   **TABLEAU 9.4**

Trend in public opinion on alcohol issues,
Canada, 1989 and 1994

Tendance de l'opinion publique sur les questions liées
à l'alcool, Canada, 1989 et 1994

	1989	1994	Change/ Ecart
ACCESS CONTROLS/CONTROLE DE L'ACCES			
Taxes on alcoholic beverages should be/			
Les taxes sur l'alcool devraient :			
increased/être augmentées	27.0%	25.4%	-1.6%
remain the same/demeurer telles quelles	46.1	44.8	-1.3
decreased/diminuées	18.1	25.4	7.3
The legal drinking age should be/			
L'âge légal pour boire de l'alcool devrait :			
increased/être augmenté	49.7	38.3	-11.4
remain the same/demeurer tel quel	44.9	54.7	9.8
decreased/diminué	2.8	4.1	1.3
Alcohol outlet hours should be/			
Les heures de vente d'alcool devraient :			
increased/être prolongées	7.2	10.9	3.7
remain the same/demeurer telles quelles	69.9	66.6	-3.3
decreased/raccourcies	17.3	16.0	-1.3
Alcohol should be sold in convenience stores/			
L'alcool devrait être vendu dans les dépanneurs :			
Yes/Oui	23.4	30.0	6.6
No/Non	73.6	66.8	-6.8
PROMOTIONS AND COUNTERPROMOTIONS/PUBLICITE ET CONTRE-PUBLICITE			
Government advertising against alcohol should be/			
La publicité gouvernementale contre l'alcool devrait :			
increased/être augmentée	61.1%	48.8%	-12.3%
remain the same/demeurer telle quelle	28.0	34.4	6.4
decreased/être diminuée	6.4	12.9	6.5
Do you think alcohol beverages should have warning			
labels about possible health hazards?/			
Pensez-vous que les bouteilles d'alcool devraient porter des mises en garde			
contre les dangers éventuels sur la santé?			
Yes/Oui	74.4	69.5	-4.9
No/Non	22.5	27.6	5.1
INTERVENTIONS/INTERVENTIONS			
Alcohol and drug prevention programs should be/			
Les programmes de prévention contre les problèmes d'alcool ou de drogues devraient :			
increased/être augmentés	81.0%	74.4%	-6.6%
remain the same/demeurer tels quels	12.8	18.0	5.2
decreased/diminués	1.1	2.6	1.5

TABLE 9.4 (concluded)

TABLEAU 9.4 (fin)

Trend in public opinion on alcohol issues, Canada, 1989 and 1994

Tendance de l'opinion publique sur les questions liées à l'alcool, Canada, 1989 et 1994

	1989	1994	Change/ Ecart
INTERVENTIONS (continued)/INTERVENTIONS (suite)			
Preventing drunken people from being served should be/			
La prévention contre la prestation d'alcool aux personnes ivres devrait :			
increased/être augmentée	82.1	75.5	-6.6
remain the same/demeurer telle quelle	10.1	15.3	5.2
decreased/diminuée	3.1	5.2	2.1
Treatment programs should be/			
Les programmes de traitement devraient :			
increased/être augmentés	74.1	64.6	-9.5
remain the same/demeurer tels quels	13.6	24.2	10.6
decreased/diminués	0.8	2.3	1.5
IMPORTANCE OF ALCOHOL ISSUES/IMPORTANCE DES QUESTIONS LIEES A L'ALCOOL			
Drinking and driving in the neighbourhood is/			
La conduite en état d'ivresse dans le quartier :			
serious or very serious/est grave ou très grave	n.a.	25.8%	s/o
a problem but not very serious/n'est pas un problème très grave	n.a.	24.7	s/o
not a problem/n'est pas un problème	n.a.	41.7	s/o
don't know/ne sait pas	n.a.	7.2	s/o
Alcohol-related domestic violence is/			
La violence domestique liée à l'alcool :			
serious or very serious/est grave ou très grave	n.a.	18	s/o
a problem but not very serious/n'est pas un problème très grave	n.a.	19.8	n.a.
not a problem/n'est pas un problème	n.a.	48	s/o
don't know/ne sait pas	n.a.	13.6	s/o
Alcohol-related public fights in the neighboorhood are/			
Les bagarres publiques liées à l'alcool dans le quartier :			
serious or very serious/sont un problème grave ou très grave	n.a.	16.7	s/o
a problem but not very serious/ne sont pas un problème très grave	n.a.	23.1	s/o
not a problem/ne sont pas un problème	n.a.	53.4	s/o
don't know/ne sait pas	n.a.	6.3	s/o
Alcohol-related problems in the workplace are/			
Les problèmes liés à l'alcool en milieu de travail :			
serious or very serious/sont un problème grave ou très grave	n.a.	7.6	s/o
a problem but not very serious/ne sont pas un problème très grave	n.a.	13.5	s/o
not a problem/ne sont pas un problème	n.a.	47.8	s/o
not applicable (e.g. homemaker)/sans objet	n.a.	26.7	s/o
don't know/ne sait pas	n.a.	3.6	s/o

Source: Health and Welfare Canada, *National Alcohol and Other Drugs Survey* (Ottawa: Health and Welfare Canada, 1990); Data obtained from the Canadian Centre for Health Information, Statistics Canada.

Santé et Bien-Etre Canada, *Enquête nationale sur l'alcool et les autres drogues* (Ottawa: Santé et Bien-être Canada, 1990); Données obtenues du Centre canadien d'information sur la santé, Statistique Canada.

TABLE 9.5   **TABLEAU 9.5**

Attitudes/Opinions about smoking by age and sex, among those aged 15 or older, Canada, February 1995

Attitudes et opinions au sujet du tabagisme selon l'âge et le sexe, chez les personnes âgées de 15 ans et plus, Canada, février 1995

		AGE/				
	TOTAL	**15-19**	**20-24**	**25-44**	**45-64**	**65+**
Estimated population (000's)/ **Population estimée (Milliers)**						
Male/Homme	11,181	993	1,023	4,875	2,938	1,352
Female/Femme	11,585	943	1,013	4,829	2,978	1,822
Total	**22,765**	**1,936**	**2,036**	**9,703**	**5,915**	**3,174**
ATTITUDES TOWARD SMOKING/ **ATTITUDES A L'EGARD DU TABAGISME**			Percentage/Pourcentage			
Health is damaged only after smoking many years/ **La santé est endommagée seulement après plusieurs années de tabagisme:**						
Male/Homme	33.2%	28.7%	26.0%	30.7%	37.8%	41.2%
Female/Femme	25.1	19.2	15.7 *	18.3	33.6	37.2
Total	**29.1**	**24.1**	**20.9**	**24.6**	**35.7**	**38.9**
Occasional smoking is risky/ **Le tabagisme occasionnel est risqué:**						
Male/Homme	59.4	65.5	65.5	61.7	54.2	53.7
Female/Femme	62.7	72.4	75.5	69.8	52.7	48.3
Total	**61.1**	**68.9**	**70.5**	**65.7**	**53.4**	**50.6**
Smoking is relaxing/ **Le tabagisme détend:**						
Male/Homme	56.8	52.6	57.6	55.7	58.9	58.2
Female/Femme	48.8	42.5	48.0	48.3	50.9	50.2
Total	**52.7**	**47.6**	**52.8**	**52.0**	**54.9**	**53.6**
Quitting is worthwhile even after smoking many years/ **Arrêter de fumer en vaut la peine, même après plusieurs années:**						
Male/Homme	91.8	87.7	93.4	95.2	88.8	87.9
Female/Femme	90.8	88.1	92.1	93.6	90.9	84.0
Total	**91.3**	**87.9**	**92.8**	**94.4**	**89.9**	**85.6**
Smoking is addictive/ **La tabagisme crée une dépendance:**						
Male/Homme	96.4	97.9	97.3	97.7	95.6	91.3
Female/Femme	97.2	97.7	97.3	98.0		
Total	**96.8**	**97.8**	**97.3**	**97.8**	**96.9**	**92.4**
Smokers can quit anytime they wanted/ **Les fumeurs peuvent arrêter comme bon leur semble:**						
Male/Homme	34.2	34.2	39.0	32.8	29.3	46.0
Female/Femme	36.2	41.8	40.9	38.6	25.8	41.0
Total	**35.2**	**37.9**	**39.9**	**35.7**	**27.6**	**43.1**

*High sampling variability./Grande variabilité de l'échantillonnage.

Source: Health Canada, *Survey on Smoking in Canada, Cycle 4* (Ottawa: Health Canada, February 1995).

Santé Canada, *Sondage sur la tabagisme au Canada, 4e cycle* (Ottawa: Santé Canada, février 1995).

Attitudes and beliefs among youth aged 12 to 19, Canada, 1994

Attitudes et croyances parmi les jeunes âgés de 12 à 19 ans, Canada, 1994

BELIEFS AND ATTITUDES/ CROYANCES ET ATTITUDES	AGE/AGE	
	10-14	15-19
BELIEFS ABOUT HEALTH EFFECTS AND SMOKING/ CROYANCES AU SUJET DU TABAGISME ET DES EFFETS SUR LA SANTÉ:		
Tobacco is additive/ Le tabac crée une dépendance	85%	96%
Tobacco smoke can harm the health of non-smokers/ La fumée du tabac peut nuire à la santé des non-fumeurs	84	96
Quitting smoking reduces damage to health/ L'arrêt du tabagisme réduit les méfaits sur la santé	47	69
Occasional smoking endangers health/ Le tabagisme occasionnel est dangereux pour la santé	62	64
Smokers can quit anytime Les fumeurs peurent arrêter comme bon leur semble	17	23
Years of smoking necessary before health affected/ Des années de tabagisme sont nécessaires avant de nuire à la santé	21	20

BELIEFS ABOUT SMOKING/	CURRENT SMOKERS[1]/ FUMEURS ACTUELS	NEVER SMOKER[2]/ JAMAIS FUMEURS
Smoking helps people relax/ Fumer aide les gens à se détendre	71	31
Smoking can help when bored/ Fumer désennuie	37	10
Nicer to date people who don't smoke/ Il est plus agréable de fréquenter des non-fumeurs	36	77
Smoking helps people stay slim/ Le tabagisme aide à garder sa ligne	31	19
Smoking is cool/ Fumer, c'est «cool»	13	4

[1] **CURRENT SMOKER** - presently smokes cigarettes either daily or non-daily.
   FUMEURS ACTUELS - fume actuellement tous les jours ou occasionnellement.

[2] **NEVER SMOKER** - Presently does not smoke cigarettes and has smoked fewer than 100 in lifetime.
   JAMAIS FUMEURS - ne fume pas à l'heure actuelle et a fumé moins de 100 cigarettes dans sa vie.

Source: Health Canada, *1994 Youth Smoking Survey* (Ottawa: Health Canada, 1995).

        Santé Canada, Sondage sur le tabagisme chez les jeunes, 1994 (Ottawa: Santé Canada, 1995).

10 Economic Aspects

10 Les aspects économiques

Highlights

★ The average Canadian age 15 or older spent $462 on alcoholic beverages in 1992/93, and the value of alcohol sales totaled more than $10.4 billion.

★ Alcohol provided employment for 15,741 Canadians in 1993 and more than $4.2 billion in government revenue in 1992/93.

★ The reduction in tobacco taxes had dramatic economic impact. After a period of substantial increases in tax revenue despite declining rates of smoking, government revenue from tobacco products declined by $896.5 million or 16.2% in 1993/94 compared with the previous year. At the same time, exports of cigarettes (widely suspected of being smuggled back into the country) dropped from $814 million in 1993 to $190 million in 1994.

★ The domestic market for the pharmaceutical industry, which employs more than 21,000 Canadians, is valued at $4.3 billion.

★ It is estimated that substance abuse cost more than $18.4 billion in Canada in 1992, representing $649 per capita, or about 2.7% of the total Gross Domestic Product. Tobacco accounts for more than $9.5 billion in costs, alcohol accounts for approximately $7.5 billion in costs, and illicit drugs account cost the Canadian economy $1.4 billion in 1992. The largest economic costs of substance abuse are for lost productivity due to morbidity and premature mortality, direct health care costs and law enforcement. There is considerable variation in the costs of substance abuse between the provinces.

Points saillants

★ Le Canadien moyen de 15 ans et plus a dépensé 462 dollars en boissons alcooliques en 1992-1993, et la valeur des ventes d'alcool ont atteint plus de 10,4 milliards de dollars.

★ Le secteur des boissons alcooliques a fourni 15 741 emplois et représenté près de 4,2 milliards de dollars de recettes gouvernementales en 1992-1993.

★ La réduction des taxes sur le tabac a eu un impact majeur sur l'économie. Après une période de hausses substantielles des recettes fiscales en dépit d'un baisse du tabagisme, les recettes gouvernementales tirées des produits du tabac ont diminué de 896,5 millions de dollars, soit de 16,2 % en 1993-1994, par rapport à l'année précédente. Parallèlement, les exportations de cigarettes (pour la plupart potentiellement réintroduites en fraude au pays) sont tombées de 814 millions en 1993 à 190 millions en 1994.

★ Le marché national de l'industrie pharmaceutique, qui emploie plus de 21 000 Canadiens, est évalué à 4,3 milliards de dollars.

★ On estime que l'abus des drogues a coûté plus de 18,4 milliards à l'économie canadienne en 1992, soit 649 dollars par habitant ou 2,7 % du produit national brut, le tabac représentant plus de 9,5 milliards, l'alcool quelque 7,5 milliards, et les drogues illicites 1,4 milliard. Les coûts économiques se traduisent principalement par une perte de productivité due à la morbidité et à la mortalité prématurée, aux coûts directs des soins de santé et à la répression criminelle. Ces coûts diffèrent sensiblement d'une province à l'autre.

Economic Aspects

by Eric Single, Canadian Centre on Substance Abuse

Economic Aspects of Alcohol

For three decades the price of alcohol increased substantially, but generally at rates similar to other consumer goods (Table 10.1). Since 1986, however, the price of alcohol has increased at a slightly faster pace than the prices for other consumer goods. In 1992/93, the cost of 10 litres of absolute alcohol as a percentage of personal disposable income increased to 2.89% from 2.78% in 1991/92, and 2.68% in 1990/91 (Table 10.2).

In 1992/93, the sale of alcoholic beverages totaled $10.43 billion (Table 10.3). Although consumption has been declining, there have been small but consistent increases in the dollar value of sales in recent years (in terms of current dollars). The dollar value of spirit sales, however, has been declining, even without taking inflation into account. On average, Canadians age 15 or older spent $246 on beer, $83 on wine and $133 on spirits in 1992/93. The highest per capita expenditure on alcohol was in the Yukon ($947) and in the Northwest Territories ($722), reflecting the higher rates of consumption in these areas.

Alcohol provided more than $3.1 billion in revenue to provincial governments in 1992/93, mainly from sales income (Table 10.5). This represents 2.2% of total provincial revenues. Federal revenue from the sale of alcohol is no longer reported, but the Department of National Revenue reported federal revenue from alcohol-related excise duties and taxes (not including revenue from sales taxes or corporate income taxes) to be in excess of $1.1 billion in 1992/93.

Alcoholic beverages have a small but positive impact on Canada's balance of trade. The value of alcohol exports in 1992/93 was $680 million, compared to $631 million for alcohol imports. Spirits are the major type of exported alcohol, but there has been a marked

Les aspects économiques

par Eric Single, Centre canadien de lutte contre l'alcoolisme et les toxicomanies

Les aspects économiques de l'alcool

Pendant trois décennies, les prix de l'alcool ont sensiblement augmenté, mais à des taux se rapprochant sensiblement de ceux des autres biens de consommation (Tableau 10.1). Mais depuis 1986, ils ont progressé à un rythme légèrement plus rapide. En 1992-1993, considéré en pourcentage du revenu personnel net, le coût de 10 litres d'alcool absolu a augmenté de 2,79 % comparativement à 2,68 % l'année précédente (Tableau 10.2).

En 1992-1993, les ventes globales des boissons alcooliques ont atteint 10,43 milliards de dollars (Tableau 10.3). En fait, malgré une régression de la consommation, la valeur monétaire des ventes a enregistré des hausses légères mais constantes au cours des récentes années (en terme de dollars courants). La valeur monétaire des spiritueux a en revanche diminué, indépendamment de l'inflation. Cette même année, les 15 ans et plus ont en moyenne déboursé 246 dollars pour la bière, 83 dollars pour le vin et 133 dollars pour les spiritueux. La plus forte dépense par habitant en matière d'alcool revient au Yukon (947 $) puis aux Territoires du Nord-Ouest (722 $), ce qui reflète les taux plus élevés de consommation d'alcool dans ces régions.

L'alcool a rapporté plus de 3,1 milliards de dollars de recettes aux gouvernements provinciaux en 1992-1993, tirées en majeure partie des ventes (Tableau 10.5). Cela constitue 2,2 % des recettes provinciales globales. Les recettes fédérales provenant des ventes d'alcool ne sont plus déclarées, mais le ministère fédéral du Revenu a établi les recettes fédérales provenant des droits et taxes d'accise associées à l'alcool (excluant les recettes

increase in the value of beer imports over the past 15 years (Table 10.6). In 1992/93, however, the value of beer exports declined to $185.9 million from $192.8 million in the previous year.

In 1993, there were 15,741 persons employed in the production of alcoholic beverages, with salaries and wages totaling approximately $744 million (Table 10.7). Following more than a decade of generally stable employment figures, the number of persons employed in alcoholic beverage production has declined each year since 1988 when there 19,754 Canadians employed in the alcohol industry.

Economic Aspects of Tobacco

The price of cigarettes relative to other consumer items generally decreased from the late 1940s until 1980, but from 1980 until the dramatic reduction in federal taxes in 1994, cigarette price increases were far greater than increases in the prices of other items (Table 10.1). In 1994 cigarette prices fell by more than 40% while the consumer price index increased 0.9%.

Government revenue from tobacco products was $4.65 billion in 1993/94, with $2.24 billion going to the federal government and $2.42 billion to the provincial governments (Table 10.8). This represents a decline of $896.5 million or 16.2% from government revenues from tobacco in the previous year. In 1993/94 tobacco taxes represented 1.7% of total federal revenues, a decline from 2.2% in the previous year, while tobacco revenue accounted for 1.6% of provincial revenues, a decline from 1.9% in 1992/93. In April of 1994, taxes ranged from $1.48 (Quebec) to $5.14 (Newfoundland) on a 25-pack of cigarettes (Table 10.9).

Tobacco exports dropped substantially in 1994, suggesting that the bulk of exported cigarettes had previously been smuggled back into Canada. Whereas exported tobacco products were valued at $814 million in 1993, exports dropped to $189.7 million in 1994. The value of imported tobacco products increased from nearly $60 million in 1993 to $70.5 million in 1994 (Table 10.10). The value of tobacco exports had

provenant des taxes de vente ou de l'impôt sur les sociétés) à plus de 1,1 milliard de dollars en 1992-1993.

Les boissons alcooliques ont un léger impact, mais néanmoins positif, sur la balance commerciale canadienne. La valeur des exportations de ces produits en 1992-1993 s'établissait à 680 millions de dollars, contre 631 millions pour les importations. Quant à la valeur des exportations de bière, elle a atteint 185,9 millions de dollars comparativement à 192,8 millions l'année précédente.

En 1993, 15 741 personnes travaillaient à la production des boissons alcooliques, représentant des traitements et salaires globaux d'environ 744 millions de dollars (Tableau 10.7). Après plus de dix ans de stabilité de l'emploi, le nombre des employés du secteur de la production des boissons alcooliques a diminué à tous les ans depuis 1988, alors que l'industrie des boissons alcooliques employait 19 754 Canadiens.

Les aspects économiques du tabac

Par rapport aux autres biens de consommation, le prix des cigarettes a généralement diminué entre la fin des années 40 et 1980, mais de 1980 jusqu'à la réduction majeure des taxes fédérales en 1994, leur prix a accusé des hausses nettement supérieures à ceux des autres produits (Tableau 10.1). En 1994, les prix des cigarettes ont chuté de plus de 40 %, tandis que l'indice des prix à la consommation a augmenté de 0,9 %.

En 1993-1994, les recettes gouvernementales sur les produits du tabac étaient de 4,65 milliards de dollars, soit 2,24 milliards pour le fédéral et 2,42 pour les provinces (Tableau 10.8), représentant une baisse de 896,5 millions de dollars, ou de 16,2 %, par rapport à l'année précédente. En 1993-1994, les taxes sur le tabac représentaient 1,7 % des recettes fédérales globales, soit 2,2 % de moins que l'année précédente, et 1,6 % des recettes provinciales, soit 1,9 % de moins que l'année précédente, En avril 1994, les taxes sur le paquet de 25 cigarettes variaient entre 1,48 $ (Québec) et 5,14 $ (Terre-Neuve) (Tableau 10.9).

increased more than eight-fold from 1989 to 1993, and it was widely suspected that much of these exports were illegally re-imported back into Canada.

The number of persons employed in processing and manufacturing tobacco products was 4,778 in 1993, with salaries and wages totaling more than $258 million (Table 10.11). The number of persons employed in the tobacco industry has declined substantially from nearly 10,000 in 1977 to fewer than 5,000 in the 1990s.

Economic Aspects of Other Drugs

More than 21,000 Canadians were employed in the manufacture of pharmaceuticals and medicines in 1992, with salaries and wages totaling more than $851 million (Table 10.12). The domestic market for pharmaceuticals and medicines was valued at approximately $4.3 billion in 1990.

Reliable estimates of the size and value of the illicit drug trade are lacking. However, the RCMP does provide information on representative street prices of illegal drugs at successive stages of trafficking (Table 10.13). In 1992, the street price was estimated to be $35 to $50 for 0.1 gram of injectable (5% to 6%) heroin, $70 to $200 for 1 gram of 60% pure cocaine hydrochloride, $10 to $50 for 1 gram of Lebanese hashish, and $30 to $50 for 1 gram of Jamaican hashish.

The RCMP also provides data on the amount of illegal drugs seized (Table 10.14). There were large increases in the quantity of seizures for almost all classes of illicit drugs. For example, 144,548 kilograms of cannabis were seized in 1993, representing an increase of 25% over the previous year.

Estimated Economic Costs of Substance Abuse in Canada

A major study of the economic costs of substance abuse to the Canadian economy in 1992 was released in 1996 (Single et al., 1996). Utilizing recently developed international guidelines for cost estimation studies (Single et al., 1995), the study first estimated the

En 1994, les exportations du tabac ont considérablement diminué, laissant croire que la majeure partie des cigarettes exportées étaient réintroduites en fraude au Canada. Considérant que les exportations de tabac se chiffraient à 814 millions de dollars en 1993, elles sont passées à 189,7 millions en 1994. La valeur des produits du tabac importés est passée de près de 60 millions de dollars en 1993 à 70,5 millions en 1994 (Tableau 10.10). Quant à celle des produits exportés, elle était de huit fois supérieure en 1993 à ce qu'elle était en 1989, et l'on a de fortes raisons de croire qu'une bonne part de ces exportations étaient illégalement réintroduites au pays.

Le nombre des personnes travaillant au traitement et à la fabrication des produits du tabac atteignait 4 778 en 1993, représentant des salaires et traitements globaux de plus de 258 millions de dollars (Tableau 10.11). Les employés de ce secteur ont sensiblement diminué, passant de près de 10 000 en 1977 à moins de 5,000 dans les années 90.

Les aspects économiques des autres drogues

Plus de 21 000 Canadiens travaillaient dans le secteur de la production pharmaceutique en 1992, représentant des salaires et traitements globaux de plus de 851 millions de dollars (Tableau 10.12). Le marché national de cette industrie s'établissait à quelque 4,3 milliards en 1990.

Il n'existe pas suffisamment d'estimations fiables en ce qui concerne la taille et la valeur du marché des drogues illicites. La GRC nous renseigne toutefois quant aux prix de ces produits dans la rue à différentes étapes de leur trafic (Tableau 10.13). Ainsi, on estime qu'en 1992 il en coûtait de 35 à 50 dollars le 0,1 gramme d'héroïne injectable (concentration de 5 % à 6 %); de 70 à 200 dollars le gramme de chlorhydrate de cocaïne (concentration de 60 %); de 10 à 50 dollars le gramme de haschich libanais; et de 30 à 50 dollars le gramme de haschich jamaïquain.

number of deaths and hospitalizations attributable to alcohol, tobacco and illicit drugs in 1992 (see Chapters 2-4 for the results of this aspect of the analysis). These morbidity and mortality estimates were the basis for examining the costs of substance abuse to the health care system and productivity costs. Other costs included costs for the administration of substance-related social welfare payments, law enforcement, prevention, research and other direct costs such as fire damage (Single et al., 1996).

It is estimated that substance abuse cost more than $18.4 billion in Canada in 1992, representing $649 per capita, or about 2.7% of the total Gross Domestic Product (Table 10.15). Alcohol accounts for approximately $7.5 billion in costs, or $265 per capita. The largest economic costs of alcohol are $4.14 billion for lost productivity due to morbidity and premature mortality, $1.36 billion for law enforcement and $1.30 billion in direct health care costs. Tobacco accounts for more than $9.5 billion in costs, or approximately $340 per capita. Lost productivity due to premature mortality accounts for more than $6.7 billion of these costs and direct health care costs due to smoking account for $2.68 billion in costs. The economic costs of illicit drugs are estimated at $1.4 billion, or $48 per person. The largest cost due to illicit drugs is lost productivity due to morbidity and premature death ($823 million), and a substantial portion of the costs ($400 million) are for law enforcement.

The results are comparable with studies in other countries (Single et al., 1996) but somewhat lower than prior estimates in Canada. The authors took a decidedly conservative approach to estimating the costs of substance abuse. Sensitivity analyses were conducted on the use of alternative measures of alcohol consumption, alternative discount rates for estimating lost income due to premature mortality and the use of diagnostic-specific hospitalization costs. It was found that the choice of a discount rate for estimating lost productivity due to premature mortality made a substantial difference to the results, while the use of alternative

La GRC fournit aussi des données sur les quantités de drogues illicites saisies (Tableau 10.14). Or ces quantités ont nettement augmenté et cela, dans la plupart des catégories. Par exemple, en 1993, on a saisi 144 548 kilogrammes de cannabis, ce qui représente 25 % de plus que l'année précédente.

Coûts économiques estimatifs de l'abus des drogues au Canada

Sont parus, en 1996, les résultats d'une importante étude sur les coûts de l'abus des drogues pour l'économie canadienne en 1992 (Single et coll., 1996). S'appuyant sur des lignes directrices internationales récemment élaborées pour les études d'estimation des coûts (Single et coll., 1995), les auteurs ont, dans un premier temps, évalué le nombre des décès et des hospitalisations imputables à l'alcool, au tabac et aux drogues illicites en 1992 (voir les chapitres 2 à 4 pour les résultats de cet aspect de l'analyse). Ils ont fondé leur analyse des coûts de l'abus des drogues pour le régime des soins de santé et des coûts de productivité sur les estimations de la morbidité et de la mortalité. Les autres coûts pris en considération étaient ceux de l'administration des prestations d'aide sociale, de la répression criminelle, de la prévention, de la recherche et des autres coûts directs tels que les dommages causés par le feu (Single et coll. 1996).

On estime que l'abus des drogues a coûté plus de 18,4 milliards de dollars à l'économie canadienne en 1992, soit 649 dollars par habitant ou 2,7 % du produit national brut (Tableau 10.15). La part de l'alcool représente quelque 7,5 milliards de dollars, soit 265 dollars par habitant. Les principaux coûts de l'alcool pour l'économie canadienne se traduisent par une perte de 4,14 milliards de dollars au titre de la productivité, imputable à la morbidité et à la mortalité prématurée, de 1,36 milliards pour la répression criminelle et de 1,30 milliard en coûts directs de soins de santé. L'abus du tabac a coûté plus de 9,5 milliards ou quelque 340 dollars par habitant. La perte de productivité due à la mortalité prématurée compte pour plus de 6,7 milliards

measures of alcohol consumption and weighting the results by diagnosis made less of a difference.

The study also examined provincial differences in the costs of substance abuse. The provincial estimates of morbidity, mortality and economic costs are not based on simple extrapolation of national results. Instead, the number of deaths and hospitalizations associated with the use of alcohol, tobacco and illicit drugs are separately estimated for each province, as well as each of the economic cost components.

The results indicate considerable provincial variations in the costs of substance abuse. In Table 10.16, it can be seen that the per capita costs of alcohol are greatest in Alberta ($285) and Prince Edward Island ($283), and lowest in Newfoundland ($199). However, expressed in terms of proportion of Gross Domestic Product (GDP), the costs of alcohol are highest in Prince Edward Island (1.67% of GDP) and lowest in Ontario and Alberta (1.02% of GDP).

As seen in Table 10.17, the costs of tobacco are highest in the Atlantic Provinces. It is estimated that smoking costs represent 2.14% of GDP ($361 per capita) in Prince Edward Island, 2.06% of GDP ($398 per capita) in Nova Scotia, 1.90% of GDP ($354 per capita) in New Brunswick and 1.86% of GDP ($294 per capita) in Newfoundland). The lowest costs due to tobacco use are in Alberta (0.99% of GDP or $277 per capita).

Table 10.18 presents the costs of illicit drug use in each province. Not surprisingly, given the higher rates of illicit drug in that province, the economic costs of illicit drug misuse are highest in British Columbia (0.24% of GDP or $60 per capita). The lowest per capita costs of illicit drug misuse are in Newfoundland ($31 per capita). Relative to GDP, the costs associated with illicit drug misuse range from 0.17% in Saskatchewan to 0.21% in Prince Edward Island and Quebec. Given the concentration of illicit drug users in Toronto and Montreal, it is somewhat surprising that the costs of illicit drug misuse relative to the GDP in Ontario (0.18%) and in Quebec (0.21%) are close to the national average (0.20%).

de ces coûts et les coûts directs des soins de santé imputables au tabagisme, 2,68 milliards. Les coûts économiques des drogues illicites sont évalués à 1,4 milliard de dollars, soit 48 dollars par habitant. Le coût le plus important imputable aux drogues illicites vise la perte de productivité due à la morbidité et à la mortalité prématurée (823 millions de dollars). Une part importante de ces coûts (400 millions de dollars) va à la répression criminelle.

Les chiffres obtenus se comparent à ceux des autres études menées dans d'autres pays (Single et coll., 1996), mais sont légèrement inférieurs aux estimations canadiennes précédentes. Les auteurs de cette étude ont pris une approche conservatrice pour estimer les coûts de la toxicomanie. Des analyses de sensibilité ont été réalisées en ce qui concerne l'application des mesures alternatives de la consommation d'alcool, des divers taux d'actualisation relatifs à l'évaluation des revenus perdus attribuables à la mortalité prématurée, ainsi que des coûts des hospitalisations associées à des certaines causes précises. Il a ainsi été observé que le taux d'actualisation retenu pour évaluer la productivité perdue à la mortalité prématurée influait considérablement sur les résultats, alors que les diverses mesures possibles de la consommation de l'alcool et l'estimation des résultats selon la cause avaient pour leur part une moins grande influence.

L'étude a aussi permis d'examiner les écarts existant entre les provinces concernant l'abus des drogues. Les estimations provinciales de la morbidité, de la mortalité et les coûts économiques ne sont pas fondés sur une simple extrapolation des résultats nationaux. Plutôt, les nombres des décès et des hospitalisations associés à la consommation de l'alcool, du tabac et des drogues illicites ont été évalués séparément pour chacune des provinces et pour chacun des aspects économiques.

Aussi, les résultats indiquent des écarts provinciaux considérables en ce qui concerne les coûts de l'abus des drogues. Selon le Tableau 10.16, les coûts de l'abus d'alcool par habitant sont les plus élevés en Alberta (285 dollars) et à l'Ile-du-Prince-Edouard (283 dollars), et les plus bas à Terre-Neuve (199 dollars). Mais lorsqu'ils

In sum, substance abuse exacts a considerable toll to Canadian society, not only in terms of illness, injury and death, but also in terms of the impact of substance misuse on the Canadian economy. Furthermore, the economic impact varies considerably between the provinces of Canada.

References

Single, E., L. Robson, X. Xie and J. Rehm, *The Costs of Substance Abuse in Canada*, Ottawa, Canadian Centre on Substance Abuse, 1996.

Single, E., B. Easton, D. Collins, H. Harwood, H. Lapsley and A. Maynard.,*International Guidelines for Estimating the Costs of Substance Abuse*, Ottawa, Canadian Centre on Substance Abuse, 1995.

sont exprimés proportionnellement au produit national brut (PNB), les coûts de l'alcool sont les plus élevés à l'Ile-du-Prince-Edouard (1,67 % du PNB) et les plus bas en Ontario et en Alberta (1,02 % du PNB).

Tel qu'il est indiqué au Tableau 10.17, les coûts de l'abus du tabac sont les plus élevés dans les provinces maritimes. Les coûts estimatifs du tabagisme par rapport au PNB sont de 2,14 % (361 dollars par habitant) à l'Ile-du-Prince-Edouard, de 2,06 % (398 dollars par habitant) en Nouvelle-Ecosse, de 1,90 % (354 dollars par habitant) au Nouveau-Brunswick et de 1,86 % (294 dollars par habitant) en Nouvelle-Ecosse. Les coûts les plus faibles s'appliquant au tabagisme reviennent à l'Alberta (0,99 % du PNB ou 277 dollars par habitant).

Le Tableau 10.18 présente les coûts de la consommation des drogues illicites dans chaque province. Les taux de consommation de ces drogues étant les plus élevés en Colombie-Britannique, il apparaîet normal que les coûts économiques de leur abus y soient également les plus élevés (0,24 % du PNB ou 60 dollars par habitant). C'est à Terre-Neuve que les coûts de l'abus des drogues illicites sont les plus bas (31 dollars par habitant). Proportionnellement au PNB, les coûts associés à l'abus des drogues illicites varient entre 0,17 % en Saskatchewan et 0,21 % à l'Ile-du-Prince-Edouard et au Québec. Vu la concentration des usagers de drogues illicites à Toronto et à Montréal, il est assez surprenant que, par rapport au PNB, les coûts de ces drogues en Ontario et au Québec se situent près de la moyenne nationale (0,20 %), soit à 0,18 % et à 0,21 % respectivement.

En fait, l'abus des drogues coûte extrîamement cher à la société canadienne, et ce, non seulement en termes de maladies, de blessures et de décès, mais aussi d'impact économique. Mais ce dernier varie considérablement d'une province à l'autre.

Ouvrages de référence

Single, E., L. Robson, X. Xie et J. Rehm, *The Costs of Substance Abuse in Canada*, Ottawa, Centre canadien de lutte contre l'alcoolisme et les toxicomanies, 1996.

Single, E., B. Easton, D. Collins, H. Harwood, H. Lapsley et A. Maynard.,*International Guidelines for Estimating the Costs of Substance Abuse*, Ottawa, Centre canadien de lutte contre l'alcoolisme et les toxicomanies, 1995.

| TABLE 10.1 | TABLEAU 10.1 |

Alcoholic beverages and cigarettes price in relation to all items, Canada, 1949 to June 1995

Prix des boissons alcooliques et des cigarettes par rapport aux prix de tous les autres produits, Canada, 1949 à 1995

YEAR/ ANNEE	PRICE INDICES/ INDICE DES PRIX			YEAR OVER YEAR CHANGE/ VARIATION D'UNE ANNEE A L'AUTRE		
	ALL ITEMS/ TOUS LES PRODUITS	ALCOHOLIC BEVERAGES/ BOISSONS ALCOOLIQUES	CIGARETTES/ CIGARETTES	ALL ITEMS/ TOUS LES PRODUITS	ALCOHOLIC BEVERAGES/ BOISSONS ALCOOLIQUES	CIGARETTES/ CIGARETTES
1949	18.5	21.1	15.9	0	0	0
1950	19.0	21.7	16.3	2.9%	2.7%	2.7 %
1951	21.1	23.4	17.6	10.7	8.0	8.2
1952	21.5	23.5	18.2	2.2	0.3	3.0
1953	21.4	23.5	15.5	-0.7	0.0	-14.4
1954	21.5	23.6	15.1	0.7	0.3	-2.8
1955	21.5	23.6	15.2	0.0	0.0	0.3
1956	21.8	23.7	15.2	1.4	0.5	0.0
1957	22.5	24.3	15.2	3.1	2.4	0.0
1958	23.1	24.7	15.2	2.7	1.9	0.0
1959	23.4	25.0	16.1	1.3	1.3	6.3
1960	23.7	25.4	16.5	1.3	1.3	2.7
1961	23.9	25.5	16.5	0.6	0.5	-0.3
1962	24.2	25.9	16.6	1.3	1.8	0.6
1963	24.6	26.1	16.6	1.9	0.5	0.0
1964	25.1	26.7	16.7	1.8	2.5	0.9
1965	25.7	26.9	17.3	2.4	0.7	3.1
1966	26.6	27.2	18.0	3.5	1.2	4.1
1967	27.6	27.7	18.8	3.7	1.7	4.5
1968	28.7	29.6	21.1	4.1	7.0	12.2
1969	30.0	30.6	22.1	4.5	3.3	5.0
1970	31.0	30.8	22.4	3.3	0.8	1.3
1971	31.9	31.3	22.9	2.9	1.5	2.1
1972	33.5	32.2	23.3	5.2	3.1	1.9
1973	36.0	33.0	24.3	7.2	2.4	4.1
1974	39.9	35.1	25.3	10.9	6.4	4.3
1975	44.2	39.4	28.3	10.8	12.3	11.7
1976	47.5	41.8	30.7	7.5	6.0	8.8
1977	51.3	44.5	33.1	7.9	6.3	7.6
1978	55.8	47.4	36.4	8.8	6.5	9.9
1979	61.0	51.1	38.3	9.2	7.9	5.2
1980	67.1	57.1	41.8	10.2	11.8	9.2
1981	75.5	64.4	47.7	12.5	12.6	14.0
1982	83.7	74.4	55.1	10.8	15.6	15.5
1983	88.5	82.0	64.9	5.8	10.2	17.9
1984	92.4	87.3	72.5	4.4	6.5	11.7
1985	96.1	92.0	85.2	4.0	5.4	17.4
1986	100.0	100.0	100.0	4.1	8.7	17.4
1987	104.4	105.5	108.5	4.4	5.5	8.5
1988	108.6	112.8	117	4.1	6.9	8.0
1989	114.0	117.9	138	5.0	4.5	18.0
1990	119.5	124.3	158	4.8	5.4	14.2
1991	126.2	133.8	208	5.6	7.6	31.6
1992	128.1	139.1	225	1.5	4.0	8.4
1993	130.4	141.9	228	1.8	2.0	1.1
1994	131.6	142.5	136	0.9	0.4	-40.1
June/Juin 1995	133.7	143.9	142	1.6	1.0	4.4

Source: Data were obtained from the Prices Division, Statistics Canada./Données obtenues de la Division des prix, Statistique Canada.

TABLE 10.2

TABLEAU 10.2

The cost of 10 litres of absolute[1] alcohol as a percentage of personal disposable income per person aged 15 or older, by beverage type, Canada and provinces, 1984-85 to 1992-93

Prix de 10 litres d'alcool absolu[1] en pourcentage du revenu net par personne, population des 15 ans et plus, selon le genre de boisson, Canada et provinces, 1984-1985 à 1992-1993

PROVINCE	1984-85	1985-86	1986-87	1987-88	1988-89	1989-90	1990-91	1991-92	1992-93
				BEER/BIERE					
Nfld./T.-N.	4.61 %	4.60 %	4.51 %	4.18 %	4.14 %	4.09 %	4.06 %	4.09 %	4.13 %
P.E.I./I.-P.-É.	3.39	3.73	3.54	3.76	3.55	3.67	3.70	3.76	3.57
N.S./N.-É.	2.81	2.82	2.93	2.96	2.92	3.10	3.19	3.27	3.22
N.B./N.-B.	3.19	3.19	3.24	3.25	3.34	3.32	3.42	3.44	3.48
Que./Québec	2.14	2.42	2.72	2.58	2.60	2.70	2.86	3.07	3.27
Ont./Ont.	1.99	2.02	2.14	2.13	2.16	2.15	2.22	2.32	2.44
Man./Man.	2.10	2.20	2.36	2.43	2.45	2.43	2.40	2.47	2.44
Sask./Sask.	2.49	2.63	2.55	2.72	2.73	2.66	2.52	2.65	2.68
Alta./Alb.	2.37	2.26	2.21	2.40	2.36	2.32	2.36	2.36	2.43
B.C./C.-B.	2.27	2.52	2.61	2.58	2.45	2.24	2.24	2.26	2.43
Yukon/Yukon	2.49	2.54	2.60	2.50	2.36	2.24	2.21	2.31	2.30
N.W.T./T.N.-O.	3.27	3.48	3.44	3.41	3.13	3.36	3.35	3.49	3.49
Canada	**2.22**	**2.32**	**2.46**	**2.44**	**2.44**	**2.43**	**2.49**	**2.60**	**2.72**
				WINE/VIN					
Nfld./T.-N.	4.75	4.50	4.42	4.27	4.46	4.26	4.28	4.08	4.09
P.E.I./I.-P.-É.	4.28	4.13	3.81	4.17	3.82	3.55	3.70	3.73	3.63
N.S./N.-É.	3.40	3.40	3.53	3.36	3.32	3.31	3.45	3.45	3.53
N.B./N.-B.	3.62	3.51	3.60	3.57	3.39	3.28	3.34	3.31	3.28
Que./Québec	3.81	3.75	3.81	3.70	3.58	3.60	3.77	3.77	3.81
Ont./Ont.	2.65	2.68	2.84	2.75	2.82	2.83	2.91	2.96	3.12
Man./Man.	2.93	2.81	3.03	3.27	3.33	3.20	3.23	3.54	3.44
Sask./Sask.	2.73	2.70	2.81	2.98	3.05	2.81	2.92	3.10	3.24
Alta./Alb.	2.63	2.42	2.73	2.92	2.79	2.68	2.76	2.88	3.02
B.C./C.-B.	2.44	2.47	2.62	2.62	2.61	2.54	2.56	2.80	2.90
Yukon/Yukon	3.03	3.13	3.20	3.45	3.07	2.83	2.85	2.61	2.40
N.W.T./T.N.-O.	4.17	4.32	4.80	4.67	4.29	4.20	4.09	3.91	3.90
Canada	**2.97**	**2.95**	**3.08**	**3.05**	**3.03**	**3.01**	**3.11**	**3.20**	**3.29**
				SPIRITS/SPIRITUEUX					
Nfld./T.-N.	3.97	3.91	3.81	3.62	3.46	3.29	3.26	3.39	3.38
P.E.I./I.-P.-É.	4.45	4.59	4.57	4.45	4.27	4.26	4.20	4.13	4.14
N.S./N.-É.	3.80	3.72	3.73	3.81	3.44	3.40	3.49	3.64	3.69
N.B./N.-B.	3.93	3.91	3.96	3.95	3.86	3.81	3.84	3.91	3.82
Que./Québec	3.37	3.48	3.69	3.52	3.43	3.32	3.27	3.30	3.34
Ont./Ont.	2.76	2.78	2.79	2.60	2.43	2.41	2.44	2.49	2.64
Man./Man.	3.21	3.11	3.33	3.12	3.03	2.89	2.85	3.05	2.99
Sask./Sask.	3.28	3.28	3.05	3.25	3.25	3.12	2.98	3.10	3.25
Alta./Alb.	2.74	2.56	2.67	2.85	2.82	2.82	2.86	2.99	3.07
B.C./C.-B.	2.93	2.96	3.02	3.00	2.98	2.88	2.90	2.93	2.94
Yukon/Yukon	3.36	3.55	3.54	3.44	3.14	3.07	3.04	3.10	2.70
N.W.T./T.N.-O.	3.67	3.62	3.79	3.48	3.22	3.08	3.24	3.22	3.44
Canada	**3.05**	**3.04**	**3.09**	**2.99**	**2.88**	**2.82**	**2.83**	**2.90**	**2.99**

TABLE 10.2 (concluded)

TABLEAU 10.2 (fin)

The cost of 10 litres of absolute[1] alcohol as a percentage of personal disposable income per person aged 15 or older, by beverage type, Canada and provinces, 1984-85 to 1992-93

Prix de 10 litres d'alcool absolu[1] en pourcentage du revenu net par personne, population des 15 ans et plus, selon le genre de boisson, Canada et provinces, 1984-1985 à 1992-1993

PROVINCE	1984-85	1985-86	1986-87	1987-88	1988-89	1989-90	1990-91	1991-92	1992-93
TOTAL ALCOHOL/ALCOOL TOTAL									
Nfld./T.-N.	4.40 %	4.30 %	4.26 %	3.99 %	3.92 %	3.81 %	3.79 %	3.84 %	3.87 %
P.E.I./Î.-P.-É.	3.87	4.09	3.95	4.05	3.84	3.88	3.88	3.89	3.78
N.S./N.-É.	3.25	3.22	3.30	3.31	3.16	3.24	3.33	3.43	3.42
N.B./N.-B.	3.45	3.44	3.50	3.49	3.50	3.46	3.54	3.56	3.56
Que./Québec	2.71	2.89	3.12	2.98	2.96	2.99	3.11	3.25	3.39
Ont./Ont.	2.34	2.36	2.45	2.37	2.34	2.32	2.38	2.46	2.59
Man./Man.	2.60	2.62	2.79	2.78	2.76	2.68	2.65	2.79	2.75
Sask./Sask.	2.85	2.91	2.79	2.97	2.98	2.87	2.75	2.87	2.96
Alta./Alb.	2.57	2.41	2.47	2.66	2.60	2.56	2.60	2.66	2.73
B.C./C.-B.	2.54	2.66	2.75	2.73	2.66	2.50	2.50	2.57	2.67
Yukon/Yukon	2.87	2.97	3.00	2.92	2.71	2.57	2.55	2.58	2.45
N.W.T./T.N.-O.	3.53	3.61	3.70	3.54	3.26	3.29	3.36	3.40	3.50
Canada	2.61	2.65	2.75	2.71	2.66	2.63	2.68	2.78	2.89

[1] For notes on conversion factors please see discussion in chapter 2./Voir les notes sur les facteurs de conversion figurant au chapitre 2.

Source: Statistics Canada, *The Control and Sale of Alcoholic Beverages in Canada 1984, 1985, 1986, 1991-92*, and *1992-93* (Ottawa: Statistics Canada, Catalogue No. 63-202, 1986, 1987, 1989, and 1993 respectively); Statistics Canada, *System of National Accounts-Provincial Economic - Accounts - Annual Estimates 1981-1991*, and *1988-1992* (Ottawa: Statistics Canada, Catalogue 13-213, 1993); Additional data was obtained from the Public Institutions Division, Statistics Canada.

Statistique Canada, *Le contrôle et la vente des boissons alcooliques au Canada, 1984, 1985, 1986*, and *1991-1992* (Ottawa: Statistique Canada, Catalogue no 63-202, 1986, 1987, 1989, et 1993 respectivement); Statistique Canada, *Système de comptabilité nationale - Comptes économiques provinciaux - Estimations annuelles 1981-1991*, et *1988-1992* (Ottawa : Statistique" Canada, Catalogue n° 13-213, 1993). Des données supplémentaires ont été obtenues de la Division des institutions publiques, Statistique Canada.

TABLE 10.3

TABLEAU 10.3

Value of alcohol sales, total and per capita aged 15 or older, Canada and provinces, 1988/89 to 1992/93

Valeur des ventes d'alcool et valeur totale, par personne, population des 15 ans et plus, Canada et provinces, 1988-1989 à 1992-1993

PROVINCE	THOUSANDS OF DOLLARS/ EN MILLIERS DE DOLLARS				PER CAPITA 15+/ PAR PERSONNE DE 15 ANS+			
	BEER/ BIERE	WINE/ VIN	SPIRITS/ SPIRITUEUX	TOTAL	BEER/ BIERE	WINE/ VIN	SPIRITS/ SPIRITUEUX	TOTAL
1988-1989								
Nfld./T.-N.	$164,211	$13,151	$77,850	$255,212	$375.7	$30.1	$178.1	$583.9
P.E.I/I.-P.-É.	23,440	3,944	19,322	46,706	233.7	39.3	192.6	465.7
N.S./N.-É.	143,371	33,734	129,749	306,854	201.0	47.3	181.9	430.2
N.B./N.-B.	121,049	21,441	69,262	211,752	210.6	37.3	120.5	368.4
Que./Québec	1,185,980	573,188	454,914	2,214,082	216.1	104.4	82.9	403.4
Ont./Ont.	1,812,889	578,505	1,241,687	3,633,081	229.7	73.3	157.4	460.4
Man./Man.	172,106	43,287	151,747	367,140	199.4	50.2	175.8	425.4
Sask./Sask.	143,982	26,697	142,589	313,268	183.7	34.1	181.9	399.7
Alta./Alb.	404,133	139,950	411,686	955,769	214.2	74.2	218.2	506.6
B.C./C.-B.	521,863	271,344	443,509	1,236,716	208.7	108.5	177.3	494.5
Yukon/Yukon	8,830	2,560	7,089	18,479	437.1	126.7	350.9	914.8
N.W.T./T.N.-O.	12,236	2,575	11,513	26,324	317.8	66.9	299.0	683.7
Canada	**4,714,090**	**1,710,376**	**3,160,917**	**9,585,383**	**221.3**	**80.3**	**148.4**	**450.1**
1989-1990								
Nfld./T.-N.	$164,373	$13,073	$79,702	$257,148	$372.0	$29.6	$180.4	$581.9
P.E.I/I.-P.-É.	24,828	4,060	19,806	48,694	246.1	40.2	196.3	482.6
N.S./N.-É.	161,898	34,083	134,257	330,238	224.8	47.3	186.4	458.6
N.B./N.-B.	127,478	22,073	70,517	220,068	219.4	38.0	121.4	378.8
Que./Québec	1,284,887	598,340	436,963	2,320,190	230.9	107.5	78.5	417.0
Ont./Ont.	1,919,825	584,822	1,250,328	3,754,975	236.8	72.1	154.3	463.3
Man./Man.	170,621	41,698	149,090	361,409	197.5	48.3	172.5	418.2
Sask./Sask.	138,346	24,770	140,402	303,518	178.0	31.9	180.6	390.5
Alta./Alb.	418,447	134,589	418,401	971,437	218.4	70.2	218.4	507.0
B.C./C.-B.	548,713	278,423	455,993	1,283,129	214.0	108.6	177.8	500.3
Yukon/Yukon	8,263	2,328	6,338	16,929	399.2	112.5	306.2	817.8
N.W.T./T.N.-O.	13,673	2,578	12,352	28,603	348.8	65.8	315.1	729.7
Canada	**4,981,352**	**1,740,837**	**3,174,149**	**9,896,338**	**229.6**	**80.2**	**146.3**	**456.1**
1990-1991								
Nfld./T.-N.	$167,102	$13,245	$81,338	$261,685	$374.2	$29.7	$182.2	$586.1
P.E.I/I.-P.-É.	25,566	4,118	19,223	48,907	252.1	40.6	189.6	482.3
N.S./N.-É.	164,485	33,323	131,261	329,069	226.7	45.9	180.9	453.5
N.B./N.-B.	131,407	22,547	70,319	224,273	224.0	38.4	119.9	382.3
Que./Québec	1,420,654	603,338	402,073	2,426,065	252.5	107.2	71.5	431.2
Ont./Ont.	1,957,983	596,958	1,191,458	3,746,399	237.3	72.3	144.4	454.0
Man./Man.	166,180	41,955	144,526	352,661	192.0	48.5	166.9	407.4
Sask./Sask.	131,234	25,840	137,677	294,751	170.7	33.6	179.1	383.4
Alta./Alb.	449,781	138,348	423,164	1,011,293	230.1	70.8	216.5	517.3
B.C./C.-B.	592,351	290,599	467,125	1,350,075	224.7	110.2	177.2	512.0
Yukon/Yukon	9,545	2,743	7,206	19,494	452.4	130.0	341.5	923.9
N.W.T./T.N.-O.	14,239	2,622	12,884	29,745	353.3	65.1	319.7	738.1
Canada	**5,230,527**	**1,775,636**	**3,088,254**	**10,094,417**	**237.5**	**80.6**	**140.2**	**458.3**

TABLE 10.3 (concluded)   **TABLEAU 10.3** (fin)

Value of alcohol sales, total and per capita aged 15 or older, Canada and provinces, 1988/89 to 1992/93

Valeur des ventes d'alcool et valeur totale, par personne, population des 15 ans et plus, Canada et provinces, 1988-1989 à 1992-1993

PROVINCE	THOUSANDS OF DOLLARS/ EN MILLIERS DE DOLLARS				PER CAPITA 15+/ PAR PERSONNE DE 15 ANS+			
	BEER/ BIERE	WINE/ VIN	SPIRITS/ SPIRITUEUX	TOTAL	BEER/ BIERE	WINE/ VIN	SPIRITS/ SPIRITUEUX	TOTAL
1991-1992								
Nfld./T.-N.	$168,890	$14,594	$80,506	$263,990	$374.2	$32.3	$178.4	$585.0
P.E.I/I.-P.-É.	25,765	3,993	18,872	48,630	254.1	39.4	186.1	479.6
N.S./N.-É.	170,161	34,764	136,330	341,255	232.5	47.5	186.3	466.3
N.B./N.-B.	132,595	22,185	68,609	223,389	223.4	37.4	115.6	376.3
Que./Québec	1,506,230	593,640	388,189	2,488,059	265.3	104.5	68.4	438.2
Ont./Ont.	2,017,268	613,683	1,149,835	3,780,786	241.5	73.5	137.7	452.7
Man./Man.	168,362	43,188	153,162	364,712	193.5	49.6	176.0	419.2
Sask./Sask.	137,252	24,973	135,991	298,216	178.9	32.6	177.3	388.8
Alta./Alb.	468,143	146,514	427,028	1,041,685	235.3	73.6	214.6	523.5
B.C./C.-B.	610,101	301,805	480,778	1,392,684	226.0	111.8	178.1	515.8
Yukon/Yukon	10,392	2,839	7,115	20,346	472.4	129.0	323.4	924.8
N.W.T./T.N.-O.	15,191	2,539	12,848	30,578	367.8	61.5	311.1	740.4
Canada	**5,430,350**	**1,804,717**	**3,059,263**	**10,294,330**	**243.5**	**80.9**	**137.2**	**461.7**
1992-1993								
Nfld./T.-N.	$168,535	$14,496	$78,761	$261,792	$370.9	$31.9	$173.3	$576.1
P.E.I/I.-P.-É.	25,360	3,857	19,339	48,556	250.8	38.2	191.3	480.3
N.S./N.-É.	168,758	33,643	134,849	337,250	229.7	45.8	183.6	459.1
N.B./N.-B.	134,107	22,139	68,557	224,803	224.9	37.1	115.0	377.1
Que./Québec	1,589,229	605,188	372,042	2,566,459	276.9	105.4	64.8	447.2
Ont./Ont.	2,004,001	641,241	1,119,113	3,764,355	237.0	75.8	132.4	445.3
Man./Man.	165,754	43,488	153,738	362,980	190.8	50.0	176.9	417.7
Sask./Sask.	134,771	24,933	136,893	296,597	176.0	32.6	178.8	387.4
Alta./Alb.	476,011	153,261	418,736	1,048,008	236.1	76.0	207.7	519.8
B.C./C.-B.	663,855	314,900	483,856	1,462,611	240.5	114.1	175.3	529.9
Yukon/Yukon	10,737	3,207	7,741	21,685	468.9	140.0	338.0	946.9
N.W.T./T.N.-O.	14,948	2,606	12,770	30,324	355.9	62.0	304.0	722.0
Canada	**5,556,066**	**1,862,959**	**3,006,395**	**10,425,420**	**246.3**	**82.6**	**133.3**	**462.2**

Source: Data were obtained from the Public Institutions Division, Statistics Canada.

Données obtenues de la Division des institutions publiques, Statistique Canada.

TABLE 10.4

TABLEAU 10.4

Value[1] of all alcohol sold, Canada and provinces, 1985/86 to 1992/93

Valeur[1] de tout d'alcool vendu, Canada et provinces, de 1985-1986 à 1992-1993

PROVINCE	THOUSANDS OF DOLLARS/MILLIERS DE DOLLARS							
	1985-86	1986-87	1987-88	1988-89	1989-90	1990-91	1991-92	1992-93
Nfld./N.-T.	$198,691	$225,770	$238,851	$255,212	$257,148	$261,685	$263,990	$261,792
P.E.I./Î.-P.-É.	41,019	42,356	44,780	46,706	48,694	48,907	48,630	48,556
N.S./N.-É.	273,601	285,178	299,209	306,854	330,238	329,069	341,255	337,250
N.B./N.-B.	187,746	194,770	203,533	211,752	220,068	224,273	223,389	224,803
Que./Québec	1,875,552	2,020,749	2,115,865	2,214,082	2,320,190	2,426,065	2,488,059	2,566,459
Ont./Ont.	2,966,885	3,218,698	3,451,124	3,633,081	3,754,975	3,746,399	3,780,786	3,764,355
Man./Man.	337,371	349,878	364,987	367,140	361,409	352,661	364,712	362,980
Sask./Sask.	297,550	302,714	310,039	313,268	303,518	294,751	298,216	296,597
Alta./Alb.	893,886	876,587	910,850	955,769	971,437	1,011,293	1,041,685	1,048,008
B.C./C.-B.	1,107,441	1,188,263	1,225,500	1,236,716	1,283,129	1,350,075	1,392,684	1,462,611
Yukon/Yukon	14,941	16,366	17,357	18,479	16,929	19,494	20,346	21,685
N.W.T./T.N.-O.	24,926	24,092	25,395	26,324	28,603	29,745	30,578	30,324
Canada	**8,219,609**	**8,745,421**	**9,207,490**	**9,585,383**	**9,896,338**	**10,094,417**	**10,294,330**	**10,425,420**

[1] All values are expressed in current dollars (ie. increases reflect the effects of inflation, tax increases etc.). Sales volumes can be found in Table 2.5./Toutes les valeurs sont exprimées en dollars courants (c.-à-d. que les augmentations reflètent les effets de l'inflation, les majorations de taxes, etc.). Les volumes des ventes figurent au Tableau 2.5.

Source: Statistics Canada, *The Control and Sale of Alcoholic Beverages in Canada 1984, 1985, 1986*, and *1992/93* (Ottawa: Statistics Canada, Catalogue No. 63-202, 1986, 1987, 1989 and 1995 respectively). Additional data were obtained from the Public Institutions Division, Statistics Canada.

Statistique Canada, *Le contrôle et la vente des boissons alcooliques au Canada, 1984, 1985, 1986, and 1992-93*. (Ottawa: Statistique Canada, Catalogue no 63-202, 1986, 1987, 1989, et 1995 respectivement). Des données supplémentaires ont été obtenues de la Division des institutions publiques, Statistique Canada.

TABLE 10.5

TABLEAU 10.5

Provincial[1,2] revenue from the control and sale of alcoholic beverages, 1987-88 to 1992-93

Recettes provinciales[1,2] provenant du contrôle et de la vente des boissons alcooliques, 1987-1988 à 1992-1993

PROVINCE	NET INCOME FROM SALES/ RECETTES NETTES SUR LES VENTES	LIQUOR SALES TAX/ TAXE DE VENTE SUR L'ALCOOL	LICENCES AND PERMITS/ LICENCES ET PERMIS	FINES AND CONFISCATIONS/ AMENDES ET SAISIES	TOTAL REVENUE/ TOTAL DES RECETTES	GOV'T REVENUE (%)/ RECETTES GOUVERNE- MENTALES (%)
1987-1988 (THOUSANDS OF DOLLARS/MILLIERS DE DOLLARS)						
Nfld./N.-T.	$38,546	$0	$40,513	$307	$79,366	3.0%
P.E.I./I.-P.-É.	9,240	$8,547	173	383	18,343	3.2%
N.S./N.-É.	108,930	0	6,480	582	115,992	3.3%
N.B./N.-B.	75,840	0	5,169	150	81,159	2.6%
Que./Québec	369,976	0	58,836	102	428,914	1.4%
Ont./Ont.	635,884	0	356,122	21	992,027	2.7%
Man./Man.	146,863	0	5,629	0	152,492	2.9%
Sask./Sask.	125,507	0	2,632	0	128,139	2.9%
Alta./Alb.	354,358	0	8,146	0	362,504	2.8%
B.C./C.-B.	333,277	0	108,496	0	441,773	3.6%
Yukon/Yukon	5,070	1,862	63	0	6,995	2.4%
N.W.T./T.N.-O.	10,353	0	131	0	10,484	1.3%
Canada	**2,213,844**	**10,409**	**592,390**	**1,545**	**2,818,188**	**2.5%**
1988-1989 (THOUSANDS OF DOLLARS/MILLIERS DE DOLLARS)						
Nfld./N.-T.	$39,952	$0	$41,691	$310	$81,953	2.9%
P.E.I./I.-P.-É.	9,223	$8,938	177	18	18,356	2.9%
N.S./N.-É.	109,283	0	6,779	550	116,612	3.0%
N.B./N.-B.	77,791	0	5,519	124	83,434	2.4%
Que./Québec	381,290	0	59,737	55	441,082	1.3%
Ont./Ont.	653,849	0	405,570	26	1,059,445	2.6%
Man./Man.	144,756	0	6,450	0	151,206	2.6%
Sask./Sask.	122,890	0	2,549	0	125,439	2.5%
Alta./Alb.	381,764	0	8,369	0	390,133	3.2%
B.C./C.-B.	345,132	0	75,002	0	420,134	3.0%
Yukon/Yukon	5,679	1,980	67	0	7,726	2.4%
N.W.T./T.N.-O.	11,392	0	139	0	11,531	1.2%
Canada	**2,283,001**	**10,918**	**612,049**	**1,083**	**2,907,051**	**2.4%**
1989-90 (THOUSANDS OF DOLLARS/MILLIERS DE DOLLARS)						
Nfld./N.-T.	$39,558	$0	$42,217	$335	$82,110	2.6%
P.E.I./I.-P.-É.	9,541	$9,328	176	20	19,065	2.8%
N.S./N.-É.	114,537	0	6,976	355	121,868	3.0%
N.B./N.-B.	81,668	0	5,860	100	87,628	2.3%
Que./Québec	387,604	0	58,264	45	445,913	1.3%
Ont./Ont.	675,536	0	434,875	28	1,110,439	2.4%
Man./Man.	138,767	0	8,227	0	146,994	2.5%
Sask./Sask.	120,665	0	1,112	0	121,777	2.1%
Alta./Alb.	384,411	0	1,836	0	386,247	3.0%
B.C./C.-B.	415,598	0	4,811	0	420,409	2.7%
Yukon/Yukon	5,856	2,031	70	0	7,957	2.4%
N.W.T./T.N.-O.	12,567	0	122	0	12,689	1.2%
Canada	**2,386,308**	**11,359**	**564,546**	**883**	**2,963,096**	**2.2%**

TABLE 10.5 (continued)

TABLEAU 10.5 (suite)

Provincial[1,2] revenue from the control and sale of alcoholic beverages, 1987-88 to 1992-93

Recettes provinciales[1,2] provenant du contrôle et de la vente des boissons alcooliques, 1987-1988 à 1992-1993

PROVINCE	NET INCOME FROM SALES/ RECETTES NETTES SUR LES VENTES	LIQUOR SALES TAX/ TAXE DE VENTE SUR L'ALCOOL	LICENCES AND PERMITS/ LICENCES ET PERMIS	FINES AND CONFISCATIONS/ AMENDES ET SAISIES	TOTAL REVENUE/ TOTAL DES RECETTES	GOV'T REVENUE (%)/ RECETTES GOUVERNE- MENTALES (%)
1990-1991 (THOUSANDS OF DOLLARS/MILLIERS DE DOLLARS)						
Nfld./N.-T.	$38,896	$0	$42,971	$339	$82,206	2.6%
P.E.I./Î.-P.-É.	9,209	$9,241	310	21	18,781	2.6%
N.S./N.-É.	109,151	0	6,894	446	116,491	2.7%
N.B./N.-B.	79,573	0	5,964	139	85,676	2.2%
Que./Québec	359,175	0	94,430	106	453,711	1.2%
Ont./Ont.	635,612	0	454,186	9	1,089,807	2.3%
Man./Man.	129,684	0	7,029	0	136,713	2.2%
Sask./Sask.	109,382	0	1,134	0	110,516	1.8%
Alta./Alb.	405,397	0	1,843	0	407,240	2.7%
B.C./C.-B.	445,299	0	5,000	0	450,299	2.6%
Yukon/Yukon	5,958	2,071	66	0	8,095	2.3%
N.W.T./T.N.-O.	14,065	0	121	0	14,186	1.3%
Canada	**2,341,401**	**11,312**	**619,948**	**1,060**	**2,973,721**	**2.1%**
1991-92 (THOUSANDS OF DOLLARS/MILLIERS DE DOLLARS)						
Nfld./N.-T.	$39,166	$0	$43,231	$353	$82,750	2.5%
P.E.I./Î.-P.-É.	9,513	$8,739	205	19	18,476	2.5%
N.S./N.-É.	113,163	0	6,728	363	120,254	2.8%
N.B./N.-B.	76,881	0	5,740	130	82,751	2.1%
Que./Québec	364,454	0	108,992	119	473,565	1.2%
Ont./Ont.	643,769	0	488,639	0	1,132,408	2.5%
Man./Man.	137,283	0	4,763	0	142,046	2.2%
Sask./Sask.	112,826	0	1,102	0	113,928	2.0%
Alta./Alb.	409,675	0	2,161	0	411,836	2.9%
B.C./C.-B.	455,547	0	4,970	0	460,517	2.6%
Yukon/Yukon	5,591	2,052	66	0	7,709	2.1%
N.W.T./T.N.-O.	14,076	0	108	0	14,184	1.2%
Canada	**2,381,944**	**10,791**	**666,705**	**984**	**3,060,424**	**2.2%**
1992-93 (THOUSANDS OF DOLLARS/MILLIERS DE DOLLARS)						
Nfld./N.-T.	$37,962	$0	$47,072	$376	$85,410	2.5%
P.E.I./Î.-P.-É.	9,438	$8,726	222	21	18,407	2.5%
N.S./N.-É.	115,557	0	6,704	280	122,541	2.8%
N.B./N.-B.	77,468	0	5,324	119	82,911	2.0%
Que./Québec	347,966	0	120,838	51	468,855	1.2%
Ont./Ont.	608,780	0	516,442	0	1,125,222	2.4%
Man./Man.	137,950	0	3,688	0	141,638	2.3%
Sask./Sask.	115,415	0	1,089	0	116,504	2.1%
Alta./Alb.	405,445	0	2,587	0	408,032	2.9%
B.C./C.-B.	517,126	0	4,970	0	522,096	2.8%
Yukon/Yukon	5,717	2,187	70	0	7,974	2.2%
N.W.T./T.N.-O.	14,188	0	527	0	14,715	1.2%
Canada	**2,393,012**	**10,913**	**709,533**	**847**	**3,114,305**	**2.2%**

TABLE 10.5 (concluded)   **TABLEAU 10.5 (fin)**

Provincial[1,2] revenue from the control and sale of alcoholic beverages, 1987-88 to 1992-93

Recettes provinciales[1,2] provenant du contrôle et de la vente des boissons alcooliques, 1987-1988 à 1992-1993

[1] Does not include revenue derived from provincial retail sales taxes./N'incluent pas les recettes provenant des taxes provinciales sur les ventes au détail.

[2] Federal revenue derived from the excise duties and taxes and import duties is no longer reported in the same source as the above information. However, information from Department of National Revenue for federal revenue from alcohol-related excise duties and taxes was:

1987-88	$1,152,200	000's of dollars
1988-89	1,117,800	"
1989-90	1,072,200	"
1990-91	1,059,200	"
1991-92	1,174,300	"
1992-93	1,100,300	"

Not included is federal revenue derived from the general sales tax (manufacturer's sales tax prior to 1991) or from corporation income taxes.

[2] Les recettes fédérales provenant des droits et taxes d'accise et des droits d'importation ne sont plus déclarées à la même source que l'information ci-dessus. Cependant, le ministère national du Revenu a fourni les données suivantes sur les recettes fédérales provenant des droits et taxes d'accise reliés à l'alcool :

1987-88	1 152 200 $	millier de dollars
1988-89	1 117 800 $	"
1989-90	1 072 200 $	"
1990-91	1 059 200 $	"
1991-92	1 174 300 $	"
1992-93	1 100 300 $	"

Sont exclues les recettes fédérales tirées de la taxe sur les produits et services (taxe de vente du fabricant avant 1991) ou de l'impôt sur le revenu des sociétés.

Source: Data were obtained from the Public Instinutions Division, Statistics Canada.

Données obtenues de la Division des institutions publiques, Statistique Canada.

TABLE 10.6	TABLEAU 10.6

Value of imports and exports of alcoholic beverages, Canada,1974-75 to 1992-93

Valeur des importations et des exportations des boissons alcooliques, Canada, de 1974-1975 à 1992-1993

YEAR/ ANNEE	(THOUSANDS OF DOLLARS/MILLIERS DE DOLLARS)							
	IMPORTS[1]/ IMPORTATIONS[1]				EXPORTS[2] OF DOMESTIC STOCK/ EXPORTATIONS[2] DES PRODUITS CANADIENS			
	SPIRITS/ SPIRITUEUX	WINES/ VINS	BEER/ BIERE	TOTAL	SPIRITS/ SPIRITUEUX	WINES/ VINS	BEER/ BIERE	TOTAL
1974-1975	$72,632	$62,938	$4,511	$140,081	$203,062	$451	$11,722	$215,235
1975-1976	76,611	86,544	6,435	169,590	238,731	325	17,341	256,397
1976-1977	73,379	83,196	7,027	163,602	226,793	552	29,612	256,957
1977-1978	90,111	124,770	8,725	223,606	278,126	497	34,557	313,180
1978-1979	108,243	160,509	26,353	295,105	293,629	1,385	49,820	344,834
1979-1980	119,308	153,905	8,827	282,040	290,989	1,374	77,046	369,409
1980-1981	119,478	157,926	32,122	309,526	318,793	739	90,085	409,617
1981-1982	148,680	174,622	12,279	335,581	343,667	1,022	112,406	457,095
1982-1983	151,906	185,423	14,427	351,756	344,370	1,100	133,559	479,029
1983-1984	135,739	171,816	18,863	326,418	375,715	1,126	142,749	519,590
1984-1985	165,309	222,226	19,947	407,482	386,715	1,070	157,866	545,651
1985-1986	153,449	218,006	51,242	422,697	345,166	1,382	172,232	518,780
1986-1987	173,073	269,717	20,011	462,801	350,918	2,136	191,439	544,493
1987-1988	151,796	281,969	28,497	462,262	353,064	2,708	187,047	542,819
1988-1989	172,381	278,273	44,557	495,211	269,273	3,157	200,375	472,805
1989-1990	200,744	356,493	68,481	625,718	396,502	1,780	197,869	596,151
1990-1991	201,418	337,471	60,552	599,441	437,085	1,111	182,863	621,059
1991-1992	197,351	347,182	56,541	601,074	437,085	1,555	192,754	631,394
1992-1993	201,197	377,261	52,661	631,119	492,782	1,331	185,925	680,038

[1] Values are based upon the prices in the country of origin./Valeurs basées sur les prix du pays d'origine.

[2] Does not include foreign products that were re-exported./Excluent les produits étrangers exportés.

Source: Statistics Canada, *Control and Sale of Alcoholic Beverages in Canada 1978, 1979, 1980, 1981, 1982, 1983, 1984, 1985, 1986, 1992,* and *1993* (Ottawa: Statistics Canada, Catalogue No. 63-202, 1980, 1981, 1982, 1983, 1984, 1985, 1986, 1987, 1989, 1993, and 1994 respectively).

Additional data were obtained from the Public Institutions Division, Statistics Canada.

Statistique Canada, *Le contrôle et la vente des boissons alcooliques au Canada, 1978, 1979, 1980, 1981, 1982, 1983, 1984, 1985, 1986, 1992,* et *1993* (Ottawa : Statistique Canada, Catalogue n° 63-202, 1980, 1981, 1982, 1983, 1984, 1985, 1986, 1987, 1989, 1993, et 1995 respectivement).

Des données supplémentaires ont été obtenues de la Division des institutions publiques, Statistique Canada.

TABLE 10.7

TABLEAU 10.7

Number of workers, and total salaries and wages in alcohol production, Canada, 1975 to 1993

Nombre des travailleurs dans la production des boissons alcooliques et total des traitements et salaires, Canada, 1975 à 1993

YEAR/ ANNEE	BREWERIES/ BRASSERIES	WINERIES/ ETABLISSEMENTS VINICOLES	DISTILLERIES/ DISTILLERIES	TOTAL ALCOHOL/ ALCOOL TOTAL
NUMBER OF WORKERS[1]/NOMBRE DE TRAVAILLEURS[1]				
1975	11,652	1,198	5,992	18,842
1976	11,632	1,159	5,708	18,499
1977	12,112	1,094	5,414	18,620
1978	11,895	1,187	5,187	18,269
1979	12,290	1,319	5,374	18,983
1980	12,342	1,313	5,509	19,164
1981	12,637	1,385	5,528	19,550
1982	12,938	1,298	5,282	19,518
1983	12,804	1,379	5,027	19,210
1984	13,318	1,339	4,790	19,447
1985	13,656	1,421	4,454	19,531
1986	13,614	1,407	4,358	19,379
1987	13,756	1,567	4,187	19,510
1988	14,162	1,496	4,096	19,754
1989	13,895	1,379	3,997	19,271
1990	12,636	1,330	3,865	17,831
1991	12,085	1,257	3,449	16,791
1992	11,737	1,222	2,857	15,816
1993	11,799	1,269	2,673	15,741
SALARIES AND WAGES (THOUSANDS OF DOLLARS)/TRAITEMENTS ET SALAIRES (MILLIERS DE DOLLARS)				
1975	$172,441	$13,219	$81,555	$267,215
1976	194,643	14,677	85,266	294,586
1977	216,875	15,670	89,551	322,096
1978	228,937	18,665	91,646	339,248
1979	262,366	22,991	104,202	389,559
1980	301,170	24,047	121,290	446,507
1981	334,316	29,170	132,112	495,598
1982	375,135	31,423	149,957	556,515
1983	411,395	35,296	151,921	598,612
1984	436,867	34,897	158,268	630,032
1985	467,445	37,716	154,356	659,517
1986	481,355	37,895	165,842	685,092
1987	502,801	46,449	168,472	717,722
1988	532,000	44,600	167,500	744,100
1989	543,900	43,800	170,300	758,000
1990	528,300	44,700	173,700	746,700
1991	556,500	45,700	169,700	771,900
1992	532,800	48,400	149,100	730,300
1993	555,900	46,900	141,300	744,100

[1] Includes administrative, office and other non-production workers./Inclut le personnel de l'administration, le personnel de bureau et tout autre personnel non affecté à la production.

Source: For 1975 to 1984, Statistics Canada, *Alcoholic Beverage Industries 1982, 1983*, and *1984* (Ottawa: Statistics Canada, Catalogue No. 32-231, 1984, 1985 and 1986 respectively); Statistics Canada, *Beverage and Tobacco Products Industries, 1985, 1986, 1987, 1988, 1989, 1990, 1991, 1992*, and *1993* (Ottawa: Statistics Canada, Catalogue No. 32-251, 1988, 1989, 1990, 1991, 1992, 1993, 1994, and 1995 respectively).

Pour 1975 à 1984, Statistique Canada, *Alcoholic Beverage Industries 1982, 1983*, et *1984* (Ottawa : Statistique Canada, Catalogue no 32-231, 1984, 1985, et 1986 respectivement); Statistique Canada, *Beverage and Tobacco Products Industries, 1985, 1986, 1987, 1988, 1989, 1990, 1991, 1992 et 1993* (Ottawa : Statistique Canada, Catalogue no 32-251, 1988, 1989, 1989, 1990, 1991, 1992, 1993, 1994, et 1995 respectivement).

TABLE 10.8

TABLEAU 10.8

Government revenue from the sale of tobacco, Canada and provinces, 1985-86 to 1993-94

Recettes gouvernementales provenant de la vente du tabac, Canada et provinces, 1985-1986 à 1993-1994

GOVERNMENT/ GOUVERNEMENT	MILLIONS OF DOLLARS[1]/MILLIONS DE DOLLARS[1]								
	1985-86	1986-87	1987-88	1988-89	1989-90	1990-91	1991-92	1992-93	1993-94
Federal/Fédéral	1,517.3	1,518.3	1,679.8	1,588.2	1,960.6	2,113.8	3,275.7	2,868.5	2,235.7
Provincial									
Nfld./N.-T.	38.9	41.0	39.8	41.1	50.6	54.1	55.3	62.4	65.0
P.E.I./I.-P.-É.	12.7	17.0	18.7	21.9	22.6	26.9	27.7	26.4	25.2
N.S./N.-É.	55.7	73.4	85.5	87.9	76.8	118.1	105.1	102.0	89.0
N.B./N.-B.	54.4	60.5	62.8	61.9	75.3	74.5	59.8	50.3	45.0
Que./Québec	640.5	692.2	647.9	675.7	628.1	693.2	592.1	411.3	372.0
Ont./Ont.	603.0	611.3	638.8	750.5	770.6	874.7	1,028.0	969.0	775.0
Man./Man.	77.8	91.8	94.0	98.8	117.0	116.2	129.9	128.0	123.3
Sask./Sask.	70.6	78.8	90.0	142.4	145.8	143.3	134.1	117.0	112.4
Alta./Alb.	100.4	110.3	183.1	212.2	235.3	275.1	322.1	315.0	315.0
B.C./C.-B.	188.6	212.2	228.0	270.7	308.2	346.7	433.4	483.0	478.0
Yukon/Yukon	2.6	4.3	4.5	4.8	4.6	4.7	4.7	5.0	7.0
N.W.T./T.N.-O.	4.4	4.7	5.4	5.3	7.9	9.3	13.5	12.6	11.4
Total	1,849.6	1,997.5	2,098.5	2,373.2	2,442.8	2,736.8	2,905.7	2,682.0	2,418.3
Total	3,366.9	3,515.8	3,778.3	3,961.4	4,403.4	4,850.6	6,181.4	5,550.5	4,654.0
TOBACCO REVENUE AS A PERCENTAGE OF TOTAL GOVERNMENT REVENUE/ POURCENTAGE DU TOTAL DES RECETTES GOUVERNEMENTALES IMPUTABLES AU TABAC									
Federal/Fédéral	1.8%	1.7%	1.6%	1.5%	1.6%	1.7%	2.5%	2.2%	1.7%
Provincial									
Nfld./N.-T.	1.7%	1.7%	1.5%	1.4%	1.6%	1.7%	1.7%	1.8%	1.9%
P.E.I./I.-P.-É.	2.6	3.2	3.3	3.4	3.3	3.7	3.7	3.5	3.2
N.S./N.-É.	1.9	2.3	2.5	2.3	1.9	2.7	2.4	2.3	2.0
N.B./N.-B.	1.9	2.1	2.0	1.8	2.0	1.9	1.5	1.2	1.0
Que./Québec	2.4	2.5	2.1	2.0	1.8	1.9	1.6	1.1	0.9
Ont./Ont.	2.1	1.9	1.8	1.8	1.7	1.8	2.2	2.1	1.6
Man./Man.	1.9	2.1	1.8	1.7	2.0	1.9	2.0	2.1	1.9
Sask./Sask.	1.8	2.1	2.0	2.9	2.5	2.3	2.4	2.1	1.8
Alta./Alb.	0.7	1.0	1.4	1.7	1.8	1.8	2.3	2.3	2.1
B.C./C.-B.	1.8	1.9	1.8	1.9	2.0	2.0	2.5	2.6	2.4
Yukon/Yukon	1.1	1.6	1.5	1.5	1.4	1.3	1.3	1.4	1.5
N.W.T./T.N.-O.	0.6	0.6	0.7	0.6	0.8	0.8	1.1	1.0	0.9
Total	1.9%	2.0%	1.9%	1.9%	1.8%	1.9%	2.1%	1.9%	1.6%
Total	1.9%	1.8%	1.8%	1.7%	1.7%	1.8%	2.3%	2.0%	1.7%

[1] Includes only revenue derived from the federal excise tax, excise duty and the specific tobacco taxes in each province./Incluent uniquement les recettes sur les droits et taxes d'accise et sur les taxes provinciales sur le tabac.

Source: Derived from data obtained from the Public Institutions Division, Statistics Canada./Données obtenues de la Division des institutions publiques, Statistique Canada.

Association of Canadian Distillers, *Annual Statistical Report 1994* (Ottawa: Association of Canadian Distillers, 1994).

TABLE 10.9   **TABLEAU 10.9**

Federal and provincial taxes per package of 25 cigarettes, Canada and provinces, April 15, 1994

Taxes fédérales et provinciales sur le carton de 25 cigarettes, Canada et provinces, 15 avril 1994

PROVINCE	SUGGESTED RETAIL PRICE/ PRIX DE DETAIL SUGGERE	FEDERAL TAXES/LES TAXES FÉDÉRALES		
		FEDERAL EXCISE TAXES/TAXES D'ACCISE FEDERALES	G.S.T./ T.P.S.	TOTAL TAXES/ TOTAL DES TAXES
Nfld./T.-N.	$7.30	$1.36	$0.43	$1.79
P.E.I./I.-P.-É.	4.12	0.83	0.27	$1.10
N.S./N.-É.	4.30	1.11	0.25	$1.36
N.B./N.-B.	4.30	1.11	0.25	$1.36
Que./Québec	2.96	0.73	0.18	$0.91
Ont./Ont.	3.13	0.78	0.19	$0.97
Man./Man.	6.14	1.36	0.38	$1.74
Sask./Sask.	6.25	1.36	0.38	$1.74
Alta./Alb.	5.43	1.36	0.36	$1.72
B.C./C.-B.	6.76	1.36	0.44	$1.80

PROVINCE	PROVINCIAL TAXES/TAXES PROVINCIALES			TOTAL TAXES/ TOTAL DES TAXES	TAXES AS A % OF PRICE/TAXES EN POURCENTAGE DU PRIX
	PROVINCIAL TAX/ TAXE PROVINCIALE TABAC	P.S.T./TAXE PROVINCIALE VENTES	TOTAL TAXES/ TAXES GLOBALES		
Nfld./T.-N.	$2.57	$0.78	$3.35	$5.14	70.41 %
P.E.I./I.-P.-É.	1.29	-	1.29	2.39	58.01
N.S./N.-É.	0.83	0.43	1.26	2.62	60.93
N.B./N.-B.	0.83	0.43	1.26	2.62	60.93
Que./Québec	0.35	0.22	0.57	1.48	50.00
Ont./Ont.	0.43	0.22	0.65	1.62	51.76
Man./Man.	2.00	0.38	2.38	4.12	67.10
Sask./Sask.	2.00	0.48	2.48	4.22	67.52
Alta./Alb.	1.75	-	1.75	3.47	63.90
B.C./C.-B.	2.75	-	2.75	4.55	67.31

Source: Based on data compiled by the Non-Smokers Rights Association.

Information fondée sur les données recueillies par l'Association pour les droits des non-fumeurs.

TABLE 10.10　　　　　　　　　　　　　　　　　　　　**TABLEAU 10.10**

Value of imports and exports of tobacco from all countries, Canada, 1968 to 1994

Valeur des importations et des exportations du tabac de tous les pays, Canada, de 1968 à 1994

YEAR/ ANNEE	IMPORTS[1]/ IMPORTATIONS[1]	EXPORTS[2]/ EXPORTATIONS[2]
1968	$9,868,000	$57,467,000
1969	10,610,000	62,856,000
1970	9,884,000	56,446,000
1971	11,254,000	57,480,000
1972	10,763,000	59,172,000
1973	17,043,000	59,311,000
1974	19,355,000	75,520,000
1975	25,155,000	72,745,000
1976	21,054,000	68,997,000
1977	22,011,000	69,043,000
1978	26,335,000	104,825,000
1979	28,835,000	145,271,000
1980	57,179,000	82,358,000
1981	32,712,000	141,042,000
1982	50,596,000	133,457,000
1983	62,948,000	118,684,000
1984	42,291,000	123,615,000
1985	32,441,000	105,398,000
1986	34,727,000	137,332,000
1987	27,113,000	139,083,000
1988	28,081,000	102,868,000
1989	26,075,000	98,073,000
1990	26,875,000	115,069,000
1991	32,804,000	266,368,000
1992	60,439,000	476,223,000
1993	59,960,000	814,030,000
1994	70,469,000	189,729,000

[1] Includes bright flue-cured unstemmed tobacco, cigar leaf unstemmed tobacco, Turkisk type unstemmed tobacco, other unspecified unmanufactured unstemmed tobacco, cigar leaf stemmed tobacco, other unspecified unmanufactured stemmed tobacco, pipe and cigarette smoking cut tobacco, cigars and similar products, cigarettes and other unspecified manufactures tobacco./Incluent le tabac blond non écoté séché à l'air chaud, les feuilles de tabac à cigare non écotées, le tabac non écoté aromatique, d'autres tabacs non écotés, non manufacturés et non précisés, les feuilles de tabac à cigare écotées, d'autres tabacs écotés, non manufacturés et non précisés, le tabac haché pour pipes et cigarettes, les cigares et autres produits similaires, les cigarettes et autres produits de tabac manufacturés et non précisés.

[2] Includes bright flue-cured unstemmed tobacco, other unspecified unmanufactured unstemmed tobacco, bright flue-cured stemmed tobacco, tobacco stems cutting scrap and waste, other unspecified unmanufactured stemmed tobacco and other unspecified manufactured cigarettes and tobacco./Incluent le tabac blond non écoté séché à l'air chaud, d'autres tabacs non écotés, non manufacturés et non précisés, le tabac blond écoté séché à l'air chaud, les déchets de la coupe des côtes de tabac, d'autres tabacs écotés, non manufacturés et non précisés, ainsi que d'autres cigarettes et tabacs manufacturés non précisés.

Source: For 1968 to 1981, these data originate from CANSIM which is the registered Trade Mark for Statistics Canada's machine - readable data base; for 1982 to 1985, Statistics Canada, *Imports by Commodities 1982, 1983, 1984* and *1985*, monthly issues (Ottawa: Statistics Canada, Catalogue No. 65-007, from April, 1982 to March, 1986); Statistics Canada, *Exports by Commodities 1982, 1983, 1984* and *1985*, monthly issues (Ottawa: Statistics Canada, Catalogue No. 65-004, from April, 1982 to March, 1986), Statistics Canada, *Exports - Mechandise Trade 1986* to *1994* annual editions (Ottawa: Statistics Canada, Catalogue No. 65-202 annual editions); Statictics Canada, *Imports - Merchandise Trade 1986* to *1994* annual editions (Ottawa: Statistics Canada, Catalogue No. 65-203, annual editions).

Pour 1968 à 1981, CANSIM, base de données informatisée de Statistique Canada; pour 1982 à 1985, Statistique Canada, *Importations par marchandises 1982, 1983, 1984,* et *1985,* mensuel (Ottawa : Statistique Canada, Catalogue no 65-007, de avril 1982 à mars 1986); Statistique Canada, *Exportations par marchandises 1982, 1983, 1984,* et *1985,* mensuel (Ottawa : Statistique Canada, Catalogue no 65-004, de avril 1982 à mars 1986); Statistique Canada, *Exportations - Commerce de marchandises 1966* à *1994,* annuel (Ottawa : Statistique Canada, Catalogue no 65-202, annuel); Statistique Canada, *Importations - Commerce de marchandises 1966* à *1994,* annuel (Ottawa : Statistique Canada, Catalogue no 65-203, annuel).

TABLE 10.11

TABLEAU 10.11

Number of workers[1], and total salaries and wages in tobacco processing and manufacturing, Canada, 1975 to 1993

Nombre des travailleurs[1] oeuvrant dans le traitement du tabac et la confection de ses produits, et total des traitements et salaires, Canada, 1975 à 1993

YEAR/ ANNEE	LEAF TOBACCO PROCESSORS/ TRAITEMENT DU TABAC EN FEUILLES	TOBACCO PRODUCTS MANUFACTURERS/ CONFECTION DES PRODUITS DU TABAC	TOTAL
NUMBER OF WORKERS[1]/NOMBRE DE TRAVAILLEURS[1]			
1975	1,329	8,357	9,686
1976	1,009	8,076	9,085
1977	838	9,085	9,923
1978	946	7,832	8,778
1979	1,000	7,690	8,690
1980	877	7,645	8,522
1981	972	7,772	8,744
1982	921	7,790	8,711
1983	802	7,308	8,110
1984	756	6,870	7,626
1985	551	6,546	7,097
1986	838	6,151	6,989
1987	561	5,387	5,948
1988	566	4,935	5,501
1989	540	4,613	5,153
1990	445	4,483	4,928
1991	492	4,318	4,810
1992	621	4,309	4,930
1993	565	4,213	4,778
SALARIES AND WAGES/TRAITEMENTS ET SALAIRES			
1975	$11,137,000	$106,195,000	$117,332,000
1976	10,355,000	115,389,000	125,744,000
1977	9,446,000	129,530,000	138,976,000
1978	11,843,000	131,438,000	143,281,000
1979	13,496,000	140,948,000	154,444,000
1980	12,876,000	157,097,000	169,973,000
1981	17,049,000	185,131,000	202,180,000
1982	18,878,000	202,769,000	221,647,000
1983	17,597,000	217,999,000	235,596,000
1984	18,760,000	221,162,000	239,922,000
1985	14,420,000	235,259,000	249,679,000
1986	21,332,000	236,571,000	257,903,000
1987	16,399,000	226,266,000	242,665,000
1988	17,200,000	213,000,000	230,200,000
1989	18,500,000	219,000,000	237,500,000
1990	15,800,000	225,800,000	241,600,000
1991	17,800,000	234,600,000	252,400,000
1992	20,900,000	242,400,000	263,300,000
1993	21,000,000	237,200,000	258,200,000

TABLE 10.11 (concluded)

TABLEAU 10.11 (fin)

Number of workers[1], and total salaries and wages in tobacco processing and manufacturing, Canada, 1975 to 1993

Nombre des travailleurs[1] oeuvrant dans le traitement du tabac et la confection de ses produits, et total des traitements et salaires, Canada, 1975 à 1993

[1] Includes administration, sale, etc./Inclut le personnel de l'administration, des ventes, etc.

Source: Statistics Canada, *Tobacco Products Industries 1981, 1982, 1983, 1984* (Ottawa: Statistics Canada, Catalogue No. 32- 225, 1983, 1984, 1985 and 1986 respectively). Statistics Canada, *Beverage + Tobacco Products Industries 1985, 1986, 1987, 1988, 1989, 1990, 1991, 1992,* and *1993* (Ottawa: Statistics Canada, Catalogue No. 32-251, 1988, 1989, 1990, 1991, 1992, 1993, and 1994, respectively).

Statistique Canada, *Industries du tabac 1981, 1982, 1983, 1984* (Ottawa : Statistique Canada, Catalogue no 32-225, 1983, 1984, 1985, et 1986 respectivement). Statistique Canada, *Industries du tabac et des boissons 1985, 1986, 1987, 1988, 1989, 1990, 1991, 1992, et 1993* (Ottawa: Statistique Canada, Catalogue no 32- 251, 1988, 1989, 1990, 1991, 1992, 1993 et 1994, respectivement).

| TABLE 10.12 | TABLEAU 10.12 |

Number of workers, total salaries and wages, and value of shipments, imports and exports in the pharmaceutical industry, Canada, 1976 to 1993

Nombre de travailleurs, salaires totaux, et valeur des cargaisons des importations et des exportations de l'industrie pharmaceutique, Canada, de 1976 à 1993

YEAR/ ANNEE	TOTAL WORKERS/ TOTAL DES TRAVAILLEURS	WAGES & SALARIES/ TRAITEMENTS SALAIRES	SHIPMENTS/ LIVRAISONS	IMPORTS/ IMPORTATIONS	EXPORTS/ EXPORTATIONS	APPARENT DOMESTIC MARKET/ MARCHÉ NATIONAL APPARENT
			(THOUSANDS OF DOLLARS/MILLIERS DE DOLLARS)			
1976	14,434	$189,069	$698,789	n.a.	n.a.	n.a.
1977	14,231	203,162	758,415	n.a.	n.a.	n.a.
1978	15,173	232,241	910,481	n.a.	n.a.	n.a.
1979	16,433	279,941	1,030,201	n.a.	n.a.	n.a.
1980	15,796	294,483	1,144,271	$225,743	$79,165	$1,290,849
1981	16,058	337,523	1,327,421	238,809	85,070	1,481,160
1982	15,260	364,590	1,457,760	267,581	103,095	1,622,246
1983	15,268	390,280	1,661,986	327,497	121,722	1,867,761
1984	15,184	418,994	1,839,822	377,903	120,147	2,097,578
1985	16,704	487,907	2,229,814	359,477	120,910	2,468,381
1986	17,127	526,952	2,489,344	447,101	144,682	2,791,763
1987	18,578	592,616	2,931,880	504,787	164,540	3,272,127
1988	19,319	651,964	3,180,422	557,222	128,196	3,609,448
1989	19,398	678,939	3,257,348	588,492	146,064	3,699,776
1990	19,876	733,556	3,581,977	709,946	181,863	4,110,060
1991	21,146	815,278	3,796,938	864,431	183,181	4,478,188
1992	21,354	851,343	4,146,955	1,192,703	261,028	5,078,630
1993	21,872	903,453	4,543,987	1,461,765	318,606	5,687,146

Source: Statistics Canada *Pharmaceuticals, Cleaning Compounds and Toilet Preparations 1982, 1983*, and *1984* (Ottawa: Statistics Canada, Catalogue 46-223, 1984, 1985 and 1986); Statistics Canada *Chemical and Chemical Products Industries 1985, 1986, 1987, 1988, 1989, 1990, 1991*, and *1992* (Ottawa: Statistics Canada, Catalogue 46-250, 1987, 1988, 1989, 1990, 1991, 1992, 1993 and 1994).

Statistique Canada *Produits pharmaceutiques, produits de nettoyage et produits de toilette 1982, 1983* and *1984* (Ottawa: Statistique Canada, catalogue 46-223, 1984, 1985 and 1986); Statistics Canada *Industries chimiques 1985, 1986, 1987, 1988, 1989, 1990, 1991*, et *1992* (Ottawa: Statistics Canada, catalogue 46-250, 1987, 1988, 1989, 1990, 1991, 1992, 1993, et 1994).

TABLE 10.13 **TABLEAU 10.13**

Representative prices for illegal drugs at successive stages of trafficking, Canada, 1992

Prix représentatifs des drogues illicites à diverses étapes de leur trafic, Canada, 1992

	PRICES FOR HEROIN THE CANADIAN MARKET/PRIX DE L'HEROINE	
WEIGHT/POIDS	NO. 4 HEROIN/HEROIN N° 4 (INJECTABLE FORM)/(A INJECTER)	NO. 3 HEROIN/HEROINE N° 3 (SMOKABLE FORM) (FORME FUMABLE)
1 kilogram/ 1 kilogramme	(pure) $120,000-$200,000	(85%) $100,000-$150,000
1 ounce (28 gram)/ 1 once (28 grammes)	(pure) $8,000-$12,000	(75%) $4,000-$6,000
1 gram/ 1 gramme	(pure) $700-$800	(45%) $200-$300
0.1 gram/ 0,1 gramme	(5%-6%) $30-$60	(45%) $35-$70

	PRICES FOR COCAINE HYDROCHLORIDE IN CANADA/PRIX DU CHLORHYDRATE DE COCAINE	
LEVEL/ETAPE	WEIGHT/POIDS	PRICE/PRIX
Wholesale/Prix de gros	1 kilogram of cocaine hydrochloride (pure)/ 1 kilogramme de chlorhydrate de cocaïne (pure)	$25,000-$65,000
Retail/Prix de détail	1 ounce (28 grams) of cocaine hydrochloride (60% pure)/ 1 once (28 grammes) de chlorhydrate de cocaïne (pureté de 60 %)	$1,000-$3,000
	1 gram of cocaine hydrochloride (60% pure)/ 1 gramme de chlorhydrate de cocaïne (pureté de 60 %)	$70-$200

	PRICES FOR LIQUID HASHISH AT SUCCESSIVE STAGES OF TRAFFICKING/ PRIX DU HASCHICH LIQUIDE
LEVEL/ETAPE	SOURCE: JAMAICA/JAMAIQUE
Source/Source 1 pound/livre	$1,250-$1,500
Traffic/Trafiquant (Canada) 1 pound/livre	$4,000-$6,500
Street/Détail (Canada) 1 ounce/once	$300-$500
1 gram/gramme	$30-$50

	PRICES FOR HASHISH AT SUCCESSIVE STAGES OF TRAFFICKING/PRIX DU HASCHICH	
LEVEL AND WEIGHT/ ETAPE ET POIDS	SOURCE AREA/SOURCE	
	LEBANON/LIBAN	PAKISTAN/PAKISTAN
Source/Source 1 pound/livre	$50-$125	$10-$40
Traffic/Trafiquant (Canada) 1 pound/livre	$1,600-$4,100	$1,600-$4,100
Street/Détail (Canada) 1 ounce/once 1 gram/gramme	$220-$900 $15-$50	$220-$900 $15-$30

TABLE 10.13 (concluded)   **TABLEAU 10.13** (fin)

Representative prices for illegal drugs at successive stages of trafficking, Canada, 1992

Prix représentatifs des drogues illicites à diverses étapes de leur trafic, Canada, 1992

PRICES FOR MARIHUANA AT SUCCESSIVE STAGES OF TRAFFICKING/ PRIX DE LA MARIHUANA					
LEVEL AND WEIGHT/ ETAPE ET POIDS	COLUMBIA/ COLOMBIE	JAMAICA/ JAMAIQUE	SOURCE AREA/SOURCE THAILAND/ THAILANDE	U.S.A./ ETATS-UNIS	MEXICO/ MEXIQUE
Source/Source 1 pound/livre	$5-$10	$100	$6-$18	$700-$900 Sinsemilla	$60-$120
Traffic/Trafiquant (Canada) 1 pound/livre	$700-$2,200	$400-$2,000	$2,500	$2,200-$3,300 Sinsemilla	$1,600-$2,500
Street/Détail (Canada) 1 ounce or unit/1 once ou dose	$75-$200	$35-$165	$25-$40 per stick/ le bâtonnet	$200-$350 Sinsemilla	$200-$250

Source: Drug Enforcement Directorate, Royal Canadian Mounted Police, *National Drug Intelligence Estimate 1993* (Ottawa: Ministry of Supply and Services Canada 1995).

Direction de la police des drogues, Gendarmerie royale du Canada, *Rapport annuel national sur les drogues, 1993* (Ottawa : Approvisionnements et Services Canada, 1995).

TABLE 10.14

TABLEAU 10.14

Type and amount of drugs seized in Canada, 1985 to 1992

Genres et quantités de drogues saisies, Canada, 1985 à 1992

DRUG/DROGUE	AMOUNT OF DRUGS SEIZED/QUANTITES SAISIES							
	1985	1986	1987	1988	1989	1990	1991	1992
Heroin/Héroïne[1] (kg)	65	48	45	69	44	65	107	117
Cocaine/Cocaïne[1,2] (kg)	170	247	283	350	959	595	1,755	5,202
Cannabis[3] (kg):								
Marihuana/Marijuana	3,765	8,314	26,475	25,164	3,744	16,033	4,426	13,722
Hashish/Haschich	18,973	17,837	23,968	7,750	2,189	67,793	33,460	15,822
Liquid Hashish/Haschich liquide	202	100	440	259	261	337	409	456
Total	**22,940**	**26,251**	**50,883**	**33,173**	**6,194**	**84,163**	**38,295**	**30,000**
Chemical Drugs(kg)[3]/Drogues chimiques[3]:								
Prescription Drugs/Drogues d'ordonnance[4]	88.954	0.091	35.179	0.454	4.201	0.002	0.006	0.683
Controlled Drugs (kg)/Drogues contrôlées (kg)								
Methamphetamine/Méthamphétamine	8.239	11.474	0.424	6.887	0.171	1.904	2.134	10.654
Amphetamine/Amphétamines	0.047	0.034	0.128	0.265	0.025	0.129	0.590	0.632
Barbiturates/Barbituriques	0.233	0.191	0.007	0.001	0.048	0.000	0.785	0.020
Other/Autres	2.937	0.524	12.117	3.841	0.026	0.888	502.058	1.239
Total	**11.456**	**12.223**	**12.676**	**10.994**	**0.270**	**2.921**	**505.567**	**12.545**
Restricted Drugs/Drogues restreintes:								
LSD (single doses/doses simples)	236,958	469,916	124,320	135,685	68,661	24,075	27,176	27,381
MDA (kg)	3.768	5.292	0.671	0.054	0.034	0.004	0.029	0.071
Other/Autres (kg)	319.810	128.713	115.308	51.293	17.485	15.480	61.289	19.893
Narcotic Control Act/Loi sur les stupéfiants								
PCP (kg)	20.191	7.212	3.212	7.287	0.464	32.026	0.979	4.123

[1] Includes seizures made by the RCMP, Canada Customs, Vancouver City Police, Ontario Provincial Police, Metropolitan Toronto Police, Quebec Police Force and Montreal Urban Community Police./Incluent les saisies effectuées par la GRC, la Douane canadien, la Police de Vancouver, la Police provinciale de l'Ontario, la Police de la région métropolitaine de Toronto, la Sûreté du Québec, et la Police de la communauté urbaine de Montréal.

[2] Seizures of cocaine by Quebec Poilice Force were not available for the year 1985./Les quantités de cocaïne saisies par la Sûreté du Québec n'étaient pas disponibles pour l'année 1985.

[3] Includes seizures made by the RCMP and Canada Customs./Incluent les saisies effectuées par la GRC et la Douane canadienne.

[4] Includes prescription drugs listed under Schedule F of the Food and Drug Act. Included in this schedule are steroids./Incluent les drogues d'ordonnance inscrites à l'Annexe F de la Loi sur les aliments et drogues, laquelle comprend les stéroïdes.

Note: Annual variations may reflect major seizures that occurred during the year and not real changes in supply./Les variations annuelles peuvent refléter les principales saisies effectuées pendant l'année, et non les changements réels de l'approvisionnement.

Source: Drug Enforcement Directorate, Royal Canadian Mounted Police, *National Drug Intelligence Estimate 1990, 1991, 1992,* and *1993* (Ottawa: Ministry of Supply and Services Canada, 1991, 1992, 1993, and 1995, respectively).

Direction de la police des drogues, Gendarmerie royale du Canada, *Rapport annuel national sur les drogues, 1990, 1991 1992, et 1992* (Ottawa : Approvisionnements et Services Canada, 1991, 1992, 1993, et 1995 respectivement).

TABLE 10.15

TABLEAU 10.15

The costs of alcohol, tobacco and illicit drugs in Canada, 1992

Coûts de l'alcool, du tabac et des drogues illicites au Canada, 1992

	Millions of dollars/Millions de dollars			
	Alcohol/ Alcool	Tobacco / Tabac	Illicit drugs/ Drogues illicites	Total ATD/ Total ATD
1. Direct health care costs: total/Coûts directs des soins de santé: total	**$1,300.6**	**$2,675.5**	**$88.0**	**$4,064.1**
1.1 Morbidity/Morbidité				
General hospitals/Hôpitaux généraux	666.0	1,752.9	34.0	2,542.9
Psychiatric hospitals/Hôpitaux psychiatriques	29.0	0.0	4.3	33.3
1.2 Co-morbidity/Co-morbidité	72.0	0.0	4.6	76.6
1.3 Ambulance services/Services ambulanciers	21.8	57.2	1.1	80.1
1.4 Residential care/Soins résidentiels	180.9	0.0	20.9	201.8
1.5 Non-residential treatment/Traitements non résidentiels	82.1	0.0	7.9	90.0
1.6 Ambulatory care: physician fees/Traitements ambulatoires: honoraires des médecins	127.4	339.6	8.0	475.0
1.7 Prescription drugs/Drogues d'ordonnance	95.5	457.3	5.8	558.5
1.8 Other health care costs/Autres coûts des soins de santé	26.0	68.4	1.3	95.8
2. Direct losses associated with the workplace/ Pertes directes associées au milieu de travail	**14.2**	**0.4**	**5.5**	**20.1**
2.1 EAP & health promotion programs/PAE et programmes de promotion de la santé	14.2	0.4	3.5	18.1
2.2 Drug testing in the workplace/Dépistage des drogues au travail	N.A.	0	2	2
3. Direct administrative costs for transfer payments/Coûts d'administration directs pour transfert de paiements	**52.3**	**0**	**1.5**	**53.8**
3.1 Social welfare and other programs/Programmes de bien-être social et autres	3.6	0	N.A.	3.6
3.2 Workers'compensation/Indemnisation des travailleurs	48.7	0	1.5	50.2
3.3 Other administrative costs /Autres coûts d'administration	N.A.	N.A.	N.A.	N.A.
4. Direct costs for prevention and research/Coûts directs de prévention et de recherche	**141.4**	**48.0**	**41.9**	**231.1**
4.1 Research /Recherche	21.6	34.6	5.0	61.1
4.2 Prevention programs /Programmes de prévention	118.9	13.4	36.7	168.9
4.3 Training costs for physicians & nurses/Coûts de formation des médecins et des infirmiers	0.9	N.A.	0.2	1.1
4.4 Averting behaviour costs/Coûts de prévention de certains comportements	N.A.	N.A.	N.A.	N.A.

TABLE 10.15 (concluded)   **TABLEAU 10.15** (fin)

The costs of alcohol, tobacco and illicit drugs in Canada, 1992

| | Millions of dollars | | | |
	Alcohol/	Tobacco /	Illicit drugs/	Total ATD/
5. Direct law enforcement costs/Coûts directs de la répression criminelle	**1,359.1**	**0.0**	**400.3**	**1,759.4**
5.1 Police/Police	665.4	N.A.	208.3	873.7
5.2 Courts/Tribunaux	304.4	N.A.	59.2	363.6
5.3 Corrections (including probation)/Service correctionnel (dont probation)	389.3	N.A.	123.8	513.1
5.4 Customs and excise/Douanes et accise	N.A.	N.A.	9.0	9.0
6. Other direct costs/Autres coûts directs	**518.0**	**17.1**	**10.7**	**545.8**
6.1 Fire damage/Dommages dus au feu	35.2	17.1	N.A.	52.3
6.2 Traffic accident damage/Dommages dus aux accidents routiers	482.8	0.0	10.7	493.5
7. Indirect costs: productivity losses/Coûts indirects: pertes de productivité	**4,136.5**	**6,818.8**	**823.1**	**11,778.4**
7.1 Productivity losses due to morbidity/Pertes dues à la morbidité	1,397.7	84.5	275.7	1,757.9
7.2 Productivity losses due to mortality/Pertes dues à la mortalité	2,738.8	6,734.3	547.4	10,020.5
7.3 Productivity losses due to crime/Pertes dues à la criminalité	0.0	0.0	N.A.	N.A.
Total/Total	**$7,522.1**	**$9,559.8**	**$1,371.0**	**$18,452.9**
Total as % of GDP/Total en pourcentage du PNB	1.09%	1.39%	0.20%	2.67%
Total per capita/Total par habitant	$265.	$336.	$48.	$649.
Total as % of all substance-related costs/Total en pourcentage de tous les coûts associés aux drogues	40.8%	51.8%	7.4%	100.0%
Range of costs under extreme assumptions, based on sensitivity analyses of alternative prevalence estimates, discount rates and Resource Intensity Weights for different diagnoses ($ billions)/ Eventail des coûts selon des hypothêses extrêmes, selon les analyses de sensibilité des diverses estimations estimationsde prévalence possibles, des taux d'actualisation et des pondérations des ressources selon leur importance, pour différentes causes (milliards de dollars)	$6.3- -$8.6	$7.8- $11.1	$1.2- $1.5	$15.3- $21.3

Source: E. Single, L. Robson, X. Xie and J. Rehm, *The Costs of Substance Abuse in Canada*, Ottawa: Canadian Centre on Substance Abuse, 1996.

E. Single, L. Robson, X. Xie et J. Rehm, *The Costs of Substance Abuse in Canada*, Ottawa : Centre canadien de lutte contre l'alcoolisme et les toxicomanies, 1996.

TABLE 10.16   **TABLEAU 10.16**

The costs of alcohol in Canadian provinces, 1992   Coûts de l'alcool dans les provinces canadiennes, 1992

Province:	B.C./C.-B.	Alta./Alb.	Sask./Sask.	Man./Man.	Ont./Ont.
Population (1000s)/Population (milliers)	**3,451.3**	**2,632.4**	**1,004.5**	**1,113.1**	**10,609.8**
	(Thousands of dollars)/(Milliers de dollars)				
1. Direct health care costs: total/Coûts directs des soins de santé: total	**$179,437**	**$123,518**	**$40,243**	**$54,469**	**$447,682**
1.1 Morbidity/Morbidité- General hospitals/Hôpitaux généraux	91,048	64,271	17,845	28,236	225,379
Psychiatric hospitals/Hôpitaux psychiatriques	0	1,931	0	273	5,738
1.2 Co-morbidity/Co-morbidité	9,841	6,947	1,929	3,052	24,361
1.3 Ambulance services/Services ambulanciers	3,777	1,016	672	805	7,651
1.4 Residential care/Soins résidentiels	30,600	19,600	9,300	10,400	46,600
1.5 Non-residential treatment/Traitements non résidentiels	9,961	7,283	2,899	2,419	31,730
1.6 Ambulatory care: physician fees/Traitements ambulatoires: honoraires des médecins	16,967	11,353	3,339	3,636	59,091
1.7 Prescription drugs/Drogues d'ordonnance	11,587	8,838	3,372	3,737	35,621
1.8 Other health care costs/Autres coûts des soins de santé	5,656	2,279	887	1,911	11,511
2. Direct losses associated with the workplace/ Pertes directes associées au milieu de travail	**1,721**	**1,313**	**501**	**555**	**5,292**
2.1 EAP & health promotion programs/PAE et programmes de promotion de la santé	1,721	1,313	501	555	5,292
2.2 Drug testing in the workplace/Dépistage des drogues au travail	n.a.	n.a.	n.a.	n.a.	n.a.
3. Direct administrative costs for transfer payments/Coûts d'administration directs pour transfert de palements	**8,889**	**6,289**	**1,134**	**1,305**	**18,008**
3.1 Social welfare and other programs/Programmes de bien-être social et autres	443	231	129	51	1,054
3.2 Workers'compensation/Indemnisation des travailleurs	8,446	6,058	1,005	1,254	16,954
3.3 Other administrative costs /Autres coûts d'administration	n.a.	n.a.	n.a.	n.a.	n.a.
4. Direct costs for prevention and research/Coûts directs de prévention et de recherche	**19,857**	**20,193**	**3,895**	**4,335**	**61,119**
4.1 Research /Recherche	1,700	3,100	260	290	13,800
4.2 Prevention programs /Programmes de prévention	18,100	17,000	3,600	4,000	47,100
4.3 Training costs for physicians & nurses/Coûts de formation des médecins et des infirmiers	57	93	35	45	219
4.4 Averting behaviour costs/Coûts de prévention de certains comportements	n.a.	n.a.	n.a.	n.a.	n.a.

TABLE 10.16 (continued)   **TABLEAU 10.16** (suite)

The costs of alcohol in Canadian provinces, 1992   Coûts de l'alcool dans les provinces canadiennes, 1992

Province:	B.C./C.-B.	Alta./Alb.	Sask./Sask.	Man./Man.	Ont./Ont.
	(Thousands of dollars)/(Milliers de dollars)				
5. Direct law enforcement costs/Coûts directs de la répression criminelle	**142,900**	**111,300**	**62,400**	**45,500**	**530,200**
5.1 Police/Police	68,900	61,700	34,700	23,400	256,500
5.2 Courts/Tribunaux	37,300	28,400	11,000	9,900	123,500
5.3 Corrections/correctionnel	36,700	21,200	16,700	12,200	150,200
5.4 Customs and excise/Douanes et accise	--	--	--	--	--
6. Other direct costs/Autres coûts directs	**61,743**	**41,417**	**18,246**	**20,519**	**200,895**
6.1 Fire damage/Dommages dus au feu	4,863	2,707	1,191	1,425	11,514
6.2 Traffic accident damage/Dommages dus aux accidents routiers	56,880	38,710	17,055	19,094	189,381
7. Indirect costs: productivity losses/Coûts indirects: pertes de productivité	**529,316**	**445,299**	**139,557**	**156,859**	**1,598,731**
7.1 Productivity losses due to morbidity/Pertes dues à la morbidité	171,053	129,565	43,645	50,968	601,860
7.2 Productivity losses due to mortality/Pertes dues à la mortalité	358,263	315,734	95,912	105,891	996,871
7.3 Productivity losses due to crime/Pertes dues à la criminalité	n.a.	n.a.	n.a.	n.a.	n.a.
Total/Total	**$943,863.**	**$749,330.**	**$265,977.**	**$283,542.**	**$2,861,926**
Total as % of GDP/Total en pourcentage du PNB	1.09%	1.02%	1.27%	1.20%	1.02%
Total per capita/Total par habitant	$272	$285	$265	$255	$270

TABLE 10.16 (continued)

TABLEAU 10.16 (suite)

The costs of alcohol in Canadian provinces, 1992

Coûts de l'alcool dans les provinces canadiennes, 1992

Province:	Que./Québec	N.B./N.-B.	N.S.-N.-E./	P.E.I./P.-E.-I.	Nfld./T.-N.
Population (1000s)/Population (milliers)	**7,150.7**	**749.1**	**920.8**	**130.3**	**581.1**
	(Thousands of dollars)/(Milliers de dollars)				
1. Direct health care costs: total/Coûts directs des soins de santé: total	**$339,978**	**$24,652**	**$46,355**	**$7,837**	**$19,843**
1.1 Morbidity/Morbidité- General hospitals/Hôpitaux généraux	187,737	8,571	18,887	1,664	10,530
Psychiatric hospitals/Hôpitaux psychiatriques	16,207	836	3,276	0	715
1.2 Co-morbidity/Co-morbidité	20,293	926	2,041	180	1,138
1.3 Ambulance services/Services ambulanciers	6,120	48	345	22	159
1.4 Residential care/Soins résidentiels	37,400	7,140	13,100	4,690	1,990
1.5 Non-residential treatment/Traitements non résidentiels	20,638	2,162	2,658	376	1,677
1.6 Ambulatory care: physician fees/Traitements ambulatoires: honoraires des médecins	25,585	2,422	2,638	398	1,643
1.7 Prescription drugs/Drogues d'ordonnance	24,008	2,515	3,091	437	1,951
1.8 Other health care costs/Autres coûts des soins de santé	1,990	32	319	70	40
2. Direct losses associated with the workplace/ Pertes directes associées au milieu de travail	**3,567**	**374**	**459**	**65**	**290**
2.1 EAP & health promotion programs/PAE et programmes de promotion de la santé	3,567	374	459	65	290
2.2 Drug testing in the workplace/Dépistage des drogues au travail	n.a.	n.a.	n.a.	n.a.	n.a.
3. Direct administrative costs for transfer payments/Coûts d'administration directs pour transfert de paiements	**14,423**	**900**	**561**	**157**	**635**
3.1 Social welfare and other programs/Programmes de bien-être social et autres	1,484	96	7	17	123
3.2 Workers'compensation/Indemnisation des travailleurs	12,939	804	554	140	512
3.3 Other administrative costs /Autres coûts d'administration	n.a.	n.a.	n.a.	n.a.	n.a.
4. Direct costs for prevention and research/Coûts directs de prévention et de recherche	**27,564**	**2,890**	**3,577**	**546**	**2,270**
4.1 Research /Recherche	1,800	190	240	46	150
4.2 Prevention programs /Programmes de prévention	25,400	2,700	3,300	500	2,100
4.3 Training costs for physicians & nurses/Coûts de formation des médecins et des infirmiers	364	0	37	0	20
4.4 Averting behaviour costs/Coûts de prévention de certains comportements	n.a.	n.a.	n.a.	n.a.	n.a.

TABLE 10.16 (concluded)

TABLEAU 10.16 (fin)

The costs of alcohol in Canadian provinces, 1992

Coûts de l'alcool dans les provinces canadiennes, 1992

Province:	Que./Québec	N.B./N.-B.	N.S.-N.-E./	P.E.I./P.-E.-I.	Nfld./T.-N.
	(Thousands of dollars)/(Milliers de dollars)				
5. Direct law enforcement costs/Coûts directs de la répression criminelle	**236,700**	**38,700**	**49,700**	**10,100**	**28,500**
5.1 Police/Police	97,900	21,200	25,400	4,500	14,200
5.2 Courts/Tribunaux	41,300	9,600	15,900	2,300	6,300
5.3 Corrections/correctionnel	97,500	7,900	8,400	3,300	8,000
5.4 Customs and excise/Douanes et accise	0	0	0	0	0
6. Other direct costs/Autres coûts directs	**141,316**	**9,841**	**12,192**	**1,753**	**7,759**
6.1 Fire damage/Dommages dus au feu	10,452	644	887	153	625
6.2 Traffic accident damage/Dommages dus aux accidents routiers	130,864	9,197	11,305	1,600	7,134
7. Indirect costs: productivity losses/Coûts indirects: pertes de productivité	**964,971**	**101,287**	**127,249**	**16,470**	**56,036**
7.1 Productivity losses due to morbidity/Pertes dues à la morbidité	364,388	36,128	44,261	5,927	27,646
7.2 Productivity losses due to mortality/Pertes dues à la mortalité	600,583	65,159	82,988	10,543	28,390
7.3 Productivity losses due to crime/Pertes dues à la criminalité	n.a.	n.a.	n.a.	n.a.	n.a.
Total/Total	**$1,728,517**	**$178,645**	**$240,092**	**$36,928**	**$115,333**
Total as % of GDP/Total en pourcentage du PNB	1.11%	1.28%	1.35%	1.67%	1.26%
Total per capita/Total par habitant	$242	$239	$261	$283	$199

Source: E. Single, L. Robson, X. Xie and J. Rehm, *The Costs of Substance Abuse in Canada*, Ottawa: Canadian Centre on Substance Abuse, 1996.

E. Single, L. Robson, X. Xie et J. Rehm, *The Costs of Substance Abuse in Canada*, Ottawa : Centre canadien de lutte contre l'alcoolisme et les toxicomanies, 1996.

The costs of tobacco in Canadian provinces, 1992   Coûts du tabac dans les provinces canadiennes, 1992

Province:	B.C./C.-B.	Alta./Alb.	Sask./Sask.	Man./Man.	Ont./Ont.
Population (1000s)/Population (milliers)	3,451.3	2,632.4	1,004.5	1,113.1	10,609.8
	(Thousands of dollars)/(Milliers de dollars)				
1. Direct health care costs: total/Coûts directs des soins de santé: total	**$297,093**	**$215,464**	**$76,233**	**$103,284**	**$1,063,610**
1.1 Morbidity/Morbidité- General hospitals/Hôpitaux généraux	177,933	135,905	47,069	69,052	677,848
Psychiatric hospitals/Hôpitaux psychiatriques	0	0	0	0	7
1.2 Co-morbidity/Co-morbidité	0	0	0	0	0
1.3 Ambulance services/Services ambulanciers	7,380	2,148	1,773	1,969	23,010
1.4 Residential care/Soins résidentiels	n.a.	n.a.	n.a.	n.a.	n.a.
1.5 Non-residential treatment/Traitements non résidentiels	n.a.	n.a.	n.a.	n.a.	n.a.
1.6 Ambulatory care: physician fees/Traitements ambulatoires: honoraires des médecins	45,228	30,261	8,900	9,692	157,513
1.7 Prescription drugs/Drogues d'ordonnance	55,499	42,330	16,153	17,899	170,611
1.8 Other health care costs/Autres coûts des soins de santé	11,053	4,820	2,338	4,672	34,621
2. Direct losses associated with the workplace/ Pertes directes associées au milieu de travail	**48**	**37**	**14**	**16**	**148**
2.1 EAP & health promotion programs/PAE et programmes de promotion de la santé	48	37	14	16	148
2.2 Drug testing/Dépistage des drogues	n.a.	n.a.	n.a.	n.a.	n.a.
3. Direct administrative costs for transfer payments/Coûts d'administration directs pour transfert de paiements	**n.a.**	**n.a.**	**n.a.**	**n.a.**	**n.a.**
3.1 Social welfare and other programs/Programmes de bien-être social et autres	n.a.	n.a.	n.a.	n.a.	n.a.
3.2 Workers'compensation/Indemnisation des travailleurs	n.a.	n.a.	n.a.	n.a.	n.a.
3.3 Other administrative costs /Autres coûts d'administration	n.a.	n.a.	n.a.	n.a.	n.a.
4. Direct costs for prevention and research/Coûts directs de prévention et de recherche	**8,390**	**3,630**	**1,400**	**1,520**	**23,000**
4.1 Research /Recherche	4,100	3,100	1,200	1,300	13,200
4.2 Prevention programs /Programmes de prévention	4,090	530	200	220	9,800
4.3 Training costs for physicians & nurses/Coûts de formation des médecins et des infirmiers	n.a.	n.a.	n.a.	n.a.	
4.4 Averting behaviour costs/Coûts de prévention de certains comportements	n.a.	n.a.	n.a.	n.a.	n.a.

TABLE 10.17 (continued)

TABLEAU 10.17 (suite)

The costs of tobacco in Canadian provinces, 1992

Coûts du tabac dans les provinces canadiennes, 1992

Province:	B.C./C.-B.	Alta./Alb.	Sask./Sask.	Man./Man.	Ont./Ont.
	(Thousands of dollars)/(Milliers de dollars)				
5. Direct law enforcement costs/Coûts directs de la répression criminelle	**n.a.**	**n.a.**	**n.a.**	**n.a.**	**n.a.**
5.1 Police/Police	n.a.	n.a.	n.a.	n.a.	n.a.
5.2 Courts/Tribunaux	n.a.	n.a.	n.a.	n.a.	n.a.
5.3 Corrections/correctionnel	n.a.	n.a.	n.a.	n.a.	n.a.
5.4 Customs and excise/Douanes et accise	n.a.	n.a.	n.a.	n.a.	n.a.
6. Other direct costs/Autres coûts directs	**2,691**	**1,211**	**494**	**593**	**6,405**
6.1 Fire damage/Dommages dus au feu	2,691	1,211	494	593	6,405
6.2 Traffic accident damage/Dommages dus aux accidents routiers	n.a.	n.a.	n.a.	n.a.	n.a.
7. Indirect costs: productivity losses/Coûts indirects: pertes de productivité	**806,043**	**508,247**	**203,701**	**248,595**	**2,580,697**
7.1 Productivity losses due to morbidity/Pertes dues à la morbidité	7,910	5,540	2,386	2,498	30,259
7.2 Productivity losses due to mortality/Pertes dues à la mortalité	798,133	502,707	201,315	246,097	2,550,438
7.3 Productivity losses due to crime/Pertes dues à la criminalité	n.a.	n.a.	n.a.	n.a.	n.a.
Total/Total	**$1,114,065**	**$728,589**	**$281,842**	**$354,008**	**$3,673,860**
Total as % of GDP/Total en pourcentage du PNB	1.29	0.99	1.34	1.5	1.31
Total per capita/Total par habitant	$322	$277	$281	$318	$346

TABLE 10.17 (continued)

TABLEAU 10.17 (suite)

The costs of tobacco in Canadian provinces, 1992

Coûts du tabac dans les provinces canadiennes, 1992

Province:	Que./Québec	N.B./N.-B.	N.S.-N.-E./	P.E.I./P.-E.-I.	Nfld./T.-N.
Population (1000s)/Population (milliers)	**7,150.7**	**749.1**	**920.8**	**130.3**	**581.1**
	(Thousands of dollars)/(Milliers de dollars)				
1. Direct health care costs: total/Coûts directs des soins de santé: total	**$661,313**	**$73,577**	**$95,020**	**$8,729**	**$50,157**
1.1 Morbidity/Morbidité- General hospitals/Hôpitaux généraux	458,321	54,564	70,693	5,280	35,761
Psychiatric hospitals/Hôpitaux psychiatriques	7	0	4	0	0
1.2 Co-morbidity/Co-morbidité	0	0	0	0	0
1.3 Ambulance services/Services ambulanciers	14,941	305	1,291	70	538
1.4 Residential care/Soins résidentiels	n.a.	n.a.	n.a.	n.a.	n.a.
1.5 Non-residential treatment/Traitements non résidentiels	n.a.	n.a.	n.a.	n.a.	n.a.
1.6 Ambulatory care: physician fees/Traitements ambulatoires: honoraires des médecins	68,199	6,456	7,031	1,061	4,379
1.7 Prescription drugs/Drogues d'ordonnance	114,987	12,046	14,807	2,095	9,344
1.8 Other health care costs/Autres coûts des soins de santé	4,858	206	1,194	223	135
2. Direct losses associated with the workplace/ Pertes directes associées au milieu de travail	**100**	**10**	**13**	**2**	**8**
2.1 EAP & health promotion programs/PAE et programmes de promotion de la santé	100	10	13	2	8
2.2 Drug testing/Dépistage des drogues	n.a.	n.a.	n.a.	n.a.	n.a.
3. Direct administrative costs for transfer payments/Coûts d'administration directs pour transfert de paiements	**n.a.**	**n.a.**	**n.a.**	**n.a.**	**n.a.**
3.1 Social welfare and other programs/Programmes de bien-être social et autres	n.a.	n.a.	n.a.	n.a.	n.a.
3.2 Workers'compensation/Indemnisation des travailleurs	n.a.	n.a.	n.a.	n.a.	n.a.
3.3 Other administrative costs /Autres coûts d'administration	n.a.	n.a.	n.a.	n.a.	n.a.
4. Direct costs for prevention and research/Coûts directs de prévention et de recherche	**9,930**	**1,050**	**1,280**	**190**	**810**
4.1 Research /Recherche	8,500	900	1,100	160	690
4.2 Prevention programs /Programmes de prévention	1,430	150	180	30	120
4.3 Training costs for physicians & nurses/Coûts de formation des médecins et des infirmiers	n.a.	n.a.	n.a.	n.a.	
4.4 Averting behaviour costs/Coûts de prévention de certains comportements	n.a.	n.a.	n.a.	n.a.	n.a.

TABLE 10.17 (concluded)

TABLEAU 10.17 (fin)

The costs of tobacco in Canadian provinces, 1992

Coûts du tabac dans les provinces canadiennes, 1992

Province:	Que./Québec	N.B./N.-B.	N.S.-N.-E./	P.E.I./P.-E.-I.	Nfld./T.-N.
	(Thousands of dollars)/(Milliers de dollars)				
5. Direct law enforcement costs/Coûts directs de la répression criminelle	**n.a.**	**n.a.**	**n.a.**	**n.a.**	**n.a.**
5.1 Police/Police	n.a.	n.a.	n.a.	n.a.	n.a.
5.2 Courts/Tribunaux	n.a.	n.a.	n.a.	n.a.	n.a.
5.3 Corrections/correctionnel	n.a.	n.a.	n.a.	n.a.	n.a.
5.4 Customs and excise/Douanes et accise	n.a.	n.a.	n.a.	n.a.	n.a.
6. Other direct costs/Autres coûts directs	**4,110**	**279**	**460**	**59**	**246**
6.1 Fire damage/Dommages dus au feu	4,110	279	460	59	246
6.2 Traffic accident damage/Dommages dus aux accidents routiers	n.a.	n.a.	n.a.	n.a.	n.a.
7. Indirect costs: productivity losses/Coûts indirects: pertes de productivité	**1,691,295**	**190,635**	**270,243**	**38,078**	**119,755**
7.1 Productivity losses due to morbidity/Pertes dues à la morbidité	30,333	2,899	3,386	310	1,881
7.2 Productivity losses due to mortality/Pertes dues à la mortalité	1,660,962	187,736	266,857	37,768	117,874
7.3 Productivity losses due to crime/Pertes dues à la criminalité	n.a.	n.a.	n.a.	n.a.	n.a.
Total/Total	**$2,366,748**	**$265,551**	**$367,016**	**$47,058**	**$170,976**
Total as % of GDP/Total en pourcentage du PNB	1.51	1.9	2.06	2.14	1.86
Total per capita/Total par habitant	$331	$354	$398	$361	$294

Source: E. Single, L. Robson, X. Xie and J. Rehm, *The Costs of Substance Abuse in Canada*, Ottawa: Canadian Centre on Substance Abuse, 1996.

E. Single, L. Robson, X. Xie et J. Rehm, *The Costs of Substance Abuse in Canada*, Ottawa : Centre canadien de lutte contre l'alcoolisme et les toxicomanies, 1996.

TABLE 10.18   **TABLEAU 10.18**

The costs of illicit drugs in Canadian provinces, 1992   Coûts des drogues illicites dans les provinces canadiennes, 1992

Province:	B.C./C.-B.	Alta./Alb.	Sask./Sask.	Man./Man.	Ont./Ont.
Population (1000s)/Population (milliers)	**3,451.3**	**2,632.4**	**1,004.5**	**1,113.1**	**10,609.8**
	(Thousands of dollars)/(Milliers de dollars)				
1. Direct health care costs: total/Coûts directs des soins de santé: total	**$10,954**	**$10,775**	**$2,512**	**$3,380**	**$30,702**
1.1 Morbidity/Morbidité- General hospitals/Hôpitaux généraux	3,772	5,435	602	1,153	12,219
Psychiatric hospitals/Hôpitaux psychiatriques0	94	0	68	1,422	
1.2 Co-morbidity/Co-morbidité	525	756	84	160	1,699
1.3 Ambulance services/Services ambulanciers	156	86	23	33	415
1.4 Residential care/Soins résidentiels	3,540	2,260	1,080	1,200	5,400
1.5 Non-residential treatment/Traitements non résidentiels	960	702	279	233	3,059
1.6 Ambulatory care: physician fees/Traitements ambulatoires: honoraires des médecins	1,063	711	209	228	3,701
1.7 Prescription drugs/Drogues d'ordonnance	704	537	205	227	2,163
1.8 Other health care costs/Autres coûts des soins de santé	234	193	30	78	624
2. Direct losses associated with the workplace/ Pertes directes associées au milieu de travail	**670**	**508**	**196**	**217**	**2,073**
2.1 EAP & health promotion programs/PAE et programmes de promotion de la santé	430	328	125	139	1,323
2.2 Drug testing/Dépistage des drogues	240	180	71	78	750
3. Direct administrative costs for transfer payments/Coûts d'administration directs pour transfert de paiements	**267**	**192**	**32**	**40**	**536**
3.1 Social welfare and other programs/Programmes de bien-être social et autres	n.a.	n.a.	n.a.	n.a.	n.a.
3.2 Workers'compensation/Indemnisation des travailleurs	267	192	32	40	536
3.3 Other administrative costs /Autres coûts d'administration	n.a.	n.a.	n.a.	n.a.	n.a.
4. Direct costs for prevention and research/Coûts directs de prévention et de recherche	**5,794**	**5,043**	**1,199**	**1,921**	**17,705**
4.1 Research /Recherche	360	730	50	50	3,300
4.2 Prevention programs /Programmes de prévention	5,420	4,290	1,140	1,860	14,350
4.3 Training costs for physicians & nurses/Coûts de formation des médecins et des infirmiers	14	23	9	11	55
4.4 Averting behaviour costs/Coûts de prévention de certains comportements	n.a.	n.a.	n.a.	n.a.	n.a.

TABLE 10.18 (continued)

TABLEAU 10.18 (suite)

The costs of illicit drugs in Canadian provinces, 1992

Coûts des drogues illicites dans les provinces canadiennes, 1992

Province:	B.C./C.-B.	Alta./Alb.	Sask./Sask.	Man./Man.	Ont./Ont.
	(Thousands of dollars)/(Milliers de dollars)				
5. Direct law enforcement costs/Coûts directs de la répression criminelle	**57,400**	**29,830**	**10,320**	**14,850**	**160,800**
5.1 Police/Police	27,100	16,500	6,200	7,800	74,300
5.2 Courts/Tribunaux	14,600	4,500	900	1,600	22,900
5.3 Corrections/correctionnel	4,600	8,000	2,900	5,100	60,200
5.4 Customs and excise/Douanes et accise	1,100	830	320	350	3,400
6. Other direct costs/Autres coûts directs	**1260**	**858**	**378**	**423**	**4,195**
6.1 Fire damage/Dommages dus au feu	n.a.	n.a.	n.a.	n.a.	n.a.
6.2 Traffic accident damage/Dommages dus aux accidents routiers	1,260	858	378	423	4,195
7. Indirect costs: productivity losses/Coûts indirects: pertes de productivité	**132,489**	**88,052**	**21,491**	**24,301**	**291,618**
7.1 Productivity losses due to morbidity/Pertes dues à la morbidité	33,805	25,886	8,641	10,059	119,145
7.2 Productivity losses due to mortality/Pertes dues à la mortalité	98,684	62,166	12,850	14,242	172,473
7.3 Productivity losses due to crime/Pertes dues à la criminalité	n.a.	n.a.	n.a.	n.a.	n.a.
Total/Total	**$208,834**	**$135,258**	**$36,128**	**$45,132**	**$507,629**
Total as % of GDP/Total en pourcentage du PNB	0.24	0.18	0.17	0.19	0.18
Total per capita/Total par habitant	$60	$51	$36	$40	$48

TABLE 10.18 (continued)   **TABLEAU 10.18** (suite)

The costs of illicit drugs in Canadian provinces, 1992   Coûts des drogues illicites dans les provinces canadiennes, 1992

Province:	Que./Québec	N.B./N.-B.	N.S.-N.-E./	P.E.I./P.-E.-I.	Nfld./T.-N.
Population (1000s)/Population (milliers)	7,150.7	749.1	920.8	130.3	581.1
	(Thousands of dollars)/(Milliers de dollars)				
1. Direct health care costs: total/Coûts directs des soins de santé: total	**$22,179**	**$1,746**	**$4,353**	**$732**	**$1,762**
1.1 Morbidity/Morbidité- General hospitals/Hôpitaux généraux	9,407	315	1,219	87	962
Psychiatric hospitals/Hôpitaux psychiatriques	1,789	41	812	0	35
1.2 Co-morbidity/Co-morbidité	1,225	44	170	12	134
1.3 Ambulance services/Services ambulanciers	307	2	22	1	14
1.4 Residential care/Soins résidentiels	4,300	830	1,500	540	230
1.5 Non-residential treatment/Traitements non résidentiels	1,990	208	256	36	162
1.6 Ambulatory care: physician fees/Traitements ambulatoires: honoraires des médecins	1,603	152	165	25	103
1.7 Prescription drugs/Drogues d'ordonnance	1,458	153	188	27	118
1.8 Other health care costs/Autres coûts des soins de santé	100	1	21	4	4
2. Direct losses associated with the workplace/ Pertes directes associées au milieu de travail	**1,392**	**146**	**180**	**25**	**113**
2.1 EAP & health promotion programs/PAE et programmes de promotion de la santé	892	93	115	16	72
2.2 Drug testing/Dépistage des drogues	500	53	65	9	41
3. Direct administrative costs for transfer payments/Coûts d'administration directs pour transfert de paiements	**409**	**25**	**18**	**4**	**16**
3.1 Social welfare and other programs/Programmes de bien-être social et autres	n.a.	n.a.	n.a.	n.a.	n.a.
3.2 Workers'compensation/Indemnisation des travailleurs	409	25	18	4	16
3.3 Other administrative costs /Autres coûts d'administration	n.a.	n.a.	n.a.	n.a.	n.a.
4. Direct costs for prevention and research/Coûts directs de prévention et de recherche	**8,511**	**886**	**1,103**	**156**	**693**
4.1 Research /Recherche	300	36	44	6	28
4.2 Prevention programs /Programmes de prévention	8,120	850	1,050	150	660
4.3 Training costs for physicians & nurses/Coûts de formation des médecins et des infirmiers	91	0	9	0	5
4.4 Averting behaviour costs/Coûts de prévention de certains comportements	n.a.	n.a.	n.a.	n.a.	n.a.

TABLE 10.18 (concluded)　　　　　　　　　　　　　　　　　**TABLEAU 10.18** (fin)

The costs of illicit drugs in Canadian provinces, 1992　　　　Coûts des drogues illicites dans les provinces canadiennes, 1992

Province:	Que./Québec	N.B./N.-B.	N.S.-N.-E./	P.E.I./P.-E.-I.	Nfld./T.-N.
	(Thousands of dollars)/(Milliers de dollars)				
5. Direct law enforcement costs/Coûts directs de la répression criminelle	**92,200**	**7,240**	**10,990**	**1,141**	**6,880**
5.1　Police/Police	52,400	4,700	5,900	700	4,000
5.2　Courts/Tribunaux	13,100	700	1,500	100	700
5.3　Corrections/correctionnel	24,400	1,600	3,300	300	2,000
5.4　Customs and excise/Douanes et accise	2,300	240	290	41	180
6. Other direct costs/Autres coûts directs	**2,889**	**204**	**250**	**35**	**158**
6.1　Fire damage/Dommages dus au feu	n.a.	n.a.	n.a.	n.a.	n.a.
6.2　Traffic accident damage/Dommages dus aux accidents routiers	2,889	204	250	35	158
7. Indirect costs: productivity losses/Coûts indirects: pertes de productivité	**206,719**	**15,009**	**19,262**	**2,593**	**8,617**
7.1　Productivity losses due to morbidity/Pertes dues à la morbidité	71,780	7,153	8,710	1,165	5,489
7.2　Productivity losses due to mortality/Pertes dues à la mortalité	134,939	7,856	10,552	1,428	3,128
7.3　Productivity losses due to crime/Pertes dues à la criminalité	n.a.	n.a.	n.a.	n.a.	n.a.
Total/Total	**$334,299**	**$25,256**	**$36,156**	**$4,686**	**$18,239**
Total as % of GDP/Total en pourcentage du PNB	0.21	0.18	0.2	0.21	0.2
Total per capita/Total par habitant	$47	$34	$39	$36	$31

Source:　E. Single, L. Robson, X. Xie and J. Rehm, *The Costs of Substance Abuse in Canada*, Ottawa: Canadian Centre on Substance Abuse, 1996.

E. Single, L. Robson, X. Xie et J. Rehm, *The Costs of Substance Abuse in Canada*, Ottawa : Centre canadien de lutte contre l'alcoolisme et les toxicomanies, 1996.

11 The Law Regarding Alcohol and Drugs In Canada

11 Les lois régissant l'alcool et les drogues au Canada

Tables

Tableaux

The Law Regarding Alcohol and Drugs In Canada

by Robert Solomon, Professor of Law, University of Western Ontario

Federal alcohol regulations

The federal government has authority over the importing and exporting of alcohol products, alcohol-related excise taxes and broadcast advertising. The broadcasting regulations prohibit a range of messages, including any that attempt to influence non-drinkers to drink; appeal to minors; associate consumption with high-risk activities; suggest consumption is associated with social acceptance, personal success, or athletic or business achievement; or violate the relevant provincial advertising law.

Provincial alcohol regulations

The control and sale of alcohol is also regulated by legislation in each province. The 10 provinces and two territories all have, to varying degrees, monopolies that control the sale of alcohol for off-premises consumption. The legislation governs the sale of alcohol in on-premises establishments, pricing, the minimum drinking age and the transport of alcohol. It also prohibits public consumption, intoxication and the sale of alcohol to intoxicated persons.

Provincial governments also have control over alcohol marketing and advertising. Typically, the provincial legislation prohibits certain marketing practices, such as price discounting, drinking contests, giving alcohol as prizes and free drinks. Most of the provincial advertising regulations prohibit lifestyle advertising, advertising that appeals to minors, advertising that depicts or encourages

Les lois régissant l'alcool et les drogues au Canada

par Robert Solomon, Professeur de droit, University of Western Ontario

La réglementation de l'alcool par le fédéral

Le gouvernement fédéral a juridiction sur l'importation et l'exportation des produits de l'alcool, les taxes d'accise et la publicité radiodiffusée reliées à l'alcool. Les règlements sur la radiodiffusion interdisent un éventail de messages, y compris tout message visant à amener les abstinents à consommer de l'alcool; s'adressant aux mineurs; associant la consommation de l'alcool à des activités à haut risque; associant la consommation de l'alcool à l'acceptation sociale, au succès personnel, ou au succès athlétique ou commercial; ou contrevenant aux lois provinciales pertinentes en matière de publicité.

La réglementation de l'alcool par les provinces

Le contrôle et la vente de l'alcool sont aussi soumis à la législation provinciale. Les dix provinces et les deux territoires jouissent chacun d'un monopole plus ou moins grand sur la vente des boissons alcooliques à consommer à l'extérieur des lieux. La législation régit la vente des boissons alcooliques à consommer sur les lieux d'achat, l'établissement des prix, l'âge légal de boire, et le transport des boissons alcooliques. Elle interdit en outre la consommation et l'intoxication en public, ainsi que la vente de boissons alcooliques aux personnes intoxiquées.

Les gouvernements provinciaux détiennent aussi le pouvoir sur la commercialisation et la publicité des

immoderate consumption, and advertising that associates alcohol with driving or other potentially dangerous activities.

As shown in Table 11.1, the legal drinking age is 19 in all Canadian provinces and territories, except in Quebec, Manitoba, and Alberta, where the minimum age is 18. However, drinking below these age limits is permitted in licensed establishments in New Brunswick and, under certain circumstances, in residences in P.E.I., Alberta, British Columbia, Ontario and Saskatchewan.

Federal drinking and driving law

There are four specific drinking and driving offences in the federal *Criminal Code* operating or having care or control of a motor vehicle while one's ability to drive is impaired by alcohol or a drug; impaired driving causing death or bodily harm; operating or having care or control of a motor vehicle with a blood alcohol level (BAL) over .08%; and failing to provide a breath or blood sample for analysis. As seen in Table 11.2, these four offences are punishable by imprisonment, heavy fines and lengthy driving prohibitions.

The scope of these offences is broad. First, there is no geographical limit on where the offences may be committed. For example, motorists have been convicted when apprehended on a private driveway or parking lot. Second, the offences apply to any "motor vehicle", which is broadly defined to include motorcycles, mopeds, snowmobiles, golf carts, and even lawn tractors. Third, these offences apply not only to those who are actually driving, but also those who merely have "care or control" of a motor vehicle. The phrase "care or control" encompasses virtually any act that could set a vehicle in motion, even accidentally. Motorists have been held to have had care or control when they used their vehicle as a place to sleep, were warming up the engine or were trying to extract their car from a ditch with a jack.

(i) **Impaired operation of a motor vehicle** The Criminal Code makes it an offence to operate a motor vehicle if one's ability to do so is impaired by alcohol or a drug. The courts have defined the term "drug" to

boissons alcooliques. Normalement, la législation provinciale interdit certaines pratiques de commercialisation, tels la réduction des prix, les concours de buveurs, la distribution de de boissons alcooliques comme prix et de consommations gratuites. La majorité des règlements provinciaux de publicité interdisent la publicité qui promouvoit un certain mode de vie, interpelle les mineurs, illustre ou encourage la consommation démesurée, et associe l'alcool à la conduite automobile ou à d'autres activités potentiellement dangereuses.

Tel que l'indique le Tableau 11.1, l'âge légal de boire est fixé à 19 ans partout au pays, sauf au Québec, au Manitoba, et en Alberta, où il est de 18 ans. Il est cependant permis de consommer avant cet âge dans des établissements autorisés en vertu d'un permis au Nouveau-Brunswick, et au foyer, dans certaines circonstances, à l'Ile-du-Prince-Edouard, en Alberta, en Colombie-Britannique, en Ontario, et en Saskatchewan.

Les lois fédérales régissant la conduite avec facultés affaiblies

Le *Code criminel* fédéral prévoit quatre infractions spécifiques concernant l'alcool au volant : conduite ou garde ou contrôle d'un véhicule motorisé sous l'influence de l'alcool ou d'une drogue; conduite en état d'ébriété causant la mort ou des lésions corporelles; conduite ou garde ou contrôle d'un véhicule motorisé avec une alcoolémie supérieure à 0,08 %; refus de fournir un échantillon d'haleine ou de fournir un échantillon sanguin. Tel qu'il est indiqué au Tableau 11.2, ces quatre infractions sont punissables d'emprisonnement, de lourdes amendes et d'interdictions de conduire à long terme.

La portée de ces infractions est vaste. Premièrement, il n'existe aucune délimitation géographique quant à l'endroit où elles peuvent être commises. Par exemple, des conducteurs ont été condamnés après avoir été interceptés dans une entrée privée ou sur un terrain de stationnement. Deuxièmement, les infractions visent tout «véhicule à moteur», dont la définition inclut aussi

include any legal or illegal substance that can cause impairment, including, for example, model airplane glue. They key issue is whether the accused's ability to drive was impaired, not whether he or she was driving in a careless or dangerous manner. Similarly, the amount of alcohol or drugs consumed is irrelevant. The courts have also adopted a broad definition of the term "impaired", which focuses on whether the driver had complete control of the vehicle.

(ii) Impaired operation of a motor vehicle causing death, and impaired operation of a motor vehicle causing bodily harm: These two new offences were introduced in 1985 to ensure that impaired drivers who caused serious accidents would be subject to a more onerous charge than impaired driving.

(iii) Operating a motor vehicle with a BAL over .08% It is a criminal offence to operate a motor vehicle with a BAL over .08%. The fact that the car was being driven safely makes no difference. Nor does it matter whether the driver appeared to be sober or whether his or her ability to drive was in fact impaired.

The amount of alcohol that someone must consume to have a BAL in excess of .08% varies from person to person, depending on such factors as weight, percentage of body fat, how quickly the alcohol was consumed, and when the person last ate. An individual's BAL can be determined by analysing samples of his or her urine, blood or breath. Although the police have the power to demand blood samples in limited circumstances, most cases involve the chemical analysis of breath samples.

The *Criminal Code* authorizes the police to use two different kinds of machines for analysing breath samples, namely "approved screening devices" (i.e., ALERTS) and "approved instruments" (i.e., Breathalyzers). If the police have complied with the *Criminal Code'}s testing procedures, the Breathalyzer results are deemed, in the absence of evidence to the contrary, to be proof of the driver's BAL.*

(iv) Refusal to provide a breath or blood sample It is a criminal offence to refuse an officer's demand for a breath or blood sample without a reasonable excuse.

bien la motocyclette, le cyclomoteur, la motoneige, ou la voiturette de golfeur, que la tondeuse à gazon. Troisièmement, ces infractions s'appliquent non seulement aux personnes qui conduisent un véhicule, mais aussi à celles qui en ont simplement «la garde ou le contrôle». L'expression «garde ou contrôle» inclut pratiquement toute action pouvant entraîner la mise en marche d'un véhicule, fusse-t-elle accidentelle. Des conducteurs ont été considérés comme ayant la garde ou le contrôle de leur véhicule alors qu'ils l'utilisaient pour y dormir, qu'ils réchauffaient le moteur, ou qu'ils tentaient de le sortir d'un fossé au moyen d'un cric.

i) Conduite en état d'ébriété d'un véhicule motorisé : Le *Code criminel* établit que quiconque conduit un véhicule sous l'effet de l'alcool ou d'une drogue commet une infraction. Les tribunaux ont défini le terme «drogue» de manière à y inclure toute substance licite ou illicite susceptible d'entraîner un affaiblissement des facultés, dont par exemple la colle pour avion miniature. L'essentiel consiste à établir si la personne accusée conduisait avec ses pleines facultés et non pas si elle conduisait d'une manière imprudente ou dangereuse. Dans cette même optique, la quantité d'alcool ou de drogue consommé est sans rapport. Les tribunaux ont en outre largement défini l'expression «en état d'ébriété», mettant l'accent sur le fait de savoir si le conducteur avait le plein contrôle de son véhicule.

ii) Conduite en état d'ébriété d'un véhicule motorisé causant la mort, et conduite en état d'ébriété d'un véhicule motorisé causant des lésions corporelles : Ces deux nouvelles infractions ont été adoptées en 1985 pour assurer que les conducteurs en état d'ébriété responsables de graves accidents puissent être accusés d'une faute plus grave que celle de conduite avec facultés affaiblies.

iii) Conduite d'un véhicule motorisé avec une alcoolémie supérieure à 0,08 % : Conduire un véhicule motorisé avec une alcoolémie supérieure à 0,08 % constitue une infraction criminelle. Le fait que le véhicule soit conduit de manière sécuritaire est sans rapport. Peu importe également que le conducteur

The essential element of this offence is the failure to comply with the officer's demand. Provided the officer had the requisite grounds for making the demand, it is irrelevant that the accused was driving safely, was otherwise innocent of any wrongdoing, or had not consumed any alcohol.

The police can demand breath samples in two situations. First, an officer may demand a breath sample for an ALERT test from any driver that the officer reasonably suspects has any alcohol in his or her body. This is not a difficult test to meet. The manner of driving, the odour of alcohol on a driver's breath, slurred speech, clumsiness, bloodshot eyes, or inappropriate responses to questions could all create a reasonable suspicion that the driver has consumed alcohol. The police need not believe that the driver is drunk, impaired or committing any offence.

Second, the police may demand breath samples for analysis in a Breathalyzer machine from any driver they have reasonable and probable grounds to believe has committed, within the last two hours, one of the other impaired driving offences.

A drinking and driving incident may also involve various other federal offences, including failing to remain at the scene of an accident or dangerous driving. In 1985, Parliament created the offence of operating a motor vehicle while prohibited from driving, or while subject to a provincial licence suspension for a federal drinking and driving offence. This offence was introduced to address the problem of impaired driving offenders who continued to drive without a licence.

Provincial laws relating to drinking and driving

The provincial highway traffic legislation is important in the apprehension, prosecution and punishment of drinking drivers. First, the provincial legislation generally gives the police the power to stop vehicles, determine if the driver has been drinking, and check the driver's licence, insurance and ownership. By observing and talking to the driver during this initial

semble sobre ou que sa capacité de conduire soit réduite ou non.

La quantité d'alcool qu'une personne doit consommer pour excéder la limite légale de 0,08 % varie chez chacune, selon divers facteurs tels le poids, le taux d'adiposité corporelle, la rapidité de consommation, et la dernière ingestion de nourriture. Il est possible de déterminer l'alcoolémie d'une personne en analysant des échantillons de son urine, de son sang ou de son haleine. Bien que la police ait le droit, dans certains cas, de demander des échantillons sanguins, elle procède le plus souvent à l'analyse chimique d'échantillons d'haleine.

Le *Code criminel* autorise la police à utiliser deux genres différents de dispositifs pour analyser les échantillons d'haleine, soit les «appareils de détection approuvés» (c.-à-d. A.L.E.R.T. ou barrage routier) et les «alcootests approuvés» (c.-à-d. les ivressomètres). Dans les cas où l'agent de la paix a effectué les tests conformément au *Code criminel*, les résultats indiqués par l'ivressomètre sont considérés, sauf preuve du contraire, comme la preuve de l'alcoolémie du conducteur.

iv) Refus de fournir un échantillon d'haleine ou un échantillon sanguin: Quiconque refuse sans motif valable d'obtempérer à la demande d'un agent de la paix de fournir un échantillon d'haleine ou un échantillon sanguin commet une infraction criminelle. Cette infraction porte essentiellement sur le refus de se conformer à la demande de l'agent. Dans la mesure où la demande de l'agent est fondée, le fait que l'accusé conduisait prudemment, était autrement innocent de toute autre faute, ou n'avait pas consommé d'alcool, demeure sans rapport.

L'agent de la paix peut demander un échantillon d'haleine dans deux cas. Il peut, dans un premier cas, demander un échantillon d'haleine et soumettre à un test d'ivressomètre tout conducteur qu'il soupçonne raisonnablement d'avoir consommé de l'alcool. L'exécution de ce test est simple. La manière de conduire, l'odeur d'alcool dégagée par l'haleine, l'empâtement de la parole, la maladresse, la rougeur des yeux, ou la non pertinence des réponses aux questions

contact, an officer can determine whether there is sufficient evidence to demand an ALERT test. Second, several provinces have created provincial licence suspensions for drivers who refuse to provide a blood or breath sample, or who have a BAL of .05% or more. Finally, most of the provinces impose lengthy licence suspensions on federal impaired driving offenders. For example, any driver convicted of a federal drinking and driving offence in Ontario is subject to a mandatory 12-month licence suspension.

Federal drug law

The two most important federal statutes dealing with illicit drugs are the *Narcotic Control Act* (NCA) and the *Food and Drugs Act* (FDA). The *Narcotic Control Act* covers cocaine, cannabis, heroin, phencyclidine, opium, and other opiates. It does not distinguish in any material way between these drugs. For example, cannabis and heroin offenders are subject to the same procedures, penalty provisions and criminal record consequences.

As seen in Table 11.3, there are six common offences under the *Narcotic Control Act* - possession, trafficking, possession for the purpose of trafficking, cultivation of opium or cannabis, importing or exporting, and "prescription shopping". (This last offence involves obtaining a narcotic from one doctor without disclosing that a prescription for a narcotic had been obtained from another doctor within the past 30 days.)

Unless authorized by statute, possession of any amount of a narcotic is an offence. No specific quantity is required for a charge of possession for the purpose of trafficking. Rather, a large quantity of drugs or other evidence of an intent to traffic, such as scales, baggies, and lists of names, may serve as the basis for laying a charge. The offence of trafficking is broadly defined to include giving, sharing, administering, transporting or sending a narcotic.

In Canada, offences are divided into two broad categories; namely, those tried by summary conviction and those tried by indictment. There are also hybrid

posées sont autant de signes raisonnables pouvant laisser croire que le conducteur a consommé de l'alcool. L'agent n'a pas besoin de croire que le conducteur est ivre, est en état d'ébriété ou a commis une infraction quelconque.

Deuxièmement, l'agent peut demander un échantillon d'haleine et soummettre à un test d'ivressomètre tout conducteur au regard duquel il a des motifs raisonnables ou probables de croire qu'il a commis, durant les deux heures précédentes, l'une des autres infractions prévues pour conduite avec facultés affaiblies.

La conduite en état d'ébriété peut aussi entraîner d'autres infractions fédérales, notamment pour défaut de demeurer sur les lieux d'un accident ou pour conduite dangereuse. En 1985, le Parlement a décrété que quiconque conduisait un véhicule motorisé pendant que touché par un interdit de conduire, ou une suspension provinciale de permis pour infraction fédérale de conduite en état d'ébriété, commettait une infraction. Cette infraction a été instituée dans le but d'empêcher les personnes condamnées pour conduite en état d'ébriété de continuer de conduire sans permis.

Les lois provinciales régissant la conduite avec facultés affaiblies

La législation provinciale régissant le trafic routier est importante pour l'arrestation, la poursuite et le châtiment des conducteurs en état d'ébriété. Tout d'abord, elle investit la police du pouvoir général d'intercepter les véhicules, de déterminer si le conducteur a consommé de l'alcool, et de vérifier le permis du conducteur et ses assurances ainsi que l'enregistrement du véhicule. En observant le conducteur et en lui parlant durant ce premier contact, l'agent de la paix peut déterminer s'il est justifié de le soumettre à un test d'ivressomètre. Aussi, plusieurs provinces ont décrété des suspensions de permis pour les conducteurs qui refusent de fournir un échantillon sanguin ou un échantillon d'haleine, ou qui présente une alcoolémie de 50 milligrammes d'alcool ou plus par cent millilitres de sang. Enfin, la majorité des provinces

offences - offences in which the prosecutor may proceed by summary conviction or by indictment. Possession and prescription shopping are hybrid offences under the *Narcotic Control Act*. If the Crown chooses to proceed summarily, the offender is liable to a maximum penalty of six months' imprisonment and a $1,000 fine for the first offence, and 12 months' imprisonment and a $2,000 fine for subsequent offences. If the Crown proceeds by indictment, the maximum penalty for possession is seven years' imprisonment. All other *Narcotic Control Act* offences are tried by indictment. The maximum penalty for cultivation is seven years' imprisonment, while trafficking, possession for the purpose of trafficking, importing, and exporting all carry a maximum penalty of life imprisonment.

Under the *Narcotic Control Act,* importing, and exporting carried a mandatory minimum sentence of seven years' imprisonment, regardless of the amount involved or other circumstances of the case. However, the Supreme Court of Canada struck down this mandatory minimum sentence, because it violated section 12 of the *Canadian Charter of Rights and Freedoms,* which prohibits cruel and unusual punishment. The court stated that this minimum might be appropriate for large-scale smuggling, heroin and other so-called "hard" drugs, and repeat offenders. However, the minimum was too broad because it applied regardless of the drug, the offender's prior criminal record or the quantity of drugs involved.

The Food and Drugs Act focuses on controls over pharmaceuticals, foods, cosmetics, and medical devices. There are two parts, however, which concern non-medical drug use (see Table 11.4).

Part III governs "controlled drugs", including amphetamines, barbiturates, and other stimulants and depressants. Offences for trafficking, and possession for the purposes of trafficking carry a maximum penalty of 10 years' imprisonment. The offence for prescription shopping carries a maximum of three years' imprisonment and a $5,000 fine. There is no possession offence.

imposent de longues suspensions de permis aux conducteurs jugés coupables d'infractions fédérales au code de la route. Par exemple, tout conducteur reconnu coupable d'une infraction fédérale pour avoir conduit en état d'ébriété en Ontario voit obligatoirement son permis suspendu pour une période de douze mois.

La législation fédérale régissant les drogues

Les deux grandes lois fédérales régissant les drogues illicites sont la *Loi sur les stupéfiants* et la *Loi sur les aliments et drogues*. La première couvre la cocaïne, le cannabis, l'héroïne, la phencyclidine, l'opium, et les autres opiacés. Elle n'établit aucune distinction matérielle entre ces drogues. Ainsi, peu importe qu'ils soient jugés pour une affaire de cannabis ou d'héroïne, les contrevenants sont soumis à la même procédure, aux mêmes peines et aux mêmes conséquences d'un casier judiciaire.

Tel qu'il apparaît au Tableau 11.3, les six infractions courantes en vertu de la *Loi sur les stupéfiants* sont : la possession, le trafic, la possession pour fin de trafic, la culture d'opium ou de cannabis, l'importation ou l'exportation, et l'obtention illégale de multiples ordonnances. Cette dernière infraction suppose que le contrevenant obtienne une drogue d'un médecin, sans lui révéler avoir déjà reçu une autre drogue prescrite au cours des trente jours précédents.

Sauf dans les cas autorisés par la loi, toute possession d'un stupéfiant, indépendamment de la quantité, constitue une infraction. Toute possession pour fin de trafic, indépendamment de la quantité, peut faire l'objet d'une accusation. En fait, la possession d'une importante quantité de drogue ou toute autre preuve d'intention de trafic, tels des balances, des sacs, des listes de noms, et d'importantes sommes d'argent, peuvent justifier une mise en accusation. L'infraction pour trafic est largement définie de manière à inclure le don, le partage, l'administration, le transport, ou l'envoi d'un stupéfiant.

Part IV governs "restricted drugs", including LSD, psilocybin and DMT. Trafficking and possession for the purpose of trafficking in "restricted drugs" carries a maximum penalty of 10 years. There is a possession offence for "restricted drugs", which is subject to a maximum penalty of three years' imprisonment and a $5,000 fine.

The *Narcotic Control Act* and *Food and Drugs Act* have been amended to include two relatively new offences: knowingly possessing property or other proceeds of any common drug offence (except the offence of possession); and knowingly dealing in such property or proceeds with the intent to conceal or convert them. This latter offence is commonly referred to as "money laundering".

In addition to these two drug statutes, other federal laws pertain to illicit drugs. Amendments to the Criminal Code make it illegal to knowingly import, export, manufacture, promote or sell illicit drug paraphernalia or literature. A court has recently struck down these provisions as they relate to drug literature. The judge held that these offences constitute an unjustifiable violation of freedom of speech as guaranteed by section 2 (b) of the *Charter of Rights and Freedoms*.

Federal tobacco legislation

Parliament enacted the first federal criminal prohibition against tobacco in 1980. This largely-ignored legislation was repealed in 1993 with the enactment of the *Tobacco Sales to Young Persons Act*. This Act makes it an offence for those who, in the course of a business, sell, give or furnish cigarettes to a person who is under 18. Offenders are subject to a fine of not more than $1,000 for a first offence, $2,000 for a second offence and $10,000 for a third offence. The Act also prohibits the placing of cigarette vending machines in any public place, other than bars and taverns. Those who sell tobacco products are required to post signs indicating that sales to those under 18 are prohibited.

Parliament has also enacted statutes that regulate tobacco marketing and restrict smoking in certain

Au Canada, les infractions se divisent en deux grandes catégories, jugées par voie de procédure sommaire ou par voie de mise en accusation. Il existe aussi les infractions hybrides, au regard desquelles le poursuivant peut choisir de procéder soit par procédure sommaire, soit par mise en accusation. En vertu de la *Loi sur les stupéfiants*, la possession et l'obtention illégale de multiples ordonnances constituent des infractions hybrides. Lorsque la Couronne choisit de procéder par procédure sommaire, le contrevenant risque une peine maximale de six mois d'emprisonnement et une amende de 1 000 dollars dans le cas d'une première infraction, et d'un emprisonnement de douze mois plus une amende de 2 000 dollars pour toute infraction subséquente. Si elle choisit plutôt de procéder par mise en accusation, la peine maximale s'appliquant pour possession est alors sept ans d'emprisonnement. Toutes les autres infractions visées par la *Loi sur les stupéfiants* sont jugées par voie de mise en accusation. La culture entraîne une peine maximale de sept ans d'emprisonnement, tandis que le trafic, la possession pour fin de trafic, l'importation, et l'exportation entraînent une peine maximale d'emprisonnement à perpétuité.

En vertu de la *Loi sur les stupéfiants*, l'importation et l'exportation sont punissables d'une peine minimale obligatoire de sept ans d'emprisonnement, indépendamment de la quantité en cause ou des autres circonstances de l'affaire. Cependant, la Cour suprême du Canada a récemment cassé cette peine minimale obligatoire parce qu'elle contrevenait à l'article 12 de la *Charte canadienne des droits et libertés*, laquelle interdit les peines cruelles et inhabituelles. La Cour a jugé que cette peine minimale pouvait convenir dans les cas de contrebande, de trafic à grande échelle, de drogues «dures» telle l'héroïne, et de récidivistes, mais l'a déclarée trop générale, puisqu'elle s'appliquait indépendamment de la drogue en cause, du casier judiciaire du contrevenant, et de la quantité concernée.

La Loi sur les aliments et drogues vise essentiellement le contrôle des produits pharmaceutiques, des aliments, des cosmétiques et des instruments médicaux. Deux

places. The *Tobacco Products Control Act* severely limits tobacco company sponsorship, and the advertising and promotion of tobacco products. It also requires tobacco packaging to carry large, prominent, health warnings. The Supreme Court of Canada is expected to hand down its decision shortly in a case challenging this legislation.

The *Non-smokers Health Act* prohibits or severely restricts smoking on aircraft, trains and ships, and in Crown corporations, federal offices, banks, and other organizations under federal control. In most cases, the Act limits smoking to designated smoking rooms or areas. A violation of the Act constitutes a summary conviction offence that is punishable by a maximum fine of $1,000 for a first offence and $10,000 for a subsequent offence.

Provincial tobacco legislation

Manitoba and Ontario have enacted provincial workplace smoking legislation. The Ontario legislation prohibits smoking in most enclosed workplaces. The legislation allows, but does not require, an employer to establish designated smoking areas. Employers are required to post signs and make "every reasonable effort" to enforce the legislation on their premises.

All Canadian jurisdictions except Alberta, Quebec and the Yukon prohibit sales of tobacco products to young people. The specifics of the legislation vary, with Ontario and Nova Scotia having perhaps the most comprehensive and stringent provisions.

Finally, the number of municipalities that have enacted smoking by-laws has increased rapidly since the mid-1980s. The scope of the prohibitions has increased, enforcement efforts have been stepped up and the penalty provisions have become more rigorous. The by-laws typically restrict or prohibit smoking in municipal offices, workplaces, restaurants, shopping malls, schools, hospitals, public transport facilities and other public places. Proprietors are often required to post signs and, in some cases, make reasonable efforts to enforce the law.

parties traitent cependant de l'usage non médical des drogues (voir le Tableau 11.4).

La Partie III régit les «drogues contrôlées», tels amphétamines, barbituriques, et autres stimulants et dépresseurs. Elle prévoit une peine maximale de dix ans d'emprisonnement pour le trafic et la possession pour fin de trafic et considère comme une infraction toute obtention illégale de plusieurs ordonnances, qui est punissable d'une peine maximale de trois ans d'emprisonnement et d'une amende de 5 000 dollars. Aucune sanction n'accompagne la possession.

La Partie IV régit les «drogues restreintes», dont le LSD, la psilocybine et le DMT. Le trafic et la possession pour fin de trafic de «drogues restreintes» entraînent une peine maximale de dix ans d'emprisonnement. La possession de «drogues restreintes» constitue une infraction punissable d'une peine maximale de trois ans d'emprisonnement et d'une amende de 5 000 dollars.

On a modifié la *Loi sur les stupéfiants* et la *Loi sur les aliments et drogues* de manière à inclure deux infractions relativement nouvelles : la possession consciente de biens ou de tout autre bénéfice résultant d'une infraction simple (sauf l'infraction pour possession) en matière de drogue; et le trafic conscient de tels biens ou bénéfices avec l'intention de les dissimuler ou de les cacher. Cette dernière infraction est couramment appelée «blanchiment d'argent».

D'autres lois fédérales traitent aussi des drogues illicites. Les modifications apportées au *Code criminel* rendent illégal le fait d'importer, d'exporter, de fabriquer, de promouvoir, ou de vendre sciemment du matériel ou de la documentation sur les drogues illicites. Un tribunal a récemment cassé ces dispositions dans la mesure où elles visent la documentation sur les drogues. Le juge a déclaré que ces infractions constituaient une violation inadmissible de la liberté de parole garantie par le paragraphe 2 b) de la *Charte des droits et libertés*.

La législation fédérale régissant le tabac

Le Parlement fédéral a adopté ses premières dispositions législatives contre le tabac dès 1908. Ces dispositions, demeurées largement ignorées, ont été abrogées par la *Loi sur la vente du tabac aux jeunes* adoptée en 1994. Selon cette loi, commet une infraction quiconque, au cours d'une activité, vend, donne ou fournit des cigarettes à une personne de moins de 18 ans. Les contrevenants sont punissables d'une amende maximale de 1 000 dollars dans le cas d'une première infraction, de 2 000 dollars dans le cas d'une deuxième infraction et de 10 000 dollars dans le cas d'une troisième. La Loi interdit en outre de placer des distributrices automatiques de cigarettes dans un lieu public autre que les bars, tavernes et brasseries. Toute personne qui vend des produits du tabac doit poser une affiche indiquant que la vente de ces produits est interdite aux moins de 18 ans.

Le Parlement a également adopté des dispositions qui réglementent la commercialisation du tabac et restreignent le tabagisme dans certains lieux. La *Loi réglementant les produits du tabac* limite sévèrement le parrainage publicitaire par les sociétés de tabac ainsi que la publicité et la promotion de ces produits. Elle exige en outre d'apposer en toute évidence sur leur emballage une mise en garde clairement lisible sur les dangers qu'ils comportent pour la santé. En septembre 1995, dans une affaire mettant en cause la validité de cette loi, la Cour suprême du Canada a annulé les dispositions de la loi qui interdisaient de faire la publicité des produits du tabac.

La *Loi sur la santé des non-fumeurs* interdit ou restreint sévèrement l'usage du tabac dans les aéronefs, les trains et les navires, ainsi que dans les locaux des sociétés d'Etat, du gouvernement fédéral, des banques, et ceux d'autres organismes relevant du fédéral. En règle générale, la Loi confine le droit de fumer à certaines pièces ou aires. Toute violation de la Loi constitue une infraction punissable par procédure sommaire et peut entraîner une amende maximale de 1 000 dollars dans

le cas d'une première infraction et de 10 000 dollars pour une infraction subséquente.

La législation provinciale régissant le tabac

Les provinces du Manitoba et de l'Ontario ont toutes deux statué sur le droit de fumer en milieu de travail. La loi de l'Ontario interdit de fumer dans la plupart des endroits fermés. Elle permet à l'employeur, sans toutefois l'exiger, d'établir des aires spécialement désignées pour les fumeurs. Les employeurs sont tenus de poser des affiches et de «faire tout effort raisonnable» pour appliquer la loi dans leurs locaux.

Au Canada, toutes les administrations provinciales et territoriales, à l'exception de l'Alberta, du Québec et du Yukon, interdisent la vente des produits du tabac aux jeunes. Les lois diffèrent selon l'administration, celles de l'Ontario et de la Nouvelle-Ecosse étant sans doute les plus exhaustives et les plus rigoureuses.

Enfin, le nombre des municipalités ayant réglementé l'usage du tabac s'est rapidement multiplié depuis le milieu des années 80. Ont suivi une plus grande portée des interdictions, le renforcement des efforts de mise en application et une plus grande sévérité des sanctions. Normalement, les règlements restreignent le droit de fumer ou interdisent de fumer dans les bureaux municipaux, les lieux de travail, les restaurants, les centres commerciaux, les écoles, les hôpitaux, les lieux de transport public et d'autres endroits publics. Les propriétaires de tels lieux sont souvent tenus de poser des avertissements et dans certains cas de faire tout en leur pouvoir pour assurer le respect des règlements.

| TABLE 11.1 | TABLEAU 11.1 |

Legal drinking age by province in Canada

Age légal de consommation, selon la province, Canada

PROVINCE	CURRENT LEGAL AGE/ AGE ACTUEL	FORMER LEGAL AGE/ AGE ANTERIEUR	DATE OF CHANGE/ DATE DU CHANGEMENT
Nfld./T.-N.	19	21	7-25-1972
P.E.I./I.-P.-É.	19	18	7-1-1987
N.S./N.-É.	19	21	4-13-1971
N.B./N.-B.	19	21	8-1-1972
Que./Qué.	18	20	7-1971
Ont./Ont.	19	18	1-1-1979
Man./Man.	18	21	8-1-1970
Sask./Sask.	19	18	9-1-1976
Alta./Alb.	18	21	4-1-1971
B.C./C.-B.	19	21	4-15-1970
Yukon/Yukon	19	21	2-1970
N.W.T./T.N.-O.	19	21	7-15-1970

Source: Adapted from Alcoholism and Drug Addiction Research Foundation, Information Centre, *Information Review: Teenage Drinking in Ontario* (Toronto: Alcoholism and Drug Addiction Research Foundation, 1978); Reginald G. Smart, *The New Drinkers - Teenage Use and Abuse of Alcohol, 2nd ed.*, (Toronto: Alcoholism and Drug Addiction Research Foundation, 1980); additional information provided by provincial liquor authorities and verified by provincial addiction agencies.

Adapté de Information Review: Teenage Drinking in Ontario, Fondation de la recherche sur la toxicomanie, Centre d'information (Toronto: Fondation de la recherche sur la toxicomanie, 1978); Reginald G. Smart, The New Drinkers - Teenage Use and Abuse of Alcohol, 2ᵉ édition (Toronto: Fondation de la recherche sur la toxicomanie, 1980). Des données additionnelles ont été obtenues des régies provinciales des alcools et vérifiées par les organismes provinciaux de toxicomanie.

TABLE 11.2   **TABLEAU 11.2**

Drinking and driving offences under the *Criminal Code*.   Infractions pours conduite avec facultés affaiblies, en vertu du *Code criminel*.

OFFENCE/PENALTY	INFRACTION/PEINE

Driving with blood alcohol over 80 mg %
 Failing to provide a breath or blood sample
    without a reasonable excuse
	Conduite avec alcoolémie supérieur à 80mg%
	 Refus de fournir un échantillon d'haleine ou de
	    sang sans motif valable

Mimimum penalty :*	Peine minimale*:

First offence:
    $300 fine and three months driving prohibition
 	
 Second offence:
    14 days imprisonment and six months driving prohibition
 	
 Subsequent offence:
    90 days imprisonment and one year's driving prohibition
	Première infraction
	    Une amende de $300 et interdiction de conduire de 3 mois
	
	 Deuxième infraction:
	    14 jours d'emprisonnement et interdiction de conduire de 6 mois
	
	 Infraction subséquente:
	    90 jours d'emprisonnement et interdiction de conduire d'un an

Maximum penalty for first, second, or subsequent offences:	Peine maximale pour la première et la deuxième infraction et toute infraction subsequente:

Summary Conviction:
    $2,000 fine, six months imprisonment and three years driving prohibition
 	
 Indictment:*
    five years imprisonment and three years driving prohibition
	Déclaration sommaire de culpabitité:
	    Amende de 2000$, 6 mois d'emprisonnement et interdiction de conduire de 3 ans
	
	 Mise en accusation*:
	    5 ans d'emprisonnement et interdiction de conduire de 10 ans

Impaired driving causing bodily harm	**Conduite avec facultés affaiblies causant des lésions corporelles**
Maximum Penalty:*	Peine maximale:*
10 years imprisonment and 10 years driving prohibition	10 ans d'emprisonnement et interdiction de conduire de 10 ans

Impaired driving causing death
 Maximum Penalty:*
    14 years imprisonment and 10 years driving prohibition
	Conduite avec facultés affaiblies causant la mort
	 Peine maximale:*
	    14 ans d'emprisonnement et interdiction de conduire de 10 ans

*In addition to these penalties the court may impose a fine of any amount	*En plus de ces peines, la tribunal peut imposer une amende d'une montant indéterminé

Source: Based on information provided by Robert Solomon.

Données fondées sur l'information fournie par Robert Solomon.

The *Narcotic Control Act*   La *Loi sur les stupéfiants*

Over 100 substances are listed in the Narcotic Control Act including cannabis, cocaine, heroin and phencyclidine.	La Loi sur les stupéfiants énumèrent plus de 100 substances, dont le cannabis, la cocaïne, l'héroïne et la phencyclidene.

OFFENCE/MAXIMUM PENALTY	**INFRACTION/PEINE MAXIMALE**

Possession
 Summary Conviction:
  First offence: 6 months and $1,000 fine
  Subsequent offence: 1 year and $2,000 fine
  Indictment: 7 years
	Possession
	 Déclaration sommairede culpabitité:
	  Première infraction: 6 mois plus une amende de 1000$
	  Délit subséquent: 1 an plus une amende de 2000$
	  Mise en accusation: 7 ans

Trafficking
  Indictment: life
	Trafic
	  Mise en accusation: perpétuité

Possession for the purpose of trafficking
  Indictment: life
	Possession pour fin de trafic
	  Mise en accusation perpétuité

Cultivation
  Indictment: 7 years
	Culture
	  Mise en accusation 7 ans

Importing or exporting
  Indictment: life
	Importation ou exportation
	  Mise en accusation perpétuité

Prescription shopping (double doctoring)
 Summary Conviction:
  First offence: 6 months and $1,000 fine
  Subsequent offence: 1 year and $2,000 fine
  Indictment: 7 years
	Ordonnances multiples
	 Déclaration sommairede culpabitité:
	  Première infraction: 6 mois plus une amende de 1000$
	  Infraction subséquente: 1 an plus une amende de 2000$
	  Mise en accusation: 7 ans

Source: Based on information provided by Robert Solomon.

Données fondées sur l'information fournie par Robert Solomon.

TABLE 11.4	TABLEAU 11.4

The *Food and Drugs Act* — La *Loi sur les aliments et la drogue*

Food and Drugs Act - Controlled Drugs (Part III, Schedule G) Schedule G contains about 15 drugs that generally have both medical and non-medical uses including: amphetamines, barbiturates and methamphetamine	**Loi sur les aliments et drogue - drogue contrôlée (Partie III, Annexe G)** L'annexe G contient à peu près 15 drogues qui peuvent s'employer dans des fins médicales et non-médicales, compris: amphétamine, acide barbiturique, et méthamphetamine
OFFENCE/MAXIMUM PENALTY	**INFRACTION/PEINE MAXIMALE**
Trafficking Summary Conviction: 18 months Indictment: 10 years	**Trafic** Déclaration sommairede culpabitité: 18 mois Mise en accusation: 10 ans
Possession for the purpose of trafficking Summary Conviction: 18 months Indictment: 10 years	**La possession pour fin de trafic** Déclaration sommairede culpabitité: 18 mois Mise en accusation: 10 années
Prescription shopping (multiple doctoring) Summary Conviction: First offence 6 months or $1,000 fine Subsequent offence 1 year or $2,000 fine Indictment 3 years or $5,000 fine	**Ordonnances multiples** Déclaration sommairede culpabitité: Première infraction: 6 mois ou une amende de 1000$ Infraction subséquente: 1 an ou une amende de 2000$ Mise en accusation 3 ans ou une amende de 5000$
Food and drugs act - restricted drugs (Part IV, schedule H) Schedule H contains about 25 drugs that generally have no medical uses including: LSD, M.D.A, and psilocybin	**Loi sur les aliments et drogue - drogues restreintes (Partie IV, annexe H)** L'annexe H contient à peu près 25 drogues qui en géneral n'ont pas de but médical, y compris: LSD MDA, et la silocybine
Possession: Summary Conviction: First offence: 6 months or $1,000 fine Subsequent offence: 1 year and $2,000 fine Indictment: 3 years and $5,000 fine	**Possession:** Déclaration sommairede culpabitité: Première infraction: 6 mois ou une amende de 1000$ Infraction subséquente: 1 an ou une amende de 2000$ Mise en accusation: 3 ans ou une amende de 5000$
Trafficking; Possession for the purpose of trafficking Summary Conviction: 18 months Indictment: 10 years	**Trafic; Possession pour fin de trafic** Déclaration sommairede culpabitité: 18 mois Mise en accusation: 10 ans

Source: Based on information provided by Robert Solomon.

Données fondées sur l'information fournie par Robert Solomon.

12 Drug-related Crime in Canada

12 La criminalité reliée à la drogue au Canada

Figures

Tables

Figures

Tableaux

Highlights

★ In 1993, there were 194,916 liquor act offences in Canada, representing 63% of offences reported under provincial statutes (excluding traffic offences).

★ There were 117,567 drinking and driving offences in Canada during 1993. The number has generally been declining since 1983. The rate per 100,000 age 16 or older has declined an average 4.6% per year over the period 1984 to 1993.

★ In 1993, there were 56,811 drug-related offences, a slight decrease of 0.6% from the previous year. Cannabis-related offences accounted for 63% of the total while cocaine-related offences accounted for an additional 22%.

Points saillants

★ En 1993, on a relevé, au Canada, 194 916 infractions aux lois sur les boissons alcooliques, représentant 63 % des infractions déclarées en vertu des lois provinciales (sauf les infractions au code de la route).

★ En 1993, on a dénombré 117 567 infractions fédérales pour conduite avec facultés affaiblies. Leur nombre a généralement régressé depuis 1983. Le taux par 100 000 habitants de 16 et plus a baissé en moyenne de 4,6 % par année de 1984 à 1993.

★ En 1993, on a enregistré 56 811 infractions liées à la drogue, soit 0,6 % de plus seulement que l'année précédente. De ces infractions, 63 % étaient reliées au cannabis et 22 % à la cocaïne.

Drug-related Crime in Canada

by Bob Williams, Minh Van Truong and Gary Timoshenko, Addiction Research Foundation

Sources of Information

This chapter deals with offences under the provincial liquor acts, federal drinking and driving legislation, and federal drug offences that fall under the *Narcotic Control Act* and *Food and Drugs Act*. For a description of the acts, types of offences and associated penalties, please see Chapter 11.

Most of the data reported in this chapter are based on police reported offences and charges recorded using the Uniform Crime Reporting system. "Offence" data represent a count of identified legal violations, while "charges" refer to the number of persons actually

La criminalité reliée à la drogue au Canada

par Bob Williams, Minh Van Truong et Gary Timoshenko, Fondation de la recherche sur la toxicomanie

Sources d'information

Ce chapitre traite des infractions aux lois provinciales sur les boissons alcooliques, des infractions aux lois fédérales régissant la conduite avec facultés affaiblies et des infractions fédérales en matière de drogue relevant de la *Loi sur les stupéfiants* et de la *Loi sur les aliments et drogues*. Pour une description des lois, des genres d'infractions et des peines connexes, se reporter au Chapitre 11.

Les données exposées dans le présent chapitre s'appuient principalement sur les infractions et les

charged in connection with the offences. In general, if a person is charged with several offences, only the most serious offence or charge is reported. This results in fewer charges than offences and the under-reporting of charges for many less serious violations.

Liquor Acts

The control and sale of liquor in Canada is regulated by legislation and enforcement policy in each province. Thus, interprovincial comparisons should be conducted with care.

In 1993, there were 194,916 liquor act offences in Canada, representing 63% of offences reported under provincial statutes (excluding traffic offences). Since 1984, the total number of offences has declined by 29% (Table 12.1).

Nationally, the rate per 100,000 population for liquor act offences in 1993 was 677.9, a decline of 7.4% from 1992. Regionally, rates of liquor act offences were highest in the Northwest Territories (4,756.8 per 100,000), the Yukon (3,003.1), and Prince Edward Island (2,746.0). The lowest offence rate was in Quebec with 31.3 offences per 100,000 population (Figure 12.1).

The number of juveniles involved in provincial liquor act offences declined 13.8% to 14,329 in 1993. This was the sixth year in a row that the rate has dropped (Table 12.2). The number of adults charged under provincial liquor acts offences was 111,727 (516.0 charges per 100,000 adults), down 13.3% from 1992. The average annual reduction in nine years between 1984 and 1993 is 5.7% (Table 12.3).

accusations déclarées par la police dans le cadre du Programme de déclaration uniforme de la criminalité (DUC). Les données des «infractions» correspondent au compte des infractions légales identifiées, tandis que celles des «accusations» correspondent au nombre de personnes réellement accusées relativement aux infractions. En règle générale, lorsqu'une personne est accusée de plusieurs infractions, seule l'infraction ou l'accusation la plus grave est déclarée. Cette mesure donne lieu à un nombre d'accusations inférieur à celui des infractions, ainsi qu'à la sous-déclaration des accusations en ce qui concerne maintes infractions moins graves.

Les lois sur les boissons alcooliques

Au Canada, le contrôle et la vente des boissons alcooliques sont de compétence et d'application provinciales. Il convient donc de faire preuve de prudence au moment de comparer les données entre les provinces.

En 1993, on a relevé, au Canada, 194 916 infractions aux lois sur les boissons alcooliques, représentant 63 % des infractions déclarées en vertu des lois provinciales (sauf les infractions au code de la route). Depuis 1984, le nombre global des infractions a diminué de 29 % (Tableau 12.1).

A l'échelle nationale, le taux des infractions aux lois sur les boissons alcooliques par 100 000 habitants, en 1993, s'établissait à 677,9, soit un recul de 7,4 % depuis 1992. Sur le plan régional, ce sont les Territoires du Nord-Ouest qui ont enregistré le taux le plus élevé (4 756,8 par 100 000), suivis du Yukon (3 003,1) et de l'Ile-du-Prince-Edouard

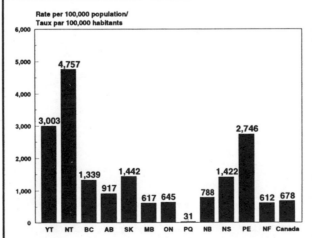

Figure 12.1   Liquor act offences, rates per 100,000 population by province, Canada, 1993

Figure 12.1   Infractions aux lois sur les boissons alcooliques, taux par 100,000 habitants, par province, Canada, 1993

In general, about 90% of the adults charged in any given year were male.

There were 5,071 reported sentenced admissions to provincial adult correctional service facilities for violating the provincial liquor acts in 1993/94 (Table 12.5). Liquor act offences accounted for 8% of all sentenced admissions to provincial correction facilities. Provincially, Quebec accounts for 88% of total sentenced admissions.

Drinking and Driving Offences

In 1993, there were 117,567 drinking and driving offences in Canada. The number of drinking and driving offences across Canada has been declining at the average rate of 3.3% per year from 1984 to 1993. The rate of offences per 100,000 population age 16 or over has also declined an average of 4.6% per year over the period 1984 to 1993 (Table 12.6, Figure 12.2). All regions of Canada, with the exception of the Northwest Territories and Saskatchewan, have experienced significant declines in the rate of drinking and driving offences. The highest rates were recorded in the Yukon (2,477), the Northwest Territories (1,655), Saskatchewan (1,248) and Alberta (1,170). Ontario and Quebec continued to have the lowest rates of drinking and driving offences at 335 and 414 respectively.

"Impaired operation of motor vehicle" offences accounted for about 91% (107,407 offences) of drinking and driving offences in 1993. Failure or refusal to provide a breath or blood sample accounted for an additional 7% (8,736 offences). The more serious offence of impaired operation of motor vehicle

(2 746,0), et le Québec le taux le plus bas (31,3 infractions par 100 000 habitants) (Figure 12.1).

Le nombre des jeunes ayant contrevenu aux lois provinciales sur les boissons alcooliques a diminué de 13,8 %, passant à 14 329 en 1993. Il s'agissait de la sixième baisse consécutive annuelle (Tableau 12.2). Celui des adultes est passé à 111 727 (516,0 accusations par 100 000 adultes), soit 13,3 % de moins qu'en 1992. La moyenne de la réduction annuelle pour la période de 1984 à 1993 est de 5,7 % (Tableau 12.3). Pour chacune des neuf années, 90 % environ des adultes accusés étaient des hommes.

En 1993-1994, on a dénombré 5 071 admissions de personnes condamnées dans les prisons provinciales pour adultes, pour infractions aux lois provinciales sur les boissons alcooliques (Tableau 12.5). Ces infractions représentaient 8 % de toutes les admissions des personnes condamnées dans ces établissements, et de ces dernières 88 % visaient le Québec.

Les infractions pour conduite avec facultés affaiblies

En 1993, le Canada a enregistré 117 567 infractions pour conduite avec facultés affaiblies et, de 1984 à cette même année, a accusé une baisse moyenne de 3,3 % par année à ce chapitre. Le taux des infractions par 100 000 habitants de 16 ans et plus a aussi diminué, soit en moyenne de 4,6 % par année durant la même période. (Tableau 12.6, Figure 12.2). Le taux de ces infractions a sensiblement régressé dans toutes les régions du Canada, sauf aux Territoires du Nord-Ouest

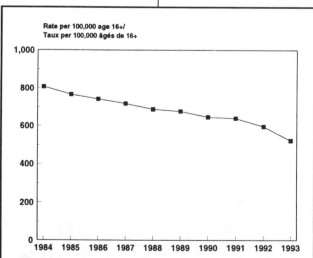

**Rate per 100,000 age 16+/
Taux per 100 000 âgés de 16+**

Figure 12.2   Drinking and driving offences, rates per 100,000 population age 16 and over, Canada, 1984 to 1993

Figure 12.2   Infractions pour conduite avec facultés affaiblies, taux par 100 000 habitants, population des 16 ans et plus, Canada, 1984 à 1993

causing death accounted for 0.2% (181 offences) of drinking and driving offences, while impaired operation of a motor vehicle causing bodily harm accounted for 1.1% (1,243 offences) (Table 12.7, Figure 12.3).

In 1993 there were 92,539 people charged with alcohol related traffic offences or 413 charges per 100,000 population age 16 and over. Men accounted for over 90% of all charges in each year from 1990 to 1993 (Table 12.8 and 12.9).

There were 13,054 sentenced admissions to provincial adult correctional service facilities for drinking and driving offences in 1993/94 (Table 12.10), accounting for 17% of all correctional facility admissions. The number increased 34.6% from the previous year, but this is primarily because Ontario reported for the first time since 1990/91.

Drug-related Crime

The interpretation of drug-related crime statistics is difficult. As noted in one of the original source materials, "a change in police reported drug offences does not mean that there was a corresponding increase or decrease in drug usage but may in fact reflect changes in police enforcement practices" (Statistics Canada, *Canadian Crime Statistics* 1990, p. 45).

In 1993, there were 56,811 drug-related offences, 0.6% higher than the level recorded in 1992 (Table 12.11). This corresponded to a rate of 197.6 per 100,000 population (Table 12.12). Offences involving cannabis accounted for 63% of the total, while cocaine offences accounted for 22%. Heroin offences increased 26.9% in 1993 and accounted for 2.8% of total drug offences. The highest rate of drug-related offences was

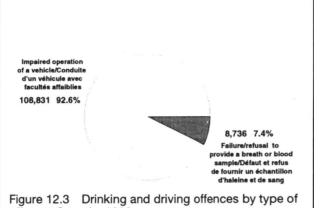

Impaired operation of a vehicle/Conduite d'un véhicule avec facultés affaiblies

108,831 92.6%

8,736 7.4%
Failure/refusal to provide a breath or blood sample/Défaut et refus de fournir un échantillon d'haleine et de sang

Figure 12.3   Drinking and driving offences by type of offence, Canada, 1993

Figure 12.3   Infractions pour conduite avec facultés affaiblies, selon le genre d'infraction, Canada, 1993

et en Saskatchewan. Les taux les plus élevés reviennent dans l'ordre au Yukon (2 477), aux Territoires du Nord-Ouest (1 655), à la Saskatchewan (1 248) et à l'Alberta (1 170), tandis que l'Ontario et le Québec continuent de présenter les taux les plus bas avec 335 et 414 infractions respectivement.

Toujours en 1993, les infractions pour «conduite avec facultés affaiblies d'un véhicule motorisé» représentaient 91 % environ (107 407 infractions) de toutes les infractions pour conduite avec facultés affaiblies; le défaut ou le refus de fournir un échantillon d'haleine ou de sang, 7 % (8 736 infractions); et les infractions plus graves, soit pour conduite avec facultés affaiblies d'un véhicule motorisé causant la mort, 0,2 % (181 infractions), et causant des lésions corporelles 1,1 % (1 243 infractions) (Tableau 12.7, Figure 12.3).

Cette même année, on a dénombré 92 539 accusations pour infractions au code de la route reliées à l'alcool, soit 413 par 100 000 habitants chez les 16 ans et plus. Pour chacune des années de la période de 1990 à 1993, les hommes constituaient 90 % de toutes les personnes accusées (Tableaux 12.8 et 12.9).

En 1993-1994, 13 054 personnes condamnées pour conduite avec facultés affaiblies ont été admises dans les prisons provinciales pour adultes (Tableau 12.10), constituant 17 % de toutes les admissions en milieu carcéral. Ce nombre équivaut à 34,6 % de plus que l'année précédente, hausse surtout attribuable au fait que l'Ontario a alors contribué au rapport pour la première fois depuis 1990-1991.

La criminalité reliée à la drogue

Il n'est pas facile d'interpréter les données statistiques de la criminalité reliées à la drogue. Comme

recorded in the Northwest Territories (591.4 per 100,000) followed by the Yukon (459.4 per 100,000) (Figure 12.4) and British Columbia (388.3 per 100,000). The lowest rate of drug offences was in Newfoundland (135.1 per 100,000).

In 1993, the number of juvenile offenders involved in drug-related offences under federal drug legislation increased 30% to 3,426 offences. This follows a period from 1986 to 1992, when the number of juvenile offenders declined an average of 7.6% per year (Table 12.13). Offences committed under the Narcotic Control Act (NCA) made up 82% of total drug-related offences. Cannabis accounted for a majority of the offences under the NCA (85.3% of its total) and 70.2% of total drug-related offences under the federal drug acts.

In 1993, 39,424 adults were charged with drug-related offences under federal legislation (Table 12.14). The rate of charges per 100,000 adults for 1993 was 182.1, 6.4% lower than the rate recorded in 1992 (Table 12.15). The territories continued to record the highest rates (611.3 charges per 100,000 adults in the N.W.T. and 441.6 in the Yukon). The lowest rate of offences occurred in New Brunswick (94.9 per 100,000 adults). As was the case with alcohol-related charges, males accounted for the majority of drug related charges in 1993 (85.7%).

It should be noted that data relating to the disposition of charges and convictions is from the Bureau of Drug Surveillance, Health Canada, and do not include convictions for offences involving cannabis. All data for 1994 in tables 12.16 through 12.20 are preliminary estimates.

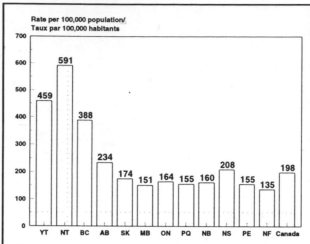

Figure 12.4　Drug-related offences under the federal legislation, rates per 100,000 population by province, Canada, 1993

Figure 12.4　Infractions reliées à la drogue commises en vertu des lois fédérales, taux par 100 000 habitants, selon la province, Canada, 1993

le précise le document original, un changement du nombre des infractions déclarées par la police en matière de drogue ne signifie pas nécessairement une hausse ou une baisse correspondante de l'usage de drogue, mais peut simplement refléter une modification des activités policières (Statistique Canada, Statistique de la criminalité canadienne, 1990).

En 1993, on a enregistré 56 811 infractions reliées à la drogue, soit 0,6 % de plus qu'en 1992 (Tableau 12.11) et un rapport de 197,6 par 100 000 habitants (Tableau 12.12). Les infractions visant le cannabis constituaient 63 % de toutes les infractions, la cocaïne, 22 %, et l'héroïne 2,8 %, soit une hausse de 26,9 % en 1993. Les taux les plus élevés ont été enregistrés dans les Territoires du Nord-Ouest (591,4 par 100 000), puis au Yukon (459,4 par 100 000) (Figure 12.4) et en Colombie-Britannique (388,3 par 100 000), et le plus bas à Terre-Neuve (135,1 par 100 000).

En 1993, le nombre des jeunes contrevenants ayant commis des infractions reliées à la drogue en vertu de la législation fédérale a augmenté de 30 %, pour un total de 3 426 infractions. Cette hausse contraste avec la période de 1986 à 1992 durant laquelle leur nombre avait diminué en moyenne de 7,6 % par année (Tableau 12.13). Quant aux infractions commises en vertu de la Loi sur les stupéfiants, elles constituaient 82 % de toutes les infractions reliées à la drogue, le cannabis étant en cause dans 85,3 % des cas et dans 70,2 % de toutes les infractions reliées à la drogue commises en vertu des lois fédérales.

Toujours en 1993, 39 424 adultes ont été accusés pour des infractions reliées à la drogue en vertu des lois

According to preliminary estimates, of the 14,153 charges that reached disposition in 1994, 10,279 (72.6%) resulted in convictions (Table 12.16). More than half (62% or 6,376) of all convictions resulted in prison sentences, while 26% were handled with fines and 7% resulted in a suspended sentence or probation.

Charges under the *Narcotic Control Act* accounted for 90% of all federal drug convictions, while convictions involving controlled drugs in the *Food and Drugs Act* (FDA) represented 10% of the total (Table 12.17). Forty-seven percent (47%) of all convictions were for possession, 32% for trafficking, 19% possession for the purpose of trafficking, 1% for multiple doctoring and 1% for importing (Table 12.18). Men accounted for 86% of all drug-related convictions (Table 12.19). Persons under age 30 accounted for 50% of the drug related convictions, while those age 30 to 39 accounted for 35% (Table 12.19).

In 1992/93, there were 782 admissions to federal adult correctional institutions for drug-related offences, up 6.8% from the year before (Table 12.21). Drug-related admissions represented 14% of all admissions to federal correctional institutions.

The number of reported thefts and other losses involving drugs controlled under the *NCA* and *FDA* declined 13% in 1994 (Table 12.23). Most thefts and losses occurred at pharmacies or hospitals, accounting for 90% of reported losses during 1994 (Table 12.23). Provincially, Ontario had the highest number of reported theft and other losses (508 cases), accounting for 52% of thefts across Canada. Table 12.24 identifies the drugs and quantities that were reported lost for the period 1987 to 1994.

The number of reported prescription forgeries decreased by 36% to 1,022 in 1994 (Table 12.25). Forgeries involving codeine accounted for 49% of all prescription forgeries in 1994.

fédérales (Tableau 12.14). Le nombre des accusations par 100 000 adultes s'établissait alors à 182,1, soit 6,4 % de moins qu'en 1992 (Tableau 12.15). Les territoires continuaient d'enregistrer les taux les plus élevés (611,3 et 441,6 accusations par 100 000 adultes dans les T.-N.-O. et au Yukon respectivement), tandis que le taux le plus bas revenait au Nouveau-Brunswick (94,9 par 100 000 adultes). Comme c'était le cas pour l'alcool, la majorité des personnes accusées étaient des hommes (85,7 %).

(Notons que les données sur le règlement des accusations et des condamnations proviennent du Bureau de la surveillance des médicaments, Santé Canada, et qu'elles n'incluent pas les condamnations pour les infractions visant le cannabis. Toutes les données de 1994 des tableaux 12.16 à 12.20 constituent des estimations préliminaires.)

Selon ces estimations préliminaires, 10 279 (72,6 %) des 14 153 accusations qui ont été réglées en 1994 ont donné lieu à des condamnations (Tableau 12.16). Plus de la moitié (62 % ou 6,376) de ces condamnations ont entraîné une peine d'emprisonnement, alors que 26 % firent l'objet d'amendes et 7 %, d'une condamnation avec sursis ou d'une peine avec probation.

Les accusations en vertu de la Loi sur les stupéfiants ont donné lieu à 90 % de toutes les condamnations fédérales en matière de drogue, tandis que les condamnations visant les drogues contrôlées régies par la Loi sur les aliments et drogues ont compté pour 10 % (Tableau 12.17). Quarante-sept pour cent (47 %) de toutes les condamnations concernaient la possession; 32 %, le trafic; 19 %, la possession pour fin de trafic; 1 %, l'obtention illégale d'ordonnances multiples; et 1 %, l'importation (Tableau 12.18). Les hommes avaient commis 86 % de toutes les condamnations reliées à la drogue (Tableau 12.19). Les personnes de moins de 30 ans étaient responsables de 50 % des condamnations reliées à la drogue, et les 30 à 39 ans, d'un autre 35 % (Tableau 12.19).

References

Statistics Canada, *Canadian Crime Statistics*, 1994 (Ottawa: Statistics Canada, Catalogue No. 82-205, 1995).

En 1992-1993, on a relevé 782 admissions dans les pénitenciers fédéraux pour des infractions reliées à la drogue, soit 6,8 % de plus que l'année précédente (Tableau 12.21). Elles représentaient 14 % de toutes les admissions enregistrées dans les pénitenciers fédéraux.

En 1994, le nombre des vols et autres pertes reliés aux drogues contrôlées régies par la Loi sur les stupéfiants et la Loi sur les aliments et drogues a diminué de 13 % (Tableau 12.23). La majorité visaient les pharmacies ou les hôpitaux, représentant 90 % des pertes déclarées pour cette année (Tableau 12.23). A l'échelle provinciale, c'est l'Ontario qui a enregistré le plus grand nombre vols et d'autres pertes (508 cas), soit 52 % des vols commis à travers le Canada. Le Tableau 12.24 indique les drogues et les quantités déclarées perdus pour la période de 1987 à 1994.

Le nombre des fausses ordonnances déclarées a diminué de 36 %, passant ainsi à 1 022 en 1994 (Tableau 12.25). Cette même année, 49 % de ces ordonnances concernaient la codéine.

Ouvrages de référence

Statistique Canada, Statistique de la criminalité canadienne, 1994 (Ottawa : Statistique Canada, Catalogue no 82-205, 1995).

TABLE 12.1   **TABLEAU 12.1**

Number and rates per 100,000 population of provincial liquor act offences, Canada and provinces, 1984 to 1993

Nombre et taux de délits contre la loi sur les alcools par 100 000 habitants, Canada et provinces, 1984 à 1993

PROVINCE	1984	1985	1986	1987	1988	1989	1990	1991	1992	1993
NUMBER OF LIQUOR ACTS OFFENCES/										
NOMBRE DE DELITS CONTRE LA LOI SUR LES ALCOOLS										
Nfld./T.-N.	5,373	5,896	5,581	6,646	6,409	6,618	5,922	5,474	5,347	3,610
P.E.I./I.P.É.	4,467	4,401	3,959	3,735	3,983	3,831	3,385	3,612	3,541	3,611
N.S./N.-É.	17,186	17,202	15,921	15,945	14,652	14,986	16,088	15,300	14,167	13,127
N.B./N.-B.	10,102	9,854	9,404	9,873	9,597	9,030	9,387	8,561	6,496	5,915
Que./Qué.	2,421	2,758	3,626	3,733	2,923	2,159	1,837	1,741	2,107	2,258
Ont./Ont.	137,483	120,449	137,399	129,255	123,650	117,652	106,851	98,035	85,440	69,357
Man./Man.	10,480	11,066	9,529	9,276	8,141	7,804	7,769	7,775	7,081	6,883
Sask./Sask.	27,876	25,699	26,423	23,911	22,490	19,889	18,160	15,248	15,721	14,464
Alta./Alb.[1]	39,989	33,927	28,711	27,402	25,983	23,660	22,291	21,843	21,616	24,414
B.C./C.-B.	17,029	14,880	16,241	23,837	20,005	22,097	31,979	40,807	43,396	47,324
Yukon/Yukon[1]	774	938	891	703	969	1,012	736	952	781	961
N.W.T./T.N.-O.[1]	1,397	1,455	1,553	1,446	1,557	1,802	1,737	1,717	2,472	2,992
Canada	**274,577**	**248,525**	**259,238**	**255,762**	**240,359**	**230,540**	**226,310**	**221,185**	**208,165**	**194,916**
LIQUOR ACTS OFFENCES PER 100,000 POPULATION/										
NOMBRE DE DELITS CONTRE LA LOI SUR LES ALCOOLS PAR POPULATION X 100,000										
Nfld./T.-N.	923.5	1,015.0	965.6	1,152.6	1,112.3	1,146.2	1,023.0	943.8	920.2	621.2
P.E.I./I.P.É.	3,517.3	3,435.6	3,071.4	2,895.3	3,068.6	2,933.4	2,584.0	2,761.5	2,717.6	2,746.0
N.S./N.-É.	1,954.1	1,937.6	1,784.7	1,779.0	1,627.6	1,652.8	1,763.1	1,666.3	1,538.6	1,422.2
N.B./N.-B.	1,396.5	1,357.1	1,292.3	1,351.5	1,309.1	1,223.6	1,263.4	1,143.6	867.2	787.7
Que./Qué.	36.4	41.2	53.8	54.8	42.6	31.1	26.2	24.6	29.5	31.3
Ont./Ont.	1,493.4	1,290.4	1,449.8	1,334.6	1,251.0	1,159.0	1,033.2	936.2	805.3	645.4
Man./Man.	975.7	1,020.4	871.0	842.9	736.9	705.5	700.9	698.4	636.2	616.8
Sask./Sask.	2,736.7	2,497.7	2,558.1	2,307.1	2,179.9	1,944.4	1,796.4	1,514.2	1,565.1	1,441.9
Alta./Alb.[1]	1,667.2	1,407.1	1,177.3	1,121.4	1,054.9	944.8	872.0	840.0	821.2	917.0
B.C./C.-B.	575.2	497.7	537.7	777.8	639.5	688.6	969.0	1,208.4	1,257.4	1,338.7
Yukon/Yukon[1]	3,198.3	3,813.0	3,592.7	2,703.8	3,615.7	3,693.4	2,628.6	3,271.5	2,586.1	3,003.1
N.W.T./T.N.-O.[1]	2,625.9	2,640.7	2,803.2	2,596.1	2,765.5	3,133.9	2,924.2	2,805.6	3,967.9	4,756.8
Canada	**1,068.3**	**958.0**	**989.3**	**963.3**	**893.7**	**842.0**	**814.3**	**786.6**	**732.1**	**677.9**

[1] Does not include provincial/territorial offences under the Intoxicated Persons Act in Alberta, the Yukon and Northwest Territories./Non-compris les délits provinciaux/territoriaux contre la loi sur les personnes en état d'ivresse en Alberta, au Yukon, et aux Territoires du-Nord-Ouest.

Source: Statistics Canada, *Canadian Crime Statistics 1984, 1985, 1990, 1991, 1992,* and *1993* (Ottawa: Statistics Canada, Catalogue No. 85-205, 1985, 1986, 1991, 1992, 1994, and 1994 respectively)./Statistics Canada, *Statistics de la criminalité du Canada 1984, 1985, 1990, 1991, 1992, et 1993* (Ottawa: Statistique Canada, Catalogue no 85-205, 1985, 1986, 1991, 1992, 1994 et 1994 respectivement).

Data for the years 1986 to 1989 were obtained from the Canadian Centre for Justice Statistics, Statistics Canada.
Les données de 1986 à 1989 ont été obtenues du Centre Canadien des statistiques judiciaires, Statistiques, Canada.

TABLE 12.2

TABLEAU 12.2

Juvenile offenders involved in provincial liquor act offences, Canada and provinces, 1986 to 1993

Nombre de jeunes délinquants/délinquantes dont le délit était contre la loi sur les alcools, Canada et provinces, 1986 à 1993

PROVINCE	1986	1987	1988	1989	1990	1991	1992	1993
	NUMBER OF JUVENILE OFFENDERS/ NOMBRE DE JEUNES DELINQUANTS/DELINQUANTES[1]							
Nfld./T.-N.	658	778	850	886	744	653	533	366
P.E.I./I.P.É.	196	222	282	300	303	414	305	258
N.S./N.-É.	379	473	571	621	666	931	644	585
N.B./N.-B.	548	712	709	796	797	879	757	727
Que./Qué.	2,132	1,904	1,880	1,182	1,531	944	1,111	917
Ont./Ont.	8,932	10,353	9,668	8,957	6,677	6,304	4,481	2,746
Man./Man.	1,818	1,635	1,528	1,531	1,473	1,699	1,544	1,300
Sask./Sask.	782	931	817	694	823	877	841	749
Alta./Alb.[2]	2,484	2,649	2,865	2,705	2,582	2,545	2,209	2,482
B.C./C.-B.	5,171	7,454	6,484	6,713	6,511	6,317	3,890	3,941
Yukon/Yukon[2]	91	89	149	166	83	144	133	116
N.W.T./T.N.-O.[2]	230	175	151	160	168	228	168	142
Canada	**23,421**	**27,375**	**25,954**	**24,711**	**22,358**	**21,946**	**16,616**	**14,329**

[1] Data include both juveniles charged and juveniles not charged./Y compris les jeunes inculpés et non inculpés.

[2] Does not include provincial/territorial offences under the Intoxicated Persons Act in Alberta, the Yukon and Northwest Territories. Non-compris les délits provinciaux/ territoriaux contre la loi sur les personnes en état d'ivresse en Alberta, au Yukon et aux Territoires-du-Nord-Ouest.

Source: Data for the years 1986 to 1989 were obtained from the Canadian Centre for Justice Statistics, Statistics Canada./Les données de 1986 à 1989 ont été obtenues du Centre Canadien des statistiques judiciaires, Statistiques, Canada.

Statistics Canada, *Canadian Crime Statistics 1990, 1991, 1992*, and *1993* (Ottawa: Statistics Canada, Catalogue No. 85-205, 19891, 1992, 1994, and 1994 respectively)./Statistics Canada, *Statistics de la criminalité du Canada 19890, 1991, 1992, et 1993* (Ottawa: Statistique Canada, Catalogue no 85-205, 1991, 1992, 1994 et 1994 respectivement).

TABLE 12.3

TABLEAU 12.3

Adults charged under the provincial liquor acts by gender, Canada and provinces, 1984 to 1993

Adultes inculpés en vertu des lois provinciales sur les alcools, selon sexe, Canada et provinces, 1984 à 1993

PROVINCE	1984	1985	1986	1987	1988	1989	1990	1991	1992	1993
MALE/MASCULIN										
Nfld./T.-N.	4,769	5,108	4,427	5,269	4,579	4,367	3,532	3,509	3,098	2,151
P.E.I./I.P.É.	3,733	3,668	3,194	2,923	3,125	2,883	2,546	2,676	2,665	2,707
N.S./N.-É.	13,810	13,989	12,979	12,738	11,416	11,860	12,612	11,535	11,026	10,038
N.B./N.-B.	8,620	7,983	7,464	7,832	7,451	6,782	6,933	5,094	4,557	4,013
Que./Qué.	1,793	1,590	2,046	2,073	2,260	2,059	1,409	1,139	970	734
Ont./Ont.	119,605	101,610	111,196	105,188	101,714	95,117	83,410	71,321	58,678	44,749
Man./Man.	6,797	7,067	5,782	5,164	4,459	4,076	3,996	4,040	3,511	3,449
Sask./Sask.	20,591	18,083	17,852	16,012	14,836	12,666	10,910	9,446	8,612	8,123
Alta./Alb.[1]	30,663	24,439	19,310	17,139	16,152	13,957	12,751	12,779	12,872	13,858
B.C./C.-B.	3,499	2,236	2,555	7,556	6,596	8,205	8,140	7,395	7,654	8,811
Yukon/Yukon[1]	424	430	397	362	429	455	339	344	313	257
N.W.T./T.N.-O.[1]	775	680	645	657	712	835	623	598	474	413
Canada	**215,079**	**186,883**	**187,847**	**182,913**	**173,729**	**163,262**	**147,345**	**129,978**	**114,430**	**99,303**
FEMALE/FEMININ										
Nfld./T.-N.	282	274	245	267	301	332	240	234	304	211
P.E.I./I.P.É.	130	146	164	159	164	130	170	120	132	179
N.S./N.-É.	727	611	586	717	613	623	712	653	644	720
N.B./N.-B.	444	467	443	487	431	403	472	401	369	309
Que./Qué.	508	420	591	411	683	565	558	401	422	311
Ont./Ont.	11,246	10,088	11,995	10,948	11,267	10,666	9,913	8,794	7,885	5,699
Man./Man.	837	882	823	742	634	566	612	643	579	598
Sask./Sask.	2,316	2,175	2,548	2,267	2,177	2,112	1,780	1,572	1,450	1,467
Alta./Alb.[1]	3,208	2,685	2,163	1,950	2,022	1,731	1,521	1,551	1,613	1,726
B.C./C.-B.	460	348	356	904	758	875	907	710	832	1,046
Yukon/Yukon[1]	87	82	71	61	77	81	59	59	51	66
N.W.T./T.N.-O.[1]	155	142	132	113	175	217	142	117	89	92
Canada	**20,400**	**18,320**	**20,117**	**19,026**	**19,302**	**18,301**	**17,099**	**15,261**	**14,370**	**12,424**
TOTAL/TOTAL										
Nfld./T.-N.	5,051	5,382	4,672	5,536	4,880	4,699	3,772	3,743	3,402	2,362
P.E.I./I.P.É.	3,863	3,814	3,358	3,082	3,289	3,013	2,716	2,796	2,797	2,886
N.S./N.-É.	14,537	14,600	13,565	13,455	12,029	12,483	13,324	12,188	11,670	10,758
N.B./N.-B.	9,064	8,450	7,907	8,319	7,882	7,185	7,405	5,495	4,926	4,322
Que./Qué.	2,301	2,010	2,637	2,484	2,943	2,624	1,967	1,540	1,392	1,045
Ont./Ont.	130,851	111,698	123,191	116,136	112,981	105,783	93,323	80,115	66,563	50,448
Man./Man.	7,634	7,949	6,605	5,906	5,093	4,642	4,608	4,683	4,090	4,047
Sask./Sask.	22,907	20,258	20,400	18,279	17,013	14,778	12,690	11,018	10,062	9,590
Alta./Alb.[1]	33,871	27,124	21,473	19,089	18,174	15,688	14,272	14,330	14,485	15,584
B.C./C.-B.	3,959	2,584	2,911	8,460	7,354	9,080	9,047	8,105	8,486	9,857
Yukon/Yukon[1]	511	512	468	423	506	536	398	403	364	323
N.W.T./T.N.-O.[1]	930	822	777	770	887	1,052	765	715	563	505
Canada	**235,479**	**205,203**	**207,964**	**201,939**	**193,031**	**181,563**	**164,444**	**145,239**	**128,800**	**111,727**

[1] See footnote 1, table 12.1/Voir renvoi 1, tableau 12.1

Source: Statistics Canada, *Canadian Crime Statistics 1984, 1985, 1990, 1991, 1992*, and *1993* (Ottawa: Statistics Canada, Catalogue No. 85- 205, 1985, 1986, 1991, 1992, 1994, and 1994 respectively).

Statistics Canada, *Statistics de la criminalité du Canada 1984, 1985, 1990 1991, 1992, et 1993* (Ottawa: Statistique Canada, Catalogue no 85-205, 1985, 1986, 1991, 1992, 1994 et 1994 respectivement).

Data for the years 1986 to 1989 were obtained from the Canadian Centre for Justice Statistics, Statistics Canada./
Les données de 1986 à 1989 ont été obtenues du Centre Canadien des statistiques judiciaires, Statistiques, Canada.

TABLE 12.4 **TABLEAU 12.4**

Adults charged under the provincial liquor acts by gender, rates per 100,000 population aged 18 and over, Canada and provinces, 1984 to 1993

Adultes inculpés en vertu des lois provinciales sur les alcools selon sexe, en taux par habitants parmi les personnes âgées, de 18 ans et plus, Canada et provinces, 1984 à 1993

PROVINCE	1984	1985	1986	1987	1988	1989	1990	1991	1992	1993
					MALE/MASCULIN					
Nfld./T.-N.	2,463.3	2,615.5	2,257.5	2,661.1	2,288.4	2,151.2	1,716.2	1,682.2	1,468.9	1,011.3
P.E.I./I.P.É.	8,388.8	8,133.0	7,019.8	6,382.1	6,778.7	6,213.4	5,463.5	5,742.5	5,731.2	5,747.3
N.S./N.-É.	4,388.3	4,370.2	4,009.6	3,906.2	3,474.1	3,569.1	3,764.8	3,415.8	3,251.5	2,948.0
N.B./N.-B.	3,388.4	3,103.8	2,877.4	2,992.7	2,821.3	2,535.3	2,562.1	1,859.1	1,654.7	1,447.2
Que./Qué.	73.8	64.8	82.5	82.4	88.9	79.8	54.0	43.3	36.6	27.4
Ont./Ont.	3,562.3	2,971.4	3,189.1	2,944.4	2,784.5	2,529.6	2,178.4	1,840.4	1,495.1	1,126.8
Man./Man.	1,772.8	1,817.2	1,467.1	1,301.4	1,117.8	1,019.3	997.3	1,003.2	872.9	855.8
Sask./Sask.	5,719.7	4,967.9	4,882.9	4,361.8	4,055.8	3,493.1	3,049.2	2,651.9	2,428.7	2,295.9
Alta./Alb.[1]	3,514.4	2,791.1	2,183.6	1,935.1	1,807.1	1,535.1	1,375.2	1,355.4	1,349.8	1,435.8
B.C./C.-B.	318.5	201.3	227.1	660.0	562.8	681.1	656.9	582.9	591.0	664.0
Yukon/Yukon[1]	4,711.1	4,673.9	4,268.8	3,693.9	4,205.9	4,417.5	3,228.6	3,156.0	2,769.9	2,159.7
N.W.T./T.N.-O.[1]	4,378.5	3,695.7	3,467.7	3,513.4	3,767.2	4,304.1	3,130.7	2,931.4	2,289.9	1,976.1
Canada	**2,304.2**	**1,975.9**	**1,959.1**	**1,877.3**	**1,755.8**	**1,616.9**	**1,437.6**	**1,253.2**	**1,091.1**	**936.2**
					FEMALE/FEMININ					
Nfld./T.-N.	144.8	140.3	123.4	133.2	148.7	161.9	115.6	111.3	143.1	98.5
P.E.I./I.P.É.	283.2	313.3	347.5	334.7	342.4	268.6	349.1	245.9	271.0	362.3
N.S./N.-É.	222.4	184.1	174.7	211.7	179.2	179.7	203.1	184.4	180.6	200.7
N.B./N.-B.	168.8	175.4	164.7	179.4	157.3	145.2	168.2	141.0	128.9	107.1
Que./Qué.	19.9	16.3	22.7	15.5	25.5	20.8	20.3	14.5	15.1	11.0
Ont./Ont.	319.9	281.9	329.1	293.4	295.2	271.2	247.2	216.6	191.8	136.8
Man./Man.	209.3	217.7	201.0	180.0	153.0	136.2	147.0	153.7	138.3	142.2
Sask./Sask.	638.4	591.7	688.8	609.2	585.8	571.7	486.7	430.3	396.8	400.7
Alta./Alb.[1]	378.3	313.0	247.9	222.5	228.2	191.8	164.9	165.2	169.6	179.1
B.C./C.-B.	41.0	30.6	30.8	76.9	63.0	70.8	71.3	54.5	62.4	76.4
Yukon/Yukon[1]	1,101.3	1,012.3	876.5	709.3	855.6	880.4	621.1	596.0	490.4	589.3
N.W.T./T.N.-O.[1]	1,026.5	898.7	825.0	701.9	1,067.1	1,284.0	811.4	650.0	491.7	505.5
Canada	**211.3**	**187.0**	**202.5**	**188.5**	**188.2**	**174.7**	**160.6**	**141.6**	**131.7**	**112.5**
					TOTAL/TOTAL					
Nfld./T.-N.	1,329.6	1,402.3	1,210.7	1,419.5	1,237.6	1,172.1	925.2	893.5	803.5	553.2
P.E.I./I.P.É.	4,355.1	4,252.0	3,702.3	3,368.3	3,540.4	3,191.7	2,871.0	2,930.8	2,938.0	2,990.7
N.S./N.-É.	2,313.0	2,290.2	2,110.3	2,069.7	1,832.6	1,885.6	1,993.1	1,761.5	1,677.7	1,538.6
N.B./N.-B.	1,800.2	1,662.1	1,544.3	1,610.6	1,512.6	1,361.1	1,382.3	984.1	877.1	763.9
Que./Qué.	47.6	41.2	53.6	49.9	58.6	51.7	38.3	28.5	25.5	19.0
Ont./Ont.	1,977.0	1,661.6	1,805.4	1,668.3	1,590.9	1,462.7	1,267.6	1,009.5	828.2	620.1
Man./Man.	996.7	1,026.6	845.4	748.5	640.7	582.4	574.3	570.3	498.2	491.4
Sask./Sask.	3,236.4	2,835.7	2,848.4	2,538.4	2,365.9	2,059.1	1,776.1	1,527.1	1,397.5	1,332.1
Alta./Alb.[1]	2,030.4	1,616.4	1,263.0	1,118.0	1,053.0	895.6	801.2	761.6	760.5	808.0
B.C./C.-B.	186.1	120.3	134.3	384.0	325.9	391.6	380.5	315.3	322.9	365.7
Yukon/Yukon[1]	3,173.9	3,141.1	2,853.7	2,459.3	2,826.8	3,028.2	2,174.9	1,937.5	1,677.4	1,398.3
N.W.T./T.N.-O.[1]	3,069.3	2,601.3	2,428.1	2,436.7	2,771.9	3,168.7	2,256.6	1,862.0	1,451.0	1,291.6
Canada	**1,281.7**	**1,104.3**	**1,107.2**	**1,060.0**	**998.2**	**924.8**	**824.8**	**686.7**	**602.0**	**516.0**

[1] See footnote 1, table 12.1/Voir renvoi 1, tableau 12.1

Source: Statistics Canada, *Canadian Crime Statistics 1984, 1985, 1990, 1991, 1992*, and *1993* (Ottawa: Statistics Canada, Catalogue No. 85-205, 1985, 1986, 1991, 1992, 1994, and 1994 respectively).

Statistics Canada, *Statistics de la criminalité du Canada 1984, 1985, 1990, 1991, 1992, et 1993* (Ottawa: Statistique Canada, Catalogue no 85-205, 1985, 1986, 1991, 1992, 1994 et 1994 respectivement).

Data for the years 1986 to 1989 were obtained from the Canadian Centre for Justice Statistics, Statistics Canada./
Les données de 1986 à 1989 ont été obtenues du Centre Canadien des statistiques judiciaires, Statistiques, Canada.

TABLE 12.5

TABLEAU 12.5

Sentenced admissions to provincial adult correctional facilities service provincial liquor act offences, Canada and provinces, 1990-91 to 1993-94

Admissions des personnes condamnées aux services provinciaux de correction pour adultes en vertu de la loi sur les alcools, Canada et provinces, 1990-91 à 1993-94

PROVINCE	ESTIMATED NUMBER OF SENTENCES ADMISSIONS[1,2]/ NOMBRE ESTIMATIF DES ADMISSIONS DE PERSONNES CONDAMNEES				PERCENTAGE OF SENTENCED ADMISSIONS RELATIVE TO TOTAL SENTENCED ADMISSIONS/ POURCENTAGE DE CES ADMISSIONS RELATIF AUX ADMISSIONS TOTALES DES PERSONNES CONDAMNEES			
	1990/1	1991/2	1992/3	1993/4	1990/1	1991/2	1992/3	1993/4
Nfld./T.-N.	61	73	53	25	3	3	2	1
P.E.I./I.P.É.	217	241	237	193	15	17	20	18
N.S./N.-.É[3]	39	107	178	165	2	5	7	6
N.B./N-B.[4]	102	67	0	111	3	2	..	3
Que./Qué.	5,022	5,145	4,195	4,464	29	25	18	18
Ont./Ont.	3,155	n.a.	n.a.	0	7	n.a.	n.a.	-
Man./Man.[5]	154	111	108	94	3	3	3	3
Sask./Sask.	n.a.	n.a.	n.a.	n.a.	n.a.	n.a.	n.a.	n.a.
Alta./Alb.	0	0	0	0	0	0	0	0
B.C./C.-B.	0	0	0	0	0	0	0	0
Yukon/Yukon	13	3	3	0	3	1	1	0
N.W.T./T.N.-O.	28	20	19	19	3	2	2	2
Canada[6]	8,792	5,766	4,793	5,071	8	8	6	4

[1] Sentenced admissions refer to the number of persons admitted to custody under a warrant of committal handed down by a court judge or magistrate. Also included are persons sentenced on one offence but who are awaiting the completion of court hearings on another charge. The total number of admissions does not necessarily represent a duplicated count of individuals since a person may be admitted, released and readmitted to custody within the same year./Admissions des personnes condamnées fait référence au nombre de personnes mises en état d'arrestation conformément au mandat de dépôt d'un juge oú magistrat de la cour. Y compris aussiont les personnes condamnées pour un certain délit mais qui attendent la fin de l'audition de la cour au sujet d'un autre délit. Le nombre total d'admissions ne représente pas forcément le nombre exact des individus admis parce que la même personne peut être admise, libérée et réadmise en état d'arrestation dans une seule année.

[2] Data have been estimated on the basis of the reported percentage of sentenced liquor act admissions relative to the total number of sentenced admissions./Les données ont été estimées d'après le pourcentage rapporté des admissions des personnes condamnées en vertu de la loi sur les alcools relatif au nombre total des admissions des personnes condamnées.

[3] The significant decrease in sentenced admissions in 1989-90 is a result of the introduction of a Fine Option Program in February 1990./La diminution importante des admissions des personnes condamnées en 1989-90 suit l'introduction du "Fine Option Program" en février, 1990.

[4] Includes only those offenders who were both admitted and released during the calender year./Y compris uniquement les délinquants admis et libérés pendant l'année civile.

[5] Excludes sentenced admissions to the Provincial Remand Centre./Non compris les admissions des personnes condamnées au centre provincial de détention préventive.

[6] Based on data from those provinces which reported in a given year./Basé sur les données des provinces qui en ont rapporté dans une année déterminée.

Source: Statistics Canada, *Adult Correctional Services in Canada 1993-94* (Ottawa: Statistics Canada, Catalogue No, 85-211, unpublished).

Statistique Canada, *Services correctionnels pour adultes au Canada, 1993-94* (Ottawa: Statistique Canada, Catalogue no 85-211, non publiées.)

TABLE 12.6　　　　　　　　　　　　　　　　　　　　　　　　　　**TABLEAU 12.6**

Number and rates per 100,000 population aged 16+ of drinking and driving offences, Canada and provinces, 1984 to 1993

Nombre et taux d'infractions routières en état d'ébriété, par 100,000 habitants parmi les personnes àgées de 16 ans et plus, Canada et provinces, 1984 à 1993

PROVINCE	1984	1985	1986	1987	1988	1989	1990	1991	1992	1993
					OFFENCES[1]/INFRACTIONS[1]					
Nfld./T.-N.	3,431	3,401	3,061	3,676	3,689	3,563	2,873	2,913	2,680	2,309
P.E.I./I.P.É.	1,776	1,604	1,381	1,189	937	785	720	867	714	772
N.S./N.-É.	7,624	6,500	5,787	5,849	5,773	4,933	5,136	4,988	4,881	4,059
N.B./N.-B.	5,001	5,080	5,567	4,998	4,447	4,941	5,183	5,216	4,983	4,459
Que./Qué.	22,475	23,767	27,009	27,973	26,395	24,500	24,014	24,965	25,457	23,563
Ont./Ont.	46,444	41,600	41,138	39,015	39,001	39,667	36,381	34,061	33,799	28,221
Man./Man.	6,978	7,437	8,401	7,289	6,375	6,103	5,672	5,794	5,481	4,677
Sask./Sask.	10,538	9,305	9,423	9,834	9,077	9,472	9,813	10,747	10,390	9,361
Alta./Alb.	31,200	31,801	29,548	29,803	29,321	32,048	31,293	32,478	25,795	23,460
B.C./C.-B.	22,547	21,370	17,965	17,284	16,982	16,606	16,280	16,818	16,675	15,412
Yukon/Yukon	757	650	597	677	980	720	660	630	568	592
N.W.T./T.N.-O.	795	795	694	781	965	991	1,053	1,250	996	682
Canada	**159,566**	**153,310**	**150,571**	**148,368**	**143,942**	**144,329**	**139,078**	**140,727**	**132,419**	**117,567**
		RATE PER 100,000 POPULATION AGED 16 AND OVER/								
		TAUX PAR POPULATION X 100,000 PARMI LES PERSONNES AGEES DE 16 ANS ET PLUS								
Nfld./T.-N.	831.4	816.6	731.8	871.5	866.6	826.9	659.6	661.1	602.9	516.6
P.E.I./I.P.É.	1,871.4	1,667.4	1,420.8	1,219.5	953.2	793.7	724.3	871.4	720.5	769.7
N.S./N.-É.	1,135.9	954.8	841.5	842.8	825.2	697.7	720.8	694.1	676.0	560.0
N.B./N.-B.	921.5	927.3	1,007.8	896.0	790.2	867.9	901.5	896.4	851.9	757.6
Que./Qué.	433.7	454.7	511.5	522.8	488.7	447.5	434.1	447.2	451.2	413.9
Ont./Ont.	648.8	571.6	554.8	513.6	502.8	497.5	448.3	414.7	406.3	335.4
Man./Man.	854.1	899.2	1,003.5	864.4	752.7	719.7	667.8	678.6	642.2	547.1
Sask./Sask.	1,395.2	1,218.1	1,227.4	1,275.5	1,181.3	1,242.9	1,302.7	1,429.9	1,384.8	1,247.8
Alta./Alb.	1,738.7	1,761.4	1,614.3	1,622.5	1,583.0	1,702.7	1,630.2	1,663.1	1,303.5	1,170.3
B.C./C.-B.	977.3	914.7	758.1	717.3	690.2	657.8	627.5	633.1	613.8	553.4
Yukon/Yukon	4,301.1	3,611.1	3,262.3	3,526.0	4,949.5	3,529.4	3,188.4	2,916.7	2,524.4	2,477.0
N.W.T./T.N.-O.	2,284.5	2,190.1	1,891.0	2,110.8	2,573.3	2,587.5	2,679.4	3,101.7	2,429.3	1,655.3
Canada	**806.4**	**765.3**	**741.3**	**719.0**	**687.7**	**676.7**	**642.5**	**642.2**	**597.2**	**524.2**

[1] For a detailed breakdown of offences for the period 1989 to 1992 see Table 12.7./L'analyse détaillée des infractions de 1989 à 1992 est présentée au tableau 12.7.

Source: Data were obtained from the Canadian Centre for Justice Statistics, Statistics Canada.

Les données ont été obtenues du centre canadien des statistiques judiciaires, Statistiques Canada.

TABLE 12.7 | **TABLEAU 12.7**

Number of alcohol-related traffic offences by type of offence and rates per 100,000 population, Canada and provinces, 1991 to 1993

Nombre des infractions routières reliées à l'alcool, selon le genre d'infraction, et taux par 100,000 habitants, Canada et provinces, 1989 à 1993

PROVINCE	OFFENCES/ INFRACTIONS			RATE PER 100,000 POPULATION/ TAUX PAR 100 000 HABITANTS			RATE PER 100,000 AGED 16+/ TAUX PAR 100 000 AGEE 16+		
	1991	1992	1993	1991	1992	1993	1991	1992	1993
TOTAL[1] ALCOHOL-RELATED TRAFFIC OFFENCES/TOTAL[1] DES INFRACTIONS ROUTIERES RELIEES A L'ALCOOL									
Nfld./T.-N.	2,913	2,680	2,309	502.2	461.2	397.3	661.1	602.9	516.6
P.E.I./I.P.É.	867	714	772	662.8	548.0	587.1	871.4	720.5	769.7
N.S./N.-É.	4,988	4,881	4,059	543.2	530.1	439.8	694.1	676.0	560.0
N.B./N.-B.	5,216	4,983	4,459	696.8	665.2	593.8	896.4	851.9	757.6
Que./Qué.	24,965	25,457	23,563	352.6	356.0	326.9	447.2	451.2	413.9
Ont./Ont.	34,061	33,799	28,221	325.3	318.6	262.6	414.7	406.3	335.4
Man./Man.	5,794	5,481	4,677	520.4	492.4	419.1	678.6	642.2	547.1
Sask./Sask.	10,747	10,390	9,361	1,067.2	1,034.3	933.2	1,429.9	1,384.8	1,247.8
Alta./Alb.	32,478	25,795	23,460	1,249.0	979.9	881.2	1,663.1	1,303.5	1,170.3
B.C./C.-B.	16,818	16,675	15,412	498.0	483.2	436.0	633.1	613.8	553.4
Yukon/Yukon	630	568	592	2,164.9	1,880.8	1,850.0	2,916.7	2,524.4	2,477.0
N.W.T./T.N.-O.	1,250	996	682	2,042.5	1,598.7	1,084.3	3,101.7	2,429.3	1,655.3
Canada	140,727	132,419	117,567	500.5	465.7	408.9	642.2	597.2	524.2
IMPAIRED OPERATION OF A VEHICLE - CAUSING DEATH/ CONDUITE AVEC FACULTÉS AFFAIBLIES CAUSANT LA MORT[1]									
Nfld./T.-N.	1	2	6	0.2	0.3	1.0	0.2	0.4	1.3
P.E.I./I.P.É.	3	1	0	2.3	0.8	0.0	3.0	1.0	0.0
N.S./N.-É.	5	4	5	0.5	0.4	0.5	0.7	0.6	0.7
N.B./N.-B.	7	7	6	0.9	0.9	0.8	1.2	1.2	1.0
Que./Qué.	46	37	42	0.6	0.5	0.6	0.8	0.7	0.7
Ont./Ont.	33	51	42	0.3	0.5	0.4	0.4	0.6	0.5
Man./Man.	12	18	10	1.1	1.6	0.9	1.4	2.1	1.2
Sask./Sask.	9	14	7	0.9	1.4	0.7	1.2	1.9	0.9
Alta./Alb.	29	17	27	1.1	0.6	1.0	1.5	0.9	1.3
B.C./C.-B.	32	29	34	0.9	0.8	1.0	1.2	1.1	1.2
Yukon/Yukon	0	0	2	0.0	0.0	6.3	0.0	0.0	8.4
N.W.T./T.N.-O.	1	2	0	1.6	3.2	0.0	2.5	4.9	0.0
Canada	178	182	181	0.6	0.6	0.6	0.8	0.8	0.8
IMPAIRED OPERATION OF A VEHICLE - CAUSING BODILY HARM/ CONTUITE AVEC FACULTÉS AFFAIBLIES CAUSANT DES LESIONS CORPORELLES[1]									
Nfld./T.-N.	17	25	38	2.9	4.3	6.5	3.9	5.6	8.5
P.E.I./I.P.É.	1	2	2	0.8	1.5	1.5	1.0	2.0	2.0
N.S./N.-É.	28	29	25	3.0	3.1	2.7	3.9	4.0	3.4
N.B./N.-B.	28	25	18	3.7	3.3	2.4	4.8	4.3	3.1
Que./Qué.	361	392	364	5.1	5.5	5.0	6.5	6.9	6.4
Ont./Ont.	421	385	290	4.0	3.6	2.7	5.1	4.6	3.4
Man./Man.	87	161	70	7.8	14.5	6.3	10.2	18.9	8.2
Sask./Sask.	45	69	84	4.5	6.9	8.4	6.0	9.2	11.2
Alta./Alb.	261	224	179	10.0	8.5	6.7	13.4	11.3	8.9
B.C./C.-B.	117	126	161	3.5	3.7	4.6	4.4	4.6	5.8
Yukon/Yukon	7	0	4	24.1	0.0	12.5	32.4	0.0	16.7
N.W.T./T.N.-O.	7	9	8	11.4	14.4	12.7	17.4	22.0	19.4
Canada	1,380	1,447	1,243	4.9	5.1	4.3	6.3	6.5	5.5

TABLE 12.7 (concluded)　　　　　　　　　　　　　　　**TABLEAU 12.7 (fin)**

Number of alcohol-related traffic offences by type of offence and rates per 100,000 population, Canada and provinces, 1991 to 1993

Nombre des infractions routières reliées à l'alcool, selon le genre d'infraction, et taux par 100,000 habitants, Canada et provinces, 1989 à 1993

PROVINCE	OFFENCES/ INFRACTIONS			RATE PER 100,000 POPULATION/ TAUX PAR 100 000 HABITANTS			RATE PER 100,000 AGED 16+/ TAUX PAR 100 000 AGEE 16+		
	1991	1992	1993	1991	1992	1993	1991	1992	1993
IMPAIRED OPERATION OF A VEHICLE - BLOOD ALCOHOL OVER 80 MG%/ CONDUITE AVEC ALCOOLEMIE SUPERIEURE A 80MG%[1]									
Nfld./T.-N.	2,591	2,349	1,873	446.7	404.2	322.3	588.1	528.5	419.0
P.E.I./I.P.É.	710	575	643	542.8	441.3	489.0	713.6	580.2	641.1
N.S./N.-É.	3,846	3,746	3,067	418.9	406.8	332.3	535.2	518.8	423.2
N.B./N.-B.	4,374	4,274	3,831	584.3	570.6	510.2	751.7	730.7	650.9
Que./Qué.	23,078	23,702	22,094	325.9	331.5	306.5	413.4	420.1	388.1
Ont./Ont.	31,056	31,093	26,016	296.6	293.1	242.1	378.1	373.8	309.2
Man./Man.	5,093	4,796	4,190	457.5	430.9	375.5	596.5	561.9	490.1
Sask./Sask.	10,125	9,801	8,885	1,005.5	975.7	885.8	1,347.1	1,306.3	1,184.4
Alta./Alb.	30,303	24,119	22,170	1,165.4	916.2	832.7	1,551.7	1,218.8	1,106.0
B.C./C.-B.	14,333	14,240	13,454	424.4	412.6	380.6	539.5	524.2	483.1
Yukon/Yukon	576	512	532	1,979.4	1,695.4	1,662.5	2,666.7	2,275.6	2,225.9
N.W.T./T.N.-O.	1,179	917	652	1,926.5	1,471.9	1,036.6	2,925.6	2,236.6	1,582.5
Canada	**127,264**	**120,124**	**107,407**	**452.6**	**422.4**	**373.6**	**580.7**	**541.7**	**478.9**
FAIL OR REFUSE TO PROVIDE A BREATH SAMPLE/ DEFAULT OU REFUS DE FOURNIR UN ECHANTILLON D'HALEINE									
Nfld./T.-N.	293	290	385	50.5	49.9	66.3	66.5	65.2	86.1
P.E.I./I.P.É.	145	133	123	110.9	102.1	93.5	145.7	134.2	122.6
N.S./N.-É.	1,068	1,070	935	116.3	116.2	101.3	148.6	148.2	129.0
N.B./N.-B.	773	648	568	103.3	86.5	75.6	132.8	110.8	96.5
Que./Qué.	1,368	1,246	995	19.3	17.4	13.8	24.5	22.1	17.5
Ont./Ont.	2,519	2,223	1,853	24.1	21.0	17.2	30.7	26.7	22.0
Man./Man.	583	482	401	52.4	43.3	35.9	68.3	56.5	46.9
Sask./Sask.	555	494	375	55.1	49.2	37.4	73.8	65.8	50.0
Alta./Alb.	1,812	1,377	1,040	69.7	52.3	39.1	92.8	69.6	51.9
B.C./C.-B.	2,262	2,198	1,680	67.0	63.7	47.5	85.1	80.9	60.3
Yukon/Yukon	43	56	54	147.8	185.4	168.8	199.1	248.9	225.9
N.W.T./T.N.-O.	63	67	22	102.9	107.5	35.0	156.3	163.4	53.4
Canada	**11,484**	**10,284**	**8,431**	**40.8**	**36.2**	**29.3**	**52.4**	**46.4**	**37.6**
FAIL OR REFUSE TO PROVIDE A BLOOD SAMPLE/ MANQUE OU REFUS DE FOURNIR UN ECHANTILLON DE SANG									
Nfld./T.-N.	11	14	7	1.9	2.4	1.2	2.5	3.1	1.6
P.E.I./I.P.É.	8	3	4	6.1	2.3	3.0	8.0	3.0	4.0
N.S./N.-É.	41	32	27	4.5	3.5	2.9	5.7	4.4	3.7
N.B./N.-B.	34	29	36	4.5	3.9	4.8	5.8	5.0	6.1
Que./Qué.	112	80	68	1.6	1.1	0.9	2.0	1.4	1.2
Ont./Ont.	32	47	20	0.3	0.4	0.2	0.4	0.6	0.2
Man./Man.	19	24	6	1.7	2.2	0.5	2.2	2.8	0.7
Sask./Sask.	13	12	10	1.3	1.2	1.0	1.7	1.6	1.3
Alta./Alb.	73	58	44	2.8	2.2	1.7	3.7	2.9	2.2
B.C./C.-B.	74	82	83	2.2	2.4	2.3	2.8	3.0	3.0
Yukon/Yukon	4	0	0	13.7	0.0	0.0	18.5	0.0	0.0
N.W.T./T.N.-O.	0	1	0	0.0	1.6	0.0	0.0	2.4	0.0
Canada	**421**	**382**	**305**	**1.5**	**1.3**	**1.1**	**1.9**	**1.7**	**1.4**

[1] Includes both motor vehicles, boats, aircraft, and vessels./Y compris les véhicules motorisés, les bateau, les avions et les vaisseaux.

Source: Data were obtained from the Canadian Centre for Justice Statistics, Statistics Canada.

Données obtenues du Centre canadien des statistiques judiciaires, Statistiques Canada.

| TABLE 12.8 | TABLEAU 12.8 |

Persons[1] charged with alcohol-related traffic offences by gender, Canada and provinces, 1991 to 1993

Personnes[1] accusées d'infractions routières reliées à l'alcool, selon sexe, Canada et provinces, 1991 à 1993

PROVINCE	MALE/MASCULIN			FEMALE/FEMININ			TOTAL		
	1991	1992	1993	1991	1992	1993	1991	1992	1993
TOTAL[2] ALCOHOL-RELATED TRAFFIC OFFENCES/TOTAL DES INFRACTIONS ROUTIERES ASSOCIEES A L'ALCOOL									
Nfld./T.-N.	2,342	2,204	1,625	125	122	112	2,467	2,326	1,737
P.E.I./I.P.É.	665	552	577	49	33	34	714	585	611
N.S./N.-É.	4,003	3,881	3,204	346	370	291	4,349	4,251	3,495
N.B./N.-B.	3,839	3,647	3,128	238	287	231	4,077	3,934	3,359
Que./Qué.	21,299	21,034	19,055	1,717	1,750	1,666	23,016	22,784	20,721
Ont./Ont.	29,476	29,322	23,786	2,194	1,973	2,391	31,670	31,295	26,177
Man./Man.	4,222	3,870	3,180	622	574	457	4,844	4,444	3,637
Sask./Sask.	6,554	5,874	4,953	1,038	1,038	855	7,592	6,912	5,808
Alta./Alb.	15,873	13,436	12,223	2,073	1,922	1,780	17,946	15,358	14,003
B.C./C.-B.	12,241	11,569	10,745	1,278	1,357	1,418	13,519	12,926	12,163
Yukon/Yukon	346	400	402	69	81	67	415	481	469
N.W.T./T.N.-O.	512	418	312	63	52	47	575	470	359
Canada	**101,372**	**96,207**	**83,190**	**9,812**	**9,559**	**9,349**	**111,184**	**105,766**	**92,539**
IMPAIRED OPERATION OF VEHICLE - CAUSING DEATH/CONDUITE AVEC FACULTES AFFAIBLIES CAUSANT LA MORT[2]									
Nfld./T.-N.	1	3	4	0	0	0	1	3	4
P.E.I./I.P.É.	2	1	0	0	0	0	2	1	0
N.S./N.-É.	2	4	5	0	0	1	2	4	6
N.B./N.-B.	5	8	4	1	0	0	6	8	4
Que./Qué.	38	33	27	1	6	3	39	39	30
Ont./Ont.	28	34	33	0	1	5	28	35	38
Man./Man.	5	13	7	1	2	1	6	15	8
Sask./Sask.	6	8	6	0	2	0	6	10	6
Alta./Alb.	13	10	13	2	0	3	15	10	16
B.C./C.-B.	22	21	28	1	1	2	23	22	30
Yukon/Yukon	0	0	2	0	0	0	0	0	2
N.W.T./T.N.-O.	0	3	0	0	0	0	0	3	0
Canada	**122**	**138**	**129**	**6**	**12**	**15**	**128**	**150**	**144**
IMPAIRED OPERATION OF VEHICLE - CAUSING BODILY HARM/ CONDUITE AVEC FACULTES AFFAIBLIES CAUSANT DES LESIONS CORPORELLES[2]									
Nfld./T.-N.	13	22	23	0	0	0	13	22	23
P.E.I./I.P.É.	0	2	0	0	0	0	0	2	0
N.S./N.-É.	24	18	23	0	3	1	24	21	24
N.B./N.-B.	19	14	17	1	3	0	20	17	17
Que./Qué.	296	303	300	31	30	26	327	333	326
Ont./Ont.	357	345	255	12	19	23	369	364	278
Man./Man.	64	134	51	7	7	8	71	141	59
Sask./Sask.	32	37	54	3	6	10	35	43	64
Alta./Alb.	128	120	110	23	18	12	151	138	122
B.C./C.-B.	82	99	122	15	9	17	97	108	139
Yukon/Yukon	3	2	3	0	0	1	3	2	4
N.W.T./T.N.-O.	2	8	5	1	0	1	3	8	6
Canada	**1,020**	**1,104**	**963**	**93**	**95**	**99**	**1,113**	**1,199**	**1,062**

TABLE 12.8 (concluded)   **TABLEAU 12.8 (fin)**

Persons[1] charged with alcohol-related traffic offences by gender, Canada and provinces, 1991 to 1993

Personnes[1] accusées d'infractions routières reliées à l'alcool, selon sexe, Canada et provinces, 1991 à 1993

PROVINCE	MALE/MASCULIN			FEMALE/FEMININ			TOTAL		
	1991	1992	1993	1991	1992	1993	1991	1992	1993
IMPAIRED OPERATION OF VEHICLE -BLOOD ALCOHOL OVER 80 MG %/									
CONDUITE AVEC UNE ALCOOLEMIE SUPERIEURE A 80 mg %[2]									
Nfld./T.-N.	2,131	1,983	1,476	110	111	101	2,241	2,094	1,577
P.E.I./I.P.É.	522	428	468	40	26	27	562	454	495
N.S./N.-É.	3,067	2,924	2,350	259	281	202	3,326	3,205	2,552
N.B./N.-B.	3,129	3,034	2,611	180	243	179	3,309	3,277	2,790
Que./Qué.	19,838	19,695	17,956	1,588	1,628	1,553	21,426	21,323	19,509
Ont./Ont.	27,183	27,182	22,053	1,975	1,758	2,207	29,158	28,940	24,260
Man./Man.	3,688	3,336	2,831	545	506	412	4,233	3,842	3,243
Sask./Sask.	6,234	5,625	4,777	982	997	823	7,216	6,622	5,600
Alta./Alb.	15,398	13,082	11,898	2,013	1,865	1,729	17,411	14,947	13,627
B.C./C.-B.	11,920	11,184	10,323	1,228	1,297	1,358	13,148	12,481	11,681
Yukon/Yukon	317	363	358	63	71	60	380	434	418
N.W.T./T.N.-O.	492	386	301	60	51	45	552	437	346
Canada	**93,919**	**89,222**	**77,402**	**9,043**	**8,834**	**8,696**	**102,962**	**98,056**	**86,098**
FAIL OR REFUSE TO PROVIDE A BREATH SAMPLE/									
DEFAULT OU REFUS DE FOURNIR UN ECHANTILLON D'HALEINE									
Nfld./T.-N.	190	188	115	15	11	11	205	199	126
P.E.I./I.P.É.	133	119	107	9	7	7	142	126	114
N.S./N.-É.	875	907	808	85	86	84	960	993	892
N.B./N.-B.	661	568	470	52	39	49	713	607	519
Que./Qué.	1,053	947	724	88	80	80	1,141	1,027	804
Ont./Ont.	1,887	1,722	1,433	205	193	153	2,092	1,915	1,586
Man./Man.	450	374	287	69	56	36	519	430	323
Sask./Sask.	278	200	114	52	33	21	330	233	135
Alta./Alb.	323	219	194	35	38	34	358	257	228
B.C./C.-B.	208	250	260	32	50	38	240	300	298
Yukon/Yukon	24	35	39	6	10	6	30	45	45
N.W.T./T.N.-O.	18	21	6	2	1	1	20	22	7
Canada	**6,100**	**5,550**	**4,557**	**650**	**604**	**520**	**6,750**	**6,154**	**5,077**
FAIL OR REFUSE TO PROVIDE A BLOOD SAMPLE/									
DEFAULT OU REFUS DE FOURNIR UN ECHANTILLON DE SANG									
Nfld./T.-N.	7	8	7	0	0	0	7	8	7
P.E.I./I.P.É.	8	2	2	0	0	0	8	2	2
N.S./N.-É.	35	28	18	2	0	3	37	28	21
N.B./N.-B.	25	23	26	4	2	3	29	25	29
Que./Qué.	74	56	48	9	6	4	83	62	52
Ont./Ont.	21	39	12	2	2	3	23	41	15
Man./Man.	15	13	4	0	3	0	15	16	4
Sask./Sask.	4	4	2	1	0	1	5	4	3
Alta./Alb.	11	5	8	0	1	2	11	6	10
B.C./C.-B.	9	15	12	2	0	3	11	15	15
Yukon/Yukon	2	0	0	0	0	0	2	0	0
N.W.T./T.N.-O.	0	0	0	0	0	0	0	0	0
Canada	**211**	**193**	**139**	**20**	**14**	**19**	**231**	**207**	**158**

[1] Includes adults and juveniles/Y compris les adultes et les jeunes.

[2] Includes both motor vehicles, boats, aircraft, and vessels/Y compris les véhicules motorisés, les bateau, les avion et les vaisseaux.

Source: Traffic enforcement data were obtained from the Canadian Centre for Justice Statistics, Statistics Canada.

Les données routières ont été obtenues du Centre canadien des Statistiques judiciaires, Statistiques Canada.

TABLE 12.9　　　　　　　　　　　　　　　　　　　　　　　　　　　　**TABLEAU 12.9**

Persons[1] charged with alcohol-related traffic offences by gender, rates per 100,000 population aged 16 and over, Canada and provinces, 1991 to 1993

Personnes[1] accusées d'infractions routières reliées à l'alcool, selon le sexe, en taux par 100 000 habitants, population de 16 ans et plus, Canada et provinces, 1991 à 1993

PROVINCE	MALE/MASCULIN			FEMALE/FEMININ			TOTAL		
	1991	1992	1993	1991	1992	1993	1991	1992	1993
TOTAL[2] ALCOHOL-RELATED TRAFFIC OFFENCES/TOTAL DES INFRACTIONS ROUTIERES ASSOCIEES A L'ALCOOL									
Nfld./T.-N.	1,065.0	992.8	728.4	56.6	54.8	50.0	559.9	523.3	388.6
P.E.I./I.P.É.	1,365.5	1,138.1	1,175.2	96.5	65.2	66.3	717.6	590.3	608.6
N.S./N.-É.	1,138.8	1,100.1	905.6	94.3	100.2	78.4	605.2	588.8	482.2
N.B./N.-B.	1,342.8	1,269.4	1,082.0	80.4	96.4	77.1	700.6	672.6	570.7
Que./Qué.	782.3	764.4	686.6	60.0	60.5	57.1	412.3	403.8	364.0
Ont./Ont.	733.6	720.7	578.2	52.3	46.4	55.6	385.5	376.2	311.1
Man./Man.	1,006.0	923.8	758.6	143.3	132.1	104.9	567.3	520.7	425.4
Sask./Sask.	1,764.2	1,588.0	1,341.9	273.1	272.9	224.4	1,010.1	921.2	774.2
Alta./Alb.	1,621.0	1,355.0	1,217.4	212.9	194.7	177.9	918.9	776.1	698.5
B.C./C.-B.	932.6	863.2	782.5	95.1	98.6	100.4	508.9	475.8	436.7
Yukon/Yukon	3,061.9	3,418.8	3,268.3	669.9	750.0	577.6	1,921.3	2,137.8	1,962.3
N.W.T./T.N.-O.	2,392.5	1,917.4	1,411.8	333.3	270.8	244.8	1,426.8	1,146.3	869.2
Canada	**941.9**	**883.8**	**756.0**	**88.0**	**84.7**	**81.8**	**507.4**	**477.0**	**412.6**
IMPAIRED OPERATION OF VEHICLE - CAUSING DEATH/CONDUITE AVEC FACULTES AFFAIBLIES CAUSANT LA MORT[2]									
Nfld./T.-N.	0.5	1.4	1.8	0.0	0.0	0.0	0.2	0.7	0.9
P.E.I./I.P.É.	4.1	2.1	0.0	0.0	0.0	0.0	2.0	1.0	0.0
N.S./N.-É.	0.6	1.1	1.4	0.0	0.0	0.3	0.3	0.6	0.8
N.B./N.-B.	1.7	2.8	1.4	0.3	0.0	0.0	1.0	1.4	0.7
Que./Qué.	1.4	1.2	1.0	0.0	0.2	0.1	0.7	0.7	0.5
Ont./Ont.	0.7	0.8	0.8	0.0	0.0	0.1	0.3	0.4	0.5
Man./Man.	1.2	3.1	1.7	0.2	0.5	0.2	0.7	1.8	0.9
Sask./Sask.	1.6	2.2	1.6	0.0	0.5	0.0	0.8	1.3	0.8
Alta./Alb.	1.3	1.0	1.3	0.2	0.0	0.3	0.8	0.5	0.8
B.C./C.-B.	1.7	1.6	2.0	0.1	0.1	0.1	0.9	0.8	1.1
Yukon/Yukon	0.0	0.0	16.3	0.0	0.0	0.0	0.0	0.0	8.4
N.W.T./T.N.-O.	0.0	13.8	0.0	0.0	0.0	0.0	0.0	7.3	0.0
Canada	**1.1**	**1.3**	**1.2**	**0.1**	**0.1**	**0.1**	**0.6**	**0.7**	**0.6**
IMPAIRED OPERATION OF VEHICLE - CAUSING BODILY HARM/ CONDUITE AVEC FACULTES AFFAIBLIES CAUSANT DES LESIONS CORPORELLES[2]									
Nfld./T.-N.	5.9	9.9	10.3	0.0	0.0	0.0	3.0	4.9	5.1
P.E.I./I.P.É.	0.0	4.1	0.0	0.0	0.0	0.0	0.0	2.0	0.0
N.S./N.-É.	6.8	5.1	6.5	0.0	0.8	0.3	3.3	2.9	3.3
N.B./N.-B.	6.6	4.9	5.9	0.3	1.0	0.0	3.4	2.9	2.9
Que./Qué.	10.9	11.0	10.8	1.1	1.0	0.9	5.9	5.9	5.7
Ont./Ont.	8.9	8.5	6.2	0.3	0.4	0.5	4.5	4.4	3.3
Man./Man.	15.2	32.0	12.2	1.6	1.6	1.8	8.3	16.5	6.9
Sask./Sask.	8.6	10.0	14.6	0.8	1.6	2.6	4.7	5.7	8.5
Alta./Alb.	13.1	12.1	11.0	2.4	1.8	1.2	7.7	7.0	6.1
B.C./C.-B.	6.2	7.4	8.9	1.1	0.7	1.2	3.7	4.0	5.0
Yukon/Yukon	26.5	17.1	24.4	0.0	0.0	8.6	13.9	8.9	16.7
N.W.T./T.N.-O.	9.3	36.7	22.6	5.3	0.0	5.2	7.4	19.5	14.5
Canada	**9.5**	**10.1**	**8.8**	**0.8**	**0.8**	**0.9**	**5.1**	**5.4**	**4.7**

TABLE 12.9 (continued)　　　　　　　　　　　　　　**TABLEAU 12.9** (suite)

Persons[1] charged with alcohol-related traffic offences by gender, rates per 100,000 population aged 16 and over, Canada and provinces, 1991 to 1993

Personnes[1] accusées d'infractions routières reliées à l'alcool, selon le sexe, en taux par 100 000 habitants, population de 16 ans et plus, Canada et provinces, 1991 à 1993

PROVINCE	MALE/MASCULIN			FEMALE/FEMININ			TOTAL		
	1991	1992	1993	1991	1992	1993	1991	1992	1993
IMPAIRED OPERATION OF VEHICLE -BLOOD ALCOHOL OVER 80 MG %/ CONDUITE AVEC UNE ALCOOLEMIE SUPERIEURE A 80 mg %[2]									
Nfld./T.-N.	969.1	893.2	661.6	49.8	49.9	45.1	508.6	471.1	352.8
P.E.I./I.P.É.	1,071.9	882.5	953.2	78.7	51.4	52.6	564.8	458.1	493.0
N.S./N.-É.	872.5	828.8	664.2	70.6	76.1	54.4	462.8	443.9	352.1
N.B./N.-B.	1,094.4	1,056.0	903.1	60.8	81.7	59.8	568.7	560.3	474.0
Que./Qué.	728.6	715.7	647.0	55.5	56.3	53.2	383.8	377.9	342.7
Ont./Ont.	676.6	668.1	536.0	47.1	41.4	51.3	355.0	347.9	288.3
Man./Man.	878.7	796.4	675.3	125.5	116.4	94.6	495.8	450.1	379.3
Sask./Sask.	1,678.1	1,520.7	1,294.2	258.4	262.1	216.0	960.1	882.6	746.5
Alta./Alb.	1,572.5	1,319.3	1,185.1	206.7	188.9	172.8	891.5	755.3	679.8
B.C./C.-B.	908.1	834.4	751.7	91.4	94.2	96.2	494.9	459.4	419.4
Yukon/Yukon	2,805.3	3,102.6	2,910.6	611.7	657.4	517.2	1,759.3	1,928.9	1,749.0
N.W.T./T.N.-O.	2,299.1	1,770.6	1,362.0	317.5	265.6	234.4	1,369.7	1,065.9	837.8
Canada	**872.7**	**819.6**	**703.4**	**81.1**	**78.3**	**76.1**	**469.8**	**442.2**	**383.9**
FAIL OR REFUSE TO PROVIDE A BREATH SAMPLE/DEFAULT OU REFUS DE FOURNIR UN ECHANTILLON D'HALEINE									
Nfld./T.-N.	86.4	84.7	51.5	6.8	4.9	4.9	46.5	44.8	28.2
P.E.I./I.P.É.	273.1	245.4	217.9	17.7	13.8	13.6	142.7	127.1	113.5
N.S./N.-É.	248.9	257.1	228.4	23.2	23.3	22.6	133.6	137.5	123.1
N.B./N.-B.	231.2	197.7	162.6	17.6	13.1	16.4	122.5	103.8	88.2
Que./Qué.	38.7	34.4	26.1	3.1	2.8	2.7	20.4	18.2	14.1
Ont./Ont.	47.0	42.3	34.8	4.9	4.5	3.6	25.5	23.0	18.8
Man./Man.	107.2	89.3	68.5	15.9	12.9	8.3	60.8	50.4	37.8
Sask./Sask.	74.8	54.1	30.9	13.7	8.7	5.5	43.9	31.1	18.0
Alta./Alb.	33.0	22.1	19.3	3.6	3.8	3.4	18.3	13.0	11.4
B.C./C.-B.	15.8	18.7	18.9	2.4	3.6	2.7	9.0	11.0	10.7
Yukon/Yukon	212.4	299.1	317.1	58.3	92.6	51.7	138.9	200.0	188.3
N.W.T./T.N.-O.	84.1	96.3	27.1	10.6	5.2	5.2	49.6	53.7	16.9
Canada	**56.7**	**51.0**	**41.4**	**5.8**	**5.4**	**4.6**	**30.8**	**27.8**	**22.6**
FAIL OR REFUSE TO PROVIDE A BLOOD SAMPLE/DEFAULT OU REFUS DE FOURNIR UN ECHANTILLON DE SANG									
Nfld./T.-N.	3.2	3.6	3.1	0.0	0.0	0.0	1.6	1.8	1.6
P.E.I./I.P.É.	16.4	4.1	4.1	0.0	0.0	0.0	8.0	2.0	2.0
N.S./N.-É.	10.0	7.9	5.1	0.5	0.0	0.8	5.1	3.9	2.9
N.B./N.-B.	8.7	8.0	9.0	1.4	0.7	1.0	5.0	4.3	4.9
Que./Qué.	2.7	2.0	1.7	0.3	0.2	0.1	1.5	1.1	0.9
Ont./Ont.	0.5	1.0	0.3	0.0	0.0	0.1	0.3	0.5	0.2
Man./Man.	3.6	3.1	1.0	0.0	0.7	0.0	1.8	1.9	0.5
Sask./Sask.	1.1	1.1	0.5	0.3	0.0	0.3	0.7	0.5	0.4
Alta./Alb.	1.1	0.5	0.8	0.0	0.1	0.2	0.6	0.3	0.5
B.C./C.-B.	0.7	1.1	0.9	0.1	0.0	0.2	0.4	0.6	0.5
Yukon/Yukon	17.7	0.0	0.0	0.0	0.0	0.0	9.3	0.0	0.0
N.W.T./T.N.-O.	0.0	0.0	0.0	0.0	0.0	0.0	0.0	0.0	0.0
Canada	**2.0**	**1.8**	**1.3**	**0.2**	**0.1**	**0.2**	**1.1**	**0.9**	**0.7**

TABLE 12.9 (concluded)

TABLEAU 12.9 (fin)

Persons[1] charged with alcohol-related traffic offences by gender, rates per 100,000 population aged 16 and over, Canada and provinces, 1991 to 1993

Personnes[1] accusées d'infractions routières reliées à l'alcool, selon le sexe, en taux par 100 000 habitants, population de 16 ans et plus, Canada et provinces, 1991 à 1993

[1] Includes adults and juveniles/Y compris les adultes et les jeunes.

[2] Includes both motor vehicles, boats, aircraft, and vessels/Y compris les véhicules motorisés, les bateau, les avion et les vaisseaux.

Source: Traffic enforcement data were obtained from the Canadian Centre for Justice Statistics, Statistics Canada.

Les données routières ont été obtenues du Centre canadien des Statistiques judiciaires, Statistiques Canada.

TABLE 12.10

TABLEAU 12.10

Sentenced admissions to provincial adult correctional service facilities for drinking and driving offences, Canada and provinces, 1990-91 to 1993-94

Admissions des personnes condamnées pour conduite avec facultés affaiblies dans les établissements correctionnels provinciaux, Canada et provinces, 1990-91 à 1993-94

PROVINCE	ESTIMATED NUMBER OF SENTENCES ADMISSIONS[1,2]/ NOMBRE ESTIMATIF DES ADMISSIONS DE PERSONNES CONDAMNEES				PERCENTAGE OF SENTENCED ADMISSIONS RELATIVE TO TOTAL SENTENCED ADMISSIONS/ POURCENTAGE DE CES ADMISSIONS RELATIF AUX ADMISSIONS TOTALES DES PERSONNES CONDAMNEES			
	1990/1	1991/2	1992/3	1993/4	1990/1	1991/2	1992/3	1993/4
Nfld./T.-N.	529	585	587	480	26	24	22	19
P.E.I./P.É.I.	709	623	403	385	49	44	34	36
N.S./N.É.[3]	308	278	330	357	16	13	13	13
N.B./N.-B.[4]	1,126	974	1,140	888	33	29	28	24
Que./Qué[5]	1,732	3,087	2,797	3,472	10	15	12	14
Ont./Ont.	5,409	n.a.	n.a.	4,385	12	n.a.	n.a.	11
Man./Man.[6]	721	481	466	408	14	13	13	13
Sask./Sask.	1,844	1,936	1,860	1,914	25	26	27	27
Alta./Alb.	2,264	2,718	2,615	2,202	11	12	11	10
B.C./C.-B.	2,193	2,331	2,119	2,098	24	23	20	18
Yukon/Yukon	61	41	6	0	14	14	2	..
N.W.T./T.N.-O.	..	..	..	..	..	..	..	..
Canada[7]	**16,896**	**13,054**	**12,323**	**16,589**	**15**	**17**	**15**	**14**

[1] Sentenced admissions refer to the number of persons admitted to custody under a warrant of committal handed down by a court, judge or magistrate. Also included are persons sentenced on one offence but who are awaiting the completion of court hearings on another charge. The total number of admissions does not necessarily represent an unduplicated count of individuals since a person may be admitted, released and readmitted to custody within the same year./Admissions des personnes condamnées fait référence au nombre de personnes mises en état d'arrestation conformément au mandat de dépôt d'un juge où magistrat de la cour. Y compris aussi sont les personnes condamnées pour un certain délit mais qui attendent la fin de l'audition de la cour au sujet d'un autre délit. Le nombre total d'admissions ne représente pas enforcément le nombre exact des individus admis parce que la même personne peut être admise, libérée et réadmise en état d'arrestation dans une seule année.

[2] Data have been estimated on the basis of the reported percentage of sentenced drinking/driving admissions relative to the total number of sentenced admissions. Les données ont été estimées d'après le pourcentage rapporté d'admissions des personnes condamnées d'infractions routières en état d'ébriété relatif au nombre total d'admissions de personnes condamnées.

[3] The significant decrease in sentenced admissions in 1989-90 is a result of the introduction of a Fine Option Program in February 1990./La diminution importante des admissions des personnes condamnées en 1989-90 suit l'introduction du "Fine Option Program" en février, 1990.

[4] Includes only those offenders who were both admitted and released during the calender year./Y comrpis uniquement les délinquants admis et libérés pendant l'année civile.

[5] Includes persons charged with dangerous driving and driving without a permit./Y compris les personnes accusées de conduite dangereuse et de conduite sans permis.

[6] Excludes sentenced admissions to the Provincial Remand Centre./Non compris les admissions des personnes condamnées au centre provincial de détention préventive.

[7] Based on data from those provinces which reported in a given year./Basé sur les données des provinces qui en ont rapporté dans une année déterminée.

Source: Statistics Canada, *Adult Correctional Services in Canada 1993-94* (Ottawa: Statistics Canada, Catalogue No, 85-211, unpublished).

Statistique Canada, *Services correctionnels pour adultes au Canada, 1993-94* (Ottawa: Statistique Canada, Catalogue no 85-211, non publiées.)

TABLE 12.11

TABLEAU 12.11

Number of federal drug offences, Canada and provinces, 1984 to 1993

Nombre des infractions reliées à la drogue en vertu des lois fédérales, Canada et provinces, 1984 à 1993

PROVINCE	1984	1985	1986	1987	1988	1989	1990	1991	1992	1993
TOTAL DRUG-RELATED OFFENCES[1]/TOTAL DES DELITS ASSOCIES A LA DROGUE[1]										
Nfld./T.-N.	756	962	743	1,030	761	798	822	666	818	785
P.E.I./I.P.É.	311	301	218	177	189	187	209	136	209	204
N.S./N.-É.	2,002	1,856	1,933	1,843	1,924	2,087	2,252	1,877	1,969	1,923
N.B./N.-B.	1,776	1,995	1,616	1,582	1,334	1,846	1,364	1,199	1,089	1,204
Que./Qué.	7,274	7,540	8,875	8,675	8,718	9,609	8,700	9,131	9,745	11,185
Ont./Ont.	19,066	19,803	19,322	22,854	22,929	27,243	23,532	21,030	17,324	17,606
Man./Man.	2,012	2,425	2,418	3,059	2,713	3,540	2,165	1,724	2,262	1,683
Sask./Sask.	2,605	2,747	2,452	3,115	1,967	1,949	2,146	1,146	1,596	1,741
Alta./Alb.	6,657	7,086	6,328	5,799	6,672	6,587	6,195	5,018	5,685	6,234
B.C./C.-B.	11,848	11,860	11,893	13,069	12,737	13,539	12,077	14,616	15,279	13,727
Yukon/Yukon	260	256	176	182	167	219	191	212	172	147
N.W.T./T.N.-O.	383	374	277	273	246	278	365	343	342	372
Canada	**54,950**	**57,205**	**56,251**	**61,658**	**60,357**	**67,882**	**60,039**	**56,123**	**56,490**	**56,811**
NARCOTIC CONTROL ACT - CANNABIS/LOI SUR LES STUPEFIANTS - CANNABIS										
Nfld./T.-N.	701	839	658	925	656	719	766	577	741	707
P.E.I./I.P.É.	251	243	171	153	151	146	161	103	170	156
N.S./N.-É.	1,763	1,637	1,658	1,494	1,552	1,538	1,668	1,234	1,402	1,460
N.B./N.-B.	1,535	1,765	1,430	1,324	1,128	1,376	1,092	883	860	911
Que./Qué.	4,369	4,482	5,128	4,620	4,048	3,559	3,696	3,625	3,778	5,083
Ont./Ont.	15,092	14,309	14,092	15,673	14,990	15,691	14,509	11,083	10,275	10,968
Man./Man.	1,717	2,003	1,653	1,685	1,566	1,584	1,662	1,367	1,382	1,315
Sask./Sask.	2,242	2,446	2,040	1,828	1,620	1,451	1,352	959	1,214	1,371
Alta./Alb.	5,767	5,871	5,150	4,624	4,716	4,825	4,582	3,641	3,920	3,693
B.C./C.-B.	9,890	9,647	9,121	10,343	9,715	9,413	8,289	9,334	9,817	9,879
Yukon/Yukon	233	222	155	154	134	183	162	171	130	121
N.W.T./T.N.-O.	357	339	258	249	208	255	331	290	316	334
Canada	**43,917**	**43,803**	**41,514**	**43,072**	**40,484**	**40,740**	**38,276**	**32,275**	**34,005**	**35,998**
NARCOTIC CONTROL ACT - COCAINE/LOI SUR LES STUPEFIANTS - COCAINE										
Nfld./T.-N.	12	11	14	22	25	44	18	38	29	27
P.E.I./I.P.É.	3	3	2	2	10	19	16	13	9	15
N.S./N.-É.	58	59	103	114	191	256	174	253	277	250
N.B./N.-B.	40	27	69	98	86	302	129	172	107	129
Que./Qué.	1,543	1,727	2,359	2,867	3,531	4,356	3,507	4,134	4,186	3,867
Ont./Ont.	1,411	1,825	2,384	3,280	4,992	7,516	5,922	7,762	4,967	4,542
Man./Man.	74	103	158	156	147	169	175	209	145	169
Sask./Sask.	43	84	72	83	79	115	83	39	41	67
Alta./Alb.	266	389	507	441	489	697	696	774	775	966
B.C./C.-B.	649	641	1,044	1,117	1,589	2,908	2,485	2,681	2,876	2,450
Yukon/Yukon	10	18	8	16	21	24	23	26	28	20
N.W.T./T.N.-O.	10	13	9	6	17	16	18	31	19	21
Canada	**4,119**	**4,900**	**6,729**	**8,202**	**11,177**	**16,422**	**13,249**	**16,135**	**13,459**	**12,523**

TABLE 12.11 (continued)　　　　　　　　　　　　　　　　**TABLEAU 12.11** (suite)

Number of federal drug offences, Canada and provinces, 1984 to 1993

Nombre des infractions reliées à la drogue en vertu des lois fédérales, Canada et provinces, 1984 à 1993

PROVINCE	1984	1985	1986	1987	1988	1989	1990	1991	1992	1993
NARCOTIC CONTROL ACT - HEROIN/LOI SUR LES STUPEFIANTS - HEROINE										
Nfld./T.-N.	0	10	0	0	1	1	0	2	0	0
P.E.I./I.P.É.	0	0	0	0	0	0	0	0	0	0
N.S./N.-É.	0	3	0	15	6	6	1	3	5	3
N.B./N.-B.	15	3	1	2	0	7	11	5	1	5
Que./Qué.	170	186	205	170	225	213	195	204	199	211
Ont./Ont.	179	273	347	269	410	425	515	604	434	621
Man./Man.	5	12	6	1	5	3	1	6	9	14
Sask./Sask.	6	5	3	5	2	4	8	0	0	13
Alta./Alb.	29	18	18	8	10	30	19	22	11	21
B.C./C.-B.	227	314	334	294	284	267	400	513	597	707
Yukon/Yukon	1	0	0	0	0	1	0	2	1	0
N.W.T./T.N.-O.	2	3	0	1	0	0	0	2	0	0
Canada	**634**	**827**	**914**	**765**	**943**	**957**	**1,150**	**1,363**	**1,257**	**1,595**
NARCOTIC CONTROL ACT - OTHER DRUGS/LOI SUR LES STUPEFIANTS - AUTRES DROGUES										
Nfld./T.-N.	7	45	33	36	45	17	9	11	12	8
P.E.I./I.P.É.	11	10	8	5	12	9	15	6	6	12
N.S./N.-É.	86	64	47	43	83	184	224	244	63	35
N.B./N.-B.	97	93	41	57	61	85	49	57	58	88
Que./Qué.	910	835	900	720	727	1,239	1,135	999	1,331	1,732
Ont./Ont.	1,425	2,344	1,555	2,527	1,631	2,713	1,921	1,014	861	830
Man./Man.	89	172	421	932	856	1,627	122	50	50	39
Sask./Sask.	195	46	167	978	126	302	522	55	179	164
Alta./Alb.	125	355	259	353	1,066	735	600	294	664	1,170
B.C./C.-B.	324	610	751	685	652	538	480	1,393	1,389	186
Yukon/Yukon	4	0	5	1	3	3	4	3	1	3
N.W.T./T.N.-O.	6	5	4	8	13	5	8	8	1	6
Canada[1]	**3,279**	**4,579**	**4,191**	**6,345**	**5,275**	**7,457**	**5,101**	**4,148**	**4,615**	**4,273**
FOOD AND DRUGS ACT - CONTROLLED DRUGS/LOI SUR LES ALIMENTS ET LA DROGUE - LA DROGUE CONTROLEE										
Nfld./T.-N.	1	7	3	3	0	0	8	8	8	17
P.E.I./I.P.É.	4	5	4	1	3	0	4	4	2	1
N.S./N.-É.	6	5	18	50	12	24	77	48	179	104
N.B./N.-B.	17	23	13	13	12	9	16	11	34	14
Que./Qué.	77	102	67	83	56	60	35	12	67	38
Ont./Ont.	375	390	325	244	316	225	192	111	323	266
Man./Man.	33	30	50	170	40	64	145	18	617	85
Sask./Sask.	16	19	24	65	19	16	126	36	130	70
Alta./Alb.	109	92	60	55	82	60	77	66	129	212
B.C./C.-B.	148	166	106	132	123	88	124	315	175	106
Yukon/Yukon	0	1	1	0	1	1	0	0	1	2
N.W.T./T.N.-O.	0	5	0	4	4	1	3	1	0	1
Canada	**786**	**845**	**671**	**820**	**668**	**548**	**807**	**630**	**1,665**	**916**

TABLE 12.11 (concluded)   **TABLEAU 12.11** (fin)

Number of federal drug offences, Canada and provinces, 1984 to 1993

Nombre des infractions reliées à la drogue en vertu des lois fédérales, Canada et provinces, 1984 à 1993

PROVINCE	1984	1985	1986	1987	1988	1989	1990	1991	1992	1993
FOOD AND DRUGS ACT - RESTRICTED DRUGS/ LOI SUR LES ALIMENTS ET LA DROGUE D'USAGE RESTREINT										
Nfld./T.-N.	35	50	35	44	34	17	21	30	28	26
P.E.I./I.P.É.	42	40	33	16	13	13	13	10	22	20
N.S./N.-É.	89	88	107	127	80	79	108	95	43	71
N.B./N.-B.	72	84	62	88	47	67	67	71	29	57
Que./Qué.	205	208	216	215	131	182	132	157	184	254
Ont./Ont.	584	662	619	861	590	673	473	456	464	379
Man./Man.	94	105	130	115	99	93	60	74	59	61
Sask./Sask.	103	147	146	156	121	61	55	57	32	56
Alta./Alb.	361	361	334	318	309	240	221	221	186	172
B.C./C.-B.	610	482	537	498	374	325	299	380	425	399
Yukon/Yukon	12	15	7	11	8	7	2	10	11	1
N.W.T./T.N.-O.	8	9	6	5	4	1	5	11	6	10
Canada	**2,215**	**2,251**	**2,232**	**2,454**	**1,810**	**1,758**	**1,456**	**1,572**	**1,489**	**1,506**

[1]The number of drug-related offences in Canada is not necessarily equal to the sum of drug-related offences in its provinces, Yukon, and Northwest Territories/Le nombre de délits associés à la drogue au Canada n'égale pas forcément le total des délits associés à la drogue dans les provinces, au Yukon, et aux Territoiries-du-Nord-Ouest.

Note: Changes in the number of drug offences reported by the police may reflect changes in police enforcement practices rather than any real increase or decrease in drug usage among the population/Des changements du nombre de délits associés à la drogue rapporté par la police peuvent refléter des changements de la pratique policière au suyet de la mise en application plutôt qu'une vraie augmentation où diminution d'usage de la drogue parmi les habitants.

Source: Statistics Canada, *Canadian Crime Statistics 1984, 1985, 1986, 1987, 1988, 1989, 1990, 1991, 1992*, and *1993* (Ottawa: Statistics Canada Catalogue No. 85-205, 1985, 1986, 1987, 1988, 1989, 1990, 1991, 1992, 1994, and 1994 respectively).

Statistique Canada, *Statistique de la criminalité du Canada, 1984, 1985, 1986, 1987, 1988, 1989, 1990, 1991, 1992*, et *1993* (Ottawa: Statistique Canada Catalogue no 85-205, 1985, 1986, 1987, 1988, 1989, 1990, 1991, 1992, 1994, and 1994 respectivement).

TABLE 12.12　　　　　　　　　　　　　　　　　　　　**TABLEAU 12.12**

Rates of federal drug offences per 100,000 population, Canada and provinces, 1984 to 1993

Infractions reliées à la drogue en vertu des lois fédérales, par 100 000 habitants, Canada et provinces, 1984 à 1993

PROVINCE	1984	1985	1986	1987	1988	1989	1990	1991	1992	1993
TOTAL DRUG-RELATED OFFENCES[1]/TOTAL DES DELITS ASSOCIES A LA DROGUE[1]										
Nfld./T.-N.	129.9	165.6	128.5	178.6	132.1	138.2	142.0	114.8	140.8	135.1
P.E.I./I.P.É.	244.9	235.0	169.1	137.2	145.6	143.2	159.5	104.0	160.4	155.1
N.S./N.-É.	227.6	209.1	216.7	205.6	213.7	230.2	246.8	204.4	213.8	208.3
N.B./N.-B.	245.5	274.8	222.1	216.6	182.0	250.1	183.6	160.2	145.4	160.3
Que./Qué.	109.3	112.7	131.8	127.5	127.1	138.3	123.9	128.9	136.3	155.2
Ont./Ont.	207.1	212.2	203.9	236.0	232.0	268.4	227.6	200.8	163.3	163.8
Man./Man.	187.3	223.6	221.0	278.0	245.6	320.0	195.3	154.9	203.2	150.8
Sask./Sask.	255.7	267.0	237.4	300.6	190.7	190.5	212.3	113.8	158.9	173.6
Alta./Alb.	277.5	293.9	259.5	237.3	270.9	263.0	242.3	193.0	216.0	234.2
B.C./C.-B.	400.2	396.7	393.8	426.5	407.2	421.9	366.0	432.8	442.7	388.3
Yukon/Yukon	1,074.4	1,040.7	709.7	700.0	623.1	799.3	682.1	728.5	569.5	459.4
N.W.T./T.N.-O.	719.9	678.8	500.0	490.1	436.9	483.5	614.5	560.5	549.0	591.4
Canada	**213.8**	**220.5**	**214.7**	**232.2**	**224.4**	**247.9**	**216.0**	**199.6**	**198.7**	**197.6**
NARCOTIC CONTROL ACT - CANNABIS/LOI SUR LES STUPEFIANTS - CANNABIS										
Nfld./T.-N.	120.5	144.4	113.8	160.4	113.8	124.5	132.3	99.5	127.5	121.7
P.E.I./I.P.É.	197.6	189.7	132.7	118.6	116.3	111.8	122.9	78.7	130.5	118.6
N.S./N.-É.	200.5	184.4	185.9	166.7	172.4	169.6	182.8	134.4	152.3	158.2
N.B./N.-B.	212.2	243.1	196.5	181.2	153.9	186.4	147.0	118.0	114.8	121.3
Que./Qué.	65.7	67.0	76.2	67.9	59.0	51.2	52.6	51.2	52.8	70.5
Ont./Ont.	163.9	153.3	148.7	161.8	151.7	154.6	140.3	105.8	96.8	102.1
Man./Man.	159.9	184.7	151.1	153.1	141.8	143.2	149.9	122.8	124.2	117.8
Sask./Sask.	220.1	237.7	197.5	176.4	157.0	141.9	133.7	95.2	120.9	136.7
Alta./Alb.	240.4	243.5	211.2	189.2	191.5	192.7	179.2	140.0	148.9	138.7
B.C./C.-B.	334.1	322.6	302.0	337.5	310.6	293.3	251.2	276.4	284.4	279.5
Yukon/Yukon	962.8	902.4	625.0	592.3	500.0	667.9	578.6	587.6	430.5	378.1
N.W.T./T.N.-O.	671.1	615.2	465.7	447.0	369.4	443.5	557.2	473.9	507.2	531.0
Canada	**170.9**	**168.9**	**158.4**	**162.2**	**150.5**	**148.8**	**137.7**	**114.8**	**119.6**	**125.2**
NARCOTIC CONTROL ACT - COCAINE/LOI SUR LES STUPEFIANTS - COCAINE										
Nfld./T.-N.	2.1	1.9	2.4	3.8	4.3	7.6	3.1	6.6	5.0	4.6
P.E.I./I.P.É.	2.4	2.3	1.6	1.6	7.7	14.5	12.2	9.9	6.9	11.4
N.S./N.-É.	6.6	6.6	11.5	12.7	21.2	28.2	19.1	27.6	30.1	27.1
N.B./N.-B.	5.5	3.7	9.5	13.4	11.7	40.9	17.4	23.0	14.3	17.2
Que./Qué.	23.2	25.8	35.0	42.1	51.5	62.7	50.0	58.4	58.5	53.6
Ont./Ont.	15.3	19.6	25.2	33.9	50.5	74.0	57.3	74.1	46.8	42.3
Man./Man.	6.9	9.5	14.4	14.2	13.3	15.3	15.8	18.8	13.0	15.1
Sask./Sask.	4.2	8.2	7.0	8.0	7.7	11.2	8.2	3.9	4.1	6.7
Alta./Alb.	11.1	16.1	20.8	18.0	19.9	27.8	27.2	29.8	29.4	36.3
B.C./C.-B.	21.9	21.4	34.6	36.4	50.8	90.6	75.3	79.4	83.3	69.3
Yukon/Yukon	41.3	73.2	32.3	61.5	78.4	87.6	82.1	89.3	92.7	62.5
N.W.T./T.N.-O.	18.8	23.6	16.2	10.8	30.2	27.8	30.3	50.7	30.5	33.4
Canada	**16.0**	**18.9**	**25.7**	**30.9**	**41.6**	**60.0**	**47.7**	**57.4**	**47.3**	**43.6**

TABLE 12.12 (continued)   **TABLEAU 12.12** (suite)

Rates of federal drug offences per 100,000 population, Canada and provinces, 1984 to 1993

Infractions reliées à la drogue en vertu des lois fédérales, par 100 000 habitants, Canada et provinces, 1984 à 1993

PROVINCE	1984	1985	1986	1987	1988	1989	1990	1991	1992	1993
NARCOTIC CONTROL ACT - HEROIN/LOI SUR LES STUPEFIANTS - HEROINE										
Nfld./T.-N.	0.0	1.7	0.0	0.0	0.2	0.2	0.0	0.3	0.0	0.0
P.E.I./I.P.É.	0.0	0.0	0.0	0.0	0.0	0.0	0.0	0.0	0.0	0.0
N.S./N.-É.	0.0	0.3	0.0	1.7	0.7	0.7	0.1	0.3	0.5	0.3
N.B./N.-B.	2.1	0.4	0.1	0.3	0.0	0.9	1.5	0.7	0.1	0.7
Que./Qué.	2.6	2.8	3.0	2.5	3.3	3.1	2.8	2.9	2.8	2.9
Ont./Ont.	1.9	2.9	3.7	2.8	4.1	4.2	5.0	5.8	4.1	5.8
Man./Man.	0.5	1.1	0.5	0.1	0.5	0.3	0.1	0.5	0.8	1.3
Sask./Sask.	0.6	0.5	0.3	0.5	0.2	0.4	0.8	0.0	0.0	1.3
Alta./Alb.	1.2	0.7	0.7	0.3	0.4	1.2	0.7	0.8	0.4	0.8
B.C./C.-B.	7.7	10.5	11.1	9.6	9.1	8.3	12.1	15.2	17.3	20.0
Yukon/Yukon	4.1	0.0	0.0	0.0	0.0	3.6	0.0	6.9	3.3	0.0
N.W.T./T.N.-O.	3.8	5.4	0.0	1.8	0.0	0.0	0.0	3.3	0.0	0.0
Canada	**2.5**	**3.2**	**3.5**	**2.9**	**3.5**	**3.5**	**4.1**	**4.8**	**4.4**	**5.5**
NARCOTIC CONTROL ACT - OTHER DRUGS/LOI SUR LES STUPEFIANTS - AUTRES DROGUES										
Nfld./T.-N.	1.2	7.7	5.7	6.2	7.8	2.9	1.6	1.9	2.1	1.4
P.E.I./I.P.É.	8.7	7.8	6.2	3.9	9.2	6.9	11.5	4.6	4.6	9.1
N.S./N.-É.	9.8	7.2	5.3	4.8	9.2	20.3	24.5	26.6	6.8	3.8
N.B./N.-B.	13.4	12.8	5.6	7.8	8.3	11.5	6.6	7.6	7.7	11.7
Que./Qué.	13.7	12.5	13.4	10.6	10.6	17.8	16.2	14.1	18.6	24.0
Ont./Ont.	15.5	25.1	16.4	26.1	16.5	26.7	18.6	9.7	8.1	7.7
Man./Man.	8.3	15.9	38.5	84.7	77.5	147.1	11.0	4.5	4.5	3.5
Sask./Sask.	19.1	4.5	16.2	94.4	12.2	29.5	51.6	5.5	17.8	16.3
Alta./Alb.	5.2	14.7	10.6	14.4	43.3	29.3	23.5	11.3	25.2	43.9
B.C./C.-B.	10.9	20.4	24.9	22.4	20.8	16.8	14.5	41.3	40.2	5.3
Yukon/Yukon	16.5	0.0	20.2	3.8	11.2	10.9	14.3	10.3	3.3	9.4
N.W.T./T.N.-O.	11.3	9.1	7.2	14.4	23.1	8.7	13.5	13.1	1.6	9.5
Canada	**12.8**	**17.7**	**16.0**	**23.9**	**19.6**	**27.2**	**18.4**	**14.8**	**16.2**	**14.9**
FOOD AND DRUGS ACT - CONTROLLED DRUGS/LOI SUR LES ALIMENTS ET LA DROGUE - LA DROGUE CONTROLEE										
Nfld./T.-N.	0.2	1.2	0.5	0.5	0.0	0.0	1.4	1.4	1.4	2.9
P.E.I./I.P.É.	3.1	3.9	3.1	0.8	2.3	0.0	3.1	3.1	1.5	0.8
N.S./N.-É.	0.7	0.6	2.0	5.6	1.3	2.6	8.4	5.2	19.4	11.3
N.B./N.-B.	2.4	3.2	1.8	1.8	1.6	1.2	2.2	1.5	4.5	1.9
Que./Qué.	1.2	1.5	1.0	1.2	0.8	0.9	0.5	0.2	0.9	0.5
Ont./Ont.	4.1	4.2	3.4	2.5	3.2	2.2	1.9	1.1	3.0	2.5
Man./Man.	3.1	2.8	4.6	15.4	3.6	5.8	13.1	1.6	55.4	7.6
Sask./Sask.	1.6	1.8	2.3	6.3	1.8	1.6	12.5	3.6	12.9	7.0
Alta./Alb.	4.5	3.8	2.5	2.3	3.3	2.4	3.0	2.5	4.9	8.0
B.C./C.-B.	5.0	5.6	3.5	4.3	3.9	2.7	3.8	9.3	5.1	3.0
Yukon/Yukon	0.0	4.1	4.0	0.0	3.7	3.6	0.0	0.0	3.3	6.3
N.W.T./T.N.-O.	0.0	9.1	0.0	7.2	7.1	1.7	5.1	1.6	0.0	1.6
Canada	**3.1**	**3.3**	**2.6**	**3.1**	**2.5**	**2.0**	**2.9**	**2.2**	**5.9**	**3.2**

TABLE 12.12 (concluded)   **TABLEAU 12.12** (fin)

Rates of federal drug offences per 100,000 population, Canada and provinces, 1984 to 1993

Infractions reliées à la drogue en vertu des lois fédérales, par 100 000 habitants, Canada et provinces, 1984 à 1993

PROVINCE	1984	1985	1986	1987	1988	1989	1990	1991	1992	1993
FOOD AND DRUGS ACT - RESTRICTED DRUGS/LOI SUR LES ALIMENTS ET LA DROGUE D'USAGE RESTREINT										
Nfld./T.-N.	6.0	8.6	6.1	7.6	5.9	2.9	3.6	5.2	4.8	4.5
P.E.I./I.P.É.	33.1	31.2	25.6	12.4	10.0	10.0	9.9	7.6	16.9	15.2
N.S./N.-É.	10.1	9.9	12.0	14.2	8.9	8.7	11.8	10.3	4.7	7.7
N.B./N.-B.	10.0	11.6	8.5	12.0	6.4	9.1	9.0	9.5	3.9	7.6
Que./Qué.	3.1	3.1	3.2	3.2	1.9	2.6	1.9	2.2	2.6	3.5
Ont./Ont.	6.3	7.1	6.5	8.9	6.0	6.6	4.6	4.4	4.4	3.5
Man./Man.	8.8	9.7	11.9	10.4	9.0	8.4	5.4	6.6	5.3	5.5
Sask./Sask.	10.1	14.3	14.1	15.1	11.7	6.0	5.4	5.7	3.2	5.6
Alta./Alb.	15.1	15.0	13.7	13.0	12.5	9.6	8.6	8.5	7.1	6.5
B.C./C.-B.	20.6	16.1	17.8	16.3	12.0	10.1	9.1	11.3	12.3	11.3
Yukon/Yukon	49.6	61.0	28.2	42.3	29.9	25.5	7.1	34.4	36.4	3.1
N.W.T./T.N.-O.	15.0	16.3	10.8	9.0	7.1	1.7	8.4	18.0	9.6	15.9
Canada[1]	8.6	8.7	8.5	9.2	6.7	6.4	5.2	5.6	5.2	5.2

[1] The number of drug-related offences in Canada is not necessarily equal to the sum of drug-related offences in its provinces, Yukon, and Northwest Territories/Le nombre de délits associés à la drogue au Canada n'égale pas forcément le total des délits associés à la drogue dans les provinces, au Yukon, et aux Territoiries-du-Nord-Ouest.

Note: Changes in the number of drug offences reported by the police may reflect changes in police enforcement practices rather than any real increase or decrease in drug usage among the population/Des changements du nombre de délits associés à la drogue rapporté par la police peuvent refléter des changements de la pratique policière au suyet de la mise en application plutôt qu'une vraie augmentation où diminution d'usage de la drogue parmi les habitants.

Source: Statistics Canada, *Canadian Crime Statistics 1984, 1985, 1986, 1987, 1988, 1989, 1990, 1991, 1992,* and *1993* (Ottawa: Statistics Canada Catalogue No. 85-205, 1985, 1986, 1987, 1988, 1989, 1990, 1991, 1992, 1994, and 1994 respectively).

Statistique Canada, *Statistique de la criminalité du Canada, 1984, 1985, 1986, 1987, 1988, 1989, 1990, 1991, 1992,* et *1993* (Ottawa: Statistique Canada Catalogue no 85-205, 1985, 1986, 1987, 1988, 1989, 1990, 1991, 1992, 1994, and 1994 respectivement).

TABLE 12.13

TABLEAU 12.13

Juvenile offenders[1] involved in federal drug offences Canada and provinces, 1986 to 1993

Jeunes contrevenants ayant commis des infractions reliées à la drogue en vertu des lois fédérales, Canada et provinces, 1986 à 1993

PROVINCE	1986	1987	1988	1989	1990	1991	1992	1993
TOTAL DRUG-RELATED OFFENCES[1]/TOTAL DES DELITS ASSOCIES A LA DROGUE[1]								
Nfld./T.-N.	63	64	80	65	76	34	39	41
P.E.I./I.P.É.	11	7	18	15	12	7	9	9
N.S./N.-É.	139	95	96	82	72	52	47	63
N.B./N.-B.	105	99	72	72	68	60	28	44
Que./Qué.	580	424	539	595	686	635	595	1,053
Ont./Ont.	1,836	1,332	1,371	1,677	1,383	972	905	1,100
Man./Man.	219	191	181	211	158	123	90	137
Sask./Sask.	187	194	144	100	84	50	51	76
Alta./Alb.	427	342	387	429	396	285	232	307
B.C./C.-B.	1,149	1,347	1,197	983	888	1,013	627	590
Yukon/Yukon	24	14	17	8	7	7	3	2
N.W.T./T.N.-O.	27	8	10	16	21	11	8	4
Canada	**4,767**	**4,117**	**4,112**	**4,253**	**3,851**	**3,249**	**2,634**	**3,426**
NARCOTIC CONTROL ACT - CANNABIS/LOI SUR LES STUPEFIANTS - CANNABIS								
Nfld./T.-N.	56	64	76	62	69	31	35	38
P.E.I./I.P.É.	10	6	16	14	6	5	9	5
N.S./N.-É.	130	86	76	74	58	41	39	54
N.B./N.-B.	102	88	65	65	65	49	27	40
Que./Qué.	421	306	371	355	440	368	304	579
Ont./Ont.	1,591	1,173	1,216	1,323	1,175	661	590	775
Man./Man.	202	175	163	195	140	117	82	125
Sask./Sask.	168	171	123	93	74	47	47	70
Alta./Alb.	399	319	358	383	356	257	208	239
B.C./C.-B.	1,050	1,250	1,099	904	778	875	492	474
Yukon/Yukon	24	12	14	5	7	4	1	2
N.W.T./T.N.-O.	26	8	10	16	21	11	8	4
Canada	**4,179**	**3,658**	**3,587**	**3,489**	**3,189**	**2,466**	**1,842**	**2,405**
NARCOTIC CONTROL ACT - COCAINE/LOI SUR LES STUPEFIANTS - COCAINE								
Nfld./T.-N.	0	0	0	0	0	0	0	0
P.E.I./I.P.É.	0	0	0	1	0	0	0	0
N.S./N.-É.	3	1	3	1	1	2	4	3
N.B./N.-B.	0	1	2	2	0	1	0	0
Que./Qué.	39	46	88	104	78	67	72	76
Ont./Ont.	32	35	65	128	119	223	217	185
Man./Man.	0	2	1	1	2	3	1	5
Sask./Sask.	1	3	1	0	3	1	0	0
Alta./Alb.	2	0	5	13	16	7	11	45
B.C./C.-B.	16	13	21	37	39	32	33	46
Yukon/Yukon	0	0	1	0	0	0	1	0
N.W.T./T.N.-O.	0	0	0	0	0	0	0	0
Canada	**93**	**101**	**187**	**287**	**258**	**336**	**339**	**360**

TABLE 12.13 (continued)   **TABLEAU 12.13** (suite)

Juvenile offenders[1] involved in federal drug offences Canada and provinces, 1986 to 1993

Jeunes contrevenants ayant commis des infractions reliées à la drogue en vertu des lois fédérales, Canada et provinces, 1986 à 1993

PROVINCE	1986	1987	1988	1989	1990	1991	1992	1993
NARCOTIC CONTROL ACT - HEROIN/LOI SUR LES STUPEFIANTS - HEROINE								
Nfld./T.-N.	0	0	0	0	0	0	0	0
P.E.I./I.P.É.	0	0	0	0	0	0	0	0
N.S./N.-É.	0	1	0	0	0	0	0	0
N.B./N.-B.	0	0	0	0	0	0	0	0
Que./Qué.	0	6	5	3	3	5	2	4
Ont./Ont.	4	2	8	2	3	0	15	33
Man./Man.	0	0	0	0	0	0	0	0
Sask./Sask.	0	0	0	0	0	0	0	0
Alta./Alb.	0	0	0	0	0	0	0	0
B.C./C.-B.	5	2	3	0	3	7	6	15
Yukon/Yukon	0	0	0	2	0	0	0	0
N.W.T./T.N.-O.	0	0	0	0	0	0	0	0
Canada	**9**	**11**	**16**	**7**	**9**	**12**	**23**	**52**
NARCOTIC CONTROL ACT - OTHER DRUGS/LOI SUR LES STUPEFIANTS -AUTRES DROGUES								
Nfld./T.-N.	3	0	0	3	2	0	0	0
P.E.I./I.P.É.	0	0	0	0	3	1	0	1
N.S./N.-É.	1	1	5	3	6	3	0	0
N.B./N.-B.	0	1	2	1	1	2	1	3
Que./Qué.	86	48	60	109	152	168	188	326
Ont./Ont.	114	30	26	153	21	14	36	38
Man./Man.	2	4	3	4	3	0	1	0
Sask./Sask.	2	11	12	5	4	1	0	3
Alta./Alb.	5	4	3	2	2	2	1	2
B.C./C.-B.	11	7	13	2	11	48	48	2
Yukon/Yukon	0	1	0	0	0	0	0	0
N.W.T./T.N.-O.	0	0	0	0	0	0	0	0
Canada	**224**	**107**	**124**	**282**	**205**	**239**	**275**	**375**
FOOD AND DRUGS ACT - CONTROLLED DRUGS/LOI SUR LES ALIMENTS ET LA DROGUE - LA DROGUE CONTROLEE								
Nfld./T.-N.	0	0	0	0	0	0	0	0
P.E.I./I.P.É.	0	0	0	0	0	0	0	0
N.S./N.-É.	0	0	2	0	2	0	0	1
N.B./N.-B.	0	1	0	0	0	0	0	0
Que./Qué.	0	0	2	0	3	1	1	7
Ont./Ont.	11	7	3	12	3	10	2	3
Man./Man.	0	1	0	0	0	1	0	0
Sask./Sask.	0	2	0	0	0	1	1	0
Alta./Alb.	1	0	1	0	2	0	1	0
B.C./C.-B.	0	1	1	1	1	2	0	1
Yukon/Yukon	0	0	1	0	0	0	0	0
N.W.T./T.N.-O.	0	0	0	0	0	0	0	0
Canada	**12**	**12**	**10**	**13**	**11**	**15**	**5**	**12**

TABLE 12.13 (concluded)

TABLEAU 12.13 (fin)

Juvenile offenders[1] involved in federal drug offences Canada and provinces, 1986 to 1993

Jeunes contrevenants ayant commis des infractions reliées à la drogue en vertu des lois fédérales, Canada et provinces, 1986 à 1993

PROVINCE	1986	1987	1988	1989	1990	1991	1992	1993
FOOD AND DRUGS ACT - RESTRICTED DRUGS/ **LOI SUR LES ALIMENTS ET LA DROGUE -LA DROGUE D'USAGE RESTREINT**								
Nfld./T.-N.	4	0	4	0	5	3	4	3
P.E.I./I.P.É.	1	1	2	0	3	1	0	3
N.S./N.-É.	5	6	10	4	5	6	4	5
N.B./N.-B.	3	8	3	4	2	8	0	1
Que./Qué.	34	18	13	24	10	26	28	61
Ont./Ont.	84	85	53	59	62	64	45	66
Man./Man.	15	9	14	11	13	2	6	7
Sask./Sask.	16	7	8	2	3	0	3	3
Alta./Alb.	20	19	20	31	20	19	11	21
B.C./C.-B.	67	74	60	39	56	49	48	52
Yukon/Yukon	0	1	1	1	0	3	1	0
N.W.T./T.N.-O.	1	0	0	0	0	0	0	0
Canada	**250**	**228**	**188**	**175**	**179**	**181**	**150**	**222**

[1] Includes both "juveniles charged" and "juveniles not charged"./Y compris les jeunes condamnés et non condamnés.

Note: Changes in the number of drug offences reported by the police may reflect changes in police enforcement practices rather than any real increase or decrease in drug usage among the population/Des changements du nombre de délits associés à la drogue rapporté par la police peuvent refléter des changements de la pratique policière au suyet de la mise en application plutôt qu'une vraie augmentation où diminution d'usage de la drogue parmi les habitants.

Source: Statistics Canada, *Canadian Crime Statistics 1984, 1985, 1986, 1987, 1988, 1989, 1990, 1991, 1992*, and *1993* (Ottawa: Statistics Canada Catalogue No. 85-205, 1985, 1986, 1987, 1988, 1989, 1990, 1991, 1992, 1994, and 1994 respectively).

Statistique Canada, *Statistique de la criminalité du Canada, 1984, 1985, 1986, 1987, 1988, 1989, 1990, 1991, 1992*, et *1993* (Ottawa: Statistique Canada Catalogue no 85-205, 1985, 1986, 1987, 1988, 1989, 1990, 1991, 1992, 1994, and 1994 respectivement).

TABLE 12.14

TABLEAU 12.14

Adults charged with federal drug offences by gender, Canada and provinces, 1990 to 1993

Adultes accusés d'infractions reliées à la drogue en vertu des lois fédérales, selon le sexe, Canada et provinces, 1990 à 1993

PROVINCE	MALE/MASCULIN			FEMALE/FEMININ			TOTAL		
	1991	1992	1993	1991	1992	1993	1991	1992	1993
TOTAL DRUG-RELATED OFFENCES/TOTAL DES DELITS ASSOCIES A LA DROGUE									
Nfld./T.-N.	388	463	544	17	30	39	405	493	583
P.E.I./I.P.É.	57	92	108	4	5	3	61	97	111
N.S./N.-É.	808	1,051	936	136	174	143	944	1,225	1,079
N.B./N.-B.	553	450	488	52	43	49	605	493	537
Que./Qué.	6,611	6,564	7,424	865	995	1,053	7,476	7,559	8,477
Ont./Ont.	12,321	12,940	12,363	2,030	2,387	2,371	14,351	15,327	14,734
Man./Man.	1,150	1,012	941	165	152	142	1,315	1,164	1,083
Sask./Sask.	691	848	970	128	138	167	819	986	1,137
Alta./Alb.	3,752	3,629	3,336	541	595	670	4,293	4,224	4,006
B.C./C.-B.	8,927	8,474	6,402	1,332	1,288	934	10,259	9,762	7,336
Yukon/Yukon	115	75	89	19	14	13	134	89	102
N.W.T./T.N.-O.	170	171	192	32	39	47	202	210	239
Canada	**35,543**	**35,769**	**33,793**	**5,321**	**5,860**	**5,631**	**40,864**	**41,629**	**39,424**
NARCOTIC CONTROL ACT - CANNABIS/LOI SUR LES STUPEFIANTS - CANNABIS									
Nfld./T.-N.	350	424	517	14	30	33	364	454	550
P.E.I./I.P.É.	47	75	87	2	3	3	49	78	90
N.S./N.-É.	643	822	776	97	119	103	740	941	879
N.B./N.-B.	403	364	397	37	39	24	440	403	421
Que./Qué.	2,419	2,364	2,963	226	283	368	2,645	2,647	3,331
Ont./Ont.	7,696	7,832	7,559	1,165	1,401	1,364	8,861	9,233	8,923
Man./Man.	916	846	747	128	104	109	1,044	950	856
Sask./Sask.	600	747	830	92	101	114	692	848	944
Alta./Alb.	2,905	2,809	2,536	314	394	362	3,219	3,203	2,898
B.C./C.-B.	5,492	4,794	4,102	696	669	483	6,188	5,463	4,585
Yukon/Yukon	101	65	74	16	12	8	117	77	82
N.W.T./T.N.-O.	152	160	180	32	38	44	184	198	224
Canada	**21,724**	**21,302**	**20,768**	**2,819**	**3,193**	**3,015**	**24,543**	**24,495**	**23,783**
NARCOTIC CONTROL ACT - COCAINE/LOI SUR LES STUPEFIANTS - COCAINE									
Nfld./T.-N.	16	20	13	1	0	0	17	20	13
P.E.I./I.P.É.	7	2	9	2	1	0	9	3	9
N.S./N.-É.	114	198	127	25	43	25	139	241	152
N.B./N.-B.	101	63	40	8	4	9	109	67	49
Que./Qué.	3,263	3,150	3,195	504	577	528	3,767	3,727	3,723
Ont./Ont.	3,874	4,040	3,656	729	764	825	4,603	4,804	4,481
Man./Man.	163	110	142	25	30	22	188	140	164
Sask./Sask.	23	17	32	2	4	2	25	21	34
Alta./Alb.	564	556	611	132	118	202	696	674	813
B.C./C.-B.	1,874	1,950	1,631	371	391	323	2,245	2,341	1,954
Yukon/Yukon	9	10	14	3	1	3	12	11	17
N.W.T./T.N.-O.	15	8	6	0	1	2	15	9	8
Canada	**10,023**	**10,124**	**9,476**	**1,802**	**1,934**	**1,941**	**11,825**	**12,058**	**11,417**

TABLE 12.14 (continued)　　　　　　　　　　　　　　**TABLEAU 12.14 (suite)**

Adults charged with federal drug offences by gender, Canada and provinces, 1990 to 1993

Adultes accusés d'infractions reliées à la drogue en vertu des lois fédérales, selon le sexe, Canada et provinces, 1990 à 1993

PROVINCE	MALE/MASCULIN			FEMALE/FEMININ			TOTAL		
	1991	1992	1993	1991	1992	1993	1991	1992	1993
NARCOTIC CONTROL ACT - HEROIN/LOI SUR LES STUPEFIANTS - HEROINE									
Nfld./T.-N.	1	0	0	0	0	0	1	0	0
P.E.I./I.P.É.	0	0	0	0	0	0	0	0	0
N.S./N.-É.	0	2	0	1	0	0	1	2	0
N.B./N.-B.	1	1	3	0	0	0	1	1	3
Que./Qué.	168	210	179	45	29	21	213	239	200
Ont./Ont.	259	307	501	59	71	82	318	378	583
Man./Man.	0	0	13	0	0	4	0	0	17
Sask./Sask.	0	0	10	0	0	3	0	0	13
Alta./Alb.	10	3	9	5	0	1	15	3	10
B.C./C.-B.	296	352	442	148	105	94	444	457	536
Yukon/Yukon	0	0	0	0	0	0	0	0	0
N.W.T./T.N.-O.	0	0	0	0	0	0	0	0	0
Canada	**735**	**875**	**1,157**	**258**	**205**	**205**	**993**	**1,080**	**1,362**
NARCOTIC CONTROL ACT - OTHER DRUGS/LOI SUR LES STUPEFIANTS - AUTRES DROGUES									
Nfld./T.-N.	2	2	3	0	0	1	2	2	4
P.E.I./I.P.É.	0	1	5	0	0	0	0	1	5
N.S./N.-É.	12	13	6	6	2	0	18	15	6
N.B./N.-B.	19	9	25	4	0	15	23	9	40
Que./Qué.	676	745	972	84	95	124	760	840	1,096
Ont./Ont.	170	410	382	33	89	62	203	499	444
Man./Man.	17	15	11	4	4	2	21	19	13
Sask./Sask.	23	52	66	16	23	37	39	75	103
Alta./Alb.	127	108	78	71	62	67	198	170	145
B.C./C.-B.	1,039	1,135	36	85	96	11	1,124	1,231	47
Yukon/Yukon	0	0	0	0	0	0	0	0	0
N.W.T./T.N.-O.	0	0	1	0	0	1	0	0	2
Canada	**2,085**	**2,490**	**1,585**	**303**	**371**	**320**	**2,388**	**2,861**	**1,905**
FOOD AND DRUGS ACT - CONTROLLED DRUGS/LOI SUR LES ALIMENTS ET LA DROGUE - DROGUES CONTROLEES									
Nfld./T.-N.	3	2	2	2	0	5	5	2	7
P.E.I./I.P.É.	0	1	0	0	0	0	0	1	0
N.S./N.-É.	0	3	4	1	3	5	1	6	9
N.B./N.-B.	1	0	3	1	0	0	2	0	3
Que./Qué.	4	12	18	2	3	4	6	15	22
Ont./Ont.	37	61	62	13	29	14	50	90	76
Man./Man.	6	11	3	3	4	2	9	15	5
Sask./Sask.	12	16	11	9	9	7	21	25	18
Alta./Alb.	20	23	25	4	13	20	24	36	45
B.C./C.-B.	57	29	20	13	8	10	70	37	30
Yukon/Yukon	0	0	0	0	0	2	0	0	2
N.W.T./T.N.-O.	1	0	1	0	0	0	1	0	1
Canada	**141**	**158**	**149**	**48**	**69**	**69**	**189**	**227**	**218**

TABLE 12.14 (concluded)　　　　　　　　　　**TABLEAU 12.14** (fin)

Adults charged with federal drug offences by gender, Canada and provinces, 1990 to 1993

Adultes accusés d'infractions reliées à la drogue en vertu des lois fédérales, selon le sexe, Canada et provinces, 1990 à 1993

PROVINCE	MALE/MASCULIN			FEMALE/FEMININ			TOTAL		
	1991	1992	1993	1991	1992	1993	1991	1992	1993
FOOD AND DRUGS ACT - RESTRICTED DRUGS/ **LOI LES ALIMENTS ET LA DROGUE - DROGUE D'USAGE RESTREINT**									
Nfld./T.-N.	16	15	9	0	0	0	16	15	9
P.E.I./I.P.É.	3	13	7	0	1	0	3	14	7
N.S./N.-É.	39	13	23	6	7	10	45	20	33
N.B./N.-B.	28	13	20	2	0	1	30	13	21
Que./Qué.	81	83	97	4	8	8	85	91	105
Ont./Ont.	285	290	203	31	33	24	316	323	227
Man./Man.	48	30	25	5	10	3	53	40	28
Sask./Sask.	33	16	21	9	1	4	42	17	25
Alta./Alb.	126	130	77	15	8	18	141	138	95
B.C./C.-B.	169	214	171	19	19	13	188	233	184
Yukon/Yukon	5	0	1	0	1	0	5	1	1
N.W.T./T.N.-O.	2	3	4	0	0	0	2	3	4
Canada	**835**	**820**	**658**	**91**	**88**	**81**	**926**	**908**	**739**

Note:　Changes in the number of drug offences reported by the police may reflect changes in police enforcement practices rather than any real increase or decrease in drug usage among the population/Des changements du nombre de délits associés à la drogue rapporté par la police peuvent refléter des changements de la pratique policière au suyet de la mise en application plutôt qu'une vraie augmentation où diminution d'usage de la drogue parmi les habitants.

Source:　Statistics Canada, *Canadian Crime Statistics 1991, 1992*, and *1993* (Ottawa: Statistics Canada, Catalogue No. 85-205, 1992, 1994, and 1995 respectively).

Statistique Canada, *Statistique de la criminalité du Canada, 1991, 1992*, et *1993* (Ottawa: Statistique Canada, Catalogue no 85-205, 1992, 1994, et 1994 respectivement).

TABLE 12.15   TABLEAU 12.15

Adults charged with federal drug offences by gender, rates per 100,000 population aged 18 and over, Canada and provinces, 1990 to 1993

Adultes accusés de délits en vertu des fédérales sur la drogue selon sexe, en taux par 100,000 habitants âgés de 18 ans et plus, Canada and provinces, 1990 à 1993

PROVINCE	MALE/MASCULIN			FEMALE/FEMININ			TOTAL		
	1991	1992	1993	1991	1992	1993	1991	1992	1993
TOTAL DRUG-RELATED OFFENCES/TOTAL DES DELITS ASSOCIES A LA DROGUE									
Nfld./T.-N.	186.0	219.5	255.8	8.1	14.1	18.2	96.7	116.4	136.5
P.E.I./I.P.É.	122.3	197.8	229.3	8.2	10.3	6.1	63.9	101.9	115.0
N.S./N.-É.	239.3	309.9	274.9	38.4	48.8	39.9	136.4	176.1	154.3
N.B./N.-B.	201.8	163.4	176.0	18.3	15.0	17.0	108.3	87.8	94.9
Que./Qué.	251.6	247.4	277.4	31.2	35.6	37.3	138.5	138.7	154.2
Ont./Ont.	317.9	329.7	311.3	50.0	58.0	56.9	180.8	190.7	181.1
Man./Man.	285.6	251.6	233.5	39.4	36.3	33.8	160.2	141.8	131.5
Sask./Sask.	194.0	239.1	274.2	35.0	37.8	45.6	113.5	136.9	157.9
Alta./Alb.	398.0	380.6	345.6	57.6	62.6	69.5	228.2	221.8	207.7
B.C./C.-B.	703.7	654.4	482.5	102.3	96.6	68.3	399.1	371.5	272.2
Yukon/Yukon	1,055.0	663.7	747.9	191.9	134.6	116.1	644.2	410.1	441.6
N.W.T./T.N.-O.	833.3	826.1	918.7	177.8	215.5	258.2	526.0	541.2	611.3
Canada	**342.7**	**341.1**	**318.6**	**49.4**	**53.7**	**51.0**	**193.2**	**194.6**	**182.1**
NARCOTIC CONTROL ACT - CANNABIS/LOI SUR LES STUPEFIANTS - CANNABIS									
Nfld./T.-N.	167.8	201.0	243.1	6.7	14.1	15.4	86.9	107.2	128.8
P.E.I./I.P.É.	100.9	161.3	184.7	4.1	6.2	6.1	51.4	81.9	93.3
N.S./N.-É.	190.4	242.4	227.9	27.4	33.4	28.7	107.0	135.3	125.7
N.B./N.-B.	147.1	132.2	143.2	13.0	13.6	8.3	78.8	71.8	74.4
Que./Qué.	92.1	89.1	110.7	8.2	10.1	13.0	49.0	48.6	60.6
Ont./Ont.	198.6	199.6	190.3	28.7	34.1	32.8	111.7	114.9	109.7
Man./Man.	227.5	210.3	185.4	30.6	24.8	25.9	127.1	115.7	103.9
Sask./Sask.	168.4	210.7	234.6	25.2	27.6	31.1	95.9	117.8	131.1
Alta./Alb.	308.1	294.6	262.7	33.4	41.4	37.6	171.1	168.2	150.3
B.C./C.-B.	432.9	370.2	309.1	53.5	50.2	35.3	240.8	207.9	170.1
Yukon/Yukon	926.6	575.2	621.8	161.6	115.4	71.4	562.5	354.8	355.0
N.W.T./T.N.-O.	745.1	772.9	861.2	177.8	209.9	241.8	479.2	510.3	572.9
Canada	**209.5**	**203.1**	**195.8**	**26.2**	**29.3**	**27.3**	**116.0**	**114.5**	**109.8**
NARCOTIC CONTROL ACT - COCAINE/LOI SUR LES STUPEFIANTS - COCAINE									
Nfld./T.-N.	7.7	9.5	6.1	0.5	0.0	0.0	4.1	4.7	3.0
P.E.I./I.P.É.	15.0	4.3	19.1	4.1	2.1	0.0	9.4	3.2	9.3
N.S./N.-É.	33.8	58.4	37.3	7.1	12.1	7.0	20.1	34.6	21.7
N.B./N.-B.	36.9	22.9	14.4	2.8	1.4	3.1	19.5	11.9	8.7
Que./Qué.	124.2	118.7	119.4	18.2	20.6	18.7	69.8	68.4	67.7
Ont./Ont.	100.0	102.9	92.1	18.0	18.6	19.8	58.0	59.8	55.1
Man./Man.	40.5	27.3	35.2	6.0	7.2	5.2	22.9	17.1	19.9
Sask./Sask.	6.5	4.8	9.0	0.5	1.1	0.5	3.5	2.9	4.7
Alta./Alb.	59.8	58.3	63.3	14.1	12.4	21.0	37.0	35.4	42.2
B.C./C.-B.	147.7	150.6	122.9	28.5	29.3	23.6	87.3	89.1	72.5
Yukon/Yukon	82.6	88.5	117.6	30.3	9.6	26.8	57.7	50.7	73.6
N.W.T./T.N.-O.	73.5	38.6	28.7	0.0	5.5	11.0	39.1	23.2	20.5
Canada	**96.6**	**96.5**	**89.3**	**16.7**	**17.7**	**17.6**	**55.9**	**56.4**	**52.7**

TABLE 12.15 (continued)

TABLEAU 12.15 (suite)

Adults charged with federal drug offences by gender, rates per 100,000 population aged 18 and over, Canada and provinces, 1990 to 1993

Adultes accusés de délits en vertu des fédérales sur la drogue selon sexe, en taux par 100,000 habitants âgés de 18 ans et plus, Canada and provinces, 1990 à 1993

PROVINCE	MALE/MASCULIN			FEMALE/FEMININ			TOTAL		
	1991	1992	1993	1991	1992	1993	1991	1992	1993
NARCOTIC CONTROL ACT - HEROIN/LOI SUR LES STUPEFIANTS - HEROINE									
Nfld./T.-N.	0.5	0.0	0.0	0.0	0.0	0.0	0.2	0.0	0.0
P.E.I./I.P.É.	0.0	0.0	0.0	0.0	0.0	0.0	0.0	0.0	0.0
N.S./N.-É.	0.0	0.6	0.0	0.3	0.0	0.0	0.1	0.3	0.0
N.B./N.-B.	0.4	0.4	1.1	0.0	0.0	0.0	0.2	0.2	0.5
Que./Qué.	6.4	7.9	6.7	1.6	1.0	0.7	3.9	4.4	3.6
Ont./Ont.	6.7	7.8	12.6	1.5	1.7	2.0	4.0	4.7	7.2
Man./Man.	0.0	0.0	3.2	0.0	0.0	1.0	0.0	0.0	2.1
Sask./Sask.	0.0	0.0	2.8	0.0	0.0	0.8	0.0	0.0	1.8
Alta./Alb.	1.1	0.3	0.9	0.5	0.0	0.1	0.8	0.2	0.5
B.C./C.-B.	23.3	27.2	33.3	11.4	7.9	6.9	17.3	17.4	19.9
Yukon/Yukon	0.0	0.0	0.0	0.0	0.0	0.0	0.0	0.0	0.0
N.W.T./T.N.-O.	0.0	0.0	0.0	0.0	0.0	0.0	0.0	0.0	0.0
Canada	**7.1**	**8.3**	**10.9**	**2.4**	**1.9**	**1.9**	**4.7**	**5.0**	**6.3**
NARCOTIC CONTROL ACT - OTHER DRUGS/LOI SUR LES STUPEFIANTS - AUTRES DROGUES									
Nfld./T.-N.	1.0	0.9	1.4	0.0	0.0	0.5	0.5	0.5	0.9
P.E.I./I.P.É.	0.0	2.2	10.6	0.0	0.0	0.0	0.0	1.1	5.2
N.S./N.-É.	3.6	3.8	1.8	1.7	0.6	0.0	2.6	2.2	0.9
N.B./N.-B.	6.9	3.3	9.0	1.4	0.0	5.2	4.1	1.6	7.1
Que./Qué.	25.7	28.1	36.3	3.0	3.4	4.4	14.1	15.4	19.9
Ont./Ont.	4.4	10.4	9.6	0.8	2.2	1.5	2.6	6.2	5.5
Man./Man.	4.2	3.7	2.7	1.0	1.0	0.5	2.6	2.3	1.6
Sask./Sask.	6.5	14.7	18.7	4.4	6.3	10.1	5.4	10.4	14.3
Alta./Alb.	13.5	11.3	8.1	7.6	6.5	7.0	10.5	8.9	7.5
B.C./C.-B.	81.9	87.6	2.7	6.5	7.2	0.8	43.7	46.8	1.7
Yukon/Yukon	0.0	0.0	0.0	0.0	0.0	0.0	0.0	0.0	0.0
N.W.T./T.N.-O.	0.0	0.0	4.8	0.0	0.0	5.5	0.0	0.0	5.1
Canada	**20.1**	**23.7**	**14.9**	**2.8**	**3.4**	**2.9**	**11.3**	**13.4**	**8.8**
FOOD AND DRUGS ACT - CONTROLLED DRUGS/LOI SUR LES ALIMENTS ET LA DROGUE - DROGUES CONTROLEES									
Nfld./T.-N.	1.4	0.9	0.9	1.0	0.0	2.3	1.2	0.5	1.6
P.E.I./I.P.É.	0.0	2.2	0.0	0.0	0.0	0.0	0.0	1.1	0.0
N.S./N.-É.	0.0	0.9	1.2	0.3	0.8	1.4	0.1	0.9	1.3
N.B./N.-B.	0.4	0.0	1.1	0.4	0.0	0.0	0.4	0.0	0.5
Que./Qué.	0.2	0.5	0.7	0.1	0.1	0.1	0.1	0.3	0.4
Ont./Ont.	1.0	1.6	1.6	0.3	0.7	0.3	0.6	1.1	0.9
Man./Man.	1.5	2.7	0.7	0.7	1.0	0.5	1.1	1.8	0.6
Sask./Sask.	3.4	4.5	3.1	2.5	2.5	1.9	2.9	3.5	2.5
Alta./Alb.	2.1	2.4	2.6	0.4	1.4	2.1	1.3	1.9	2.3
B.C./C.-B.	4.5	2.2	1.5	1.0	0.6	0.7	2.7	1.4	1.1
Yukon/Yukon	0.0	0.0	0.0	0.0	0.0	17.9	0.0	0.0	8.7
N.W.T./T.N.-O.	4.9	0.0	4.8	0.0	0.0	0.0	2.6	0.0	2.6
Canada	**1.4**	**1.5**	**1.4**	**0.4**	**0.6**	**0.6**	**0.9**	**1.1**	**1.0**

TABLE 12.15 (concluded)   **TABLEAU 12.15** (fin)

Adults charged with federal drug offences by gender, rates per 100,000 population aged 18 and over, Canada and provinces, 1990 to 1993

Adultes accusés de délits en vertu des fédérales sur la drogue selon sexe, en taux par 100,000 habitants âgés de 18 ans et plus, Canada and provinces, 1990 à 1993

PROVINCE	MALE/MASCULIN			FEMALE/FEMININ			TOTAL		
	1991	1992	1993	1991	1992	1993	1991	1992	1993
FOOD AND DRUGS ACT - RESTRICTED DRUGS/ LOI LES ALIMENTS ET LA DROGUE - DROGUE D'USAGE RESTREINT									
Nfld./T.-N.	7.7	7.1	4.2	0.0	0.0	0.0	3.8	3.5	2.1
P.E.I./I.P.É.	6.4	28.0	14.9	0.0	2.1	0.0	3.1	14.7	7.3
N.S./N.-É.	11.5	3.8	6.8	1.7	2.0	2.8	6.5	2.9	4.7
N.B./N.-B.	10.2	4.7	7.2	0.7	0.0	0.3	5.4	2.3	3.7
Que./Qué.	3.1	3.1	3.6	0.1	0.3	0.3	1.6	1.7	1.9
Ont./Ont.	7.4	7.4	5.1	0.8	0.8	0.6	4.0	4.0	2.8
Man./Man.	11.9	7.5	6.2	1.2	2.4	0.7	6.5	4.9	3.4
Sask./Sask.	9.3	4.5	5.9	2.5	0.3	1.1	5.8	2.4	3.5
Alta./Alb.	13.4	13.6	8.0	1.6	0.8	1.9	7.5	7.2	4.9
B.C./C.-B.	13.3	16.5	12.9	1.5	1.4	1.0	7.3	8.9	6.8
Yukon/Yukon	45.9	0.0	8.4	0.0	9.6	0.0	24.0	4.6	4.3
N.W.T./T.N.-O.	9.8	14.5	19.1	0.0	0.0	0.0	5.2	7.7	10.2
Canada	**8.1**	**7.8**	**6.2**	**0.8**	**0.8**	**0.7**	**4.4**	**4.2**	**3.4**

Note: Changes in the number of drug offences reported by the police may reflect changes in police enforcement practices rather than any real increase or decrease in drug usage among the population/Des changements du nombre de délits associés à la drogue rapporté par la police peuvent refléter des changements de la pratique policière au suyet de la mise en application plutôt qu'une vraie augmentation où diminution d'usage de la drogue parmi les habitants.

Source: Statistics Canada, *Canadian Crime Statistics 1991, 1992*, and *1993* (Ottawa: Statistics Canada, Catalogue No. 85-205, 1992, 1994, and 1995 respectively).

Statistique Canada, *Statistique de la criminalité du Canada, 1991, 1992*, et *1993* (Ottawa: Statistique Canada, Catalogue no 85-205, 1992, 1994, et 1994 respectivement).

TABLE 12.16

TABLEAU 12.16

Disposition of charges under federal drug acts, Canada, 1988 to 1994

Disposition des accusations en vertu des lois fédérales sur la drogue, Canada, 1988 à 1994

DISPOSITION	1988	1989	1990	1991	1992	1993	1994
TOTAL DISPOSITION OF CHARGES/DISPOSITION TOTALE DES SENTENCES							
Fine/Amende	4,317	4,356	3,994	3,610	3,515	3,067	2,699
Suspended sentence probation/ Sentence suspendue probation	867	1,020	1,067	1,539	1,250	1,125	1,004
Absolute discharged/Libération inconditionêlle	82	64	57	35	62	63	64
Conditional discharge/Libération conditionêlle	335	181	255	162	204	126	98
Prison/Gaol	4,473	6,047	6,598	7,016	8,183	7,666	6,376
Other guilty/Autres coupables	24	13	27	15	23	34	38
Dismissal/Rejetée	331	468	518	487	456	365	311
Withdrawn/Retirée	1,591	2,302	3,278	2,623	2,718	2,174	2,004
Stay of proceedings/Arrêt des procédures	1,084	1,125	1,108	1,293	1,214	1,183	1,139
Acquitted/Acquitté	337	365	426	439	472	502	419
Sine die	0	2	1	6	0	1	0
Bench warrant issued/Mandat d'arrestation	1	3	0	2	1	2	1
Total/Totaux	**13,442**	**15,946**	**17,329**	**17,227**	**18,098**	**16,308**	**14,153**
UNDER THE NARCOTIC CONTROL ACT (EXCLUDING CANNABIS) VERTU DE LA LOI SUR LES STUPEFIANTS (NON COMPRIS LE CANNABIS)							
Fine/Amende	3,513	3,756	3,420	3,112	3,116	2,687	2,342
Suspended sentence probation/ Sentence suspendue probation	697	897	941	1,414	1,099	982	819
Absolute discharged/Libération inconditionêlle	57	45	39	21	48	48	47
Conditional discharge/Libération conditionêlle	281	150	222	131	170	100	80
Prison/Gaol	3,734	5,375	5,967	6,529	7,692	7,265	6,014
Other guilty/Autres coupables	16	7	14	9	12	21	9
Dismissal/Rejetée	254	418	438	431	406	323	274
Withdrawn/Retirée	1,243	1,961	2,839	2,299	2,432	1,909	1,778
Stay of proceedings/Arrêt des procédures	745	878	899	1,094	1,031	1,011	1,011
Acquitted/Acquitté	291	327	392	395	446	458	384
Sine die	0	2	1	6	0	1	0
Bench warrant issued/Mandat d'arrestation	1	1	0	2	1	1	1
Total/Totaux	**10,832**	**13,817**	**15,172**	**15,443**	**16,453**	**14,806**	**12,759**
UNDER THE FOOD AND DRUGS ACT - CONTROLLED DRUGS/ VERTU DE LA LOI DES ALIMENTS ET LA DROGUE - DROGUES CONTROLEES							
Fine/Amende	73	19	20	16	9	29	32
Suspended sentence probation/ Sentence suspendue probation	33	8	32	17	22	5	7
Absolute discharged/Libération inconditionêlle	0	0	0	0	0	0	2
Conditional discharge/Libération conditionêlle	8	0	1	0	3	0	0
Prison/Gaol	130	163	74	46	56	41	74
Dismissal/Rejetée	28	15	25	10	12	3	3
Withdrawn/Retirée	76	37	65	34	46	40	52
Stay of proceedings/Arrêt des procédures	81	92	32	36	53	32	15
Acquitted/Acquitté	11	12	3	9	10	12	12
Total/Totaux	**440**	**346**	**252**	**168**	**211**	**162**	**197**

TABLE 12.16 (concluded)　　　　　　　　　**TABLEAU 12.16** (fin)

Disposition of charges under federal drug acts,
Canada, 1988 to 1994

Disposition des accusations en vertu des lois fédérales
sur la drogue, Canada, 1988 à 1994

DISPOSITION	1988	1989	1990	1991	1992	1993	1994
UNDER THE FOOD AND DRUGS ACT - RESTRICTED DRUGS/ VERTU DE LA LOI DES ALIMENTS ET LA DROGUE - DROGUES D'USAGE RESTREINT							
Fine/Amende	731	581	554	482	390	351	325
Suspended sentence probation/ Sentence suspendue probation	137	115	94	108	129	138	178
Absolute discharged/Libération inconditionêlle	25	19	18	14	14	15	15
Conditional discharge/Libération conditionêlle	46	31	32	31	31	26	18
Prison/Gaol	609	509	557	441	435	360	288
Other guilty/Autre coupables	8	6	13	6	11	13	29
Dismissal/Rejetée	49	35	55	46	38	39	34
Withdrawn/Retirée	272	304	374	290	240	225	174
Stay of proceedings/Arrêt des procédures	258	155	177	163	130	140	113
Acquitted/Acquitté	35	26	31	35	16	32	23
Sine Die	1	0	2	1	0	0	0
Bench warrant issued/Mandat d'arrestation	0	2	0	0	0	1	0
Total/Totaux	**2,171**	**1,783**	**1,907**	**1,617**	**1,434**	**1,340**	**1,197**

Note:　Does not include convictions involving cannabis/Non compris les condamnations associées au cannabis.

Source:　Bureau of Drug Surveillance, Health Canada, unpublished data.
　　　　Bureau de la surveillance des médicaments, Santé Canada, non publiées.

TABLE 12.17   **TABLEAU 12.17**

Drug-related convictions under the federal drug acts, Canada and provinces, 1985 to 1994

Condamnations associées à la drogue en vertu des lois sur la drogue, Canada et provinces, 1985 à 1994

PROVINCE	1985	1986	1987	1988	1989	1990	1991	1992	1993	1994
TOTAL CONVICTIONS (EXCLUDING CANNABIS)/CONDAMNATIONS TOTALES (NON COMPRIS LE CANNABIS)										
Nfld./T.-N.	73	41	38	69	109	41	50	36	35	27
P.E.I./I.P.É.	13	26	11	6	15	13	10	8	10	11
N.S./N.-É.	100	116	151	120	159	148	150	160	221	116
N.B./N.-B.	70	70	84	91	97	88	120	109	93	82
Que./Qué.	2,122	2,455	2,665	3,621	4,047	3,818	4,572	5,666	5,749	4,516
Ont./Ont.	2,066	2,063	2,936	3,193	3,820	4,520	4,368	3,821	3,151	2,733
Man./Man.	335	425	312	365	346	259	256	259	180	189
Sask./Sask.	153	156	169	288	238	196	155	149	136	96
Alta./Alb.	677	783	825	913	1,044	1,070	888	1,047	770	716
B.C./C.-B.	1,040	1,174	1,297	1,411	1,782	1,826	1,782	1,950	1,716	1,768
Yukon/Yukon	14	16	13	13	14	12	20	17	6	7
N.W.T./T.N.-O.	16	13	3	9	10	7	6	15	14	18
Canada	**6,679**	**7,338**	**8,504**	**10,099**	**11,681**	**11,998**	**12,377**	**13,237**	**12,081**	**10,279**
NARCOTIC CONTROL ACT (EXCLUDING CANNABIS)/LOI SUR LES STUPEFIANTS (NON COMPRIS LE CANNABIS)										
Nfld./T.-N.	43	17	9	42	93	26	22	15	15	9
P.E.I./I.P.É.	1	0	4	2	7	7	2	2	5	2
N.S./N.-É.	45	51	80	70	113	92	123	127	192	93
N.B./N.-B.	33	30	41	59	77	41	86	77	67	52
Que./Qué.	1,851	2,168	2,382	3,351	3825	3607	4390	5450	5462	4215
Ont./Ont.	1,568	1,565	2,309	2,688	3410	4052	4008	3481	2912	2507
Man./Man.	240	324	193	236	239	158	167	196	131	159
Sask./Sask.	59	54	78	181	133	141	99	93	91	58
Alta./Alb.	386	455	504	594	761	820	692	911	666	584
B.C./C.-B.	674	825	963	1,062	1553	1644	1612	1762	1550	1615
Yukon/Yukon	6	10	4	6	11	9	12	11	2	5
N.W.T./T.N.-O.	10	5	1	7	8	6	3	12	10	12
Canada	**4,916**	**5,504**	**6,568**	**8,298**	**10,230**	**10,603**	**11,216**	**12,137**	**11,103**	**9,311**
FOOD AND DRUGS ACT - CONTROLLED DRUGS/LOI DES ALIMENTS ET LA DROGUE - DROGUES CONTROLEES										
Nfld./T.-N.	0	0	0	0	0	0	5	0	0	1
P.E.I./I.P.É.	0	0	0	0	0	0	0	0	0	0
N.S./N.-É.	0	6	0	1	0	0	0	0	0	0
N.B./N.-B.	1	1	2	1	1	0	0	0	0	1
Que./Qué.	8	19	14	6	4	5	6	19	18	6
Ont./Ont.	63	106	89	60	22	57	3	18	9	39
Man./Man.	5	9	33	32	21	23	21	9	8	9
Sask./Sask.	2	0	3	30	53	4	13	15	20	16
Alta./Alb.	26	36	35	79	66	29	21	17	10	28
B.C./C.-B.	31	30	26	35	23	9	10	12	10	15
Yukon/Yukon	0	0	0	0	0	0	0	0	0	0
N.W.T./T.N.-O.	0	0	0	1	0	0	0	0	0	0
Canada	**136**	**207**	**202**	**245**	**190**	**127**	**79**	**90**	**75**	**115**

TABLE 12.17 (concluded)   **TABLEAU 12.17** (fin)

Drug-related convictions under the federal drug acts,
Canada and provinces, 1985 to 1994

Condamnations associées à la drogue en vertu des lois
sur la drogue, Canada et provinces, 1985 à 1994

PROVINCE	1985	1986	1987	1988	1989	1990	1991	1992	1993	1994
	FOOD AND DRUGS ACT - RESTRICTED DRUGS/ LOI SUR LES ALIMENTS ET LA DROGUE - DROGUES D'USAGE RESTREINT									
Nfld./T.-N.	30	24	29	27	16	15	23	21	20	17
P.E.I./I.P.É.	12	26	7	4	8	6	8	6	5	9
N.S./N.-É.	55	59	71	49	46	56	27	33	29	23
N.B./N.-B.	36	39	41	31	19	47	34	32	26	29
Que./Qué.	263	268	269	264	218	206	176	197	269	295
Ont./Ont.	435	392	538	445	388	411	357	322	230	187
Man./Man.	90	92	86	97	86	78	68	54	41	21
Sask./Sask.	92	102	88	77	52	51	43	41	25	22
Alta./Alb.	265	292	286	240	217	221	175	119	94	104
B.C./C.-B.	335	319	308	314	206	173	160	176	156	138
Yukon/Yukon	8	6	9	7	3	3	8	6	4	2
N.W.T./T.N.-O.	6	8	2	1	2	1	3	3	4	6
Canada	**1,627**	**1,627**	**1,734**	**1,556**	**1,261**	**1,268**	**1,082**	**1,010**	**903**	**853**

Note: Does not include convictions involving cannabis/Non compris les condamnations associées au cannabis.

Source: Bureau of Drug Surveillance, Health Canada, unpublished data.

Bureau de la surveillance des médicaments, Santé Canada, non publiées.

TABLE 12.18

TABLEAU 12.18

Drug-related convictions under the federal drug acts by section, Canada, 1986 to 1994

Condamnations associées à la drogue en vertu des lois fédérales sur la drogue selon article, Canada, 1986 à 1994

SECTION/ARTICLE	1986	1987	1988	1989	1990	1991	1992	1993	1994
TOTAL CONVICTIONS (EXCLUDING CANNABIS)/ **CONDAMNATIONS TOTALES (NON COMPRIS LES CANNABIS)**									
Possession/Possession	3,749	4,141	4,850	5,813	5,740	5,135	5,587	5,217	4,859
Trafficking/Trafic	1,243	1,551	2,400	2,886	3,453	4,114	4,691	4,246	3,266
Possession for purpose of trafficking/ Possession en vue du trafic	1,349	1,580	1,769	2,148	2,102	2,107	2,381	2,416	1,985
Importing/Importation	37	45	46	62	57	71	92	91	83
Multiple doctoring/ Ordannances multiples	960	1,187	1,033	772	646	950	486	111	86
Total	**7,338**	**8,504**	**10,098**	**11,681**	**11,998**	**12,377**	**13,237**	**12,081**	**10,279**
NARCOTIC CONTROL ACT (EXCLUDING CANNABIS)/ **LOI SUR LES STUPEFIANTS (NON COMPRIS LES CANNABIS)**									
Possession/Possession	2,756	3,099	3,960	5,108	5,040	4,516	5,056	4,735	4,353
Trafficking/Trafic	893	1,201	1,971	2,539	3,187	3,884	4,449	4,045	3,029
Possession for purpose of trafficking/ Possession en vue du trafic	904	1,103	1,363	1,802	1,714	1,811	2,079	2,136	1,760
Importing/Importation	37	45	46	62	57	71	92	91	83
Multiple doctoring/ Ordannances multiples	914	1,120	958	719	605	934	461	96	86
Total	**5,504**	**6,568**	**8,298**	**10,230**	**10,603**	**11,216**	**12,137**	**11,103**	**9,311**
FOOD AND DRUGS ACT - CONTROLLED DRUGS/ **LOI SUR LES ALIMENTS ET LA DROGUE - DROGUES CONTROLEES**									
Trafficking/Trafic	81	60	98	70	28	19	33	24	72
Possession for purpose of trafficking/ Possession en vue du trafic	80	75	71	67	58	44	32	36	43
Multiple doctoring/ Ordannances multiples	46	67	75	53	41	16	25	15	0
Total	**207**	**202**	**244**	**190**	**127**	**79**	**90**	**75**	**115**
FOOD AND DRUGS ACT - RESTRICTED DRUGS/ **LOI SUR LES ALIMENTS ET LA DROGUE - DROGUES D'USAGE RESTREINT**									
Possession/Possession	993	1,042	890	705	700	619	531	482	506
Trafficking/Trafic	269	290	331	277	238	211	209	177	165
Possession for purpose of trafficking/ Possession en vue du trafic	365	402	335	279	330	252	270	244	182
Total	**1,627**	**1,734**	**1,556**	**1,261**	**1,268**	**1,082**	**1,010**	**903**	**853**

Note: Does not include convictions involving cannabis/Non compris les condamnations associées au canabis.

Source: Bureau of Drug Surveillance, Health Canada, unpublished data.

Bureau de la surveillance des médicaments, Santé Canada, non publiées.

TABLE 12.19
TABLEAU 12.19

Drug-related convictions under the federal drug acts by age and sex, Canada, 1991 to 1994

Condamnations associées à la drogue en vertu des lois fédérales sur la drogue, selon âge et sexe, Canada 1991 à 1994

AGE	MALE/HOMMES				FEMALE/FEMMES				TOTAL			
	1991	1992	1993	1994	1991	1992	1993	1994	1991	1992	1993	1994
TOTAL CONVICTIONS (EXCLUDING CANNABIS)/CONDAMNATIONS TOTALES (NON COMPRIS LE CANNABIS)												
< 15	20	15	8	32	1	7	9	5	21	22	17	37
15 - 19	689	798	804	793	125	125	128	96	814	923	932	889
20 - 24	2,226	2,340	2,148	1,737	350	395	346	235	2,576	2,735	2,494	1,972
25 - 29	2,673	2,722	2,465	1,807	431	526	410	401	3,104	3,248	2,875	2,208
30 - 39	3,557	3,691	3,410	3,083	708	710	592	519	4,265	4,401	4,002	3,602
40 - 49	1,053	1,186	1,135	1,070	147	215	204	135	1,200	1,401	1,339	1,205
50 - 59	206	289	253	186	35	81	35	43	241	370	288	229
60+	31	38	59	76	8	11	9	5	39	49	68	81
Unknown/ Unçonnu	76	69	59	49	41	19	6	7	117	88	65	56
Total	**10,531**	**11,148**	**10,341**	**8,833**	**1,846**	**2,089**	**1,739**	**1,446**	**12,377**	**13,237**	**12,080**	**10,279**
NARCOTIC CONTROL ACT (EXCLUDING CANNABIS)/LOI SUR LES STUPEFIANTS (NON COMPRIS LE CANNABIS)												
< 15	15	6	4	18	1	4	5	1	16	10	9	19
15 - 19	458	534	540	473	101	111	110	73	559	645	650	546
20 - 24	1,867	1,972	1,858	1,486	324	372	335	217	2,191	2,344	2,193	1,703
25 - 29	2,450	2,547	2,309	1,686	406	493	393	383	2,856	3,040	2,702	2,069
30 - 39	3,395	3,557	3,293	2,957	678	697	580	504	4,073	4,254	3,873	3,461
40 - 49	1,005	1,154	1,079	1,039	140	208	196	131	1,145	1,362	1,275	1,170
50 - 59	201	277	245	182	35	81	34	43	236	358	279	225
60+	28	35	57	66	8	10	9	4	36	45	66	70
Unknown/ Unçonnu	64	61	52	42	40	18	4	6	104	79	56	48
Total	**9,483**	**10,143**	**9,437**	**7,949**	**1,733**	**1,994**	**1,666**	**1,362**	**11,216**	**12,137**	**11,103**	**9,311**
FOOD AND DRUGS ACT - CONTROLLED DRUGS/LOI DES ALIMENTS ET LA DROGUE - DROGUES CONTROLEES												
< 15	0	0	0	0	0	0	0	0	0	0	0	0
15 - 19	0	1	1	4	0	0	0	1	0	1	1	5
20 - 24	8	9	7	20	3	2	3	2	11	11	10	22
25 - 29	6	9	11	21	2	20	6	3	8	29	17	24
30 - 39	19	22	8	28	9	3	1	5	28	25	9	33
40 - 49	26	12	27	18	1	3	5	1	27	15	32	19
50 - 59	2	7	4	3	0	0	0	0	2	7	4	3
60+	1	2	1	8	0	0	0	0	1	2	1	8
Unknown/ Unçonnu	1	0	0	0	1	0	1	1	2	0	1	1
Total	**63**	**62**	**59**	**102**	**16**	**28**	**16**	**13**	**79**	**90**	**75**	**115**

TABLE 12.19 (concluded)

TABLEAU 12.19 (fin)

Drug-related convictions under the federal drug acts by age and sex, Canada, 1991 to 1994

Condamnations associées à la drogue en vertu des lois fédérales sur la drogue, selon âge et sexe, Canada 1991 à 1994

AGE	MALE/HOMMES				FEMALE/FEMMES				TOTAL			
	1991	1992	1993	1994	1991	1992	1993	1994	1991	1992	1993	1994
FOOD AND DRUGS ACT - RESTRICTED DRUGS/ **LOI DES ALIMENTS ET LA DROGUE - DROGUES D'USAGE RESTREINT**												
< 15	5	9	4	14	0	3	4	4	5	12	8	18
15 - 19	231	263	263	316	24	14	18	22	255	277	281	338
20 - 24	351	359	283	231	23	21	8	16	374	380	291	247
25 - 29	217	166	145	100	23	13	11	15	240	179	156	115
30 - 39	143	112	109	98	21	10	11	10	164	122	120	108
40 - 49	22	20	29	13	6	4	3	3	28	24	32	16
50 - 59	3	5	4	1	0	0	1	0	3	5	5	1
60+	2	1	1	2	0	1	0	1	2	2	1	3
Unknown/ Unçonnu	11	8	7	7	0	1	1	0	11	9	8	7
Total	**985**	**943**	**845**	**782**	**97**	**67**	**57**	**71**	**1,082**	**1,010**	**902**	**853**

Note: Drug-related convictions involving cannabis are not included in this table/Non compris dans ce tableau les condamnations associées au cannabis.

Source: Bureau of Drug Surveillance, Health Canada, unpublished data.

Bureau de la surveillance des médicaments, Santé Canada, non publiées.

TABLE 12.20 **TABLEAU 12.20**

Convictions by sentence and gender,
Canada, 1992 to 1994

Condamnations selon sentence et sexe,
Canada, 1992 à 1994

SENTENCE/SENTENCE	MALE/MASCULIN			FEMALE/FEMININ			TOTAL		
	1992	1993	1994	1992	1993	1994	1992	1993	1994
UNDER THE NARCOTIC CONTROL ACT/VERTU DE LA LOI SUR LES STUPEFIANTS									
Fine/Amende	2,632	2,282	2,045	484	405	297	3,116	2,687	2,342
Suspended sentence probation/ Sentence suspendue/probation	636	613	538	463	369	281	1,099	982	819
Absolute discharged/ Libération inconditionelle	38	41	37	10	7	10	48	48	47
Conditional discharge/ Libération conditionelle	114	76	66	56	24	14	170	100	80
Time/Prison:									
< 1 month/mois	1,362	1,224	1,059	347	310	293	1,709	1,534	1,352
1- 6 months/mois	2,117	1,892	1,641	368	298	240	2,485	2,190	1,881
6-12 months/mois	1,177	1,267	998	140	103	104	1,317	1,370	1,102
1-2 years/ans	1,013	1,047	771	46	85	69	1,059	1,132	840
2-3 years/ans	566	514	414	41	21	25	607	535	439
3-4 years/ans	229	236	194	15	10	9	244	246	203
4-5 years/ans	115	69	70	5	8	7	120	77	77
5-6 years/ans	51	52	42	7	3	1	58	55	43
6-7 years/ans	15	33	28	2	3	1	17	36	29
7-8 years/ans	17	11	6	1	3	1	18	14	7
8-9 years/ans	17	21	6	3	2	1	20	23	7
9-10 years/ans	6	9	6	1	5	0	7	14	6
10-20 years/ans	19	24	5	3	1	0	22	25	5
20+ but not life/Prison de 20 ans et plus mais non à vie	1	8	0	0	0	0	1	8	0
Time indefinite/Prison indéterminé	7	5	15	1	1	8	8	6	23
Other/Autres	11	13	8	1	8	1	12	21	9
Total/Totaux	**10,143**	**9,437**	**7,949**	**1,994**	**1,666**	**1,362**	**12,137**	**11,103**	**9,311**
UNDER THE FOOD AND DRUGS - CONTROLLED DRUGS/ VERTU DE LA LOI DES ALIMENTS ET LA DROGUE -DROGUES CONTROLEES									
Fine/Amende	8	25	30	1	4	2	9	29	32
Suspended sentence probation/ Sentence suspendue/probation	3	1	5	19	4	2	22	5	7
Absolute discharge/ Libération Inconditionelle	0	0	1	0	0	1	0	0	2
Conditional discharge/ Libération conditionelle	3	0	0	0	0	0	3	0	0
Time/Prison:									
< 1 month/mois	11	2	17	0	4	0	11	6	17
1- 6 months/mois	11	10	17	5	2	6	16	12	23
6-12 months/mois	12	7	7	3	0	1	15	7	8
1-2 years/ans	12	9	13	0	2	1	12	11	14
2-3 years/ans	2	3	6	0	0	0	2	3	6
3-4 years/ans	0	1	3	0	0	0	0	1	3
4-5 years/ans	0	1	2	0	0	0	0	1	2
5-6 years/ans	0	0	0	0	0	0	0	0	0
6-7 years/ans	0	0	1	0	0	0	0	0	1
Total/Totaux	**62**	**59**	**102**	**28**	**16**	**13**	**90**	**75**	**115**

TABLE 12.20 (concluded)

TABLEAU 12.20 (fin)

Convictions by sentence and gender,
Canada, 1992 to 1994

Condamnations selon sentence et sexe,
Canada, 1992 à 1994

SENTENCE/SENTENCE	MALE/MASCULIN			FEMALE/FEMININ			TOTAL		
	1992	1993	1994	1992	1993	1994	1992	1993	1994
UNDER THE FOOD AND DRUGS - RESTRICTED DRUGS/ **VERTU DE LA LOI DES ALIMENTS ET LA DROGUE - DROGUES D'USAGE RESTREINT**									
Fine/Amende	367	329	297	23	22	28	390	351	325
Suspended sentence probation/ Sentence suspendue/probation	121	123	151	8	15	27	129	138	178
Absolute discharged/ Libération inconditionelle	12	14	14	2	1	1	14	15	15
Conditional discharge/ Libération conditionelle	30	24	18	1	2	0	31	26	18
Time/Prison:									
< 1 month/mois	112	73	74	10	5	6	122	78	80
1-6 months/mois	164	132	105	15	4	5	179	136	110
6-12 months/mois	70	64	56	2	3	0	72	67	56
1-2 years/ans	45	51	30	1	2	0	46	53	30
2-3 years/ans	14	13	9	0	0	0	14	13	9
3-4 years/ans	1	10	3	0	0	0	1	10	3
4-5 years/ans	1	2	0	0	0	0	1	2	0
5-6 years/ans	0	1	0	0	0	0	0	1	0
Other/Autres	6	10	25	5	3	4	11	13	29
Total/Totaux	**943**	**846**	**782**	**67**	**57**	**71**	**1,010**	**903**	**853**

Source: Bureau of Drug Surveillance, Health Canada, unpublished data.

Bureau de la surveillance des médicaments, Santé Canada, non publiées.

TABLE 12.21

TABLEAU 12.21

Sentenced admissions[1] to federal adult correctional institutions for federal offences[2], Canada, 1986-87 to 1992-93

Admissions[1] dans les pénitenciers fédéraux pour adultes en vertu les lois fédérales[2], Canada, 1986-87 à 1992-93

OFFENCE/DELIT	1986/7	1987/8	1988/9	1989/90	1990/1	1991/2	1992/3
NUMBER OF SENTENCED ADMISSIONS[3]/ **NOMBRE DES ADMISSIONS DES PERSONNES CONDAMNEES**							
Narcotic Control Act/ Loi sur les stupéfiants	337	439	481	598	644	732	782
Food and Drugs Act/ Loi sur les aliments et drogues	37	40	n.a.	n.a.	n.a.	n.a.	n.a.
Total	**374**	**479**	**481**	**598**	**644**	**732**	**782**
SENTENCED ADMISSIONS AS A PERCENTAGE OF TOTAL SENTENCED ADMISSIONS/ **TAUX DES ADMISSIONS DE PERSONNES CONDAMNES PAR RAPPORT AUX ADMISSIONS GLOBALES**							
Narcotic Control Act/ Loi sur les stupéfiants	9	11	12	14	15	15	14
Food and Drugs Act/ Loi sur les aliments et drogues	1	1	..	..	..	..	..
Total	**10**	**12**	**12**	**14**	**15**	**15**	**14**

[1] Sentenced admissions refer to the number of persons admitted to custody under a warrant of committal handed down by a court, judge or magistrate. Also included are persons sentenced on one offence but who are awaiting the completion of court hearings on another charge. The total number of admissions does not necessarily represent an unduplicated count of individuals since a person may be admitted, released and readmitted to custody within the same year./ Admissions des personnes condamnées fait référence au nombre de personnes mises en état d'arrestation conformément au mandat de dépôt d'un juge ou magistrat de la cour. Y compris aussi sont les personnes condamnées pour un certain délit mais qui attendent la fin de l'audition de la cour au sujet d'un autre délit. Le nombre total d'admissions ne représente pas forcément le nombre exact des individus admis parce que la même personne peut être admise, libérée et réadmise en état d'arrestation dans une seule année.

[2] Includes persons sentenced and admitted to custody whose most serious offence was an offence under the Narcotic Control Act or the Food and Drugs Act./Y compris les personnes condamnées et mises en détention préventive dont le délit le plus grave était contre la loi sur les stupéfiants ou la loi sur les aliments et la drogue.

[3] Data have been estimated on the basis of the reported percentage of sentenced admissions relative to the total number of sentenced admissions./ Les données ont été estimées d'après le pourcentage rapporté des admissions des personnes condamnées relatif au nombre total des admissions les personnes condamnées.

Source: Statistics Canada, *Adult Correctional Services in Canada 1992-93* (Ottawa: Statistics Canada, Catalogue No, 85-211, unpublished).

Statistique Canada, *Services correctionnels pour adultes au Canada, 1992-1993* (Ottawa: Statistique Canada, Catalogue no 85-211, non publiées.)

TABLE 12.22

TABLEAU 12.22

Sentenced admissions[1] to provincial adult correctional service facilities for service drug-related offences, Canada and provinces, 1990-91 to 1993-94

Admissions pour infractions[1] reliées à la drogue dans les prisons provinciales pour adultes, Canada et provinces, 1990-91 à 1993-94

PROVINCE	ESTIMATED NUMBER OF SENTENCED ADMISSIONS[2]/ NOMBRE ESTIME D'ADMISSIONS DES PERSONNES CONDAMNEES[2]				PERCENTAGE OF SENTENCED ADMISSIONS RELATIVE TO TOTAL SENTENCED ADMISSIONS/ POURCENTAGE D'ADMISSIONS DES PERSONNES CONDAMNEES RELATIF AU NOMBRE D'ADMISSIONS TOTALES DES PERSONNES CONDAMNEES			
	1990/1	1991/2	1992/3	1993/4	1990/1	1991/2	1992/3	1993/4
Nfld./T.-N.	102	122	133	152	5	5	5	6
P.E.I./I.P.É.	29	28	24	11	2	2	2	1
N.S./N.-É.	154	171	178	192	8	8	7	7
N.B./N.-B.[3]	137	101	122	111	4	3	3	3
Que./Qué.	693	1,646	1,865	1,984	4	8	8	8
Ont./Ont.	3,606	n.a.	n.a.	3,986	8	n.a.	n.a.	10
Man./Man.[4]	257	185	215	188	5	5	6	6
Sask./Sask.	295	223	207	213	4	3	3	3
Alta./Alb.	1,029	1,132	1,189	881	5	5	5	4
B.C./C.-B.	914	1,014	1,060	932	10	10	10	8
Yukon/Yukon	17	12	10	0	4	4	3	..
N.W.T./T.N.-O.	9	20	28	28	1	2	3	3
Canada[5]	**7,242**	**4,654**	**5,030**	**8,678**	**6**	**6**	**6**	**7**

[1] Sentenced admissions refer to the number of persons admitted to custody under a warrant of committal handed down by a court judge or magistrate. Also included are persons sentenced on one offence but who are awaiting the completion of court hearings on another charge. The total number of admissions does not necessarily represent an unduplicated count of individuals since a person may be admitted, released and readmitted to custody within the same year./ Admissions des personnes condamnées fait référence au nombre de personnes mises en état d'arrestation conformément au mandat de dépôt d'un juge où magistrat de la cour. Y compris aussi sont les personnes condamnées pour un certain délit mais qui attendent la fin de l'audition de la cour au sujet d'un autre délit. Le nombre total d'admissions de représente pas forcément le nombre exact des individus admis parce que la même personne peut être admise, libérée et réadmise en état d'arrestation dans une seule année.

[2] Data have been estimated on the basis of the reported percentage of sentenced drug-related admissions relative to the total number of sentenced admissions./Les données ont été estimées d'apres le pourcentage rapporté d'admissions des personnes condamnées de délit associé à la drogue relatif au nombre total des admissions des personnes condamnées.

[3] Includes only those offenders who were both admitted and released during the calender year./Y compris uniquement les délinquants admis et libérés pendant l'année civile.

[4] Excludes sentenced admissions to the Provincial Remand Centre./Non compris les admissions des personnes condamnées au centre provincial de détention préventive.

[5] Based on data from those provinces which reported in a given year./Basé sur les données des provinces qui en ont rapporté dans une année déterminée.

Source: Statistics Canada, *Adult Correctional Services in Canada 1992-93* (Ottawa: Statistics Canada, Catalogue No, 85-211, unpublished).

Statistique Canada, *Services correctionnels pour adultes au Canada, 1992-93* (Ottawa: Statistique Canada, Catalogue no 85-211, non publiées.)

TABLE 12.23

TABLEAU 12.23

Reported thefts and other losses involving narcotics and controlled drugs, Canada and provinces, 1985 to 1994

Vois et autres pertes déclarés concernant les stupéfiants et les drogues contrôlées, Canada et provinces, 1985 à 1994

PROVINCE	1985	1986	1987	1988	1989	1990	1991	1992	1993	1994
REPORTED THEFTS AND OTHER LOSSES BY PROVINCE/ VOLS ET AUTRES PERTES DECLARES, SELON LA PROVINCE										
Nfld./T.-N.	7	4	4	2	2	9	6	6	8	6
P.E.I./I.P.É.	0	0	2	1	2	1	2	7	2	2
N.S./N.-É.	35	25	27	15	12	17	17	17	26	21
N.B./N.-B.	13	12	11	9	3	6	6	9	7	6
Que./Qué.	195	210	216	323	288	255	265	192	192	144
Ont./Ont.	345	438	475	495	553	633	629	671	530	508
Man./Man.	74	71	71	38	44	47	43	51	57	82
Sask./Sask.	86	67	51	38	38	42	32	41	30	27
Alta./Alb.	156	252	127	131	129	162	222	218	157	98
B.C./C.-B.	116	155	184	116	140	126	138	103	101	77
Yukon/Yukon	0	0	4	2	2	5	8	9	5	2
N.W.T./T.N.-O.	0	0	0	0	0	0	3	2	0	0
Canada	**1,027**	**1,234**	**1,172**	**1,170**	**1,213**	**1,303**	**1,371**	**1,326**	**1,115**	**973**
REPORTED THEFTS AND OTHER LOSSES BY SOURCE OF LOSS/ VOLS ET AUTRES PERTES DECLARES, SELON LA SOURCE										
Pharmacies	751	853	781	734	751	884	899	804	680	486
Practitioners/Praticiens:										
Office/Bureau	7	6	1	6	12	6	7	11	7	14
Medical Bag/ Trousse Médicale	1	0	3	2	1	1	3	0	0	0
Hospitals/Hôpitaux	177	248	269	278	286	293	375	405	369	394
Licensed Dealers/ Distributeurs Autorisés	70	108	98	136	152	107	77	77	50	65
Other/Autres	21	19	20	14	11	12	10	29	9	14
Total	**1,027**	**1,234**	**1,172**	**1,170**	**1,213**	**1,303**	**1,371**	**1,326**	**1,115**	**973**

Source: Bureau of Drug Surveillance, Health Canada, unpublished data.

Bureau de la surveillance des médicaments, Santé Canada, non publiées.

TABLE 12.24

TABLEAU 12.24

Reported thefts and other losses involving narcotic and controlled drugs by quantity and type of drug taken, Canada, 1987 to 1994

Vois et autres pertes, déclarés concernant les stupéfiants et les drogues contrôlées, selon la quantité et le genre de drogue, Canada, 1987 à 1994

TYPE OF DRUGS/ GENRE DE DROGUE		NARCOTIC DRUGS/STUPEFIANTS							
		1987	1988	1989	1990	1991	1992	1993	1994
Anileridine/Aniléride									
Tab./Co.		22,765	15,335	17,584	17,531	15,264	17,809	16,931	10,934
Inj.	mLs/ml	592	12	97	176	25	163	27	133
Cocaine/Cocaïne									
Liq.	mLs/ml	172	33	123	225	50	97	87	88
Powder/Poudre	gms/g	702.709	269.300	356.740	319.840	300.671	184.000	80.000	89.955
Codeine/Codéine									
Tab./Co. & Cap		726,104	573,078	609,804	863,095	627,013	915,014	535,798	474,278
Inj.	mLs/ml	143	96	408	604	70	544	60	551
Liq.	mLs/ml	231,010	195,576	262,977	294,792	284,540	219,335	224,179	168,234
Powder/Poudre	gms/g	332.110	286.650	224.496	161.007	1,154.500	53.000	180.000	44.900
Diphenoxylate/Diphénoxylate									
Tab./Comp.		119,893	48,031	42,028	64,109	45,600	38,308	42,856	23,164
Liq.	mLs/ml	8,597	5,155	4,760	4,740	4,556	1,630	4,380	560
Heroin/Héroïne									
Powder/Poudre	gms/g	0.000	0.000	0.000	0.000	30.000	0	0	0
Hydrocodone									
Tab./Co.		15,098	14,557	12,895	16,908	11,614	8,949	8,795	3,769
Liq.	mLs/ml	909,465	851,134	996,399	991,049	827,033	300,793	307,507	116,976
Hydromorphine									
Tab./Co.		27,381	26,121	42,173	56,302	48,098	55,890	51,328	35,190
Inj.	mLs/ml	380	432	212	5,403	1,243	2,452	775	5,151
Liq.	mLs/ml	0	0	0	900	2,770	1,230	3,121	1,699
Powder/Poudre	gms/g	0.000	0.000	0.000	0.000	0.400	1.000	35.400	0.000
Supp.		231	85	40	208	98	15	128	76
Levorphanol									
Tab./Co.		10,305	7,387	8,988	8,026	3,959	4,430	2,374	1,134
Inj.	mLs/ml	31	0	10	0	1	0	90	0
Meperidine/Mépéridine									
Tab./Co. & Cap		71,364	57,537	44,202	45,609	61,853	70,084	54,309	34,622
Inj.	mLs/ml	9,424	8,021	3,857	10,144	4,858	6,429	8,795	3,233
Methadone/Méthadone									
Tab./Co.		100	0	29	30	0	0	0	0
Liq. Mixture/Melange	mLs/ml	0	981	180	19,636	4,432	1,366	8,627	1,887
Powder/Poudre	gms/g	257.000	81.210	106.688	248.136	277.239	251.200	983.200	15.215
Morphine									
Tab./Co.		27,744	45,908	53,913	69,249	78,073	97,568	94,309	57,766
Inj.	mLs	3,599	2,136	3,720	3,350	2,856	8,168	26,690	3,213
Liq.	mLs/ml	84,306	96,772	68,330	60,247	60,750	65,189	43,981	20,457
Powder/Poudre	gms/g	468.136	214.962	201.750	182.480	157.000	114.900	77.600	23.630
Supp.		363	341	85	681	318	662	839	120
Nabilone									
Cap.		296	164	40	30	200	204	224	250

TABLE 12.24 (continued)   **TABLEAU 12.24** (suite)

Reported thefts and other losses involving narcotic and controlled drugs by quantity and type of drug taken, Canada, 1987 to 1994

Vois et autres pertes, déclarés concernant les stupéfiants et les drogues contrôlées, selon la quantité et le genre de drogue, Canada, 1987 à 1994

TYPE OF DRUGS/ GENRE DE DROGUE		NARCOTIC DRUGS/STUPEFIANTS (continued/suite)							
		1987	1988	1989	1990	1991	1992	1993	1994
Normethadone									
Tab./Co.		95	0	0	0	0	0	0	0
Liq.	mLs	5,554	3,750	5,349	3,620	3,852	3,000	2,265	994
Opium									
Tab./Co. & Cap		3,265	1,522	3,585	2,265	1,877	1,090	478	188
Inj.	mLs	112	10	1	1	0	405	12	0
Liq.	mLs	14,778	9,669	7,500	10,543	9,144	4,675	4,000	1,972
Supp.		221	164	62	131	93	246	39	192
Oxycodone									
Tab./Co.		299,711	315,547	305,946	340,694	305,225	307,248	223,872	156,657
Powder	gms	0	0	0	0	2	0	0	0
Supp.		223	290	958	399	373	678	205	85
Pentazocine									
Liq.	mLs	0	0	20	10	0	0	0	0
Tab./Co.		78,949	61,357	43,383	42,593	47,567	35,172	37,412	15,628
Inj.	mLs	866	516	468	105	683	485	211	45
Propoxyphene/Propoxyphène									
Tab./Co. & Cap		59,650	43,163	42,745	38,444	37,988	34,857	39,834	25,980
Others/Autres									
Tab./Co.		25	100	0	10	0	0	4	50
Inj.	mLs	634	1,412	366	422	1,044	852	15,741	365
Liq.	mLs	5,402	722	39	300	3	576	412	56
Powder/Poudre	gms	0.000	0.000	0.000	1.260	0.000	3.500	5.690	0.203
Supp.		72	24	6	12	30	18	24	12
		CONTROLLED DRUGS/DROGUES CONTRÔLÉES							
Amphetamine/Amphétamine									
Tab./Co. & Cap		7,306	5,101	5,092	6,160	7,232	8,638	6,794	5,579
Powder/Poudre	gms	0.000	1.000	0.000	0.000	0.000	0	0	0
Diethylpropion/Diéthylpropion									
Tab./Co.		8,735	8,096	15,093	12,072	10,216	8,390	7,170	6,248
Fluoxymesterone/Fluoxymésterone									
Tab./Co.		0	0	0	0	0	0	123	250
Methaqualone/Méthaqualone									
Tab./Co. & Cap		8,445	8,301	8,814	4,589	1,517	60	287	145
Methylphenidate/Méthylphénidate									
Tab./Co.		56,629	53,903	56,822	67,581	59,677	51,356	45,246	36,112
Inj.	mLs	0	18	0	0	0	20	0	0
Liq.	mLs	500	0	0	0	0	0	0	0
Oxymetholone/Oxmétholone									
Tab./Co.		0	0	0	0	0	0	200	200
Phentermine									
Liq.	mLs	0	0	0	0	30	0	0	0
Cap.		21,373	13,030	23,374	23,918	26,424	17,162	14,240	7,975

TABLE 12.24 (concluded)　　　　　　　　　　　　　**TABLEAU 12.24** (fin)

Reported thefts and other losses involving narcotic and controlled drugs by quantity and type of drug taken, Canada, 1987 to 1994

Vois et autres pertes, déclarés concernant les stupéfiants et les drogues contrôlées, selon la quantité et le genre de drogue, Canada, 1987 à 1994

TYPE OF DRUGS/ GENRE DE DROGUE		CONTROLLED DRUGS/DROGUES CONTRÔLÉES (continued/suite)							
		1987	1988	1989	1990	1991	1992	1993	1994
Secobarbital/Sécobarbital									
Tab./Co. & Cap		26,110	16,320	16,596	16,006	10,380	8,954	9,393	3,546
Inj.	mLs	0	0	0	0	0	0	0	0
Secobarbital & Amobarbital/ Sécobarbital et amobarbital									
Cap.		20,898	15,040	10,259	6,806	4,156	4,607	4,072	770
Testosterone									
Inj.	mLs	0	0	0	0	0	46	359	16,001
Liq.	mLs	0	0	0	0	0	14	15	108
Powder/Poudre	gms	0	0	0	0	0	0	3.000	0
Tab./Co.		0	0	0	0	0	0	60	0
Other Barbiturates/Autres Barbituriques									
Tab./Co. & Cap		239,148	149,805	186,725	228,354	121,771	150,592	136,118	69,267
Inj.	mLs	89	181	289	3,098	352	942	280	43
Liq.	mLs	13,982	45,825	48,431	45,485	13,262	13,801	4,052	6,018
Powder/Poudre	gms	125.00	43.00	135.00	100.11	15,739.00	0	25.000	2.880
Supp.		252	132	456	338	1,560	432	507	72
Other Controlled Drugs/ Autres Drogues Contrôlées									
Tab./Co. & Cap		840	510	0	430	70	353	151	527
Inj.	mLs	20	40	123	22	63	487	71	152
Liq.	mLs	200	200	100	20	0	4	0	0
Powder/Poudre	gms	255.000	257.000	123.000	3.000	42.694	23	0	0
Other Steroids/Stéroïdes									
Inj.	mLs	0.000	0.000	0.000	0.000	0.000	24	39	33
Tab./Co.	mLs	0.000	0.000	0.000	0.000	100	4,800	50	30

Source: Bureau of Drug Surveillance, Health Canada, unpublished data.

Bureau de la surveillance des médicaments, Santé Canada, non publiées.

TABLE 12.25 **TABLEAU 12.25**

Number of reported prescription forgeries[1] by province and type of drug, Canada, 1986 to 1994

Nombre des fausses prescriptions[1] déclarées, selon la province et le genre de drogues, Canada, 1986 à 1994

PROVINCE	1986	1987	1988	1989	1990	1991	1992	1993	1994
Nfld./T.-N.	10	4	5	12	10	8	19	10	8
P.E.I./I.P.É.	0	0	0	37	31	2	2	5	0
N.S./N.-É.	11	17	17	5	4	18	5	5	11
N.B./N.-B.	59	14	5	6	32	28	3	9	2
Que./Qué.	437	572	360	440	428	393	320	286	90
Ont./Ont.	786	1,153	1,132	1,372	1,111	1,097	1,216	1,127	668
Man./Man.	168	108	99	105	17	104	94	70	76
Sask./Sask.	99	40	3	14	5	10	14	10	3
Alta./Alb.	66	47	91	98	156	534	348	238	206
B.C./C.-B.	261	232	229	166	95	160	162	68	8
Yukon/Yukon	5	3	0	0	2	5	1	0	0
N.W.T./T.N.-O.	0	0	0	0	0	1	0	0	0
Canada	**1,902**	**2,190**	**1,941**	**2,255**	**1,891**	**2,360**	**2,184**	**1,828**	**1,072**

TYPE OF DRUG/GENRE DE DROGUE
Narcotic Drugs/Stupéfiant:

	1986	1987	1988	1989	1990	1991	1992	1993	1994
Anileridine/Aniléride	11	113	68	25	2	17	52	68	7
Codeine/Codéine	562	769	530	737	715	1,083	1,002	782	498
Diphenoxylate/ Diphénoxylate	2	1	1	4	0	0	1	0	1
Hydrocodone	229	108	268	249	106	98	82	112	53
Hydromorphone	70	49	156	74	56	205	159	86	69
Levorphanol	0	0	0	0	0	1	0	4	0
Meperidine/Mériridine	41	56	49	101	96	174	109	119	54
Methadone/Méthadone	32	128	0	0	9	2	3	0	0
Morphine	3	6	37	37	7	63	67	37	30
Oxycodone	398	577	441	678	552	483	495	345	280
Pentazocine	111	69	54	39	53	48	16	25	29
Propoxyphene/ Propoxyphène	20	35	24	31	43	31	40	13	1
Other/Autres	1	5	2	0	1	1	0	1	0
Total	**1,480**	**1,916**	**1,630**	**1,975**	**1,640**	**2,206**	**2,026**	**1,592**	**1,022**

TABLE 12.25 (concluded)

TABLEAU 12.25 (fin)

Number of reported prescription forgeries[1] by province and type of drug, Canada, 1986 to 1994

Nombre des fausses prescriptions[1] déclarées, selon la province et le genre de drogues, Canada, 1986 à 1994

PROVINCE	1986	1987	1988	1989	1990	1991	1992	1993	1994
Controlled Drugs/Drogue Contrôlée:									
Amphetamine/ Amphétamine	2	1	0	0	1	3	0	5	0
Diethylpropion/ Diéthylpropion/	99	30	51	73	63	29	34	17	11
Methaqualone/ Méthaqualone	38	52	67	68	11	0	0	0	0
Methylphenidate/	162	96	99	30	31	32	28	38	3
Méthylphénidate/ Phentermine	27	19	46	51	40	34	43	21	15
Secobarbital Sécobarbital	77	68	37	22	12	33	29	54	7
Secobarbital & Amobarbital/ Sécobarbital Amobarbital	1	2	7	13	8	7	2	1	0
Other Barbiturates/Autres Barbituriques	16	6	4	23	68	15	15	12	8
Other/Autres	0	0	0	0	17	0	0	0	0
Fluoxymesterone/ Fluoxymestérone	0	0	0	0	0	0	2	2	1
Methyltestosterone/ Méthyltestosterone	0	0	0	0	0	0	0	2	0
Oxymetholone/ Oxymétholone	0	0	0	0	0	0	0	38	3
Testosterone/ Testostérone	0	0	0	0	0	1	3	38	2
Other steroids/ Autres stéroïdes	0	0	0	0	0	0	2	7	0
Total	**422**	**274**	**311**	**280**	**251**	**154**	**158**	**235**	**50**

[1] Includes both forgeries that were filled and forgeries that were not filled./Incluent les fausses ordonnances exécutées.

Source: Bureau of Drug Surveillance, Health Canada, unpublished data.

Bureau de la surveillance des médicaments, Santé Canada, non publiées.

E pilogue: Information Gaps and Implications to Research

by Eric Single and Diane McKenzie, Canadian Centre on Substance Abuse and Robert Williams, Addiction Research Foundation

Introduction

This volume gives a national picture on alcohol and other drug use in Canada. The tables and figures have been selected from formal systems for collecting and reporting information on morbidity, mortality, crime and sales of legal drugs. Some of the most recent national surveys were also included. New information became available on the mortality, morbidity and economic costs attributed to the use of alcohol, tobacco and illicit drugs (Singer et al., 1996).

Despite an enormous amount of data available in Canada, a number of major gaps exist. There is little or no information on how much of a street drug is used safely and how much leads to problems. The patterns and problems associated with multiple drug use and situational influences that lead to heavy drinking and heavy drug use are not well documented either. Drug seizures give the only information on the availability of illicit drugs. Treatment data are limited to cases reported in the health care system and are more a function of the availability of services than patient need. Information about other critical forms of intervention such as self-help groups are not available. This lack of information about alcohol and drug problems and their solutions in Canada limits our ability to develop well targeted and timely responses to need.

E pilogue : Les lacunes d'information et leurs incidences sur la recherche

Eric Single et Diane McKenzie, du Centre canadien de lutte contre l'alcoolisme et les toxicomanies, et Robert Williams, de la Fondation de la recherche sur la toxicomanie

Introduction

Le présent ouvrage brosse un tableau national de la consommation de l'alcool et des autres drogues au Canada. Les tableaux et les figures présentées proviennent de systèmes officiels de collecte et de déclaration de données sur la morbidité, la mortalité, la criminalité et les ventes des drogues licites, ainsi que de certaines des enquêtes nationales les plus récentes. De nouvelles informations ont récemment été rendues disponibles sur la mortalité, la morbidité et les coûts économiques imputables à la consommation de l'alcool, du tabac et des drogues illicites.

Bien que nous disposions, au Canada, de masses considérables de données, d'importantes lacunes persistent. Il existe peu d'informations, sinon aucune, indiquant par exemple la quantité d'une drogue de la rue qu'il est possible de consommer sans courir de danger. Les profils et les problèmes associés à l'usage de multiples drogues et aux contextes qui mènent à une forte consommation d'alcool et de drogues sont aussi mal documentés. La seule information sur la disponibilité des drogues illicites provient des saisies de drogues. Les données sur le traitement sont pour leur part limitées aux cas déclarés au moyen des systèmes des soins de santé et renseignent davantage sur la disponibilité des services que sur le besoin du patient. Quant à d'autres genres d'intervention majeurs, tels les groupes d'entraide, il n'existe aucune donnée. Ce manque d'information sur les problèmes d'alcool et de

Underlying dimensions of information gaps

There are a number of underlying reasons for these information gaps:

STIGMATIZATION: In order to reintegrate alcohol or drug dependent persons back into society, there is a tendency to diagnose their problems in terms of the presenting problem rather than the underlying substance abuse. The illegal status of street drugs makes users reluctant to discuss their patterns of use and seek treatment when they need it. This situation also prevents developing reliable data on the production and trade of drugs.

INADEQUATE REPORTING SYSTEMS: Some weaknesses in Canadian alcohol and drug information are from deficiencies in the official reporting systems. Only some provinces have a triplicate prescription system; those without such a system have little information on the prescribing practices of doctors and consumption of licit drugs in the population. Similarly, the statistics on alcohol-and drug-related morbidity are limited to hospital-based treatment settings.

Some reporting systems do not give detailed information on their classification criteria and their procedures for collecting information. Routinely collected statistics can be strongly affected by changes in procedures or legal status without any real change in the prevalence or incidence of a problem. The introduction of breathalyzers influenced impaired driving statistics. The user of these statistics must be aware of the procedures by which the information is obtained, and alert to any technological advances or other events that influence the results. Perhaps most importantly, routinely collected statistics and surveys are limited in that they do not tap the interactions among alcohol and other drug use.

LACK OF COORDINATED REPORTING PROCEDURES: Information about some drug-related activities (drug seizures) is maintained by different organizations and generates statistics that vary greatly. These

drogues répondre adéquatement et en temps opportun aux divers besoins.

Causes profondes des lacunes d'information

Les lacunes d'information relevées s'expliquent par plusieurs causes sous-jacentes :

LA STIGMATISATION : Dans l'optique de la réintégration des alcooliques et des toxicomanes dans la société, on a tendance à diagnostiquer leur problème immédiat plutôt que les causes profondes de leur abus. En outre, vu le caractère illégal des drogues de la rue, ceux qui les consomment hésitent à discuter de leurs habitudes de consommation et à s'adresser aux services de traitement dont ils ont besoin. Une telle situation empêche également d'obtenir des données fiables sur la production et le commerce des stupéfiants.

L'INSUFFISANCE DES SYSTÈMES DE DÉCLARATION : Certaines faiblesses de l'information canadienne sur les problèmes d'alcool et de drogues découlent de lacunes dans les systèmes officiels de déclaration. Seules quelques provinces ont adopté le système d'émission des ordonnances en trois exemplaires. Celles qui ne disposent pas d'un tel système possèdent peu de données sur les pratiques de prescription des médecins et sur la consommation des drogues licites par la population. De la même façon, les données sur la morbidité reliée à l'alcool et aux drogues sont limitées aux services de traitement des hôpitaux. Certains systèmes de déclaration ne fournissent aucune information détaillée sur leurs critères de classification et leurs procédés de cueillette des données. Les données statistiques recueillies régulièrement peuvent être largement influencées par une modification de ces procédés ou du statut légal, sans que les facteurs prévalence ou incidence n'accusent de véritable changement. C'est le cas notamment des statistiques sur la conduite avec facultés affaiblies, qui ont été influencées par l'introduction de l'alcootest. Il importe que l'utilisateur de ces statistiques connaisse les procédés de cueillette et soit informé de tout progrès technologique ou de tout autre fait

inconsistencies lead to questions about the validity of enforcement statistics. Other difficulties in estimating the size and nature of the under ground economy of illicit drugs in Canada may be overcome if these organizations worked with other countries to formalize coordinated reporting procedures.

PREDOMINANT CONCEPTS OF ALCOHOL AND OTHER DRUG PROBLEMS: Another reason for gaps in information relates to how problem use is conceptualized. Our concepts of dependence and their contribution to overall problem levels have evolved significantly over the past years. Thirty years ago, the major alcohol problem was seen as "alcoholism". Now, it is recognized that many drinking problems happen at levels well below those associated with dependence. Similarly, the lack of data on patterns and levels of use for illicit drugs stems from its legal status as criminal activity. Because it is illegal, any use is viewed as a problem and detailed information that characterizes patterns of use and dosage is often neglected.

Even our notion of which substances should be included in a report on substance abuse is constantly changing. Thirty years ago, this report would not have contained any information on tobacco use. We now know that tobacco accounts for more deaths than any other psychoactive substance. By the same token, this report does not include information on caffeine; 30 years from now, it might do so.

Implications for future research

Given these information gaps and their underlying causes, the following recommendations are offered for improving our information base:

IMPROVED COMMUNICATION: There should be improved communication among research, treatment and enforcement specialists and organizations. The CCSA National Clearinghouse on Substance Abuse provides an electronic network of resource centres across Canada which should be expanded. Other means for improving communication were suggested by an expert panel

susceptible d'influer sur les résultats. Mais le plus important est peut-être de se rappeler que les données statistiques recueillies régulièrement, ainsi que les enquêtes, sont limitées en ce sens qu'elles ne tiennent pas compte des interactions entre la consommation de l'alcool et celle des autres drogues.

L'ABSENCE DE PROCÉDURES DE DÉCLARATION COORDONNÉES : L'information sur les activités reliées à la drogue (saisies de drogues) est tenue à jour par nombre d'organismes et donne lieu à des statistiques fort différentes les unes des autres. Ces incohérences soulèvent des questions quant à la validité des statistiques sur la mise en application de la loi. Il est par ailleurs difficile à l'heure actuelle d'évaluer l'importance et la nature de l'économie souterraine que représentent les drogues illicites au Canada, difficulté qui pourrait être résolue si ces organismes joignaient leurs efforts à ceux des autres pays afin d'harmoniser les procédures officielles de déclaration.

LES CONCEPTS PRÉDOMINANTS DE L'ALCOOLISME ET DES AUTRES TOXICOMANIES : Une autre cause à l'origine des lacunes d'information relevées a trait à la manière dont on perçoit le problème de l'abus. Notre conception de la dépendance et de sa contribution aux différents aspects du problème a considérablement évolué au cours des dernières années. Il y a trente ans, on percevait l'«alcoolisme» comme le principal problème d'alcool. Aujourd'hui, il est généralement admis que de nombreux problèmes d'alcool interviennent bien avant ceux associés à la dépendance. De façon similaire, le manque de données sur les habitudes et les niveaux de consommation des drogues illicites s'explique du fait qu'elle soit juridiquement considérée comme une activité criminelle. Vu son caractère illégal, toute consommation est perçue d'office comme un problème, et l'on néglige donc souvent de recueillir l'information qui permettrait de préciser les profils de consommation et les dosages.

Même le choix d'inclure telles ou telles substances dans les rapports pertinents évolue constamment. Il y a trente ans, le présent rapport n'aurait contenu aucune information sur l'usage du tabac. Or, nous savons

on substance abuse commissioned by the National Health Research Development Program:

"Efforts should be directed toward establishing archives and data banks for maintaining, classifying and retrieving data from surveys and other studies concerning substance use and abuse. Such material can be used for secondary analysis, including meta-analytic research. To this end, and where applicable, computer-readable data sets should be required, along with the final report of funded studies." (Andrews and Single, 1993: 2).

EXPANSION OF RESEARCH DESIGNS: As noted at several points in this report, there is a need to consider a variety of data sources to obtain a complete picture of alcohol and other drug use in Canada. Many of the information gaps will require nontraditional methods to supplement the aggregate statistics and survey data. Ethnographic, observational and non-traditional methods should be encouraged, particularly where there is a lack of basic description of the nature and extent of problems. Effects of changes in social policy should be assessed, to make information more relevant to government decision-makers.

IMPROVE METHODOLOGIES FOR ESTIMATING UNDERGROUND ECONOMIES: Methods for assessing the availability of illicit drugs should be expanded and refined in collaboration with other international jurisdictions. Ideally, a collaborative effort by drug intelligence experts and social researchers would advance this work quickly. Other underground economies should be examined as well, including special studies on the unrecorded consumption of licit drugs such as alcohol and tobacco.

ATTENTION TO SPECIAL POPULATIONS: There is a particularly need for better information on the nature and extent of substance abuse in certain segments of the population. In particular, special attention should be given to street youth, women, Aboriginal peoples, elderly and illicit drug users.

For the next edition of the Canadian Profile, a number of new studies will generate new data.

aujourd'hui que le tabac est responsable de plus de décès que toute autre substance psychotrope. Dans cette même optique, le présent rapport n'inclut aucune information sur l'usage de la caféine, alors que dans trente ans, il en contiendra peut-être.

Incidences sur les recherches futures

Compte tenu de ces manques d'information et de leurs causes profondes, il est recommandé d'améliorer la base d'information en appliquant les recommandations suivantes :

AMÉLIORER LES COMMUNICATIONS : Il convient d'améliorer les communications entre les spécialistes et les organismes des secteurs de la recherche, du traitement et de la justice. A ce titre, il conviendrait d'élargir le réseau électronique des centres de ressources au Canada exploité par le Centre national de documentation sur l'alcoolisme et les toxicomanies du CCLAT. D'autres formules d'amélioration ont été proposées par un comité d'experts chargé de l'abus des substances dans un rapport d'étude commandé par le Programme national de développement de la recherche en matière de santé :

"Il faut s'attacher tout particulièrement à établir des archives et des banques de données, afin de mieux conserver, classer et repérer les données des enquêtes et des autres études portant sur l'usage et l'abus des substances. Une telle documentation peut servir à des fins d'analyse secondaire, y compris la recherche méta-analytique. Dans cette optique, et chaque fois que cela est possible, il y aurait lieu de demander, en même temps que le rapport final des études subventionnées, des ensembles de données informatisés." (Andrews et Single, 1993: 2).

Elargir les protocoles de recherche : Tel qu'il a été souligné à plusieurs reprises dans le présent rapport, il importe de puiser à plusieurs sources de données si l'on veut brosser un tableau complet de l'usage de l'alcool et des autres drogues au Canada. Pour parer aux lacunes d'information, il faudra souvent compléter les données

During 1994, the Federal government undertook the Canadian Alcohol and Other Drug Survey which examined many new dimensions of alcohol and drug use. A series of national epidemiology studies on illicit drugs monitor problems in several Canadian cities and estimates the number of injection drug users in the population.

The challenge for the future is clear. Programming and policy depends on better information on substance abuse to improve in the future, especially under the increasing financial constraints of government.

References

Andrews, F. and Single, E., 1993. "Substance Abuse Research and Funding Priorities: Report of a National Workshop", Ottawa: Canadian Centre on Substance Abuse.

Single, E., Robson, L., Xie, X., Rehm, J., *The Costs of Substance Abuse in Canada*. Ottawa: Canadian Centre on Substance Abuse, 1996.

statistiques d'ensemble et les données des enquêtes en recourant à des méthodes non traditionnelles. Or, il convient à ce chapitre de favoriser les méthodes ethnographiques, observationnelles et non traditionnelles, en particulier lorsque l'on ne dispose pas d'un énoncé fondamental complet de la nature et de l'étendue des problèmes. Il y a également lieu d'évaluer les changements dans les politiques sociales, de façon à rendre l'information plus utile aux décideurs gouvernementaux.

AMÉLIORER LES MÉTHODOLOGIES D'ÉVALUATION DES ÉCONOMIES SOUTERRAINES : Il importe d'élargir et de raffiner les méthodes servant à évaluer la disponibilité des drogues illicites en collaboration avec d'autres autorités internationales. De manière idéale, la participation conjointe des experts antidrogue et des chercheurs sociaux permettrait de conclure rapidement un tel projet. Il conviendrait également d'examiner d'autres économies souterraines et de mener des études spéciales sur la consommation non enregistrée des drogues licites telles l'alcool et le tabac.

S'INTÉRESSER DAVANTAGE AUX POPULATIONS SPÉCIALES : Il convient tout spécialement d'obtenir une meilleure information sur la nature et l'étendue de l'abus des substances dans certains segments de la population. Nous pensons en particulier aux jeunes de la rue, aux femmes, aux Autochtones, aux aïénés et aux usagers de drogues illicites.

En ce qui concerne la prochaine édition de Profil canadien, soulignons que plusieurs nouvelles études fourniront de nouvelles données. En 1994, le gouvernement fédéral a amorcé l'Enquête nationale sur l'alcool et les autres drogues, au cours de laquelle on s'est penché sur de nombreux nouveaux aspects de la consommation de ces produits. Une série d'études épidémiologiques sur les drogues illicites permet en outre de suivre l'évolution des problèmes dans plusieurs grands centres urbains canadiens et d'évaluer le nombre de toxicomanes par injection au pays.

Le défi à relever est clair. La qualité future des programmes et de leur orientation repose sur

l'amélioration de l'information, surtout dans le contexte de restrictions budgétaires de plus en plus sévères imposées par les gouvernements.

Ouvrages de référence

Andrews, F. et E. Single, 1993. *Substance Abuse Research and Funding Priorities: Report of a National Workshop*, Ottawa : Centre canadien de lutte contre l'alcoolisme et les toxicomanies, 1993.

Single, E., L. Robson, X. Xie et J. Rehm, *The Costs of Substance Abuse in Canada*, Ottawa, Centre canadien de lutte contre les toxicomanies, 1996.

Medical Conditions and Diagnostic Categories

All morbidity and mortality data included in this report are classified according to the 9th Revision of the International Classification of Diseases (ICD-9) which was put into effect in Canada in 1979. Below is a list of the medical conditions that were used in this publication and the corresponding ICD-9 category.

Nutritional Deficiencies:

Alcoholic pellagra..265.2

Mental Disorders:

Alcoholic psychoses 291

Drug withdrawal syndrome 292.0

Drug psychoses..292

    paranoid and/or hallucinatory states induced

      by drugs 292.1

    pathological drug intoxication.....................292.2

    other..292.8

    unspecified 292.9

Alcohol dependence syndrome 303

Drug dependence...304

    morphine type..304.0

    barbiturate type.......................................304.1

    cocaine 304.2

    cannabis 304.3

    amphetamine type and other

      pyschostimulants....................................304.4

    hallucinogens 304.5

    other..304.6

    combinations of morphine drug with other

      type...304.7

    combinations excluding morphine type

      drug...304.8

    unspecified 304.9

Nondependent abuse of alcohol 305.0

Nondependent abuse of drugs (excluding

    alcohol)... 305.1-9

    tobacco 305.1

Catégories des conditions médicales et des diagnostics

Toutes les données sur la morbidité et la mortalité incluses dans le présent rapport sont classifiées selon la neuvième édition de la Classification internationale des maladies (CIM-9), adoptée par le Canada en 1979. La liste ci-après énumère les conditions médicales utilisées dans la publication, accompagnées du CIM-9 correspondant.

Maladies de la nutrition

Pellagre alcoolique 265.2

Troubles mentaux

Psychoses alcooliques...291

Psychoses dues aux drogues 292

    syndrome de sevrage de drogue....................292.0

    états délirants et hallucinatoires dus aux

      drogues..292.1

    forme pathologique d'intoxication par les

      drogues..292.2

    autres 292.8

    sans précision..292.9

Syndrome de dépendance à l'alcool 303

Pharmacodépendance...304

    type morphinique.....................................304.0

    type barbiturique......................................304.1

    type cocaïnique..304.2

    cannabisme..304.3

    type amphétaminique et autres stimulants...304.4

    hallucinogènes...304.5

    autres 304.6

    association de drogue de type morphinique

      avec autre substance...............................304.7

    association ne comprenant pas de drogue de

      type morphinique....................................304.8

    sans précision..304.9

Abus d'alcool sans dépendance.........................305.0

Abus de drogues sans dépendance (excluant

    l'alcool).. 305.1-9

Intoxication par médicaments et produits
biologiques

**Toxic Effects of Substances Chiefly
Nonmedicinal as to Source:**

EXTERNAL CAUSE OF INJURY
(Used only in classification of deaths)

**Intoxication par des substances
essentiellement non médicinales à l'origine**

**Accidental Poisoning by Drugs, Medicaments
and Biologicals:**

CAUSES EXTERIEURES DE TRAUMATISMES (utilisées seulement dans la classification des décès)

Poisoning by barbiturates E980.1

Poisoning by other sedatives and
hypnotics E980.2

Poisoning by tranquillizers and other
psychotropic agents E980.3

CAUSES OF DEATH INDIRECTLY DUE TO ALCOHOL

Neoplasms 140-239

Diseases of the circulatory system 390-459

Diseases of the respiratory system 460-519

Motor vehicle accidents E810-E838

Accidental falls E880-E888

Accidents caused by fire and flames E890-E899

Accidental drowning and submersion E910

Suicide and self-inflicted injury E950-E959

Homicide and injury purposely inflicted by
other persons E960-E969

CAUSES OF DEATH INDIRECTLY DUE TO SMOKING

Neoplasms 140-239

Hypertension disease 401-405

Ischaemic heart disease 410-414

Cerebrovascular disease 430-438

Chronic bronchitis 491

Emphysema 492

Asthma 493

Reference

World Health Organization, International
Classification of Diseases, 1975 Revision, 2 Vols.
(Geneva: World Health Organization, 1977).

Suicide et traumatisme infligé par soi-même

Empoisonnement par analgésiques,
antipyrétiques et antirhumatismaux E950.0

Empoisonnement par barbituriques E950.1

Empoisonnement par autres sédatifs et
hypnotiques E950.2

Empoisonnement par tranquillisants et autres
agents psychotropes E950.3

Traumatismes et empoisonnements causés d'une manière indéterminée quant à l'intention

Empoisonnement par analgésiques,
antipyrétiques et antirhumatismaux E980.0

Empoisonnement par barbituriques E980.1

Empoisonnement par autres sédatifs et
hypnotiques E980.2

Empoisonnement par tranquillisants et autres
agents psychotropes E980.3

CAUSES DES DECES INDIRECTEMENT CAUSES PAR L'ALCOOL

Tumeurs 140-239

Maladies de l'appareil circulatoire 390-459

Maladies de l'appareil respiratoire 460-519

Accidents de véhicules à moteur E810-E838

Chutes accidentelles E880-E888

Accidents provoqués par le feu E890-E899

Noyade et submersion accidentelles E910

Suicide et traumatismes provoqués par
soi-même E950-E959

Homicide et traumatismes faits par une autre
personne, avec l'intention de blesser ou de
tuer E960-E969

CAUSES DES DECES INDIRECTEMENT CAUSES PAR L'USAGE DU TABAC

Tumeurs 140-239

Maladies hypertensives 401-405

Cardiopathies ischémiques........................ 410-414

Maladiesires cérébrales.............................. 430-438

Bronchite chronique 491

Emphysème 492

Asthme..493

Ouvrage de référence

Organisation mondiale de la santé, Classification internationale des maladies, Révision 1975, 2 volumes (Genève : Organisation mondiale de la santé, 1977).

Table Index

Index des tableaux

(References are to table numbers)

(Les numéros ont référence aux tableaux)